EMPIRE
of
SHADOWS

ALSO BY GEORGE BLACK

Casting a Spell: The Bamboo Fly Rod and the American
Pursuit of Perfection

The Trout Pool Paradox: The American Lives of Three Rivers

Genocide in Iraq

Black Hands of Beijing: Lives of Defiance in
China's Democracy Movement (with Robin Munro)

The Good Neighbor: How the United States Wrote the History of
Central America and the Caribbean

EMPIRE

of

SHADOWS

The Epic Story of Yellowstone

GEORGE BLACK

St. Martin's Press

New York

www.stmartins.com

Library of Congress Cataloging-in-Publication Data

Black, George, 1949–
    Empire of shadows: the epic story of Yellowstone / George Black.—1st ed.
        p. cm.
    Includes bibliographical references.
    ISBN 978-0-312-38319-0 (hardcover)
    ISBN 978-1-4299-8974-9 (e-book)
    1. Yellowstone National Park—History.   2. Yellowstone National Park—Discovery
and exploration.   I. Title.
    F722.B53 2012
    978.7'52—dc23   2011041351

First Edition: March 2012

10   9   8   7   6   5   4   3   2   1

CONTENTS

AUTHOR'S NOTE

One day in the summer of 2010, as I was chatting with the Yellowstone National Park archivist and historian Lee Whittlesey about the challenges of writing a revisionist history, he handed me a quotation from the distinguished Western historian Elliott West, which he kept pinned to the wall of his office: "The use of 'revisionist' has always struck me as odd. We historians are all in the revision business, aren't we? If we don't ask new questions and work toward some fresh understanding, what's the point? Treating past historians respectfully is our obligation; revising and building on what they have done is our job."

This, then, is a revisionist history, and it seeks to ask new questions about the nineteenth-century West. My intention has not been to pull back the curtain on the dark side of Yellowstone, although some readers may well see it that way. Rather, it is an account, starting with Lewis and Clark and ending with the last spasms of the Indian wars, of how the intertwined paths of settlement, exploration, violence, and institution-building all converged toward the "discovery" in 1870 of the most remote, inaccessible, and mythic corner of the Western frontier.

It is a story of men at a particular moment in history, of individuals who acted not only according to the dictates of their own character but within the values, culture, and institutions of their time, with all their attendant passions, ambitions, ideals, fears, and uncertainties. Strange contradictions arise in people during times like these, when societies are in the process of being redefined. Principled citizens justify acts of extreme violence, and ruthless military men develop a passion for education and knowledge. Retiring city-dwellers become intrepid explorers, and venal businessmen display unexpected bursts of altruism.

Historians often warn against "presentism"—the danger of relying on contemporary values to pass moral judgment on people of a different time. A certain amount of presentism is probably inescapable, but I have done my best to place my characters in the fullness of their historical context—the decade following the Civil War—with all its contradictions. At the heart of my story is a great paradox: that no matter how deeply flawed these characters may be as individuals, no matter how mixed their motives, and no matter how much damage they caused along the way, the paths they opened led to one of the true glories of American history—the creation of the world's first national park. In that sense, the epic of Yellowstone is a quintessentially American story, of terrible things done in the name of high ideals, and of high ideals realized by dubious means.

At first it felt presumptuous for a foreign-born New Yorker to write about a period and a place that has already filled so many bookshelves. But the more time I spent in and around Yellowstone, the more I was struck by the fact that while some of the friends I made there were natives of Montana or Wyoming, the majority were not. They came from Pennsylvania and upstate New York, from Michigan and Arkansas, from Virginia and New Jersey, from Oklahoma and Ohio. All of us are drawn to this place, I think, by the same magnetic force that worked on the nineteenth-century settlers and explorers—the sheer wonder of the landscape of mountains, rivers, and skies, the sense that something primordial is still present and available to us.

I am deeply indebted to these friends for whatever virtues this book may possess. In particular I thank Paul Schullery, Kim Allen Scott, and Lee Whittlesey, who know these places more intimately than I ever will and read drafts of this manuscript with care and insight. Many others have offered generous support and companionship along the way, or enriched my travels with their insights into particular corners of the Yellowstone land-scape. They include Linda Baker, Doug Barasch, Frances Beinecke, Glenn Brackett, Peter Carey, Emily Cousins, Louise Desalvo, Gerald Doane, Jason Doane, Dr. Wilton Doane, Bob Doerk, Maya Dollarhide, John Echohawk, Mike Foster, Janet Gold, Bruce Gordon, Andrew Graybill, Laurie Gunst, Phil Gutis, Karl Hepner, Darrell Kipp, Jack Lepley, Jesse Logan, Amy McCarthy, Forrest McCarthy, Wally MacFarlane, Bill McKibben, Dick Manning, Marlene Deahl Merrill, Peter Messina, Cullen Murphy, Jane Pargiter, Karen Perszyk, Philip Perszyk, Ken Robison, Paulette Running Wolf, Tracy Stone-Manning, Meredith Taylor, Laura Wright Treadway, Tom Turiano, L. J. Turner, Louisa Willcox, and Lesley Wischmann.

Librarians and archivists are one of our society's unsung treasures, and I am grateful to Jodie Foley, Lory Morrow, Zoe Ann Stolz, and their colleagues at the Montana Historical Society in Helena; Patricia Engbret-son at Montana State University in Bozeman; Colleen Curry, Anne Foster, Bridgette Guild, and Jackie Jerla of the Yellowstone National Park Heri-tage Research Center; Alison Purgiel at the Minnesota Historical Society; and the staffs of the American Heritage Center at the University of Wyo-ming, Laramie; the Museum of the Mountain Man in Pinedale, Wyo-ming; the Butler Library at Columbia University, New York; the Beinecke Library at Yale University; and the incomparable room 315 at the New York Public Library.

These are tough times in the world of publishing, and I am endlessly appreciative of the wisdom and friendship of my agent, Henry Dunow, who has now held my hand through three very different books. For his sharp critical eye and warm support of this project, I am grateful to my editor at St. Martin's Press, Michael Flamini. Vicki Lame, Eric Meyer, and John Morrone shepherded the manuscript effortlessly through the pro-duction process. Rob Grom, Michelle McMillian, and Baker Vail have made the book beautiful as well as, I hope, readable.

My special good fortune is to share my life with Anne Nelson, whose loving support and acute insights as a writer and editor have helped this book along in innumerable ways. She, David, and Julia remain the rock on which everything else is founded.

It is grand, gloomy, and terrible; a solitude peopled with fantastic ideas, an empire of shadows and of turmoil.

—Lieutenant Gustavus Cheyney Doane, Second U.S. Cavalry,
on the Black Canyon of the Yellowstone,
August 26, 1870

THE VIEW FROM MOUNT WASHBURN

Nathaniel Pitt Langford left Helena a day ahead of the rest of the party. There were two important if unpleasant pieces of business to take care of before his unlikely group of explorers set off for the upper Yellowstone. He had chafed for five years to reveal the truth about this most inaccessible corner of the frontier, to settle once and for all the swirl of rumors about its hallucinatory wonders. Another day would not matter.

Langford was an expert horseman who had ridden alone for thousands of miles across the forbidding landscapes of Montana Territory with a shotgun strapped to his saddle, and he made a formidable impression. He was a handsome man of thirty-eight, with a black beard so dense that birds might have nested in it, a high forehead, a downturned mouth, and an intense, blazing stare. Most of the extant photographs capture his fierce charisma, though they also suggest an absence of humor, the self-righteousness of a man with strong and fixed ideas, and a taste for melodrama.

It was mid-August of 1870, but in one of those capricious turns in the weather that are so common in the Northern Rockies, Langford was caught in a snowstorm near the Three Forks of the Missouri. He bedded down there in the home of a retired army major, one of a straggle of cabins that some wishful thinker had called Gallatin City.

Steeped in the history of the territory, Langford knew that this was
the heart of the old fur-trapping country, where Jim Bridger, the most
celebrated of the mountain men, and two generations of trappers had
fought the implacable Blackfeet over beaver pelts. Usually they had come
out the worse from these encounters, tomahawked, riddled with arrows,
dismembered.

Langford knew from the journals of Lewis and Clark that he was
walking in their footsteps. President Jefferson's Corps of Discovery had
stopped at the Three Forks for two days in July 1805, and it had been one
of the most discouraging junctures in their two-year journey. Despite the
help of their sixteen-year-old Shoshone guide, Sacagawea, they had failed
to make contact with her tribe. The girl was carrying a six-month-old
baby and was barely recovered from a life-threatening illness that Lewis
had treated with laudanum and saltpeter. Clark was in wretched shape,
his feet torn to bleeding shreds from days of tramping over prickly pear
and needle grass. Yet Lewis reveled in the glory of the landscape, the "extensive and beautifull plains and meadows which appear to be surrounded
in every direction with distant and lofty mountains."

From their source among the unexplored snowpeaks of the upper Yellowstone, the forks of the Missouri River meandered northward across the
broad, lush valley. Lewis named them for the leaders of the young country: Secretary of State James Madison, Treasury Secretary Albert Gallatin,
and "that illustrious personage Thomas Jefferson President of the United
States." Later, as the expedition made its way south, Lewis, a Royal Arch
Mason, would name three of the Jefferson's tributary streams to honor the
president's virtues and the values of freemasonry—Philanthropy, Philosophy, and Wisdom.[1]

On his second morning out of Helena, when the storm had abated,
Langford set out for Fort Ellis, two miles east of the small town of
Bozeman and the starting point for the Yellowstone expedition. But he
had to deal first with the unhappy situation at the local masonic lodge. Like
so many of the leading men of Montana, Langford was a dedicated mason,

creator of the first lodge in the territory and proud to trace his lineage back to Meriwether Lewis. The masonic community in Bozeman, however, was riven by internal dissension, and Langford saw no alternative but to order the town's lodge closed until some amicable solution could be found.

Next day, two lieutenants from the Second Cavalry accompanied him to the fort. In his diary,[2] Langford names one of them as Bachelor, though this was almost certainly James Batchelder, who would play a small but important part in the events that followed. The commanding officer, Brevet[3] Lieutenant Colonel Eugene M. Baker, was waiting to meet Langford to discuss the contentious matter of a military escort. Langford's diary says nothing of his feelings about Baker, but the colonel was not an easy man to like. He was a harsh disciplinarian, a notorious alcoholic, and behind his back men called him "Piegan Baker," for his slaughter of 173 members of that Blackfeet tribe on the Marias River seven months earlier. But Baker was a favorite of "Little Phil" Sheridan, the Civil War hero who now commanded the Division of the Missouri. And the army, all the way up to its commander in chief, William Tecumseh Sherman, had stood firm behind Baker in the face of the storm of condemnation of the massacre by Eastern humanitarians.

Although the colonel's superiors had spoken at first of providing a whole company of cavalry, he told Langford bluntly that he could spare only six men for the expedition—a lieutenant, a sergeant, and four enlisted men. On the other hand, Baker was prepared to assign the best of all his officers to lead the escort, a hero of the Piegan campaign named Gustavus Cheyney Doane, who had dreamed since his college days of becoming America's greatest explorer.

At thirty, Cheyney Doane—he abhorred the name Gustavus—was an imposing if inelegant figure. The tallest officer at the post, he wore his black hair to the shoulders and sported a drooping walrus mustache that was spectacular even by the standards of the time. Socially awkward among his fellow officers, Doane was endlessly attentive to his men, who would follow him blindly through any privation. But he was also a man with a respectable degree of book learning and a solid grounding in the natural sciences.

Langford had now taken care of all the practical arrangements for the expedition, but protocol demanded that he wait until the following day, August 21, when its titular head, General Henry Dana Washburn, would arrive with the rest of the party and formalize the agreement with Colonel Baker. Washburn had distinguished himself in the late war, breveted a brigadier general under Phil Sheridan in the pitiless Shenandoah Campaign. He was a man of fine judgment and impeccable reputation, a diplomat, a skilled manager of tangling egos and flaring tempers. But the war had left him consumptive, and his recent appointment as surveyor general of Montana was seen by some as an invalid posting.[4] As the exploration continued, his stamina would become a source of anxiety to the rest of the party.

There were nineteen of them in all: nine of the leading men of Montana Territory, Lieutenant Doane's six-man escort, two packers, two cooks—"unbleached Americans of African descent"—and a black dog of apparently limited intelligence named Booby. And while it was officially the Washburn Expedition, everyone recognized that Langford and Doane were its de facto leaders—Doane its pathfinder, and Langford its organizing dynamo, promoter, and publicist. Though they were unaware of it, the two men's paths had been converging for years. Now they had become entwined, first through a murder, then through a massacre, and at last, with their meeting at Fort Ellis, through their shared hunger for exploration, discovery, and fame.

On August 29, the eighth day out, the explorers had their first whiff of sulfur. It emanated from some bubbling springs at the mouth of a creek that plunged into the turquoise waters of the Yellowstone, through a chasm edged with "spires, pinnacles, towers, and many other capricious objects." There they pitched camp for the night. The weather continued to display all the vagaries of the late summer season in the mountains: The snowstorm at the Three Forks had given way to ninety-two-degree sunshine at Fort Ellis, and then a soaking downpour at the Bottler brothers' ranch, the last rough outpost of civilization. Now, a bitterly cold night had frozen the water in their buckets.

But their spirits had risen after the unsettling portents of the first few days. A bout of food poisoning had kept one man confined to his tent at the Bottlers' ranch. Perhaps a surfeit of corn and wild berries was to blame. Or perhaps it was the canned peaches, a particular delicacy. There was a nervousness about hostiles, warnings from other frontiersmen that some of the party were likely to lose their hair. Two hunters encountered on the trail told of finding the bleached skeletons and severed heads of two miners killed two years earlier.

While the sick man lay sweating in his blankets, a band of a hundred Indians had watched the party from a high bluff across the river. To Langford, especially, they had a menacing aspect. "For me to say that I am not in hourly dread of the Indians when they appear in a large force, would be a braggart boast," he wrote in his diary. He was grateful for the party's rifles, accurate at long range, and their plentiful supply of ammunition. But Lieutenant Doane, with wide experience in such matters, appeared unconcerned. The horsemen on the bluff were friendly Crows, he said, not the fearsome Blackfeet from the north, nor the Shoshone, both tribes cowed now by force of arms, nor the Sioux, who, despite repeated alarums, had never been known to venture this far to the west, into the valley of the upper Yellowstone. The Crows, as Langford surely knew, were more prone to horse theft than to murder.

Not that Langford himself was any stranger to violence. He had always seen himself as one of that elite of educated and ambitious men who would bring civilization to the frontier—and the frontier did not civilize easily. Tribes like the Blackfeet and the Sioux, who had ranged freely for centuries across their ancestral buffalo lands, were the most obvious impediment. But there were other obstacles, too, as men like Langford sought to build the institutions of law and order. Their methods were peremptory; in the absence of government authority in the Montana gold camps, where Langford had come to seek his fortune, those who disrupted the new civic order with robbery and murder were likely to find themselves hanging from the nearest tree. The Montana goldfields gave birth to the largest episode of vigilante violence in American history, and Langford was one of those who guided it.

W ith Doane invariably riding first, the explorers had found much to write about in the days since leaving Fort Ellis. They marveled at a singular formation of red rock that they mistook for cinnabar and named "the Devil's Slide"; they picked their way across a bleak, boulder-strewn stretch of country that one member of the party called "the Valley of Desolation"; fighting vertigo, they peered down into three successive canyons, each more unfathomable than the last; and now they had stumbled upon this group of malodorous sulfur springs.

Langford and Doane kept the most detailed diaries, although most of their companions made notes of their own. Some would publish newspaper and magazine accounts of the expedition, while the jottings of others are best described as perfunctory. Langford's business partner, Samuel Hauser, though a successful Helena banker and a future governor of Montana after the territory acquired statehood, seemed scarcely literate. Each day he scrawled a few misspelled words in a dull pencil. Contemplating the snowcapped spectacle of the Absaroka mountains, where the two unfortunate prospectors had been killed, he managed just this: "cenery supurb."

The camp above the sulfur springs was at 6,500 feet, but the mountain they proposed to climb today towered more than 3,000 higher. They broke camp at eight o'clock, though not all of them joined the trip. Among the three who stayed behind was a bright and self-effacing young Helena lawyer named Cornelius Hedges, a close friend of Langford's and another prominent mason. He was an improbable explorer, slightly built and something of a hypochondriac. Let the others make the ride up the mountain, Hedges said; his horse was tired, and he would climb instead to the top of a beetling cliff that overlooked the campsite, to savor the view of the Yellowstone and update his journal.

At the foot of the mountain, the riders diverged from the Indian trail that Lieutenant Doane had been following for the past several days. The ascent from here was steep and rough, through stands of timber, across meadows of late-blooming wildflowers where grizzly bears began to forage at this time of year for berries and whitebark pine nuts, over bare rocks and ravines, past the tree line and the snow line. At the summit, they took measurements with an aneroid barometer, although the numbers varied widely. Perhaps not all the members of the party were familiar with the workings of the instrument. Hauser, a former civil engineer with a talent for triangulation, estimated their altitude at 10,700 feet. Less, Langford said; about 9,800. Doane fixed the figure at 9,966 feet. Yet while there was disagreement about the altitude, there was no dispute about the name. By common acclaim, they dedicated the mountain to their ailing general, who had surprised them all by riding alone to the summit on the previous day. It would be Mount Washburn.[5]

"The view from the summit is beyond all description," Doane wrote. His whole field of vision was rimmed by mountains: to the east, the dark, white-tipped mass of the Absarokas; to the west, the forested slopes and chiseled rock faces of the Madison and Gallatin ranges; straight ahead to the south, the sheer-sided silhouette of the distant Tetons. A pellucid lake, dotted with islands, occupied the middle ground.

The Grand Canyon of the Yellowstone cut a ragged line across the open landscape, and twenty miles beyond it, a column of smoke rose hundreds of feet above the trees. They took it for a forest fire, not an uncommon occurrence after summer lightning strikes, until someone remarked that the smoke seemed to be rising in regular puffs, as if it was being expelled from the earth with great force. As they concentrated on the sight, their senses sharpened in the cold, thin air, they convinced themselves that this smoke was also making a sound, a low roar—although at such a distance this might have been an aural illusion. The meaning of the curious sight began to dawn on them: a cheer went up; hats were thrown in the air. They had found a geyser.

As Doane took in the view, he became aware of other plumes of white, more and more of them. Some appeared in a sudden spurt of steam; others formed lazy, drifting clouds. He was looking, astonished, at dozens of geysers and hot springs, scattered all across the great circular basin. The scene put him in mind of the Alleghenies, with the iron and coal furnaces going full blast. While the others took their measurements and raised their hurrahs, Doane alone seemed to understand the totality of what he was seeing. All this was the vast crater, the caldera, of an extinct volcano. And that meant that everything they had heard—the campfire yarns spun by Jim Bridger and the mountain men, the wild exaggerations of the gold prospectors, the tales told by the Jesuit fathers of their travels with the Blackfeet to a place they called the "land of many smokes"—all of it was true.

Over the days that followed, Doane recorded the explorers' progress conscientiously in his journal, covering page after page in his bold, sloping hand. It was the first coherent record of the sights that tens of millions would flock to see—the canyons and falls of the Yellowstone, the shimmering lake, the mud pots and geyser basins. Doane's report was a masterpiece of crisp, clear observation. Before the next year was out, it would be favorably compared to the journals of Lewis and Clark; within two, it would be instrumental in the creation of one of the nation's greatest icons.

On March 1, 1872, as President Ulysses S. Grant signed the bill establishing the world's first national park, the army was at work on its official history of the Second Cavalry. It traced each proud episode, from the hunting down of the Seminoles in the Everglades in the late 1830s, through the heroic fights against the Confederacy at Bull Run and Manassas, to the Piegan affair of 1870, in which the central role of Lieutenant Doane in destroying the hostile village on the Marias was singled out for special praise.

The history was written by an elite group of colonels and generals, but remarkably they asked Doane, a mere lieutenant, to contribute a chapter of his own in which he would recount his memories of the Yellowstone expedition.[6] Violence, exploration, and civilization were to be woven together in the army's salute to this young officer, as they were in the history of the West.

Doane wrote with pride:

It is something to break down the barriers of the unknown; to behold the mists of darkness fade; to marshal the videttes of the vanguard of progress; to form the crest of that wave of civilization which sweeps onward, invincible and without ceasing, through the breadth of a great continent, until it meets the reflux tide from the broad Pacific slopes.

As for Yellowstone:

When the park shall have been made accessible to the pleasure-seekers of the world, it will be a satisfaction not to be derived from wealth nor honors to have been in some degree concerned in the discovery and development of a new source of pleasure and instruction for the human race.

This was an official history, and as such it called for decorum. But in the normal run of things, this kind of modesty was not a quality that marked the lieutenant's character. In his own mind, Doane was not "in some degree concerned" in the creation of Yellowstone; he would always be "the man who invented Wonderland."

Part One

PATHFINDERS

"A KNOLEDGE OF THESE PEOPLE"

1805–1806

They had soldiered together, and they were nominally co-captains of the Corps of Discovery, but Meriwether Lewis and William Clark could hardly have been more contrasting personalities. The redheaded Clark was the elder by four years. He was an experienced frontiersman and Indian fighter, with a talent for mapmaking and navigation, a natural command of men, and an open, genial character. Lewis was a child of privilege, scion of one of the first families of Virginia, and personal secretary to the president, whom he regarded as a virtual father figure. But there was an awkward formality about Lewis, and he had a "martial temper." Above all he was a manic depressive, veering wildly from limitless excitement to dark feelings of impotence and failure that would eventually lead him to suicide. The episodes of euphoria sometimes made him reckless, and on the homeward leg of the journey, in the summer of 1806, he made a critical misjudgment, ignoring the warnings of people to whom he should have paid close attention.

In the matter of their contact with Indians, Jefferson's instructions to Lewis and Clark[1] had been detailed and explicit. The president wrote, "The commerce which may be carried on with the people inhabiting the line you will pursue, renders a knoledge of these people important."

What that meant in practice was that Lewis and Clark were to acquaint themselves with the names and numbers of the tribes they encountered; their languages, occupations, and peculiarities of law and custom; their characteristic diseases and remedies; how they dressed and what they ate; the extent of each tribe's territory; and the state of intertribal relations. Jefferson continued, "Considering the interest which every nation has in extending & strengthening the authority of reason & justice among the people around them, it will be useful to acquire what knowledge you can of the state of morality, religion & information among them, as it may better enable those who endeavor to civilize & instruct them."

The president was clear that violence was to be avoided wherever possible: "In all your intercourse with the natives treat them in the most friendly & conciliatory manner which their own conduct will admit." If the explorers ran into an overwhelming display of hostile force, they should retreat. This was a matter of simple pragmatism. Engagement would risk, at the very least, loss of the data collected by the expedition, while turning back to give a full reporting of the number and disposition of hostiles would allow future explorers to return with the proper amount of hardware.

This is not to say that Lewis and Clark went ill-equipped. On the contrary, they carried the largest arsenal that had ever been seen west of the Missouri. The threat of violence was implicit in the act of exploration, and certainly in Jefferson's intent to civilize. The Corps of Discovery was a military expedition, under military discipline. The explorers were uninvited guests in an unknown land, and any tribe they encountered was assumed to be hostile until proven otherwise. To a belligerent tribe seeking dominance over its neighbors, what greater temptation than the rifles, powder horns, bullet molds, gunsmith's tools, knives, and tomahawks that Lewis had commissioned from the United States arsenal at Harpers Ferry? The basic truth about weaponry is that it is an enticement to violence as well as a safeguard against it. Or put another way, Lewis and Clark, and many subsequent explorations of the West, proved Chekhov's first iron law of theater: Hang a pistol on the wall in the first act, and it is sure to be fired before the final curtain.

Miraculously, however, it took more than two years for the point to be proved. In the meantime, there were incidents and near-incidents. As the expedition labored upstream on the Missouri in September 1804, a group of Teton Sioux chiefs, after downing a glass or two, or three, of whiskey on the explorers' keelboat, expressed their dissatisfaction with Lewis's gifts of peace medals, coats, and hats, and refused to be put ashore without more, while warriors milled around on the bank with their bows strung. Lewis ordered the boat's swivel gun loaded with musket balls and held a lighted taper over the fuse until they dispersed. Three days later, there was a second, similar episode, this time because a gift of tobacco was considered insultingly meager. But on both occasions the offended chiefs backed down, the warriors put away their arrows, and the fuse of the swivel gun remained unlit.[2]

Lewis's temper almost got the better of him nineteen months later, as the party headed back up the Columbia from the Pacific and spent several days in the country of the Chinooks. The captain had mixed feelings about these people. On one hand he was disdainful of their general demeanor ("low and ill-shaped . . . badly clad and illy made"). On the other, he had to acknowledge that they were peaceable sorts ("the greatest harmoney appears to exist among them"). But the Chinooks were inveterate petty thieves, and that drove Lewis to distraction. They stole an ax; they stole a lump of lead; they tried to steal a tomahawk from Private John Colter, who was not a man to trifle with; they stole Lewis's black dog, Seaman, which almost pushed him over the edge. It was not clear whether the thieves intended to eat the dog, as many tribes did.

One of the Chinook chiefs apologized. He tried to explain the problem of tribal authority; there were limits to the discipline a chief could impose, and there was not much he could do if a few hotheaded young men yielded to temptation. Lewis had to understand that the village as a whole wanted peace. But Lewis didn't really understand, and few whites would. Friendly and/or powerless chiefs, and young warriors who saw theft and violence as a display of valor and a source of prestige: This would be a running theme for the rest of the century and the root of one violent confrontation after another.

As if to underline the chief's point, the thieving continued. Tomahawks and knives went missing in the night. Lewis threatened beatings. A saddle disappeared, and a buffalo robe. Then he caught a man red-handed, as he tried to liberate an iron socket from a discarded canoe pole. He flew into a rage and told the village that "I would shoot the first of them that attempted to steal an article from us." He went beyond this to the threat of collective punishment, informing the Chinooks "that I had it in my power at that moment to kill them all and set fire to their houses." But then he summoned all his self-control, no doubt contemplating the political consequences of acting out his threat, and the Corps of Discovery moved on toward the territory of a tribe about whom Lewis felt differently.[3]

Lewis and his companions got on well with many of the tribes, to be fair. As Clark noted in his journal, "A cuirous custom . . . is to give handsome squars to those whom they wish to show more acknowledgments to." The men of the corps, he reported in March 1805, were "generally healthy except Venerials Complaints which is verry Common amongst the natives and the men Catch it from them."[4]

The explorers had a mutual love affair with the Mandans, whose amiable welcome made their villages a favored stopover for generations of European and American adventurers on the upper Missouri. Lewis liked the Arikara, too, and the Clatsops. He found the Wallawallas "the most hospitable, honest, and sincere people that we have met with in our voyage."[5] The Flatheads were friendly. The Shoshone were "frank, communicative, fair in dealing, generous with the little they possess, extreemly honest, and by no means beggarly."[6] And of course there was Sacagawea, herself a Shoshone, freed from slavery among the Hidatsa.

But no tribe stood in quite such high regard as the Nez Perce. There is disagreement about how the tribe acquired its odd name. Some of them appear to have indeed pierced their noses and ornamented them with dentalium shells, which they acquired in trade with the tribes of the Pacific Coast. Other authorities say the name is a mistranslation of sign language. The Plains tribes indicated the Nez Perce by passing the index finger over the nose with a slashing motion; this was a sign of bravery, denoting people who did not flinch even if an arrow came that close.

Lewis and Clark also attested to this bravery, but they spoke too of the gentleness of the Nez Perce men, as well as the intelligence and attractiveness of the women. The explorers found the Nez Perce to be proud, dignified, reserved, slow to anger, attentive to personal cleanliness. Their language contained no profanity. They were orators, who settled their disputes by a prolonged search for consensus. The tribe was famous for its horse breeding and its horsemanship.

There were perhaps four thousand Nez Perce when the Corps of Discovery encountered them, divided into a number of small, autonomous bands. The men hunted and fished for salmon and cutthroat trout; the women gathered berries and dug camas roots, which they pounded into flour for bread that gave Lewis chronic gas and diarrhea. Buffalo were gone from the plateau country west of the Rockies by the time the expedition arrived, so the Nez Perce crossed the mountains each summer to hunt the great herds on the plains of what is now Montana. It is this knowledge of the high passes that explains the tribe's warm relationship with Lewis and Clark. The Nez Perce knew the way across the Continental Divide, and they knew the dangers that lurked on the other side. Captain Lewis took their advice on the first count, and ignored it on the second.

The most daunting moment of the outward journey occurred in September 1805 when the captains contemplated the sheer granite wall of the Bitterroots. "The most terrible mountains I ever beheld," remarked Sergeant Patrick Gass.[7] The Columbia River and the Pacific Ocean lay somewhere on the far side. They bought some fresh horses from a friendly band of Flatheads. With the help of the expedition's translator, George Drouillard (Drewyer, for the most part, in Lewis's journals, or sometimes Drulyard), son of a French-Canadian father and a Shawnee mother, Lewis constructed a summary Flathead vocabulary. The tribe spoke in a guttural fashion that led Lewis to think they might be the descendants of Prince Madoc and a wandering band of Welshmen. Jefferson subscribed to the theory that such a tribe was out there, somewhere in the Western wilds.

The Corps of Discovery had better horses now, but the "emince Dificuelt Knobs" remained to be conquered. On Lolo Creek, at a campground they called Travelers' Rest, a group of hunters went out to supplement the party's dwindling rations as it prepared for the crossing. John Colter, the soldier who would later withhold his tomahawk from the larcenous Chinooks, brought back three Indians who said they lived on the other side of the mountains. They were Nez Perce, and they indicated a trail across the divide that would take the explorers to their villages in six days. It took eleven in reality, and they were the worst days of the whole trip, beset by snowdrifts, hailstorms, dysentery, fallen timber, the eating of a colt when the rest of the food ran out, and the loss of Clark's writing desk when a packhorse fell forty feet down a precipice.

The elderly chief of the Nez Perce villages was Twisted Hair, a "Chearfull man with apparent Siencerity." He offered hospitality, traded food for trinkets, knives, and tobacco, and allowed the men to lie up for more than a week while Clark treated their intestinal troubles with salt pills and other emetics. Clark wrote that his modest doctoring abilities "raised my reputation and gives those nativs an exolted oppinion of my skill as a phisician." Most important, the Nez Perce made no move to relieve the ailing and vulnerable explorers of their weapons, despite having no more than a couple of defective rifles with which to defend themselves against hostile tribes.

In early May 1806, Lewis and Clark were back from the western sea, and as they prepared to recross the Bitterroots the friendship between the whites and the Nez Perce was cemented. It would endure for more than half a century until it was finally betrayed by settlers, soldiers, and the lust for gold.

While the Nez Perce had declined the opportunity to steal the explorers' guns, they had no objection to being armed as part of a larger geopolitical compact. Lewis laid this out in the stump speech he gave to all the tribes, sweetened by the medals and the flags and the trade trinkets. The Nez Perce would accept an American-dominated system of trading posts and agree to live in peace with their neighbors; in exchange they would be given a guarantee of security, with guns and ammunition to protect themselves. The Nez Perce pointed out only one flaw with this scheme, but it was a serious one. The Blackfeet would never stand for it.

Violent resistance was built into that tribe's creation myth, and they were well supplied with weapons from traders in the British possessions to the north. When Napi, Old Man, was done with fashioning the prairies, the mountains, and the forests, he marked the ground and told the Blackfeet, "This is your land. It is full of animals and other things which I have given you. Let no other people come into it. When others cross the line, take your bows and arrows, your lances and your battle axes, and keep them out. If they remain, trouble will come."[8]

The Corps of Discovery's second crossing of the mountains was no easier than the first. By early June the captains were eager to be on the move, but the Nez Perce pointed up at the peaks, observing that the winter snowfall had been prodigious, and counseled a few more weeks of patience. Clark was inclined to heed their advice. "I Shudder with the expectation with great dificuelties in passing these Mountains," he wrote.[9] Lewis was having none of it; he pronounced this a "delightfull season for travelling" and decided they should proceed without a guide. He was wrong on both counts. The snow turned out to be fifteen feet deep, and there was no grass for the horses. For the first time in two years the explorers were forced to retrace their steps. Lewis sent Drouillard back to the Nez Perce villages for help and the captains cooled their heels in camp for a week. Clark seems to have found a silver lining in the "great dificuelties" of the crossing, since a child with reddish hair, who later became a familiar figure to Montana settlers, was born about nine months later, the outcome of Clark's dalliance with a Nez Perce woman.

Eventually Drouillard returned with three young men who agreed to see them safely across. The plan was for the expedition to split into two groups when it got back to Travelers' Rest, the first time it had ever risked such a step, and to reassemble about six weeks later at the confluence of the Yellowstone and the Missouri. Clark would take one group and head down the Yellowstone. Lewis, with the rest of the party, would follow the Nez Perce trail along the Blackfoot River and into the buffalo country. Once they reached the Great Falls of the Missouri, the Lewis party would subdivide again. One group would stay on the big river to dig up a large cache of supplies the explorers had left there the previous year and prepare for Clark's portage around the falls. Lewis, with half a dozen volunteers, would explore "at every hazard" the Marias River, which entered the Missouri from the northwest. Lewis named it for his cousin, Maria Wood. Originally, then, it was Maria's River, but the apostrophe fell away with time.

Clark's route was longer than Lewis's but easier, and he made steady, uneventful progress, up the Bitterroot and over the divide, across the broad, lovely valley of the upper Big Hole with the Beaverhead peaks to his right, until he found himself back at Camp Fortunate, where Sacagawea had been ecstatically reunited with her fellow Shoshone the previous summer. From there, northeast along the Jefferson River to the Three Forks, and thence eastward across the fertile valley of the Gallatin, through a twisting gap in the mountains that would later be called the Bozeman Pass, until he finally struck the Yellowstone near the site of the present-day town of Livingston, where the river makes a big ninety degree turn to the east.

It seems strange that a man with Clark's instincts would disregard three separate opportunities to explore the sources of the Madison, the Gallatin, and the Yellowstone itself. Strange stories were already in circulation about the spectacular landscapes and bizarre natural phenomena in the high country where the three rivers had their origins. Fur traders in St. Louis had heard tales of spouts of boiling water in the area as early as 1803.[10] Clark wrote in his journal that the Yellowstone had "a considerable fall" high in the mountains, but then crossed out the reference with an enigmatic "no." At the big bend, the river emerges from the corridor of Paradise Valley as a broad, leisurely riffle, flanked by the peaks of the Absarokas and the Gallatin Range. It offers no particular deterrent at that point to the explorer. Early in the trip, the Hidatsa had told Lewis and Clark that the Yellowstone was navigable almost to its source, which was roughly accurate, give or take fifty miles. So was Clark tempted? Apparently not. His journal notes only that, "The Roche [the Roche Jaune, that is, or Yellow Stone] passes out of a high rugid mountain covered with snow."

It is irresistible to speculate about what might have happened if Lewis and Clark had left St. Louis a couple of years later than they did. That would have given them time to be apprised of a curious report that was submitted to Jefferson in October 1805 by General James Wilkinson, "the admirable trumpeter," military governor of Louisiana Territory. In this the general informed the president that he had "a Savage delineation on a Buffaloe Pelt, of the Missouri & its South Western Branches. . . . among things a little incredible, a volcano is distinctly described on Yellow Stone River."[11] Jefferson, after all, had particularly ordered the captains, as part of their inventory of Louisiana's geological and mineral resources, to be alert to any signs of volcanic activity. The temptation to pursue such a fantastic story would surely have been powerful.

Three years after the Corps of Discovery returned home, William Clark had collated even more fragments of information and hearsay about the mysterious upper Yellowstone. In about 1809, he added to his notes, "At the head of this river the nativs give an account that there is frequently herd a loud noise, like Thunder, which makes the earth Tremble, they State that they seldom go there because their children Cannot sleep—and Conceive it possessed of spirits, who were averse that men Should be near them."[12] Merely a footnote, but the first recorded entry in a durable canard: that Indians were driven by fear or superstition to avoid the upper Yellowstone.

In July 1806, however, no matter how strong the temptation, a ninety degree diversion to the south simply did not figure in Clark's plans. Everything was for eastward, to the rendezvous with Lewis, and home before winter.

2

THE TERRIBLE PAHKEES

1806

The Nez Perce guides took their leave of Lewis on July 4, 1806. It was the thirtieth anniversary of American independence, but the guides appeared in no mood for celebration. It was not an easy parting, Lewis recorded in his journal: "These affectionate people our guides betrayed every emmotion of unfeigned regret at seperating from us." They tried to put a brave face on things, telling Lewis that he really had no further need of their services. But not far beneath the surface confidence it was obvious that the guides had no desire to run into a hostile war party. They warned Lewis particularly of the fearsome Pahkees.

The origins of the word *pahkee* are murky. One explanation is that it is a generic term that the northwestern tribes used to connote "enemy." But other scholars say it refers to one of the three tribes that made up the Blackfeet nation or confederacy, some identifying it with the Siksika, or Northern Blackfeet, and others with the Piegans.[1] Pahkee, Piegan, Piedgan, Piikani, Peekanow, Pekan, Pikenow, Pekannekoon, Pikiraminiaouch, etc. The common root, *pa'kskikaho*, apparently means a muddy place. In Cree, *pikan* or *pikakamiw*, muddy or turbid water. Thus, to the early fur traders, the Muddy River Indians. John Ewers, the authoritative modern historian of the Blackfeet, offers a different explanation. Piegan (Pay-gán): a people who possessed poorly dressed or torn robes.² The trappers who encountered the Blackfeet in the field had their own term for the tribe—Bug's Boys. Bug, that is, as in the Devil.³

From the descriptions he heard of the tribe, Lewis formed the clear impression that "they are a vicious lawless and reather abandoned set of wretches. I wish to avoid an interview with them if possible."

In exploring the Marias River, Lewis was acting on Jefferson's desire to fix the boundary of upper Louisiana as far to the north as possible, in order to assert American dominance over the lucrative fur trade and compete with the British for access to the Columbia, by way of which all those glossy beaver skins would make their way to the markets of Asia. The 1783 Treaty of Paris had set the borderline between the newly independent nation and the British possessions at 49° 37' N.⁴ But could it be pushed 23 minutes farther north? Did the headwaters of the Marias, or any of its tributaries, extend to the 50th parallel? Answering that question would almost inevitably present the opportunity, perhaps even the necessity, of an interview with the Blackfeet.

"The whole face of the country as far as the eye can reach looks like a well shaved bowlinggreen," Lewis wrote as they trekked up the valley of the Marias, "in which immence herds of buffaloe were seen feeding attended by their scarcely less numerous sheepherds the wolves."⁵ This was what the Blackfeet called the "Ground-of-Many-Gifts," carpeted with grass, timothy, and blue grama for grazing, and home not only to buffalo and wolves but to prairie chickens, jackrabbits, wild turkeys, prairie dogs, bears, antelope, foxes, beavers, and otters.⁶

The trip was already attended by troubling omens. There were horrendous swarms of mosquitos on the Missouri. On the Sun River, seven of Lewis's seventeen horses were stolen by Indians. As a result, he had not only split his party in two as planned; he had set off up the Marias with only three companions instead of six—Drouillard/Drulyard/Drewyer as translator, and the Field brothers, Joseph and Reubin, both expert woodsmen and hunters, good with a gun. At every hazard, indeed. *Reckless* would be a better word, because they were now in Piegan country.

The Piegans had the most southerly range of the three Blackfeet tribes—roughly between the Milk and Teton rivers—and they were known to range very far indeed, once they had horses. Some versions have them traveling as far south as Taos and Santa Fe, even into Old Mexico proper, and as far north as the Yukon.[7] They boasted of having "the best legs in the mountains."[8] They roamed routinely in the country between the Three Forks and the upper Yellowstone in search of beaver.

The Piegans were especially renowned for their aggressiveness, but the other two Blackfeet tribes also had a sanguinary reputation, as the name of one—the Bloods or Kainah ("many chiefs")—suggests.[9] The German explorer Prince Maximilian von Wied, visiting the northern plains in the 1830s, said they acquired this name after returning blood-smeared from a massacre of Kutenai. Others offer a more mundane explanation, that the Cree called them Bloods for their habit of painting their faces and robes with red earth. The name of the third tribe, the Siksika ("black-footed people") seems to be less controversial; it refers to the discoloration of their moccasins, either from deliberate blackening or from walking through the ashes of prairie fires.[10]

In appearance, the Blackfeet were impressive: "tall Apollos, with large eyes and straight black hair," which they often cut off, leaving only a thick scalp lock. Their faces were swarthy and weatherbeaten by the north wind. They plucked their beards meticulously. George Catlin painted a Piegan warrior named Eagle Ribs, whom he encountered at the fur-trading post of Fort McKenzie, near the mouth of the Marias, in 1832. He is captured in a belligerent stance, one arm crooked on his hip, the other hand holding a decorated lance and a pair of medicine bundles. He wears a painted shirt decorated with the scalps of eight white men. Blackfeet women were also renowned for their handsome looks, despite being "inclined to corpulence."[11]

At the time of Lewis's arrival in the Blackfeet country, the three tribes numbered around fifteen thousand. The Piegans were the largest, having finally rebounded from a devastating epidemic of smallpox—the "white scabs"—which they contracted during a raid on a Shoshone camp in 1781.[12] Since then, the Piegans had decimated the Shoshone and driven them westward, deriding them as "miserable old women whom they could kill with sticks and stones."[13]

The young men were essentially beyond the control of their chiefs. The cult of the warrior, of the stealthy ambush and the commando-style raid, of revenge killings and mutilations (from which women and children were not exempt), was instilled early in young males. Older men and women might tire of these endless cycles of violence, which they could do little to stop, and crave restraint, collective security, and communal solidarity. This, however, was not an aspect of tribal life that white explorers and settlers often encountered or had much interest in hearing about.

Horses—"sky dogs" to the Piegans—were the key to their military dominance of the Northern Plains. Buffalo runners and warhorses brought status and economic security. They were the bride price, the favored gift in religious ceremonies, the object of the raid. They brought young men the jolting adrenaline of the hunt. The uses of the buffalo they hunted are the stuff of legend. Food obviously—especially the hump and tongue, the meat eaten fresh or dried and mixed with berries, fat, and wild peppermint to make pemmican. But hides, skins, bones, horns, hair, sinews, internal organs, blood, and fat all had their uses, all the way down to the scrotum, which was used as a stirrup cover, and the penis, which was boiled to make glue.

As they advanced up the Marias, Lewis, Drouillard, and the Field brothers kept a nervous eye out for the terrible Pahkees. They passed the Piegans' favored winter campsites in the river hollows, where the bands would hunker down for months in temperatures that sometimes dropped below the point at which mercury freezes in the thermometer. Lewis was much impressed by their fortitude.

Where Cut Bank Creek and the Two Medicine River converge to form the Marias, the four men took the right-hand, northern fork, still heading for the elusive 50th parallel. But on the fifth day, July 21, it became obvious that Cut Bank Creek was trending west, even slightly south, as it emerged from the mountains that the Blackfeet called "the backbone of the world."[14] Lewis halted the march, demoralized. "I now have lost all hope of the waters of this river ever extending to N Latitude 50 degrees," he wrote. If manic depression helps explain his reckless exploration of the Marias, this place, which he called Camp Disappointment, was where his mood hit bottom. The weather was foul, cold, and rainy, and the lowering cloud cover made it impossible to determine his longitude with any accuracy. There was no food until the hunters managed to shoot down some passenger pigeons that flew over on July 24.

The little party stayed at Camp Disappointment for four days, every hour of which increased the risks of a hostile encounter. As they prepared to head back to the Missouri, Drouillard reported heavy Indian sign, including a campsite abandoned perhaps ten days earlier and trampled by large numbers of horses. Lewis wrote in his journal: "We consider ourselves extreemly fortunate in not having met with these people." This was a premature conclusion.

The events of the following evening, July 26, unspooled in cinematic fashion.

Lewis climbed to the top of a bluff overlooking the Two Medicine. Drouillard had gone ahead, following the river bottom. Suddenly Lewis saw a movement a mile away and grabbed his spyglass: a group of Indians, with thirty horses. They had not spotted him; they appeared to be watching Drouillard intently. "This was a very unpleasant sight," Lewis would write later, laconically. "From their known character I expected that we were to have some difficulty with them."[15]

However, Drouillard's exposed position ruled out any thoughts of concealment or evasion, so Lewis decided to put his best foot forward and approach the Indians in a friendly manner. Joseph Field displayed the American flag. The Indians milled around, chattering nervously. Lewis walked ahead alone to greet them. One of the Piegans rode forward, then wheeled around and galloped back to the group. More milling. Eventually there was a handshake. Lewis presented one of the young men with a peace medal, another with a flag, a third with a handkerchief. The medal bore the embossed likeness of Thomas Jefferson on one side, clasped hands and a crossed tomahawk and peace pipe on the reverse.

The conversation, mediated by Drouillard, took a friendlier turn after that, and the parties prepared a camp for the night on a narrow stretch of bottomland, beneath three large cottonwoods. The Field brothers would sleep on the ground by the campfire. The Piegans rigged up a rough shelter of skins, and Drouillard and Lewis bedded down with them. They talked late into the night, and the young men showed themselves to be "extreemly fond of smoking."

Over tobacco, each side learned more about the other. The Piegans— there were eight of them—were part of a larger party that was encamped on the Marias, half a day's ride away. Another large group was out hunting buffalo. These bands did a brisk trade with the British forts on the Saskatchewan, obtaining "arm amunition sperituous liquor blankets & c in exchange for wolves and some beaver skins." Lewis decided it was time to make his pitch or, more accurately, to drop his bombshell. He had been to the big waters where the sun sets and invited all the tribes he had met along the way to join him in a great trading alliance. He had restored intertribal peace and promised guns for self-protection. The same deal, augmented with gifts of tobacco and horses, was now on offer to these new friends. He asked them to pass along an invitation for their chiefs to visit the Great Father in Washington. The Shoshone and the Nez Perce, now united in friendship, were already among the lucky beneficiaries of this arrangement.

Telling someone that you have just agreed to arm and unite their mortal enemies is not generally the best way to win their trust. However, these particular Indians, who were very young and probably more interested in stealing horses and chasing girls than in realpolitik, said all the right things about wanting to live in peace and harmony and passed the pipe around some more. But no doubt they filed away the particulars of Lewis's pitch for a later report back to their tribal decision-makers.

In the gray light of dawn Lewis was awakened by a clamor of angry voices. Joseph Field, drowsy or complacent at the end of his watch, had laid his rifle down on the ground. One of the Indians had grabbed it, and he had Reubin's weapon, too. Another Piegan had seized Lewis's own rifle. Drouillard was struggling with a third, and Lewis heard him cry, "Damn you let go my gun!" The rest were making off with the horses, and Lewis understood immediately that losing them would be tantamount to a death sentence to four white men stranded without food or weapons in this hostile territory. The Field brothers gave chase to the man who had stolen their guns, and Joseph brought him down. It was the man to whom Lewis had given the medal the evening before. Before the thief could wriggle free, Reubin Field plunged a knife into his chest. He heard the breath whistle out through the man's punctured lung.

Lewis, who had retained his pistol, confronted the Piegan who was holding his rifle. He ordered the thief to drop it, and surprisingly the man did so. Drouillard wanted to shoot him on the spot, but Lewis said no. Instead, he concentrated on recovering the panicked horses, pursuing the rest of the thieves into one of the small box canyons, or "nitches," that cut into the steep bluffs. Trapped in the cul-de-sac, one of the Indians threw himself behind a mushroom-shaped rock and took aim at Lewis. But Lewis shot first, hitting the man—or boy, more likely—in the abdomen.[16] The Piegan fired back but missed. This was not surprising, since he was probably armed with a trade musket accurate only to a few yards. And besides, he had just been shot in the stomach. Even so, it was close, Lewis wrote: "[B]eing bearheaded I felt the wind of his bullet distinctly."

Did the young Piegan die? Certainly Lewis believed so. In a letter to an unsigned addressee, written two months after the event, he said his party "killed two of them."[17] And recall that in the Civil War, more than half a century later, abdominal gunshot wounds were notoriously fatal in the absence of field medicine. However, other sources say the evidence is inconclusive, and the victim himself has never been identified.[18]

About the second Indian there is less dispute. His name was He That Looks at a Calf, and he was assuredly dead.[19]

Back at the campfire, Lewis burned the Piegans' possessions—bows and arrows, buffalo-hide shields, and so forth—and rounded up some of their horses to supplement his own. He retrieved the American flag. But in a moment of taunting anger he left the Jefferson peace medal around the neck of He That Looks at a Calf, "that they might be informed who we were." And with that final gesture, Lewis, Drouillard, and the Field brothers galloped back to the Missouri, covering 120 fearful miles in 24 hours.

The incident on the headwaters of the Marias was the first ever armed conflict between official representatives of the U.S. government and the tribes of the Northern Plains,[20] and over the succeeding decades it passed into frontier mythology. Washington Irving started the legend in *Astoria,* his account, published in 1835, of John Jacob Astor and the Rocky Mountain fur trade. According to Irving, the Blackfeet "conceived an implacable hostility to the white men, in consequence of one of their warriors being killed by Captain Lewis."

In fact, it may not have been the killing itself that accounted for the decades of rage that ensued. Killings were a fact of life. You lost one, you killed one or more of theirs in return. In truth the skin color of the adversary in itself made very little difference. The larger source of the enduring hostility was the plan that Lewis had laid out to the Piegans in camp that night: an end to the Blackfeet monopoly on firearms and an alliance between the whites and the tribes on the far side of the divide, all in the context of an American-dominated trading alliance on the Northern Plains.

Lewis's plan set in motion a long and complex chain of events that would culminate only in the winter of 1870, with another, much more serious encounter, just a few miles away on the same Marias River, between another band of Piegans and another explorer—but this time accompanied by the full might of the U.S. Cavalry. And that final outburst of violence would in turn clear the path for white men at last to penetrate the long-rumored mysteries of the upper Yellowstone.

3

ALL FOR A BEAVER HAT[1]

1807–1810

Those who executed Lewis's plan for a great fur-trading empire were men of almost unfathomable physical hardiness, ingenuity, instinct, and self-reliance, men whose lives intersected at every turn—through competition, battle, death, and even sometimes marriage—with the world of the Piegans.

Jim Bridger was the greatest of them, and among all the mountain men of the West only Kit Carson (with whom Bridger traveled often) could match his reputation. Born in 1804, the son of a tavern-keeper, Bridger had been an illiterate teenaged roustabout on the St. Louis waterfront, and until the end of his life an "X" was the best he could manage by way of signature. But his eyes strayed constantly up the sluggish Missouri to the country that Lewis and Clark had explored, and in time he came to know it better than any man alive.

Even before Bridger, there was John Colter, a veteran of the Corps of Discovery, the man who had stood up to the tomahawk thief during Lewis's furious and almost fatal encounter with the Chinooks. Even though his three-year enlistment still had two months to run, Colter asked permission to leave the party just five days after Lewis and Clark joined forces again at the Great Falls of the Missouri. On the morning of the reunion, Lewis encountered two trappers heading upriver. Colter liked the sound of their plans, and on August 17, 1806, the captains granted his request for an early discharge.

Colter was seldom mentioned in the early volumes of Lewis and Clark's journals, and the few references are less than flattering. The captains described him as a barely literate Virginian, a drunk, with a tendency to disputatiousness and violence. In March 1804, even before the expedition set off, he was confined to quarters for ten days for going AWOL. This turned out to be on account of a bender at a whiskey shop on the disreputable outskirts of St. Louis. But in later journal entries the picture softened, and it became apparent that Colter merited respect, especially as a hunter of uncommon skill.

By the time he took to the fur trade, everyone seemed to admire him. He was described by a fellow trapper as being five feet ten inches tall, with "an open, ingenious (sic), and pleasing countenance of the Daniel Boone type. Nature had formed him, like Boone, for hardy indurance of fatigue, privations, and perils."[2] One of his biographers, a man with a florid pen, calls him a "Ulysses of the Rockies . . . driven by some overmastering power, some irresistible daemon of adventure."[3] Yet elsewhere he is spoken of as "a shy, quiet, and reserved man who had little to say about anything."[4]

In the winter of 1807–1808, in the employ of a St. Louis fur trader named Manuel Lisa, Colter embarked on an epic solo journey. As an "expectant capitalist,"[5] which William Clark was not, he followed the path that Clark had declined to take, into the valley of the upper Yellowstone. Where he went exactly cannot be ascertained. He was not a diarist or a thinker or an emissary of the president. He was just a man looking for beaver, which were all the rage in those days in London, Paris, and New York for the making of hats for gentlemen of the upper crust. But Colter did leave enigmatic, if debatable, marks of his passage that were found decades later, and back in St. Louis in 1808 he gave Clark some rudiments of a map of his travels.

Manuel Lisa intended to be the first to reap the profits of the fur trade on the upper Missouri, sustained by a network of purchased tribal loyalties. In the spring of 1807 he assembled a party of forty-two men, guided by George Drouillard. Colter joined the group after a chance encounter on the Platte River, and with these two veterans to guide him, Lisa opened a trading post in October of that year on the Yellowstone, at the mouth of the Bighorn. (Clark had made a note as he passed the spot: "Good place for fort here & c and here the beaver country begins.") Lewis, who had done business with the Spaniard, heartily detested him. In fact, pretty much everyone seems to have detested Lisa. Quarrelsome, greedy, dark-humored, unprincipled, he appears to have had virtually no redeeming qualities as a human being, though many as a businessman.

Lisa's party was in Crow country now, and over the winter months he dispatched Colter and Drouillard as emissaries to inform that tribe and any others they might meet that his fort was open for business. Lewis's encounter on the Marias had established a principle that would define the century: Exploration plus "civilization" leads to violence. Over the ensuing three years, Lisa's overtures to the Crows would take this logic to the next level. This was what happened when white men made pacts with the enemies of the Blackfeet, which was another way of saying just about every other Indian within a three-hundred-mile radius.

So John Colter, carrying his thirty-pound pack of trade goods, traveled into the Crow lands to make friends. In the country flanked by the Bighorns and the Absarokas, the Crows believed that the First Maker had given them the most beautiful place on earth, fertile, rich in game of all kinds, with snowy mountains and sun-drenched plains and a healthy and varied climate.[6] How they came here is a matter of conjecture.[7] Sometime between 1500 and 1700 they split from the Hidatsa of North Dakota, who were sedentary agriculturalists, and began two waves of westward migration. The reasons for the split are obscure. One theory is that it arose from a dispute between two squaws over who would get the half-digested vegetable stomach contents of a buffalo. Improbable as it sounds, this appears to have been a prized delicacy. Crow oral tradition says that the migration then followed a large, counterclockwise sweep through Alberta to the Great Salt Lake and thence to the Bighorns, passing through a place "where there is fire," which another ethnohistorian refers to as "land-of-the-burning-ground." The upper Yellowstone? Perhaps.

Somewhere along the way the Crows encountered the French and acquired horses, which gave them the means of hunting buffalo on the Montana plains and thus created an immediate point of friction with the Blackfeet. The Crows had two names for their new white acquaintances. One was *Beta-awka-wahcha*, or Sits on the Water, for the inordinate amount of time these eccentric newcomers spent in canoes. The other was *Mah-ish-ta-schee-da*—Yellow Eyes, perhaps because the first white man they encountered was suffering from jaundice.[8] The French in turn called them *les beaux hommes* or *gens des corbeaux*—People of the Crow. In fact this is a mistranslation of the tribe's own name for itself—*Apsáalooke*, or children of the large-beaked bird, later rendered by the whites as Absaroka. Thus the Absaroka mountains, the snow-laden peaks that Clark had described when he arrived at the big bend of the Yellowstone. The sobriquet of *beaux hommes* also stuck; Crow men were "decidedly prepossessing," wrote one mid-nineteenth-century trader, "perhaps the handsomest body of Indians in North America. They are tall, straight, well-formed, with bold, fierce eyes, and as usual good teeth." The men were also notorious dandies, with extravagant costumes and body paint, and pompadours raised high and shiny with bear grease.

Colter's route has been endlessly debated, on the basis of much conjecture and little hard evidence. Eventually, when he returned to St. Louis, both he and Drouillard passed on data from their travels to William Clark, though his celebrated 1810 and 1814 maps, with a chicken-scratch line marking Colter's journey, raise more questions than answers. The consensus is that he traveled in a large figure eight, the western portion being much the larger. Over the Pryor Mountains to the Sunlight Basin and the forks of the Shoshone River, which the Indians called the Stinkingwater, and south to the Wind River Valley, a favorite wintering spot of the Crows. From there westward to Jackson Hole and the three Tetons, the first white man to see either. A little back-and-forth along the upper Snake River, then northeast to Yellowstone Lake, and after that, with an Indian guide or two along the way no doubt, Crow or Shoshone, down and across the Yellowstone River, along an old Indian trail to the broad Lamar Valley, Soda Butte Creek, the Clark's Fork of the Yellowstone, and back again via the Stinkingwater and the Sunlight Basin to Lisa's fort at the mouth of the Bighorn. Or vice versa. Whether Colter traveled clockwise or counter-clockwise is unknowable; there are no directional arrows on Clark's maps.

How much did Colter see of the fantastic landscapes of the upper Yellowstone? There is no evidence that he passed through the main geyser basins.[9] William Goetzmann thinks he followed the west bank of the Yellowstone almost as far north as Mammoth Hot Springs and then turned east up the Lamar Valley. How and where he crossed the thunderous river is not explained. Aubrey Haines, the national park's own longtime historian, is categorical, arguing that a notation on Clark's map—"Hot Springs Brimstone"—can refer only to the sulfur beds at Tower Fall and "leaves little doubt that John Colter passed that way."[10] Robert Utley agrees that the Virginian "became the first white man to explore part of what later fell within Yellowstone National Park" and that he "probably marveled at the giant chasms and falls of the Yellowstone River." *Probably.* More recent historians continue to debate the matter with inconclusive passion.

Two pieces of physical evidence add a little to the story, though only indirectly, since both were found outside the western boundary of the park. In 1889 a group of three hunting guides—including one with the novelistic name of Tazewell Woody, who later guided Teddy Roosevelt in the Rockies—scraped the bark off a large pine tree near the mouth of the present-day Coulter Creek, a tributary of the Snake River, and uncovered a carved "X," five inches high, and below that the smaller initials "J. C."[11] Woody and his companions reported their find to the government, who promptly chopped down the tree, considered putting it in a museum, and then somehow contrived to lose it. Then, in 1931, a father and son clearing timber near the Wyoming-Idaho state line, about twenty miles north of Teton Pass, unearthed a piece of weathered rhyolite, carved into the rough shape of a human head in profile and inscribed on one side "1808" and on the other "John Colter." Such things always carry the scent of a hoax, but the rhyolite story at least appears to stand up to scrutiny.[12]

That just leaves the legend of "Colter's Hell." The trapper himself didn't coin this term; again it was Washington Irving, the tale-spinner. In his 1837 *Adventures of Captain Bonneville*, Irving concocted the story that Colter, traveling along the Stinkingwater, "gave such an account of its gloomy terrors, its hidden fires, smoking pits, noxious streams, and the all-pervading 'smell of brimstone' that it received, and has ever since retained among trappers, the name of Colter's Hell." This appears to be a story from whole cloth, though it is correct in one particular: The location of Colter's Hell is an area of thermal activity on the Shoshone River, west of the present-day city of Cody, Wyoming, partly submerged today beneath the waters of the Buffalo Bill Reservoir.

A more curious aspect of Colter's Hell is that the legend was later elaborated on by someone who should have known better. In 1895, the engineer and army officer Hiram Chittenden, in one of the first significant book-length accounts of Yellowstone, decided to appropriate Colter's gloomy terrors as part of the creation myth of the national park. Chittenden wrote that "Colter's description" (or, more accurately, Irving's invention) "undoubtedly referred in large part to what he saw in the Yellowstone and Snake River Valleys." In the 1930s Colter's biographer, the one with the florid pen, took matters a step further. Irving had it wrong, he said. The hidden fires and noxious pits weren't on the Stinkingwater at all, but in the volcanic caldera of the Yellowstone.[13] All this nonsense is long discredited, but creation myths are tenacious things, and casual journalists continued for decades to equate Colter's Hell with Yellowstone.

I n the spring or early summer of 1808, John Colter came upon a band of several hundred Flatheads and/or Crows in the Gallatin Valley. About fifteen miles south of Three Forks, a huge war party of Blackfeet materialized and attacked them. Colter was severely wounded in the leg but managed to take cover in a thicket and hold off his assailants with

rifle fire. How were the Blackfeet to interpret this but as a serious provocation, and in many respects a more flagrant one than Lewis's skirmish
with the Piegans two years earlier? A group of four white men traveling
on their own and responding to the theft of their weapons and horses
was one thing; a white man fighting on the same side as a mortal enemy
was another.

Matters quickly went from bad to worse. Later that summer, Colter was
trapping beaver along the Jefferson River with an old comrade from the
Corps of Discovery, John Potts. This was an arduous business, even in summertime temperatures: Wade into the target area to avoid leaving a scent,
plant a submerged steel trap, fix a chain to it, attach the chain to a stake
plunged firmly into the riverbed, bait the trap with an overhanging stick
smeared with castoreum, the oily, yellow-orange-brown, bitter-smelling
substance that is secreted by a pair of glands between the animal's anus and
genitals. And wait.

Colter and Potts were engaged in these toilsome operations when they
heard a loud drumming sound. Potts identified this as a herd of buffalo.
Unfortunately he was mistaken. It was another war party of Blackfeet,
several hundred strong.

There are two accounts of what ensued, varying slightly in their particulars.[14] The Blackfeet ordered the two trappers ashore and told them to
strip naked. Colter complied. Potts accused him of cowardice, probably
the first time anyone had made that charge. Potts remained in his canoe,
so the warriors shot and wounded him. When he fired back, "he was made
a riddle of"—Colter's words. Alternatively, Potts *did* come ashore as ordered. Colter grabbed his gun, then tossed it back to Potts, at which point
the Indians let loose with bows and arrows. The outcome was the same: a
riddle.

The Blackfeet then hacked Potts's dead body to pieces, ripped out his
heart, lungs, and entrails, and flung them in Colter's face. Colter stood
there naked and bespattered with blood while the chief of the party considered how the warriors might have more sport with their second captive
than they had had with the first. Again the two versions diverge slightly.
Either Colter was told to walk away, and the Indians' purpose only

dawned on him slowly, or the chief asked him if he was a fast runner, and Colter, sensing what was afoot, lied and said no. Whichever is the case, once he had a decent head start the Blackfeet came sprinting after him en masse. Colter kept his lead for six miles over a prairie of prickly pear cactus, until his tormentors' lead runner was close on his heels. Then Colter halted abruptly and turned to face his attacker, who stumbled in his surprise and snapped his spear. Colter seized the business end and plunged it into the Indian.

With the rest of the party still in pursuit, and blood now streaming from his nose, Colter made a final dash for the Jefferson, plunged in, and swam either into a beaver lodge or beneath a mat of driftwood. His pursuers reached the spot, prowled around on the bank, even walked out onto the driftwood or beaver lodge to search the water, while Colter observed them through cracks in the branches. He stayed in the water all night until finally they abandoned the search. It is easy to imagine their rage at this point, to have been outsmarted twice in a matter of months by this same apparently indestructible white man.

Stark naked—or perhaps carrying a blanket taken from the man he had killed—John Colter set off for home. He walked for seven days, or perhaps it was eleven, subsisting on a starchy tuberous root called *Psoralea esculenta*, or prairie turnip, until he reached Lisa's fort, some 250 miles distant.

How much of this is real and how much embroidered? After all, we have only Colter's word for it, and some of the details feel like a stretch. But the story became one more compelling addition to the mythology of the West. Memory, as they say, always smiles on the highest bidder.

Colter's trapping adventures lasted for two more years, until the spring of 1810, when Lisa built a second fort at the confluence of the Jefferson and Madison rivers, in the richest part of the beaver country. This decision was equal parts reckless and naïve: reckless for obvious reasons, naïve because Lisa still seemed to harbor some notion of engaging in friendly trade with the Blackfeet.

He should have been disabused of this idea when the Blackfeet killed and mutilated two more trappers that April, members of a party of eighteen that again included Colter. This was enough for the Virginian, who declared, "Now if God will only forgive me this time and let me off I *will* leave the country day after tomorrow—and be damned if I ever come into it again." George Drouillard, however, refused to back down. Indeed he only became more audacious, asserting that the best way to catch beaver was to go out on your own. "I am too much of an Indian to be caught by Indians," he said. This philosophy served him well on the first two occasions, but not on the third. A party of trappers who still believed in safety in numbers discovered Drouillard's body on the trail, disemboweled, decapitated, and dismembered.[15]

After Colter retreated to St. Louis and gave his account of events, Reuben Lewis reported to his brother, Meriwether, that it was "probably impossible to trap on this river"—presumably meaning the Jefferson. "We have already lost 5 men to this Nation [the Blackfeet] and I fear for the lives of those who are going to try the experiment again."

Yet even with Drouillard dead and Colter back in St. Louis (where he died, perhaps of jaundice, soon after serving in the War of 1812), the experiment continued. Even as it wove the imperatives of economic expansion, exploration, and violence more tightly together, the pursuit of *Castor canadensis* was simply too lucrative to be abandoned.

4

THE BIG KNIVES

1811–1840

From St. Louis, men fanned out across the northern Rockies in pursuit of beaver and in search of a passage across the continent easier than the one discovered by Lewis and Clark, and preferably free of the ferocious Blackfeet. After 1811 many of them entered into the employ of John Jacob Astor, the German immigrant who had begun his career by opening a fur shop in New York and went on to become the richest man in America.

The Astorians threaded their way through the highest passes in the Absarokas, the Wind River Mountains, the Gros Ventre Range. Arduous passages led them to the raging canyons of the Snake River, the rich valleys of the upper Green River, the fertile expanses of Jackson Hole and Pierre's Hole, and the three abrupt peaks that they called the Pilot Knobs but later would be known as the Tetons. The name is something of a mystery.[1] Nothing could less resemble the shape of a woman's breast—a *téton*—given by legend to these sawtooth mountains by French trappers, who were presumably both imaginative and homesick for the real thing. It is strikingly similar, however, to the Shoshone word *Teewinot*, or "many pinnacles," the modern name for the sixth highest mountain in the Teton range.

The fact that these early trappers never stumbled upon the volcanic

caldera of the upper Yellowstone seems almost perverse. They reached
the perimeter; they could hardly have come closer. On more than one occasion, a right turn rather than a left would have brought them there—
due north along the Snake, rather than west across the Teton Pass by a
well-trodden Indian trail; or an equally straightforward route north from
Pierre's Hole across the Targhee Pass, one of the gentler crossings of the
Continental Divide, and from there up the Madison River. But none of
them ever penetrated the upper Yellowstone; perhaps it was fear of the
Blackfeet that dictated all those left turns and about-faces.

By the end of the 1820s the beaver trade was dominated by two big
companies, locked in increasingly bitter competition. The more formal of
the two, with an infrastructure of forts, trading posts, salaried officials,
and regional divisions, was Astor's American Fur Company; the other
operated on a looser business model and went by a variety of names and
shifts in ownership until eventually it became the Rocky Mountain Fur
Company. It was the brainchild of the lieutenant governor of Missouri,
William H. Ashley, and its distinctive feature was the unengaged "free
trapper."

In March 1822, Ashley posted a notice in St. Louis, asking for a hundred
"enterprising young men" to join his adventure. The volunteers included an
orphan-turned-ferryman-turned-blacksmith's apprentice-turned-keelboat
hand who answered to the name of Jim Bridger. At seventeen, Bridger was
shy and withdrawn, embarrassed by his lack of education, and uncomfortable with the other, more rambunctious rivermen. But he had learned one
vital skill in the blacksmith's shop: "A gun to him," says his first biographer,
"was as personal as a jacket."[2]

During his first journeys up the Missouri, Bridger began to display
the qualities that defined his life, an unusual mixture of natural deference to his superiors and easy command of his subordinates. Somewhere
along the way, he acquired a nickname—"Old Gabe." The man who gave
it to him was another of Ashley's recruits, a cerebral twenty-two-year-old
New Yorker named Jedediah Smith ("the knight in buckskin"), who carried a Wesleyan hymnal wherever he went. What Smith had in mind, it
seems, was Bridger's resemblance to the Angel Gabriel, who "had the

mythical duty of revealing Jehovah's will and purpose."[3] Despite their
differences of personality, education, and background, the men shared two
things in common: They were as much explorers as trappers, and both
were instinctive cartographers. As a kind of unlettered polymath, strad-
dling the next four and a half decades as fur trapper, hunter, guide, army
scout, Indian fighter, and explorer and mapper of new territories, Bridger
had no equal.

A friend described Bridger, once he had shed his youthful shyness, as

> . . . a very companionable man. In person he was over six feet
> tall, spare, straight as an arrow, agile, rawboned and of power-
> ful frame, eyes gray, hair brown and abundant even in old age,
> expression mild, and manners agreeable. He was hospitable
> and generous, and he was always trusted and respected.[4]

Another contemporary adds that he was

> a model for a sculptor or painter, by which to express the per-
> fection of graceful strength and easy activity. . . . To sum up, his
> bravery was unquestionable, his horsemanship equally so, and
> as to his skill with the rifle, it will scarcely be doubted, when we
> mention the fact that he had been known to kill twenty buffa-
> loes by the same number of consecutive shots.[5]

Among white men, the fur trappers had this country to themselves, for a
military exploration in 1820 had concluded that the land between the
Platte River and the Canadian border, and from Iowa to the Rockies, was
unfit for human habitation, worthless for agriculture. There would be no
officially sanctioned settlement of the West, not yet.

There may have been a thousand trappers altogether. The majority
were Canadian, French-Canadian, or Creole. Perhaps a quarter were
Americans. They made a striking picture: skeletal horse, saddle blanket,
beaver traps, smelly containers of castoreum, buffalo robe, leggings, leather
breeches, fur cap, moccasins, hatchet, powder horn, bullet pouch, and gun.

They lived on meat, unsalted, boiled, roasted or raw, as much as ten pounds of it a day when the hunting was good—buffalo, beaver, brown bear, grizzly bear, deer, elk, pronghorn antelope, mountain sheep. They were always in debt. For protection against the Blackfeet they sought safety in numbers, traveling in loose packs of forty to sixty men.

The Rocky Mountain Fur Company, established in 1830 by five men including Jim Bridger, lost seventy men in twelve years.[6] A grizzly bear pounced on Jedediah Smith on the Powder River, at the edge of the Crow country, threw him to the ground, smashed his ribs, clawed his head, scarred him for life. "This gave us a lisson on the charcter of the grissly Baare which we did not forget," wrote James Clyman, who sewed him up. Having survived that encounter, Smith finally succumbed in 1831 to a party of Comanches on the Santa Fe Trail.

Traveling in company with Bridger, Hugh Glass of the American Fur Company bumped into a grizzly sow even more ferocious than Smith's. He was "tore nearly to peases," said Daniel Potts, and left to die by his companions. But Glass managed to crawl two hundred miles to Fort Kiowa on the Missouri, surviving on roots and marrow from the bones of a dead buffalo and bent on revenge against those who had abandoned him. The episode left a rare stain on Bridger's character, since he had been part of that group. But while he remained enraged at the others, Glass decided to forgive Bridger on grounds of his youth, and perhaps in recognition of the basic decency of his character.

For as long as they survived, the mountain men mapped the West in ways both formal and informal; they made overnight fortunes and lost them just as quickly; and they gathered each summer for an annual "rendezvous." The first of these was in 1825. Presided over by Ashley, it was held on the Henry's Fork of the Snake River, which they called Randavouze Creek. After that the location varied from one year to the next, the preferred spots being the valleys of the upper Green River, the Wind River, and the Popo Agie, and Pierre's Hole on the west side of the Tetons. The numbers attending the rendezvous swelled from one year to the next. Trappers brought their pelts; traders from St. Louis brought supplies for the following season. The mountain men held horse-riding and target-shooting contests, drank themselves unconscious on medicine water, howled at the moon, gambled away their money, and told campfire tales that no one believed but equally no one could disprove.[7] After this annual bacchanal, which could last for weeks or even months, they rode their hangovers back into the mountains for another year of living by their wits.

Stories of the trappers' adventures, and of the vast herds of big game in the northern Rockies, even spread to the European aristocracy. Jim Bridger offered himself as a guide to the first and most celebrated of these visiting sportsmen. For several seasons in the 1830s, Sir William Drummond Stewart, son of the 17th Lord of Grandtully and 5th Baronet of Murthly Castle in Perthshire, Scotland, a man with an outsize nose, a weak mouth, and an Errol Flynn mustache, attached himself to the Rocky Mountain Fur Company.[8] Sir William had come to America after impregnating a maid and falling out with his brother, who had inherited their late father's titles and estates. He traveled with three manservants, two dogs, and wagons laden with canned meats and sardines, plum pudding, preserved fruits, coffee, fine tobacco, cheeses, and a selection of brandies, whiskey, and wines. At the 1837 rendezvous, he presented Jim Bridger with the full dress uniform of Britain's elite Life Guards regiment, which included a steel cuirass and white-plumed helmet. Bridger put it on over his buckskins and rode up and down. The reactions of the trappers and the Indians in attendance may be imagined.[9]

Indians came to the rendezvous for the first time in 1826, Nez Perce and Shoshone for the most part, and then Flatheads, all bringing their women and children. In their full immersion in the wilderness, the trappers took the Native Americans as their teachers and role models. Many took Indian wives, and if they didn't take wives they took short-term substitutes. Joe Meek, "the wittiest, saltiest, and most shameless wag and jester that ever wore moccasins in the Rockies," married the daughter of a Nez Perce chief. Jim Bridger married three times—first a daughter of a Flathead chief, then an Ute whose name is lost to us, and finally Little Fawn, also known as Mary, daughter of the celebrated Shoshone chief Washakie.

Bridger was a master of sign language and spoke Blackfoot and Crow. The Crows are said to have given him the name of Blanket Chief, either because his Flathead wife had made him a multicolored one to use on special occasions or, more prosaically, because he was just a man in charge of some blankets. It was the Crows who showed him the way to the South Pass, of which he was the joint discoverer in 1824. Hooking around the southern tip of the Wind River Range, this would become the key to the Oregon Trail and the great westward migration. Later that year Bridger was the first European-American to record the existence of the Great Salt Lake.

The web of social and economic relationships forged at the rendez-vous between the trappers and the Crows and the Nez Perce, the Sho-shone and the Flatheads, could only be taken by the Blackfeet as a further declaration of hostile intent. Having said which, it has to be acknowl-edged that there was a double-edged quality to the attitude of the Black-feet, and particularly of the Piegans, toward the "Big Knives," as they called the white interlopers.[10] In 1830, a certain Kenneth McKenzie—there were many transplanted Scots among these people—overcame his trepidation and sent a delegation up the Marias River, retracing Meriwether Lewis's journey until he arrived, whether he knew it or not, within a mile or two of Camp Disappointment. The Piegans had not seen any white men in this area for a quarter of a century, but the group McKenzie eventually encountered on Badger Creek turned out to be surprisingly amiable. Al-low the American Fur Company to build a fort at the mouth of the Ma-rias, he proposed; in return there would be gifts and trade goods. When the Piegans arrived at the appointed spot, they found a stockaded post al-ready in place. The gifts pleased them, especially the two hundred gallons of whiskey, enough for three days in an alcoholic haze. The trader James Kipp—a name later famous in the Blackfeet country—called the place Fort Piegan.[11]

So it was not a case of blind hatred toward the Big Knives. The Black-feet had already come to a modus vivendi with the Canadian and British traders on the northern side of the line—the "Real Old Man People." Now a similar arrangement was worked out with the trading posts of the

American Fur Company on the upper Missouri—Fort McKenzie, Fort Union, and eventually the most important of them all, Fort Benton. Food, guns, ammunition, and kegs of white men's water flowed in one direction; from the other came peltry of all sorts—not just beaver, but pronghorn, bear, deer, elk, fox, marten, mink, otter, skunk, wildcat, wolf, and buffalo robes. The first intermarriages followed, often accompanied by gifts of prize horses to influential local chiefs.

Static trading posts offering mutual benefit were one thing. The roaming mountain men were another. With hindsight it isn't hard to see how cooperation at one end of the economic food chain led to violence at the other. The trade in furs gave the Piegans a level of material security their ancestors had never imagined. Prosperity meant horses, which meant mobility. Greater mobility brought more opportunities for commando raids and horse theft. More horses, more military prowess, a continuing cycle of territorial expansion, until ever-larger Blackfeet hunting parties were ranging far to the south, beyond the Three Forks country and into the uppermost reaches of the Yellowstone, the "land of many smokes," where they encountered the Big Knives at work, hand in glove with the tribe's historic enemies and competing directly for control of the richest beaver streams. This was intolerable. The attitude of the Blackfeet was put concisely to the Indian agent John Sanford in 1832: "If you will send Traders into our Country we will protect them & treat them well; but for Trappers—Never."[12]

The Astorians had never found the upper Yellowstone, but Jim Bridger and his cohort did. He got there for the first time in 1825 or 1826, when he was still only twenty-one years old, and returned at least eight and perhaps nine times over the next quarter of a century. Twice, in 1834 and again in 1850, he came in company with Kit Carson. The upper Yellowstone was not a prime trapping destination. The climate was too cold, the season too short, the beaver too few, their skins of inferior quality.[13] But at least a few men went there each year, spurred in the first instance by the tales that Bridger told and then by the accounts that circled around the campfire, dressed up with bells and whistles, at each year's rendez-vous. And by the time the beaver boom ended in 1840 the trappers had seen, described, and at least in crude fashion mapped every one of the region's salient features—Yellowstone Lake, the Grand Canyon, the Up-per and Lower Falls, the main geyser basins, the Lamar Valley, and Mam-moth Hot Springs, which some of them called the Sulphur Mountain.

The first written account dates from 1827, in the form of a letter from Daniel Potts, one of the original Ashley expedition, to his brother in Pennsylvania. Potts, "dayly harrased by the Black-feet," went first to the West Thumb of Yellowstone Lake, where he felt a "tremendious trem-bling" of the earth, heard "an explosion . . . resembling that of thunder," and saw boiling springs "of most beautiful fine clay . . . throw[ing] particles to the height of from twenty to thirty feet." Journeying upriver "for the purpose of accumalating a few more Bever . . . we were met plumb in the face by a large party of Black-feet Indians." In another encounter, a much bigger group of Blackfeet opened fire on the trappers' camp, killing three friendly Shoshone who were accompanying them.[14]

More narratives followed. In 1833, Warren Angus Ferris, an articulate New Yorker working for the American Fur Company, rode with two Pend d'Oreilles—close relatives of the friendly Flatheads—into what must have been one of the geyser basins. "When I arose in the morning," he wrote, "clouds of vapor seemed like a dense fog to overhang the springs, from which frequent reports or explosions of different loudness, constantly as-sailed our ears."[15] Along with his diaries, Ferris also drew a remarkably accurate and well-proportioned map of his travels, on which he marked Yellowstone Lake, the Madison and Gallatin rivers, the "Burnt Hole" and "Volcanoes."[16]

The most lyrical record was left by Osborne Russell of Maine, who made five trips to Yellowstone until he, too, was set upon by a ferocious group of Piegans on Pelican Creek, a tributary of Yellowstone Lake, barely escaping with his life. In 1835 Russell wrote of the Lamar Valley,

> There is something in the wild romantic scenery of this valley which I cannot nor will I attempt to describe; but the impres-

sions made upon my mind while gazing from a high eminence on the surrounding landscape one evening as the sun was gently gliding behind the western mountain and casting its gigantic shadows across the vale were such as time can never efface from my memory.

While Russell's descriptions had the ring of Keats and Wordsworth, it was the "shameless wag and jester" Joe Meek who left the most melodramatic accounts. Like Daniel Potts, Meek was on the run from the Blackfeet. In the summer of 1829, at the age of nineteen, he joined a party of trappers on the Popo Agie River, on the headwaters of the Bighorn, at the first of two rendezvous that were held that summer. From there the group went west to the Henry's Fork of the Snake River, joining forces with Bridger and Jedediah Smith. Somewhere on the Henry's Fork the party was attacked by a large band of Piegans. Several horses were lost, several men wounded. William Sublette, another of the principals of the Rocky Mountain Fur Company, led part of the group north into the Gallatin Valley, then crossed the mountains to the Yellowstone. Confident that they had shaken off the Piegans, Sublette decided to pitch camp and rest up on a flat piece of ground between the river and the curious rock formation that was first known as Red Streak Mountain but would later be called the Devil's Slide. But here the Piegans attacked again, this time killing two trappers.

In the confusion of flight, young Joe Meek became separated from the rest of the party. He struck out to the south again, upriver, looking for a way back to the Bighorns and the hospitable lodges of the Crows. He found the trail his companions had taken but kept his distance from it, fearful of attack or detection. For the same reason he resolved not to fire his gun or light a fire, even though it was November now, and snow was falling. He trudged on through "the horrible and monotonous solitude of the wilderness," feeling that "the bravest man is wretchedly nervous in the solitary presence of sublime nature."

On the fourth morning, Meek ascended a mountain to orient himself. The whole country spread out beneath him seemed to be burning, with countless craters spouting steam and throwing off (at least in Meek's hyperactive imagination) blue flames and molten brimstone. "The morning being clear," a nineteenth-century author wrote, "he thought himself reminded of the city of Pittsburgh as he had seen it on a winter morning a couple of years before."[17]

Meek made it home safely, but the hostile encounters with the Blackfeet continued. (Not that the belligerence was all one-sided. The trappers had moved aggressively into an area that they knew was highly prized by the Blackfeet, and Kit Carson recalled that, "[W]e determined to trap wherever we pleased, even if we had to fight for the right.")[18] In October 1832, Jim Bridger himself survived one of the worst attacks. It came on top of the most violent summer yet. The rendezvous was in Pierre's Hole that year, in the shadow of the Tetons. Furs were in increasingly short supply. The rivalry between the American and Rocky Mountain companies had turned ugly; they were competing with each other for the same beaver on the same streams, and everyone was competing with the Blackfeet. The rendezvous was the biggest yet—four hundred mountain men and almost two hundred lodges of Nez Perce and Flatheads. On July 18, a powerful force of Indians attacked the camp. They were actually Gros Ventres, the only close allies of the Blackfeet, but the trappers were not interested in such fine distinctions. Accounts of the battle of Pierre's Hole vary widely, but one widely circulated version has five trappers dead, seven Nez Perce, one man of mixed race, and twenty-six "Blackfeet."[19]

Three months later, on the headwaters of the Jefferson, a party of Blackfeet fell on a group of trappers that included the diarist Warren Ferris and a West Point–educated employee of the American Fur Company named William Henry Vanderburgh. Ferris took a bullet in the shoulder from "the lightning and thunder of at least twenty fusils." Vanderburgh was gunned down and his skull cleaved open with a hatchet. The Blackfeet then chopped off his arms, defleshed his body, and dumped the pieces in the river.[20]

Eleven days after that, another war party of one hundred—or perhaps it was the same one—encountered Bridger and his companions on the upper Madison. There were friendly overtures this time, it appears; a white flag, an offer to smoke. But whether intended or accidental (Bridger is said to have cocked his rifle at some hint of a threat), the encounter turned into another fight, and he came away from it with an arrow lodged in his back and another in his hip.[21] One of the arrowheads remained there as a souvenir until the rendezvous of 1835, when it was excavated by the celebrated missionary Marcus Whitman, who had come looking for Flatheads and Nez Perce who had yet to receive the blessings of Christianity.[22] The arrowhead measured three inches, a good deal of iron to carry around in the body for thirty-four months.

The remaining exchanges of violence between the Blackfeet and the Big Knives were more in the nature of a brutal postscript, followed by a twenty-year hiatus. Five trappers died in the course of a two-day siege of their corral at the northern end of Yellowstone Lake in 1839.[23] And up north at the trading posts, where relations had been more amicable—there, too, the peace was threatened in 1844, when the thoughtless killing of a cow, or a pig, escalated into the full-blown massacre and scalping of a group of Blackfeet at Fort McKenzie, near the mouth of the Marias, a river that seemed destined to have its history written in bullets and corpses.[24]

By that time, however, two separate events had drawn a line under this period of frontier history. For the first time in decades the Blackfeet had more pressing preoccupations than fighting. They had seen the first fearsome auguries in 1833, with a total eclipse of the sun and a riot of shooting stars.[25] Four years later a 119-ton American Fur Company side-wheeler called the *St. Peters* chugged up the Missouri toward Fort McKenzie. The post's young Scots-Irish bourgeois, Alexander Culbertson, who traced his lineage directly to Mary Queen of Scots, heard that the boat had been spreading the "Small Pox" hither and yon, decimating the Mandans, the Hidatsa, the Arikara, and the Assiniboines on its journey west, and pleaded with the hundreds of assembled Piegans and Bloods to stay away from the vessel. To no avail. Fifty-one people at the post fell sick; more than half of them died. Culbertson, who had been "variolated" with the live virus, survived.[26]

Business at Fort McKenzie dried up in the weeks following the outbreak, and Culbertson set forth to discover the reason. In the Three Forks country, he came upon an encampment of Piegans, "a silent, stinking village. Hundreds of rotting corpses were strewn about. . . . It was like another Assyrian host that the Angel of Death had overwhelmed in a night."[27] By the time the white scabs had run their course, six thousand had perished, almost two-thirds of the entire Blackfeet Nation.

Meanwhile, the beaver extravaganza was over; the best streams were trapped out and silk was the new rage in London and New York—a shift in fashion that Astor had foreseen years earlier. In July 1840, the trappers gathered at the confluence of Horse Creek and the Green River for the last of their rendezvous. "Come," said Doc Newell to Joe Meek, "we are done with this life in the mountains—done with wading in beaver dams, and freezing or starving alternately—done with Indian trading and Indian fighting. The fur trade is dead in the Rocky Mountains, and it is no place for us now, if it ever was."[28]

5

BRIDGER'S FORT

1840–1850

With its diversified trade in skins, the American Fur Company was much better placed than its competitors to ride out the decline of the beaver boom. Buffalo robes, shipped downriver to St. Louis from Fort Union at the mouth of the Yellowstone and Fort Pierre in present-day South Dakota, became the cornerstone of the company's fortunes. Three people dominated this trade: Alexander Culbertson; James Kipp, who had built Fort Piegan and was described as "the most picturesque man on the frontier"; and Malcolm Clarke,[1] who came west to join Culbertson in the winter of 1840–1841. These men stood at the unstable intersection of commerce, exploration, and violence. All three married Blackfeet women, and they acted as mediators, seeing both sides of the cultural argument as few others ever did, and, while constantly surrounded by violence, understanding that patience and compromise were the most useful tools for avoiding it.

At the trading posts, Culbertson, Kipp, and Clarke played host to visiting politicians, army officers, artists, Jesuit missionaries, fossil hunters, railroad surveyors, and dignitaries from Europe. The painter George Catlin was the first of these guests. He came in 1832, hopping aboard the steamship *Yellow Stone,* which the Blackfeet called Fire Boat That Walks on Water, for its inaugural voyage, and creating an incomparable documentary record of Piegan warriors and medicine men in full regalia.

In 1843 it was the turn of John James Audubon. Culbertson took him hunting; Audubon returned the compliment by painting portraits of Culbertson and his beautiful, dark-eyed seventeen-year-old Blood wife, Natoyist–Siksina', or Holy Snake Woman, whom others described as "present[ing] the most striking illustrations of high civilization which these tribes of the interior are capable of attaining."[2] Visitors often compared her to Sacagawea.

Audubon agreed to sleep in a tepee at Fort Union and wore moccasins because they were more comfortable than boots. He even managed to summon up some kind words for Natoyist-Siksina''s refined manner, but his enthusiasm waned when she broke open a buffalo skull, scooped out the brains, and ate them raw. For the rest of the Indians, he felt no ambivalence at all. He considered them "miserably poor, filthy beyond description"—not entirely surprising, one might think, in people who had just been devastated by smallpox. But Audubon had no compassion; he was more interested in visiting the seven-year-old mass burial grounds and doing a little grave robbing in the name of science. With a little effort, the skull of one old chief, White Cow, "was twisted off in a moment, under jaw and all."[3]

In the long run, Malcolm Clarke had an even greater influence on events than Culbertson and Kipp. He bestrode the Piegan heartland from the Sun River to the Marias for the next quarter-century like no other white man, and in the end it was the complexities of his life and personality that would lead to the eventual, terrible detonation of violence between the whites and the Blackfeet.

What we know of Clarke comes mainly from his sister Charlotte and his daughter Helen, known as Nellie. A lucid writer, she was a tall, strikingly handsome woman with deep-set black eyes, and proud of her mixed heritage and her Blackfeet name, Paiota-pamakan Omuksikimi, or Came Running Back.[4] Nellie left a remarkable portrait of her father. Born in

1817, the son of a military officer, he grew up in Fort Wayne, Indiana, but moved shortly afterward to Fort Snelling, a lonely outpost at the junction of the Mississippi and Missouri rivers, and from there to Cincinnati. His sister describes "a handsome, bright-eyed, brave, and venturesome boy" who seems to have spent most of his time bareback riding, wolf hunting, and getting into fistfights, when he wasn't declaiming lines from *Julius Caesar* and showing precocious levels of chivalry to young women.

His only aspiration at this point was to become a professional soldier, like his father. At seventeen he was admitted to West Point, where he was a classmate and friend of William Tecumseh Sherman. His brief stay was mainly remembered for his exaggerated sense of personal honor, which flared easily into violence. One friend says that when a fellow cadet insulted him, Clarke grabbed the man by the collar and beat him with a rawhide whip. He was court-martialed, but according to one source, avoided expulsion after the personal intervention of President Andrew Jackson. His sister Charlotte insists, however, that he refused to apologize and agreed to leave—as a matter of honor.[5]

This reputation for violence in the name of aggrieved honor followed Clarke wherever he went. After leaving the military academy he went south to fight for Texas independence. On the way, he paused to lead a mutiny on a ship from New Orleans to Galveston and threw the captain, whom he accused of a want of consideration for his passengers, in irons. When General Sam Houston learned of the incident, he praised the "beardless boy" for his initiative and dismissed all charges against him. An ecstatic crowd carried Clarke on their shoulders through the streets of Galveston.

Once he arrived on the upper Missouri as a man of twenty-three, it was much the same story. He planted a tomahawk in the skull of Alexander Harvey, a brutal man who had ordered the 1844 massacre at Fort McKenzie and, by some accounts, scalped the victims and licked the blood off his knife to taunt the survivors. (Harvey survived Clarke's attack, barely.) Some years later, Clarke succeeded in putting three fatal bullets in Owen McKenzie, the mixed-blood son of the fort's founder, for some obscure drunken slight delivered aboard a keelboat. ("It would be somewhat singular," says Nellie Clarke with a daughter's indulgence, "if a man with as strong characteristics as Malcolm Clarke should pass through life without making enemies."[6])

Strong characteristics, indeed. Contemporaries used all sorts of contradictory adjectives like shrewd, tough, stubborn, eloquent, quick-tempered, domineering, arrogant, honorable, punctilious, straightforward, and generous to describe Clarke. It is also generally agreed that he was one of the few traders not addicted to rotgut whiskey.

In 1844, Clarke married a full-blood seventeen-year-old Piegan girl, Kahkokina (or Coth-co-co-ma, in Nellie's rendering).[7] Whatever the spelling, the name meant Cutting-Off-Head-Woman. The union produced four children—Nellie was the eldest—who were sent off to Ann Arbor, Cincinnati, and points east at the appropriate age to receive a proper education.

Particularly relevant to the events that unfolded later is that the marriage connected Clarke to the All Chiefs band of Piegans, the head of which was a perpetually angry man named Mountain Chief, who would in time become supreme chief of the tribe.[8] Like many renowned warriors, Mountain Chief drew his mystique from a singular vision. Reaching manhood, a young Piegan retreated alone to a remote and dangerous spot—a precipice, a burial ground, a place infested by grizzlies, an island haunted by the Su-ye-tup-pi, the Underwater People—where he fasted and prayed for four days, sleeping two nights on his left side and two on his right. Sometimes an animal, a secret helper, would appear to him in a vision. In the case of Mountain Chief, it was a mountain squirrel, which told him that he could never be killed by bullets.[9]

The Piegans evidently regarded Clarke with a mixture of awe, fear, and respect. The first name they gave him was White Lodgepole, a tribute to his stature and erect bearing. But then he carried out the unprecedented feat of killing thirty grizzly bears in a single month, four of them on a single day before breakfast. So he became Ne-so-ke-i-o, Four Bears. Clarke's loyalty to the territorial claims of the Blackfeet became famous in later years as the settlement of Montana Territory gathered speed. "When the Whites come in and try to take the Indians' land," he told his son Horace, a year younger than Nellie, "stand by your mother's people."[10]

Jim Bridger traveled to Fort Union for the first time in 1844 to visit his old rivals from the American Fur Company, although it took him a long way from home. After the collapse of the beaver trade, Bridger had shown his business acumen by setting up a trading post at a critical point on the new Oregon Trail. Fort Bridger, as he called it, was in western Wyoming, halfway between the South Pass and the Great Salt Lake, in country that he knew intimately from the old rendezvous days.

Bridger had acquired a fellow veteran of the fur trade as his business partner, a stylish Spaniard named Louis Vasquez, who liked to ride around the country in a coach and four. "Bits of aristocratic elegance clung to him in the mountains like cottonwood fluff," writes the historian Bernard DeVoto. The establishment that Bridger and Vasquez built in 1843 lay in friendly Shoshone country, on a small island among the braided channels of Black's Fork of the Green River. There was lush grass all around for grazing, giving way to sagebrush and then pine on the higher slopes, and cut here and there by cobbled streams of snowmelt. Beyond the plateau were the Uinta Mountains and the uncompromising landscape of the Bridger Badlands—"a desert to the agriculturist, a mine to the paleontologist, and a paradise to the artist," wrote the explorer John Wesley Powell in 1869, on his way to make the first descent of the Colorado River.[11]

Fort Bridger itself was a humble affair, a single cabin, eight feet high, of logs, willow and dogwood brush, and mud. Nearby were a couple of dozen scruffy lodges—squaw men, their Shoshone wives, naked children and dogs underfoot. Visiting parties of Indians came to exchange robes, skins, meat, and clothing for flour, sugar, powder, lead, blankets, butcher knives, spirits, coffee, and hats. Appearances notwithstanding, Bridger's enterprise prospered. The emigrants necessarily traveled with plenty of cash, and by the time they reached the fort they had been on the road long enough to have plenty of material needs: food, supplies, blacksmithing, wagon repairs. Fort Bridger was the last chance to replenish stocks before the arduous crossing of the Great Salt Lake Desert.

From this new base, Bridger ranged far and wide, developing the multiple skills and personae that made him one of the archetypal figures of the frontier, part Natty Bumppo, part Kit Carson, part Buffalo Bill, and more versatile than any of them. He was the human bridge that spanned the successive eras of the Western experience, from the ascendancy of the mountain men to the great military-scientific explorations of the years preceding the Civil War and the eruption of the final, defining phase of the Indian wars on the Northern Plains.

Everyone had to pass through the fort, it seemed, from the Donner Party, who ignored, or misconstrued, Bridger's advice and blundered into a nightmare of starvation and cannibalism,[12] to a group of refugees who had been hounded from their churches in Missouri and Illinois and were now headed westward to found a new Zion. They called themselves the Church of Jesus Christ of Latter Day Saints, or Mormons. Bridger was invited to join their leader, Brigham Young, in his tent, together with his Council of Twelve Apostles. He promised Young he would find his earthly paradise near the Great Salt Lake and told him how to get there.[13] Young had already heard of the place from the writings of the great explorer of the 1840s, John C. Frémont—the "Pathfinder." But Bridger heaped scorn on Frémont's maps; his own, even if crudely drawn, were incomparably more accurate; his topographical memory was close to infallible.

The California gold rush turned the stream of emigrants into a torrent. In the course of two seasons, tens of thousands of forty-niners passed through Fort Bridger, making its owners prosperous men, though no one would have known it from the frugal way in which Bridger lived. And with the emigrants came the army. The Regiment of Mounted Riflemen arrived first, charged with securing the Oregon Trail; in their wake came the topographical engineers and explorers, led by Captain Howard Stansbury and Lieutenant John W. Gunnison.

Guided by Bridger, Stansbury located the pass that would eventually carry the Union Pacific west through Shoshone country to the Great Salt Lake. Gunnison, meanwhile, mapped the southern part of Brigham Young's new Zion and listened enthralled to Jim Bridger's tales of Yellowstone. "His graphic sketches are delightful romances," the young officer wrote.

> With a buffalo-skin and piece of charcoal, he will map out any portion of this immense region, and delineate mountains, streams, and the circular valleys called "holes," with wonderful accuracy . . . He gives a picture, most romantic and enticing, of the head-waters of the Yellow Stone. A lake sixty miles long, cold and pellucid, lies embosomed among high precipitous mountains. One side is a sloping plain several miles wide, with clumps of trees and groves of pine. The ground resounds to the tread of horses. Geysers spout up seventy feet high, with a terrific hissing noise, at regular intervals. Waterfalls are sparkling, leaping, and thundering down the precipices, and collect in the pool below. The river issues from this lake, and for fifteen miles roars through the perpendicular kanyon at the outlet. In this section are the Great Springs, so hot that meat is readily cooked in them, and as they descend on the successive terraces, afford at length delightful baths. On the other side is an acid spring, which gushes out in a river torrent; and below is a cave which supplies "vermilion" for the savages in abundance.[14]

Wherever else Bridger traveled, the upper Yellowstone was the magnet that constantly drew him back. In 1846, now in his mid-forties, he set off from Fort Bridger on what was initially conceived as a trading mission to the Crows and the Sioux, but along the way took on something of the character of a tourist excursion. One of the participants was a man named James Gemmell, who recalled many years later:

> We camped for a time near the west arm of the [Yellowstone] lake and here Jim Bridger proposed to show me the wonderful

spouting springs at the head of the Madison. Leaving our main camp, with a small and select party we took the trail by Snake Lake (now called Shoshone Lake) and visited what have of late years become so famous as the Upper and Lower Geyser basins. There we spent a week and then returned to our camp, whence we resumed our journey, skirted the Yellowstone and Mammoth Hot Springs, which appeared as wonderful to us as had the geysers. Here we camped several days to enjoy the baths and to recuperate our animals.[15]

Four years later, Bridger went to the upper Yellowstone again, this time with Kit Carson, mentoring a group of twenty would-be trappers, who appeared not to have heard the news about the end of the beaver trade.[16] Bridger was no longer *acquiring* his exploring skills, in other words, but *applying* them, as a guide to others. And with each new group he led, each new willing ear he found among the wayfarers at Fort Bridger, the tales he told about the headwaters of the Yellowstone acquired the proportions of legend, until a new generation of explorers became obsessed with reaching the place he described, the last and most myth-laden white space remaining on the map of the American West.

{ 6 }

FAKELORE

1851

No white man had better relations with the native peoples of the northern Rockies than Jim Bridger. Everyone remarked on it. Crows, Nez Perce, Flatheads, Southern Shoshone: Most of the tribes on the perimeter of the Yellowstone Plateau were well disposed toward the old mountain man, with the signal exception of the Blackfeet (who hated almost everyone).

Bridger's close ties with the tribes produced mixed reactions from other whites. Gunnison, the army explorer, remarked that Fort Bridger had a "most eligible position for a commanding influence" over the tribes of the region. "If a humane policy is the proper one," he wrote (implying some ambivalence about the idea), "then here is the place for a pacificator, and the interposition of good offices to prevent their internecine contests."[1]

Brigham Young, meanwhile, got on well with the pacificator at first, but his attitude soon cooled to the point of paranoia, seeing plots by the tribes who were being displaced from their ancestral lands by his disciples. "I believe I know that Old Bridger is death on us," the Mormon patriarch wrote, "and if he knew 400,000 Indians were coming against us, and any man were to let us know, he would cut his throat."[2]

Bridger did indeed play a crucial mediating role as Indian-white relations deteriorated with the disruptive passage of so many emigrants. The

Oregon Trail—the "Great Medicine Road"—had sliced the buffalo plains in two, infuriating the tribes whose lives depended on the herds. So the Great Father called them together at Fort Laramie in 1851 to discuss their grievances, and Bridger acted as the government's chief interpreter and go-between, narrowly averting a crisis caused by the arrival of a large, uninvited group of Shoshone headed by his new father-in-law, the great chief Washakie.

The government promised peace and annuities; insisted on the white man's rights to traverse Indian territory and protect that passage with a series of forts; mapped out tribal hunting grounds with clearly demarcated boundaries; and demanded that each tribe elect a single chief with authority to make binding agreements—as well as to punish any hotheaded brave who attacked a white settler. Boundaries? Maps? Authority? Binding agreements? Several of the Great Father's stipulations had the Indians looking at one another with puzzlement, but they went through the motions that were required of them, aided by Jim Bridger's adept shuttle diplomacy.

The official map of the tribal spheres of influence was drawn by the Flemish Jesuit Father Pierre-Jean De Smet, who had traveled down to Laramie from the fur trading post of Fort Union in the company of his good friend Alexander Culbertson. The Crows, despite their small numbers, came out of it best, with a vast expanse of the Yellowstone and Bighorn country. To their east, the "Sioux or Dacotah" were granted a somewhat smaller portion. The Blackfeet got the land between the Missouri and the Continental Divide, though its lines were drawn more tightly than they would have drawn themselves had they been in the business of mapmaking. Smaller areas went to the lesser tribes to the northwest and northeast. The Shoshone fell into a cartographic vacuum, since, with the exception of Washakie's band, they didn't show up for the talks.

The mountain man and the Jesuit had known each other for a decade, and De Smet had heard the story of the Blackfoot arrowhead lodged in Bridger's back and its painful extraction by Dr. Whitman. *Stuck in there for three years!* the Jesuit exclaimed. *Did it suppurate much?* Bridger answered laconically, *In the mountains meat never spoils.*[3]

The Jesuit had his own experience of the Blackfeet by this point, and it was a singular one. Like Lewis and Clark, like Bridger and the other fur trappers, De Smet had not found it hard to befriend the Crows, the Nez Perce, and the Flatheads. But unlike any other white man, the Jesuit had also built a certain degree of trust with their ferocious adversaries. He first learned about the Blackfeet in 1840, when he was told of a group of Christianized Flatheads kneeling to pray before a battle with them. "The Blackfeet are the only Indians of whose salvation we would have reason to despair," the Jesuit wrote, "for they are murderers, thieves, traitors, and all that is wicked."[4] Yet a year later, on Christmas Day, 1841, he baptized his first five Piegans.

A footnote is in order, however. These first converts were not representative of the Piegans as a whole, but members of a large, quasirenegade band in the Three Forks area known as the Small Robes, who had forged friendly ties with the Flatheads. So separate were their lives from the Piegan mainstream that De Smet considered them a distinct tribe.

Several hundred more baptisms followed as the Jesuits patiently expanded their influence down the Missouri and into the heart of the Blackfeet country. De Smet taught them a prayer which he had translated into their language:

> *God almighty;*
> *Piegans are all his children.*
> *He is going to help us on earth;*
> *If you are good, he will save your soul.*

If you are good. The motives of the converts were actually a little more complicated than they might have seemed. De Smet was shrewd enough to see what was going on beneath the professions of piety. Christianity to the Blackfeet was less a doctrinal matter than a new and powerful form of war medicine; accept the God of the Black Robes, and you will be in a better position to annihilate your enemies.[5] The arguments for conversion gained even greater force in 1846, when a Crow war party wiped out an entire camp of Small Robes, killing all the men and boys and taking two hundred women and children captive.[6]

During the gathering at Fort Laramie, the demarcation of tribal territories was not the only mapping exercise that interested De Smet. He also quizzed Bridger about the most salient features of the upper Yellowstone plateau, together with their precise location. Bridger's account was so clear and detailed that the priest was able to fix the geographical coordinates with some accuracy—"between the forty-third and forty-fifth degrees of latitude and the one hundred and ninth and the one hundred and eleventh degrees of longitude, that is between the sources of the Madison and the Yellowstone."[7] Here, De Smet concluded, was "perhaps the most marvelous [spot] of all the northern half of this continent." Following Bridger's descriptions, he wrote:

> Bituminous, sulphurous and boiling springs are very numerous in it. The hot springs contain a large quantity of calcareous matter, and form hills more or less elevated, which resemble in their nature, perhaps, if not in their extent, the famous springs of Pambuk Kalessi, in Asia Minor, so well described by Chandler. The earth is thrown up very high, and the influence of the elements causes it to take the most varied and most fantastic shapes. Gas, vapor, and smoke are continually escaping by a thousand openings from the base of the summit of this volcanic pile; the noise at times resembles the steam let off by a boat. Strong subterranean explosions occur, like those in "Colter's Hell."[8]

The sources for what was now known of Yellowstone—lake, canyon, falls, geysers, hot springs, location—could hardly have been more credible: a promising young army engineer and explorer (at a time when topographical engineers, not combat troops, were considered to be the military elite), and the most celebrated of the Black Robes, a man known as an explorer as much as a priest, and with a reputation for knowing more about the Northern Rockies than any man of his time other than Jim Bridger. De Smet even had a map now to complement the rougher ones sketched earlier by the educated trappers Jedediah Smith and Warren Ferris.

The problem with Bridger's authority was that he also had a second, conflicting reputation as a teller of tall tales. His own psychology and sense of humor played a part in this. The more his listeners gawped in disbelief, the more he embroidered. If they found it impossible to believe in a cliff of black obsidian, which the Indians used to make tools and arrowheads, then Bridger would give them a mountain of transparent glass; if the hot springs of the Firehole were too much to credit, Bridger would explain that the water, ice-cold at its source, was heated by friction because it ran so fast over the riverbed; if the audience couldn't swallow the idea of petrified trees, why, let them hear about petrified rabbits and sage hens and petrified birds singing petrified songs, and bushes laden with walnut-size diamonds, rubies, and emeralds. Münchhausen would have been proud of the mountain man's whoppers.[9]

Which version of Bridger to believe? That was the problem. Even Gunnison, after all, had suggested a caveat in characterizing these stories as "delightful romances." The mountain man, by all accounts, was uncouth, overfond of alcohol, an illiterate, the kind who used words like *dogond* and *dur'n* and said *ef* instead of *if.* And that meant that there were three possible interpretations of his tales. *It can't be true*—it's just Old Gabe shooting his mouth off. *Could it be true?*—after all, who could make this stuff up? *It must be true*—if men like Gunnison and De Smet vouched for its authenticity.

It can't be true; it might be true; it must be true. In the end only the professionals, the leading men of the frontier, would be in a position to sort it all out, and that was the story of Yellowstone for the next twenty years.

At the same time as making a major contribution to geographical knowledge of the upper Yellowstone, De Smet also helped give birth to an enduring myth: that Native Americans were terrified of the place and for that reason avoided it. The first hint of this had been William Clark's note, written more than forty years earlier, recording the rumor that they "Conceive it possessed of spirits, who were averse that men Should be near them."[10] Now the Jesuit elaborated on the theme.

> The hunters and the Indians speak of it with a superstitious fear, and consider it the abode of evil spirits, that is to say, a kind of hell. Indians seldom approach it without offering some sacrifice, or at least without presenting the calumet of peace to the turbulent spirits, that they may be propitious. They declare that the subterranean noises proceed from the forging of war-like weapons: each eruption of earth is, in their eyes, the result of a combat between the infernal spirits, and becomes the monument of a new victory or calamity.[11]

But what Indian would have known about the forging of weapons with hammers and anvils and fire?[12] Also, De Smet was grafting elements of Christian theology, like the idea of Hell, onto a culture to which such concepts were alien. (The only exception, to be fair, were those small tribes that had been visited by Christian missionaries. So, for example, the trapper Warren Ferris had given an account of an unnamed companion's travels in 1833 with two Pend d'Oreilles, who "could not by any means be induced to approach [the geysers]. . . . They believed them to be supernatural and supposed them to be the production of the Evil Spirit. One of them remarked that Hell, *of which he had heard from the Whites* [italics added], must be in that vicinity.")

It does seem odd, however, that the fur trappers would be the first to spread the myth that primitive superstition kept the Indians away from the upper Yellowstone. After all, they had been having ugly encounters with the Blackfeet in and around the area of the future national park for decades. The trappers' accounts of these confrontations also made it clear that any more systematic exploration and mapping of the area would have to wait until the Blackfeet and other hostiles were cleared from the plateau and pushed back from its perimeter.

Whatever its transparent defects, the superstition myth persisted into the late twentieth century. It was certainly convenient to those who would later turn the volcanic caldera into a "pleasuring ground" for tourists. Yellowstone was a pristine wilderness, and that defining idea was helped along by the fiction that it had never been touched by human hands, and especially not by dirty ones. Passed down from the trappers to the Jesuits, and from there to the first historians of the national park, the myth was cemented sulphurously in place by generations of park tours, guidebooks, and volumes of what the cultural historian Peter Nabokov and the anthropologist Lawrence Loendorf call "fakelore."[13]

Granted, with its high elevation, long, subzero winters, and limited growing season, the upper Yellowstone didn't lend itself to permanent habitation—with the exception of one small band of Shoshone known as the Sheepeaters. But in fact quite a few tribes, including other branches of the Shoshone, crisscrossed the plateau with some frequency, for reasons both religious and pragmatic.[14]

The Shoshone were a particularly complicated people. Culturally they were a mix of Plains and Great Basin tribes, diverse in their attitude toward white incursions, a social labyrinth of dialects, dispersed bands, and economic hierarchies that ranged across a skinny, elongated triangle that encompassed parts of Wyoming, Utah, Idaho, and Montana, and had as its apex the plateau of the upper Yellowstone. Their elaborate social stratification was basically determined by what food you ate and how you got a hold of it. At the top of the pyramid, the buffalo eaters; in the middle, the deer eaters and the salmon eaters; at the bottom, the root diggers and those who depended for their survival on mountain sheep, which forced them to the higher and more inhospitable altitudes.

A large portion of the Yellowstone fakelore derives from these Sheepeaters, a small, reclusive group ostracized by the rest of their tribe. Lacking horses, reliant on dogs to drag around their travois, and consequently vulnerable to enemies, the Sheepeaters—who probably never numbered more than four hundred—retreated into the rocky fastnesses of the Absarokas and the Wind River Range for much of the year. Their reputation for timidity swelled in the telling into a portrait of wretched Stone Agers, low on the evolutionary scale, a "deteriorating, half-miserable-animal, half-miserable-man type . . . too despicable to be worth raiding or hunting down, even by lusty young Blackfeet, Crow, or Sioux braves hell-bent for scalps."[15] The French trappers called them *Les dignes de pitié*. Those deserving of pity.

But the trappers' accounts of their meetings with the Sheepeaters cast doubt on this caricature. Osborne Russell, who left the most lyrical record of the upper Yellowstone, bumped into members of the tribe in the Lamar Valley in 1834 or 1835. They traded amicably, and Russell seemed enchanted with them. They were "neatly clothed in dressed deer and sheepskins of the best quality and seemed to be perfectly happy." They had gorgeous bows made of ornamented sheep horn. Clearly they were no slouches as hunters. They drew the trapper a map of their territory on a piece of bleached elk skin. Their domain seemed idyllic. "I almost wished I could spend the remainder of my days in a place like this," Russell wrote, "where happiness and contentment seemed to reign in wild romantic splendor surrounded by majestic battlements which seemed to support the heavens and shut out all hostile intruders." True, this has the ring of a man who lived in the age of Wordsworth. But even allowing for that, it hardly squares with the image of squalid, feebleminded Paleolithics.

It's clear today from archaeological evidence and oral history that the Blackfeet, Flatheads, Pend d'Oreilles, Kutenai, Gros Ventres, and Assiniboines, all coming from the north, penetrated the mountainous perimeter of the upper Yellowstone at will, and that other Shoshone groups came and went freely on the southern and western sides.[16] Despite the multiple intertribal animosities, some scholars suggest that the Yellowstone plateau may have functioned as a kind of demilitarized zone. Obsidian Cliff, in particular, where the black, glassy rock made excellent tools and arrowheads and was widely traded,[17] had that pacific reputation. Nabokov and

Loendorf, however, see this as another piece of fakelore: "Approach-the-rocks-but-avoid-the-waters."

Indian attitudes seem to have varied from one tribe to another, but most appear to have regarded the geyser basins with awe and respect, as a place suited to vision quests and other spiritual practices. The Crows called the geysers *Bide-Mahpe* or *Bimmaaxpée*—sacred or powerful waters.[18] The Shoshone term was *bow-we-ran*, or steaming water, and they either treated the hot springs as a natural Jacuzzi to ease their rheumatism and aching bones or gulped the liquid down as a specific against ulcers and gallstones. The Sheepeaters, meanwhile, saw the Absarokas as the domain of the spirits. They had quite a roster of these, many of them malignantly inclined: *Tundzoavits*, "rocky-skinned ghosts"; *Pandzoavits*, "water ghosts" who lived in the hot springs and lakes and drowned people in order to eat them; *Tundzoavaip*, the "stone-ghost woman," who had an alarming taste for the flesh of babies.[19]

The Bannock and the Northwestern Shoshone took reverence a step further, using hot springs as burial places, especially for their chiefs: a quick and direct path to a better world. A Mormon traveling through Shoshone country in eastern Utah in 1855 came upon a warm saltwater spring that contained "six Indian bodies standing bolt upright and crusted over with the salty deposit in this lake, giving them the appearance of mummies. It was evident that they had heavy weights attached to their lower extremities, thus keeping them perpendicular with their heads three or four feet below the surface of the water." He described this sight, with striking restraint, as "curious."[20]

The highest status among the Shoshone was accorded to the buffalo hunters. But by the 1830s their lives, too, had became more difficult, and that drove them more and more into the upper Yellowstone—though as a transit route rather than a place of permanent residence. The most significant of these groups were the Bannock—an odd word that is a corruption of their own name for themselves: the *Bana'kwut* or *Banai'ti* (half a dozen variants exist). Some authorities say the name means "water people"; others that it refers to their favored upswept hairstyle.[21] Most whites disliked and mistrusted the Bannock. Though few in number, they were notoriously fractious, rivalling the Crows as horse thieves and the Blackfeet as pickers of fights.

Tribal differentiation becomes difficult in the case of the Bannock. Unlike their immediate neighbors, the Northwestern Shoshone, they spoke a Northern Paiute language; they were a little taller perhaps, slim and sinewy, superb horsemen. Otherwise there were few meaningful distinctions, and over time there was a virtual cultural fusion between the two groups, who took to referring to themselves in modern times as the Sho-Ban. To confuse matters further, nineteenth-century whites tended to lump them all together as "Snakes"—a name that derived from the undulating hand movement they used as an identifying sign.

Technology and mobility, in the form of the horse and the trade rifle, had given the Blackfeet new power; for the Bannock they proved to be a temporary blessing and then a curse. The Blackfeet could hunt at will among the vast bison herds of the upper Missouri. But the herds on the Snake River Plain were much smaller, and by about 1840 the newly mobile Bannock had all but annihilated them. That left them a variety of options for "going to buffalo," most of them unappealing. The shortest and fastest route—down the Madison Valley to the Three Forks of the Missouri—was basically an invitation to be ambushed by the Blackfeet. Instead they chose a path through the upper Yellowstone that was somewhat circuitous but much safer from attack. In places along the so-called Bannock Trail, the marks of generations of travois are still visible today.

The trail was "not a fixed and invariable treadway," says the Yellowstone historian Aubrey Haines, "but rather, a series of rambling parallels."[22] It wound its way eastward from Idaho through the Targhee Pass to the Madison Canyon and zigzagged over the Gallatin Range to the Gardner River and Mammoth Hot Springs. From there, the route crossed the Yellowstone at the Sulphur Beds ford above Tower Fall (where John Colter probably crossed the river), continued through the "wild romantic splendor" of the broad Lamar Valley and so up Soda Butte Creek to the

Clarks Fork of the Yellowstone, until the two-hundred-mile journey ended in the open buffalo country below. This journey took the Bannock to the edge of the Crow lands—admittedly no prospect of a friendly welcome there—but it was still more appealing than risking what Meriwether Lewis would have called an "interview" with the Blackfeet.

For these arduous journeys, the Bannock sought safety in numbers, traveling with various permutations of Flatheads, Nez Perce (during their intermittent truces), and even Eastern Shoshone—not normally their best of friends. Starting around 1840, the Bannock made this trek each fall for more than twenty years, until their Yellowstone migrations ended with the Montana gold rush, when the anger of Mormons, soldiers, and miners coalesced to terrible effect.

7

MAN PICKING UP STONES RUNNING
1853–1858

Government explorers had largely neglected the West for the four decades after Lewis and Clark, and Washington didn't get serious about exploring and mapping until 1838, when it created the Army Corps of Topographical Engineers. Even then, much of what the corps did was not really *exploration* in the strict sense of the word. It rarely involved the discovery of the unknown; rather, it was an effort to collect, codify, and in general professionalize and make public the private, anecdotal data that the likes of Bridger and his fellow trappers had acquired from firsthand experience. For his part, Bridger found that this gave him a pleasant and decently paid new line of employment, as he helped the army address the big questions: Where were the best routes for wagon trails and railroads? Where was the mineral wealth located? Which was the best agricultural land? Who lived there already, and what were their attitudes to newcomers? In other words, what were the military and strategic considerations involved in taking that land, turning it to productive use, and making it secure for settlement?

As these questions were asked and answered, economic development, scientific research, the seductive lure of exploration, and the imperatives of national security became inseparable. This necessarily meant that there would be dirty work to be done, yet at West Point in the 1840s and 1850s the cream of each year's class were not so much the tacticians of combat as the practical men. And while the dashing John C. Frémont, "the Great Pathfinder," may have been the romantic archetype of the explorer, the kind who could stir a young boy's imagination, just as important were the men who could lay a road, string a telegraph cable, grade a railroad, throw a bridge.[1] The Corps of Topographical Engineers in turn acted as a point of convergence for mountain men, Indian fighters, and a new cadre of professional scientists who were beginning to emerge from the great intellectual centers of the East—the Smithsonian Institution, Harvard and Yale, the Philadelphia Academy of Natural Sciences—and who now set out with their military companions and protectors to comb the mountains, prairies, and badlands for specimens, everything from pressed flowers and promising lumps of coal to the skulls of mastodons and Indians.

The first great civilian-military exploring partnership was between Lieutenant Gouverneur Kemble Warren and Ferdinand Vandeveer Hayden. They worked together for two years, making an odd couple. Thin-faced, with a luxuriant mustache, dark-complected, with deeply lined features and hair worn long and combed rather foppishly forward over the ears into small cowlicks, Warren had some similarities to Frémont: the same impetuous dash, the physical courage, the conceit, the intolerance of mediocrity, the love of art, literature, and women. As a soldier he was the beau ideal: ramrod-straight, a lover of the regimented life, something of a martinet.

He had graduated second in his class from West Point, and engineering was apparently in the family genes; his sister, Emily, married Washington Roebling of Brooklyn Bridge fame, and when her husband fell sick with caisson disease, she took over the work on the great span herself and saw it to completion. Lieutenant Warren's expert cartography would make the army's great synthetic map of the West in 1857, drawing on every tale the mountain men had told and every inch the seven great transcontinental railroad surveys had traced with their odometers and theodolites.

Hayden shared Warren's dash and his wordly tastes (especially where women were concerned), but little else. He was born illegitimate in West-field, Massachusetts, in 1829. His father was a shiftless alcoholic; his mother rejected him and sent him to live with relatives. These shaming facts Hayden covered up in his biography, while inventing others more flattering. For his whole life he was driven by demons. At Oberlin Medi-cal College, some classmates detested him for his blatant ambition: "He fairly ran when he walked that he might reach something." Others found the impetuous enthusiasms more appealing: "A jolly good fellow is Hayden, who always falls desperately in love several times a month." And he acted on it physically, it appears, the beginnings of a career of romances and brothel encounters that would eventually lead to his death from "locomo-tor ataxia," the diagnosis that Victorian physicians used, like drapes over the legs of a piano, to conceal the shame of tertiary syphilis.[2]

There are hints of all this in his appearance, although the numerous photographs that exist of Hayden leave a lot of room for interpretation. He was a handsome man, but not excessively so, with regular, well-formed features, but for oddly shaped ears that look as if they have lost their bot-tom third to a careless razor. Hair worn long, but neatly combed and parted; hooded eyes that can look melancholy or self-regarding; a mouth that some would see as sensual, others as carrying a hint of cruelty.

Hayden's education coincided with the birth of a new American sci-ence, no longer a poor cousin to the European school. The era of the gen-eralist, often trained in medicine (as Hayden had been), was evolving steadily into the age of the specialist, branching out with advanced train-ing and practical experience into geology, botany, ornithology, paleontol-ogy, zoology, and so forth. It called for a new scientific elite, and brought forth men with egos to match.[3]

From an early age Hayden had a genius for self-promotion and the astute cultivation of powerful sponsors. James Hall, the famous geologist at New York's Albany Institute, was the first. Normally irascible and de-ceitful, criticizing everyone, resenting everyone, Hall for some reason took a shine to Hayden and stoked his ambition. To this first patron, Hayden quickly added a second, Spencer Fullerton Baird of the Smithsonian, an impresario of the natural sciences who was busy putting together a network of hard-driven young specimen collectors. Hayden begged to be sent fossil hunting in the badlands of Dakota Territory. To Hall he wrote, "With all modesty, I think I should exceed even your expectations, for obstacles have no terror to me and I trust never will have." And to Baird, "Were it necessary to accomplish my purposes, I could live as the Wild Indian lives, and endure any amount of exposure and toil without a murmur."[4]

And what did the Wild Indians think of all this? According to an often-told tale, they thought Hayden was mad. On a fossil-hunting trip to the Black Hills, the young geologist-paleontologist was intercepted by some suspicious Sioux. He was carrying a bag. The Sioux told him to empty it. Rocks tumbled to the ground. Culturally disposed to pity and respect for the insane, they gave one another looks and sent him on his way. Thereafter they called him Man Who Picks Up Stones Running. The story sounds too good to be true, and perhaps it is.[5] But there is little doubt about Hayden's passion for rocks. He is said to have jumped to his feet one night during a campfire conversation and exclaimed, "Geology is like the Bible, a sermon in every verse!"

In the summer of 1853, Hayden teamed up with Hall's principal assistant, Fielding Bradford Meek, and the two men clanked off together into the White River Badlands, loaded down with their picks, shovels, crowbars, geologist's hammers, sledgehammers, blasting powder, compasses, hand lenses, alcohol bottles, insect nets, and screw-top cans for specimens. Two months later, they clanked their way out again with all manner of mineral samples, plants, birds and bird's eggs, pickled reptiles, fishes, amphibians, small mammals and pelts, and more than a hundred vertebrate skulls, including that of the extinct *Titanotheres*, a relative of the rhinoceros.

The following spring Hayden was back on the upper Missouri, alone this time, mesmerized by the blinding light, the great emptiness, and the bizarre rock formations that suggested the ruined castles of Europe and the towers and minarets of the Holy Land. This time he dragged out fully six tons of fossils, before overwintering with Alexander Culbertson and the traders of the American Fur Company at Fort Pierre.

Amateur citizen-scientists were still a valuable source of data, and Culbertson, with years of experience hosting European and American visitors, was one of the best. He knew the badlands between Fort Pierre and Fort Laramie like his own front porch, and the specimens he sent back east to the Philadelphia Academy were described as "instrumental in the birth of the science of vertebrate paleontology in North America."[6]

Hayden spent his idle hours that winter churning out reams of correspondence to his sponsors in the East, designing strategies to map the entire Upper Missouri Basin from the Platte to the Yellowstone, teaching the local children their alphabet, and compiling—at Baird's behest—vocabularies of the local tribes.

In early 1855, as soon as the weather broke, he was off again, a man who could rarely sit still. Over the winter, Baird had tried to put him in touch with the impetuous but prodigiously talented Lieutenant Warren, hoping that Hayden could attach himself to a full-scale military expedition. But Warren dropped in on Fort Pierre to see Hayden while he was off on one of his solo adventures, either foraging for fossils or lobbying government officials to put him in charge of a planned geological survey of the whole of the vast Nebraska Territory. So the meeting was deferred, and Warren hastened to join his commanding officer, Brevet General William S. Harney. Warren was assigned to the general as chief topographical engineer, on a mission where exploration and punitive violence were glued together like Siamese twins under a single joint command. It was not that Warren himself was inherently ill-disposed toward Native Americans. In fact he rather liked the Sioux. But he agreed that there was little alternative but to "brush them aside" as a necessary part of the march of science and civilization.[7] *Brush them aside*: a mild term for what followed, which Hayden ended up missing by an accident of timing.

Man Who Picks Up Stones Running was now in the territory of the Brulé Sioux, and that occasioned some nervousness. He wrote to Baird complaining of the "rascally Indians" and wondering if he was safe to continue his work. "Perhaps I shall have to give it up until the government sends troops up here and wipes out two or three hundred of them," he said. His fears had some foundation, ever since the trifling matter of an ox that had gone astray the previous summer as a result of the carelessness of a Mormon emigrant. A Minneconjou Sioux named High Forehead had come upon the wandering beast and put a bullet through it, with an eye to dinner. The chief of High Forehead's band offered to make restitution for the offense, but the army at Fort Laramie was having none of it. Nothing less than a show of force would do, and an exceedingly stupid and headstrong young lieutenant named John L. Grattan was dispatched with twenty-nine men, an inebriated interpreter, and two howitzers to do the business, which he described as going to "crack it to the Sioux." In the event, it was the Sioux who cracked it to Grattan, wiping out his entire command.

General Harney was not the man to see this as the sorry outcome of a subordinate's foolishness; for him, it was an intolerable affront to military honor. Harney was a Tennesseean, six foot four, powerfully built, a natural athlete, with long, flowing white hair and beard to match. Jefferson Davis said that he was "physically, the finest specimen of a man I ever saw." He was as profane and violent tempered as he was intelligent and ambitious. On one occasion he beat a slave woman to death with a length of rawhide.[8] To the killers of Lieutenant Grattan, and to any other Sioux who happened to find himself (or herself) sharing tipi space, he took much the same approach. So off he marched up the Platte River from Fort Leavenworth with six hundred men, declaring that, "By God, I'm for battle—no peace." Warren mapped the way.

The Sioux had been warned that anyone remaining to the north of the North Platte would be regarded as a hostile, occupying the nineteenth-century equivalent of a free-fire zone. For some reason a chief named Little Thunder ignored this advice, and while his camp undoubtedly housed individual braves who were implicated in recent acts of violence, the chief himself had never shown any aggressive intent and had the friendship medals and the pieces of paper with white men's scribbles on them to prove it. These didn't help him much when he came out of his tent on September 3, 1855, to greet Harney with a white flag and an offer to parley. The two men shouted at each across a forty-foot divide (the general refusing to come any closer to shake hands), but after half an hour he decided there was nothing further to be gained by jawing.

When the smoke cleared, "squaw killer" Harney counted eighty-six Sioux corpses and five wounded, a striking ratio. "I never saw a more beautiful thing in my life," said one cavalryman of the massed charge. The pursuit of survivors reminded another of a buffalo hunt, high entertainment. Looking for souvenirs, soldiers took their knives and sliced the pubic hair off dead women.

Engineer Warren was appalled by the carnage, which left "wounded women and children crying and moaning, horribly mangled by the bullets." He made a litter to evacuate a woman whose baby was dead. He fetched water from the creek to bathe the wounds of a young boy. He found a little girl wandering among the bodies and gave her a piece of chocolate. But Warren's scruples counted for little in the scheme of things. Harney's action at Ash Hollow—or Blue Water, the name that eventually stuck— was an innovation in military strategy, an attack on a static camp that provided the template for most of the mass killings of succeeding years. And if it involved women and children, well, so be it. Not only was it impossible to distinguish who was who when you were firing into crowded tipis to forestall resistance; it was also notorious that women carried out many of the worst atrocities against captured or wounded soldiers. As for the children, the old dictum applied: Nits make lice.

For the Sioux, it was a lesson not easily forgotten. A Lakota later told Warren, "If they went to war again, they would not yield so easy as they did before."

Warren and Hayden finally joined forces on April 1, 1856, and spent the summer of 1856 upriver at Fort Union. With the Sioux temporarily pacified, the two men turned their attention to the flora, fauna, and fossils of the Yellowstone and Powder River country.

Hayden, who by this time knew more about the paleontology of the Northern Plains than any man alive, had signed on as the expedition's geologist and naturalist. Warren offered him an annual salary of $1,000. And as their guide, almost inevitably it seems, Warren had hired Jim Bridger.

Old Gabe, over fifty now, had been on one of his prolonged jaunts as guide to the aristocracy, leading the mobile entourage of the stout, bald-headed Irish nobleman Sir St. George Gore, 8th Baron of Magherabegg in County Donegal. Gore put the earlier excesses of Sir William Stewart in the shade. Forty servants; ox wagons and mule wagons; twenty-one horse-drawn French carts painted a fetching shade of red; a linen tent with a striped lining and a brass bedstead; one vehicle for his guns and two for his fishing tackle and his personal fly-tier. The baron had an invariable routine: rise late, have the servants select some toothsome morsel for breakfast, bathe, prepare for the day's sport. For two seasons, with Bridger as his guide, he roamed from the Yellowstone to the Colorado, seemingly intent on the single-handed extermination of the Rocky Mountains population of large carnivores and ungulates. His tally ran to 2,000 buffalo, 1,600 elk and deer, 105 grizzly bears, uncounted pronghorn and small game. Most were left on the ground to rot.

Of an evening, Sir St. George would invite Bridger to his tent for a glass of wine and a story. He liked to read aloud from Sir Walter Scott and Shakespeare, although his guest found the Bard of Avon "a leetle too highfalutin.'" Bridger preferred the adventures of Baron Münchhausen, even though "he be dogond ef he swallered everything that there Baren Mountchawson said, and he thout he was a dur'n liar." On reflection, however, Bridger wondered how his accounts of his own experiences would sound "ef writ down in a book."[9]

Warren, Hayden, Bridger, and Gore met at Fort Union in July 1856. Warren took a liking to the 8th Baron's red-painted wagons and persuaded him to sell several of them to the scientific exploration before returning to Ireland. In camp at night, Bridger regaled the army engineer and the paleontologist with his stories of spouting geysers, mud volcanoes, boiling rivers, and petrified trees. "Wonderful tales, that sharpened the imagination of the whole party," said Hayden, who was almost certainly hearing them for the first time.[10] He resolved immediately to see this mix of geology and sorcery for himself.

Hayden and Warren spent two years at their task, adding considerably to the tonnage of specimens shipped back to the Smithsonian and the Philadelphia Academy. Warren, drawing heavily on Bridger's recollections, completed his comprehensive map of the West, the best that had yet been made. But the frictions between Hayden and Warren and their monumental egos put a strain on the expedition. The lieutenant's "egotism and tyrannical disposition are his ruin," Hayden wrote to Fielding Bradford Meek. Warren responded by accusing the geologist of mendacity and dereliction of duty. "I intend now either to whip him or shoot him, or else consider myself no more a gentleman," Hayden fumed in a letter to Baird at the Smithsonian.[11]

What happened next, however, remains something of a puzzle. With Warren's map in hand, with its mysterious references and tantalizing blank spaces in the upper reaches of the Yellowstone, the government decided to organize the first official exploration of the area. Warren would have been the most natural person in the world to lead it, but for reasons unknown he accepted an offer to be an assistant professor of mathematics at West Point. The Yellowstone job went instead to a man who was his opposite in every way.

8

TERRA INCOGNITA

1859–1860

W arren's successor, Captain William Franklin Raynolds, was a plodding desk jockey, a narrow-minded
evangelical, hitherto best known for supervising the
construction and repair of lighthouses. He did, how-
ever, have the good grace to acknowledge his own shortcomings, noting his
"entire want of previous preparation" for the trip to the upper Yellowstone,
and he had enough acuity to keep the rest of the group together—Bridger
as guide, Hayden as naturalist.[1]

Much had changed for Jim Bridger in the previous seven years. His
tentative friendship with Brigham Young had turned to rabid suspicion
on the part of the Mormon patriarch, and in the summer of 1853 Young
dispatched a posse to arrest Old Gabe for treason. Affidavits charged that
he had "sold or furnished hostile Indians with ammunitions and etc."[2]
Bridger had been forewarned and fled to Fort Laramie, so the Mormons
occupied the abandoned trading post, and he never did get it back.

But four years later he got a kind of indirect revenge, and in a new
role. He had been trapper, explorer, guide, and trader. Now he signed on
as a scout for combat troops, with the honorary rank of major.

An army captain described Bridger at this point as being "about sixty
years of age, tall, thin, wiry, with a complexion well bronzed by toil and

exposure, with an independent, generous and open cast of countenance indicative of brave and noble impulses." This was not entirely accurate; Bridger was only fifty-three, not sixty, when he signed on, but the toil and exposure had obviously aged him as well as bronzing him.

The federal government's grievances against Brigham Young had piled up in the decade since his arrival in Utah. His followers insisted on polygamy, rejected the authority of the federal government, and were bent on setting up an independent theocracy that they called Deseret. Federal officials fled the new Zion in fear of their lives. So in went the army, with Jim Bridger agreeing to guide the soldiers to Utah through the South Pass for five dollars a day plus grub.

Young declared martial law and vowed scorched-earth resistance, and the Mormons burned several army supply trains, one of which was accompanied by a twelve-year-old bullwhacker named William F. Cody (the "Buffalo" part came later). In September, amid the hysteria over the approach of federal forces, a Mormon militia, dressed as Indians and joined by a contingent of Paiute, attacked a wagon train of emigrants and slaughtered 120 of them at Mountain Meadows in southern Utah. Having already occupied Fort Bridger, the Mormons now put it to the torch, and the army was forced to encamp for the winter in the ruins, digging around for wild onions to ward off scurvy and keeping up morale with fantasies of lascivious Mormon women thankful for their release from the harems of Deseret.

As a fight it didn't amount to much in the end, more jaw than war. Young backed down in the end, and President James Buchanan issued a full pardon to all concerned. The captive wives did not seem especially grateful to their rescuers. A reporter for the *New York Herald* summed it up: "Killed, none; wounded, none; fooled, everybody."

With the end of hostilities, Old Gabe asked for his honorable discharge from the army and went back to the farm he maintained in Little Santa Fe, Missouri. There he found a new baby, William, but a dead wife, carried off in childbirth. Another season in the mountains would be his refuge from grief.

Almost as soon as the Yellowstone explorers left St. Louis, Captain

Raynolds conceived an intense dislike for Ferdinand Hayden, both for the man and his mandate. The captain insisted on discipline; Hayden ignored it. The wagons, army property for goodness sake, always seemed to be burdened down with chunks of rock and old animal bones. It appeared to Raynolds that "the Expedition had been fitted out simply to build up the Smithsonian Institution," whereas the true purpose of the army's investment of $160,000 was "more Military and Geographical."

Raynolds's orders were quite similar to those Jefferson had issued to Lewis and Clark more than fifty years earlier:

> The objects of this exploration are to ascertain, as far as practicable, everything related to the numbers, habits and disposition of the Indians inhabiting the country, its agricultural and mineralogical resources, its climate and the influences which govern it, the navigability of its streams, its topographical features, and the facilities and obstacles which the latter present to the construction of rail or common roads, either to meet the needs of military operations or those of emigration through, or settlement in, the country.

To spell this out more concretely: What was the best route from the East to the mineral wealth of the West? From the Yellowstone Basin (sure to attract new settlers, and sooner rather than later) to the South Pass? From Fort Laramie to the fur-trading center of Fort Benton on the upper Missouri, and thence to the new road that Lieutenant John Mullan and his team of engineers were mapping from Minnesota to Puget Sound? And what would be the national security implications of driving these new roads through the hunting grounds of the Sioux and the Blackfeet?

And then, finally, there remained the great enigma of the upper Yellowstone, the empty space on Warren's map that might as well have been labeled "Here Be Dragons." Raynolds was charged, once and for all, "to ascertain the truth or falsehood" of the legends of the mountain men, a challenge that kindled a rare spark of passion in the stolid lighthouse engineer.

Though he couldn't stand Hayden, Captain Raynolds was full of respect for the guide he called "the old man of the mountains," and seemed to take his Yellowstone tales at face value. In his journal, which is careful, conscientious, and usually fretful about something, Raynolds wrote:

> Bridger, in one of his recitals, describes an immense boiling springs that is a perfect counterpart of the Geysers of Iceland. As he is uneducated, and had probably never heard of the existence of these natural marvels elsewhere, I have little doubt that he spoke of that which he had actually seen.

After leaving St. Louis by steamer in May 1859, the expedition's first stop was the old American Fur Company trading post at Fort Pierre, where Hayden had spent the winter with Alexander Culbertson five years earlier. But before the serious exploring could begin, Raynolds had another task: to enforce the terms of the treaty that General Harney had negotiated with the Sioux six months after Blue Water.

As soon as the steamer docked, Raynolds ordered the local chiefs to assemble for "a talk." He had been asked to evaluate the "numbers, habits and disposition" of the tribes he met on his journey, and he made quick, terse judgments. Their numbers were modest. Their habits were repellent. Their disposition was fair to middling.

Fifty Sioux showed up to hear him lay out his terms, "decked in full court dress, with feathers and paint in profusion." This display did nothing to impress the captain, who also went "behind the scenes" at the trading post to observe the chiefs in less formal mode. He found them dressed in filthy loincloths, worn buffalo robes, and greasy blankets, "lying about on the floor in all conceivable postures, their whole air and appearance indicating ignorance and indolence." The scene "produced an ineffaceable impression upon my mind, banishing all ideas of dignity in the Indian character, and leaving a vividly realizing sense of the fact that the red men are savages."

Raynolds approved thoroughly of Harney's "severe chastisement" of the Sioux at Blue Water—as, we may infer, did Hayden. But Raynolds was perplexed by the treaty that followed, which obliged him to dole out supplies, clothing, and firearms. He felt such generosity was a mistake: "This is simply offering a premium for future outrages, and lessens the savage's appreciation of the power and majesty of the government." In case the Sioux had any misconceptions about that majesty, Raynolds laid on "an occular [sic] demonstration of the improved quality" of the weapons carried by his escort.

He then demanded unhampered passage through the Sioux lands. A Hunkpapa chief named Bear Rib protested; Harney had promised that no whites would travel through his lands. No need for concern, said Raynolds, I'm an explorer, not a land-grabber; the Great Father simply likes to send people like me out to inspect the far corners of his realm. But that didn't satisfy Bear Rib. What would happen if some of our young warriors were to bother you? he asked. How can we guarantee keeping every last one of them under control?

"I replied," Raynolds wrote in his journal, "that the President would undoubtedly hold the entire nation responsible if I should be molested." Less than four years after Blue Water, there was no need for him to spell out the implied threat.

Leaving Fort Pierre, the explorers skirted the northern edge of the Black Hills until they reached the confluence of the Powder and the Yellowstone rivers. They saw signal fires on the hilltops at night, and rumors reached them that a war party of 350 Sioux was planning an ambush. But Raynolds was confident in the effect of his "occular demonstration," and no attack materialized.

Guided by Bridger, they continued by a circuitous route into the Crow country, where they picked up a guide called Robert Meldrum, an old friend of Culbertson and Malcolm Clarke, who had lived among the friendly tribe for thirty years, spoke their language fluently, and was also, like Bridger, familiar with the upper Yellowstone. So now there was a second set of travelers' tales to while away the long evenings in camp.

The Crow chiefs professed lasting friendship, as long as the whites did not settle permanently on their lands. "We have never killed a white man," said Two Bears, who stopped by Raynolds's tent, wearing pants, shirt, and hat, and made himself thoroughly at home. Raynolds was pleased by the chief's wardrobe. In fact, he was tentatively pleased by the Crows as a whole, noting that they were "of much lighter color than the Sioux, and have a less savage and repulsive expression." He was fascinated, at least at first, by the vain and exotic displays of their chiefs and warriors: their skin leggings, ornamented with brightly painted porcupine quills; the regal tricorn headdress; the beaded, ermine-fringed wrap, which reminded him of a Mexican serape; the faces caked with vermilion war paint; the hair worn long, even to the knees, compacted with gum and bear grease and daubed with splotches of white paint. But the more he saw of the Crows, the more the fascinated anthropologist gave way to the censorious moralist. "Their personal cleanliness is disgusting, and their bodies are covered with vermin," he confided to his journal. "Nothing was safe that they could steal, and their licentiousness was beyond conception."

Eventually Raynolds found the Crows too annoying for words and doubled the night guard on the camp to keep them at a distance. He spent a lot of his time being annoyed by one thing or another, irritated by the rolling sagebrush plains, frustrated by the quicksands at the river crossings, fractious about the lack of good water and forage. He pronounced "the entire district . . . unfit for the home of the white man."

The expedition proceeded through the deep-cut valleys and annoying side gulleys of the Powder, Tongue, and Bighorn rivers. Raynolds continued to be upset by Hayden's disdain for discipline and his solo forays into the wild, one of which kept him absent for three days. Then the lieutenant in charge of the military escort staged a mini-mutiny, telling Raynolds that he had no intention of taking orders from an engineer, only a line officer. (After their return, Raynolds ordered the man court-martialed, but to his chagrin the court upheld the junior officer's interpretation of army regulations.)

By mid-October, as the long nights began to draw in, Raynolds, Hayden, and Bridger had described a large counterclockwise loop and found themselves at Deer Creek, in the vicinity of present-day Casper,

Wyoming. There wasn't much here but some unfinished buildings belonging to the Indian Agency of the Upper Platte. Raynolds found a rough cabin that had been abandoned by a Mormon emigrant, and the party hunkered down to wait for spring. "We are totally shut up with cold and snow," Hayden wrote to Meek. "Thermometer 30° below zero. We are going to have a hard winter." At least there was a weekly mail delivery, a tenuous link with civilization, and Baird sent care packages from Washington via the newly inaugurated Pony Express that included the latest issues of *Harper's Weekly, Century* magazine, and other Eastern specifics against the disease of boredom. Seven glacial months in close proximity to each other were not what either Raynolds or Hayden would have chosen, though Jim Bridger, who had certainly seen worse, remained his usual unflappable self and recycled his full repertoire of Yellowstone stories. "Some of these Munchausen [sic] tales . . . [were] altogether too good to be lost," Raynolds wrote in one of his less ponderous moments.

Otherwise the topographical engineer sat and fretted and prayed and considered paths to self-improvement. "May I have grace to live more in accordance with my professions and may I be the means of doing something in my Master's cause," he wrote in his journal. He took astronomical observations and practiced on his flute. He worried about the ornery mood among the troops. He worried about how much they were drinking. He worried about his urinary tract infection. He debated theology with a hapless group of German Lutherans who were on their way to open a mission among the Crows but also found themselves stranded at Deer Creek for the winter. They were "god-fearing and devoted men, but ignorant of the world as of our language, and in consequence poorly fitted for the labors they have undertaken." Poorly fitted, indeed. The Lutherans never did reach the Crows. In the springtime, their leader was murdered by the Sioux, and the rest of them retreated to Iowa, asking directions in German.

The high point of Raynolds's week was always Sunday. Week after week he thumped his Bible and ordered three pistol shots to be fired in lieu of church bells. "I find that entire party eagerly anticipate throughout the week the welcome rest of the Sabbath," he wrote with a large degree of wishful thinking, "and upon Monday morning our labors are resumed with renewed vigor, an illustration of the physical advantages of this heaven-appointed day of rest." In other entries Raynolds displayed the stoic qualities of the true martyr. "Read the Service as usual at 9 o'clock," he told his journal. "Attendance not as good as I would like, yet hope it may be the means of doing good."

Hayden did his best to sit still for the occasional sermon and maintain a façade of civility—no profit in doing otherwise—but he regarded Sundays mainly as a waste of good fossil-hunting time. Raynolds spent considerable energy trying to make him see the error of his ways but made little headway. He sighed to his journal that Hayden "seems to live only for the world and worldly fame. . . . I fear his whole aim is this world's rewards," not those of the hereafter. Which was basically true.

Hayden began to wonder if his previous military partner had been so bad after all, and vented his feelings in letters to Meek and Baird back east. "Capt. R. is an old <u>fogie</u>," he wrote. "This man has not the tithe of the good sense or intellect of Warren." Which was also basically true. "I am not happy on this trip. My Christian Captain is in trouble with someone all the time. About all he cares for is to get back with his wife. I don't think I shall ever go out again unless Warren were to go."

For now, though, Hayden and Raynolds were stuck with each other, and on May 10, 1860, with spring finally in the air, they broke camp and headed west toward the Wind River Valley for the final leg of their journey to the geyser basins.

Two weeks later, at the junction of the Wind and the Popo Agie, Raynolds divided the party in two. Lieutenant Henry Maynadier took one group north down the Bighorn to the Yellowstone, where he was to retrace, in reverse, the route that William Clark had taken in 1806, as far as the Three Forks of the Missouri, the heart of the old fur-trapping country. Raynolds, Hayden, and Bridger would make for the headwaters of the Wind, crack the mysteries of the upper Yellowstone, and rejoin Maynadier at the Three Forks on June 30. Barely a month. Leaving winter camp at Deer Creek so late had created enormous time pressures, for Raynolds had orders to reach the Canadian border in time to observe a total solar eclipse in the middle of July.

Time was not the only problem. The winter snows had been the heaviest in memory and still lay thick on the ground. Bridger was sick. Up to this point, whenever the old man raised a question about the party's route, Raynolds had bowed to his advice "out of deference to his remarkable knowledge of the country." Approaching the upper Yellowstone, however, Raynolds turned mulish. He told Bridger that he intended to proceed straight up the Wind River, over the mountains, and voilà, Yellowstone Lake. The old man seems to have bitten his tongue. Perhaps after a year of the captain's company, he relished the idea of watching the man make an ass of himself.

They went on, flanked by mountains that were "aesthetically magnificent, but practically foreboding." Up ahead to the right were the first of the Absarokas. The exact route they took in their attempt to cross the Continental Divide is not entirely clear from the markings on Raynolds's map or from his diary. The captain reported that they were confronted by a sheer basalt ridge, "rising not less than 5,000 feet above us, its walls apparently vertical with no visible pass or even cañon"—almost certainly the forbidding walls of rock that stretch from the Breccia Cliffs and the Pinnacle Buttes to the towering finger spire of the Ramshorn.[3] Raynolds and Hayden rode to the head of the winding Dunoir Valley, but that looked no more promising.

Raynolds was despondent. "Triumphantly and forcibly," Bridger said, "I told you you could not go through. A bird can't fly over that without taking a supply of grub along." Raynolds had no alternative but to admit defeat, "mentally conced[ing] the accuracy of the information of the 'old man of the mountains.'"

For some reason they failed to do the obvious thing, which was to keep following the Wind to its source. That would have brought them to the easiest of the crossings of the divide (though in this season nothing would have been easy)—the Togwotee Pass. Instead, they pitched camp, much discouraged, at the head of the great natural amphitheater of the

Wind. Scattered all around were hundreds of discarded Shoshone lodge poles from a winter camp, no doubt left behind by Chief Washakie's people. So soon after the death of his wife, the chief's daughter, the melancholy setting probably did nothing to improve Bridger's mood.

They struggled on the next day with painful slowness. Raynolds climbed alone to a new vantage point, wriggling over the deep snow on all fours to avoid falling through the icy crust. Sometimes it gave way beneath his weight, and he plunged in, neck deep. Seeing nothing useful, he returned to camp, soaked and exhausted by his labors. They were well above nine thousand feet now. Next day, more wading through fields of mud and late snowdrifts and swollen streams. Even Bridger didn't seem to know what to do next. "My guide seems more at a loss than I have ever seen him," Raynolds wrote.

They headed back to the southwest, crossing Union Pass in the Wind River Range, and dipping down along the Fish Creek drainage to the brick-red hills of the Gros Ventre valley, which the tribe of that name used for their annual migrations to the buffalo grounds. Here the captain insisted on halting for his customary observance of the Sabbath; Hayden went off in search of specimens. When they started off again on Monday, the mood of the escort began to turn ugly: "A spirit of insubordination and discontent was . . . manifest among the men," Raynolds wrote.

The captain was now "exceedingly anxious to reach the upper Yellowstone." On June 5, they conferred again—"a full discussion of the question in all its bearings." Somewhere short of the confluence of the Gros Ventre and the Snake, they made a right turn. Bridger said they were following an old trappers' route he had taken once before, up to Two Ocean Pass, where he had seen a river that split in two, one fork to the Pacific and the other to the Atlantic, giving him more tales to tell, of trout swimming in both directions in the same piece of water. From that crack in the divide, it was all downhill, just a few miles, to the broad valley at the head of the Yellowstone that trappers, who used it often, called the Thorofare.

On June 7, Raynolds resolved to strike out for the pass with a small party of nine, to "pick out some path by which we may if possible find our way across [the mountains], and accomplish our purpose." They floundered around in the drifts, constantly forced downward as they tried to ascend, tumbling into snow-choked crevasses "in a style at once ridiculous and exhausting." Raynolds ordered the men to stay back and pressed on to the divide, alone. What he saw there must have been like a blow to the gut: the glittering meander of the Yellowstone headwaters, above the lake, but many miles of thick snow and rugged slopes between him and his destination.[4] Stretching away in the middle distance to the east of the lake was a row of ten-thousand-foot-plus summits that in later years would be called Colter Peak, Mount Langford, and Mount Doane. There was no way to bring the whole party up here. The pack animals would surely perish; perhaps they all would. "My fondly cherished schemes of this nature were all dissipated . . . by the prospect before us," Raynolds wrote. His mission had failed, yet Christian charity prevailed; he laid no blame on Bridger. "These little errors in matters of detail, upon his part, are not remarkable, as it is 15 years since he last visited this region."[5]

Eventually, Raynolds would draw a map of his 1860 journey. It shows the plateau of the upper Yellowstone as a great void encircled by crenellated battlements, like a child's sandcastle representation of a medieval fortress.

B y June 9, the party was on the banks of the Snake, looking up at "the snow-covered peaks of the Great Teton, dazzling in the clear atmosphere, with the reflected rays of the newly risen sun." The ordeal was far from over. They still had to get across the big river, its braided channels swollen and angry with spring snowmelt. Bridger made a bullboat for the crossing, weaving its frame from willow branches, covering it with the buffalo skin from his tipi, waterproofing it with pine resin. They fought their way over in relays, losing one member of the military escort, who was swept away and drowned. Finally they made it to the other side. Three days for the crossing, and now it was June 16; they had forfeited the better part of ten days to the snow and to their miscalculations. Only two weeks remained to reach the rendezvous with Maynadier at the Three Forks.

Even so, they might still have reached the upper Yellowstone, at least in theory. After the crossing of the Snake and the Teton Pass, which Bridger knew well, the travel was somewhat easier, and the expedition made good time along the Henry's Fork. One of the hunters shot a bear, and the explorers dined on fresh meat for the first time in a week. When they reached Henry's Lake they made camp again, and Hayden went off on another of his side forays, accompanied this time by the party's topographer, J. D. Hutton. They came back with interesting news. They had ridden five miles to the divide—today's Targhee Pass—and looked down on the valley of another good-size river, which Raynolds, no doubt after consulting Warren's map, called the Burnt Hole. In fact it was the Madison.[6]

From this vantage point, Hayden said, he had seen a second pass on the far side of the valley. Bridger listened to the description and nodded; yes, that one led to the Gallatin. Between it and the upper Yellowstone there were no more mountains to be crossed. Given his obsession with reaching the geyser basins, Raynolds's only comment seems an odd statement of priorities: "If this is true, these passes unquestionably offer the best route for a transcontinental railroad." In fact, the distance from the Targhee Pass to the junction of the Madison and the Firehole was no more than twenty-five miles, most of it over flat country, with just a short stretch of canyon. They might have covered that distance in a day; certainly no more than two. But rather like William Clark in 1806, standing at the big bend of the Yellowstone and considering the "high rugid mountain" to his south, Captain Raynolds was looking at his watch. An appointment to keep with Lieutenant Maynadier; orders to observe the solar eclipse; a last opportunity missed.

To be fair, Raynolds and Bridger may have been confused as well as pressed for time. They were dealing with a major geological and topographical conundrum, after all: How could the Madison, the Gallatin, the Yellowstone, and the Snake—in other words, the paths to the Missouri and the Columbia—all rise in a single volcanic plateau, their sources no more than a few miles apart?

So Raynolds turned left. But what if he had turned right? For that matter, what if he had left winter camp a couple of weeks later, giving enough time for the snow in the high passes to melt? What if he hadn't been so stubborn about trying to cross the Absarokas? What if Bridger hadn't lost his bearings on the way to Two Ocean Pass? What if the army hadn't been so interested in a solar eclipse?[7]

What if? The perennial question of history.

Raynolds came back from the Yellowstone with a daunting task: how to digest hundreds of pages of often peevish journal entries, full of annoying Indians and unobserved Sabbaths, into a concise form fit for publication by the government. A year wasn't enough, and the report languished. With the Civil War, explorations of the West by topographical engineers became an unaffordable luxury. For Raynolds, the war was just one more annoyance, "scattering my assistants [and] seriously interfering with my work." He saw field service with the Sixth Ohio Volunteer Cavalry and returned to Detroit as a lighthouse engineer after the war, worrying once again about things like the efficiency of Fresnel lenses and the correct temperature for preheating lard oil for use in the lamps.

In the end it took him more than six years to finish his report. He submitted it to the army in July 1867, acknowledging "its many and great imperfections"; a year later it was published as a Senate document. It did confirm that there was a viable wagon road from central Wyoming to the Yellowstone along the base of the Bighorns, but that was old news. By 1867 thousands of prairie schooners had taken this trail, and the army was embroiled in a traumatic three-year war with the Sioux to keep it open—the only Western war it ever lost.

The upper Yellowstone remained an unsolved riddle, and on the crucial question of its physical character, Raynolds was dead wrong—strangely so, since he had been traveling in the company of the country's best-known geologist and its most famous guide. Speculating about the "burning plains" that he had heard Bridger describe, Raynolds wondered if they might be volcanic, but decided that they were "more probably burning beds of lignite similar to those on Powder River."

Any melancholy Raynolds may have felt about his failure is concealed beneath his Christian resignation. He does allow himself a single *what if*... Had they waited another month before trying to cross the mountains, the snow would have melted, and it might all have been different, even fairly painless. "I cannot doubt, therefore," he wrote, "that at no very distant day the mysteries of this region will be fully revealed, and though small in extent, I regard the valley of the upper Yellowstone as the most interesting unexplored district in our widely expanded country."

But for now, he wrote, it would have to remain "a terra incognita."

Part Two

CIVILIZERS

9

SAVAGERY, BARBARISM, CIVILIZATION

1860–1862

Whatever explorers like Raynolds and Hayden might think, East Coast politicians had spent decades heaping scorn on the terra incognita. "Mountains wholly impassable," one senator said. "Irreclaimable and barren," said another; "rock-bound, cheerless, uninviting." "What do we want with this vast, worthless area, this region of savages and wild beasts?" Daniel Webster asked.[1] Perhaps it might serve one day as a penal colony, a newspaper editor suggested, as England used Australia's Botany Bay. By 1860, the whole vast territory that would later be known as Montana was still devoid of whites, save only for a couple of Jesuit missions, a scattering of isolated fur-trading posts, and a handful of solitary prospectors. Anyone seeking to change that situation, to explore the region's impassable mountains and exploit its unknown resources, would have to settle once and for all the problem of the implacable tribes that stood in the way.

By the early 1860s, there was some awareness among the better educated pioneers and military officers of an emerging body of social theory suggesting how that obstacle should be dealt with. These ideas were rooted in the European Enlightenment and elaborated in the United States by scholars like Lewis Henry Morgan and Edward Burnett Tylor, who divided all human societies into three clearly defined stages: Savagery, Barbarism,

and Civilization. Savages had the bow and arrow, fire, the clay pot; barbar-
ians grew crops, domesticated animals, worked in metal; civilized man
created the written alphabet and moved smoothly from there to the cen-
tralized state, the acquisition of land and material wealth, the railroad, the
hunger for gold.

If these ideas legitimized the subjugation of native peoples in Africa,
Asia, and North America, this was not based on a belief that skin color
made them innately inferior—cranial examination had shown that their
brains were equal in size and capacity to those of white men, and since the
laws of evolution were applicable to all cultures, they, too, would inevitably reach that state of grace that Morgan and Tylor called "civilization."
The problem was that in the meantime, they tended to do inconveniently
savage things, such as failing to understand the concepts of private land
ownership and Christian morality. And that, sadly, meant dealing with
them with a certain amount of unavoidable harshness—for their own
good.

The final outcome of this evolutionary process would be the extinction
of the savage culture, preferably by fair means but if necessary by foul. A
not untypical statement of this philosophy of generous genocide came
from Lieutenant John Mullan, who mapped out the first wagon road
through the Blackfeet country of Montana, a project that he completed in
1863. "The Indian is destined to disappear before the white man," Mullan
wrote, "and the only question is, how it may best be done, and his disappearance from our midst tempered with those elements calculated to pro-
duce to himself the least amount of suffering, and to us the least amount of
cost."[2]

The strategy for accomplishing this was the reservation, where the
Indians would emerge from savagery by first learning barbarian skills
such as growing vegetables and then moving on to the rudiments of civilization by sitting in rows in the schoolhouse with shorn locks and reciting their ABCs. However, for a recalcitrant tribe like the Blackfeet, the
terms of the discussion were very different.

The fur trader Alexander Culbertson, with his cross-cultural perspective, urged the lieutenant to get past the stereotypical view of the tribe as

"predatory and intractable savages," but Mullan was having none of it. They were "hell-hounds" and "devils," he raged. "[O]ur military force should be sent among them, put every man, woman and child to the knife, burn down their villages, and thus teach the nation that, since persuasion will not, force must and shall, effect [t]he ends we have in view." The Blackfeet "had better by far be totally exterminated, than thus left to prowl the mountains, murdering, plundering, and carrying everything before them."[3]

The final confrontation with the Blackfeet would come soon enough, but the first tribe that found itself in the way of permanent white settlement was the Nez Perce. Even as Raynolds, Hayden, and Bridger slogged their way through the mud and snow of the Absarokas, irresistible tides of miners were pouring into the river valleys of Idaho Territory, on the west side of the Continental Divide. A popular song of the time went like this: "They say there is a land/Where crystal waters flow/O'er beds of quartz and purest gold/Way out in Idaho!"[4]

The Nez Perce had lived in relative harmony with the whites since their encounter with Lewis and Clark more than half a century earlier.[5] A good proportion of the tribe had been Christianized by a fierce-eyed, black-bearded missionary named Henry Spalding, a vindictive man whose techniques for bringing the tribe to Jesus included beatings and whippings, as well as the translation of parts of the Bible into the Nez Perce language. Spalding alienated many, but his methods worked on an elderly chief named Tuekakas, or Old Joseph.

Pressure on Indian lands had preceded permanent settlement, of course, with the movement of emigrants along the Oregon Trail and the first glimmering of the idea of driving a railroad across the Northern Plains. In 1855, Governor Isaac Ingalls Stevens of Washington Territory, the first government emissary to explore the Blackfeet country since Meriwether Lewis, had offered a proposal to several northwestern tribes—the Flatheads, Pend d'Oreilles, Kutenai, Nez Perce, and Blackfeet. For the sake of their own peace and security, they would confine themselves to reservations that would keep them well away from the new white transit routes;

refuse to do so, and the settlers would take their land willy-nilly. The consequences, inevitably, would be violent.

The smaller tribes living around Flathead Lake and the present-day Glacier National Park raised no real objections to this scheme. Being blessedly gold-free, these remote mountains presented no real temptation to outsiders. In a separate agreement, Stevens gave the troublesome Blackfeet the right to hunt freely as before as far south as the Three Forks of the Missouri, leaving their reservation boundaries deliberately fuzzy. This ambiguity worked well enough for a few years, but it also sowed the seeds of worse future conflict as the pace of white traffic and settlement increased.

The Nez Perce, meanwhile, signed away a third of their territory, but neither this nor their acceptance of Jesus was enough to bring them a quiet life. By the summer of 1860 there were five thousand white settlers on Nez Perce lands. The new town of Lewiston accounted for two thousand of them, a number in which drunks, whores, gamblers, and murderers were generously represented. These were not people who sat around reading Morgan and Tylor. Like their counterparts elsewhere on the mining frontier, they liked to get straight to the point. A newspaper editor in Boise suggested distributing blankets infected with smallpox to the Nez Perce, a circumstance that had proved so salutary against the Blackfeet in 1837.[6]

The number of miners in Idaho swelled to fifteen thousand before the first soldiers arrived to establish a modicum of order.[7] But successive treaty demands cut the Nez Perce reservation by more than 80 percent.[8] This was presented as an act of kindness on the part of the whites; if the entire tribe would assemble in these new confines, the soldiers could protect them. About one-third of the tribe accepted this reasoning, but Old Joseph tore up the meaningless piece of paper he had received from Governor Stevens in 1855.

The old chief survived until 1871, when he was succeeded as leader of the nontreaty Nez Perce by his handsome and meditative son, Young Joseph, more properly known as Heinmot Tooyalakekt, or Thunder Traveling to Loftier Mountain Heights. On his deathbed, Old Joseph told him:

Always remember that your father never sold his country. You must stop your ears whenever you are asked to sign a treaty selling your home. A few years more, and the white men will be all around you. They have their eyes on this land. My son, never forget my dying words. This country holds your father's body. Never sell the bones of your father and your mother.[9]

Old Joseph's skull was disinterred some years later by parties unknown. The curious were permitted to view it in a dentist's office in the town of Baker, Oregon.

There was gold on the east side of the Continental Divide, too, and, as it turned out, in much greater quantities. As early as 1840, in the summer of his first encounter with the Piegans, Father De Smet had seen a gleam of color in a brushy stream named Alder Gulch, deep in the old beaver-trapping country and no more than eighty tantalizing miles from the western gateway to the Yellowstone caldera. But the Black Robe said nothing of his find for twenty years, judging with some reason that news of gold drove men to moral degeneracy and madness.[10]

But gold strikes cannot be kept quiet forever, and in the spring of 1858 a pair of adventurous brothers named Granville and James Stuart heard the rumors and settled on a creek near the present-day town of Deer Lodge. They planted a garden, raised a few cattle, traded trinkets with the Indians, grumbled when the Blackfeet stole their horses, and for four long, shivering Montana winters kept their minds sharp by reading Shakespeare and Byron, a French translation of the Bible, a history of Napoleon's army, and Adam Smith's *The Wealth of Nations*.[11]

In 1862 the brothers built their first sluices, though it was hard work for meager rewards. More hopeful prospectors began to trickle in as the mining booms in California, Nevada, and Colorado entered their decline. These newcomers panned each new stream as they proceeded northward, until, on July 28, 1862, a party of men from Denver hit pay dirt on a grasshopper-infested creek that ran through scrubby sagebrush country into the Beaverhead River. By fall there was a small town of about five hundred rough souls there. They called the new settlement Bannack, misspelling the name of the Shoshonean tribe, the Bannock, who roamed in the vicinity. A rough-hewn wooden sign was posted nearby to direct newcomers. Lettered in wagon-tar, it read:

Tu grass Hop Per diggins
30 myle
Kepe the Trale nex the bluffe.

One of the first Easterners to keep the "Trale nex the bluffe" was Nathaniel Pitt Langford. He described himself as "a plain substantial man," but this is only half-accurate; plain he was not.[12] Like many of the diarists and letter-writers who created the core record of the frontier generation, Langford was deeply conscious of his role in writing the first draft of history,[13] and he wrote as copiously as any of them, cranking out letters that covered a dozen, fifteen, twenty pages of foolscap at a time in an elegant, slanting copperplate hand.

Langford was born in Oneida County, New York, the eleventh of thirteen children. In 1854, at the age of twenty-two, he left the family home in Utica to start a new life in the frontier settlement of St. Paul, Minnesota. His character, as it emerges from a torrent of correspondence with his closest friend, a shy-sounding young man named Will Doolittle, is a welter of contradictions. He is ambitious, energetic, pompous, verbose, sentimental, moralistic, passionate, self-regarding, sometimes sociable and sometimes solitary, constantly interested in some comely woman he has met, given over to manly physical activity, hardheaded in business—the alpha male in all respects. At other times he is whimsical, affectionate, given to bad puns. He signs himself Nat, or Gnat, sometimes NPL. Throughout his life, close friends and family will call him Tan.

"Perhaps you think me wildly ambitious—a schemer, but never an executor; a dreamer—no realizer," he wrote to Doolittle, barely a month after reaching Minnesota. "If it has been true in the past, it is (I believe) true no longer. Once my thought was like my sight, was bounded by a few surrounding hills; <u>now</u> a continent is the field.[14]

Langford relished the rough-and-ready masculine informality of people on the frontier, amid the smell of fresh-sawn lumber, where "the conventionalities of refined society have not deadened the heart."[15] But at the same time, like so many settlers of his kind, he began to dream of importing the ordered framework of civilization—the church, the school, the courthouse, the town meeting—into these raw communities.

As he embarked on his business career, Langford was preoccupied with his sense of honor—and with letting the world know about it. "I see every day, more and more, the paramount importance of being governed by the strictest integrity, even in the smallest matters of business,"[16] he told Doolittle. Yet he could not resist—never would be able to—a certain boastfulness, couched in the most solemn expressions of modesty. Telling Doolittle of a killing he had made in a land deal, he wrote, "Will, this last sentence looks very gas-y, but I would not write it to any one but to you. I do not write it because I want to <u>blow</u>."[17] Of course not.

Other crucial facets of Langford's character came into focus during his eight years in St. Paul. By twenty-three, he was a partner in the politically well-connected banking house of Marshall & Co., and his letters home began to fill with tales of profitable investments. At twenty-five, with two partners, he was in a position to invest $50,000 in the newly established North Pacific Rail Road Company, already seeing the strategic importance of railroad land grants to the civilizing and prosperity of the frontier. At twenty-seven, he became master of the local masonic lodge in St. Paul.[18] At twenty-eight, when the house of Marshall failed, his eyes began to turn westward. And at thirty, a year into the Civil War, an opportunity arose in which patriotism, ambition, and the lure of wealth came into perfect alignment.

Western gold was critical to Lincoln as a source of funding for the war effort.[19] By the early summer of 1862 the northern offensive had bogged down, the Army of the Potomac forced to suspend its assault on Richmond. Troops stationed on the frontier were tugged in two directions;

they were badly needed in the East, yet at the same time the emigrant routes and the roads to the goldfields had to be kept open, with more of the task falling on militias and volunteers who were much less disciplined and were prone to indiscriminate violence.

Unfortunately for Lincoln, the gold camps were filled with secessionist ideologues. They called their new settlements Dixie, Fort Sumter, Confederate Gulch. For the biggest camp of all the "Seceshes" would choose the name Varina, in honor of the wife of Jefferson Davis, until a local judge overruled them and ordered it changed to Virginia City, hedging his bets.

The Homestead Act of 1862 encouraged good Union men to move to the Western frontier as a counterweight, and soldiers on the access road exacted oaths of loyalty from travelers, whether sincerely sworn or not. For those coming from the upper Midwest, like Langford, the most direct route—cutting seven hundred grueling miles off the Oregon Trail—was the new wagon road that Lieutenant John Mullan had mapped out from Minnesota to Fort Benton, the head of navigation on the Missouri and Montana's major gold-shipping center.

The task of conducting the first wagon train fell to James L. Fisk, a spirited young captain in the 3rd Minnesota Regiment of Volunteers.[20] Langford wasted no time in presenting his credentials to Fisk: "To come straight to the matter," he wrote,

> I would like some important and prominent position—and I feel that I can render invaluable aid, in many ways. My business talent and energy would fit me for any important position; and I presume you know enough of these without my speaking of them . . . I feel competent to do myself and yourself credit, in anything I undertake, and can anyone serve you better?

Fisk took him on as "second assistant and commissary," which in effect made Langford third in command. The Northern Overland Expedition left St. Paul on July 7, 1862, with 117 men, 13 wives, 168 oxen, 8 mules, 14 horse trains, 13 pack animals, 17 cows, an assortment of mutts, a brass mountain howitzer, an armed escort of 40, and a half-breed Chippewa guide named Pierre Bottineau, who had worked for the American Fur Company and liked to grease his boots with oil of peppermint.[21]

The journey took them through the territory of the Sioux and the Blackfeet, and while the temper of the Blackfeet was uncertain, the Sioux were openly hostile. Eastern migration to Minnesota had put immense pressure on the Dakota Sioux, who had retaliated with a murderous rampage through the pioneer settlements in the summer of 1862. In December of that year thirty-eight of them were hanged, to this day the largest mass execution in American history.

Langford despised Indians from the first, describing the Sioux in terms strikingly similar to the journal entries of Captain William Raynolds at Fort Pierre. "Most miserable people," Langford wrote, deploring their "coarse, black visages" and finding them "naturally indolent." He continued unforgivingly, "They are becoming every year less in number and soon will all be gone. This is their fore-ordained doom. . . . They can no more live with civilized white men, than can the buffalo, or elk, or bear."[22]

The Fisk expedition made steady time across the open country, constantly on guard against attack, but there were no hostile encounters. At the Fort Union trading post on the upper Missouri the party was joined by the trader Robert Meldrum, who had helped guide Raynolds and Hayden through the Crow lands in the summer of 1859. They bumped into a party of suspicious Assiniboines, but bought them off with the gift of some buffalo carcasses. In the Blackfeet country, they breathed a little easier after an amicable dinner with a once hostile but now conciliatory Piegan chief named Little Dog.

The greater dangers were the barrenness of the land, the lack of fresh water, the constant sickness, the existential dread of traveling without a map and with no way of knowing how long it would take to reach their destination, fourteen hundred miles distant on the far side of the Continental Divide. They saw herds of buffalo so vast that Langford was reminded of the flocks of passenger pigeons he had seen darkening the sky over St. Paul. A couple was married on a velvety patch of prairie. A child was born. Langford formed a lasting friendship with a man by the name of David Folsom, a New Hampshire Quaker six years his junior, who had been a schoolteacher in St. Paul.

Langford and Fisk knew nothing of the gold strikes on Grasshopper Creek; their destination was the Salmon River in Idaho, the "river of no return." But when it reached the Rocky Mountains, the party halted. It was late September, they were fourteen weeks out of St. Paul, and winter was fast approaching. Their provisions were almost gone, the cattle were too exhausted to go on, and the most arduous part of the journey was still to come. The nearest known settlement was Salt Lake City, four hundred miles away across high mountain passes that would soon be choked by snow, "beset for the entire distance by hostile Indians";[23] which mainly meant roving bands of Blackfeet raiders.

When the Fisk train reached the Continental Divide, Langford invited the two other masons in the party to collect the Bible, square, and compass and join him on a nearby hilltop. It was a pivotal moment in his life, and in the history of Montana. Freemasonry had a long and conflicted history in the United States. Discredited in the 1820s by charges of secrecy, conspiracy, and atheism, it had steadily rebuilt its reputation in the years leading up to the Civil War. Masons now stressed their patriotism, fellowship, and charitable deeds, and if they still insisted on closed and arcane rites, let them be thought of not as a secret society but as a society with secrets. In Montana their role would be crucial. Tracing their lineage proudly back to Meriwether Lewis, those who would build its institutions, impose law and order, and explore the remotest corners of the territory were masons, almost to a man.

On the hilltop, it was a quiet evening under a rising moon. Langford, more versed in masonic ritual than his companions, acted as Worshipful Master as the three men joined hands and declared the establishment of the first Lodge of Master Masons in Montana. A painting by the twentieth-century artist Olaf Seltzer memorializes the scene. Two men stand on a rock. One has his head bowed, as if in prayer. The second, arms folded, carries a weapon at his belt. Several feet above them Langford stands erect, a commanding presence. He wears an immaculate dark suit and holds his hat in one hand. He has a long, dense black beard. Behind him, towering peaks stretch away into the distance. It is a classic Western genre piece, though executed with skill.[24]

Most of the exhausted Fisk party stayed put at the divide, trying their luck on a nearby creek just south of the present-day city of Helena. But a man they met on the trail had spoken of a new settlement that went by the name of Grasshopper, or Bannack, where a rich strike had been made two months before. Langford and two others volunteered to make a reconnaissance[25] and rode off into the unknown, convinced, in Langford's later account, that they faced "the certainty of death in its most horrid form if they fell into the clutches of a band of prowling Blackfeet."[26]

On the first day out, they pitched camp in a narrow canyon "not ten rods wide," although they knew that this contravened the most basic rule of traveling in Blackfeet country: always find a campsite at least half a mile from the trail to minimize the risk of ambush. Langford awoke at three in the morning, covered in five inches of fresh snow. "[Our] fire lighted up the canyon with a lurid gloom and mantled the snow-covered trees with a ghastly radiance," he wrote. "The black smoke of the burning pitch rolled in clouds through the atmosphere, which seemed to be choked with the myriad snowflakes." From somewhere above him, he heard a neighing sound, obviously a human counterfeit; then, from below, a similar response. He roused his companions and quickly unhitched the horses. Out of the swirling snow came forty or more Blackfeet warriors, each holding a gun.

> Their faces hideous with war paint, their long ebon hair floating to the wind, their heads adorned with bald-eagle's feathers, and their knees and elbows daintily tricked out with strips of antelope skin and white feathery skunks' tails, they seemed like a troop of demons which had just sprung out of the earth, rather than beings of flesh and blood.

The leader of the raiding party seemed to give the signal for attack, but there was confusion in the ranks and a series of incomprehensible exchanges. The chief appeared furious and began making violent gestures.

From the response of the warriors Langford surmised that their guns were wet and their firing caps useless.

This is the kind of detail that sometimes nags at the reader of Langford's memoirs, which are filled with moments of high Victorian melodrama: forty guns, and every last one of them disabled by the weather? Whatever the case, the warriors put away their firearms and drew bows and arrows, but by that time Langford and his companions had maneuvered the horses into a defensive circle and were using them as improvised breastworks. Langford offers another surmise here: that the Indians declined to fire because they risked killing the horses, the theft of which was presumably their main objective. More hesitation, a long moment of suspense, and then the Indians wheeled on their mounts and galloped off into the storm.

As so often, Langford is giving us a perennial of frontier literature: the narrow escape from a fate worse than death. And if his account is to be taken at face value, this was the first of many such episodes as he honed his career as Montana pioneer, civilizer, and eventual explorer of the Yellowstone.

10

ROADS PAVED WITH GOLD

1863

In the first winter of Nathaniel Langford's residence in Bannack, the total population of Montana was 670, of whom 59 were "respectable females." These numbers are recorded in a publication of the period entitled "A List of All Persons (Except Indians) Who Were in What Is Now Montana During the Winter of 1862–1863."[1] Bannack alone accounted for 369 of the men and 33 women. How many of the latter were "respectable" is not noted. The men listed include such worthies as Whiskey Bill, Wild Cat Bill, Bummer Dan, Old Phil the Man Eater, and Geo. Hillerman, "The Great American Pie-Biter." Twenty-seven of the men are recorded as having died violent deaths. Had alcohol not had such a bad effect on a fellow's aim, the number might have been higher.

Placer mining (the word derives from the Spanish *placera*: alluvial sand) is an arduous job but one that requires no particular skills. Once "the color" is located, it's a matter of long, and for most people fruitless, days of digging, sluicing, and panning. But on Grasshopper Creek almost anyone had a real shot at unimaginable wealth. It was said that a miner could uproot a piece of sagebrush and shake out a dollar's worth of gold. Within four years, the diggings in Bannack and Virginia City, followed by Confederate Gulch and Last Chance Gulch—site of the future city of Helena—may have yielded $100 million.[2] Only California produced more.

Of all the trails to Montana, the easiest was from the south, through Utah. But as in Idaho, there was an obstacle that had to be cleared away first. This time it was not the Nez Perce but the Shoshone.

This was the Shoshone-Bannock heartland, centered on the fertile Cache Valley. Unfortunately for the Sho-Ban, the valley's fertility made it a prime target for the new Mormon immigrants to Utah. Brigham Young had seemed well-disposed to Indians at first, believing them to be direct descendants of the tribes of Israel. "Better to feed them than fight them," he said. But when well-intentioned theology runs up against a competition for natural resources, it is usually the loser.

By 1855, Mormon settlers had begun to move into the rich bottomlands of the Bear River, an old haunt of the fur trappers and a favored site for Shoshone winter camps. The settlers not only frightened away the game, they began selling cattle to the Shoshone that had been fattened on the same grass the tribe used to graze its horses. For the Shoshone, it was no longer a matter of feed or fight; it was fight or starve. But Indian resistance only invited visits from the Mormon militia known as the Minute Men, and the cycle of violence grew worse.[3]

By the summer of 1860 hundreds of wagons were headed for the valley; people talked of "Cache Valley Fever." Rage mounted on one side, hysteria on the other. News of Shoshone attacks on settlers mutated into rumors of wholesale massacre,[4] while the raiders responded to the worsening food shortages by treating the new Pony Express stations and stage stops like unlocked grocery stores. Bear Hunter, chief of the Cache Valley band of Shoshone, urged restraint on his angry young men, but as far as they were concerned their honor and manhood were at stake.

After the gold strikes on Grasshopper Creek in 1862, the trails through the Cache Valley swarmed not only with Mormon settlers but with prospectors, itinerant merchants, assorted lowlifes—and soldiers, who now arrived to protect the strategically important conduit for gold for the Union Army.[5] With so many regular troops tied up in the East, Lincoln had no alternative but to rely on loyal volunteers, and those were men not generally known for their discipline or restraint.

Not that "restraint" was a word one would immediately associate with

Colonel Patrick Connor, commanding officer of the Second California Volunteer Cavalry, which was sent in to pacify the Cache Valley.[6] Connor, born in Ireland on St. Patrick's Day, 1820, was a hard and bitter man with soul-piercing eyes and razor-edged black side-whiskers, clean-shaven at the chin. His second-in-command, Major Edward McGarry, is best described as an alcoholic psychopath.[7] Connor's orders to him were straightforward: "Destroy every male Indian whom you may encounter in the vicinity of the late massacres. This course may seem harsh and severe, but I desire that the order may be rigidly enforced, as I am satisfied that in the end it will prove the most merciful." McGarry saluted smartly and began the systematic execution of prisoners. Running out of trees large enough to hang them, he shot them instead.

Far from being cowed, the Shoshone only stepped up their reprisal raids, and once they started killing miners bound for Montana a final detonation of the crisis became inevitable.[8] The chief justice of Utah Territory issued an arrest warrant for three Shoshone chiefs, including Bear Hunter, whose band was by now huddled, stationary, in its winter camp on the Bear River. But mere arrest was too tame for Connor's tastes. "I determined," he said, "although the weather was unfavorable to an expedition, to chastise them if possible." And chastise them he did.[9]

What he proposed was a tactical novelty; the first great military strike on an Indian winter camp. The Shoshone had hunkered down in a narrow defile on the east bank of the Bear River, thick with willows, sheltered below a bluff and warmed by some nearby hot springs. There were seventy-five lodges in the camp—some six hundred souls perhaps—and the camp was well-defended with ditches, breastworks, and escape routes.

Connor ordered the California volunteers well-munitioned to deal with this "miniature Sebastopol."[10] "Forty (40) rounds of carbine ammunition and thirty (30) rounds of pistol ammunition, per man." Sixteen thousand rounds in total; almost thirty chances at each man, woman, and child. Conducted by a Mormon guide, the soldiers advanced on the Shoshone camp through deep snow. Seventy-five suffered frostbite. Whiskey rations froze in their canteens. "Whiskers and moustache [were] so chained together by ice that opening the mouth became most difficult," said one soldier.

They arrived on the rock-hard banks of the Bear River at dawn on January 29, 1863, and despite the element of surprise met resistance and displays of bravado that infuriated Connor. He responded with mass slaughter and mass rape, even of women who were already dead and dying. The worst was reserved for Bear Hunter, the war chief turned conciliator, who was shot, kicked, whipped, and tortured in a variety of imaginative ways. "Because he would not die or cry for mercy, the soldiers became very angry," a survivor said years later. "One of the military men took his rifle, stepped to a burning campfire and heated his bayonet until it was glowing red. He then ran the burning hot metal through the chief's ears."[11]

The body count was straightforward enough on the army side, each casualty well accounted for "down to name, how wounded, when died, where buried, and with what eulogy."[12] On the Shoshone side, calculations were more complicated, and the numbers ranged widely, from 90 to 368 dead. Connor himself said 224 dead, without distinction as to age and sex. Whatever the true number, the *Deseret News* said that Connor's volunteers had "done a larger amount of Indian killing than ever fell to the lot of any single expedition of which we have knowledge."[13]

Verdicts on the event varied according to interest and perspective. The Mormons hailed Connor's action as "an intervention of the Almighty." The Montana miners adopted a new motto: Kill every Snake Indian in sight.[14] Connor himself was promoted to the rank of brigadier general.

And then there was the larger verdict of those who understood the full strategic significance of the killings on Bear River. Writing many years later, when many if not most Western settlers and military officers had softened their views, Nathaniel Langford wrote of the slaughter of the Shoshone: "The example to be salutary, must be terrible, and [Connor] contemplated nothing less than the destruction of the entire band.... This victory removed at once and forever the greatest impediment in the way of emigration to the new Territory." And, he might have added, it also removed a great impediment to his own ambitions.

. . .

All manner of men flocked to Bannack over that winter and the following spring, and the banks of Grasshopper Creek sprouted hundreds of crude timber cabins and shanties, tents and brush wickiups. But among the hordes of unskilled, illiterate placer miners and militant secessionists, there was also the nucleus of Montana's future elite—men who were drawn here by the promise of a quick fortune, the chance to prove their virility in this harsh corner of the frontier, and the opportunity to create a political order out of nothing. One early twentieth-century historian described the communities they built as "the ganglia of Civilization, comparable to Roman Colonies."[15]

There were several dozen of these men, but within their ranks a handful emerged—the elite within the elite—who would explore and map the remotest corners of this new territory, blazing paths that would eventually lead them to the blank, battlemented fortress of the upper Yellowstone that Captain William Raynolds had drawn in 1860. Langford was at the heart of this group, but around him were men like David Folsom, his Quaker schoolteacher friend from the Fisk expedition; Samuel Hauser, an ambitious young engineer and would-be entrepreneur from Kentucky who eventually became Langford's business partner; John Bozeman, "a great mountain pathfinder and Indian fighter," several inches over six feet, 225 pounds, a gambler, an amusing raconteur, and a favorite with the ladies, who abandoned his wife and three small children to join the gold rush and never saw his family again; and a self-effacing Virginian in his mid-forties, Walter Washington De Lacy, who could trace his lineage all the way back to 1172 and the first Norman governor of Ireland under King Henry II.

Hauser, who gave up his job on the Missouri-Pacific Railroad to join the hunt for the huge windfall profits that were offered by the virgin frontier and, unlike conventional business opportunities in the East, required no real capital investment or overhead.[16] His personality fit the times to perfection: ruthlessly competitive, willful to the point of reck-lessness, with a "tendency to procrastinate when the bill came due."[17]

Hauser had taken the steamboat *Emilie* from St. Louis to Fort Benton. He noted with satisfaction in his diary that the one-hundred-dollar fare had done a good job of social pruning; there were three doctors, two en-gineers, two ministers of religion, and a professor in the company, and "a large proportion of the balance are Gentlemen." They whiled away the long, dull days on the Missouri sitting on deck, reading, playing cards, dominoes, and checkers, and writing in their journals.[18]

In the early spring of 1863 Hauser joined a party of twenty-three pros-pectors led by James Stuart, the Shakespeare-reading pioneer of Gold Creek, to extend the search for color into the valley of the Yellowstone. In the event, they found more Indians than gold, and in particular received some instructive lessons in the contradictory temper of the Crows.

Their first encounter was on April 25, near the mouth of the Stillwater River, when a group of painted and pompadoured Crow rode up to the miners' camp with shouts of "Absaroka!" and a cheerful "How d'ye do!," a greeting they had learned from the whites.[19] After the two parties had bedded down together, the Crows spent most of the night trying to help themselves to anything that wasn't nailed down; they "would steal the world-renowned Arabs poor in a single hour," Stuart wrote later.

A week later, however, at the mouth of the Bighorn, where Stuart and Hauser had sketched out a provisional town site, there was a much more serious incident. This time there were no friendly how d'ye do's, only a fusillade from out of the darkness that killed four horses and mortally wounded two men. One of them had been sharing a blanket with Hauser, who woke up with blood streaming from his own chest. It was another episode from a dime novel: a bullet to the heart had struck a thick pock-etbook that he carried in his breast pocket and then lodged harmlessly over a rib.

He and Stuart identified their attackers as Crows, but it's possible they were Sioux.[20] This was contested territory between the two tribes, and a couple of days earlier the prospectors had passed some Sioux burial plat-forms. Furthermore, opening fire without provocation on a party of travelers was totally out of character for the Crows. On his deathbed, the great chief Arapooish, or Rotten Belly, had told his warriors, "Go back to my people with my dying words. Tell them ever hereafter to keep peace with the whites." And they prided themselves on having done so.[21]

A smaller group, led by William Fairweather, had split off from the main party and had their own adventures with a Crow war party, which captured them, took them back to a large camp of 180 tipis, and subjected them to a ceremony that was equal parts menacing and incomprehensible. While a medicine man chanted and drummed, the eight men were obliged to walk in endless circles around a sacred bush. Fairweather didn't think much of this, so he uprooted the bush and began beating the medicine man about the head with it. This apparently convinced the Crows that this eccentric white man had powerful medicine, and they sent the prospectors on their way.[22] Fairweather and his men then proceeded to a small creek lined with green alders, where they started digging around under a shelf of rimrock. On the first day they found small quantities of gold, enough for tobacco money. By the end of the second day, they had amassed $150 worth, and it was of unusual purity, much better than the gold in Idaho. Within months, Alder Gulch was home to ten thousand people, with the largest concentration in the new boomtown of Virginia City. In later years, Fairweather liked to ride through the streets drunk, tossing nuggets of gold in all directions. He said it amused him to see the children and the Chinese grubbing for it in the dirt.[23]

Virginia City was the second major settlement in Montana, and John Bozeman would now establish the third, which in time would become the most important to the explorers of the upper Yellowstone. He left Bannack at about the same time as Stuart and Hauser, but traveled in a different direction, and in search of a different source of wealth. Bozeman didn't think only of immediate profit; he had the eye of a grander strategist. Like Langford, he grasped the shortcomings of the existing routes from the States to the goldfields: The journey upriver from St. Louis to Fort Benton, and from there across the Blackfeet country, was long and dangerous. Although the road north through Utah was now secure, that portion of the Oregon Trail worked best for people coming from the West; for the main emigrant traffic from the East the trail remained slow and tedious, the wagon masters carrying maps that showed long, barren stretches with no reliable grass, wood, or water. Bozeman set out to find a more direct alternative.

Jim Bridger had much the same idea, and at much the same time. While Bozeman's trail cleaved to the east side of the Bighorns, Bridger's retraced much of the route he had shown Raynolds and Hayden four years earlier: to the west of those mountains and north to the Yellowstone. The Bozeman Trail up the Powder River had good grass and water but lots of hostile Indians. Bridger's route offered the reverse mix: The forage wasn't the best, but these were Crow lands, and the road was relatively safe from attack. Those who took it became known as "Bridger's Pilgrims."

Bozeman's first wagon train left the North Platte on July 3, 1863. Almost immediately he ran into trouble when a band of unsmiling Sioux told him to turn back. The wagon masters did as they were told, but Bozeman and nine others decided to disregard the warning. It took them almost two months to get back to the gold camps, traveling mainly by night, and they almost starved along the way.

But as Bozeman followed the Yellowstone back upriver and emerged from a narrow pass that now bears his name, he had a kind of entrepreneurial epiphany: Miners didn't just need pickaxes and shovels; they would also benefit from a change of diet. Beef, bear meat, and molasses grew monotonous. The settlers needed bread, fruit, and vegetables, and here, spread out like a pool table before him between the pass and the Three Forks of the Missouri, were hundreds of square miles of rich, black alluvial soil. Bozeman saw waving wheat and apple trees and potato fields, well watered by the Gallatin River and its east fork. A man could make a more reliable living here than he could through the crapshoot of placer mining. Bozeman selected a town site the following spring and went back to the Platte to pick up another season's worth of emigrants. On Christmas Eve, 1864, the first hotel in the new settlement of Bozeman opened with a ball.[24]

. . .

alter De Lacy, meanwhile, left Virginia City on August 3, 1863, mounted on a horse named Muggins, which had one blue eye, one black eye, and a schizophrenic personality to match. While Bozeman, Hauser, and Stuart had all headed east, De Lacy rode south into Idaho, with the goal of reaching the Snake River and Jackson Hole.[25]

A Catholic-educated civil engineer, "a splendid draftsman and a scientist of no mean repute," De Lacy had taught foreign languages at West Point and acquired the honorific rank of colonel for his exploits in the Mexican War and the Indian conflict in Washington Territory in the 1850s. He had also worked under Lieutenant John Mullan to grade the wagon road through the Blackfeet country.[26] By his own account, De Lacy was one of the few men in his group of prospectors (whom he referred to as the "Forty Thieves") who could hold his liquor or write his name, and he duly found himself elected their leader.[27] Despite his scientific credentials, this trip made no pretense of being a serious piece of exploring: "There was not a telescope, and hardly a watch, in the whole party," De Lacy recalled. It was a search for gold, pure and simple, though it was no more successful in this respect than the Stuart-Hauser expedition.

By the time De Lacy reached the Snake, a month later, he had made a lot of sketches but had barely a sniff of gold, and so, like Stuart, allowed his party to split up into several smaller groups that would take their own chances. De Lacy, with his remnant thieves, resolved to make his way back to Alder Gulch via the Madison River. So he rode north through dense timber to a large lake that for years afterward bore his name,[28] across the naked and forbidding Pitchstone Plateau, and down to an open basin filled with smoke.

One of De Lacy's companions, an otherwise forgotten individual named John C. Davis, told a reporter twenty years later, "When we first came in sight we thought the steam from the geysers was the smoke from a large Indian camp. [We] never dreamed that we were on the threshold of a great discovery. We left after a few hours without any of the party paying attention to the surroundings."[29]

This offhandedness is unconvincing, and De Lacy himself seemed quite impressed by what they had seen. "The ground sounded hollow beneath our feet, and we were in great fear of breaking through, and proceeded with great caution," he wrote later. "The water of these springs was intensely hot, of a beautiful ultra-marine hue, some boiling up in the middle, and many of them of very large size, being at least twenty feet in diameter and as deep."

Leaving the spectacle behind, De Lacy followed the Firehole River north, then turned west through the canyon of the Madison. He arrived back in Virginia City after seven weeks in the saddle, the first educated Easterner ever to have seen the bizarre wonders of the Yellowstone geyser basins.

{ II }

A NOOSE PENDANT

1863–1864

As these fingers of exploration reached out into the surrounding wilderness, Nathaniel Langford and Sam Hauser set about making money. Hauser opened the first smelter in Montana. Langford set up a sawmill and lumberyard that allowed the miners to replace their brush shelters with log cabins. At the end of 1864 he obtained the concession to operate a wagon road from Virginia City to the mouth of the Yellowstone, with a spur that led to the small new mining camp of Emigrant Gulch, recently discovered by a party of "Bridger's Pilgrims" and deeper into the upper Yellowstone valley than any previous white settlement. Langford also began to flex his political muscles, establishing himself as the leading Republican in the gold camps, president of the Union League of Bannack.[1]

Deeply conscious of their role as the advance guard of civilization, it flattered Langford and his friends to think that there was little between them at one end of the sociological spectrum and the hordes of draft dodgers, whores, and criminals at the other. "Middling people do not live in these regions," said the Englishman Thomas Dimsdale, a portly, florid, Oxford-educated schoolmaster and freemason[2] who launched a newspaper in Virginia City in 1864, even though he sometimes had to publish on lavender-colored cotton rag for want of newsprint.[3]

The next problem was to establish law and order. The camps were inherently lawless, "with no vice unrepresented," wrote Langford.[4] But this was not only because so many of the inhabitants had little to do but drink, gamble, and fornicate; there were also deeper structural reasons. There was still no federal law governing the mining of precious metals; that would not come until 1872. The camps were nominally part of Dakota Territory, but the territorial capital, Yankton, was more than a thousand miles away and no one there even knew of Bannack's existence for many months. "Napoleon was not more of an exile on St. Helena," Langford wrote. He did not learn of the battles at Antietam or Fredericksburg or the Second Bull Run—all of them in the latter third of 1862—until the following spring, when the first mails got through.

The Civil War was yet another source of problems. The seceshes had no intention of bending to federal law, if and when it arrived. They went wild at news of these Union defeats, and drunken horsemen set fire to the Stars and Stripes. Two years later, Lincoln's assassination prompted dancing in the streets, and a notice was posted on the door of Dimsdale's *Montana Post* that read, in part:

> *Old Abe has gone to Hell!*
> *Hurrah for Jeff Davis!*

During the first eighteen months of the Montana gold rush, Langford wrote later, the camps were equally divided between law-abiding citizens and "roughs," and "it was doubtful who possessed the mastery."[5] No one would question that the camps were, to put it mildly, rambunctious places. According to one new arrival, Virginia City "present[ed] a wild western air not seen in any other place in the country."[6] The main street was a mile long, with eight hotels, six billiard halls, four or five gambling houses, three dance halls, a generous number of brothels, and saloons beyond counting.[7] "Mr. Al K. Hall" was a permanent companion to these entertainments, variously served up as Lightning, Tarantula Juice, Tanglefoot, or Forty-Rod (because a man who had drunk it could knock you down at that distance with his breath). The standard recipe, according to

Granville Stuart, involved "a quantity of boiled mountain sage, two plugs tobacco steeped in water, box cayenne pepper, one gallon of water."

In the hurdy-gurdy houses, dancers could pull in twenty-five dollars in an evening, and after the prancing was over they could earn "fabulous sums for their purchased favors."[8] The minister "lectures on the evils of such places with considerable force," wrote Dimsdale, whose memoirs have moments of waspish Oxonian humor, "but his attention is evidently more fixed on the dancers than on his lecture."[9]

The streets swarmed with miners, gamblers, Indians, singers and dancers, horse traders, athletes, acrobats and contortionists, itinerant actors, minstrels, soothsayers and fortune-tellers, mediums and magicians, quack purveyors of patent medicines to cure venereal diseases. Drunks sprawled in the gutters. Chinese prostitutes could be bought in the Virginia City market for six hundred dollars apiece, with the customary discount for paying in gold. The other Chinese, laborers, launderers, and cooks, were universally despised. The miners couldn't abide the caterwauling of their music, the stink of their incense, the way they wore white instead of good Christian black at their funerals and laid out food for the dead. The things eaten by the living were an equal abomination; John Chinaman was said to favor rats fried in axle grease. "Don't kill 'em unless they deserve it," wrote another early newspaper, the *Montanian*. "But when they do—why, kill 'em lots."[10] The Chinamen, that is, not the rats.

While the low sort went to burlesques with titles like *The Frisky Cobbler*, the better class of citizen turned out for performances of *Romeo and Juliet* and *The Merchant of Venice* by Jack Langrishe's itinerant People's Theatre. "We had a number of fine balls attended by all the respectable people," said Granville Stuart. "Young people danced the waltz, schottish, varsovian, and polka," while "older ones stuck to the Virginia reel and quadrille." Dressed in freshly starched shirtfronts, men danced in pairs, since there were ten of them to every woman. No drinking was allowed.

Even in the hurdy-gurdies, not all the "soiled doves" were whores. Many women limited their evenings to lurching around the dance floor in the arms of some besotted miner with hands like an octopus, realizing that they could earn more that way in a week than an Eastern shopgirl could earn in two months. Besides, after dancing their feet to blisters many of them wanted nothing more than a good night's sleep.

The nominal forces of law and order were led by Sheriff Henry Plummer, whose singular disadvantage as a law-enforcement officer was that he was also the leader of a gang of road agents who had fled from Idaho after three of them were hanged by vigilantes.[11] Now they came to Bannack like flies to honey.

By the time Plummer arrived, he was known to have killed five men, starting with the husband of a girlfriend and another man encountered in a whorehouse. He was a celebrated gunslinger, said to be the fastest in the northern Rockies, although skeptics said his speed was greater than his accuracy. In that respect, Langford's Quaker friend David Folsom had the greater renown: It was said that he had once hit all five spots on the five of diamonds with consecutive shots. Yet Plummer was also "a man of the most insinuating address and gentlemanly manners," said Thomas Dimsdale,[12] and by the summer of 1863 he had been elected sheriff of the newly created Madison County.

Some remarked on his impassive manner, thin features, and cold, reptilian eyes, but Langford was charmed. Plummer "possessed great executive ability," he wrote, with

> a power over men that was remarkable, a fine person, polished address, and prescient knowledge of his fellows. . . . In demeanor he was quiet and modest, free from swagger and bluster, dignified and graceful. He was intelligent and brilliant in conversation, a good judge of men, and his manners were those of a polished gentleman.[13]

Whatever Langford thought of Plummer, the trust probably did not flow in the other direction, since Langford had already stuck his neck out to bring to justice one of the sheriff's most unsavory associates, a certain

Charley Reeves. In January 1863, the month of the Bear River massacre, when the miners' rage against the Shoshone was at its height, this Reeves had acquired—bought? stolen? who knows?—a woman of the Sheepeater band. He seems to have abused her without mercy, and she fled to the shelter of a local chief, encamped outside Bannack. Reeves rounded up a couple of the town drunks, chased her down, and used the chief's tipi for target practice, killing four people: the chief himself, a lame boy, a papoose, and a Frenchman. In Dimsdale's telling, the drunks declared that "if the d———d cowardly white folks on Yankee Flats were afraid of Indians, they were not."

Even though three of the four victims were Indians, Bannack clamored for a miners' court to try Reeves and his accomplices, the standard procedure in the absence of constituted legal authority. But miners' courts had a tendency to degenerate into mob scenes, and Langford, summoned by messenger from his sawmill, argued for a trial by jury. It's possible that his motives were mixed; in the absence of justice, one of Langford's fellow-Minnesotan migrants worried, "a thousand armed savages may pounce on us at an unlooked for moment."[14] But Langford's memoirs speak only of his devotion to justice. "Mounting a bench," he remembered,

> I reminded [the miners] of the constitutional provision which secured to every one accused of crime a trial by jury. It was a law of the land, as applicable on this as on any other occasion. The men were probably guilty; if so, the fact should be proved; if not, they had the right by law, on proving it, to an acquittal.[15]

The trial turned into a mob scene, regardless, which Langford compared to the chaotic early days of the French Revolution. There were yells of "String 'em up!" and "To the scaffold!" Pistols and knives were waved in the air, obscenities shouted. There were threats that no member of the jury would survive a month if they returned a guilty verdict. The defendants asked for Langford to be appointed foreman, apparently confident that his high-minded insistence on constitutional norms was their guarantee of freedom. When the vote came in, it was 11 to 1 for acquittal, but

Langford was the sole dissenter. Furthermore, he demanded the death penalty. More uproar, frantic deliberations, and in the end a fudged compromise: The men would be banished from Bannack and their property confiscated. But within days they shuffled back to town with a hangdog look; it was cold out there, and there was nothing to eat. No one had the heart to send them away again.[16]

While the sentences didn't stick, the threats and reprisals went on. By midsummer, only seven of the twenty-seven men involved in the trial as judge, prosecutor, witness, or juror were left alive in the territory. Eight or nine had been murdered, and the rest had fled. Langford says that he was marked after the trial as the road agents' prime enemy and that he never went anywhere without a loaded gun.[17] Someone took a potshot at him in Virginia City, grazing an eyeball, and he spent two weeks in a darkened room, temporarily blinded by an infection.

August 1863 brought the first outrider of government authority to the mining camps, in the person of a U.S. marshal from Idaho Territory, who invited Langford to run for the territorial legislature. He declined the honor; his political ambitions were tied up with the idea to create a separate territory east of the Bitterroots, which would eventually be called Montana. But he was happy to lend his good offices to the search for a deputy, and since the government wanted someone politically reliable the matter was put before the Union League, of which Langford was president. The vote was thirty to none for Henry Plummer.

Years later, Langford wrote that he and Sam Hauser already had their doubts about the man, though this has the ring of post-facto wisdom. Encountering Plummer on the street one day, Langford suggested a chat. He remembers that they sat on an ox-shoeing frame. He told the sheriff that he had had second thoughts and was overruling the vote of the Union League, to which Plummer responded with "many oaths and epithets" and threats of revenge.

The worst wave of robberies and murders began soon after that, in the fall. It was the season for travel, before the worst of the snows set in and the gold camps were cut off from the outside world. Trains of freighters brought in supplies for the long winter; miners who had hit pay dirt went home to bank their new wealth; those who had come up empty-handed returned to their families in the States. Filled with ravines, gullies, timber thickets, and other convenient hiding places, the lonely road between Bannack and Virginia City and the desolate four-hundred-mile stretch south to Salt Lake City were an open invitation to crime, infested by masked men with sawn-off shotguns. Over a period of two or three months, Dimsdale says, the road agents killed 102 people, and Langford and Hauser were next on their list.

They almost accomplished their goal, at least if Langford's memoirs are to be believed—always a question. In November 1863, he set off for an extended trip to the East, traveling with a Mormon freighter out of Salt Lake. He had properties to visit in Kansas and political ambitions to promote in Washington, where he hoped to pay a call on President Lincoln. Hauser said he would join him, and the two of them agreed to do a favor for their friend James Stuart by delivering fourteen thousand dollars in gold dust that he and a business partner owed to creditors in St. Louis. Sheriff Plummer, at his most ingratiating, offered Hauser a red scarf to wear, hoping that he would "find it useful on the journey these cold nights"—a melodramatic detail that Langford took to be a way of identifying him as a target.

Langford says he barely slept that night, bedded down on the frozen ground under a buffalo robe. Walking around at 3 A.M. to stamp the numbness out of his feet, he surprised a group of masked men, who galloped off in the direction of Bannack after Langford exhibited his shotgun. He says that the men were later identified as Plummer and three of his gang, though it is never explained how this was established.[18] Another miraculous escape from black-hearted villainy.

For the rest of the way to Salt Lake, Langford sat next to the garrulous driver, listening to his passionate lectures about the revelations of Joseph Smith and the teachings of Brigham Young. The Mormon noted that his black-bearded companion carried his shotgun cocked on his lap the whole way, each barrel loaded with a dozen revolver balls. Langford enjoyed a lively theological debate with the teamsters, whom he found "simple-hearted, affable and unsophisticated, with bigot faith in their creed." One of the Mormons remarked to another that the intense young man with the shotgun "talked mighty fine . . . and I rather think it would trouble Brigham Young himself to say nicer things." Langford had been reciting a passage from *Paradise Lost,* describing the meeting of Satan and Death at the gates of Hell.

In the Mormon capital, Langford was besieged by gentiles bearing tales of persecution and promised to relay their complaints to the federal government, even to the president himself if such a thing were possible. As it turned out, such a thing *was* possible. Langford met with Lincoln sometime in the early months of 1864, at least once and perhaps twice.[19]

He found the president in a somber mood. As Langford gave his account of the Mormon abuses, Lincoln "sat almost motionless, with body inclined forward, and eyes directed to the floor, for the space of over half a minute." Then he looked up and said that with a great and bloody war on his hands, he would have to put off the Mormon problem for another time. He took his leave of the visitor from the distant gold camps with a parable:

> I am like the old farmer out in Illinois. He and his boys had been grubbing the stumps, and clearing out the bushes from a large field before putting in the spring crop, and all the stumps had been cleared out except one—a large one with spreading roots, in which was a large hornet's nest, so that they could have a clear field for the plow—but the old man said it was getting late in the season and that it was time to get the seed into the ground. "Boys," said he, "that stump and hornet's nest ought to come out, but we have so much other work on hand that we'll have to plow around it this year." . . . So it is with me. That Utah hornet's nest ought to be rooted out—but there is more important work on hand just now, and we'll have to plow around it this year.

Langford's own more pressing concern was to lobby the federal government for a proper sytem of governance in the mining region. Who was to collect taxes? Regulate property disputes? Settle estates? Impose the criminal law? With Hauser and Stuart, he demonstrated the wealth of the new camps by pouring bags of gold onto the floor of the House of Representatives and illustrated their need for law and order with lurid tales of the Plummer gang.

A bill to separate the land east of the Bitterroots from Idaho Territory went to the Senate on March 30. There was an element of comic opera to the debate. "The name of this new territory—Montana—strikes me as peculiar, [as if] borrowed from some novel," said the noted abolitionist Senator Charles Sumner of Massachusetts, who had once been caned to within an inch of his life on the Senate floor for his passionate denunciation of slavery. But other senators calmed him by saying it was bona fide Latin, and that no one could doubt that the place was indeed mountainous.

The deeper debate, however, touched the rawest nerve of American politics—race. Would negroes have the right to vote in this remote place that no Eastern politician had ever seen? A purely academic question, some scoffed: There wasn't a black face for hundreds of miles around. Not so, said Senator Morton S. Wilkinson of Minnesota. His good friend Mr. Nathaniel Pitt Langford of St. Paul had reported that there were a fair number of negroes in the gold camps, some of them prosperous and respectable; one black prospector was said to be worth $50,000. The franchise should therefore be extended to "every male citizen of the United States and those who have declared their intention to become such."

There was an uproar, as Langford watched from the Senate gallery and considered his self-inflicted dilemma. Insisting on the black vote, the most incendiary of all issues, might well derail Montana's territorial independence, not to mention his own political ambitions. More grievously, if the battle over Montana's status was allowed to become a referendum on voting rights, it might be the rock on which Lincoln's fall campaign for reelection would founder.

The quick-witted Langford sent his business card to Senator James R. Doolittle of Wisconsin, asking for an urgent audience. When they were done, the senator rose for a two-hour stemwinder. He was delighted to tell his honorable friends that a solution was at hand; the gentleman from Montana had just given him the welcome news that the wealthy negro in question was now in fact deceased! Sighs of relief from the chamber.

Was this expediency in the service of a higher cause? Or personal ambition over moral principle? Langford's behavior frequently raises questions of this sort. Whatever the case, a final bill went forward, and the president signed it into law on May 26. Within six months Langford was appointed tax collector for the new territory—a much more adventurous job than the name implies.[20]

M eanwhile, back in the gold camps, George Ives was the first to hang.

Much like Plummer, he had been regarded as "a suave, prepossessing fellow . . . progressive and intelligent."[21] Stuart and Hauser had found him wholesome enough to invite along on their prospecting expedition in the spring, and he had survived the attack at the mouth of the Bighorn. But now he was charged with the robbery and murder of a popular young Dutchman named Nicholas Tiebolt, whose frozen body had been discovered in a patch of sagebrush.

The trial was another chaotic affair, disrupted by a mob of Ives's defenders, who had to be held back at gunpoint. Fifty-eight minutes after a guilty verdict was returned, Ives was led to the scaffold. He said he refused to die with his boots on, so they gave him a pair of moccasins. But he found that his feet were too cold in these, put the boots back on, and was duly strung up.

His executioners decided that if they were truly set on extirpating the menace of the Plummer gang, there could be no more cumbersome and unruly trials. "Some shorter, surer and at least equally equitable method of procedure was to be found,"[22] wrote Thomas Dimsdale. The slippery phrase, of course, being "equally equitable."

Whether the formation of a vigilance committee was the product of a single meeting is a matter of debate.[23] Probably there were several. Their

They hanged Red Yager on January 4. He broke down in sobs and begged for mercy, then tripped and fell off the stool into the snow. His last words were, "Good bye boys; God bless you. You are on a good undertaking."

Ned Ray cursed and clawed at the rope until his fingers had to be pried loose.

Buck Stinson, the barber, twisted his head at an odd angle and took several minutes to die.

Dutch John Wagner asked how long it took a man to die by hanging, since he had never seen it done before.

Clubfoot George Lane "seemed to think no more of the hanging than a man would of eating his breakfast."

Jack Gallagher went to his death in a cavalry officer's overcoat trimmed with beaver fur, screaming obscenities.

George Shears, who was was taken up a ladder with the noose around his neck, said, "Gentlemen, I am not used to this business, never having been hung before. Shall I jump off or slide off?" Told to jump, he did so with perfect sangfroid.

Boone Helm, an unpleasant Kentuckian who survived a freezing trek through Utah in the winter of 1859 by eating the legs of a companion who had starved to death, swore he was innocent and died with a shout of "Hurrah for Jeff Davis!"

"Greaser" Joe Pizanthia, the only Mexican in the gold camps, never reached the rope. After he opened fire on his captors, they blasted his cabin apart with a mountain howitzer, riddled him with one hundred bullets, and burned the body. The soiled doves picked through the ashes to extract the gold from his teeth.

Henry Plummer himself went out with a bravura performance. He whimpered and pleaded his innocence, then abruptly altered his tone and cried out, "I am too wicked to die. I cannot go blood-stained and unforgiven into the presence of the Eternal. Only spare me, and I will leave the country forever." Finally, as the noose was made ready, he took off his necktie and tossed it nonchalantly to a sobbing admirer in the crowd, saying, "Here is something to remember me by."

By the end of 1864, the Montana vigilantes had hanged thirty-two men. By 1867 they had dealt with another twenty-five. It was the biggest episode of vigilantism in American history.

For some of the victims, death was not sufficient indignity. Clubfoot George Lane's distinguishing feature was dug up and put on public display. Some said Jack Gallagher's head was boiled and skinned and given to the masons of Virginia City to be used in their unspeakable rites. Rumors swirled around the fate of Sheriff Plummer's skull. Some said it was exhumed by drunks and deposited on the back bar of the Bank Exchange Saloon in Bannack, others that it was sent back East to an unnamed learned institution, so that scientists could try to decipher the phrenological origins of evil.

TALES OF THE CHIEF GUIDE

1864–1867

T he third of the great Montana gold strikes came in July 1864, in a place the prospectors called Last Chance Gulch. The name suggests a novel by Louis L'Amour, but as a town took shape around the diggings more sober men would call it Helena.[1]

Virginia City had never quite escaped its rollicking origins, but from the start Helena was different, the product of rapid infusions of the capital that had been amassed on Grasshopper Creek and Alder Gulch. Within a year there was running water, pumped in through log tubes from a pair of nearby creeks. All the attributes of a real town followed: a library and a historical society, plush gentlemen's brothels like Chicago Joe's, Christian temperance groups and townswomen's morality drives. St. Vincent's Academy attended to the deportment of young ladies of the better class.[2] Along the gulch there were imposing cut-stone mansions, home to prominent citizens like Samuel T. Hauser and Nathaniel P. Langford, owners of the First National Bank of Helena, successor to the house of S. T. Hauser & Co. of Virginia City.

For all their personal closeness, Hauser and Langford were men of very different character. When Hauser traveled up the Missouri to Montana, he was already mentally at his destination; the operative question was how soon he could start making his fortune. He was a relatively uncomplicated man who looked at money in linear fashion: get in on the ground floor of each promising new source of profit—gold, smelters, banks, railroads; cut corners where possible and make backroom deals where necessary; use the wealth and connections acquired as a springboard to political influence.[3]

Not to say that Langford was uninterested in money or influence, far from it, but his vision was both more romantic and more strategic. The wild, unexplored landscapes around the gold camps nourished his love of drama, as did near-death experiences at the hands of road agents and Blackfeet war parties. He wanted to know these places, map them, master them, and at the end of the day bring them within the embrace of civilization. It was not until the end of the Civil War in April 1865 that the national taste for exploring the West was switched on again like a spotlight, but Langford was already playing out the same impulses in his own untamed backyard.

As the environmental historian Roderick Nash has observed, the word *wilderness* has always had two distinct meanings to Americans. On the one hand, there was *wildeor,* as described in *Beowulf:* a place where savage and fantastic beasts inhabit a dismal region of forests, crags, and cliffs. On the other, there was the nineteenth-century West, where the "occupation of wild territory . . . proceed[ed] with all the solemnity of a providential ordinance."[4] Langford would have nodded in agreement.

Nothing fired his imagination more than the rumors he had begun to hear, within months of arriving in Bannack, "of wonderful phenomena in the region where the Yellowstone, Wind, Snake, and other large rivers take their rise."[5] He was also familiar with the report that Lieutenant John Mullan had submitted to Congress in 1863, which mentioned reports from Native Americans of geysers and "an infinite number of hot springs."[6] And he had seen the map that the engineer-explorer Walter De Lacy had drawn, based on his accidental visit to the geyser basins in that same year.

. . .

Even before he met Jim Bridger, who was the source of so many of these rumors, Langford was paying close attention to the new emigrant trails that the old mountain man and John Bozeman had blazed from the North Platte to the goldfields. He grasped the importance of their efforts from every perspective: as a strategic asset to the government, a problem of national security, and a great business opportunity. And like a general at a sand table, he began to map out his ideas.

At the beginning of 1864, he wrote to Congressman Ignatius L. Donnelly of Minnesota to say that the Montana gold camps "may be made to yield annualy [sic] sufficient to pay the interest on a national war debt of 2,000,000,000"—if the gold could be brought out expeditiously.[7] The Bozeman and Bridger trails were the answer, he said; shaving hundreds of miles off the old Oregon Trail, they would attract thousands of new emigrants in the coming spring. This he could say with confidence, as the result of his extensive consultations with "old mountaineers . . . fur trappers, and others."

The army would have to protect the trails, however. Langford suggested building two forts as a bulwark against the Sioux, one on the Missouri and the other at the mouth of the Bighorn. Perhaps two smaller ones farther up the Yellowstone, in case of trouble with the Crows. Most whites saw the larcenous tribe as a nuisance rather than a menace, but for whatever reason Langford always seemed to harbor some special anxiety about the Crows and their twelve hundred dandified warriors.[8] He thought five hundred "mounted infantry" should be about right to keep them in line.

As the prairie schooners stacked up at Fort Laramie in the spring of 1864, Langford shifted his focus to logistics. What supplies would the emigrants need? Would there be a demand for stagecoaches and telegraph lines to service the spur roads? What difficulties were posed by the river crossings? By the end of the year, he had chartered the Missouri River and Rocky Mountain Wagon Road and Telegraph Company and inaugurated

ferry services on the Bighorn, the Clarks Fork of the Yellowstone, and the
Yellowstone itself,[9] and by early 1865 he had formed a working relationship with the two great trailblazers themselves. He wrote to Hauser:

> We have interested Bozeman, and have sent both him and
> Brydger [sic] down to Laramie to bring through the emigra-
> tion by our route, and have made an assessment for building
> ferry-boats.[10]

Now there was no need for Langford to hear the outlandish tales of the
upper Yellowstone secondhand. He could get them direct from the source.
His friend and would-be explorer David Folsom also met Old Gabe at
about this time, when one of the first wagon trains to use the Bridger Trail
reached Virginia City. At first he found Bridger oddly reticent. But then, he
said, "I uncorked a jug of Indian whiskey, and when I uncorked the whiskey I uncorked Jim."[11] And out poured the stories: glass mountains, petrified birds, washing laundry in the steaming headwaters of the Madison.

Of course, Langford and Folsom had the same problem as anyone who
listened to Bridger: What to believe? The old man was something of a celebrity by now—his fame had reached a national audience, thanks to the writings of a picaresque individual who used the nom de plume Ned Buntline.[12]
To Buntline's readers, Old Gabe was a colorful character from a dime novel,
but Langford knew him as a skilled professional, and while he acknowledged that "his narrations were generally received with many grains of allowance by his listeners,"[13] he himself did not dismiss them so easily.

He was particularly struck by Bridger's account of seeing "a column of
water as large as my body, spout as high as the [Virginia City] liberty pole
(about 70 ft.)"—Old Faithful, perhaps. At first he was skeptical; was this
just another tale from Münchausen? However, "The more I pondered
upon this statement, the more I was impressed by the probability of its
truth." The description sounded just like the geysers in Iceland, Langford
thought, and the famously unlettered Bridger was unlikely to have heard
of those. "I was therefore inclined to give credit to his statement, and to
believe that such a wonder really did exist. Determined to visit it."[14]

· · ·

By 1866, Langford was asserting "exclusive ferry rights" on the emigrant trails,[15] charging a toll of ten dollars per wagon (negotiable). But the Bozeman Trail in particular was now in deep trouble. It was by far the more heavily trafficked of the two routes, but just as Bridger had warned, while Bozeman's forage was better, security was a nightmare. In the three years since the opening of the trail, violence to the east and to the south had filled the Powder River country with rage. After the Sioux uprising in Minnesota in 1862, the army had driven the tribe relentlessly westward, inflicting terrible losses. The Lakota, who had taken the worst mauling, were now led by militant chiefs like Sitting Bull, Gall, and Rain in the Face of the Hunkpapa, and the Oglala's Crazy Horse and Red Cloud. On the Powder River, they joined forces with the Northern Cheyenne, who were no less hostile to the whites, and a new influx of Southern Cheyenne from Colorado, who were bent on revenge for the recent outrage perpetrated by the messianic preacher-warrior Colonel John M. Chivington.[16]

On the advice of General Patrick Connor, hero of the Bear River two years earlier, Chivington's First Colorado Cavalry had hit the Cheyenne at the end of November 1864, in the deep cold of winter. The body count has never been firmly established, but it was at least 150, perhaps 200. Chivington said it might have been 500, or maybe it was 600; in any event, a matter of indifference to him. He was also unconcerned that the camp he had struck belonged to a friendly chief, Black Kettle, who had run up a white flag and the Stars and Stripes over his tipi. When the killing was over, Chivington's soldiers had excised women's genitals and strung them across the stage of a Denver theater to loud applause.[17] The Eastern humanitarians wrote furious editorials about this barbarity; the *Rocky Mountain News* wrote furious editorials about the Eastern humanitarians. The surviving Cheyenne packed up their tents and fled north to the Powder River. Black Kettle survived the attack, although George Armstrong Custer would get him four years later.

The new Sioux-Cheyenne alliance created the greatest fighting force ever assembled on the Northern Plains, putting intolerable pressure on the Bozeman Trail. "There is not one foot of road but what we have to guard our trains, and it uses up troops beyond all conception," said General Grenville Dodge, commander of the Division of the Missouri.[18] To make matters worse for the emigrants, the army had never built the permanent forts that Langford had recommended.

Cleaning up the mess called for two kinds of men: one with specialized combat skills and another who knew every inch of the terrain. To lead the expedition, the army chose the reliably ruthless General Connor, and with him came Jim Bridger, hired as his chief guide at ten dollars a day—twice what the army had previously paid him.

To put it mildly, they made an odd couple. Although it was summertime and he no longer had the demented Major McGarry at his side, Connor basically foresaw a replay of Bear River. "You will not receive overtures of peace or submission from the Indians," he ordered his men, "but will attack and kill every male Indian over twelve years of age."[19] Bridger told General Dodge that he thought holding on to the Powder River country was more trouble than it was worth, but he continued to do his usual conscientious job in his usual good-natured way, plotting the route of march, spinning his yarns to the paper-collar officers, and gathering intelligence from the Crow scouts.

The unhappy Crows had found themselves in the middle of all these crosscurrents of migration, violence, and revenge. Legend said that the First Maker had given the tribe the most beautiful country on Earth, but the gift came with a corollary: He would also test their courage by surrounding that country with ferocious and much more numerous enemies—Blackfeet to the west, Sioux and now Cheyenne to the east.[20] However, the Crows' vulnerability had also given them skills that the army found useful. Because they were always alert to danger, they made excellent scouts. They worked well in small teams. Fear and hatred made them utterly ruthless. In agreeing now to act as "an extra regiment of cavalry," the Crows were given rich opportunities for glory, plunder, and revenge, unrestrained by any formal military discipline.[21]

Connor was given 750 men to pacify the Bozeman Trail. It was half the number he had requested: just enough to make a fight of it, not enough to win. He built a crude fort and named it after himself, but to all intents and purposes it was indefensible. His supply wagons got stuck in the mud and had to be abandoned; half a century later some cowhands found the wheels and collected the iron rims for scrap.[22] The enemy was elusive. By early September, the first Wyoming snows had begun, and Connor was relieved of his command. Bridger told a local reporter that he had nothing but contempt for the general. "He thinks that our mode of hunting savages with mounted men and wagon trains is simply absurd," the reporter wrote, "since it results only in heavy loss of animals and unnecessary exposure of troops."[23]

Nevertheless, Bridger signed up for another tour of duty the following June, with the honorary rank of major.[24] He was sixty-one now, "somewhat bowed with age" and "somewhat gray." The Indians no longer called him Blanket Chief; now it was Big Throat, an allusion to the pronounced goiter he had developed.[25] But up the Bozeman Trail he went again with more mounted men, more wagons, numerous officers' wives and children, a thirty-piece brass band, an assortment of easy chairs and rocking chairs, this time under the command of a Yale-educated colonel named Henry Carrington, who might have been happier with a career as a schoolmaster.

The colonel's wife, Margaret, who left one of the classic accounts of army life on the frontier, was enchanted by the old man. "He was invariably straightforward, truthful, and reliable," she wrote. "His sagacity, knowledge of woodcraft, and knowledge of the Indian was wonderful, and his heart was warm and his feelings tender whenever he confided or made a friend."[26]

At Bridger's request, the baggage train carried the complete works of Shakespeare, which the illiterate guide had read aloud to him at night. He was indignant at the murder of the two young princes in the Tower, Margaret Carrington recalled, and, "Upon positive conviction that the text was properly read to him, he burned the whole set, convinced that 'Shake-speare must have had a bad heart and been as de———h mean as a Sioux, to have written such scoundrelism as that.' "

"James Bridger had a head full of maps and trails and ideas all of the utmost value to the expedition," she wrote elsewhere.[27] But whatever her husband may have thought of the maps and trails, he seems to have ig-nored his chief guide's ideas. Instead, he seemed intent on compounding the problems Connor had created. He built three forts—Reno, Phil Kearny, and C. F. Smith—but all the military huffing and puffing provoked the Sioux more than it intimidated them. Bridger said that the exposed loca-tion of Fort Phil Kearny in particular, Carrington's headquarters, was an act of folly. But who cared about the advice of a sixty-one-year-old with a goiter, when there was glory to be won by men half his age?

This was certainly the view of a headstrong young captain named Wil-liam J. Fetterman, who is remembered for one of the more unfortunate one-liners in the annals of the West: "With 80 men I could ride through the whole Sioux nation." Hearing this infamous boast, Carrington said later, Bridger exclaimed, "Your men who fought down South are crazy! They don't know anything about fighting Indians!"[28]

There is endless debate about what actually happened to Fetterman on December 21, 1866.[29] Did he ride out against the Sioux with 80 men under his command, or was it 82, or 83, or 84? Who was mainly to blame for what ensued? Was it Fetterman himself, for his arrogance? Or Car-rington, the dithering commanding officer? Or even the newly appointed head of the Division of the Missouri, General William Tecumseh Sher-man, who had encouraged Carrington and his officers to take their wives and children up the Bozeman Trail, promising "a pleasant garrison life in the newly opened country, where all would be healthful, with pleasant service and absolute peace"?[30]

Whatever the answers, the basic facts are not in dispute. Fetterman and every man under his command rode into an ambush and were slaughtered, the worst debacle ever suffered by the frontier army until the Little Bighorn, ten years later.

Even more significant, from the point of view of those hearing the news in the new frontier settlements of Montana, were the varied forms of torture and mutilation to which Fetterman's men had been subjected. These more than evened the score for Sand Creek and cemented in place the settlers' darkest fears of the alien Other. The dreadful details were enumerated in Colonel Carrington's official report.

> Eyes torn out and laid on the rocks; noses cut off; ears cut off; chins hewn off; teeth chopped out; joints of fingers; brains taken out and placed on rocks with other members of the body; entrails taken out and exposed; hands cut off; feet cut off; arms taken out from sockets; private parts severed and indecently placed on the person; eyes, ears, mouth and arms penetrated with spear-heads, sticks and arrows; ribs slashed to separation with knives; skulls severed in every form, from chin to crown; muscles of calves, thighs, stomach, breast, back, arms, and cheek taken out; punctures upon every sensitive part of the body, even to the sole of the feet and palms of the hand.[31]

Bridger knew full well that the forts on the Bozeman Trail had to be abandoned and said as much. But by now he had "twinges of rheumatism in his stiffening legs and blank stares in his dimming eyes," and Carrington's successor let him go disdainfully, saying that he had no need of another guide and "[paid] no heed to rumors about attacks."[32] Sioux war parties promptly launched two more—the so-called Wagon Box and Hayfield fights—in the summer of 1867. Further confirmation, if such were needed, that the army of the West was as often led by fools as by villains.

But eventually the army did do what the old mountain man had recommended. As an emigrant route the Bozeman Trail was finished, and so was Nathaniel Langford's dream of making his fortune from it. The Sioux declared that they would be happy now to reserve their guns for buffalo, since they could "chase soldier and drive away with sticks."[33] Jim Bridger asked for his final discharge on September 23, 1867, and went back to his family farm in Missouri, this time more or less for good. His advice, as usual, had been right, but he was an old man now, and no one listened to old men.

{ 13 }

THE LEADING MEN

1865–1867

I n the first of the gold camps, the nucleus of an elite group of leading citizens and would-be explorers had formed around men like Nathaniel Langford and Sam Hauser, John Bozeman and Walter De Lacy. With the discovery of gold in Last Chance Gulch, a stream of new arrivals had swelled their ranks.

Beyond a doubt, the most extravagantly colorful of them was Thomas Francis Meagher, acting governor of the new territory. "Meagher of the Sword," they had called him back in Ireland, an orator and freedom fighter who had gone to France in 1848 for a crash course in revolution; was tried for sedition by Queen Victoria and sentenced to be hanged, beheaded, and quartered; had his sentence commuted to life imprisonment in Tasmania; escaped from there on a ship bound for Brazil; came to New York to practice law; defended slavery and spoke out for the South after Fort Sumter; then turned his coat to the North and commanded a famously reckless and casualty-prone Irish brigade before being relieved of duty on account of his fondness for strong liquor.

David Folsom, Langford's old companion from the Fisk expedition, was one of many who followed the trail from the first camps to the new diggings in Helena. No longer the retiring Quaker schoolteacher, he was known now as a crack shot who liked to go grizzly bear hunting with

Langford, and an enthusiastic amateur naturalist who had spent the winter of 1864–1865 collecting samples for the Smithsonian.

A blustery Maine native named Charles W. Cook, known familiarly as the Captain, an old school friend of Folsom's and fellow Quaker, also came seeking "the painted glories of Montana" in 1864, driving a hundred head of cattle from Denver and "exchang[ing] a steer for his scalp" with some aggressive Sioux and Cheyenne on the way to Fort Bridger. Now Cook established a ditch-digging company in Confederate Gulch, a few miles east of Helena, in the cluster of ramshackle huts known ambitiously as Diamond City, and was master of that settlement's masonic lodge.

But of all those whose names would later be associated with the upper Yellowstone, none was more important than a young lawyer, Cornelius Hedges, a small, neatly groomed, physically frail man of thirty-three for whom no one seems to have had a bad word.[1] "Thoughtful, kind, charitable, ever ready to heed the call of the unfortunate, without selfishness or guile,"[2] was a typical description. By coincidence, Hedges was a native of the small town of Westfield, Massachusetts—also the birthplace of the explorer-geologist Ferdinand Vandeveer Hayden, who was two years his senior. Though the son of a blacksmith and farmer, Hedges was a graduate of Yale and Harvard Law. He taught Bible classes. Almost inevitably he was a mason, yet another in the secretive group that dominated Montana politics.

In 1856, Hedges left the East for Independence, Iowa, where he opened a law office and edited the local newspaper. But he had a poor head for business, and by 1864 his law practice was floundering. It was time to join the rite of passage to the West. He left home in April, traveling west past Des Moines, Council Bluffs, and Omaha before following the North Platte to Fort Laramie, where he was delighted to find that the commanding officer was a Royal Arch Mason. At Laramie, Hedges joined the third of the huge wagon trains that departed for the goldfields in the second half of May.

Hedges walked all the way, with his wife Edna and two young children traveling in the family's wagon. He kept a meticulous diary of the trip, covering the pages in a tiny, compulsive script with a blunt pencil. He records that he fished a little, suffered bouts of diarrhea, read Proverbs and the Book of Ruth. He had never fired a gun in his life, but he brought along four—three rifles and a revolver—for "a fancied sense of security." He also cut his hair very short, "lest in some unlucky time a 'red skin' might try to remove his scalp."[3] In the event, he encountered just one in the course of the eighty-two-day journey. He drew his pistol on the man, who threw his hands up, cried "Good injun!" and ran away.[4]

The train met up with Bridger at the Yellowstone and crossed the river in time to celebrate Independence Day on the north bank. Within a week they were in Virginia City, and by May 20, Hedges had a job, shoveling mine tailings for six dollars a day in gold dust. But the prospects were bleak. "Have had many thoughts about going home," he wrote in his diary on May 24. "Claims working out, hands discharged, pilgrims coming in, prices going up, wages coming down." His sleep was disturbed, he recorded two weeks later: "Had troubled dreams . . . I was halloing in my sleep, was trying to warn John about Indians."

As winter drew in, he passed the long evening hours playing checkers and committing to memory the Book of James. Despite the efforts of the vigilantes, he found "every sort of dissipation and crime" in Virginia City, although he took some comfort in the fact that, "in such a Devil's hot bed were scattered a few seeds of Masonry."[5] He had further episodes of diarrhea and colic, took liver pills, smoked too much, felt "blue." He still seems the unlikeliest of adventurers, although there were the first signs of a new turn of mind in a broadening of his reading matter: *The Colorado Exploring Expedition, 1857–1858*, by Lieutenant J. C. Ives of the Army Corps of Engineers, Heine's *Travel Pictures*, a book on the Malay Archipelago. Later he would read the travel journals of Father De Smet and Louis Agassiz's account of a journey to Brazil.

In January, midway through this dark and demoralizing first winter, Hedges decided it was time to up stakes and try his luck in Last Chance Gulch. He got there on the thirteenth, but it was the same story, lots of gold but too many people chasing it. Within days he abandoned his mining ambitions, deciding instead to hang up his shingle as a lawyer because "there was nothing else to do."[6] Meagher of the Sword offered him the post of District Attorney, but he turned it down, thinking he could do better in private practice. "I mean to do anything honest and respectable that I can make the most money at," he wrote to his parents.[7]

David Folsom and Charles Cook, both fellow masons, were among his first clients. "We have a large number of masons here," he told the folks back home, "probably more than a hundred."[8] Masonry became the center of his life, and by May he had been elected master of the Helena lodge. By the time he was done, he had piled up more masonic honors than anyone in the territory, even Langford: Thrice Illustrious Master, Illustrious Order of the Red Cross, Orders of the Knights Templar and the Knights of Malta, Most Worshipful Grand Master of the Grand Lodge of Montana, Grand Commander of the Grand Commandery, Grand Secretary of the Grand Chapter of the Royal Arch Masons, Grand Secretary of the Grand Chapter of Miriam Chapter No. 1, member of the Algeria Temple, High Priest, Scottish Rite Mason, and so on.[9]

He also made his forays into politics. Although he had placed his hopes in General George McClellan, "Little Mac," in the 1864 election and lamented Lincoln's victory ("more war, debt & disaster"), it was Hedges who ran up the Stars and Stripes in Helena to celebrate Lee's surrender at Appomattox, and then stood guard all night over the flag, armed with a rifle, in case the seceshes tried to tear it down.

Amid this sudden whirl of activity, Hedges made two enduring friendships. The first was with Langford, "a friend I esteem above almost all here."[10] Later, he would name one of his sons Langford Hedges, though the child died in infancy. The other notable friendship is first recorded in a diary entry for March 20, 1865: "Malcolm Clark [sic] stayed over night. Had long conversation with him—he is an old mountaineer—been in mountains twenty-four years."

The meeting with Malcolm Clarke, whom Hedges promptly took on as a client, created the first link between the new civic elite of the gold camps and the old aristocracy of the fur trade on the upper Missouri. The fiery and charismatic Clarke—the famous Four Bears who had dominated the Piegan country and married into the band of the militant

Mountain Chief—had moved to the Helena area with his wife, Cutting-Off-Head Woman, just a few months earlier, after the liquidation of the American Fur Company. During the Civil War, according to his son Horace, he had been offered a generalship but turned it down. A second and more politically sensitive offer followed: an appointment as special government emissary to the Northern Plains tribes, "to council [sic] and keep the Indians from going to war as the Indians well knew that the great conflict between the North and South would call for all the available men in the Northern States and territories, and that it was an opportune time to attack and rob the settlers." This offer he accepted, and he kept the Blackfeet from open hostilities until the end of the war.[11]

The lives of those few settlers who crossed ethnic lines were inevitably tangled, and Clarke's was more tangled than most. No white man had ever been so fully embraced by the Blackfeet, or perhaps by any Native Americans. He mediated disputes small and large, within tribes, among tribes, and between the tribes and the whites. It was even said that the Piegans had offered to make him their supreme chief, another offer he declined. He had controlled the fur trade up and down the Marias River, one of the most dangerous places on the entire frontier, through sheer force of personality. None of the early mountain men—not John Colter, not Jim Bridger—outstripped him in physical courage and resourcefulness.

Yet Clarke also cut a figure in Helena society. He became an intimate of cultured men like Langford, Hedges, and the mapmaker Walter De Lacy. He was one of the founders, in 1865, of the Montana Historical Society.[12] And he had always insisted that his family receive the best of educations back in the States.

He had taken them to Ann Arbor, Michigan, in 1857—Nellie, the eldest; her two brothers, Nathan and Horace; and a boy named Ne-tus-che-o, a sixteen-year-old relative of Clarke's wife. Clarke had tried briefly to make a new life for himself in the Midwest, but the lure of the Blackfeet country was too powerful, and after less than a year he went back, taking Ne-tus-che-o with him. He saw his children in Ann Arbor just once a year while they went to school. Nellie wrote that his visits "flashed upon us like meteors, bright, beautiful, and brilliant."[13]

Now, at the age of forty-seven, Malcolm Clarke embarked on a new life, abandoning the world of fur for the world of ranching. His new home was twenty-five miles or so north of Helena, enclosed by sheltering hills at the head of the canyon of the Little Prickly Pear, which the Blackfeet called Wolf-Also-Jumped-Creek. The land was good for raising horses and sheep, and the nearby ranches were an important source of food for the new gold camp. The Clarke ranch was close enough to the Blackfoot country for his Piegan friends and relatives to visit at will—yet far enough from Helena that their arrival would not bring an armed mob onto the streets. Some of the ranch buildings still stand, just before the interstate highway and the abandoned railroad tracks of the Burlington Northern enter the narrow canyon.

By now Nellie had completed her education in the East and rejoined her father. She had blossomed into a tall, handsome young woman whose features clearly showed her mixed lineage, of which she was proud. She set about civilizing the place. One pictures family daguerrotypes, heavy velvet drapes, antimacassars. She always seemed to have something on the stove. Her brother Horace had come home, too. He appears to have inherited much of the turbulent character of his father, who had wanted him at various times to enter the priesthood or go to West Point. Horace rebelled, ran away from his home in Cincinnati, and eventually made his way back to Montana, still a teenager, traveling alone. The Piegans gave him a name that captured his personality: Man Who Stands Alone With His Gun. There were also two younger daughters in residence. The elder, perhaps ten or eleven years old, was Isabel. The younger, name unrecorded, was the result of Malcolm Clarke's second marriage to another Piegan woman, name also unrecorded.[14]

Clarke turned his new home into a profitable stage stop and bunkhouse. An easy day's ride from Helena, it made a convenient resting place for the first night before a traveler set off (with the benefit of daylight) on the dangerous road to the head of navigation at Fort Benton. Clarke also acquired the concession to operate a tollgate at the entrance to the Little Prickly Pear canyon, a red rock defile with a particularly ugly reputation. The country around the Clarke property, Langford wrote, was "favored by nature with every facility for ambuscade . . . there is hardly a spot of the entire distance after entering the foothills, twelve miles from Helena, where a successful attack could not be made on the unsuspecting traveller."[15]

Langford and Clarke became great friends. "He was to my mind a man of the highest sense of honor," Langford wrote. Yet the relationship, given Langford's unforgiving view of Native Americans, must have had its wrinkles. "It was a common saying among the citizens of Helena where I lived," he went on, "that Malcolm Clarke was more of a friend to the Indians than to the whites." Langford himself seems to have recorded only one single positive view of an Indian, but it was a striking one, involving an elderly man with light-colored hair who was something of a fixture around the town. Langford photographed him in 1866 or 1867.

"He was very proud of his paternal ancestry," he wrote, "and, when accosted, would straighten his body to its full height and strike his chest with his open palm, exclaiming as he did so: 'Me Clark!' Then extending his arm he would ask for tobacco." The man was no relation to Malcolm Clarke—the name lacked the final "e." He was, in fact, the son of William Clark, born to a Nez Perce mother.[16]

These new friendships between Hedges, Langford, and Clarke seem improbable: a fragile New England lawyer, a self-dramatizing businessman, and a man who had killed four grizzly bears before breakfast. But the realities of life on the frontier—the harshness, the exoticism, the absence of law and order, the immersion in wilderness, the fear of Indian attack and other kinds of violence—worked radical transformations. People were thrown together who would never have met under other circumstances. Roles were reversed. Men like Clarke, who knew the intimate realities of tribal life firsthand and had actual experience with violence, became the most tolerant. Those who came from a more peaceable and sophisticated background in the States often found that fear quickly hardened their moral arteries.

Another of Hedges's Eastern-educated friends, E. B. Nealley, attorney general of Virginia City, wrote in the new *Atlantic* magazine in Boston:

These regions are held by the Blackfeet, who, with their off-shoots, the Bloods, Gros Ventres, and Piegans, are the most formidable Indians of Montana. . . . The noble Indians of history and poetry do not exist among the Indians of to-day. You seek in vain for Logan and Pocahontas, for Uncas or Minne-haha. The real Indians are cruel and treacherous, lazy and filthy, crafty and ungrateful.[17]

These lines could have been written by so many white men—Captain Raynolds, Ferdinand Hayden, Nathaniel Langford himself. *Cruel, treacherous, lazy, filthy*: the repetition of the same adjectives seems dictated by some central script.

Had he remained in Massachusetts, a Harvard and Yale man like Hedges might have turned into one of those Eastern humanitarians who wrote editorials deploring the harsh oppression of the Indians. Instead, within six months of arriving in Montana, he and many like him had become exterminationists. "The Indians are making trouble on the Plains," he wrote to his mother in July 1865, meaning the Blackfeet. "I hope the last Indians will be killed this season."[18]

Langford had moved to Last Chance Gulch within a few days of Hedges's arrival, having been appointed Collector of Internal Revenues for Montana the previous December. But Virginia City, stuck away in a remote corner of the territory, made a poor base of operations. Helena, by contrast, lay at a crossroads leading to Montana's main population centers, none of them more than 150 miles distant: south to the older gold camps; west to the Deer Lodge Valley; north up the Missouri to the Great Falls and Fort Benton; and southeast to the rich new farmlands around Bozeman. Helena was an excellent location, then, for a man like Langford who would be spending a lot of time on horseback.

Being a federal tax collector in 1860s Montana was anything but a dull desk job. A lot of improvisation was involved: for several months Langford had no copy of the tax law, no letterhead, no direct means of communicating with Washington. To put it mildly, there was plenty of scope for conflicts of interest between the public servant and the private entrepreneur. The writ of the federal government did not run far in the wilds of the Northern Rockies, and Washington did not honestly expect to bring in much in the way of taxes. Langford was told to aim for twenty-five thousand dollars a year, but he was confident he could bring in four times that amount—if the government would agree to pay him a commission of 25 or 30 percent. "That will bring us out all right," he wrote to his partner Sam Hauser. But he warned that if Hauser ever referred to the matter in writing he should choose his wording carefully, "so that it will not be understood by any one else."[19] This was not illegal perhaps—such practices were not uncommon in the remoter territories—but it smells of a man who knew he was treading close to the ethical line.

Instead of law and letterhead, Langford had his wits, his taste for adventure and confrontation, and his double-barreled shotgun. His first deputy tax collector was murdered by a party of Blood Indians at the mouth of the perpetually dangerous Marias River, and Langford says he himself "ran the risk of losing my scalp on two different occasions," though he gives no particulars.

Later, he would calculate that in fourteen years as collector of revenues and later as federal bank examiner, he had traveled seventy-four thousand miles. Most of this was alone on horseback, carrying bulging pouches of gold dust in his saddlebags. A smaller portion was by stagecoach, sitting up front with the driver, well-armed, dressed in overalls, furs and rubber topcoat, open to the elements and to the constant risk that road agents might mistake him for the coach guard. He encountered them more than once and described the incidents in his correspondence with his usual self-regarding flair for melodrama and an occasional flash of humor.

"Does them gun barrels look pretty big?" a road agent asked in the course of one attempted holdup.

Staring down the barrels in question, Langford says,

> I replied that I could not readily recall a time when gun barrels looked quite as large as they did at that moment, and that

although neither the moon nor the stars were very bright, yet
I was quite sure I could read the advertisements on a page of
the *New York Herald* which they had used for gun wadding.[20]

Unrepentant seceshes, who had no intention of paying federal taxes, were
an even more persistent headache. "I was in a Territory more disloyal as a
whole, than Tennessee or Kentucky ever were," Langford wrote. "Four-
fifths of our citizens were <u>openly declared</u> secessionists."[21] He divided
them into two categories: the angry miners and the "Gentlemen Secesh,"
whose guns were likelier to have pearl handles and to be worn concealed.
The second group made him more nervous. But he faced them down
repeatedly—again, if his own accounts are to be taken at face value.[22]

"<u>He</u>, from whom all power comes, gave me the courage to do right
even when swift destruction threatened," Langford wrote. Thus divinely
guided, he brought dozens of indictments against tax evaders. On one
occasion, he provoked a riot in the streets of Virginia City by impound-
ing all the liquor, tobacco, and cigars in town against unpaid taxes. If the
offenders continued in their delinquency, he would personally thrash
them: "The refractory have learned from experience, that I will not be tri-
fled with. These men <u>shall</u> have respect for me, if I flog it into them. They
may hate me, and curse and abuse me, but they <u>shall not</u> despise me."[23]

With road agents on one side, secessionists on the other, and Blackfeet
raiders a constant menacing presence, Langford's work immersed him in
a culture of violence. It was a constant threat but also a constant temptation for those who sought to uphold law and order. Which is the essential
problem with violence: It takes on its own logic and momentum.

In theory, the mass hangings in Bannack and Virginia City had been a
measure of last resort, taken in the absence of a functioning legal system. But Helena should have been different. By the time Langford arrived, an official legal system was in place, and he was closely associated
with the men charged with its functioning, men like the new chief justice, Hezekiah Hosmer, a partner in Langford's wagon road company.

There was no further need, then, for citizens to take the law into their own hands. At least in theory.

Judge Hosmer empaneled his first grand jury in December 1864 and declared that the time had come to abandon vigilante justice. He lavished praise on those who had cleaned up the gold camps but told them their job was done: "Let us then erect no more impromptu scaffolds, let us inflict no more midnight executions." He warned the vigilantes that if they refused to disband, they would be charged with "a highly penal offense."[24]

This turned out to be a toothless threat. On June 6, 1865, a gambler named Keene shot dead another named Slater—"in a very ungentlemanly way," according to the fastidious Cornelius Hedges. Keene was chased down by a crowd of several hundred and brought to Hedges's cabin.[25] Before more formal proceedings could begin, Hedges was drawing up the man's will. The mob selected a "jury" of twelve, which promptly passed the death sentence, and at eleven thirty the next morning the murderer was taken to a lone pine tree on Dry Gulch, where he asked for a glass of whiskey and then cried, "Let her rip."

The hanging of Keene marked the birth of the Helena Committee of Safety, and Cornelius Hedges was present at the creation. As in the gold camps, masons were the backbone of the Helena vigilantes. As members of a highly organized and secretive group, they were singularly well-suited to their task. "While it was by no means true that every Vigilante was a Mason," Hedges wrote, "it might be said without serious deviation from the exact fact that every Mason in those days was a Vigilante."[26] Hedges, Langford, Folsom, and Cook were all members of the executive committee of the reborn vigilante movement.[27]

The Lone Pine in Helena became their impromptu scaffold, where "the habeas corpus and the criminals were suspended simultaneously," Hedges wrote drily.[28] A few months later, when a ne'er-do-well named James Daniels was sentenced to four years imprisonment for manslaughter, Acting Governor Meagher decided to exercise clemency. This did not sit well with the vigilantes, and when Daniels had the audacity to come back to Helena with the pardon in his pocket, Hedges regarded it as a "contemptuous disregard of justice" and "an insult to the law." So it was off to the Lone Pine again, where the hangmen left the pardon pinned to the victim's back, together with a message to the chief executive suggesting that he refrain from any more blunders of this kind. Hedges wrote that the implied threat "produced terrible excitement in executive circles and called forth threats of calling out the militia and declaring martial law, but it all ended in a prolonged drunk."[29]

Hosmer and his two fellow justices huddled in emergency session to discuss this fresh outbreak of "night-time life-taking." But they decided to turn a blind eye. After all, one of the other judges reasoned, the vigilantes "can attend to this branch of jurisprudence cheaper, quicker, and better than it can be done by the courts." Hosmer's vow seven months earlier to end vigilantism was already a dead letter.[30]

This branch of jurisprudence: an interesting choice of words. The executions went on, with Langford playing an ever more central role, raising funds for the vigilantes' activities even as he served as an official of the federal government, sworn to uphold the Constitution.[31] Toward the end of 1865, he wrote his old Utica friend Will Doolittle a detailed account of Helena's efforts to quell crime. Two men had been lynched just the day before. "The Vigilance Committee have hung 15 or 20 of them lately," Langford said, "and upwards of a hundred suspected persons left Last Chance Gulch the day after notices were posted in the streets." The reference to his personal role is ambiguous, even coy. The events surrounding the vigilante killings seemed like a dream, he told Doolittle, "all of which I saw, and part of which I was."[32]

By the beginning of January 1867, Langford's mask was off. "The vigilantes have just been reorganized," he wrote to Doolittle. "I have been solicited to take the position of 'chief,' but have not the time, for the responsibility of chief is very great." However, he freely admitted, "An executive committee of 10 try all offenders. I am one of that Committee. The only crimes we punish, are horse stealing, highway robbery and murder. We have nothing to do with petty crimes. The committee inflict but one punishment;- Death."[33] Langford was always a great underliner.

But the backlash had begun. The territorial courts had been in operation for two years now, and Judge Hosmer had tried once already to tell
the vigilantes that enough was enough. Now that sentiment began to
spread among ordinary citizens. In March 1867, after another hanging, a
notice went up in the Highland mining district:

> We now, as a sworn band of law-abiding citizens, do hereby
> solemnly swear that the first man that is hung by the Vigilan-
> tes of this place, we will retaliate five for one. . . . We are all
> satisfied that in times past, you did some glorious work, but
> the time has come when law should be enforced. Old fellow-
> members, the time is not like it was. . . . We know you all. We
> are American citizens, and you shall not drive, or hang, whom
> you please.
>
> (signed) FIVE FOR ONE[34]

Yet Langford and Hedges remained largely unrepentant. "Helena has
never forgotten what it owes to the vigilantes," Hedges wrote in an undated history of the early days of the town. The Helena vigilantes, he
wrote, "for nearly a year and still for some time after the courts had been
organized and *were in full working order* [emphasis added], meted out
rude but effective justice, and kept lawlessness and violence in wholesome
fear and check." But Hedges was slippery with his facts. He stated that the
vigilance committee's "last regular business was the hanging of Daniels,
March 2nd, 1866." But as Langford makes clear, the killings went on long
after this, and Hedges himself was very likely involved in the decision-
making process.[35] The last vigilante hanging in Helena was not recorded
until April 1870.

Langford himself, writing more than thirty years after the event, did
acknowledge that there had been errors, mentioning in particular the
execution of Daniels. "This, at least," he wrote, "was one case where the
Vigilantes exceeded the boundaries of right and justice, and became themselves the violators of law and propriety. . . . And I will here take occasion

to say that this was not an isolated instance. . . . As soon as this order of things was understood by the people, the Vigilante institution was brought to an end." Langford says nothing of his own, privately admitted role in ordering the executions. And his last word on the subject is the same as that of Hedges: "Let those who would condemn these men try to realize how they would act under similar circumstances."[36]

14

MISSION IN THE SNOW

1865

As Cornelius Hedges approached his thirty-fourth birthday on October 28, 1865, he began to think of a good way to celebrate. A trip perhaps. He was accustomed by now to the rigors of the Northern Plains but he worried about his safety on the wild roads around Helena. He especially worried about the Black-feet, who continued to roam across most of the vast territory north from Helena to the Canadian line and west to the glaciers of the Continental Divide, the "Backbone of the World."

The Blackfeet had never lost their reputation for ferocity, and no neighboring tribe was safe from what Governor Isaac Stevens of Washington Territory called "their warlike and treacherous character."[1] Even the legendary fur trader Alexander Culbertson, who had married a Blood woman and was as sympathetic to the Blackfeet as any white man, was under no illusions, warning Stevens that, "It is evident the day is far off when the Blackfeet will turn the Sword into the Ploughshare."[2]

The representatives of the Great Father had taken another stab at a treaty in 1855, four years after the previous one, and gathered the Piegan, Blood, and Siksika chiefs together in a grove of cottonwoods on the banks of the Missouri. It seems to have been a fairly good-natured affair. Stevens told them that the white man would be free to run roads and telegraph lines through the Blackfeet lands, and to build military outposts if he so desired. In return Stevens promised to punish any infractions by white settlers. The government would also build schools for the Blackfeet, as well as any additional institutions that might "in other respect promote their civilization and Christianization." Stevens advised the Blackfeet to take up farming and acquire a taste for beef, a challenging notion to people who regarded buffalo tongue and hump meat as the choicest delicacies. There would also be annuities, starting right away with some beneficial additions to the tribal diet: sugar, coffee, and flour. The chiefs dumped the sugar into the Missouri and lapped up the sweetened water. They tried the coffee but didn't much care for the bitter taste. The flour at least provided some amusement; they threw it up in the air and were highly entertained by the sight of the white powder floating slowly to the ground.[3]

The chiefs raised no objections to the terms of the treaty, perhaps because the idea of white men settling in their sphere of influence must still have seemed quite theoretical. Apart from the trading posts of the American Fur Company, with which the Blackfeet were happy to do business, there was no fixed white presence. But the chiefs added the usual caveat: whether or not they accepted the Great Father's terms, no one could promise to control the headstrong young braves.

Yet the peace with the whites held, more or less, for about seven years. Little Dog, the head chief of the Piegans, made a conscientious effort to avoid violence and even dabbled in farming. In 1859 the Jesuits opened a mission on the Teton River near the town of Choteau, in the heart of Piegan country, and spent the winter learning the language.

However, two monumental events that Stevens could not have foreseen overturned all the treaty's assumptions. The first was the outbreak of the Civil War, and the second was the finding of the color—the discovery of gold—on Grasshopper Creek, which affected the Blackfeet as grievously as it had the Shoshone. The wagon train that Langford rode in on in 1862 was the first of many that rumbled their way across the tribal hunting grounds. The Blackfeet had at least seen some mutual advantage in dealing with the fur traders who had settled here during the preceding thirty years, but all the benefits of the Gold Rush flowed in one direction.

Meanwhile, the war in the East robbed the frontier of many of its more competent public servants, such as the Blackfeet agent, Major Alfred Vaughan, a well-respected (if usually intoxicated) Virginian.[4] The administration of Indian affairs passed instead to a string of venal racists like Gad Upson, who regarded the Blackfeet as "degraded savages" and thought the best thing to do with them was to souse them in whiskey. Another of these revolving-door agents told Washington that he expected trouble because "not a few" of the gold rush migrants were men who would not "be tolerated in any civilized society."[5] By the spring of 1865, when the Blackfeet broke their winter camps, people in Helena and Fort Benton were openly using the word *war*.

The rituals of the new season began with the first spring thunderstorm and the medicine pipe ceremony. The buffalo calved, and the horses fattened on the fresh grass. There was more variety in the diet as women dug for roots in the thawing ground. At the trading posts, the winter's haul of buffalo robes was baled up and shipped downriver to the markets of the East.[6] Within weeks, bands of young men began to assemble for the summer hunt, where they would collect buffalo tongues for the Sun Dance in August. Carrying their war medicine—a feather, a necklace, a special shirt—other braves, especially from the poorer lodges, galloped off to increase the size of their horse herds. And the white men's horses, which were larger and stronger, were a more tempting prize than the smaller ponies that could be appropriated from the Flatheads, the Shoshone, or the Crows.

There was an unpleasant game of tit-for-tat violence during these months, born of proximity, temptation, and fear. The most serious incident came in May, when a war party of Bloods massacred ten woodcutters at the mouth of the Marias; one of them was Nathaniel Langford's deputy tax collector, Frank Angevine, who was found scalped and mutilated at the base of a cottonwood tree.[7] The only survivor was a mixed-race, multilingual eighteen-year-old named Joe Kipp, known to the

Blackfeet as Raven Quiver, whose father had founded the Fort Piegan trading post in 1830.[8] The young man would play a more important role in the events of the next five years than anyone could have imagined.

After that, another season's annuities failed to arrive, and there was a lethal epidemic of measles. The Blackfeet blamed the whites for poisoning them and attacked the agency farm. None of this came close to any reasonable definition of war. Yet it alarmed the authorities enough that Langford's old friend James Stuart was asked to raise a civilian militia. However, by the time he had scraped together a halfhearted force of fifty men, the miscreants had escaped across the Canadian line, always handy in these situations.[9]

It was time for a more restrictive treaty, Washington decided, and new talks were scheduled for early November at Fort Benton. The host would be the unsavory agent Gad Upson, who carried the government's instructions. His fellow negotiator would be Acting Governor Thomas Meagher. Judge Lyman Munson would accompany the delegation as secretary, and on October 5, he invited his friend Cornelius Hedges to join them. Hedges had no official standing and might not have time to stay at Fort Benton for the talks, but as a birthday treat the trip was irresistible.

The basic purpose of the new treaty was simple: the Blackfeet would give up all their lands south of the Teton and Missouri rivers to make way for the rising tide of miners and settlers, and for a future railroad. This strict physical separation of the races was essential, said agent Upson, since physical encounters "had a tendency to create in their ignorant minds a jealousy and prejudice against the whites amounting in several instances to open hostilities, and resulting in bloodshed to both parties."[10]

Judge Munson, who seems in general to have been a more enlightened man, saw this backdrop of violence rather differently. "Whites would murder whites for plunder, scalp and mutilate their victims, and then report it as an Indian massacre, to be followed by similar outrages upon the Indians," he wrote. "The Indians were more sinned against than sinning."[11]

The rest of the party that traveled to Fort Benton included the former Virginia City vigilantes X. Beidler and Neil Howie, both of them now deputy U.S. marshals, and Malcolm Clarke, who was asked to act as translator and cultural mediator. Clarke was uniquely equipped to play this role after the recent spasms of violence. The Blood chief, Calf Shirt, brother-in-law to Alexander Culbertson and sometimes known as Impervious to Bullets, had told Clarke: "There is something about you which steals away our hearts against our inclinations. I hate all white men, but I hate you less than any white man I have ever known." This from the leader of the war party that had murdered Langford's deputy, Frank Angevine, and his fellow woodcutters just weeks earlier.[12]

The group left Helena on October 20. "We were well-mounted and equipped," Hedges said. "The weather was delightful and we anticipated a splendid and enjoyable excursion."[13] He raced his horse across the flat country and admired the beauty of the dark pines outlined against the yellow fall cottonwoods. They reached Clarke's ranch in the late afternoon and "found him at home surrounded by children and Indians." Nellie presided over a splendid dinner; oysters, sardines, cocktails, champagne. Afterward there was "sparkling conversation" as Clarke regaled them with tales of his adventures and showed off his collection of Indian bows. That night they slept "under a shed, provided for horses."

Next morning they decided to skirt the dangerous canyon of the Little Prickly Pear and instead follow the Mullan Road over the rugged hills. Although Clarke was planning a toll road through the canyon, construction work had not yet begun, and the following spring he would sell the concession to Warren Caleb Gillette, a man of French Huguenot extraction with an extravagant set of side-whiskers, already well-known in the territory as a merchant, expert woodsman, and would-be explorer. In Helena, Gillette had opened an office next door to Langford and Hauser's First National Bank, and the three men had struck up a warm friendship.[14]

The second day dawned fair, but then came an abrupt change in the weather, common enough in Montana in October. With the snow coming down in earnest, the riders took shelter in the cabin of one Paul Vernet, a

Canadian of mixed race, where they dined on a mountain sheep brought in by a Piegan hunter named Iron, who had been baptized by the Jesuits and wore the scapular and beads. Vernet lent Meagher a battered copy of Shakespeare. Outside the cabin, the storm raged, while the acting governor, appropriately enough, whiled away the evening reading *The Tempest*.[15]

The following day it was worse, a whiteout. Meagher compared the journey to Napoleon's retreat from Moscow. It was no weather for camping out, and Clarke, "a sincere and active friend of the Jesuit fathers," suggested they try to make it as far as the site of the new St. Peter's Mission.[16] Meagher, the only other Catholic in the party, thought this a fine idea.[17] Clarke, "understanding 'Indian,'" enlisted Iron as a guide.

Blinded by the snow, they blundered along, lost among the sudden outcrops of rock—Skull Butte, Black Butte, Fishback Butte, Haystack Butte, Birdtail Butte—until suddenly they heard a watchdog bark in the white darkness and the voices of men. Work on the Jesuit mission had just begun. The new St. Peter's, Meagher reported, "consisted, architecturally, of an Indian tent or tepee, capable of accommodating sixteen people in Indian fashion." Parked outside was "a commodious ambulance of rather an elegant air and finish," which had been donated to the Jesuits by General William Harney, the "squaw killer" of Blue Water.[18]

Frozen to the bone, the travelers squatted around the fire, while the Jesuits fetched bacon, bread, and coffee. Eventually they bedded down, with ropes of horsehair around the door of the tipi to deter rattlesnakes. But they found it impossible to sleep in the choking smoke and spent the rest of the night huddled on the ground outside.

Next morning, they struck out for the old mission on the Missouri, a few miles above the Great Falls, accompanied by a young Belgian Jesuit, Father Xavier Kuppens, who had established the first Catholic church in Helena earlier in the year and was now supervising the construction at Birdtail Butte. The blizzard blew worse than ever, and Hedges was so cold that he bound his feet with strips torn from his blankets. "It needed a most experienced guide to find the way in the blinding snow storm, but such a one we had in Mr. Clarke," he wrote.[19]

The Jesuits' former home lay on flat ground dominated by a huge table rock that the Piegans used as a pishkun, where buffalo were driven over the edge to their deaths. The site was being abandoned for a number of reasons, Kuppens explained. The drought that summer had caused the crops to fail; there were rumors of new gold strikes on the nearby Sun River, which would bring a predictable stampede of miners; and after the killing of the ten woodcutters on the Marias, the Jesuits were anticipating further violence.[20]

The party spent the next two days at the old mission, resting up after their ordeal. "We were in condition to appreciate our royal entertainment," said Hedges, "feasting on the fat of the land and from reserved stores rarely opened." Meagher of the Sword told his tales of revolution in France, rebellion against Queen Victoria, prison in Tasmania, escape to Brazil. Judge Munson found him "a charming conversationalist with a wonderful store of experiences, garnered from travels in all quarters of the globe." An old Canadian trader, François "Crazy" Vielle, stopped by and added colorful yarns of his own. But the most captivating stories of all were told by Father Kuppens.

The young Belgian was a protégé of Father De Smet's, still just twenty-seven and only two years ordained. He was no ordinary man, according to his Jesuit biographers. "Whether he was taming wild bronchos [sic], swimming the icy waters of dashing streams, or venturing amid flying bullets between lines of hostile miners in attempts to reconcile them, he met all hazards of the new country with an open fearlessness."[21]

By his own account, Kuppens had led a "nomad life" with the Piegans after his arrival at St. Peter's. He sat in the tents of their chiefs and listened to tales of their exploits. He was especially entranced by their reports of the wonders of the upper Yellowstone, though he must surely have heard something on the subject already from his mentor, De Smet, who had compared notes years earlier with Jim Bridger and prepared strikingly accurate maps of "the most extraordinary spot and perhaps the most marvelous of all the northern half of this continent."[22]

"I do not know that the narrator[23] always adhered strictly to facts," Kuppens wrote, "but making allowance for fervid imagination there was sufficient in the tale to excite my curiosity and awaken in me a strong desire to see for myself this enchanted if not enchanting land." Sometime in early 1864 he asked to be taken there.[24]

A group of Piegans offered to take him along on their spring buffalo hunt. They followed what was clearly a familiar route to the southwestern corner of their hunting range and ended the journey by showing Kuppens the "chief attractions" of the Yellowstone caldera, "the Grand Cañon, hot and cold geysers, variegated layers of rock, the Fire Hole, etc."[25]

Kuppens wrote,

> [Meagher's] interest was greatly aroused by my recital and perhaps even more so, by that of a certain Mr. Viell [sic]—an old Canadian married to a Blackfoot squaw—who during a lull in the storm had come over to see the distinguished visitors. When he was questioned about the Yellowstone he described everything in a most graphic manner. None of the visitors had ever heard of the wonderful place. Gen. Meagher said if things were as described the government ought to reserve the territory for a national park. All the visitors agreed that efforts should be made to explore the region and that a report of it should be sent to the government.[26]

A national park. Can the Jesuit's memory be trusted?[27] His account was written more than thirty years after the fact, when the concept was well-established. If Meagher did indeed use the phrase, he was the first person ever to do so. Even if he didn't, Meagher, Hedges, Clarke, and their companions were the first men since the failure of the Raynolds expedition five years earlier to discuss an exploration of Yellowstone with enough authority to deliver a report to the government. But one other thing was clear. Unless you were a trusted individual—a Jesuit priest, a fur trader who had married into the tribe—it would be dangerous for an official party of white men to venture into this fabulous region while Piegan hunting parties still ranged freely there.

Taking their leave of the Jesuits, the party pressed on toward Fort Benton, stopping for one last night on the way to camp under the stars at the Great Falls. What better way to celebrate a birthday? The spot was famous as one of the natural wonders of the West, and Hedges would have been familiar with the vivid descriptions in the journals of Lewis and Clark. The portage of the falls had been one of the great dramas of the westward journey of the Corps of Discovery, and on the way back east they were the point of rendezvous after Lewis's violent and abortive exploration of the Marias River. Lewis had all sorts of adventures at the falls, in fact. A grizzly bear chased him into the water. A wolf, or perhaps a bobcat or a mountain lion, attacked him. He was charged by three buffalo bulls, which pulled up short at the last moment. "It now seemed to me that all the beasts of the neighborhood had made a league to distroy me," he wrote, "or that some fortune was disposed to amuse herself at my expence." Nonetheless, he considered the falls "a truly magnificent and sublimely grand object which has from the commencement of time been concealed from the view of civilized man."[28]

Hedges was enraptured. "We visited the Great Falls on my birthday & slept soundly to the music of the Great Cataract," he wrote to his parents on his return to Helena.[29] But it was almost time for him to go home; business called. Although he went on with the treaty negotiators as far as Fort Benton, the Indians "were very dilatory about coming in" and he could not stay long enough to witness their grand assembly.[30]

Thousands of Piegans, Bloods, and Gros Ventres eventually straggled in, although the Siksika for some reason never showed up.[31] What Hedges missed, Judge Munson wrote, was "a panoramic scene of tribal costume, interlaced with painted faces and fantastic paraphernalia of tribal ornaments, requiring the graphic touch of a painter's brush on canvas, to convey a realistic impression, nowhere to be reproduced by pen and ink descriptions."[32]

The Blackfeet sat around a huge square where the annuity goods were laid out for display. The vanity of the chiefs was flattered by seating them in armchairs in the front row. Meagher showed his respect—or perhaps it was condescension?—by refusing to accept their customary offering of buffalo robes, telling them that they were too poor to be giving gifts to a government official on full salary.[33]

To describe the talks as *negotiations* would be a fairy tale. With the young Joe Kipp acting as translator, the chiefs were simply asked to set their marks to a set of terms precooked in Washington. In addition to the usual annuities, each of the chiefs would get an annual payment of $250 if the terms of the treaty were upheld, with the promise of added bonuses for those who "show themselves most worthy of favor."[34]

On November 16, eighteen Piegans made their X's, including the normally aggressive Mountain Chief and a more conciliatory chief named Heavy Runner. Fourteen Gros Ventres scrawled their marks, and so did nine Bloods. They all vowed that, "Perpetual peace, friendship, and amity shall hereafter exist between the United States and the Black-foot Nation and Tribes of Indians parties to this treaty." And they agreed to new reservation boundaries that would pen them back north of the Teton and Missouri rivers. In return, Governor Meagher and Agent Up-son promised to "protect said Indians against depredations and other unlawful acts, which white men, travelling, or passing through said reservation may commit." Of the ceded land, 640 acres were granted to the Jesuits for their new mission, and Malcolm Clarke got another plot of the same size. They received these tokens of the government's grati-tude "on account of their long residence, liberality, and valuable faithful services, in keeping the peace between the government and the Black-foot Nation of Indians."

But the 1865 treaty suffered from all the usual failings, a mixture of naïveté, disingenuousness, and bad faith: the pretense that these reso-nant abstractions, the lines drawn on a map, the future timetables, the talk of hoes and ploughshares, had any real meaning to the Blackfeet;

that the chiefs had any real intention of complying with terms that the other side routinely broke; and that the young warriors would pay any attention one way or the other. Every treaty, with every tribe, was subject to these illusions, but when a tribe was under such pressure that its very existence was at risk, as was now the case with the Blackfeet, the illusions would have especially terrible consequences.

15

CALL TO ARMS

1866–1867

There are times when people push, or are pushed, too far, and things begin to fall apart. A new line is drawn on a map. One man steals a horse; another takes one drink of whiskey too many. An insult is magnified, and the reprisals escalate. Personal grudges bleed into larger political grievances. Prejudice breeds fear, and fear feeds prejudice.

Demagogues seize hold of these unstable moments. Moderate men chafe at the absence of order and find themselves invoking extreme remedies that end in outbursts of collective madness. This had been the story of the Montana vigilantes. Now that story was repeated, as the treaty line of white settlement pushed the Blackfeet farther and farther north, and the crisis that ensued involved many of the same cast of characters.

In early 1866, as the Black Robes had feared, hundreds of white prospectors poured into the valley of the Sun River, driven by rumors of new gold strikes. They brought with them the usual innate hostility to the original inhabitants of the land, but they also came whooping with triumphalism after the signing of the new treaty at Fort Benton. Its terms seemed too good to be true. The fearsome Piegans and Bloods had agreed to give up a vast expanse of territory—space for new mines, farms, secure transportation routes—and asked for almost nothing in return. The accommodating chief Little Dog was learning to use gardening tools. He even went so far as to send his hunters out in the snow to bring in antelope meat for a group of prospectors stranded in a snowstorm. To many Piegans, the word for this was not *accommodating,* but *supine,* even *treasonous.*

Their anger exploded over an incident involving a man named John Morgan.[1] Four Piegans showed up one day at Morgan's cabin on the Sun River. Although the demeanor of his visitors was friendly enough, he soon grew irritated by their presence and called in some fellow prospectors to evict them. This they accomplished by shooting one and hanging the other three from a nearby tree.

The cycle of reprisals was inevitable. A Piegan war party came looking for Morgan, who had sought sanctuary with the Jesuits. The Piegans attacked the mission, so friendly to them for so long, killing a herder. On April 27, the very day of its planned inauguration, the Jesuits abandoned their new mission at Birdtail Butte and took refuge on the far side of the Continental Divide, among the friendly Flatheads. Father De Smet, the tribe's evangelizer and champion for a quarter of a century, retired to St. Louis, brokenhearted. "A fresh and furious war has broken out between the whites and the Blackfeet, in which the whites again have given the first provocation." he wrote with anguish. "Often wronged, insulted and outraged beyond measure by the whites," the Indians would now "dig up the war-hatchet and utter the cry of vengeance against the pale-faces."[2]

A band of Piegans, inflamed by Fort Benton's ready supply of white man's water, set upon the hapless chief Little Dog with butcher knives, murdered him, and mutilated his corpse. Then more whites were killed, including a nephew of Kit Carson. Citizens banded together and presented a petition to the redoubtable vigilante X. Beidler in Helena, demanding the formation of a militia.

Inter- and intratribal alliances shifted and broke with the strain. Piegan against Piegan, Blood against Blood, and now Blackfeet against Gros Ventres, their only traditional allies. In 1866 or 1867—accounts vary—militant

Piegans murdered at least three hundred Gros Ventres and Mountain Crows,[3] the highest body count ever recorded in a single battle among the tribes. The world of the Blackfeet was disintegrating, the chiefs' tenuous authority over the young men was slipping away, and the Commissioner of Indian Affairs in Washington decided there was no point in submitting the recent Fort Benton treaty for ratification—which made the chiefs wonder in turn why they should take the agreement seriously. And in this spiralling sequence of calamities Acting Governor Thomas Meagher saw an opportunity for his own greater glory.

At Meagher's insistence, the first soldiers came to the Blackfeet country in July 1866, two companies of the 13th Infantry encamped at the mouth of the Judith River, out in the middle of nowhere. Compared to the forts that were being built to protect the Bozeman Trail, Camp Cooke was a paltry affair; even so, a threshold had been crossed, the official theater of hostilities expanded.

In Helena, respectable citizens like Cornelius Hedges were muttering about extermination. In Fort Benton, Blackfeet scalps were accepted as legal tender in the bars.[4] And now the web of fear, rumor, and violence spread south to the small town that John Bozeman had built in the Gallatin Valley.

The valley was a beautiful and, by frontier standards, a peaceable place. Indians had always called it the Valley of the Flowers, and now it was beginning to fulfill the promise that Bozeman himself had made, that its black soils and rich grass would transform it into "the garden of Montana."[5]

The small town of Bozeman had its lively moments—German beer was brewed there, and sometimes there were pistol shots in the dead of night. But there was also a brass band and a choral society, and the first sermon had been preached within weeks of the first lot being platted. Those who lived in Bozeman—all one hundred of them—were as a general rule less likely to give free rein to their passions than those who labored to flush gold from the streams, or braved the risks of trapping and trading for furs, or fought the road agents and the displaced battles of the Civil War in the gold camps.

Indians could often be found encamped around the town, especially in the summer months. While no one much cared for them, the attitude seems to have been more one of distaste than overt hostility. Sarah Jane Tracey, an early settler, wrote in her diary, "The windows would be darkened by their dusky faces begging for biscuits, heap hungery or when the doors were opened we would find them sitting all around the door steps begging for everything. Meat, old clothes, soap, any other thing."[6]

The most frequent visitors were the Crows, but others also passed through Bozeman on their way to the buffalo grounds, traveling groups of basically friendly Nez Perce, Flatheads, and Kutenai who stopped to trade blankets and buffalo robes for novelties like umbrellas. Bannock and Shoshone visited, too, and most of them had learned at least the outward signs of friendship after the trauma of Bear River in 1863.[7]

But there was always a thread of nervousness among the white residents. Most had traveled the Bozeman or Bridger trails and even if they had no direct experience of violence, they were likely to have witnessed its aftermath—the scalped corpses, the graves torn open by wolves. These undercurrents of anxiety curdled into outright terror at the end of December 1866, when word came of the massacre of Lieutenant Fetterman and his eighty soldiers on the Bozeman Trail, with men castrated, disemboweled, eyes torn from their sockets. There was no need this time for the rumor mill to exaggerate.

Tales of torture and mutilation had long formed part of the settler's mental picture of Indian culture, and scalping was the classic morbid trope of the Western imagination. The settlers took little comfort from the fact that tribal adversaries received the same treatment as whites, or that whites themselves often resorted to scalping—witness the currency accepted in the bars of Fort Benton. Indeed all the evidence suggests that scalping had been a universal constant since the time of Bodo Man, a predecessor of *Homo sapiens* in Ethiopia, through the Parthians in Herodotus and the soldiers of Xenophon, to the indigenous peoples of the Caribbean and the Spanish conquistadores.[8] But the good people of Bozeman were not sitting around in their cabins reading Herodotus for historical perspective.

The torture of living prisoners was less common among the northwestern tribes than among those east of the Mississippi, although, as the remains of Fetterman and his men showed, the dead were fair game. The Crows seemed to have a particular fondness for dragging the corpses of their adversaries around camp by a rope tied around the neck, until the unfortunate victim disintegrated—rather in the manner of Achilles and Hector, except without the chariot. Women were responsible for many of the most egregious abuses, a further shock to Christian sensibilities. One French fur trader described women wielding their knives on battlefield corpses and then doing a kind of victory lap around their lodges, wearing severed penises around their necks as ornament.[9] For men, stuffing a man's genitalia into his dead mouth was part practical joke and part spiritual ritual, designed to ensure that the victim entered the next life in the same humiliated condition in which he had left this one.[10] The world beyond would be a harmonious place, and a man with no arms or legs or sexual organs would be unlikely to disturb the peace. Different tribes made their own ritual marks: A visiting British ethnologist named Dr. William Bell noted that the corpse of a certain Sergeant Wyllyams, killed in 1867, had been disfigured in ways that were deserving of scholarly interest: arm muscles slashed (Cheyenne), nose slit (Arapaho), throat cut (Sioux).[11]

If the settlers needed further proof that they were dealing with unfathomable aliens, it was the fact that the Indians did many of these things not only to others, but to themselves. Most famously, there was the excruciating self-torture of the Sun Dance, practiced each year at the summer solstice by the Sioux, the Blackfeet, the Crows, and most of the Northern Plains tribes.

Most Montana pioneers would have heard the anecdotes, and the more educated might well have read the extraordinary letters that George Catlin wrote from the Mandan villages on the upper Missouri in 1832, where he was allowed to witness, and even to paint, the ceremony. After fasting for several days, young men, skewered through incisions in the pectoral muscles, were hoisted by ropes to hang six or eight feet off the ground, while people hung heavy weights—bows and quivers, shields, buffalo skulls—from their extremities. What horrified Catlin most as he painted the scene was that he was unable "to detect anything but the pleasantest smiles as they looked me in the eye, while I could hear the knife rip through the chest, and feel enough of it myself, to start involuntary and uncontrollable tears over my cheek."[12]

Seeing in the ceremony a reflection of Britain's dark ages, Catlin subscribed to the theory—which had also been espoused by Thomas Jefferson, who passed it on to Lewis and Clark—that the Mandans were the descendants of Prince Madoc of Wales, who had supposedly sailed to America in 1170.[13]

So when news reached Bozeman of the Fetterman massacre and mutilations, fear of the alien Other had stacked up plenty of dry kindling, to which the politicians and newspapermen were happy to add the lighted match.

The *Helena Herald,* which spoke for the town's respectable Republican opinion, summed up the prevailing sentiment—and fanned the fires—in an editorial published in the hysterical month of January 1867. "Revenge— extermination; a rigid enforcement of grape, shrapnel, canister, fire, sword and bayonet, is the only treatment we can recommend for those untamable, treacherous, savage fiends of earth."[14]

The violence continued through the spring of 1867, marked by two events that spoke to the explosive state of relations between the whites and the Blackfeet and the increasingly unstable dynamics within the tribes themselves. Each event involved an individual who was a towering presence in the territory. One involved a murder, the other what seemed to be a minor family quarrel, with no more serious violence than a slap in the face with a riding whip. But it was the slap in the face that proved, in the course of time, to have the more devastating consequences.

It's hard to say exactly when the episode took place. Malcolm Clarke's daughter, Nellie, tells us only that it was "one sunshiny morning, in the spring of 1867," which, given the vagaries of the Montana weather, might mean March or might mean the end of June. It revolved around a family visit to the Clarke ranch on the Little Prickly Pear.

The most complicated member of Clarke's complicated family was Ne-tus-che-o, his Piegan relative by marriage, whom he had taken East for an education.[15] The young man belonged to the most militant and powerful of the Piegan bands, that of Mountain Chief.[16] His given name meant Owl Child, but people also called him Pete—so Pete Owl Child, or, when the army later turned its beam on him, simply Peter. Culturally displaced, thin-skinned, and desperate to prove his manhood, he quickly acquired a reputation for moodiness and violence. At some point he married a woman from the band of Heavy Runner, a man friendlier to the whites, which complicated his life still further. He seems to have become a kind of pariah, unwelcome in any lodge, especially after he murdered his Piegan father-in-law.[17]

In the three years since his arrival, Clarke's ranch and bunkhouse had become a prosperous place. Blackfeet visitors dropped in as they pleased. Nellie, now twenty-one, was always hospitable. So when Owl Child turned up that spring morning with his entourage—wife, mother, sister, and brother—there was no question of turning him away. Despite his unsavory ways, he was family.

After a week or so, the angry young man woke to find his horses gone. The thieves had left tracks with the marks of horseshoes, which suggested that they were white men. Such a theft raised complicated questions of honor. Stealing horses from a Piegan village was no great drama: You simply went out and found the thief, stole some of his horses in return, killed him if necessary. But the theft of horses from a white man's house while you were enjoying his hospitality—that imposed a serious obligation on the host to make restitution.

Clarke searched diligently for the horses but found no trace of them. According to Langford, who got much of the story from Nellie, Owl Child's wife and mother needled him, saying that he was "a coward and a woman for submitting so tamely to the offence."[18] Not many young Piegan males would have been able to withstand that kind of taunting from their womenfolk, let alone one of Owl Child's temperament. So it was not entirely surprising that one rainy night, with Clarke away from home, the young man absconded with most of his host's herd.

As soon as Clarke returned, he and his son Horace, still a teenager, took off in pursuit. They finally caught up with Owl Child in the camp of Mountain Chief, where he rode out to meet them mounted on one of Horace's favorite horses. Horace, who had obviously inherited his father's incendiary temper, dragged the Piegan from his saddle, called him a dog, and struck him across the face with his riding whip. Clarke raised his gun but was surrounded by a dozen or more Piegans. "Instant death to himself and his son, would have been the penalty, had he fired," says Langford, milking the drama in his usual fashion. Clarke called Owl Child an old woman. What seemed to inflame him even more than the loss of his horses was the theft of a favorite spyglass. But somehow the fracas was smoothed over; no doubt the tribal elders intervened.

This at least is the story as we have it from Nellie Clarke and from Langford. Other accounts are different. Horace Clarke said the bad blood began some time earlier, when he tried to restrain Owl Child from slashing his wife with a hunting knife. Among the Blackfeet, it was said that Malcolm Clarke had slept with—perhaps even raped—Owl Child's pretty Piegan wife, or at least tried to. When events unraveled later, this explanation of the grudge between the two men was favored by Mountain Chief and Heavy Runner, the Piegan chiefs on each side of the marriage.[19]

April brought another act of violence, 150 miles away on the banks of the Yellowstone. The victim this time was the great trailblazer John Bozeman.

Bozeman was not one to be unnerved by Indian troubles. He was one of life's natural explorers and adventurers, endowed with great physical courage—he had to be, in order to have blazed a wagon trail through unsettled Sioux country. He was famous for his good judgment, although known on occasion to have slippery ethics. A friend recalled that, "His sense of honor in some directions was terribly sensitive, while in other directions his conscience was very elastic." Which could just as easily have been a description of his friend and sometime business partner Nathaniel Langford.[20]

Above all, Bozeman was "a natural speculative genius," and it may be that his interest in the prosperity of the town he founded, rather than any real fear of an Indian invasion, inspired a letter he composed to Meagher on March 25. "General," he wrote,

> We have reliable reports here that we are in imminent danger of hostile Indians and if there is not something done to protect this valley soon, there will be but few men and no families left in the Gallatin Valley. Men, women and children are making preparations to leave at an early day. If you can make any arrangements to protect them, they will stay; if not, the valley will doubtless be evacuated.[21]

Meagher was now in his second eccentric stint as the "acting one" in the governor's mansion. He immediately saw his opportunity for glory and on April 9, dispatched a telegram to Ulysses S. Grant, General-in-Chief of the Army: "The greatest alarm reasonably prevails . . . Danger is immanent [sic]."

A few days later, Bozeman did something that seems reckless and entirely out of character: He agreed to accompany a friend, the local merchant Thomas Cover, on a mission to negotiate a contract with the army to reprovision Fort C. F. Smith and Fort Phil Kearny on the Bozeman Trail—a trip that took them down the Yellowstone and into the teeth of the supposed insurgency. At the mouth of Mission Creek, just east of the present-day town of Livingston, the two men were roasting venison over a campfire when a group of five Indians appeared some distance away, traveling on foot, one leading a pony. Not to worry, Bozeman said: They were Crows. One of them was even a personal acquaintance. Cover nonetheless suggested shooting them, just to be on the safe side. The putative Crows invited themselves to dinner, but as the little party sat chewing on the venison, Bozeman supposedly whispered to Cover, "I am fooled, they are Blackfeet." Cover says he went for his pistol, but one of the Indians opened fire on Bozeman and then shot him from behind, wounding him in the shoulder. Cover returned fire and killed one of the Crows, or Blackfeet, or whatever they were. The rest fled, carrying the dead man with them.

Cover's story has more holes than a prospector's gold sieve. There was no trace of a disturbance at the crime scene, no Indian sign, no evidence of a struggle, no blood other than Bozeman's. Nothing was taken; Bozeman's gun and watch were still lying there by his body. And why would five Blackfeet be wandering around without their horses in the territory of the Crows, their worst enemies? A friend noticed later that the bullet had entered Cover's shoulder from the front, not the back. There were powder burns around the entry wound, suggesting a shot from close range. Rumor was that Bozeman had been paying attentions to the merchant's wife.

But what matters in these instances is not what happened, but what people choose to believe happened—and Montanans were in no mood to question a version of events that confirmed all their worst fears and prejudices. Popular opinion laid the murder to the vicious Blackfeet, and some said that the killers included the Piegan Mountain Chief and three of his sons.[22] So the *Helena Herald* cranked up the press for another round of headlines.[23]

Killing of Col. Bozeman and Wounding of
Thomas Cover by the Blackfeet Indians!
The panic upon the Gallatin settlers!
Their apprehensions of a general attack upon their homes!
Their appeal to Gov. Meagher and the people of the Territory!
War Meeting at the Court House!
Rally! Rally!! Everybody!!!

Meagher fired off another telegram to Washington on April 27, this one jointly signed with Hedges's friend Judge Hezekiah Hosmer: "Our territory in serious danger from the Indians. Richest portion already invaded. Citizens murdered."

Washington was unimpressed. "Meagher in Montana is a stampeder, and can always with a fair show of truth raise a clamor," wrote Secretary of War Edwin M. Stanton to General William Tecumseh Sherman, who was now in charge of all military operations in the West.[24]

"The biggest humbug of the age," declared the former Flathead agent, Augustus Chapman; whites traveling through the Blackfeet country did not "apprehend any more danger from hostile Indians than they would in Washington city."[25] General Alfred Terry, the straight-backed lawyer-soldier in charge of the Department of Dakota, felt that Bozeman's murder, while serious, appeared to be an isolated event. "Nothing which has happened within this territory during this spring and summer, in my judgment, justified the alarm which has been felt," he reported.[26]

All true enough, but Sherman still faced a dilemma. As a soldier, he found it unhelpful when settlers tossed around words like "exterminate"; reality tended to be more nuanced. And like many senior officers, he had seen this game played before—there was nothing these frontier towns liked more than to exaggerate the dangers they faced, demand protection by the army, and then reap the economic benefits of a permanent military presence. Soldiers were not only good customers for local businesses; when things were quiet, they were also handy at building roads, digging irrigation ditches, and stringing up telegraph wires—all at no cost to the beneficiaries.

At the same time, it was hard for Sherman to give the governor of a United States territory a flat "no." He offered a compromise answer: the army would build two forts in Montana. Fort Shaw, on the Sun River near the old Jesuit mission, was commissioned in June; Fort Ellis, two miles east of Bozeman, at the end of August. There would now be a permanent military presence at the northern gateway to the upper Yellowstone, a development that would have enormous significance for future explorers.

Pending arrival of these regular troops, the government would send weapons enough for Meagher to equip eight hundred volunteers—to be distributed only "if Indians enter the Valley of the Gallatin."[27] *Enter* the valley? Or just *threaten* to enter it? Meagher paid no heed to the semantic distinction.[28] Nor did the merchants of Bozeman, who cheerfully set about supplying the militia with horses, boots, provisions, whiskey, whatever they needed, confident of reimbursement by the U.S. Treasury. "Montana's Picnic," some called it.[29]

By the time Sherman's reply came, Meagher was already handing out commissions like candy. The old vigilante enforcer X. Beidler was placed in charge of recruiting. One Thomas Thoroughman found himself in charge of the militia and an overnight brigadier general. The engineer and mapmaker Walter De Lacy, who had seen some of the wonders of the upper Yellowstone in 1863, was made a colonel and dispatched to scout suitable locations for a fort. He found a good spot eight miles east of Bozeman, and the acting governor named it for his wife: Fort Elizabeth Meagher. *Stockade* would have been more accurate. Thirty miles down the Yellowstone, a second makeshift "fort" was also named out of spousal loyalty: Camp Ida Thoroughman.[30]

But it was all sound and fury signifying very little. Meagher and his men cantered back and forth across the Blackfeet country and did their best to look menacing. The weapons promised by Sherman chugged their way slowly up the Missouri to Fort Benton, where they were due to arrive at the end of June, together with the infantrymen who would establish Fort Shaw. But by that time Meagher himself recognized that the brouhaha was winding down—a fact for which, entirely in character, he took the credit. On June 15, he wrote to his father, "I am satisfied that having acted promptly . . . no mischief will accrue to the Territory from the spirit that animates the savages on our borders."[31]

With one piece of excitement over, a man of Meagher's character cast around for another. And at this time, in this place, the thoughts of an adventurous man turned easily from violence to exploration. Meagher went on, "I shall [now] . . . take to certain explorations, with the assistance of the Good Fathers from which some material advantage will probably eventuate."[32]

The meaning of this seems unambiguous. Meagher was clearly thinking of the unexplored upper Yellowstone, which he had presumably discussed again with his friend Father Kuppens since first hearing the Jesuit's account of his trip with the Piegans at the snowbound mission a year and a half earlier. As for the "material advantage," there is a hint of

what Meagher had in mind in a dispatch from the *Frontier Index,* an obscure newspaper that was published out of a mobile railcar: "A few years
more and the U.P. Railroad will bring thousands of pleasure seekers,
sightseers and invalids from every part of the globe, to see this land of
surpassing wonders."[33]

By the middle of 1867, the Yellowstone rumors had spread far and
wide, and the idea of a formal exploration had become serious and specific. Inspired by the stories he had heard from Jim Bridger, Nathaniel
Langford had been proposing an expedition for more than a year, though
he remained apprehensive of the Indian threat. The Montana legislature
had commissioned Walter De Lacy to make a map of the known features
of the upper Yellowstone in 1865, and in 1867, when he wasn't galloping
about as a cardboard colonel in the militia, he drew another. Another
candidate for the proposed expedition was a bespectacled, middle-aged
gentleman named Truman Everts, who worked with Langford as Assessor of Internal Revenue and had been a strident voice calling for the establishment of a militia. A third was Chief Justice Hosmer.[34]

By the end of June, when Meagher set off to pick up his guns at Fort
Benton, the little group of explorers had begun active preparations for
their trip. The *Montana Post* carried this announcement: "The expedition
to the Yellowstone country mentioned a short time since is now organized, and it is the intention of the party to start from the camp on
Shields River [Camp Ida Thoroughman] in about two weeks." Two weeks.
Enough time, in other words, for General Meagher to take care of his
business in Fort Benton and hand over his caretaker governorship to his
successor. The *Post* continued:

> The expedition will be gone some three weeks and will go up
> the river as far as Yellowstone Lake. A number of gentlemen
> have expressed a desire to join the party. We refer those in Hel-
> ena to General Thoroughman, who will be at that city on Mon-
> day, and will give all desired information. Parties who have
> leisure to make this fascinating jaunt can ascertain particulars
> from Judge Hosmer or T. C. Everts.[35]

Fascinating jaunt is an odd phrase to describe a serious exploration of unknown and forbidding territory, but perhaps that is how they saw it.

So Meagher rode to Fort Benton to pick up Sherman's surplus muskets with the upper Yellowstone on his mind. He was not a well man, however, and hardly fit for three weeks in the wilderness: A lifetime of alcohol abuse, a couple of months in the saddle, a bad case of dysentery had all taken their toll. A friendly merchant on the sternwheeler *G. A. Thompson* plied him with several glasses of blackberry wine, a common remedy for the "summer complaint." Some said this was the prelude to a night of heavy drinking, others that the governor was stone-cold sober, others that he was depressed, others still that he was in fine spirits. Whatever the truth, late that night there was the sound of splintering wood, a splash, a cry. *Man overboard!* And that was the last anyone saw of Meagher of the Sword, though Langford put up a one-thousand-dollar reward for anyone who found the body. The governor's wife, Elizabeth, is said to have haunted the banks of the Missouri for weeks, waiting vainly, like Penelope, for her husband to return.[36]

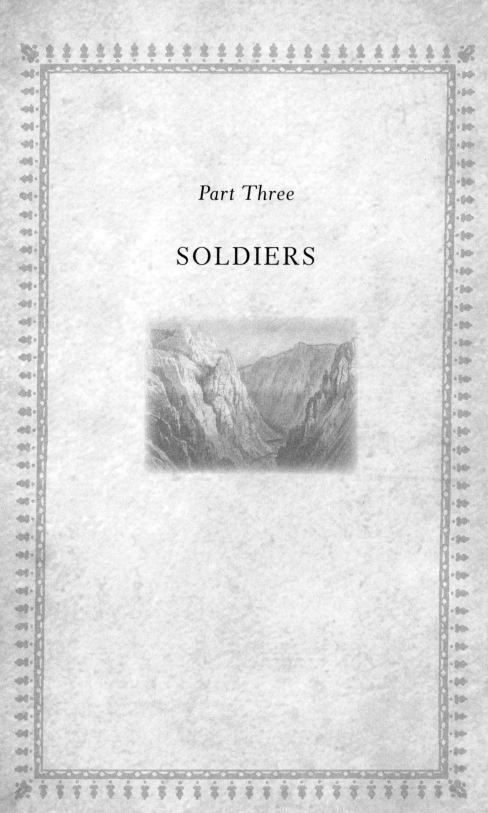

Part Three

SOLDIERS

16

PATHS OF GLORY

1860–1868

Since his youth, Gustavus Cheyney Doane had dreamed of becoming a soldier and an explorer.[1] His family traced its pedigree back to a John Done, who arrived in the New World in 1629 or 1630, and was a leading man in the Plymouth Colony—one of the few to merit the title of "Mr.," which was reserved for high-ranking officials, schoolmasters, members of the clergy, and men of wealth or nobility. Tradition says the Doanes, or Dones, came originally from Wales.[2]

Cheyney, as he came to call himself, loathing the name Gustavus, belonged to one of the more improvident branches of the family. His father, a carpenter, moved around a lot and had a knack for losing money. He was a narrow man, authoritarian but at the same time ineffectual. From the small lead-mining town of Galesburg, Illinois, just east of the Mississippi, Solomon Doane took his family to St. Louis, and then, in 1846, when his son was six, he struck out for Oregon. The Doanes were among the thousands who passed through Fort Bridger that summer, part of the same year's migration that brought both Francis Parkman and the Donner Party to the West. After three unproductive years, the family moved again, along with half the white population of Oregon, to join the California gold rush. But it was another round of failure, as it was for so many

in that scramble for instant wealth, leaving no alternative for Solomon
Doane but a life of hardscrabble farming.

This peripatetic childhood nurtured a complicated and contradictory
character. The young Cheyney was obstinate, practical, militant, ambitious, with a passion for horses and the farm boy's talent for all things me-
chanical. "It seemed he could make anything he saw anyone else make," his
brother George said.[3] As he grew a little older, he developed a love of "the
martial spirit" and a contempt for the "would-be philanthropists and
Quakers" who opposed it; "success belongs to the quickest and the bravest,"
he wrote, not to the namby-pamby East Coast humanitarians.

He dreamed of going to West Point,[4] but ended up at the University of
the Pacific in Santa Clara, California. The first institution of higher learning in California, the college had been founded by Methodists in 1853,
supposedly "to counter the potentially negative effects on the youth from
association with the alleged immorality of the gold rush miners known as
the 49ers."[5] This elite education was his mother's doing; she was evidently
intent on turning out a son who would not be a failure like his father.

Doane was slovenly and profane, resentful of social superiors, an intellectual contrarian. He left behind a sheaf of college essays, and they are all
uncompromising passion, nothing held back. He saw California as a place
"throbbing with latent energy," and was thrilled to be on the spot to witness
"the magical disappearance of the aborigines . . . a wandering, profligate,
and degraded race . . . into whose brains never entered a thought of anything great or glorious."[6] But there was evidence of scholarship, too. He
emerged from four years of study with a solid grounding in Latin and
Greek, mathematics and physics, geology and mineralogy, botany and zoology, philosophy, religion and government. His particular enthusiasm was
for geology, which he described as "the fulminating star of all Sciences."[7] He
graduated with a modest reputation as a writer.

Most important, Doane had vaulting ambitions of becoming a great
explorer. At the University of the Pacific, along with his love of
things practical and martial, he demonstrated a passion for wild places

and their character-building possibilities. In essays or "orations" with titles like "The Beauties of Nature" and "The Eloquence of Solitude," he declared that encounters with wilderness opened up "a new and more blissful existence." He wrote that he yearned for "the desert wilds," for "the unexplored region of dark oblivion."

> Rich are the enjoyments and valuable the numerous lessons of instruction which accrue to a thoughtful mind while sojourning in the midst of uncultivated nature. . . . In those deep solitudes and awful cells . . . we wander alone in the deep mountain gorges, where beetling crags hang in mid air above us threatening direst destruction to all those who pass beneath. . . . That lone wilderness . . . breathes forth . . . that peculiar elevating sense of internal exaltation.[8]

His yearning to become an explorer seems to have begun with the same adolescent hero-worship that many young Californians would have felt for "The Great Pathfinder," John C. Frémont, the signal figure in the mapping of the far West in the 1840s. Years later Doane wrote:

> [E]xplorations furnish a source of reputation wherein the rewards are, and ever have been, more than commensurate with the efforts put forth. . . . A single exploration by a junior officer [Frémont] in 1846[9] carried him afterward successively to a seat in the United States Senate, the possession of a princely estate, a candidature for the Presidency, and the command of the Western army at the commencement of a great war [against Mexico]. The field is open still. This invasion does not require exalted rank. A poor subaltern, yet unknown, while traversing with weary steps the barren wilderness or scaling the mighty summits from which the waters part and flow, may stumble, under fortune's favor, upon some new discovery, the merit of which will secure to him all that history vouchsafes to greatness—a paragraph in the encyclopedia of the human race.[10]

Frémont would have represented a model of many things to Doane: the marriage of soldiering and exploration, manliness and physical courage, the expansion of scientific knowledge, romantic self-aggrandizement, public recognition, political success, and material wealth—all of which were aided greatly in Frémont's case by a handsome, gifted, and socially well-connected wife.[11] But what he neglects to mention is Fremont's recklessness and the fact that he eventually crashed and burned, dying near-destitute and all but forgotten.

The call of the martial life was just as strong as the lure of the wilderness, and within a year of graduation from the College of the Pacific Doane became a soldier, though the first phase of his military career can most charitably be described as checkered.

The Civil War had its units of legend—the great cavalry regiments, the Army of the Potomac. And then there were the ragged sideshows like the California One Hundred. The One Hundred were a group of Union volunteers, formed after secessionists in San Francisco threatened a breakaway "Pacific Republic" and rosily described by recruiters as an "elite equestrian corps." Doane joined the unit at the end of October 1862 and was awarded the yellow chevrons of a sergeant. The impression he made on his fellow soldiers seems to have been one part imposing, one part clownish. One described him as "a tall, rawboned individual, not very tidy in his appearance with an appetite which required at least two men's rations to satisfy and a very dry wit. He rode a pinto horse that was the smallest in the Company, in riding which his feet would come very near the ground."[12]

Assigned to the Second Regiment of the Massachusetts Cavalry, the Californian equestrians made their seasick way to Boston via Panama, sustained by rancid salt pork ("Cincinatti chicken") and maggoty rice, on ships optimistically named the *Golden Age* and *Ocean Queen*. When they arrived, they were promptly thrown into action as counterinsurgency specialists, defending the outskirts of Washington against the Partisan Rangers of the dashing and audacious Colonel John S. Mosby, the "Gray

Ghost." Doane's unit came close to capturing Mosby, who would have been a prize of prizes. Instead, heroism degenerated into comic opera. After another fruitless pursuit of the Gray Ghost, Doane became separated from his unit and was captured by a group of Partisan Rangers, surrendering his weapon and offering no resistance. But he showed a characteristic flash of ingenuity when his captors demanded to know which unit he was attached to. Knowing that "Massachusetts" was one of the more incendiary words in the Confederate vocabulary, Doane affected a thick German accent and said "New York Volunteers." This marked him as a "dumb Dutchman," not worth taking into custody. The rangers gave him a kick in the behind and told him to get lost.[13]

This was not the end of the story, however. Surrendering without a fight was considered to be "conduct prejudicial to good order and military discipline" and it cost Doane his stripes at a court-martial. He left no record of his reaction, but presumably it was not good; this was a man with a fierce sense of pride and the thinnest of skins.

From the California One Hundred Doane passed to the Mississippi Marine Brigade, an even less romantic riverborne unit charged with hunting down Confederate guerrillas. Rehabilitated and newly commissioned as a first lieutenant, Doane saw more action this time than he had during his thankless pursuit of Mosby. "I had the honor to command either the advance or rear guard in eight actions," he wrote later in his service record, the most significant being the battle of Chicot Lake in June 1864, a disastrous encounter that cost the Union 180 casualties and has been compared to the Charge of the Light Brigade.

Like the California One Hundred, the Marine Brigade was notionally an "elite" force, but its particular talents seem to have been looting and burning, raping and pillaging. General Alfred Ellett, in overall command, complained that the unit was a gang of

> ... [r]egular finished highwaymen who do not hesitate to put
> a pistol to the head of any man or woman they find and de-
> mand "his money or his life," or seize a woman and throw her

down and search her person for jewelry, or violate her if so
inclined. They are certainly the most reckless fiends that I
ever heard of.

What was Doane's role in this mayhem? For the most part, elegantly
written reports that glossed over the abuses committed by the men under
his command. He would build much of his career around this singular talent as a writer, and General Ellett was the first to spot it. "He makes a very
good officer," Ellett wrote. "I like him very much. He has right good sense
and can send in a better official paper than any officer of his battalion."[14]

War grants young men permission to shed the minimum standards of
civilized conduct, and postwar reconstruction offers unique opportunities for profit and self-advancement. If the first phase of Doane's military
career had been buffoonish, and the second sordid, the third had elements
of both, plus a dose of recklessness that verged on the criminal.

Doane received his honorable discharge at Vicksburg on January 23,
1865, and in May he settled in Yazoo City, Mississippi, which had been
burned to the ground by Union forces a year earlier. He spent three eventful
years there, a proto-carpetbagger. He opened a mercantile business, but it
did not thrive. He married Amelia Link, the nineteen-year-old daughter of
a wealthy Canadian-born slave- and plantation-owner. Letters from home
brought the news that his father had fallen into another economic black
hole, and then that he had fallen into a black hole of a more permanent kind
after cutting off his big toe with a rusty axe and contracting lockjaw.

Then, in a nine-month flurry of appointments after the passage of the
Reconstruction Acts in March 1867, there were the stirrings of a political
career for Cheyney Doane, first as registrar of new voters, next as justice
of the peace, and finally, in December, at the age of twenty-seven, as
mayor of Yazoo City. Along the way, however, there was an excess of bad
judgment, another constant in Doane's career. There was a narrowly
avoided duel with a political rival, more Keystone Cops than Hamilton-
Burr.[15] At one public assembly, he stood to deliver a thirty-two-page oration ("A Republican Speech Addressed to the Working Men of the
South") that drew on all the flourishes of classical rhetoric he had learned

at the University of the Pacific, but his Ciceronian effort was broken up by a rock-throwing mob. Finally, after Doane had created a critical mass of enemies, there was humiliation, resignation as mayor, and flight with Amelia to Illinois, with $4,000 in his pockets. The amount raises eyebrows, given the failure of his mercantile business, the floods that washed out a cotton crop he had planted, and the loss of Amelia's father's fortune, but Doane's biographer, Kim Allen Scott, surmises that it had something to do with the fines that officials like Doane could levy against freedmen who carried unlicensed weapons.[16]

Doane's sojourn in Illinois lasted only a few weeks, and the soldiering life called to him again. In June 1868, after pulling some strings from his old days in the California One Hundred, he secured a letter of recommendation to the new Secretary of War, Major General John M. Schofield, supporting his candidacy as an officer in the regular army.[17]

He reported to Carlisle Barracks in Pennsylvania for the examination and passed easily. Doctors no doubt prodded and poked him according to the standard instructions for dealing with a new recruit, which called on them to

> ... examine him stripped; to see that he has free use of all limbs; that his chest is ample; that his hearing, vision, and speech are perfect ... [and that he does not have false teeth]; that he has no tumors, or ulcerated or extensively cicatrized legs, no rupture or chronic cutaneous affection; that he has not received any contusion, or wound of the head, that may impair his faculties; that he is not a drunkard; is not subject to convulsions; and has no infectious disorders ... [especially venereal], nor any other to unfit him for military duty.[18]

On August 1, 1868, duly certified as both intelligent and healthy, Cheyney Doane had the commission he craved as a second lieutenant in the Second Regiment of the United States Cavalry.

But his first assignment was remote from any dreams of becoming a second Frémont. It was a dreary posting as quartermaster at Fort Russell, in the bleak flatlands of eastern Wyoming. He craved combat but instead had to pay out wages, order supplies, maintain inventories of weapons and uniforms, and worry about keeping the peace among the new railroad-town rabble of Cheyenne—the "end-of-the-track horde"—tedious duties that were interspersed with spells of trudging back and forth along the South Platte in fruitless pursuit of invisible Indians.[19] "Traveled a distance of 60 miles," said a typical report from his commanding officer. "Operated against the Sioux, Cheyennes, and Arapahoes. No results."[20]

But even these futile forays into the surrounding country convinced Doane that he had all the skills an explorer needed. "In country I had never seen before and which was imperfectly mapped," he wrote later, "I never once failed in my course either in darkness or daylight though I had seen veteran officers who have served there for years entirely lost." He claimed to have requested permission at this time to be the first man to explore the canyons of the Colorado, presumably by launching a boat at the new railroad bridge over the Green River, near the site of many of the old trappers' rendezvous. The request was denied, and the honor went instead to the one-armed Civil War hero, Major John Wesley Powell, no doubt adding insult to a man who already had a tendency to feel a sharp sense of injury.[21] Powell set out from the Green River bridge on May 14, 1869, but by that time Cheyney Doane had received new orders that would change his life.

17

THE LOST TRIBES OF THE
SECOND CAVALRY

May–July 1869

I n the early morning of May 19, 1869, Brevet Colonel Albert Gallatin Brackett mustered four companies of the Second Cavalry at
Carter's Station in Wyoming. His parents had named him for Jefferson's Secretary of the Treasury, but perhaps some senior officer
with a sense of humor had ordered his new posting, which was to a
freshly built fort in Montana's Gallatin Valley.

Just nine days earlier, the laying of the Golden Spike had marked the
completion of the transcontinental railroad, and to reach their assembly
point Brackett's troops had ridden the new rails more than three hundred miles from the boisterous town of Cheyenne. Carter's Station lay at
the intersection of the old Oregon Trail and the Union Pacific. The old
Fort Bridger, transformed now into a permanent army base, was just
twelve miles away.

The cavalry's destination was Fort Ellis, 437 miles to the north according to Colonel Brackett's final odometer reading. The fort was named
for Brevet Brigadier General Augustus van Horne Ellis, who had taken a
bullet in the forehead at Gettysburg, and it was the lasting legacy of Acting
Governor Thomas Meagher's Blackfeet panic two summers earlier. Originally it had been assigned two companies of infantry, soon raised to
three. But against agile, mounted Indian raiders, infantrymen were worse

than useless, and the *Montana Post* derided them as "laborers, ignorant of drill, undisciplined in fight."[1] So when a fresh spate of attacks unnerved the territory in the spring of 1869, it was time for the mounted cavalry to come riding over the hill.

The six-week march to Fort Ellis would take Colonel Brackett and his men northward over high desert and sagebrush flats, through fertile river valleys and high mountain passes. On a good day they might make twenty miles; on a rough one barely five.

The officer corps of the frontier army ranged from gentleman-scholars and aristocratic playboys to strutting martinets and out-and-out psychopaths like John Chivington, of Sand Creek notoriety. Factionalism, jealousy, and patronage were rampant. Alcoholism was rife and usually indulged. Officers subscribed to a rigid caste system, but this was honored as often in the breach as in the observance, and the brevet system of honorary promotions made the pecking order even more complicated. Many officers saw themselves, especially after the Civil War, as the incorruptible lineal descendants of medieval knights, although, as one historian has remarked, medieval chivalry never saw much contradiction in the slaughter of infidels.[2]

Even by the motley standards of the officer corps, Colonel Albert Brackett was an odd duck. He was a veteran of Polk's Mexico campaign of 1846–1848, which he memorialized in doggerel newspaper verse:

> *O those noble men of yore*
> *Who went to win a name*
> *That should last forevermore*
> *In the sacred hall of Fame!*

He had served with distinction in the Civil War, leading a cavalry force at Bull Run, but after being badly wounded in Arkansas his career had taken a quieter turn. He was an amateur ornithologist who got tangled up in an acrimonious dispute with John James Audubon over the nocturnal habits of the goatsucker—the kind of arcane debate that often consumed nineteenth-century naturalists. He was also a sometime military historian, author of a standard history of the U.S. Cavalry and a how-to manual for cavalrymen.[3] The colonel's polymath skills even extended to ethnography; self-taught in the Shoshone language, he had written a study of the religion and customs of the tribe.[4] On matters of Indian policy, he held progressive opinions. He had a benign view of Native American women, for example, who were regarded by most of his peers as squalid and shiftless creatures, all well and good for fur trappers and mountain men, but beneath the dignity of officers on a *mission civilisatrice*. (Exceptions permitted, of course, frontier posts being lonely places.) But Brackett admired Indian women for their constant hard work and believed that their lives were "unquestionably far happier than the do-nothing, thankless, dyspeptic life led by a majority of American women."[5]

Fifteen officers rode to Montana under Brackett's command. Companies F, H, and L each went with the regulation captain and two lieutenants; Company G traveled a man short. A surgeon, an adjutant, an engineer, and a quartermaster made up the numbers. But the only officer to whom the colonel devoted any attention in his conscientious daily journal was Gustavus Cheyney Doane.

No one could have missed the second lieutenant in a crowd. At twenty-nine years old, he stood well over six feet tall and weighed two hundred pounds. Private William White, who served under him, described him as "erect in carriage, but rather awkward in motion, had a big bony frame covered with powerful sinews without a pound of superfluous flesh."[6] Doane had an uncommonly large nose and a sharply jutting chin. His black hair grew stiff and straight, and he wore it to the collar or below. His great, luxuriant mustache was a remarkable adornment even by the extravagant standards of the period, swooping far below the chin, part walrus and part Fu Manchu.

Few would have thought Doane handsome, and fewer still would have thought him cultivated in manners. Even though he neither drank nor smoked, Private White went on, "The language he used was not delicate. His manner of speech was loud, rough, slow and drawling. Some of the more polished officers looked upon him as being objectionably uncouth. But it seemed his ample stock of native common sense and his utterly honest and brave heart more than compensated for all deficiencies in mental elegance."[7]

Less than a year after his commission, Doane already had a reputation for leadership, scholarship, and practical frontier skills. He could find a trail, hitch a mule, and pitch a tent better than anyone. "A thorough caval-ryman," said a comrade of the Second; "The best field soldier I have ever known" was the view of Hugh Lenox Scott, another dragoon, who went on to become army chief of staff in World War I and knew a thing or two about field soldiering.

Doane also stood out from the pack because he traveled with his wife, the former Amelia Link of Yazoo City, the only woman in a column of more than two hundred uniformed men. One night the troops pitched camp at some hot springs that were reputed to be haunted, because the ground nearby trembled and shook with volcanic activity. The chivalrous Brackett named the place Amelia's Springs. She was a charming woman by all accounts, "but ill-suited by temperment [sic] to frontier conditions and [her husband's] impetuous condition." The marriage would not last.[8]

Although it was May, the first few days of the march to Montana were a misery of hail, rain, and snow, the road close to impassable. An Irish recruit complained that the mud was so deep that there was "noth-ing of [his horse] left above ground but his ears." After a week or so, the going became easier, but even when the mounted column made good time, it had to spend frustrating hours, even whole days, in camp waiting for the cumbersome ox train to catch up.

Lieutenant Doane seems to have strayed from the main party at will. He went off in search of bighorn sheep and killed a fine ram; he was at-tacked by a pair of eagles while attempting to rob their nest; he rode out to visit a Shoshone camp and came back with a badger, which greatly amused Colonel Brackett.[9] The impression is of a man who chooses to operate by his own rules and gets away with it by virtue of his competence and his sheer gall.

Moving steadily north through Utah, Brackett's men crossed paths with Major General Winfield Hancock—"Hancock the Superb," men called him—the newly appointed commander of the Department of Dakota, on an extended tour of inspection of military bases west of the Missouri.

The column came upon small, scattered Mormon settlements and frequently passed the graves of emigrants. On June 3, they crossed a stream named Thomas's Fork, where the infamous outlaw Boone Helm, who had been hanged five years earlier by the gold camp vigilantes, had eaten a dead companion's leg and wrapped the other up in an old flannel shirt to eat later. Nathaniel Langford called him "one of those hideous monsters of depravity whom neither precept nor example could have saved from a life of crime."[10]

Brackett's men passed through the Bear River Valley, the scene of the carnage inflicted by Colonel Connor and Major McGarry six years earlier. Nine hundred head of Texas cattle passed them, on the way to California. Mormon homesteaders brought eggs to supplement the trout for dinner. A party of Chinese were encountered, heading south from the mines. More Shoshone rode by, friendly ones from the band of Chief Washakie, Jim Bridger's father-in-law, "dragging their property with them on lodge poles which are strapped to the saddles of their ponies in a manner peculiar to themselves."

By this time the cavalry had completed two-thirds of its march to Fort Ellis and was almost at the Montana-Idaho line. The weather had turned foul again—two days of heavy rain interspersed with hail—and the line of peaks to the east had been wreathed in thick cloud. But now the sky cleared, and a line of jagged peaks stood revealed: the Tetons. Beyond their impenetrable barrier and a little to the north lay the caldera of the upper Yellowstone. It was only fifty miles away, but it might have been a thousand. Brackett, who seems to have had little feeling for the sublime, recorded the sight in his journal without noticeable emotion. "The 'Three Tetons,' celebrated land mark in this country," he wrote. "[T]hey are high mountains with large pinnacles reaching upward."

In later years Cheyney Doane would see the Tetons more than once. Viewing them by moonlight from a point farther north, on the Snake River, he would describe them more lyrically.

> There are no foothills to the Tetons. They rise suddenly in rug-ged majesty from the rock strewn plain. Masses of heavy for-ests appear on the glacial debris and in parks behind the curves of the lower slopes, but the general field of vision is glittering glaciated rock. The soft light floods the great expanse of the valley, the winding silvery river and the resplendent deeply carved mountain walls.

Doane's reaction to his first sight of the Tetons is not recorded, though it may be imagined. Had he read Raynolds's report of the failed 1860 ex-pedition, which was finally published in July 1868? If so, did he give a thought to the terra incognita beyond the peaks? The conclusion seems irresistible. After all, he was a man of letters, in relative terms; the report was the work of a fellow army officer and had been published just two weeks before Doane received his own commission as a lieutenant. Now he found himself posted to an army base within a day's ride of the Yel-lowstone. Jim Bridger's tales of the upper Yellowstone had spread far and wide, and its mysteries had become something close to an obsession for the leading men of the territory. Raynolds, Hayden, and Bridger were surely names that would have been familiar to any aspiring explorer.

Cheyney Doane rode across the Continental Divide on the summer solstice, Monday, June 21, 1869. It was a brilliant sunny day after a freezing night. "Thus far," his commanding officer wrote in his journal the following day, "Montana has fully sustained its name, as it is the most mountainous region ever beheld." The column had just ridden through the Island Park caldera, the result of an eruption of the Yellowstone supervolcano two million years ago. The upper Yellowstone plateau was much closer now, directly to their east, and Colonel Brackett made notes on the strange geology of the region: "Volcanic scoria to the right, left and front on all mountain ridges and on the plains. A great volcanic region once on fire for thousands and thousands of miles." An exaggeration, perhaps, but an allowable one in these exotic surroundings.

After crossing the Red Rock River the cavalry made fifteen or twenty miles a day through open country, sometimes beautiful, sometimes desolate. Four more days brought them to creeks lined with the detritus of worked-out gold diggings, and at last to Virginia City. The town was much smaller now than it had been in its heyday, but Brackett admired it as "an evidence of American enterprise, built as it is far away from the great marts of commerce." He especially liked the Masonic Hall, an imposing building of cut stone, where the pillars of local society gathered. In the evening the soldiers—or perhaps it would have been the officers only—went to a play in Virginia City's theater, where the celebrated Jack Langrishe had brought his peripatetic company at the height of the gold rush. Next morning the friendly locals begged the soldiers to stay longer, but Brackett was anxious to move on and reach Fort Ellis "as soon as practicable." No time-wasting Sabbaths for this officer.

On June 30, the column stopped by the Gallatin River. It was mustering day, the last of the month, and Colonel Brackett was pleased by his inspection. In matters of discipline and instruction, he gave his officers and men a rating of "excellent." In military appearance and condition of weapons and clothing, he classified them as "good," despite forty-four days on the road in mud, dust and rain.[11]

The next day they covered the last eleven miles of their journey, an easy ride over rich, flat agricultural land to Fort Ellis, which they found nestled on the sinuous east branch of the Gallatin at the foot of what is now called the Bridger Range. The fort was nothing much to look at, just a ramshackle collection of wooden huts with roofs of packed dirt. The army considered it a hardship posting, and the troops who were unlucky enough to be sent there were sometimes mocked as "the lost tribes of the Second Cavalry." But Colonel Brackett was in fine humor, his appreciation of the fort's creature comforts no doubt colored by forty-three straight nights of sleeping on the ground or in the back of a wagon.

Over the next few days, the colonel took stock of the strategic situation. He was, after all, despite all the poetry and the ornithology and the linguistics, the commanding officer of a combat unit. "The fort is made of logs and surrounded with palisades with two blockhouses at diagonal corners," he wrote with satisfaction. "It is small, compactly built, and seems well adapted for frontier protection."

Everything looked peaceful. The outgoing commanding officer, Captain Robert S. La Motte of the 13th Infantry, told him sniffily that "one Company of Cavalry would be sufficient at this point," and that this was all he had asked for.[12] The town of Bozeman was full of Indians, but they did not seem to be the threatening kind.[13] Some Crows encamped near the fort had ridden off in haste as the soldiers approached, but it turned out to be over a trifling incident. A young Crow had stabbed a white man; the white man had returned the favor; neither wound had proved fatal. Some friendly chiefs visited Brackett later to assure him that the offender had been punished with expulsion from their camp.

Nothing to report, the colonel wrote to his superiors a week after his arrival: "I cannot hear of any difficulties in this section of the country, nor has there been any since early in the spring."

Satisfied that everything was under control, Brackett found delicious opportunities for bird-watching. Dippers, grebes, flycatchers, goldeneyes, and catbirds congregated on the wetlands around the East Gallatin; juncos, finches, crossbills, grosbeaks, and siskins gathered in the pines; ruby-crowned kinglets, red-naped sapsuckers, yellow-rumped warblers, red-breasted nuthatches, Bohemian waxwings, and western tanagers passed through on their seasonal migrations; a dozen species of raptors rode the thermals over the Bridger Range.

To the east of the fort, the Bridgers pressed up against the first outriders of the Gallatin Range to form the Bozeman Pass. Just beyond the pass, a well-worn horse trail headed southeast over the hills, providing a direct route to the upper Yellowstone by cutting off the great bend of the river where William Clark had paused during his homeward journey in 1806. At the wooded crest, the rider came upon a sudden view across Paradise Valley to the steep wall of the Absarokas, before making the descent along a steep, sparkling trout stream—Trail Creek.

The little creek flowed into the big river near the rudimentary settlement known as Emigrant Gulch, where a group of Bridger's Pilgrims had found gold in 1864. The mines had been briefly abandoned in 1867, during the Blackfeet panic, but they had started up again in a small way, a few thousand dollars worth of dust a year. Other prospectors had made modest strikes in the forbidding, grizzly-ridden country between the Yellowstone and the naked Precambrian rock of the Beartooth Plateau. Much of what we know about these episodes comes from the diary of a Southern adventurer named Bart Henderson, a determined personality with a fondness for strong drink, who left a compelling journal describing his travels.[14]

He set off from Deer Lodge with three companions on August 12, 1867, carrying Walter De Lacy's map and two bottles of whiskey, already "two sheets in the wind and the third fluttering," and traveled south over the Snake River plain to Jackson Hole and from there to the upper Yellowstone via Two Ocean Pass—a route that Jim Bridger had trodden more than once and that he had tried and failed to reach again with the Raynolds expedition in 1860. When the Henderson party struck Yellowstone Lake, one member was momentarily confused by De Lacy's map and formed the conviction that they had reached the Pacific. Near the lake, they saw fresh Indian sign and took pains to avoid it. "We pronounced them Blackfeet and they meant no good to those they met," Henderson wrote.[15] From here they made their way north, passing through "a wonderful country of lava and boiling springs" and eventually seeing the Upper Falls of the Yellowstone, the Grand Canyon, and Mammoth Hot Springs. Henderson hacked off a saddlebag full of mineral specimens before following the river downstream and returning to Bozeman.

To Bridger's stories of steaming rivers, waterspouts as high as flagpoles, and trout that swam in both directions, men like Henderson now added details of their own. Their tales were, at a minimum, highly colored, but newspaper editors lapped them up and packaged them in their best high Victorian frontier prose. "The prospectors have given [the upper Yellowstone] the significant name—'Hell'!" wrote the inimitable *Montana Post*. "They declare that they have been to that 'bad place' and even seen the 'Devil's Horns'! but through the interposition of Providence (not to speak profanely), their 'souls have been delivered.'"[16]

Gold inspires constant forward motion in the men who seek it, and Bart Henderson, with a variety of companions, searched high and low. In the wild country twenty miles or so northeast of the Grand Canyon of the Yellowstone, they found the color "in every gulch and sag." This was still perilous country—in the summer of 1869 the severed heads of two miners were found impaled on their picks in a camp that had been torn apart by Indians—Blackfeet, Arapaho, Crows, no one could say. But over the next few years, the dauntless Henderson continued to travel all over the upper Yellowstone, finding more gold and trading hides with the Sheepeaters, before finally establishing a ranch just west of the present-day town of Gardiner.

One of the men who found the prospectors' mutilated bodies was a German hunter named Frederick Bottler, one of three bachelor brothers—the others being Philip and Henry—who established themselves on the west bank of the Yellowstone, across from the Emigrant mines, in the summer of 1868.[17] People called it the Bottler Ranch, but in reality it functioned less as a ranch than as a rest and supply center for itinerant miners and hunters who came to Paradise Valley in pursuit of elk, antelope, and bear.[18]

By the time the Second Cavalry arrived in July 1869, then, most of the elements were in place for a more formal and systematic exploration of the mysteries of the upper Yellowstone. Every literate man in Bozeman,

Helena, and Virginia City would have heard the stories. Access to the valley was more secure than it had ever been in the past. There was a well-trodden shortcut east over the mountains from Bozeman, the rudiments of permanent settlement, a place for provisions and logistical support, and a critical mass of reports which the leading men of the territory now resolved to put to a more educated test than the miners and hunters could offer.

"Owing to the fact that this class of men had gained a reputation for indulging in flights of fancy when recounting their adventures," wrote Langford's Quaker friend David Folsom, "these reports were received with considerable incredulity, until it was noticed that however much the accounts of the different parties differed in details there was a marked coincidence in the description of the most prominent of the features.[19] As Folsom said, it was a matter of class. Whatever the prospectors and the mountain men might say, the upper Yellowstone was "still to the world of letters a terra incognita."

The only serious obstacle that remained was the Blackfeet. They had stood in the way of the fur trappers and the gold rush, and now they were a distraction, and sometimes a direct threat, to those who were hoping to explore the upper Yellowstone. Langford had laid more plans for an expedition in 1868, but once again these remained at the level of a general discussion, "the most potent factor in the abandonment of the exercise being the threatened outbreaks of the Indians in the Gallatin valley."[20]

To those who lived on the perimeter of the Blackfeet country, Colonel Brackett's complacency about the security situation was a puzzle. Just weeks before the cavalry arrived in Montana, a group of settlers on the Musselshell River had fought off a Piegan war party and killed ten, prompting another round of incendiary editorials in the *Montana Post*. "Men rendered desperate by such provocations are not likely to stand on nice points of postmorten (sic) etiquette," the paper declared.[21] The breaches of etiquette on this occasion had included decapitating the dead Indians and displaying their severed heads on stakes as a warning to others of their tribe. "How long, how long will the blood of innocent murdered men cry out?" the *Post* went on. "How long will the butchery of good citizens by these bloody fiends invoke the curses of western people upon a government that wantonly fails to protect its citizens from a savage foe?[22]

To carry forward its plans for the upper Yellowstone, then, the world of letters would need some additional guarantees of safety from the world of arms, and that meant forging a relationship with Colonel Brackett and his officers—especially any among them who shared the taste for exploration.

18

THE FORT AT THE END
OF THE WORLD

July 1869

L ieutenant Doane established himself right away as a commanding figure, by all accounts the best liked of the fifteen officers
on the post. Most kept aloof from the ordinary soldiers, but
Doane treated them as near-equals and was fiercely protective
of their interests. He was regarded as incorruptible.[1] He had boundless
energy and unparalleled skills as a frontiersman. He was adventurous to
the point of recklessness. "He appeared not to know any feeling of fear
under any circumstances," said Thomas Leforge, who later served under
Doane as a scout.[2]

Doane spent most of his first two months at Fort Ellis on detached
duty, charting a possible wagon route between the fort and the mouth of
the Musselshell River. This was still dangerous territory—it was where the
severed heads of the ten Piegans had been impaled on stakes in May—and
the army had some notion of building another fort there to reinforce the
existing garrisons.[3] That plan was abandoned, but Doane's exploration
and description of the route enhanced his growing reputation, both as a
pathfinder and a writer of lucid, detailed field reports.

He had the ability to turn any assignment, no matter how tedious,
into a creative challenge. One complaint about Fort Ellis was that the

barracks had been foolishly constructed out of green logs. After two years of drying out and contracting, the walls were full of drafty cracks, intolerable in a Montana winter. Doane was given orders to seal the gaps. When his superiors returned from a trip to Virginia City, they found that he had torn the barracks apart and was rebuilding them from scratch. He had broken every rule in the book, and the men loved it. Higher ranks were forced to swallow his insubordination and praise his initiative.[4] It was classic Doane: Armed with his education and his arrogance, if he thought he knew better than his commanders, he would simply disregard them—and usually he got away with it.

At the same time, he was a ferocious disciplinarian when a member of his own troop stepped out of line.

> The offender would be commanded to step forward, where-upon a perfectly uninterrupted flow of vituperation would boom forth from the Lieutenant in a voice clearly heard by the assembled company, and many inhabitants of the fort. In Doane's usage, the most choice brand of army language was lifted above the level of crude profanity, and became a sting-ing, biting, flesh rending lash and to avoid it men were known to desert the army.[5]

Like any officer, he had his favorites. No one was closer or more loyal to him over the years than Private Daniel Starr, a thirty-five-year-old veteran from Oregon who was on his third enlistment. Starr seems to have had much of Doane in his manner. "He scolded and stormed at other awkward youngsters, but he was always kind to me," said William White. Doane himself described Starr as

> [a] man of powerful voice and massive form . . . [who] could turn his hand to any work. A man of infinite jest and humor, and reckless beyond all conception. He was already a celebrity in Montana on account of his uproarious hilarity, daring, and wild adventures—always a volunteer in anything which prom-

ised a new field and basis of new stories of the most ludicrous and most exaggerated character.[6]

For the most part, life at Fort Ellis was monotonous, uncomfortable, full of petty irritations. In 1867, the U.S. Army had a paper strength of almost fifty-seven thousand men.[7] But two years later, with Ulysses S. Grant in the White House, a parsimonious Congress cut the force to thirty-seven thousand; the following year it would be drawn down by a further seven thousand, leaving twenty-five regiments of infantry, ten of cavalry, and five of artillery thinly spread over a vast expanse of territory and charged with a hodgepodge of missions. Ragamuffin new frontier communities like those in Montana made multiple demands of the soldiers and never seemed content with the results. The troops had to protect ungrateful and unruly settlers, build and guard their railroads, wagon roads, and telegraph lines. They had to be as adept with axes, shovels, and spades as they were with rifles and sabers.[8]

Most soldiers on the frontier never saw combat, facing a highly mobile enemy that was elusive to the point of invisibility. Their experience consisted in the main of "scouting" and "reconnaissance," terms that put a professional-sounding sheen on the reality of trudging back and forth over an alien landscape under burning sun or in driving snow, slowed by cumbersome supply trains, bedding down among scorpions, rattlesnakes, tarantulas, and all manner of biting insects, guided by no coherent doctrine.

Peter Koch, a Danish immigrant who came to Fort Ellis to work in the post store in 1870, described the rank-and-file soldiers as a "rough sort altogether." In the words of one cavalryman, the assortment included "the Danbury hatter, watchmaker, sailor, counterhopper, shoemaker, tailors, doctors, lawyers, dentists, pumpkin rollers, preachers, [and] . . . the bowery boy."[9] Irish and German immigrants predominated. Some were highly educated; many were illiterate. There were temperance zealots and chronic drunks; spendthrifts and skinflints; poets and street fighters.

A new private under Colonel Brackett's command would have started at $16 a month, but in 1871 Congress reduced that meager figure to $13

for the first two years of a five-year enlistment, rising by dollar incre-
ments to $16 by year five. After all the deductions for the barber, the laun-
dress, and the Soldiers' Home in Washington, a soldier might return to
civilian life with savings of $70, perhaps $100 if he minded his pennies
and didn't drink.

Not that many stuck it out to the end. The "Three D's"—death, desertion, and discharge—saw to that. (One could make an argument for five
"D's," in fact, by adding drink and disease to the list.) Annual turnover in
the army was anything from 25 to 40 percent, and desertion took the
heaviest toll. For some, it was simple opportunism. Joining the army was
a way to get free transportation to the Western frontier; once you were
there, you could slip away to seek your fortune as a miner, or find work
on a railroad crew, and chances were no one would ever track you down.
(A third of Colonel Brackett's troops had done the disappearing act before the column reached Fort Ellis.) For others desertion was a response
to capricious punishments by brutal officers, primitive living conditions
in barracks infested with lice, bedbugs, and rats, or a diet dominated by
Cincinnati chicken that was often green with mold and unsalted hardtack so stale it had to be soaked and fried before it became semiedible.[10] It
was said with some reason that army cooks got rid of more soldiers than
did the Indians.

Fort Ellis did have one advantage over other posts. The Gallatin Valley
was incredibly fertile, more and more of it crisscrossed now by four-foot
irrigation ditches, and the post took advantage of the excellent soil and
water to grow its own potatoes, cabbage, beets, lettuce, and radishes. So
at least there was no scurvy. From their ranch in Paradise Valley, the Bottler brothers kept the fort supplied with beef, elk, and antelope steaks.
Cavalryman William White said that sometimes Fort Ellis's problem was
that there was too much food, not too little.

There was no scurvy, perhaps, but at the same time there was no
shortage of other reasons for a trip to the sick bay, mostly associated with
female companionship. "It was a common saying in the 1870s that [post
surgeons] had nothing to do but confine laundresses and treat the clap,"
says the historian Don Rickey. About one in twelve soldiers on the fron-

tier had a venereal disease, though the remedies available to the post surgeon—Epsom salts and iodine—were not much help.[11] Compliant Indian women were often enough encamped nearby. Bozeman, ten minutes away on horseback, had its prostitutes, although soldiers, with their miserable pay, were even lower in the pecking order than cowboys and miners, and much lower than stagecoach drivers.

For a town of barely one hundred people,[12] Bozeman was a community of some social complexity. There were Northerners and Southerners, Democrats and Republicans, a Methodist preacher, the odd secesh. There were lumbermen, barley malters, saloon keepers, pea canners, fruit growers, railroad boosters, and real estate promoters, a couple of Chinese to do the laundry and cook their mysterious food, and a black musician-cum-barber named Samuel Lewis. Bozeman's attitude toward the soldiers' off-duty shenanigans can be seen either as small-town hypocrisy or as reasonable pragmatism. People might be offended by the sight of men roaring out of the saloons and hookshops, but they brought money into the local economy.

Otherwise a soldier's entertainments were meager, dominated by card games—three-card monte, faro, blackjack, seven-up, penny-ante poker. Cavalryman White observed wryly that, "Some soldiers were evidently professional gamblers who had joined the Army for the prime purpose of making money at gambling."[13] Other than that, there was only the occasional visit from a minstrel show; Saturday-night dances where the laundresses were always in demand, but most of the soldiers ended up hoofing it with each other; and the singing of sentimental Irish ballads and old Civil War chestnuts like "Marching Through Georgia" or "The Girl I Left Behind Me" to the accompaniment of harmonica, banjo, and the odd fiddle.[14]

There was a pound of plug a month, and of course there was liquor, which was not limited by any army regulations. The post sutler, whose store functioned as a makeshift saloon, sold whiskey, brandy, wine, and fifty-cent beer in quart bottles packed in straw.[15] Payday was a riot of drunken brawls. Officers did their drinking in a separate room, away from the rank and file. "A certain West Point lieutenant" at Fort Ellis became famous for his sprees; one captain was a notorious alcoholic who ended up committing suicide.[16] But Cheyney Doane was an exception to the rule; despite his rough-and-ready manners, he rarely if ever touched a drop.

The senior ranks of the army were deeply ambivalent about their role on the Western frontier. The dirty, scattered business of taming remote Indian tribes had none of the grand moral purpose of the late hostilities between North and South. Some officers wanted to return to the ideals of heroism and service; but the Civil War had also bred habits of unspeakable brutality, and others saw a posting to the West as an opportunity to apply the wartime philosophy of extermination in a new theater.

To the dismay of the Montana settlers, the government had recently (if briefly) embarked on a new Indian policy, one that emphasized conquest by kindness. The policy shift was accompanied by a wholesale change in command, from the highest echelons of power in Washington, D.C., to the most remote outposts on the frontier. At its apex was a triumvirate of Civil War heroes: General Ulysses S. Grant, who assumed the presidency in March 1869; General William Tecumseh Sherman as General-in-Chief of the Army; and at the head of the Division of the Missouri, based in Chicago, the newly promoted Lieutenant General Philip H. Sheridan—"Little Phil."

Sheridan had three huge military departments within his jurisdiction, stretching from the Canadian border to the desert Southwest. (Two more—Texas and the Gulf—would be added later.) The northernmost of these, the Department of Dakota, was commanded by General Winfield Scott Hancock, who made his headquarters in Nathaniel Langford's hometown of St. Paul, Minnesota. Hancock's department in turn included a number of military districts. One of these was Montana, whose commander, based at Fort Shaw on the Sun River, was an idiosyncratic French aristocrat, Brevet Major General Philippe Régis de Trobriand. Even though Colonel Brackett at Fort Ellis commanded twice as many men— the largest contingent of troops in the department—he was low man on this pole. The last in this array of officers, though not actually part of the chain of command, was the long-bearded General Alfred Sully, scourge of the Sioux in Minnesota and now Montana's Superintendent of Indian Affairs.[17]

Sheridan commanded about eleven thousand troops in 1869, of whom perhaps one-quarter were in the Department of Dakota, sprinkled like pepper grindings over the vast, empty prairies of Minnesota and the Dakotas, and the plains, mountains, and badlands of Montana Territory.[18] The number of Indians they had to worry about is a matter of conjecture. The historian Robert Utley says that in the mid-nineteenth-century the buffalo-hunting tribes of what would later be the Division of the Missouri numbered about seventy-five thousand.[19] Disease and drink had done effective work in reducing them. "Turn it as we may," said an army doctor, "three things, which have done the most to make the Indian what he is today, are not the state, the church, and the army—they are *alcohol, syphilis,* and *smallpox.*"[20]

As part of the effort to bring peace to the Northern Plains, the army had acknowledged one rare defeat, abandoning the indefensible forts on the Bozeman Trail (a belated admission that Jim Bridger had been right all along). That concession to the Sioux was granted by a peace commission headed by General Sherman and riddled, in the view of many army officers, with milquetoast humanitarians. These officers deplored the tone of the commission's report to President Andrew Johnson in January 1868, which brimmed with compassion for the dispossessed Indian:

> His hunting grounds are as dear to him as is the home of childhood to the civilized man. He, too, loves the streams and mountains of his youth. To be forced to leave them breaks those tender chords of the heart which vibrate to the softer sensibilities of human nature, and dried up the fountains of benevolence and kindly feeling without which there is no civilization.[21]

But there was military pragmatism here as well as Christian charity. Abandoning the Bozeman Trail might seem like a humiliating defeat, but it was more a loss of face than a loss of assets. The transcontinental railroad through Wyoming and Utah was scheduled for completion within months, opening up a much more efficient and more easily defended supply route to and from the Montana goldfields. The old trails that Bozeman and Bridger had blazed in 1863 had become redundant. And the railroad, cleaving the plains in two, would drive the buffalo one step closer to extinction. The less the Indians could rely on that staple food supply, the more they would be attracted to life on the reservation—which was really the point of the whole exercise.

Phil Sheridan had been Sherman's field commander in Kansas in 1868, and extending the peace process south of the Platte had been much harder. Sheridan was embroiled in a particularly nasty little war against the Cheyenne, who had been in a state of fury since Colonel Chivington's barbaric attack at Sand Creek four years earlier. The fighting in Kansas ended up destroying the peace commission, which met for the last time in Chicago in October 1868. "Too many scalps have disappeared from the heads of their legitimate owners to make it safe to prolong this policy," Sherman told the man from *The New York Times*. The army's overriding obligation was to protect the settlers and emigrants, Grant said, even if that meant the extermination of every tribe.[22] In the case of the Cheyenne, Phil Sheridan was not shy about obliging.

Sheridan was a man of the cavalry, the core of his military doctrine forged in the Shenandoah Valley.[23] He was a strange little man: runty, graceless, with black hair plastered down over a head of such peculiar shape that men joked his hat would never stay on. By the end of the Civil War his weight was down to 115 pounds.[24]

But he was a winner, and men, even when they laughed at him, adored him as a leader in battle. He was "a persevering terrier dog, honest, modest, plucky, and smart enough," Sherman thought. Grant said he "has no equal as a general, living or dead." By 1864, Little Phil's dash to rejoin his troops at the battle of Cedar Creek had made him a folk hero. In celebration of that event, the poet (for want of a better word) Thomas Buchanan

Read composed "Sheridan's Ride," a piece of patriotic doggerel that was drummed into generations of schoolchildren.

> . . . *Then striking his spurs with a terrible oath,*
> *He dashed down the line 'mid a storm of huzzas,*
> *And the wave of retreat checked its course there, because*
> *The sight of the master compelled it to pause.*

Together, Grant, Sherman, and Sheridan redefined American military doctrine, casting the civilian population and infrastructure as a strategic target. Sheridan was the most enthusiastic practitioner of this philosophy of total war. "Give the enemy no rest," Grant told him. "If the war is to last another year, we want the Shenandoah Valley to remain a barren waste."[25] So Sheridan's troops put barns, corncribs, smokehouses, mills, factories, and railroads to the torch. People called it "the Burning." Soldiers were encouraged to loot cattle, sheep, hogs, and horses. Sheridan called it foraging. If the victims complained, let them be told they had brought it on themselves by giving aid and comfort to the enemy.

Sheridan defined total war as a humanitarian act, an apparent oxymoron. In one of his reports from the field, he put the matter succinctly:

> I do not believe war to be simply that lines should engage each other in battle, and therefore do not regret the system of living on the enemy's country. These men or women did not care how many were killed, or maimed, so long as war did not come to their doors, but as soon as it did come in the shape of loss of property, they earnestly prayed for its termination. As war is a punishment, if we can, by reducing its advocates to poverty, end it quicker, we are on the side of humanity.[26]

Add racial animus to this mix, add the loss of life to the loss of property, and you have the doctrine that Sheridan took to the Plains Indians. Like many officers, he had a certain fascination with Native Americans as one

more of the bizarre phenomena a man encountered in the West—
"marvels, freaks, and exotics, all the more interesting because they were
sometimes dangerous," in the words of the great historian of exploration,
William H. Goetzmann.[27] But that did nothing to restrain his philosophy of war. Extermination as compassion: The maxim might have been
poker-burned on the kitchen wall of every settler in Montana.

Sherman ordered Sheridan to strike the Cheyenne in deep winter,
promising that he would neither micromanage nor second-guess him.

> Go ahead in your own way and I will back you with my whole
> authority. If it results in the utter annihilation of these Indians,
> it is but the result of what they have been warned again and
> again. . . . I will say nothing and do nothing to restrain our
> troops from doing what they deem proper on the spot, and will
> allow no mere vague general charges of cruelty and inhuman-
> ity to tie their hands.[28]

It isn't entirely clear where Sherman or Sheridan got their notion of
winter war. Perhaps they were thinking of Patrick Connor's rampage
against the Shoshone on the Bear River in January 1863, or the campaign
that Kit Carson and General James Carleton conducted against the Na-
vajo exactly a year later.[29] It was still a controversial idea, and Jim Bridger
came out of retirement in Missouri to warn Sheridan that marching
troops and horses into battle in the depths of a plains winter was madness. But Sheridan ignored the old man's advice, in the belief that the
same numbing cold and heavy snow that would impede his troopers were
also what put the Indians at a disadvantage, since they were immobilized
in their camps with their women and children. The soldiers were better
fed and better clothed, and their grain-fed horses were more dependable
at this time of year than the Indians' emaciated, grass-fed ponies.[30]

To punish the Cheyenne, Sheridan chose his favorite officer, Lieutenant Colonel George Armstrong Custer. At dawn on November 27, 1868,
Custer's cavalry struck a Cheyenne village on the Washita River in twelve
inches of wet snow, with the band blasting out as much of their com-

mander's signature "GarryOwen" as they could get through before their lips froze to their bugles. The chief of the village was Black Kettle, an aging, weary peace chief who had been through all this once before at Sand Creek, where he had naïvely imagined that displaying an American flag would be enough to establish his bona fides. Chivington had ignored the Stars and Stripes, but Black Kettle somehow got away. On the Washita, he was not so lucky. He got a bullet in the back. So did his wife, riding away desperately on the same horse. A hundred and three Cheyenne in all died on the Washita; the number of these who were women and children was disputed. Custer ordered his men to burn everything in the camp and shoot all the horses, then left the field as the band played "Ain't I Glad to Get Out of the Wilderness."[31]

Sheridan had no patience for the columns of ink spilled by humanitarians in the East. Be they newspaper editors or be they bishops, he regarded his critics as

> . . . the aiders and abetters of savages who murdered, without mercy, men, women and children; in all cases ravishing the women sometimes as often as forty and fifty times in succession, and while insensible from brutality and exhaustion forced sticks up their persons, and in one instance, the fortieth or fiftieth savage drew his saber and used it on the person of the woman in the same manner.[32]

Beyond the sexually charged histrionics, however, Sheridan knew his doctrine had been vindicated. Total war worked, and so did winter campaigns. Flags of truce were no obstacle; collateral damage—all those dead women and children on the Washita—was inevitable. Let the humanitarians squawk.

Grant had always backed Sheridan to the hilt. But as the eighteenth president, he became the leader of all Americans, not just the ones in uniform. With the Sioux and the Cheyenne now apparently quiet and the complaints of the peace faction rumbling away in the background, he decided it was time to change course. On the cold, drizzly morning of March 4, 1869, in his brief inaugural address, Grant laid out the bare bones of his new Peace Policy. In language that departed radically from his exterminationist orders less than a year earlier, he announced, "The proper treatment of the original occupants of this land—the Indians—is one deserving of careful study. I will favor any course toward them which tends to their civilization and ultimate citizenship."[33]

The central premise remained the same, however, undergirded by the new social science of Lewis Henry Morgan and Edward Burnett Tylor: Raise the Indians out of savagery, coax them through the transitional stage of barbarism, and finally absorb them into the mainstream of civilization. The instrument of uplift, as before, was the reservation, located well away from white settlements and transit routes, where the Indians would be schooled in peaceful pursuits.

As Sheridan knew perfectly well, the reservation idea was riddled with contradictions. The system was predicated on the separation of "good" from "bad" Indians. Those who remained outside were by definition bad, and the jurisdiction of the Indian supervisors and agents stopped at the reservation edge. Beyond that the military would remain the sole arbiter of who was who. But the Indians by and large didn't want to go near the reservations, in large part because the agents so often failed to deliver the food and annuities that had been promised. Young braves had no respect for boundary lines, and the chiefs had little or no control over them. Individuals and small groups found in the no-go areas might be hunting, gathering berries, visiting friends, just looking around the country, minding their own business. The rules of tribal society, based on kinship and group identity, meant that the Indians tended to move from one place to another in large bands of mixed age, gender, and attitude. So the distinction between "good" and "bad" Indians was meaningless. That was the lesson of all those dead women and children on the Washita. Sheridan's view was that if the Indians refused to move to the reservations voluntarily, the only way to get them there was by brute force—which was what the reservation system had ostensibly been designed to avoid.

L ike most other tribes, the Blackfeet had absolutely no interest in being penned up in an ever-shrinking corner of their ancestral hunting grounds. The conflict with them had simmered for years; it was the reason Montana had two new forts. But now, within weeks of Cheyney Doane's arrival in Montana, more serious hostilities erupted, presenting Phil Sheridan with his first crisis on the Northern Plains.

But who was to deal with the problem? His officers in the Department of Dakota were a snakepit of clashing personalities. He detested Hancock, his departmental commander, for a brutal but botched campaign against the Cheyenne in 1867.[34] He also loathed Sully, Montana's aristocratic Superintendent of Indian Affairs and his temperamental opposite in every way (except for a shared fondness for whiskey). The only senior officer Sheridan seemed to respect was de Trobriand at Fort Shaw, but Grant disliked the man, and there were whispers that the Frenchman's assignment to this coldest and most remote of the frontier forts was punishment for the criticisms he had voiced of Grant's management of the Army of the Potomac.[35] As for Albert Gallatin Brackett at Fort Ellis, well, no one seemed to think much about him one way or another. He was competent, well enough liked, and he certainly knew a lot about birds. But the Blackfeet problem called for someone with a stiffer backbone.

After just five months in the job, Brackett was eased out. Little Phil's choice to replace him was Brevet Colonel Eugene Mortimer Baker,[36] a man of very different character who had served under Sheridan in the Shenandoah Campaign. Sheridan liked him, and so did Cheyney Doane. Under Brackett, Doane had cultivated the art of doing end runs around his superiors. But realizing his ambitions as soldier and explorer would require a commanding officer who could act as both patron and protector, and in Colonel Baker he found exactly what he needed.

19

A DEATH IN THE FAMILY

July–August 1869

In his first few weeks at Fort Ellis, Colonel Brackett had devoted a good deal of his energy to a variety of noncombat-related duties. Surveyors had set out in July 1869 to map the future Northern Pacific Railroad, which would follow the course of the Yellowstone, traverse the Bozeman Pass, and eventually reach Puget Sound; once the engineers reached Fort Ellis in late August they would need army protection for their foray into Sioux and Blackfeet territory. At the same time, plans for an expedition to map once and for all the mysteries of the upper Yellowstone were back on the agenda of the leading men of Helena; these explorers too would require a military escort, as well as a reliable base for supplies and logistics. On June 24, Hancock the Superb, commander of the Department of Dakota, paid his first visit to Helena and agreed in principle to provide what they needed as soon as the Second Cavalry brought the garrison at Fort Ellis up to strength.[1]

The expedition was to include "citizens from Helena, Virginia City, and Bozeman, accompanied by some of the officers stationed at Fort Ellis, with an escort of soldiers." The prospective explorers had even fixed a date. They "would leave Bozeman about the fifth of September for the Yellowstone country, with the intention of making a thorough examination of all the wonders with which that region was said to abound."[2]

There is no full list of the participants, but Langford's Quaker friend David Folsom mentioned Horatio Nelson Maguire, the future editor of the *Pick and Plow* newspaper in Bozeman, as well as a certain Mr. Clark, who was "connected with some mining operations" (almost certainly a reference to William Andrews Clark, "a tight, white, starched little man" who later became one of the country's greatest mining barons).[3]

The expedition now had a kind of operational hub in the office of the U.S. Surveyor General for Montana. The engineer-explorer Walter De Lacy, who had drawn the best available maps of the upper Yellowstone, was already working there. In July the new surveyor general himself arrived after a perilous ten-week journey up the Missouri that included the loss of all his possessions when his boat ran aground on a sandbank north of Fort Benton and was attacked by Indians—probably Blackfeet or Gros Ventres—as the crew struggled to refloat it.

Henry Dana Washburn had impeccable political and military connections. He was six feet tall, with blue eyes, a light complexion, and light brown hair that he wore swept back from a high forehead. Although slimly built and in fragile health, he is said to have been a commanding presence. Cornelius Hedges called him "a man with the largest manly sympathies; a man with much less of the divine image effaced than usual."[4] Born in Vermont in 1832, Washburn had accomplished more by the age of thirty-seven than most men do in a lifetime. After a stint as a schoolteacher, he studied at Oberlin, where he was a classmate of Warren Gillette, who now operated the dangerous toll road next to Malcolm Clarke's ranch.[5] After that, Washburn took a law degree in New York and was commissioned a lieutenant colonel in the Indiana Volunteer Infantry.

During the Civil War, he fought at the siege of Vicksburg, but came away from the battle with a serious case of consumption. He continued to serve, however, joining Phil Sheridan for the brutal Shenandoah Campaign, and eventually being breveted major general. When the war ended, Washburn was elected to two successive terms as Republican congressman for Indiana. But health problems continued to plague him, and in April 1869 Grant appointed him surveyor general of Montana—a move that may have had as much to do with the restorative air of the Rockies as with his surveying experience.

Of all the would-be explorers, the only one not on the spot was Nathaniel Langford, who by this time had become a very big fish indeed in the pond of territorial politics. He had spent the previous winter in Washington, D.C., burnishing his reputation and contacts, and in January 1869, just before leaving office, President Andrew Johnson had named him governor of Montana.[6]

This was not as straightforward as it sounds, however, given the partisan labyrinth of territorial politics.[7] In its four years as a territory, Montana had already had three governors, two Republicans and one Democrat—Thomas Meagher. Further complicating this sectarian stew, anyone trying to govern Montana had to contend with its nonvoting territorial delegate to the 40th Congress. Langford's good friend Wilbur Fisk Sanders, the former vigilante prosecutor known to his enemies as "the Mephistopheles of Montana politics," had lost the election to a militant Democrat, James Michael Cavanaugh. "Our Jim" was a silver-tongued Irish orator and a rabid member of the "nits make lice" school of Western thought. In fact, it was he, not Phil Sheridan, as commonly believed, who probably gave birth to the most famous of all frontier proverbs—"the only good Indian is a dead Indian." This, at any rate, is what he said during one typical 1868 rant against the Blackfeet:

> I have never in my life seen a good Indian (and I have seen thousands) except when I have seen a dead Indian . . . I believe in the policy that exterminates the Indians, drives them outside the boundaries of civilization, because you cannot civilize them.[8]

Sadly for Langford, President Johnson's timing was terrible. Nothing was less likely to advance a man's political ambitions than the patronage of a lame-duck president who had just survived a brutal impeachment battle over his mishandling of Reconstruction. Congress refused to ratify the appointment, and the post of governor remained vacant until Grant filled it permanently in April.[9]

The restless and ambitious Langford, whose term as collector of inland revenues had just ended and whose political ambitions were now stymied, needed a fresh challenge. He turned his eyes, as so many did in those days, to the railroad. The prospect of a northern route to the Pacific had excited him from the moment he arrived in Minnesota in 1855 and began buying up railroad stocks and acquiring land grants along the track of the Union Pacific. Like his wagon road enterprise with Bridger and Bozeman, railroads offered both the pursuit of profit and the opportunity to realize grand strategies of development, civilization, and a further reduction of the Indian threat.

Early in 1867, with the Bozeman Trail no longer a going concern, Langford and Sam Hauser's First National Bank of Helena had made its first overtures to the investor who promised to make the Northern Pacific a reality: the great banking house of Jay Cooke and Co. of Philadelphia.[10] Cooke was a national icon by this time, a devout Christian, an opponent of slavery, rich as Croesus, "the financier of the Civil War." He viewed the building of the Northern Pacific as a comparable challenge, which he proposed to take on as "God's chosen instrument."[11] For someone with Cooke's instincts, it was hard not to be bewitched by the potential rewards of the Pacific Northwest, as described to him in a letter from his associate Samuel Wilkeson: "Such timber—such soil—such orchards— such fish—such climate—such coal—such harbors—such rivers! . . . Jay—we have the biggest thing on earth. Our enterprise is an inexhaustible gold mine."[12]

In the early summer of 1869, just weeks after the completion of the Union Pacific, two groups of Northern Pacific officials set out to inspect the proposed route, one starting from each end. The first, which departed from the railroad's eastern terminus at St. Paul, seems to have been as much political junket as engineering survey. The guest of honor was

William R. Marshall—as in Marshall and Co., where Langford had taken his first step up the economic and political ladder at the age of twenty-three. The bald-headed former banker was now the Republican governor of Minnesota, and Langford attached himself to his party, together with an assortment of railroad executives, investors, ministers of religion, teamsters, servants, and Indian guides. Pimps, gamblers, and whores also tagged along. Together they tramped through the wastes of Minnesota behind the peppermint-scented boots of Pierre Bottineau, who had guided Langford and the Fisk wagon train to Montana in 1862. As a survey, it was a farce. Men fell neck-deep into the black muck. Cheapskate contractors used wood to fill the bogs and sinkholes. Pilings had to be sunk fifty or sixty feet into the squelching ground.[13] Langford and Marshall stayed together until they hit the Missouri at Fort Stevenson, where the governor turned for home, and Langford hopped on a riverboat for Fort Benton. By the second week of August he was back in Helena, having been invited by Folsom to join the Yellowstone expedition that was leaving on September 5.[14]

The second surveying party, led by Cooke's chief engineer, William Milnor Roberts, set out eastward from Walla Walla in Washington Territory. By the middle of August they, too, had reached Helena. At a reception in their honor, the new territorial governor—the Republican James M. Ashley, who had led the impeachment proceedings against Andrew Johnson—told the audience to thunderous applause: "One thing is unquestioned—the Northern Pacific must be built!"[15] But when?

From Helena, the Roberts party zigzagged to Fort Benton, then to Fort Shaw, then back to Helena, and finally to Fort Ellis at the end of August. At Fort Shaw, they made what must have seemed like a straightforward request for a contingent of soldiers to escort them through the Blackfeet country, up the Dearborn River to the Cadotte Pass, close to where Meriwether Lewis had crossed the Continental Divide on his journey to the Marias. But de Trobriand shuffled his feet, muttered about fresh Indian troubles, and said he could only spare six infantrymen. At Fort Ellis they got much the same response from Colonel Brackett: seven cavalrymen, but only as far as the mouth of Paradise Valley. Everyone seemed on edge—and with good reason.

The trouble erupted just a couple of weeks after Colonel Brackett's complacent report that the territory was at peace. But like any outburst of violence, its roots went deeper.

Sherman's peace commission and Grant's peace policy left all sorts of loose ends, notably that there was still no treaty of any kind with the Blackfeet. In September 1868, the government gave it one last try. The veteran trader Alexander Culbertson and the brandy-loving Indian agent, Major Vaughan, were sent out to round up as many willing Blackfeet chiefs as they could. At least fifty, perhaps as many as one hundred, showed up for the talks in Fort Benton. Langford says that two of his close friends, Malcolm Clarke and the former vigilante enforcer X. Beidler, went along as witnesses.[16] The terms were much the same as they had been three years earlier. This time several of the more militant chiefs scrawled their Xs on the paper, including Calf Shirt, the reputedly indestructible chief of the Bloods, and Clarke's relative, Mountain Chief, the most powerful of the Piegan leaders. But the fate of these negotiations were the same as before; the treaty was never ratified by a Congress that had weightier things on its mind, like the impeachment of the president.

The settlers were not in the mood for any further nonsense. When Mountain Chief petitioned the government to remove certain troublesome white men from the area, a group of furious whites insulted and abused him in the streets of Fort Benton.[17] In the continued absence of a treaty, the Blackfeet felt themselves unconstrained by any formal obligations, and the young men had lost none of their taste for thievery. The more settlers, the more horses, the greater the temptation. The safety of the Canadian line was barely a day's ride away, and any stolen horse could be easily traded on the other side for weapons, ammunition, and white man's water.

Clarke, according to his daughter Nellie, spent much of that winter and the following spring in Mountain Chief's camp.[18] His younger son, Nathan, went with him. Clarke had two things on his mind, one personal and one political, and he and the Piegan leader "had many confidential chats." He found Mountain Chief in an ugly frame of mind. "I despise the whites," he said, in Helen's rendering. "They have encroached on our territory; they are killing our buffalo, which will soon pass away; they have treated my nation like dogs; and hereafter I shall no longer be responsible for the depredations which may be committed by my young men."

With the tempestuous Owl Child, things went more smoothly. The feud over the stolen horses and the spyglass two years earlier seemed forgotten. "During the winter, Ne-tus-cho (sic) slept in the same lodge as Clarke, ate from the same dish, and smoked the same pipe," Langford reports. "Their intimacy was apparently as friendly as ever." When he left in the spring, Clarke presented his young relative with a horse, and Owl Child promised in return to recover some horses that had been stolen from Clarke by Blood raiders. Give my regards to Horace and Nellie, Owl Child said in farewell.

Fort Benton had become a lethal place for visiting Indians, its streets pickled in whiskey and violence, and in May the Blackfeet agency was moved to the Teton River, seventy-five miles away. But in mid-July a small wagon train was ambushed near Fort Benton, and two herders were killed. Two of the attackers were hanged. The assumption was that they were Blackfeet, but it turned out that they were River Crows. Killing white men was an extreme rarity for that tribe, but the attack was laid to alcohol. No matter; one dead Indian was as good as another. Several days later, Mountain Chief sent his elderly brother, Rock Old Man, and a fourteen-year-old Blood boy to Fort Benton on some unspecified business. A gang of whiskey traders set upon them in the street and gunned them down.

The news of the killings reached Mountain Chief's camp when a number of white traders were in residence, Langford says. The chief told them they could leave unmolested, but that he couldn't speak for his young men, who were "angry and hungry for revenge."[19]

General Sully, Montana's Superintendent of Indian Affairs, wrote to Washington to express his outrage and alarm, denouncing "the cowardly

murder of an old man and a boy."[20] He could identify and arrest the per-
petrators in a heartbeat, he said, but he knew that no court in the territory would ever convict them. The settlers' devotion to the rule of law was
highly selective. "It is a wonder to me that open war with the Indians has
not broken out already," Sully wrote. Even with the new reinforcements
at Fort Ellis, he fretted that there were not enough troops to control the
volatile situation.

On August 7, there was a total eclipse of the sun—the worst of auguries to the tribe, bringing back memories of the sign that had preceded
the scourge of the white scabs in 1837.[21]

August 17 was a beautiful midsummer day.[22] "The birds sang—the sun
shone, and the stream gurgled on," Nellie Clarke remembered. It was a
normal workaday Tuesday at the Clarke ranch on the Little Prickly Pear.
Malcolm was out looking for some stock who had wandered away from
the unfenced property, browsing for bunchgrass. Nathan, the younger of
the two boys, had ridden off in search of yet another batch of stolen horses.
Nellie busied herself with household tasks.

At about seven o'clock, Malcolm Clarke returned; his seventeen-year-
old ranchhand, a Piegan boy named Jackson, had found the errant cows.
A quiet domestic evening followed. After dinner, Clarke challenged his
daughter to a game of backgammon, something they both enjoyed. The
two younger girls curled up on the floor with Horace, engrossed in a picture book. The elderly Black Bear, mother of Cutting-Off-Head-Woman,
dozed in a chair.

In the middle of the third round of backgammon, they heard the
sound of dogs barking in the yard. "It must be some belated Indians,"
Clarke said, without apparent concern. Even though it was past nine, this
was not an uncommon occurrence. Sometimes the visitors even helped
themselves to one or two of Clarke's guns; they liked to go outside to
shoot them off for entertainment.

Nellie, Horace, and the younger girls went to investigate. The visitors
turned out to be Owl Child and "three stalwart Blackfeet." They exchanged
warm greetings. Helen teased Owl Child: "Oh-oh, our horses are again
stolen!" The young Piegan smiled and shook her hand. He and Horace

exchanged a kiss of peace on the lips, further evidence that their old quarrel was in the past. Nellie offered to fix the visitors something to eat.

The other three men were introduced as Eagle's Rib, Bear Chief, and Black Bear (no relation to Clarke's mother-in-law; the name is coincidental). They explained that a fifth man was waiting in the yard: Black Weasel, son of Mountain Chief, who was too bashful to enter the house. Eventually he was coaxed inside. Clarke welcomed him warmly, saying that he was "one of the finest Indians I have ever known." For some reason he was nicknamed Shanghai—on account of his great height, Nellie said, though the logic for this is obscure. The family expressed its condolences for the death of Black Weasel's uncle at Fort Benton.

After they had eaten, Clarke filled his meerschaum and passed it around. Perhaps whiskey was also poured. After a good spell of time had passed in these ritual preliminaries, they arrived at the point: to what did the family owe this gratifying surprise? Owl Child said that they had come, as promised in the spring, to return the horses stolen by the Bloods. Nellie frowned; somehow this rang false to her. The mood of the gathering had turned distinctly peculiar. Owl Child sat with a blanket over his lap, as if concealing something. Eagle's Rib wandered about the room fingering things; Nellie found his behavior unnerving and offensive. Bear Chief began creeping around in a way that reminded her of "Bulwer's description of the crookbacked Richard III." Inexplicably, Black Weasel put his head in his hands and appeared to be weeping.

By now it was close to midnight, and Owl Child suggested that Horace accompany Bear Chief down to the canyon where his father's stolen horses were waiting to be returned to the corral. Horace looked around for his gun, but Nellie asked him why he thought he needed it, since he was among friends—oddly though they might be behaving. So the two young men left together, chatting, apparently in high good humor. Horace, who seemed not to share his sister's unease, rode ahead. But as they entered the canyon he heard the click of a trigger behind him and spun around in his saddle. Bear Chief tried to pass it off as a joke; mock gunplay was a well-known test of nerve among young Piegans, a proof of manhood. But then, bizarrely, the Indian began singing a death song in the Crow language. "A Blackfoot would never sing to one of his own blood in an enemy's tongue if he did not bear him mortal hatred," Nellie said. Before Horace could react, the Piegan shot him. The bullet struck Horace on the right side of his nose and exited below the left ear. He fell from his horse, became entangled in his lariat, and was dragged for several yards as Bear Chief fired again. This time the shot went wide. Three or four more braves emerged from the dense willows by the creek and stripped young Clarke of his possessions, leaving him for dead. Why they refrained from scalping him is something of a mystery, but Nellie speculated later that it was from some sense of respect for a man who shared their Piegan blood.

Back at the house, Nellie heard the gunfire from the canyon. Her younger sister, Isabel, tried to run outside, but Owl Child grabbed the girl and threatened to kill her if she didn't get back inside. In the confusion, Nellie heard Horace groaning in the yard, "Father, I am shot!" and then more gunfire from the rear of the house. Pandemonium. As many as two dozen Indians were milling around outside now, firing off their rifles and yelling. The women were screaming. The horses had stampeded. All this "rendered the night hideous beyond all parallel," wrote Langford with his usual sense of melodrama. "Nellie said it fairly made the blood curdle in her veins. Stronger hearts have quailed under less appalling terrors."

What awaited her at the back of the house was worse. Her father lay dead on the ground. Eagle's Rib had shot him in the chest, and Owl Child had added the coup de grace—a slashing blow to the forehead with a tomahawk.[23]

In a panic, Nellie and old Black Bear dragged Horace back inside and laid him on the table. He was bleeding badly from the face, vomiting up his own blood. All his sister could think to do to staunch the flow was to press a plug of tobacco into the open wound, but it seemed to have some beneficial effect. Black Weasel, still tearful, took little Isabel aside and said, "I did not think [Ne-tus-che-o] would do it."

The women and girls retreated to Nellie's room, pulling Horace along with them. One grabbed a knife, one a hatchet. As they hurried inside, another bullet shattered a window pane. Cutting-Off-Head-Woman barricaded the door behind them. After a while all was quiet, and Nellie decided to risk lighting a candle. But then she heard the attackers return and blew it out again. They ransacked the house, smashing mirrors, chairs, and tables, stealing food, ripping open sacks of flour. There was a debate. One voice argued in favor of killing the whole family; another said kill Cutting-Off-Head-Woman and take the daughters captive. "Let us finish the work we came to do," said Owl Child, rattling the door of Nellie's room in its frame. But Horace had recovered sufficiently now to position himself behind the door with the hatchet, and the barricade held firm. At last they heard Black Weasel say, "We have shed enough blood for one night," and after that there was silence.

At 5 A.M., first light, Nellie ran to the house of the nearest neighbor, three-quarters of a mile away. She rousted the man out of bed and told him to check on Horace's condition and then ride to Helena, find a doctor, and bring help.

"The citizens of Helena had often anticipated an Indian irruption from this direction," Nathaniel Langford wrote in his subsequent account of the event,

> and at noonday on the 18th of August 1869, were thrown into consternation by the intelligence that on the previous night, Malcolm Clark [sic], who lived twenty four miles away among the foot hills on the Benton road, had been murdered at his ranche by Blackfeet, one of his sons mortally wounded, and his daughters, three in number, carried away into captivity. To this was added the unwelcome tidings that the foot hills were swarming with the red devils, and the long expected invasion was at hand. I immediately consulted with some friends, as to the expediency of attempting a rescue of the children and was so fortunate as to obtain the cooperation of Mr. Andrew J. Simmons and Mr. J. X. Beidler.[24]

Simmons and Beidler, he says elsewhere, were "two men as resolute as can be found here, and armed with 2 Henry and 1 Spencer rifles, and our revolvers, we started."[25]

Like so many of Langford's narratives, this one raises some eyebrows. A full-scale Blackfeet invasion in the air, the hills aswarm with "red devils," and three men with rifles—even individuals as redoubtable as Langford and the celebrated vigilante X. Beidler—are going to ride into their midst to rescue three kidnapped children?

By the time Langford and his companions reached the Clarke ranch, the doctor had already arrived. He had good news about Horace. Remarkably, the bullet from Bear Chief's gun had passed only through soft tissue. The young man's injury was more ugly than life-threatening; there might be some scarring, but no lasting damage.

Leaving Beidler in charge of matters at the ranch, Langford rode down to the toll house that Warren Gillette operated at the mouth of the canyon. He found the family that lived there, the Wilkinsons, frightened out of their wits and with not a weapon in the house, and agreed to stay the night for their protection.

Next day, at three in the afternoon, the mourners gathered around the gravesite. All the men clutched their rifles, glancing nervously at the surrounding hills for signs of trouble. Nellie Clarke described the mood in just a few words: "Everything tender, sad, and mystic." And in the absence of a clergyman, Langford himself performed the funeral service.

20

THE WORLD OF LETTERS
AND THE WORLD OF ARMS

September–October 1869

W hen Langford returned home on August 20, taking the surviving members of the Clarke family back to Helena in an ambulance, the last thing on his mind was the Yellowstone expedition, which was due to set off in two weeks.

"[A] score of the brightest luminaries in the firmament of Montana" were supposed to take part, but as the departure date approached one after another of them dropped out, citing pressing business engagements. More likely is that they got cold feet when word reached Helena that in view of the Blackfeet emergency, Fort Ellis could no longer provide the escort of cavalrymen that General Hancock had promised.

In the end, the party dwindled to three.[1] Its titular leader was the blustery, impetuous, womanizing Mainer, Charles W. Cook—the "Captain." The second member was Langford's old friend David Folsom, who'd known Cook from childhood and since arriving in Montana had blossomed from retiring Quaker schoolteacher into grizzly bear hunter, dead shot, and expert woodsman. The third was a middle-aged Dane, William Peterson, who worked for Folsom and Cook at the Boulder Ditch Company in Diamond City, east of Helena, an enterprise that supplied water for the hydraulic gold-mining operations in Confederate Gulch.

Peterson had the kind of exotic résumé that a lot of people had in Montana in those days. He had signed on as a cabin boy on the Danish island of Bornholm in 1834, and his subsequent maritime adventures were the stuff of fiction. Peterson traveled from Iceland to Havana to Odessa to Santos, Brazil (where most of the crew died of yellow fever), to Calcutta to Dublin to Naples to Galveston to New York to Southampton (after saving six men from drowning in a shipwreck). In 1860 he wound up in New York again, got a job on a ship that sailed around Cape Horn to San Francisco and Oregon, joined the gold rush to the Idaho mines, and finally wound up in Diamond City, by which time he had developed all sorts of practical skills that made him invaluable as a factotum for the Yellowstone trip. "'Wonder what's at the head of the Yellowstone?" Peterson wrote in his own laconic account of the expedition. "But Indian [sic] were bad."[2]

As one after another of the participants dropped out in the wake of the Malcolm Clarke crisis, Cook declared, "If I could get one man to go with me, I'd go anyway." Peterson said, "Well, Charley, I guess I can go as far as you can." That left Folsom. "Well, I guess I can go as far as both of ye's," he said, and so off they went. Their destination: "the Falls, Coulter's [sic] Hell and Lake, and the Mysterious Mounds."[3]

Diamond City thought they had taken leave of their senses. As they rode out of town on September 6, neighbors offered half-humorous, half-nervous fare-thee-wells. *If you get into a scrap, remember I warned you . . . It's the next thing to suicide . . . Good-bye, boys, look out for your hair . . .*

They traveled by way of the Three Forks of the Missouri, the heart of the old beaver country, where so many of the original trappers had lost their hair to the Blackfeet. Cook brought a pair of French field glasses; Folsom a pocket compass and thermometer; Peterson two stout balls of twine. Their other supplies included three repeating rifles, three Colt revolvers, and three sheath knives; one double-barreled shotgun; ammunition; a pick, shovel, and pan in the event of finding gold; fishing tackle; five pairs of blankets; two buffalo robes; an axe; a camp kettle; a coffeepot; two frying pans, three tin cups, and four tin plates; three knives, forks, and spoons; and the map drawn and revised by Walter De Lacy, who was now working in the territorial surveyor's office. Reaching Bozeman, they stocked up on 175 pounds of flour, 25 pounds of bacon, a ham, 30 pounds of sugar, 15 of ground coffee, 10 of salt, 10 of dried fruit, 50 of potatoes, a dozen boxes of yeast powder.[4] These were practical men.

They tried to recruit more adventurers in Bozeman but found no takers. The expedition "has assumed proportions of utter insignificance," Folsom wrote bitterly, "and of no importance to anyone in the world except the three actors themselves." It seemed to puzzle him that anyone should be concerned for their own safety, since "whoever located [Fort Ellis] displayed strategic talent of a high order, for no Indian would have the temerity to attack it so near the settlements."

From the fort, they headed over the low saddle of Chestnut Mountain and down Trail Creek, taking the well-established route to the Emigrant mines in Paradise Valley. Thirty-nine miles from Bozeman they arrived at the Bottlers' ranch. Although the brothers had been there for about a year, the buildings were still crude. But the antelope and elk hides piled up outside were testament to their skill with a rifle.

From there the party picked up an Indian trail that followed the west bank of the Yellowstone. They remarked on the curious natural features of the landscape, like the parallel red rock walls on "Cinnabar Mountain," which later became known as the Devil's Slide, and the deep, swirling waters of present-day Yankee Jim Canyon.[5] The trip was uneventful until they reached the mouth of Tom Miner Creek, where they encountered two old women crushing and drying chokecherries outside a primitive wickiup. Sign language established that they were Sheepeaters. The women made hand gestures; ten fingers at a time, three times. The meaning of this only became clear two days later, when they ran across a lone Indian herding horses. He indicated an encampment of thirty tipis, which put the three explorers immediately on their guard. "We halted on the spot and held a council of war," Folsom wrote. "We overhauled our packs, tightened the cinches of our saddles, put new caps upon our revolvers, filled our bullet pouches with cartridges for our rifles, and putting on a bold front started forward." But the Indians gave them no trouble, only annoyance when one of them followed the party for several miles begging for matches and ammunition. The "captain" asked if there were any women in the tipis; perhaps he meant it as a joke, perhaps not.

The three men continued upriver until they reached the confluence with the fast, rocky Gardner River. Here the travois marks diverged, one path following the Yellowstone and the other the Gardner. They kept to the big river and crossed a low ridge, the Black Canyon of the Yellowstone off to their left. They gasped at the monumental basalt columns and horizontal bands of multicolored rock at the head of the canyon, then came upon Tower Fall and Tower Creek, where they saw and smelled their first hot springs. "All the crevices were lined with beautiful crystals of sulphur, as delicate as frost-work," Folsom wrote. They loaded up with mineral specimens, too many to carry. Cook, always headstrong, took one chance too many while investigating the steam vents, and narrowly escaped falling into a chasm where Folsom's thermometer registered the temperature as 194 degrees—only five or six degrees below boiling point at this altitude.

They coaxed their horses across the river at the Bannock Ford. Fortunately it was late in the season now, September 16, and the water was shallow. On the east side, rather than heading directly upriver to the falls of the Yellowstone, they struck out for some reason through what the trapper Osborne Russell had called the "wild romantic splendor" of the Lamar Valley, and then cut across the beautiful Mirror Plateau. The two mountains across the river to the west would be known in later years as Folsom Peak and Cook Peak.

Until now it had all seemed something of a lark, but on the Mirror Plateau they seemed suddenly to feel their isolation and vulnerability. The exotic became frightening. They lay awake in the pitch darkness listening to the bugling of elks, the roaring of mountain lions, the howling of wolf packs. A storm dumped six inches of snow on them. But then the weather cleared, and the rocky peaks of the Absarokas "glistened like burnished silver in the sunlight," restoring their spirits.

Trending southwest toward the river again, they saw dense clouds of steam rising over the downed jackstraw pines and stumbled upon a group of foul-smelling mud springs of various colors. One was full of a slimy yellow-green compound with the consistency of hasty pudding. This they christened the Chemical Works.[6]

Eighteen miles farther on, one of the saddle horses pulled up abruptly on the edge of a sheer drop. They had reached the Grand Canyon. "I sat there in amazement, while my companions came up," Cook wrote, "and after that, it seemed to me it was five minutes before anyone spoke." Like every early explorer, and like most present-day visitors for that matter, he groped for words: "Language is inadequate to convey a just conception of the awful grandeur and sublimity of this masterpiece of nature's handiwork." Using Peterson's balls of twine, they lowered weights to estimate the drop. For the Upper Falls, their calculations were extraordinarily accurate: they measured 115 feet; in fact it is 109. The Lower Falls, where the string disappeared into billowing plumes of mist, were tougher to estimate. They came up with 360 feet instead of the actual 308.

And so they continued, crossing the river from east to west and back again, wondering at the hollow, rumbling ground around the Mud Volcano and the Dragon's Mouth Spring, where the explosions could be heard half a mile away, until they reached Yellowstone Lake—"one of the most beautiful places we had found fashioned by the practised hand of nature, that man had not desecrated." Presciently, Folsom wrote that, "We felt glad to have looked upon it before its primeval solitude should be broken by the crowds of pleasure seekers which at no distant day will throng its shores." At the farthest point of their outward journey, Folsom chiseled their names and the date on a piece of rock and set it into a tree trunk by the lakeside. This souvenir of their passage has never been found.

Cook, Folsom, and Peterson never did see Old Faithful or the "Mysterious Mounds," but the homeward leg of their trip brought them to the northern tip of Shoshone Lake, across the divide separating the Snake and the Madison rivers, into the Lower Geyser Basin just in time to see an eruption of the Great Fountain Geyser, the Firehole River, the rainbow-hued Excelsior Geyser, and out again at last to civilization via the Madison. They arrived home on October 11, after a thirty-six-day journey, more than half of it within the boundaries of the future national park.

David Folsom had said that exploring the upper Yellowstone was all a matter of class—that the "world of letters" needed to validate the outlandish rumors spread by the mountain men and the miners. This they had accomplished to a considerable extent, but to very little public effect.

Langford was eager to hear every detail of what the three explorers had seen, and he and Hauser invited them to the First National Bank to present their report to the leading men of Helena. But seeing unfamiliar faces, Folsom lost his nerve: Would people actually *believe* what he told them? Langford says that his friend "maintained an ominous silence, as if he doubted the evidence of his own senses."[7] Admittedly, Langford could vouch for Folsom's bona fides, but none of the three explorers was really considered a charter member of the Helena elite. Cook was seen as a picaresque character with a credibility problem. That left only Peterson, and who would give much weight to the account of an unlettered Danish handyman?

Horatio Nelson Maguire, the future publisher of the *Pick and Plow*, Bozeman's first newspaper, was intrigued enough to ask Folsom and Cook for their diaries and promised that with his excellent contacts with editors in the East he would do his best to find them a home.[8] But the *New York Tribune* and *Harper's* both treated the reports as if they were a tale of alien abduction, sniffing that "they had a reputation they could not risk with such unreliable material." Lippincott in Philadelphia simply said, "We do not deal in fiction." Finally, in July 1870, the *Western Monthly*, an obscure Chicago periodical, agreed to publish a heavily truncated version of the diaries, which had all the public impact of a tree falling in the forest.

Folsom was not done, however. Over the winter of 1869–1870, he went to work in the U.S. surveyor's office under General Washburn. He gave the general a copy of his diary and helped Walter De Lacy revise and update his map. There were even suggestions, many years later, that Folsom had spoken of some kind of public ownership of the upper Yellowstone. According to Cook, he "made the definitive statement to General Washburn that he hoped to see the Government step in and prevent private settlement."[9] If true, this was the first time that anyone had put forward such an idea since the conversation four years earlier at the snowbound Jesuit mission among General Meagher, Cornelius Hedges, Malcolm Clarke, and Father Francis Xavier Kuppens.

As for Langford, he needed no further persuading of the significance of the expedition. Cook said later that Langford took him aside and told him "in a jocular way that they [Langford, Hauser, and Washburn] were going up to see that country we lied so much about."[10]

The larger truth is that the expedition's reports were drowned out by the panic over the Blackfeet.[11] In the camps of the Piegans, the murder of Malcolm Clarke was the subject of intense debate. What should be done about Owl Child? The militant Mountain Chief, father of Eagle's Rib, washed his hands of the whole affair. It was a personal matter, no concern of his. Heavy Runner, a chief much friendlier to the whites, was camped on Two Medicine River, close to the place where Meriwether Lewis had his fatal encounter with the Piegans in 1806. He was warned of white reprisals, but like Mountain Chief he shrugged them off. If the whites wanted revenge, they should hunt down Owl Child.

Furthermore, many Blackfeet had heard the rumors about Clarke's unwanted advances to the Piegan renegade's wife and felt the killing of the white man was justified. "Much as I hated Owl Child," said Bear Head, a young man whose father had been murdered by the young hothead, "I had to admit he had had good right to kill this fire-hearted, quarrelsome man. Four Bears [Clarke] had tried to steal his woman. . . . In no other way could Owl Child have wiped out that terrible disgrace."[12]

Nellie Clarke had the shrewdest reading of the murder: While Owl Child's real motives were personal, he had taken advantage of the turmoil that followed the killing of Mountain Chief's brother as a convenient smoke screen. Langford, too, clearly understood that the murder was rooted in a personal grievance, but he did nothing to stem the tidal wave of rage that swept through Helena and the other white settlements, for which Indian family quarrels were an irrelevance. This was race war.

The New North West ran a detailed account of the murder and editorialized:

> Verily, the day of reckoning will come. The wrath of an injured people will burst forth and overtake the red fiends, who are petted and fed by the government that they may be the better enabled to burn and pillage our unprotected settlements, and murder unoffending men, women and children.[13]

The Helena Herald struck a similar note, but the editors were encouraged by the arrival of such a distinguished military man as General Washburn, who had already "touched the popular heart on the Indian question. . . . he is just our sort."[14] A week later, the Herald declared:

> That we are now on the verge of a general Indian outbreak no sensible or intelligent man who understands the situation can deny . . . We are well satisfied that with a force of four or five regiments armed and equipped in accordance with General Sully's mode of Indian warfare, he would soon put an end to these outrages, and give the "red devils" a whipping that would last for all time to come.[15]

Sully's "mode of Indian warfare" was a reference to his murderous suppression of the Sioux in the wake of their 1862 uprising in Minnesota. But his failures against the Cheyenne had dimmed his reputation, and he lost his command to Custer, who despised him. (Sully had "marched up the hill and then, like the forces of the king of France, marched them down again," the boy general wrote later.[16]) Now Sully was reduced to being territorial commissioner of Indian affairs, which put him outside the military chain of command, and to the dismay of the men of Helena, he did nothing to leap to their defense. Instead, he took soundings from people whose judgment he had reason to trust more. The legendary fur trader Alexander Culbertson, a man of sixty now, had spent the summer among the Blackfeet, and he told Sully that "my knowledge of their character for a great many years will not permit me to think that there exists a general hostile feeling among them; on the contrary these depredations have been committed by a portion of the young rabble over whom the chiefs have no control, and nothing but the strong arm of the government can control."[17]

General de Trobriand rode out from Fort Shaw to assess the situation for himself, but Helena didn't get much satisfaction from him either. His skepticism about the Blackfeet threat was even echoed in a letter to Sheridan from Sherman, who was wary of settlers who cried wolf: "Somehow I regard the clamor in Montana as identically the same as occurred two years ago, the same Indians, the same men, and the same stories."[18]

Baron and Brevet General Philippe Régis Denis de Keredern de Trobriand was in every sense the wild card in this tortured affair.[19] He was a physically imposing man, balding, with piercing eyes, a long, forked, and carefully manicured goatee, and what can only be described as an aristocratic demeanor. He had a lineage to rival Walter De Lacy's (one of de Trobriand's ancestors, a man of Irish descent, had won fiefdoms in Brittany in 1385, fighting for Jean de Montfort) and a coat of arms with one of the more striking heraldic mottoes: *Trop brillant pour être terni*—shining too bright to be tarnished. His father was an officer in Napoleon's army who had fought at Moscow in 1812 and had more lives than a cat. Wounded on eleven separate occasions, he somehow survived to become a brigadier general.

The young Régis took a law degree in Paris in 1837 and went to work for the Ministry of the Interior, but took a break to write a thinly veiled *roman à clef* entitled *Les Gentilshommes de l'Ouest*, which dealt with an obscure episode in French monarchical politics. The critics spoke well of the young man; a distinguished literary future was predicted. In 1841 he crossed the Atlantic and began to write Tocquevillian commentaries for the French papers on American life and customs. Introduced to society by Washington Irving, he spent several "years of silk and gold" in New York, studying painting, music, and history, with an interlude at the Bourbon court in Venice. Back in New York again in 1847, he wrote opera criticism and founded a literary magazine, *La Revue du Nouveau Monde,* which published poetry by distinguished figures like Théophile Gautier, Alphonse de Lamartine, and Alfred de Vigny.

There was something about watching the Sixth Massachusetts Regiment marching through the streets of New York in 1861, de Trobriand said later, that stirred some atavistic desire for military service. He may be the only man in history to have put on a uniform for the first time at the age of forty-five and risen within four years to the breveted rank of major general—the only Frenchman besides Lafayette ever to rise so high. Along the way he fought at Fredericksburg, Chancellorsville, and Gettysburg. Sheridan admired him, although Grant turned against him after he retired to France at the end of the war to work on his highly critical two-volume *Quatre Ans de Campagne à l'Armée du Potomac.* With that memoir almost completed, he was recalled to active duty in 1867 as a colonel in the 31st Infantry. A month earlier he had been rubbing shoulders with the crowned heads of Europe at the *Exposition Universelle* in Paris; now, at fifty-one, he found himself on a Missouri River steamer bound for Fort Stevenson, in the desolate wilds of Dakota Territory, the heart of Sioux country. "From the brilliant peaks of civilized life," he wrote, "I was to plunge straight into the dark pit of savage existence."

There are few things in frontier literature more atmospheric than the journals de Trobriand kept at Fort Stevenson. They capture the great flat emptiness of the country, the raging storms, the boredom, the flashes of fear. He painted landscapes and portraits of Indians in the manner of George Catlin, tinged with the romance of the noble savage that he had picked up from reading Rousseau and Chateaubriand.[20]

But while he had come to the West relatively free of prejudices, he soon acquired them, becoming a kind of equal-opportunity misanthrope. He deplored the Indian Bureau—"a vast association of thieves who make their fortune at the expense of the redskins and to the detriment of the government."[21] He despised the whiskey traders for opening up a "Pandora's box" of violence on the Plains, and he despised the Indians for succumbing to white man's water. They were doomed to die out, he said, in "the chain of eternal progress."[22] "Oh, Chateaubriand!" he lamented to his diary, "Where is your noble savage?"[23]

It took de Trobriand a full two weeks to complete his investigation of the Blackfeet situation. At Fort Ellis, he was disturbed to find that Lieutenant Doane and his men were still off exploring the new route to the Musselshell River, leaving the fort in poor condition to react to a military threat. In Helena, he talked at length to all sorts of people, who would certainly have included Nathaniel Langford and the Clarke family. From this he concluded, correctly, that Clarke's murder was no more than "the bloody denouement of a long-standing family quarrel." He reported to Hancock:

> The Blackfeet, the Pend d'Oreilles, the Bloods, and even part of the Piegans, remain perfectly quiet. . . . The responsibility of the recent hostilities and depradations seems therefore to rest on a band of Piegans and some roaming vagabonds of different tribes, acting on their own hook, and independently of their own people, as is often the case in Indian country. . . . This is not altogether very formidable.[24]

Yet even this cool response left a loophole—*part* of the Piegans—large enough for a regiment of cavalry to be driven through under the right circumstances.

De Trobriand was hugely irritated by the kind of civilian overreaction army officers had seen too many times before. "Of course there was a cry for more troops and a corresponding blame upon the government for leaving the frontier so unprotected," he wrote to Hancock. But he didn't have enough soldiers at his disposal to scour thousands of square miles of northern Montana for a handful of Piegan renegades. As if he needed further convincing, he traveled the roads through the Gallatin Valley and from Helena to Fort Benton and found everything tranquil. He saw unarmed families going about their business in ox-drawn wagons, perfectly unconcerned, and even a farmer's wife strolling along the road alone with her carpetbag.[25]

None of this calmed the panic in Helena, especially after another dead body turned up just eight miles from town. The victim this time was one James Quail,[26] a masonic friend of Langford's, and his murder jolted even the normally skeptical General Sully into a bout of anxiety. Relying on nothing more than the wild rumors from Helena, the general fired off a note to Indian Commissioner Ely Parker in Washington: Quail's body had been mutilated; he was riddled with arrows; nine Indians had been seen prowling in the vicinity; the Blackfeet were "daily becoming more bold in their depredations." De Trobriand investigated the incident later and found that all of this was nonsense; Quail had almost certainly been murdered by white robbers.[27]

Be that as it may, Helena was still in a lather. On September 27, Langford again served in lieu of a clergyman, officiating at Quail's funeral with full masonic honors as Cornelius Hedges stood by him at the graveside. Two nights later Langford chaired an emergency meeting of furious citizens. They debated three alternatives: Send in the army; raise a volunteer militia; or send out a posse to arrest Clarke's murderers, since Nellie and Horace had identified all five of them by name. The police chief of Helena favored a militia and said he would be delighted to lead it, on the sole condition that his men receive a bounty for each scalp they lifted.[28]

But the majority opted for the army, and two days after the meeting they wrote to de Trobriand that, "[u]nless suppressed, and that speedily," the depredations of the Blackfeet

will culminate in a general massacre of our outlying settlements and the consequent abandonment and ruin of so much of our fair Territory." Their demands: "to ask you, as chief of military command, to put into the field two hundred cavalry, or as many as you have available for that purpose, and drive to their reservations and homes the squads or bands of Indians now scattered throughout the Territory.

The petition was signed by a committee of six, including General Henry Dana Washburn, Sam Hauser, and Malcolm Clarke's neighbor Warren Gillette.[29]

A week later, the formal legal machinery was cranked into motion. A grand jury of merchants, storekeepers, miners, saloon keepers, clerks, and jewelers—including another would-be Yellowstone explorer, a freighter named Benjamin Stickney—accused the Blackfeet of "a declaration of war on the whites of Montana" and declared that, "Ours is a contest between civilization and barbarism."[30] With this resonant document, which they submitted to the president, the secretary of war, and the general-in-chief of the army, went indictments against five named individuals: Pete Owl Child, Eagle's Rib, Bear Chief, Black Bear, and Black Weasel.[31]

De Trobriand was unmoved. *Do I really have to repeat everything I told you a month ago?* He walked Washburn, Hauser, Gillette, and the rest of their committee through the limitations of his command: He had been in Montana for only three months; he barely had enough troops to garrison Fort Shaw, let alone send them off on this wild-goose chase; the newly arrived cavalry units at Fort Ellis were still at half-strength. With all the aristocratic hauteur he could muster, he wrote, "[G]entlemen, there is a French proverb that says that 'the prettiest girl can give but what she has.' So with any military commander."[32]

But even if he *did* have the troops, he sighed, as if lecturing a classroom of particularly obtuse schoolchildren,

Let us see the facts as they are, and without exaggeration. The first fact which I think must be admitted by all is that there is

actually *no Indian war* [italics in original] in the Territory.
Depredations are committed, even murders are committed,
but by whom? By a handful of roaming thieves and murderous red vagabonds, being principally of the Piegan tribe, and
doing mischief not in any concentrated force, but in small
parties of a few men.... The capture or death of these few
men is the principal object to be arrived at, and would, in my
opinion, suffice to restore security in the Territory. This is
what I propose to do as soon as possible through a cavalry
expedition; and to that effect, instructions will be sent without delay to the post commander at Fort Ellis.

This left very little for the leading men of Helena to do but wait and
grumble. On October 22, Langford left for the States for the winter.[33] He
took Nellie Clarke with him and left her with her aunt in Minneapolis.
Horace and Nathan took over the running of the family ranch.

From Minnesota Langford went on to Washington on a mission that
seems quixotic in the extreme. In a cryptic note written many years
later, he says that since any attempt to arrest Owl Child and his accomplices "would have been resisted by the whole tribe, thus bringing a general Indian war," he was asked by his fellow citizens to go to the capital
to see if the federal government would fund a posse to hunt down
Clarke's killers. Apparently he put this idea to several influential senators, but "they thought this should not be done, and the matter ended
there."[34] A mystery.

However, the crisis was far from over. In Chicago, Phil Sheridan
had been monitoring the situation closely and reading the small print
in de Trobriand's reports. *This is what I propose to do as soon as possible.* That was what the Frenchman had said. Sheridan made his opening move on October 21, the day before Langford's departure for the
East. It was less than a year since Custer's action on the Washita, and
Sheridan was clearly interested in a repeat performance. He wrote to
Sherman's adjutant,

I think it would be the best plan to let me find out exactly where these Indians are going to spend the winter, and about the time of a good heavy snow I will send out a party and try and strike them. About the 15th of January they will be very helpless, and if where they live is not too far from Shaw or Ellis we might be able to give them a good hard blow, which will make peace a desirable object.[35]

The adjutant's reply, dated November 4, was the merest formality: "I have the honor to inform you that your proposed action . . . for the punishment of these marauders, has been approved by the General of the Army."[36]

21

FORTY-FOUR BELOW

December 1869–January 1870

A most excellent man, who may be intrusted with any party you may see fit to send out." That was what Sheridan said to Hancock about Colonel Eugene Mortimer Baker, after meeting with him in Chicago to review the Piegan problem before Baker took up his new post at Fort Ellis in December 1869.[1] Baker was a West Point graduate, class of '59, a man with a "very strong and vigorous mind, as well as a marvelously powerful and perfect physique."[2] He was fiercely loyal to the cavalrymen under his command, whom he called his "busters." He and Sheridan were old comrades in arms; as a captain, Baker had served under Little Phil in the Shenandoah and had taken part in a dozen or more merciless battles, including Gettysburg. He was at Appomattox for Lee's surrender. He was breveted twice for gallant and meritorious conduct. But the Civil War hardened him, as it did so many.

As a young lieutenant in the First Cavalry he had seen prewar action against the western Shoshone in Nevada. From the field reports he submitted at this early stage of his career, one could almost take him for a humanitarian, warning that if the government failed to provide food for the starving tribe it would face an outbreak of violence—an accurate assessment of the situation that eventually led to the Bear River Massacre in 1863.

After the war he went west again, serving this time under the most famous Indian fighter of all, General George Crook, during the so-called Snake War of 1867–1868 in Oregon and Idaho against the Shoshone, the Bannock, and the Northern Paiute.[3] At Fort Ellis, Baker brought a radical and immediate change of tone. Colonel Brackett had run its affairs in conscientious but unimaginative fashion. Under Baker, there was an idiosyncratic mix of slovenly informality and brutal discipline.

Lieutenant Doane's favorite soldier, Private Daniel Starr, described Baker as "a hard-hearted man . . . big, powerful, hardy, carried his strong body in erect, soldierly manner." And Starr also offered a likely explanation for the numerous "sick leaves" that showed up on Baker's service record, including one of five months immediately preceding his assignment to Fort Ellis. "He was a hard drinker, and he was tolerant of alcoholic excesses among his soldiers," Starr said. "In fact, his rough and common ways, his familiar mingling with his subordinates, did much toward bringing them into forgetfulness about some of the reprehensible traits of his character."[4]

Life at the fort during the three years of Baker's command has been described in detail by two men. One was Private William White. The other was a young Dane, Peter Koch, the Latin- and Greek-speaking son of "a solemn, pipe-puffing Lutheran minister,"[5] who arrived in Bozeman in 1870 and took a position as an assistant in the sutler's store at Fort Ellis.

Baker's officers, Koch said, were "infested by that intolerable stuck-up pride which so many of the officers of the regular army have, and which makes them look down on all civilians (unless they have plenty of money) as inferior beings." For special parades—an inspection by a superior officer from St. Paul or Chicago, or a visit from some political dignitary— the men of the Second Cavalry would turn out in full dress uniform: belted, yellow-braided jacket; helmet with double visor and crest with an emblazoned eagle, a yellow plume, and a long, triple-braided cord, also yellow, that encircled the helmet and hung down the left side of the body.[6] Otherwise, officers rarely wore insignia of rank or regulation uniform, and ordinary soldiers were left to dress according to their personal whim.[7]

Koch wrote that drill was "something unknown." On inspection day, the officers limited themselves to "inspecting a few bottles of Champagne and some cigars, which is altogether one of the most important duties every day." Yet despite Baker's own weakness for alcohol, Koch said he had no tolerance for roaring drunks and subjected them to his own brutal form of discipline.

> The officer of the guard would send a squad of men and march the worst ones away to the guardhouse where they had some tied up by the thumbs, some by the arms, some a la spread eagle, one fellow, whom they couldn't manage in other way, bucked and gagged and laid out into the snow for four hours.[8]

Meanwhile, in Chicago, Washington, and St. Paul, and at Fort Shaw, the debate over the Piegans continued. It involved the rationales and rationalizations of military men locked up in various kinds of ideology, doctrine, and misperception, and a curious reversal of roles between General Sully and General de Trobriand.

Sully had evidently been alarmed by Sherman's authorization of military action and immediately began to backpedal. "It appears to be the impression among those acquainted with these Indians that they do not intend a general war," he wrote on November 16, a little belatedly. The political reality, of course, was that Sully himself was being cut out of the loop; the military forces in Montana were not his to command.

For his part, General de Trobriand continued for a while to pour scorn on the idea of a larger conflict. He dismissed the idea that Langford's friend James Quail had been killed by Blackfeet: There were no arrows in the body, no scalping, no sign of mutilation. None of his horses had been stolen, and stealing horses, for heaven's sake, was what the Blackfeet lived for.[9] On November 26, he sent General Hancock a detailed analysis of the location and disposition of each of the three Blackfeet tribes. Almost all of the Bloods and the Siksika were in the British possessions now and inclined to peace. The only Piegan camp within striking distance was that of Heavy Runner, a well-known friend of the whites.

Heavy Runner had what amounted to a blood feud with Owl Child, who was the only real problem: "That Peter is the worst ruffian among the Indians," de Trobriand reported. Indeed, he went as far as to propose enlisting the friendly chief's help to hunt down the man. But where was Peter? The best bet was in the camp of Mountain Chief, way up on the Milk River, near the Canadian borderline. And therefore, de Trobriand said, "I do not see, so far, an opportunity for striking a successful blow."[10] *So far* being the operative words.

Nothing could be worse, he concluded, than to act hastily and hit the wrong camp—"to chastise [Heavy Runner's band] for offenses for which they are not guilty." His suggestion was to lull the guilty parties into a trap: Wait quietly until deep midwinter, when they would return to the Marias River country, "supposing that we will let bygones be bygones."

In Chicago, Phil Sheridan was mightily confused by all these conflicting signals. Sully had been yelping about a general war, on the basis of which Sherman had given permission for a military strike. Now he seemed to have come around to de Trobriand's view that "the condition of Indian affairs is by no means alarming." What was going on here? To answer the question, Sheridan turned to a trusted friend, Major General James A. Hardie, the army's Inspector General for the Division of the Missouri. However much he might dislike Indians, Sheridan didn't see the need for unnecessary killing. Before Hardie left for Montana, he told him, "If there is any danger of Indians being molested who are friendly, you are authorized to suspend all operations under the orders emanating from the General-in-Chief."

From de Trobriand's perspective, what happened over the next few weeks, before Hardie reached Fort Shaw, was less a change of heart than a change of circumstances. It started with the weather. This was already shaping up to be Montana's most bitter winter in years, and the buffalo herds had begun to move south and east from the border. So did the Piegan camps, following them—something that did not occur normally until well after the first of the year.

Despite the Arctic temperatures of the Northern Plains, winter camp was usually a relaxed place.[11] Dispersed bands came together in large numbers. Friendships were renewed; stories shared. Children zipped back and forth on the ice on sleds with buffalo rib runners. Periodically the young men went out on a two- or three-day hunt—it was a particularly good time of year for this, in fact, even in subzero temperatures, because the buffalo coats were long and shaggy; they made good, warm clothing and bedding and fetched high prices from the traders.[12]

The choice of location was up to the chief of each band. Normally it was a sheltered river bottom, where stands of cottonwood offered fuel for campfires and browse for the ponies. Drinking water came from holes cut in the ice. The Marias, the most important of all the rivers that flowed through the Blackfeet country, was particularly favored, since it wandered and zigzagged for miles between high, dark bluffs and badlands, each bend constituting a natural windbreak. The best spot of all was the so-called Big Bend, about thirty-five miles east of the spot where Meriwether Lewis had clashed with the Piegans. To the north, defining the Canadian horizon, were the three evenly spaced mounds of the sacred Sweetgrass Hills, the middle one rising in a perfect Mount Fuji cone.[13] A flat sagebrush bottom stretched for hundreds of yards on each side of the river, making a perfect campground.

By mid-December de Trobriand had learned that Mountain Chief had moved his lodges to the Marias, and with the glacial weather was likely to stay there for a while. What he did not know yet was that for the second time in three decades the Piegans had been invaded by the white scabs. When Hardie learned of this in early January, he totally misinterpreted the impact of the epidemic: "The smallpox . . . is thought by some to have had the effect to intensify hostility of many of the Blackfeet against the whites, to whom they attribute the introduction among them of the disease."[14] Nothing could have been farther from the truth; the response of the Piegans to the white scabs was to hunker down in terror in their buffalo robes amid the stench of death.

De Trobriand was already under pressure from his superiors to act. Hancock had written to him from St. Paul in the first week of December to reiterate Sheridan's proposal for a strike in mid-January. Now the distinguished Frenchman grasped the moment:

Indian affairs in this Territory have assumed, quite recently, a
new aspect, which is much more favorable to the execution of the
plan of the Lieutenant General [Sheridan] for a winter expedition
against the Piegans than could have been expected at this season
of the year. . . . There they are within easy reach, and I propose to
seize the opportunity and strike as soon as we are ready.[15]

As if they were needed, he went on to offer additional grounds—thin
and cynical ones—for launching an attack. In the course of a few days in
December, a group of hunters was ambushed forty-five miles from Fort
Shaw, with one fatality; thirty mules were stolen; a ranch at Dauphin Rapids on the upper Missouri was ransacked and provisions taken. Compared
with the murder of Malcolm Clarke, these incidents were trivial, but the
timing was opportune. "It is my firm belief," de Trobriand announced,
"that they are greatly encouraged by their past impunity, and that it has
become necessary to inflict a punishment on the guilty parties."[16]

As the Frenchman's position hardened, the hapless Sully scurried forward, backward, and sideways in an effort to regain some control over
the rapidly unraveling situation. He wrote urgently to Hancock, proposing the muster of a force of three hundred volunteers, which he, Sully,
would personally command. This was a bizarre suggestion, as any wet-
behind-the-ears second lieutenant would have understood. Sully worked
for the Indian Bureau now, and his advice on military strategy was about
as relevant as the local saloon keeper's.

Next he proposed diplomacy. He would go to the Blackfeet agency on
the Teton River to demand that whatever chiefs he could assemble hunt
down Pete Owl Child and deliver him to justice. De Trobriand agreed to
provide an armed escort for Sully's thirty-five-mile ride, no doubt with a
raised eyebrow and a Gallic shrug.

Sully called his summit meeting for New Year's Day. The amiable
Heavy Runner made an appearance. So did Little Wolf and Big Lake, both
Piegans. The fourth man to show up was Gray Eyes of the Bloods. The
messengers Sully had sent out were apologetic; they had found all the
other tribal leaders prostrate in their tipis, in an alcoholic stupor. Sully

told the four sober chiefs that the government was committed to war and that the British government had given the army permission for hot pursuit across the border. It was a preposterous bluff, but presumably the chiefs were ignorant of the subtleties of *Napikwan* diplomacy. Sully gave them an ultimatum: Bring in Owl Child and his cronies and all the stolen stock within two weeks, or face the consequences. The chiefs made all the familiar and reasonable protests: They were innocent, they had no power over the young men, they hated Owl Child as much as the whites did. But yes, of course, if by any chance they stumbled across him, they would be more than happy to kill him as requested. General Sully gave Heavy Runner a piece of white paper; it was a safe-conduct pass, he explained, to show that he was a loyal friend of the army. "I hope my mission to the Piegans and Bloods may be a success," he reported to Washington on January 3, 1870, "yet I am not over-sanguine."[17]

As the deadline approached, a couple of Blackfeet boys retrieved a few stolen horses and mules, but there was no trace of Owl Child. In a panic, Sully improvised his most eccentric idea yet: Why not take Mountain Chief hostage along with "about half-dozen other principal men of his band"?[18] Hardie asked de Trobriand what he thought of this idea. "An impracticability," he replied—Trobriandese for plain silly. Very little was left now of Sully's shredded reputation as an Indian fighter.

Major General Hardie reached Helena on January 5, and arrived at Fort Shaw two days later. By the 13th, looking at his watch, he had made up his mind, though the reasoning in his final report to Sheridan was, to say the least, questionable. He began with the careful objectivity that had made his name as an investigator. His assessment of the settlers from the East, who had raised the clamor for war, was especially astute:

> In Montana, as in most of our other Territories, where there are Indians, there are two classes of people. One is that of the citizen interested in the settlement, growth, prosperity, and civilization of the country . . . the other class is connected with the Indians in some way, either through trade or intermarriage & c. or belonging to the Indian service. The former class is naturally

timid as respects Indian disturbances . . . they dread their savage neighbors . . . The complete subjection of the Indians is absolutely essential to their sense of security. The other class have generally not so much fear from the Indians.[19]

Nathaniel Langford would probably have taken exception to the word *timid,* but in other respects Hardie's description perfectly characterized men like Cornelius Hedges, Sam Hauser, and Langford himself.

Hardie agreed with de Trobriand that the majority of the Piegans were disposed to peace, and that the only problem was Owl Child and his cohort. Nonetheless, Hardie decided that the time had come to draw a line in the sand. Sheridan wanted an attack; so did de Trobriand; so did the new commanding officer at Fort Ellis. "I think chastisement is necessary," Hardie wrote. "In this Colonel Baker concurs."

> The duty of providing security for the lives and property ofthe citizens of Montana . . . is imperious. To shrink from what the occasion called for as necessary, no matter how severe, is to incur responsibility for future massacres of men, women, and children, for the destruction of homes and the plunder and ruin of the settlements.

Why? one is entitled to ask, reading Hardie's enumeration of the case for war:

July 16, 1869: Two men killed (not by Blackfeet, but by drunken Crows, who were promptly hanged).

Early August: A government supply train attacked, one white fatality, 20 oxen stolen, four Indians killed in the ensuing gunplay.

August 17: Malcolm Clarke murdered (in a family feud).

September 27: James Quail murdered (by whites).

December 13: One hunter killed.

December 16: Thirty government mules stolen.

December 22: Property wantonly destroyed at a ranch.

Total accounting over a six-month period: Six dead white men (only three killed by Piegans, and the most important of those in a family quarrel). On the other side, six dead Blackfeet, including Mountain Chief's elderly brother, and two hanged Crows. Four cattle stolen, 20 oxen, 30 mules.

Let slip the dogs of war.

On January 13, Hardie submitted his recommendations to Lieutenant General Sheridan. Two days later, the reply came back from Chicago: "If the lives and property of the citizens of Montana can best be protected by striking Mountain Chief's band, I want them struck. Tell Baker to strike them hard."[20]

The planners of the operation added only one caveat, which Sheridan had already communicated to Hardie. *Where* Baker struck was as important as *how* he struck: It had to be the right target, the village of Mountain Chief, whose hostility to the whites was well-known. An important clarification, however: Sparing an innocent camp was not the same thing as sparing innocent individuals in a hostile one. The tactics of a winter strike, especially at the favored time of first light, made that distinction impossible. The Indians would be defenseless, often still asleep; the most efficient way of preempting resistance was to fire indiscriminately into the lodges without knowing who was inside; and besides, in line with the doctrine of total war formulated in the Shenandoah, just as important as killing people was destroying the infrastructure of their survival—the tipis, the clothing and blankets, the food stores, the horses. Under such circumstances, women, children, and old people were inevitably going to die.[21]

De Trobriand seeems to have felt some misgivings about Sheridan's philosophy of war, to judge from the draft of a letter he wrote to Hardie:

There lies the difficulty—that is, how to discriminate in the field among the Indians when our men come upon them if they happen to be intermixed around the trading post and on

the banks of the Marias, as is the case now. Of course, no effort will be neglected towards that discrimination; but who
can say how successfully?

As the Montana historian Ben Bennett adds acerbically: Who indeed?[22]

In any event, de Trobriand had second thoughts about anguishing
over this too publicly, for he deleted this passage from the letter he finally
sent. And in other moments of handling the Piegan crisis, he showed no
moral qualms at all. The Frenchman normally disliked the cavalry, but
he recognized its utility in a winter campaign, where "[t]he confessed aim
is to exterminate everyone, for this is the only advantage of making the
expedition."[23]

Before making his final recommendations to divisional headquarters,
Hardie had insisted on one final step to make sure that the right target
was selected. De Trobriand should send out a reliable scout to pinpoint
the location of Mountain Chief's hostile camp. The ideal candidate for
this delicate mission was Joe Kipp, son of the legendary James Kipp, who
had opened the first trading post with the Piegans on the Marias River
forty years earlier. Joe—known to the Piegans as either "Choe Keepah" or
Raven Quiver—was twenty years old, a handsome young man with his
white father's coloring and his Mandan mother's good looks. He had
joined the army as a seventy-five-dollar-a-month scout and interpreter
just a few months earlier, attached to the 13th Infantry at Fort Shaw.

Kipp went off fully confident that he could distinguish Mountain
Chief's camp from that of Heavy Runner. To someone as familiar with
Piegan life as Kipp was, this did not present a great challenge. Each camp
had its own unique features, not least of which were the distinctive designs on a chief's tipi; it was a bit like telling the difference between a
house with a red door and another with a green one. Kipp returned to
Fort Shaw on January 12, and reported that Mountain Chief was encamped on the sagebrush flats at the Big Bend of the Marias. There was
no doubt about it. The only drawback was that Owl Child, the ostensible
target of the operation, was not there; he was holed up in a Blood camp
on the other side of the Canadian line.[24] By this time, however, hunting

down Malcolm Clarke's murderer was no longer really the point. *Owl Child? Who was that again?* one imagines Colonel Baker saying.

Baker arrived at Fort Shaw on January 14, with the four companies of the Second Cavalry from Fort Ellis. Company F was led by Cheyney Doane, who had taken charge of the company after the court-martial of its commander.[25] For a second lieutenant with less than two years of experience to lead a company into a major action was nothing short of astonishing. The other three company commanders all outranked him; one was a rising star from West Point, one a twenty-five-year veteran, and one a hero of Gettysburg.[26]

The cavalry had left Fort Ellis twelve days earlier. Along the way they collected a contingent of troops who had been on detached duty in Diamond City, then stopped at the Clarke place on the Little Prickly Pear to pick up Horace and Nathan, who attached themselves to the column seeking to avenge their father's death. A neighbor of the Clarkes, Joe Cobell, rode over to join the party as an additional guide: He was an Italian immigrant and former hunter for the American Fur Company, famously good with a rifle, married to a sister of the friendly Piegan chief Little Dog. Helena buzzed with rumors: Where were the soldiers going?

At Fort Shaw, de Trobriand gave Baker his marching orders. Travel in total secrecy. Ride by night, sleep by day. Do not molest the friendly camp of chief Heavy Runner. However, "Beyond these general instructions it is deemed unnecessary to add anything. The details as to the best way to surprise the enemy and to carry on successfully the operation is confidently left to your judgment and discretion, according to the circumstances and to your experience in such expeditions."[27]

It took four days to prepare the troops for departure: 10 officers, 207 cavalrymen, 55 mounted infantry and another 75 on foot, with Joe Kipp as scout. The weather was the worst in living memory. The temperature plunged far below zero. In places the snow lay three feet deep on the ground. The men pulled on their winter combat clothes and stuffed their forty-pound packs with essentials.

Captain Simon Snyder of the Fifth Infantry, who took part in a similar midwinter offensive against Crazy Horse and the Oglala Sioux, wrote,

> I am now wearing two flannel and a buckskin shirt, one pair of drawers, trousers of buckskin and a pair of army trousers, two pairs of woolen socks, a pair of buffalo overshoes and big boots, a heavy pair of blanket leggings, a thick blouse and heavy overcoat, a heavy woolen cap that completely covers my head, face and neck, except nose and eyes, and still I am not happy.

The soldiers "looked more like a large body of Esquimaux than like white men and U.S. troops," wrote another participant in that campaign.[28]

On the morning of Wednesday, January 19, the troops at Fort Shaw moved out. Mercury freezes at minus thirty-eight degrees Fahrenheit. On the eve of departure, presumably with the aid of a spirit thermometer, someone measured the temperature as forty-four below.

22

A CASE OF MISTAKEN IDENTITY

December 1869–January 1870

Many things go into the unfolding and resolution of a tragedy: most famously, of course, the human flaw, but also human error, misdirection, accidents of timing, how words are used and interpreted. Regarding the climax, Aristotle talks of "a fatal or painful action like death on the stage, violent physical pain, wounds, and everything of that kind," which together evoke pity and terror. The outcome of a tragedy, when all its elements have played out to their conclusion, always appears inevitable.[1]

The Second Cavalry's two-week journey to the banks of the Marias in subzero temperatures was an epic of physical endurance, made more remarkable by the frontier army's haphazard standards of drill and training and the egregious levels of alcohol abuse. Not a man was lost.[2]

By January 22, they had reached the Dry Fork of the Marias, close to the point where it is crossed today by Interstate 15.[3] Here Colonel Baker sent a small detachment up the Marias to guard a fur-trading post run by a man named Riplinger.

At daybreak on the 23rd, a Sunday, after another brutal night march, they came upon a single lodge belonging to a Piegan named Gray Wolf; there were only a handful of people inside, and several were stricken by smallpox, said Private John Ponsford.[4] Baker learned that the big camp he was looking for was eight or ten miles downriver, and told Doane, his most trusted officer, to gallop ahead with Company F and pinpoint the exact location. Halfway, Doane encountered more Indians—two women on ponies and two young men on foot. One of them was a twelve-year-old named Bear Head, who had been sent out with a number of other boys to round up the horses that had strayed from the main camp at the Big Bend.[5]

Many years later, Bear Head told an interviewer: "One of the seizers came and grasped my arm; spoke; tapped his lips with his fingers. I was not to speak; shout. He was a chief, this seizer, had strips of yellow metal on his shoulders, had a big knife, a five-shooter pistol." Given the context, he can only have meant Doane.

The company advanced silently with their prisoners. The river was concealed at this point in a deep ravine, but after a while Doane saw ponies grazing and wisps of smoke rising from the tipis. Advancing to the top of a bluff, he counted thirty-two lodges spread out on the flats on both banks of the river, some two hundred feet below. The bluffs were steep and deeply scored, cut by gullies and ravines, dark and cindery, topped with patches of stunted cactus and wind-seared grass.[6]

The camp seemed silent, the smoke holes giving the only sign of life, although perhaps there was the growling of dogs and the moans of small-pox victims, for by this time the deaths had begun, a few each day. The Piegans would say later that most of the young men had left the day before on a hunt, leaving the camp all but undefended.[7] Private Ponsford saw large herds of buffalo in the distance, toward the Sweetgrass Hills, black forms against a fresh fall of snow.

As the rest of Baker's troops approached and took up positions, aiming their .50 caliber rifles at the tipis, every fourth man left to hold the horses, Doane ordered Company F to storm down the bluffs, cross the frozen river, and take up positions at the perimeter of the camp to prevent anyone escaping to the north. A sergeant and six men drove off the Indians' pony herd. It was a rough descent, and one of the horses fell as it charged down a ravine, breaking a trooper's leg.

Baker prepared to issue orders to the main body of troops. He "had made known the paramount feature of his military policy, when he announced as a motto, 'Nits Make Lice,'" said Private Starr. "This was the customary way of indicating that children were not to be spared. With this general-extermination idea impressed upon the troops, the camp was quickly surrounded."[8] Baker's plan of attack appeared to be proceeding by the book, but there was just one flaw. It was the wrong camp.

The most prosaic explanation is that the buffalo herds had moved again; others say Mountain Chief had gotten wind of the attack in advance.[9] But Blackfeet oral history said that Mountain Chief had a dream in which he was lying on the ground as people fired on him—and for this reason decided to shift to another spot a few miles downstream.[10] Whatever the reason, the smallpox-ridden camp of Chief Heavy Runner had moved onto the site on the Big Bend that Mountain Chief had vacated, just a few days after Joe Kipp returned to Fort Shaw with his intelligence pinpointing the location of the hostile and friendly bands.

The commotion of the cavalry charge had broken the torpor of Heavy Runner's camp.[11] Spear Woman said later that the chief told everyone to be calm, that he would go outside and show the seizers his safe-conduct pass, the "name paper," he had been given by General Sully three weeks earlier.[12]

Up on the bluffs, Joe Kipp was squinting down at the tipis in the steely gray light of the early morning, when the sudden, awful realization came upon him. The designs on the lodges were not those of Mountain Chief. He rushed over to Baker, yelling that he had to abort the operation. Baker's response was to have Kipp seized by two guards and threaten to have him shot if he uttered another word.

Kipp says the colonel was drunk at this point and had no idea what he was doing. Author Robert Ege, a military historian and Custer expert who is Baker's principal apologist, offers some specious arguments to dispute this.[13] For one thing, Baker had been sober enough to order a detachment of soldiers to guard a nearby fur-trading post (the previous day); for another, he had not opened fire on Gray Wolf's lodge (which would presumably have alerted every Indian for miles). But even Ege concedes in the end that Baker "may have been drunk." It was a frigid night, after all, and a tense situation.

Kipp remained categorical on the point, as did Horace Clarke, whose father's death had been the cause of all this in the first place. In a sworn affidavit to the Indian Claims Commission in 1920, he said Baker's incapacity was "an undeniable fact." Later he added that, "Because of the intense cold, both officers and men had "tried to keep their spirits up by taking spirits down." When Kipp tried to convince Baker of his mistake, "that 'officer and gentleman' had been too long in conference with John Barleycorn to heed the warning."[14]

Heavy Runner emerged from his tipi, holding up General Sully's paper. Some say he began to cross the frozen river. Wherever he was, the paper was as useless as the American flag Black Kettle had displayed at Sand Creek, or the peace medal Little Thunder had offered General Harney at Blue Water. A single shot rang out, hitting the Piegan chief in the chest. The troops, absent any clear command from Baker, took this as their signal to open fire. Doane wrote later that the fusillade lasted an hour, though other accounts say it was less.

On the north bank of the Marias, Doane's company chased down anyone trying to escape and dispatched them with revolvers. Others went around tipi by tipi, finishing off any wounded who remained inside. "Corporal Etheridge distinguished himself in killing Indians," Doane said, "taking great risks by standing in front of the lodges and firing into the doors." This tactic produced the only fatality of the day on the army side, when a Canadian-born private named Walton McKay pulled open the flap of a tipi to do the business and was shot dead—the only instance of gunfire from a Piegan, according to Joe Kipp, though others must surely have defended themselves with bows and arrows. The soldiers then collapsed the tipis and set fire to them, burning to death those who remained alive inside.

Ege, again straining in Baker's defense, insists that there was shooting from the Piegan side, but no one else mentions this, not even Doane, who makes it clear that the main risk to his men came from the enfilading fire from the bluffs.

Every testimony by a survivor of the massacre concurs that the able-bodied men of the camp had gone out on a buffalo hunt, as they sometimes did even in deepest winter, and did not return until the next day. Joe Kipp told the same story. Again, Ege disputes this, since the soldiers had seen no buffalo on their way from Fort Shaw. But presumably, as Private Ponsford had noted, this was because the herds were ranging to the north and east of the camp, on the broad prairie between the Marias and the Sweetgrass Hills.

For years no one knew, or at least cared to say, who had fired the shot that killed Heavy Runner and set off the slaughter. But eventually the scout Joe Cobell, an expert marksman, confided to his Piegan wife that, well, yes, he had been the shooter; the motive was revenge for the theft of some horses by members of Heavy Runner's band. He positively gloated over it, she said. But the personal may also have been entangled with the political, just as it had been in the killing of Malcolm Clarke. Cobell's wife was sister to Mountain Chief, and attacking Heavy Runner's camp was the most effective way imaginable of shielding the man who had been the real target of Baker's expedition.

Many years after the massacre, a Piegan named George Bull Child made a hide painting of the scene. The image shows a perfect circle of eleven tipis. Nine of them are painted with dream images; two are black. Within the circle, splayed out like the hands on a clock face, are the bodies of men, women, children, and infants in cradleboards. Six seizers are charging on horseback, with firesticks pointed at the tipis. George Bull Child has addressed the incomprehensible, conjuring symmetry out of chaos.[15]

When the killing was over, Colonel Baker instructed Doane to remain in the camp with his company and clean up. The remainder of the force, almost three hundred men, would continue on to the camp of Mountain Chief, which Baker had now been told was four miles downstream. In the end, he found it was considerably more.[16] When they arrived, they found seven abandoned lodges, burned them, and bivouacked for the night. For twenty-four hours or so, Doane was the sole officer in charge of the massacre site.

With Kipp and Cobell, he rounded up the survivors and counted the dead. There were 173 bodies, Doane recorded, and more than 100 survivors—some said 140—mostly women and children, who were packed into a couple of tents. All their possessions—buffalo robes, bedding, medicine bundles, cooking utensils, and other household goods, and more than a ton of meat and pemmican—were heaped in piles and set ablaze.

The custom of the Blackfeet and many other northwestern tribes was to leave the bodies of the dead aboveground, so that the soul could ascend more easily to the spirit world.[17] In the case of a chief like Heavy Runner, the body would be dressed in its most elaborate finery and set on a raised platform in the center of the lodge. The man's favorite horse would be decorated with representations of his most heroic war exploits and then ritually killed. When Doane's men confirmed Heavy Runner's identity after examining his "name paper," they dug a shallow grave in the frozen earth and buried him.[18] Whether this reflected some degree of respect or remorse or whether, in the knowledge of Blackfeet customs, it was intended as a sign of contempt, is hard to say.

Eight young Blood males who had shared the Piegan camp, as often happened, were kept under guard with the rest of the survivors. At last darkness fell, a little after five. The rest of the night, Doane wrote later, was "made hideous [by] the sentinels firing at intervals . . . the groans of the wounded, the howling of dogs, fire breaking out in the woods, and the stampeding of the pony herd in a tremendous windstorm." At some point, said the twelve-year-old Bear Head, "I heard a sound, as if someone was cutting up meat with an axe, and I heard a grunt. I looked around and could see by the firelight one of the Bloods lying on the ground with his head split open." All the prisoners had been killed.

Private Dan Starr later gave his version of the event. The officer in charge—Doane, in other words[19]—"lost control of his temper. He issued an order: 'Kill them—every---- ---- one of them.'" The guards readied their weapons, but Doane said, "No, don't use your guns. Get axes and kill them one at a time." Starr, according to the author Thomas Marquis, who recorded his testimony, was one of the executioners. However, Marquis wrote, "He never indicated to me that he felt any prickings of conscience on account of his action in the affair . . . The killing of an Indian, under any circumstances and in any manner, was regarded as an act so commendable as to approach the status of a stern duty."[20]

Starr says that when Baker and the main troop returned at about ten the next morning, Doane reported that the prisoners had been "killed while trying to escape. The report was not questioned. The true case was well understood, but nobody talked openly about it."

By this time, it had become clear to Doane that he had a smallpox camp on his hands. Baker ordered the men to rustle up a few boxes of bacon and hardtack, and the troops rode away, leaving the survivors to fend for themselves with these meager provisions, either to find their way to another Piegan camp, or to Fort Benton, some eighty miles distant. Temperatures were still far below zero, and an uncounted number died.

Next day, at Riplinger's trading post, the colonel assembled those Blood chiefs who could be found and told them that the annihilation of Heavy Runner's camp should serve as a warning. No more trouble, or the same thing would happen to them. With that, he ordered the troops to return to base. On January 29, they reached Fort Shaw, where the infantry units remained. By February 6, the Second Cavalry was back at Fort Ellis. They had been in the field for eighteen days. "Total distance marched 612 miles," Colonel Baker noted blandly in his annual Report of Operations.

23

HEROES OF THE HOUR

January–March 1870

Yesterday had news of Indian fight," Cornelius Hedges noted in his diary entry for January 29. On the same day, Sheridan passed on the glad news to Sherman: de Trobriand has reported that "the expedition is a complete success . . . most of the murderers and marauders of last summer are killed. . . . I think this will end Indian troubles in Montana."[1]

Helena feted the victors, and when the windows of the banqueting room were flung open, de Trobriand told his daughter in a tour de force of vanity,

> . . . immediately there commenced a serenade in my honor beneath torches. The crowd called me to the balcony. There I was on my stage, my entrance applauded, acclaimed and introduced to the citizens by the favorite orator of the place. I astonished the natives by an improvised talk which was interrupted twenty times by applause, and when my peroration ended, three hurrahs and a "tiger" for General Trobriand, Trobian, Troben, Trobridge, Trobin, and all the other indescribable names.[2]

The *Helena Herald* saluted "the annihilation of the most murderous company of red devils" by the unpronounceable Frenchman.[3] An un-

When this portrait was made in 1866, the twenty-six-year-old Gustavus Cheyney Doane was mayor of Yazoo City, Mississippi. *(Merrill G. Burlingame Special Collections, Montana State University)*

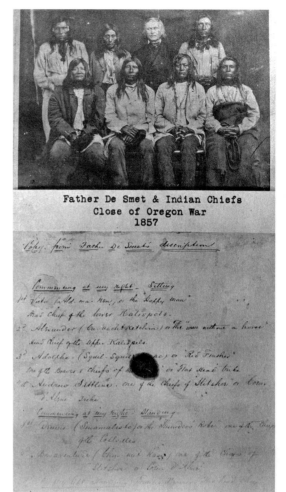

Father De Smet & Indian Chiefs
Close of Oregon War
1857

The Flemish Jesuit father Pierre-Jean de Smet, surrounded here by chiefs from the Kalispell, Flathead, and Coeur d'Alene tribes, was the first to bring Christianity to the Blackfeet. *(Montana Historical Society Research Center—Photograph Archives, Helena, Montana)*

Pictured here at about the time of the 1870 Yellowstone expedition, Nathaniel Pitt Langford had already achieved celebrity in Montana Territory as a businessman, aspiring politician, and vigilante leader. *(Montana Historical Society Research Center—Photograph Archives, Helena, Montana)*

Trapper-scout-explorer Jim Bridger knew the Northern Rockies better than any other white man and was famous for his tall tales of the wonders of the upper Yellowstone. *(Denver Public Library)*

Crossing the Continental Divide at Mullan Pass in 1862, Nathaniel Langford presided over the first masonic gathering in Montana. *(Painting by Olaf Seltzer; photograph by George R. Lane/Grand Lodge of Montana)*

Although the federal court system was now operating and he had been pardoned by acting governor Thomas Francis Meagher, drifter James Daniels was hanged by vigilantes in Helena in 1865. *(Montana Historical Society Research Center—Photograph Archives, Helena, Montana)*

As commander of the Division of the Missouri after 1869, General "Little Phil" Sheridan brought to the Northern Plains the brutal military tactics he had pioneered during the Shenandoah Valley campaign five years earlier. *(National Archives)*

The murder of retired fur trader Malcolm Clarke by a Piegan relative was the trigger for the Marias massacre in January 1870, which in turn paved the way for the exploration of the upper Yellowstone. *(Montana Historical Society Research Center—Photograph Archives, Helena, Montana)*

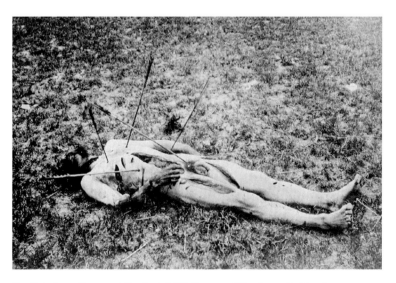

English-born Sergeant Frederick Wyllyams of the Seventh Cavalry was killed and mutilated in a battle with Cheyenne Dog Soldiers in 1867. *Harper's Weekly* later published a slightly sanitized engraving of this scene, shocking Eastern sensibilities and leading to calls for more aggressive policing of the frontier. *(Library of Congress/Smithsonian Institution)*

From the bluffs in the foreground, troops of the Second Cavalry opened fire on Piegan Chief Heavy Runner's encampment on the Big Bend of the Marias River, while Company F, commanded by Lieutenant Cheyney Doane, stormed the camp, burning the tipis and shooting their occupants. In the background are the Sweetgrass Hills, sacred to the Blackfeet. *(George Black)*

Piegan artist George Bull Child, painting in the 1930s, depicted the Marias massacre on a deer hide. Heavy Runner is the figure half-exposed in the upper center of the picture; most of the other victims are women and children. *(The L. D. and Ruth Bax Collection, 1985. 106. Photograph © Denver Art Museum 2010. All rights reserved.)*

In this 1870 engraving in *Harper's Weekly*, entitled "An Indian Peace-Offering," Piegans bring the head of Pete Owl Child, murderer of Malcolm Clarke, to General Philippe Régis de Trobriand, seated right. *(New York Public Library Digital Gallery)*

William Henry Jackson made this photograph of Nathaniel Langford in 1872, shortly after Langford's appointment as the first superintendent of Yellowstone National Park. *(Yellowstone National Park Museum Collections and Photo Archives)*

All available evidence suggests that Langford's close friend Cornelius Hedges was the man mainly responsible for the idea of creating the world's first national park. *(Montana Historical Society Research Center–Photograph Archives, Helena, Montana)*

Jackson photographed the officers at Fort Ellis, Montana Territory, in the summer of 1871. The post commander, the alcoholic Colonel Eugene M. Baker, leans against the railing, center right. Lieutenant Cheyney Doane, wearing the sash of officer-of-the-day, is fourth from the left. *(Photograph by William Henry Jackson, Yellowstone National Park Museum Collections and Photo Archives)*

The 1870 Yellowstone expedition was nominally led by the ailing General Henry Dana Washburn, who died just four months after the explorers returned to Helena. *(From* Diary of the Washburn Expedition to the Yellowstone and Firehole Rivers in the Year 1870, *by Nathaniel Pitt Langford)*

Truman Everts, at fifty-four the oldest member of the 1870 expedition, survived for thirty-seven days in the wilderness after becoming separated from the rest of the party near Yellowstone Lake. *(Montana Historical Society Research Center–Photograph Archives, Helena, Montana)*

Nathaniel Langford joined the 1872 Hayden survey of the upper Yellowstone and the Tetons. He stands here on the terraces at Mammoth Hot Springs, armed with a geologist's hammer. *(Photograph by William Henry Jackson, Yellowstone National Park Museum Collections and Photo Archives)*

Ferdinand Vandeveer Hayden, center, at the height of his fame in the 1870s. Photographer William Henry Jackson, who accompanied the geologist on several of his surveys of the West, is seated on the right. *(Scotts Bluff National Monument)*

In 1875, Cheyney Doane guided Secretary of War William Belknap on a tour of the national park. This portrait is from a published account of the trip by General W. E. Strong. *(Merrill G. Burlingame Special Collections, Montana State University)*

Doane, riding here at the head of the column, took command of the military escort to the 1871 Hayden expedition to the upper Yellowstone. *(Photograph by William Henry Jackson, Yellowstone National Park Museum Collections and Photo Archives)*

With the end of the Indian Wars, the image of the bloodthirsty savage gave way to an idealized picture of the noble Red Man. In this 1903 magazine cover, a warrior welcomes tourists to the national park, now guaranteed to be free of Indians. *(Yellowstone National Park Museum Collections and Photo Archives)*

Chief Joseph—or Thunder Traveling to the Loftier Mountain Heights—in exile with his family after the defeat of the Nez Perce in 1877 by Colonel Nelson Miles. *(Cabinet card by F. M. Sargent, Washington State History Museum)*

Crow chiefs, with their distinctive pompadours, meet with a government delegation in 1880. Medicine Crow, seated second from left, had served as a scout under Doane in 1876–1877. *(National Museum of the American Indian, Smithsonian Institution, P03423)*

named paper, quoted in de Trobriand's memoirs, reported "a terrible and fatal blow at the impudent and bloody marauders . . . When he struck, he struck so wisely and forcibly that although every band of outlaws was destroyed, not one friendly Indian was injured."[4] Where this information came from, or whether the writer believed it, is a mystery.

The same papers named three officers as the heroes of the hour: General de Trobriand, as the "head and projector" of the operation; Colonel Baker, as its "right arm"; and Lieutenant Doane, as its principal executor.

The *New North West* also singled out Doane in its weekly news roundup, which recorded the progress of civilization on the frontier and its occasional setbacks. Its February 11 edition included these snippets:

> Bozeman has a dancing school. New and handsome buildings are going up all over the city. Bozeman has a literary club.

> Ah Chow, the alleged murderer of John R. Hitzer, has been apprehended, hung at night on the Pine Tree, at Helena, and the execution attributed to the Vigilantes.[5]

> Langrishe puts on an opera bouffe on Thursday evening—Gran Duchesse, Can Can, etc.

> Lieut. Pease says the small-pox is raging fearfully among the Bloods and Piegans on the Marias, and that they are dying at the rate of six or eight per day.

> "Will the Indians remain quiet now, do you think?" asked an anxious settler of Lieutenant Doane, of the cavalry, when the expedition was returning from the Marias. "Well, I can't say," returned the Lieutenant, "but there are certainly one hundred and seventy-three very good arguments in favor of their remaining quiet, lying out on the Marias!"

In the handwritten record of his army service that Doane prepared many years later, he described himself as "First and last man in Piegan Camp

January 25th [sic] 1870. . . . Greatest slaughter of Indians ever made by U.S. Troops." Clearly he did not mean this as a criticism.

Was his statement accurate? The highest figures ever given were 220, which de Trobriand cited in one of his letters without giving a source, and 217, which was the number Joe Kipp told the Indian Claims Commission he had counted on the field.[6] But Doane's body count of 173 would certainly put the Marias massacre among the two or three worst of the Indian wars, and it is beyond a doubt the least remembered.

No one ever had a clear idea of how many Cheyenne were murdered by John Chivington at Sand Creek—the only massacre ever officially condemned by the army; estimates ranged from 69 to several hundred. On the Bear River, the best guess is that Patrick Connor killed about 250 Shoshone. On the Washita, Custer said 103, but then upped the number to 140 or more; the Cheyenne said 30 or 38, perhaps for reasons of morale. At Wounded Knee in 1890, some say 146 died; others think it was closer to 300.

But there is another point, not without significance. In each of these incidents, soldiers died in considerable numbers: 24 at Sand Creek, 21 at Bear River, 21 at Washita, 29 at Wounded Knee. Massacres, battles, call them what you will—these sound like events where people fought back. On the Marias, by contrast, there were 173 Piegan corpses, one dead soldier, and one with a broken leg.

The larger debate about the Marias—and it turned into a very large debate indeed—concerned the innocence or guilt of the victims, and how they broke down by age, sex, and state of health. General Sully, the Indian Commissioner, was the first to raise these awkward questions. Already fearing that the massacre "may possibly excite the [Blackfeet] nation to open war," he asked de Trobriand on February 1, "How many of these killed were men? It has been reported to me that there were only twenty or thirty, the rest women and children. These reports come from citizens, half-breeds, and Indians." Which just about covered every category of the population of Montana, with the exception of soldiers.

Citizens, half-breeds, and Indians? the French aristocrat wrote back on February 3, as if he had discovered something unpleasant on his shoe. He told Sully to put no stock in "idle rumors and false reports spread by some whiskey traders in [Fort] Benton . . . and by other croakers to whom the peace of the Territory and the security of its residents are of little or no weight."[7]

Next to weigh in, on February 8, was the Blackfeet agent, Lieutenant W. A. Pease. Based on information received from the Piegans themselves, Pease told Sully that 219 people had been in the camp at the time of the attack. Forty-six had survived: 18 women and 19 children under three who had been spared by the soldiers, and nine young men who escaped. Pease not only concurred with Doane's body count of 173 but broke that number down with a specificity that was matched in no other report:

> 33 were men, of these 15 only were such as are called by them young, or fighting, men; these were between the ages of twelve and thirty-seven. The remaining 18 were between the ages of thirty-seven and seventy; 8 of the latter were between the ages of sixty and seventy; 90 were women—35 between the ages of twelve and thirty-seven, and 55 between the ages of thirty-seven and seventy. The remaining 50 were children, none older than twelve years and many of them in their mother's arms.[8]

In the face of the numbers from Sully and Pease, the defense shifted. All right, perhaps there had been a significant number of women and children among the dead, but such was war. "Not an unusual event when towns are destroyed, yet sad enough," Captain Lewis Thompson of the Second Cavalry wrote in a regimental history. *Things like that we know must be/After a famous victory.*[9]

The *Chicago Tribune*, Sheridan's hometown paper, went after two controversial questions at once: the deaths of women and children, and the identity of the camp that had been hit—since de Trobriand had just acknowledged in his letter to Sully that it was not Mountain Chief's. Referring to Heavy Runner by his alternate name, Bear Chief, the *Tribune* came up with this, in which everything but the words *and* and *but* is made from whole cloth:

There is no doubt but that Bear Chief and his warriors killed
Clarke . . . He was bloodthirsty and cruel in his disposition
and exerted himself greatly to stir up feeling among his people
against the whites. . . . The Indians are reported to have fought
desperately, men, women and children joining the battle. . . .
In Indian fights, where all fight, the killing of a few women and
children is inevitable.

The paper illustrated this truism with a droll anecdote about a Dutchman
who shot an Indian during an action against the Cheyenne and was surprised to discover that she was a woman: "Beats me, dat, all now. I tot he
vas a man, he shoot so tam vell."[10]

The defense of Colonel Baker's action gained greater force when word
spread that two other Piegan subchiefs, Big Horn and Red Horn, who had
been on a list of those accused of "depredations," were among the dead, having attached themselves to Heavy Runner's camp in the usual Piegan way,
different bands mixing together promiscuously as they prepared for winter.

B y now, however, these arguments were rallying the faithful rather
than convincing the skeptics. And when Vincent Colyer, secretary
to the Board of Indian Commissioners, presented Agent Pease's information from Indian sources as a matter of established fact, the East Coast
was outraged. A verse of doggerel captured the mood of many members
of Congress and editorial writers.

> *Women and babes shrieking awoke*
> *To perish 'mid the battle smoke,*
> *Murdered, or turned out there to die*
> *Beneath the stern, gray, wintry sky.*[11]

"I only know the names of three savages upon the Plains: Colonel
Baker, General Custer, and at the head of all, General Sheridan," said the
abolitionist Wendell Phillips.[12]

"I shall wash my hands of all responsibility for this system of warfare. It cannot be justified here or before the country; it cannot be justified before the civilization of the age, or in the sight of God or man," added Congressman Daniel Voorhees of Indiana.[13]

From Montana, meanwhile, came the same kind of retort that had come from the Denver papers after Eastern condemnations of Sand Creek. The *New North West* was typical, deploring "all the namby-pamby, sniffling old maid sentimentalists of both sexes who leave most of their brains on their handkerchiefs when under excitement."[14]

Phil Sheridan was less interested in examining the charges of the critics than in suffocating them in invective. Singling out the egregious Vincent Colyer, and taking much of his language directly from the tirades he had delivered after Custer's action on the Washita, he added new pornographic flourishes.[15] The victims of the savages had not been gang-raped forty or fifty times, but fifty or sixty. Sticks had been forced up their persons after death, as well as when they were alive, and in one case far along in pregnancy. The fact that no such charge had ever been leveled against a Piegan or any other member of the Blackfeet, in more than sixty years of on-again, off-again conflict, was irrelevant. All Indians were collectively guilty of such atrocities, and anyone questioning whether a particular Indian might have been killed in error was in effect endorsing the gang-rape of white women.

William Tecumseh Sherman condemned his fellow general, Sully, for speaking out of turn, even though Sully had not communicated his doubts publicly but merely asked for the army to find out more about what had happened. Yet to his partial credit, Sherman insisted that the storm of criticism in Congress could not be wished away, only answered with hard facts. Where was Baker's formal report of the incident?

A good question. Baker had brought the cavalry back to Fort Ellis on February 6, but Sheridan heard nothing from him until more than a month later, when a bare-bones description of the action arrived. This was dated February 18, but oddly Sherman did not see it until March 8.[16] Baker's report was not sent to divisional headquarters in Chicago but to a lowly aide to de Trobriand at Fort Shaw[17]—so one inference is that de Trobriand may have dragged his feet in passing along the message.

Sherman was still not satisfied, and by now anger against the massacre had even reached the *Chicago Tribune,* the newspaper that Sheridan read every morning and up to this point a staunch propagandist for the operation on the Marias. In two successive editorials, the *Tribune* said that, "The account given by Vincent Colyer did not by any means present the worst features of the affair. There is nothing in the records of the Indian Office which surpasses the atrocities detailed in this paper." It cited Sully's "grave doubt whether the band surprised and murdered had taken any part in the late depredations" and added that "the affair is looked on at the Interior Department as the most disgraceful butchery in the annals of our dealings with Indians."[18]

Sherman demanded the facts from the three central actors in the Piegan affair—Sheridan, de Trobriand, and Baker. But each of them responded with something close to insubordination, and all three got away with it.

Sherman to Sheridan, March 12:

> I think Colonel Baker should have reported more exactly the number, sex, and kind of Indians killed; and in view of the severe strictures in Congress on this act as one of horrible cruelty to women and children, I wish you would require, by telegraph, Colonel Baker to report specifically on this point.[19]

It took ten days for Sheridan to pass along this message from his commanding officer. During that delay, he did two things, which at first blush seem contradictory.

First he brought Inspector General Hardie back into the picture, instructing him to get more information from de Trobriand.

Hardie to de Trobriand, March 16:

> State to me by telegraph if the band of Piegans struck by Baker was guilty. How do you know of their guilt? How do you presume Baker knew state, age, sex and condition of people killed.

Send for young [Horace] Clarke. Get his affidavit. I want also
Joseph Kipp's affidavit. Send them by mail.

De Trobriand to Hardie, March 20:

> The band of Piegans struck by Baker was guilty. Lots of mur-
> derers and thieves among them. . . . Baker never knew the
> state, age, sex, or condition of the Indians killed. How could
> he? . . . You request me to send for young Clarke and get his
> affidavit, and you mention that you also want Joe Kipp's affi-
> davit, but you don't say about what. Is it about the murder of
> Mr. Clarke by the Indians, and about Horace Clarke being
> treacherously shot himself by Mountain-Chief's son? Or is it
> about the papers of the father found on the bodies of some of
> the Piegans killed by our men on the Marias?[20] Is it to the ex-
> tent of the falsehood of Lieut. Pease in his report and to the
> real number of women and children killed? . . . A number [of
> women] were actually murdered by their husbands in order to
> save them (as they imagined) from the tortures among white
> men which are inflicted upon white women when captured by
> those red fiends.

This was a response of breathtaking cynicism and evasiveness. Affidavits
from the men who could testify to Baker's drunken incapacity and the mistaken identification of the camp? Open that can of worms, de Trobriand
was insinuating to Hardie, and through him to Sheridan, and everyone
would regret it.[21]

Second, Sheridan played his own most brazen trump card, implicat-
ing Sherman himself in the slaughter on the Marias as the author of its
doctrinal logic.

Sheridan to Sherman, March 18:

> The responsibility is not with the soldier, but with the people
> whose crimes necessitate the attack. During the [Civil] war,

did anyone hesitate to attack a village or town occupied by the enemy because women and children were within its limits? Did we cease to throw shells into Vicksburg or Atlanta because women and children were there?[22]

That did the trick. Sherman to Sheridan, March 24:

> It is, of course, to be deplored that some of our people prefer to believe the story of the Piegan massacre, as trumped up by interested parties at Benton, more than a hundred miles off, rather than the official report of Colonel Baker, who was on the spot, and is the responsible party. I prefer to believe that the majority of the killed at Mountain Chief's camp were warriors.[23]

Of course everyone knew by this point that it hadn't been Mountain Chief's camp at all, but Sherman must have understood the game that was being played. Perhaps at some level he was even amused by the temerity of his old comrade-in-arms in checkmating him in this way.

With full political cover from Sheridan and de Trobriand, Baker now at last played his own hand. It included an unheard-of assault by a brevet lieutenant colonel on the integrity of a full general.

Baker to Sheridan, March 27:

> I am satisfied that the following numbers approximate as nearly to the exact truth as any estimate can possibly be made; that the number killed was one hundred and seventy-three. Of these there were one hundred and twenty able men, fifty-three women and children. . . . The reports published in the eastern papers, purporting to come from General Alfred Sully, are wholly and maliciously false; if he has given authority to these slanders, I can only suppose it is that attention may be drawn away from the manifest irregularities and inefficiency that mark the conduct of Indian affairs under his direction in this Territory. . . . All the officers of this com-

mand ask at the hands of the authorities is a full and complete investigation of the campaign, and less than this cannot, in justice, be conceded to them.[24]

Baker surely knew that his demand for an investigation was a bluff no one would call. Indeed, the very next day, Sherman closed the book on the affair, writing to Sheridan, "You may assure Colonel Baker that no amount of clamor has shaken our confidence in him or his officers."[25]

For the leading men of Montana, Sherman's decision spelled relief and vindication. They assembled once again in the Helena courthouse, drafted a statement, and had it published in the *Chicago Tribune*, even though that paper had turned 180 degrees in its own view of the massacre. Montana Territory deplored the "severe and unjust censure" heaped on Baker for "the recent chastisement of the Piegan Indians on the Marias River." Such Eastern criticisms, they declared, were "based upon a misinterpretation of facts, and still more upon a misunderstanding of the true Indian character."

"After diligent investigation of the facts concerning the so-called massacre," the statement continued, the men of Helena resolved:

1. That, in our judgment, the long-continued and oft-repeated acts of murder and pillage committed by this tribe of Indians, counting among the victims some of our noblest and worthiest citizens like the lamented Angevine and Borhees,[26] and culminating in the murder of our eldest and most respected citizen, the late Malcolm Clark [sic], under circumstances of peculiar atrocity and treachery, demanded signal and exemplary punishment.

2. That the cowardly nature of the Indian renders it necessary to seek him in his camp, among his squaws and children, when confined by the rigors of the season, and fight him in his own favorite chosen style.

3. That in our opinion it is the first and highest duty of the government to effectually protect its citizens in all places, at all times, and at any cost; to encourage the hardy adventurer who seeks to develop the resources of the country, and assure to him complete safety in person, property and family; and whatever severity of retaliation is necessary to this end should not be accounted barbarity, but true kindness to those who deserve it.

4. That, in our opinion, Colonel Baker and his command discharged a disagreeable duty faithfully, and deserve the commendation and gratitude of the whole country, as they already have of every good citizen of Montana, who can now breathe, sleep, and travel with a fuller sense of security than ever before since entering the Territory.

    [. . . .]

7. That we disclaim all cruel and vindictive feeling against the Indian, but as all the past history of our country has shown him to be a robber and murderer by inclination and education, we believe our government should rigidly confine him in reservations at a distance from white settlements, and compel him to cultivate the soil and earn his bread as the Lord has commanded, by the sweat of his brow.

    Resolved, That the thanks of the people of this Territory are eminently due to Brevet Lieutenant Colonel E. M. Baker; to Brevet Brigadier General R. De Trobriand; to Major General W. S. Hancock, Lieutenant General P. H. Sheridan and General W. T. Sherman for the humane desire they have manifested in the protection of the lives of the people of this Territory, and for the determination they have evinced to make the American flag a terror to evil-doers and a protection to those who do well, and to cause it to be respected at home as well as abroad.

    Presented, on behalf of the citizens of Helena, by the chairman of the Committee on Resolutions, Cornelius Hedges.[27]

General Sully, dissident, vilified, and discredited, was still concerned. Whatever its other effects, the massacre on the Marias had left President Grant's Peace Policy in tatters. The commander of the action would ever after be known as Piegan Baker—though never to his face. So would the slaughter quieten the Blackfeet or rouse them to all-out war?[28]

He need not have worried. A Christianized Piegan named Three Persons, for his belief in the Holy Trinity, told Sully that there was no fight left in the tribe; their terror and demoralization had only grown worse with the ravages of smallpox and the death of many of the women and children who had been abandoned in Heavy Runner's camp.[29] Alexander Culbertson visited the Piegans in the Sweetgrass Hills in July and found the tribe decimated by disease. Yet to his surprise they showed no resentment toward the whites, "whom they know are the whole cause of their misfortune."[30]

The army scout Joe Kipp was overcome by remorse at the events on the Marias. Later he married Martha, or Double Strike Woman, one of the daughters of Heavy Runner, a child at the time of the massacre and one of the survivors. Kipp's reputation is still mixed among the Piegans. Some remember him as a deeply compromised figure, who went on to become a successful whiskey trader and acquired the nickname Merchant Prince of the High Missouri. Others praised him as "the strongest, truest friend that the Pikuni ever had" and "our strongest protector, our most powerful shield against the wiles of the whites."[31]

As for Pete Owl Child, whose feud with Malcolm Clarke had triggered this orgy of violence in the first place, he, too, fell victim to the white scabs about two weeks after the massacre on the Marias. "To bring him in alive was troublesome," Colonel de Trobriand wrote in his memoirs, "and finding his death too lingering, they hastened the end by cutting off his head which was brought in a bag to prove the sincerity of their desire for peace."[32]

Part Four

EXPLORERS

24

THE SPOILS OF WAR

May–August 1870

I
n early May of 1870, a month after the book was closed on all criticism of Colonel E. M. Baker, Little Phil Sheridan decided it was time to make a tour of inspection of his Western forts and offer his personal congratulations to the heroes of the Marias.

Despite his exalted rank, Sheridan had to travel rough like anyone else. He transferred from the Union Pacific to a stagecoach at Corinne, Utah, a noisy, rollicking railroad town full of gamblers, bull-whackers, and mule-skinners. From Corinne it was a sixty-six-hour overland journey to Helena, and the overnight accommodations along the way were primitive. On May 15, his third night on the road, Sheridan stopped at Parsons Bridge on the Jefferson River and bedded down in a crude log shed, roughly partitioned into a kitchen and eatery, and a stable. Another of the overnight guests was an "old mountaineer" named Atkinson, of whom nothing else is known. Over dinner, Atkinson regaled the famous general with vague, secondhand stories, gleaned from aging fur trappers, of mud pots and hot springs, petrified forests and black glass mountains, great herds of elk and pronghorn protected from hunters by their remoteness and the high altitude. Sheridan was riveted.

He arrived at Helena the following day and was greeted, after the great victory over the Piegans, "like a Roman conqueror." Cornelius Hedges welcomed the general personally and arranged for the reception in his honor to be a fund-raiser for the town's new library, of which he was president.[1] Sheridan addressed a crowd of a thousand, promising the army's enduring support for the people of Montana and predicting that the Northern Pacific Railroad, soon to become a reality, would be the key to their future prosperity. The town danced until dawn.

However, the general decided to cut short his planned inspection tour, for on his arrival in Helena he received news of the imminent outbreak of war between France and Prussia. The temptation to travel to the battlefield as an observer, accompanying the army of Kaiser Wilhelm, was too much to resist. But while he ended up staying in Helena for only two days, the conversation with Atkinson the mountaineer was fresh in his mind, and he used the time to arrange a meeting with David Folsom, Charles Cook, and William Peterson to learn more of their Yellowstone adventures the previous year.

Their accounts had already helped inspire a couple of small-bore expeditions that spring, though both had an element of farce. The day after Sheridan left town, the *Helena Herald* carried a report by one Charles Sunderlee, who claimed that he and four others had just returned from the upper Yellowstone, where they had witnessed the mass suicide of a group of thirteen Crow braves and five women who drove their raft over the Lower Falls. His account has all the finest qualities of fakelore: The Crows had no use for boats and rarely went near the water, and the tribe had no cultural tradition of suicide.[2]

At about the same time, a buckskin-clad former trapper and all-around venturesome spirit named Philetus Norris set out to make a preliminary exploration of the upper Yellowstone with the Bottler brothers (whom he described as "moral, temperate, and industrious mountaineers").[3] Norris and Frederick Bottler got as far as Electric Peak, by the present-day northern entrance to the national park. From the eleven-thousand-foot summit they scanned the country ahead of them through field glasses. But before they could proceed much farther, Bottler, who was still recovering from a grievous mauling by a grizzly bear, fell into a swollen tributary of the

Yellowstone, the Gardner, and nearly drowned. So back they went to the Bottlers' ranch.[4]

Abortive though they were, these misadventures were part of the general momentum toward a more systematic exploration of the upper Yellowstone. And having listened attentively to the men of Diamond City, Sheridan was persuaded to throw the weight of the army behind the enterprise. He wrote in his memoirs, "I authorized an escort of soldiers to go that season from Fort Ellis with a small party to make such superficial exploration as to justify my sending an engineering officer with a well-equipped expedition the next summer to scientifically examine and report upon this strange country."[5]

Nathaniel Langford had not been present in Helena to greet Sheridan; for the second year in a row, he had spent the winter in Minnesota and on the East Coast. However, before returning to Montana he stopped to pay his respects to Hancock the Superb at the army's departmental headquarters in St. Paul and outlined his plans for the summer expedition. The general expressed his strong support and promised a military escort, although his reasons seem to have been different from Sheridan's. Langford does not mention any interest on Hancock's part in geysers and mud pots, but instead says that he "expressed a desire to obtain additional information concerning the Yellowstone country which would be of service to him in the disposition of troops for frontier defense."[6]

Langford's other stop that spring was in Philadelphia. On June 1, with his passion for the Northern Pacific increasing, he and Charles Cook made a pilgrimage to Ogontz, the home of the legendary banker Jay Cooke, the main backer of the enterprise. (Cooke had named the place for an aging Huron chief who often slept in the family barn during the financier's boyhood in upstate New York.) Ogontz was perhaps the most extravagant private mansion in the country. Cooke had designed the estate himself: two hundred acres with brooks, floral walks, a deer park, an aquarium, pools and fountains, a farm. There were mock Roman ruins, a family mausoleum. Inside the vast, seventy-five-thousand-square-foot marble building there were fifty-three rooms, three hundred paintings, five hundred gas outlets, a private telegraph system, statues, tapestries, stained glass.[7] Langford was invited to stay the night.

The two men—the supplicant from the West and the tycoon who saw himself as "God's chosen instrument"—found that they had a marvelous convergence of interests. Like Phil Sheridan, Langford saw the Northern Pacific as the key to Montana's future prosperity—not to mention his own. For Cooke, the shrewd and well-connected almost-governor of the territory had the smell of an effective local propagandist. And now Langford was offering him a new enticement: the Northern Pacific, he suggested, could carry thousands of curious Easterners to view the wonders of the upper Yellowstone once they were laid bare, and he himself was proposing to lay them bare within a matter of months.[8] By early July Langford was back in Helena, ready to proceed.

The circumstances were now such that the explorers could set out with confidence, knowing that with Sheridan and Cooke behind them they had the personal support and sponsorship of two of the most powerful men in the United States. They could also rest assured that the perimeter of the great volcanic caldera was secure for the first time since white men had arrived in these latitudes.

Inside the ring of mountains, the Sheepeaters were a small and innocuous presence. To the east of the Absarokas, the Crows, despite their annoying taste for thievery, continued to profess loyalty to the army and friendly feelings toward whites in general. Farther to the East, along the middle Yellowstone, there was peace, or at least a cease-fire pro tem, with the Sioux. Down in the valley of the Wind River, Chief Washakie's Eastern Shoshone had long been hospitable to emigrants, trappers, even Mormons. To the northwest, the Flatheads, the Pend d'Oreilles, and other smaller tribes were largely Christianized and confined to their reservations. The same was true, for the most part, of the Nez Perce. To the southwest, in Utah and Idaho, the Northwestern Shoshone and the Bannock had never recovered from the trauma of the Bear River Massacre. And now the army had silenced the most persistent adversary of all—the Blackfeet, who had stood in the way of every explorer since the days of Lewis and Clark: the scourge of John Colter and the early fur trappers; an object of fear for the leading men of Helena; a menacing distraction for the soldiers newly arrived at Fort Ellis.

"Talking with parties about a Yellowstone expedition," Cornelius Hedges noted in his diary for July 8. Five days later, he conferred a masonic degree on Warren Gillette, who added his own name to the list of explorers. Two days after that, word reached Helena of General Hancock's support—a relief to Hedges, who was still more nervous than any of his fellow adventurers about an Indian threat.

By August 1 or thereabouts, Langford says, the plans had taken definite shape. The "parties" at this point numbered around twenty, but over the next couple of weeks several men begged off for one reason or another. The oddest of the dropouts was James Stuart, one of the original discoverers of gold in Montana. On the face of it he was the most dauntless of the twenty original explorers, considered by Langford to be "a man of large experience in such enterprises as that in which we were about to engage."[9] Stuart, along with Sam Hauser, had led the party of prospectors into their fatal encounter with the Crows, or Sioux, or whoever they were, in the spring of 1863.[10] Stuart remained convinced that the attackers had been Crows, and that may account for the strangely nervous tone of a letter he addressed to Langford and Hauser on August 9.

> [Benjamin] Stickney wrote me that the Yellow Stone party had dwindled down to eight persons. That is not enough to stand guard, and I won't go into that country without having a guard every night. From present news it is probable that the Crows will be scattered on all the headwaters of the Yellow Stone, and if that is the case, they would not want any better fun than to clean up a party of eight (that does not stand guard) and say that the Sioux did it, as they said when they

went through us on the Big Horn. It will not be safe to go into
that country with less than fifteen men, and not very safe with
that number.[11]

Yet Stuart was a man of mercurial temperament, and in the course of
the same three-paragraph letter, he first pulled out of the party and then
pulled in again. "I am just d———d fool enough to go anywhere that anyone else is willing to go, only I want it understood that very likely some of
us will lose our hair," he concluded. And by the time he sealed the enve-
lope, he had been given an update, presumably by Stickney, which led
him to add a PS: "Since writing the above, I have received a telegram saying 'twelve of us going certain.' Glad to hear it—the more the better. Will
bring two pack horses and one pack saddle."

But then another reversal, and this time it was definitive. Stuart received a jury summons, from which the court declined to excuse him.
"This was a sore and discouraging disappointment both to Hauser and
myself," Langford wrote, "for we felt that in case we had trouble with the
Indians Stuart's services to the party would be worth those of half a
dozen ordinary men."[12] Nonetheless, Langford and his companions took
a deep breath and decided that if it were not now, it might be never.

And so they assembled, these men of their time and their place in
history. In the end there were nine of them. "I question if there was
ever a body of men organized for an exploring expedition, more intelligent or more keenly alive to the risks to be encountered than those then
enrolled," Langford wrote.[13] Cornelius Hedges was more focused on the
strangeness of what lay ahead; were these rumored wonders real? "I think
a more confirmed set of sceptics never went out into a wilderness than
those who compose our party,"[14] he wrote in his journal.

They were men with large egos, "each of whom counted himself a host,"
said Hedges, "all unusually self-sufficient and self-reliant, and singularly
disposed to individual judgment."[15] Closely clustered in age, most of
them were freemasons; six of the nine, including all of the most notable

members of the expedition, had been leading players in the violent process of suppressing the Blackfeet and civilizing the frontier.

General Henry Dana Washburn, thirty-eight, was the titular head of the party, a man Hedges saw as having the gravitas and diplomatic skills to unite the potentially fractious group and to do so "with no articles of war to aid in the enforcement of discipline"; a man who had "touched the popular heart on the Indian question" in the wake of the Malcolm Clarke affair; a member of the Helena citizens committee that had so strenuously urged Colonel de Trobriand to chastise the Piegans.[16]

Deference to rank made Washburn the official leader and day-to-day manager of the expedition, but Langford, also thirty-eight, was its "spark plug" (in Aubrey Haines's phrase): businessman, politician, leader of the resurgent vigilantes in Helena, the man who had read the service over Clarke's grave.

Hedges was the quietest and most self-effacing of the group, another thirty-eight-year-old, Clarke's lawyer, Harvard and Yale-educated, pillar of the masonic lodge, Bible student, yet active member of the Helena vigilantes, exterminationist, and author of the citizens' resolution praising Sheridan and Baker for their salutary action on the Marias.

Hauser, thirty-seven, banker, businessman, speculator,[17] and vigilante, was also a signatory, with Washburn, of the citizens' petition to de Trobriand.

Warren Gillette, thirty-eight, the expert woodsman in the party, was a merchant, freighter, Malcolm Clarke's neighbor and friend, and another signatory to the petition.

Benjamin Stickney, thirty-one, in charge of logistics and supplies, was a Helena storekeeper, rugged outdoorsman, member of the grand jury that had indicted Pete Owl Child.

That left three.

The most surprising of them was Truman Everts. Assessor of Internal Revenue for Montana Territory until February 1870,[18] Everts had been on the point of returning to the East with his daughter Bessie, the belle of Helena, but decided at the last moment to stay and join the Yellowstone adventure. At fifty-four, he was by far the oldest member of the group.

Walter Trumbull, twenty-four, assistant to Everts, brought powerful political connections as the son of Illinois Senator Lyman Trumbull, author of the Thirteenth Amendment to the Constitution outlawing slavery.

Last, and by all accounts least of the nine, was Jake Smith, forty, former butcher, speculator, failed owner of a tannery, hustler, practical joker, a man who did not suffer fools gladly—but was often taken for one himself. He and Langford were chalk and cheese: Langford was grave, thin-skinned, took himself very seriously; Smith was exuberant, earthy, acted as if he didn't have a care in the world. Langford described him as "constitutionally unfitted to be a member of such a party of exploration."[19] But Smith came anyway, not being the kind to take no for an answer.

Which left only one question: Who would command the military escort? There was no lack of candidates among the midranking company commanders at Fort Ellis, but again, as had happened on the Marias, they were passed over in favor of the much younger Second Lieutenant Cheyney Doane, Colonel Baker's favorite. There is no written order from Baker to say that this was in recognition of the lieutenant's services against the Piegans or his ambitions as an explorer, but it's hard to avoid that inference. Yet Doane also did some extraordinary political lobbying of his own. As on countless other occasions throughout his career, he simply sidestepped the formal chain of command and went straight to the top.

On August 12, he addressed a strikingly presumptuous letter to Washburn that suggests he had already been cultivating powerful civilian patrons—businessmen and judges—as well as military ones. There was not a hint of deference.

Dear Sir

Your kind favor of the 9th ult—came yesterday—and I reply—at the first opportunity for transmittal. Judge [Hezekiah] Hosmer was correct as regards my earnest desire to go on the trip proposed—but mistaken in relation to my _free agency_ in the premise. To obtain permission for an escort will require an order from Genl Hancock—authorizing Col. Baker—to make the detail.

If Hauser and yourself will telegraph at once on rec't to Genl Hancock at Saint Paul, Minn—stating the object of the expedition & c and requesting that an order be sent to the Comdg officer at Fort Ellis, M. T. to furnish an escort of an officer and five men—it will doubtless be favorably considered—and you can bring the reply from the office when you come down or send it before—if answer comes in time. Col. Baker has promised me the detail if authority be furnished. And by your telegraphing instead of him—the circumlocution at Dist Hdqrs will be obviated. I will reimburse you the expense of the messages which should be _paid both ways_ to insure prompt attention.

I will be able to furnish Tents and camp equipage better than you can get in Helena—and I can furnish them without trouble to your whole party.

Hoping that we can make the trip in Company I have the honor to be

> Your Obdt Servant
> G. C. Doane
> Lt. 2nd Cavalry, U.S.A.

Please let me know what steps you take in the matter as soon as convenient.[20]

Events moved rapidly now. In Helena, General Washburn packed a copy of the diaries of David Folsom and Charles Cook, together with their detailed instructions on particular campsites and compass bearings, and the latest revised version of De Lacy's map.[21] At nine o'clock on the morning of August 17, a year to the day after the murder of Malcolm Clarke, the explorers gathered outside Washburn's office on Main Street, and in the afternoon they rode out of town, accompanied by the last members of the expedition—two packers, Elwyn Bean and Charles Reynolds,[22] and two cooks, "African boys," remembered only as Nute and Johnny. Each man, except presumably for the cooks and packers, carried a needle carbine, a cartridge belt, two revolvers, and a hunting knife. "When mounted and ready to start, we resembled more a band of brigands than sober men in search of natural wonders," Langford recalled.[23]

Next morning, he rode on ahead of the main party, looking to deal with some unspecified dispute that had arisen at the Masonic Lodge in Bozeman. He reached Fort Ellis on the 20th, leaving the rest of the group to catch up with him later. They took their time, spending the first night at Nick Greenish's Half-Way House; next morning, said the *Helena Herald,* "several of the party . . . were 'under the weather' and tarried in the gay Metropolis until 'night drew her sable curtain down.' "[24] On the 19th, after riding through a surprising early snowstorm, they took an elegant supper at Campbell's Hotel in Gallatin City; some of the younger members of the party (presumably Trumbull and Stickney) paid a call on certain young women of the town.[25] In Bozeman, there was more of the same: a lavish dinner hosted by two prominent local families and a musical recital by Mrs. Emma Wilson, who was gifted with such a remarkable voice that even the transient Indians clustered around to hear her sing.[26] Later that night, there was one last send-off: a champagne nightcap at the Guy House, social hub of Bozeman, with Baker, Doane, and other officers from Fort Ellis in attendance. This time the town's black barber, Samuel Lewis, provided the entertainment, accompanying his singing with guitar and banjo.[27]

Evidently there was some kind of awkwardness the next day with Colonel Baker, some misunderstanding about the size of the escort. Hedges had noted in his diary on August 15, that they had "had word from Hancock he gives us escort of a whole company."[28] But Sheridan had drawn the distinction between a "small party" that would conduct a "superficial exploration" and a professional "engineering officer who would return with a well-equipped expedition" the following year. And now Baker was insisting that he could spare no more than six men. The majority were "out in the field fighting the Indians," according to Langford; he mentions the Sioux, although that seems implausible, and there is no record of such a fight.[29] Even so, six soldiers would bring the total strength of the party (excluding packers and cooks) to fifteen—James Stuart's magic number—and Langford for one seems to have felt this was enough.[30]

> A venture with so small a number into a country infested by savages, would seem desperate, but with us, in Montana where it is not uncommon for men, singly to brave risks as daring, our outfit was regarded as sufficient. We were entirely satisfied with it—not because it was strong enough to engage in successful combat with such bands as generally prowl through that region of the Rocky Mountains, but for the reason that among our number were several men of large experience— familiar with all the tricks of Indian craft and sagacity.[31]

Doane, as familiar with these tricks as any man in the territory, named five veterans of the Piegan campaign to his detail. They were a representative cross section of the frontier army: Sergeant William Baker was a typical Irish NCO of the old school; Private George McConnell, Doane's orderly, was a farm boy from Indiana; Private Charles Moore, Canadian-born, was an amateur sketch artist; Private John Williamson was a hearty and resourceful outdoorsman; and Private William Leipler was a German maker of pianofortes.[32]

Doane was instructed to prepare a written report of the trip, something he was famously good at, and to make a map. But the modest supplies issued to the escort—thirty days' rations and one hundred rounds of ammunition per man—suggests that the physical scope of the expedition was quite narrowly circumscribed.[33] According to Walter De Lacy, General Hancock's intent was "to determine by exploration the location of the lake and falls of the Yellowstone."[34] Not a word about geysers.

And so, on the morning of August 22, 1870, joined by a black dog named Booby who belonged to one of the packers, the explorers set off for the terra incognita.

25

GRAND, GLOOMY, AND TERRIBLE

August 22–29, 1870

Like any group, the explorers had their own internal hierarchy. Washburn, Langford, and Doane were the natural leaders. Hedges, Hauser, and Gillette formed the middle tier, with Hauser's background as an engineer making him especially useful in measuring heights and calculating dimensions. The two youngest members of the group, Stickney and Trumbull, were less conspicuous, and so was Truman Everts—at least at first. Langford's nemesis, Jake Smith, played the smallest role of all, seeming to regard the whole adventure as a mobile card game. Hauser, Gillette, Stickney, and Trumbull were his poker cohorts. Hedges and Washburn joined in when a more genteel game was suggested, like whist. Hedges, Langford, and Washburn were the intellectuals of the party. Hedges whiled away the evening hours reading old copies of *Harper's* magazine by firelight; Langford liked to recite inspirational poems from memory; General Washburn offered his reflections on the Franco-Prussian War.

The majority of them kept journals.[1] Most were thumbnail notes, scribbled in a pocketbook. But Doane's ran to twenty thousand words or more, and Langford's was twice that length, although what has been handed down is actually the reconstruction, written many years later, of a diary that was lost and then found in a box of old papers. Or so Langford says. Then it was lost again, this time forever; a mystery. This tangled history means that much of what he says about the expedition has to be approached with care. How much of it is an accurate transcription of his original diary (assuming such a thing existed), and how much is ex post facto embellishment? *Caveat lector.*[2]

Langford dwells more than any of the other diarists on the internal dynamics of the group, their quirks of character, the tensions and conflicts, the particular friendships. Washburn, Doane, and above all Hedges were his own preferred companions. Doane's journal, meanwhile, is a much more scrupulous and clear-eyed account of the expedition. He had a job to do—this was an official report to the War Department—and he took it very seriously. A journal of exploration, he wrote, should be "a faithful delineation. Such a report one likes to travel by—truthful, plain, and unembellished; a simple narrative of facts observed. It gives evidence of a correct eye and a sound judgment; of capacity for the work undertaken."[3]

Doane drew above all on the knowledge of basic geology—"the fulminating star of all Sciences"—that he had acquired at the University of the Pacific. But he also describes moments of pure rapture, inspired by the Yellowstone wilderness, of the kind he had written about in his college orations. He seems to have had little interest in the rest of the party as individuals. His journal rarely mentions any of his companions by name, other than in his description of a single episode that almost cost him his sanity and even, at least in Langford's estimation, his life.

The explorers rode out of Fort Ellis at 11 A.M. and struck the well-beaten trail to the mines that had first been worked by Bridger's Pilgrims six years earlier. In one of those abrupt changes of weather that come so often in Montana, the snow of three days earlier had given way to blazing sunshine. By noon, the thermometer showed ninety-two degrees. The path took them over a gentle divide, and they made camp on the headwaters of Trail Creek, where they feasted on serviceberries they had picked along the way. To raise funds for a game of 21, Jake Smith set down his hat and invited everyone to take potshots at it from twenty yards, a quarter a shot.[4] Langford stood guard that first night with Hedges. "I am especially pleased at being assigned to duty with so reliable a coadjutor," he noted, "a man who can be depended on to neglect no duty."[5] Smith complained that posting guard was a waste of time.

The second day brought them into the broad, radiant expanse of Paradise Valley, and they rode as far as the Bottlers' ranch, across the river from the Emigrant mines. All of the diarists struggled to convey the majesty of the country, the meandering river backed by the unbroken, snow-capped wall of the Absarokas, with lightning and hailstorms dancing over Emigrant Peak, broken by sudden flashes of sunlight that illuminated every crevice, gully, and sparkling stream. Hedges likened the silhouette of one mountain to a crouching bear, another to a sphinx. Hauser was lost for words; the best he could manage was "cenery supurb."

As they rode through the glacier-sculpted valley, Doane made his first notes on the geology of the surrounding mountains.[6] "Approaching the river," he wrote, "the country became more and more volcanic in appearance, with large masses of trachyte lava cropping out from the high ridges." Largely trachyte and andesite, the Absarokas were born of debris from the great volcanic eruptions of the Eocene, between 40 million and 50 million years ago. To the north, the 80-mile-long range shades into the 12,000-foot Beartooth Plateau; to the south, the sheer breccia cliffs that stood in the way of the Raynolds-Hayden-Bridger expedition in 1860 give way to the Wind River Range, which soars even higher. The volcanic rocks of the Absarokas weather into soils that are rich in magnesium, calcium, iron, and potassium and efficiently store water and nutrients, and Doane remarked on the lush greenery in the foothills and the dense forests of pine on the upper slopes.

On their way upriver, the party divided for the first time, with Doane and Washburn going ahead and keeping an eye out for Indians. But it was Hauser and Stickney, riding out to hunt antelope, who spotted them: a hundred or more Crows watching the pack train from the shelter of a high bluff. The sighting triggered all of Langford's old instincts for drama.

This early admonition of our exposure to hostile attack . . .
has renewed in our party the determination to abate nothing
in our vigilance, and keep in a condition of constant preparation. With our long-range rifles and plenty of ammunition, we
can stand off 200 or 300 of them, with their less efficient
weapons, if we don't let them sneak up on us in the night. If
we encounter more than that number, then what? The odds
will be against us that they will "rub us out," as Jim Stuart
says . . . for me to say that I am not in hourly dread of the Indians when they appear in large force, would be a braggart
boast.[7]

That night, the Indians vanished, driven off by a rainstorm, Langford
thought. Doane was unperturbed by the incident. They were Crows; at
worst, horse thieves. Langford was not entirely reassured, especially
when the Bottlers reported that there was an encampment of twenty-five
lodges farther up the valley. And he implied, oddly, that it was only that
evening, in the face of the Indian menace, that General Washburn was
elected leader of the expedition.[8]

It was not the easiest of nights. The guards fretted about the Crows;
the rain hammered down; and everyone had to sleep "heads and tails" in
the large tent that Doane had brought from Fort Ellis. Everts was laid up
sick—too many serviceberries on Trail Creek, Hedges thought, or perhaps it was the corn they had eaten at the Bottlers. But their hosts were
endlessly hospitable, even if none of the diarists could agree on how to
spell their name.[9] But Bottler is the one that stuck.

Next afternoon, when the rain finally stopped, the explorers set off
again, leaving the feverish Everts behind to recover and catch up with
them later. Doane took stock of the country around them and was greatly
impressed. He noted that the Bottlers and the miners were no longer the
only residents of the valley. Other small settlements had sprung up, and
cattle were grazing freely on the rich bunchgrass. The soil was fertile, and
there were limitless possibilities for irrigation. The residents told him that
the winters were exceptionally mild by Montana standards.

The going was easy at first, but became more arduous as the walls of what was later known as Yankee Jim Canyon[10] closed in on the river, forcing them to ride in single file, high above the thunderous green rapids. There were all sorts of new geological features for Doane to catalogue along the way, from the outcrops of ancient granite in the canyon itself—Precambrian rocks that are some of the oldest in North America—to a vertical red stratum of Mesozoic sedimentary rock, exposed by the erosion of softer material, that he wrongly supposed to be cinnabar. Surprisingly they did not stop to take a close look at this striking phenomenon, but they gave it a name that is still used today: the Devil's Slide.[11]

Doane had an eye for the smallest details: Indian sign, the abandoned prospect holes of miners, fragments of petrified wood and obsidian, clumps of wild cherry trees gnawed and broken by grizzly bears, small riverbank cedars "yielding most beautiful material for small cabinet work, and of a nature susceptible of an exquisite polish." The fishermen in the party—Hedges seems to have been especially skilled—caught large cutthroat trout at will and savored them for supper. "Grasshoppers are their peculiar weakness," Doane wrote, "and using them for bait, the most awkward angler can fill a champagne basket in an hour or two."

The following evening, August 25, after riding across sagebrush and alkali flats that offered little nourishment for the horses, they pitched camp at the confluence of the Yellowstone and the Gardner rivers, where Fred Bottler had come close to drowning in the spring. Two wandering hunters joined them for the night. Four days out of Fort Ellis, the expedition had now reached the northern gateway of the future national park.

Next morning they forded the Gardner. Even though it was late summer, normally a time of low water, the small, boulder-strewn river was in spate from the recent rains, and several of the pack animals were nearly knocked off their feet. Crossing the Gardner meant that the explorers would entirely miss one of the most dramatic sights of the upper Yellowstone—the "mysterious mounds" of Mammoth Hot Springs—

even though they were only five miles away. Instead they headed eastward, using the Yellowstone as their compass.

Once again the party split in two, this time for the whole day.[12] Doane left camp early with Truman Everts and the resourceful Private Williamson. The three men rode for several miles over what the lieutenant described as "a high rolling prairie" until they struck a heavy Indian trail leading upriver. They came upon an abandoned colt, a further indication of the proximity of the Crows, and eventually, near a small lake, they spotted an abandoned encampment of fifteen wickiups. The plateau around the camp had been recently burned—by the Indians, Doane thought, "to drive away the game," although it might just as well have been the result of a lightning strike.

For the remaining members of the expedition it was a singularly tedious day. They cut away from the bend of the big river and took a second, less distinct Indian trail, which Langford immediately regretted. Doane seemed to have taken the easier, if longer, of two trails, one that the Crows used for their families and their heavily laden packhorses. The main group was following a more direct but difficult route which, Langford surmised without any particular evidence, "the war parties use in making their rapid rides." This forced the riders and the pack train to cross several granite ridges and hack their way through heavy timber. No one found much to like in the landscape. It was "very rough and destitute of beauty," wrote Hedges. "Country very rough and barren has a little the appearance of the bad lands of the Mo river," said Gillette. Someone called it the "Valley of Desolation." They made only six miles that day before halting, frustrated and exhausted. Langford and Hauser rode out from camp and finally located Doane's trail, but darkness was coming in and it was too late to follow.[13]

The lieutenant, too, found the journey taking on a more somber character that day, though for different reasons. He, Williamson, and Everts were the only ones to see the Black Canyon of the Yellowstone, which takes its name from the dark outcrops of gneiss and schist, metamorphosed remnants of Precambrian rock. For the first time, the objective tone of Doane's journal dissolved in the emotion of the moment. Staring down into the canyon, he was overwhelmed. It was everything he had yearned for in his college essays and orations.

> Standing on the brink of the chasm, the heavy roaring of the imprisoned river comes to the ear only in a sort of hollow hungry growl, scarcely audible from the depths, and strongly suggestive of demons in torment below ... Everything beneath has a weird and deceptive appearance. The water does not look like water, but like oil. . . . In the clefts of the rocks down, hundreds of feet down, bald eagles have their eyries, from which we can see them swooping still farther into the depths to rob the ospreys of their hard-earned trout. It is grand, gloomy, and terrible: a solitude peopled with fantastic ideas, an empire of shadows and of turmoil.[14]

After leaving the rim of the Black Canyon, Doane's group had struck the old Bannock Trail, which made for an easy ride across the northern edge of Blacktail Deer Plateau, an open, rolling expanse of grass and sagebrush dotted with ponds and patchy groves of pine and aspen.

Wildflowers were everywhere. Doane did not name them, but the end of August in Yellowstone would have meant late-blooming species— groundsel, goldenrod, Engelmann's aster, all splashing the ground with shades of yellow that echo the first tinge of color on the aspens. The fall rut was just beginning, bull elk shedding their velvet, spraying urine, clashing antlers; pronghorn antelope building their harems; grizzlies foraging for late berries and pine nuts, digging up squirrel caches, and starting to think about building their dens for hibernation. Private Williamson brought down a pronghorn, dressed it, and left it on the trail for Langford's group to find.

Doane's little group continued for another five or six miles, joined again by the two hunters they had met on the Gardner, skirting the confluence with the East Fork of the Yellowstone—today's Lamar River— and across the aptly named Pleasant Valley, until at last, near dark, they came to a flat piece of ground by a stream that cascaded vertically into the big river between towering pinnacles of rock. Doane called it Hot Spring Creek, and the evening breeze brought him the first whiff of sulfur.[15]

I n the morning, the lieutenant had plenty of time to investigate the rotten-eggs smell wafting up the creek bed from the Yellowstone while he waited for Langford and others to catch up. He rode over to the Lamar first, noting "diminished volcanic action, calcareous mounds being frequently seen, which had originated in the action of hot springs." Following the precipitous Indian trail to the mouth of Hot Spring Creek he found a series of bubbling seeps that contained more sulfur than they could carry in solution and were surrounded by bright yellow in-crustations. He measured their temperature; some were boiling, others cool.

Moving downriver, Doane studied the unique configuration of the Narrows, the lower mile or two of the Grand Canyon of the Yellowstone, a dramatic, multicolored layer cake spanning several different geological eras separated by hundreds of millions of years. Rising from the lower part of the perpendicular canyon walls were eroded columns and spires of volcanic breccia, as ancient as the Absarokas; above, twin rows of hex-agonal jointed basalt columns, the product of cooling and contracting lava flows from the second eruption of the Yellowstone supervolcano about 1.3 million years ago, sandwiched between broad bands of river sediment, and the whole thing topped off with a shallow frosting of gla-cial till. Doane ascribed the brilliant yellow coloration of the canyon to an excess of sulfur, but this was one of the rare occasions when his college geology studies let him down: In fact the rock is hydrothermically altered volcanic rhyolite, also known as limonite.[16]

Sometime in the early afternoon the main party straggled in, saddle-sore, a little cranky. The horses had been unruly, spooked by the linger-ing smoke from the fires on the Blacktail Deer Plateau. Gillette's packhorse had broken loose in the night and charged through the camp, entangling Langford in its lariat and dragging him along the ground for twenty yards until he slammed his head into a log, fortunately a rotten one. Washburn had been on guard duty and now seemed "somewhat fatigued," Langford wrote—a first hint, perhaps, of the general's frailty. They all needed a day off, and the campsite Doane had chosen, perched high above the Yellowstone and overhung by a beetling cliff, was a good place for some rest and recreation.[17] Truman Everts named it Camp Comfort, and the party stayed there for two days. Hedges and Gillette kept them well-supplied with big trout. Thanks to the hunters, a side of venison sizzled over the fire. Jake Smith, inevitably, pulled out a deck of cards.

On the morning of August 28, the two hunters made their farewells, off in pursuit of game and gold. A quarter of a mile upstream, they crossed the Yellowstone by the old Bannock Ford, where a small island divides the river into two shallow channels—the same route John Colter had presumably followed in 1807. The Crows had gone that way a short time earlier, Doane noted, with not a sign of hostility from first sighting to last.

After the day of rest at Camp Comfort, there was a palpable change in the mood of the expedition, a shifting of gears. There had been curiosities and minor adventures and mishaps during the first week; now there was spectacle, wonder, and revelation.

While he waited for the others to come into camp, Doane clambered his way upstream along the narrow, rocky gorge of Hot Spring Creek until he reached its vertical plunge over what he called an "amygdaloid ledge"—a shelf of basalt in which minerals have been deposited in the almond-shaped gas bubbles trapped in the cooling volcanic rock. On either side of the fall, eroded spires and pinnacles as much as a hundred feet tall, "very friable, crumbling under slight pressure." Doane was entranced by these sentinel rocks, by the icy rush of the stream, by the dense, green carpeting of moss that flourished in the clouds of spray. "Nothing can be more chastely beautiful than this lovely cascade, hidden away in the dim light," he wrote in his journal.

The others were similarly enthralled when they saw the waterfall the following day. They named it, measured it, and Private Moore sketched it—the first of a number of crude, schematic drawings he made that would have a significant impact on the outside world in the months after the expedition returned. Members of the party used a variety of methods to determine the height of the falls. Benjamin Stickney and Bean the packer lowered a stone plummet, and came up with 105 feet. Gillette said 113. Hauser, the trained engineer, used triangulation, assisted by Langford, and estimated 115.[18]

Washburn's description of the rocks surrounding the falls—"like some old castle with its turrets dismantled but still standing"—suggested the name they finally came up with, after a debate that prompted a mild, nineteenth-century kind of locker-room humor. The rule had been that no member of the party should name any natural feature after himself. Trumbull had proposed Minaret Falls, logical enough, and that carried the initial vote. But Hauser deemed this a covert violation of the ground rules; Trumbull was known to have a sweetheart in St. Louis named Minnie Rhett. Hauser countered with Tower Fall, and that carried the recount. Trumbull and others groused later that this was not as innocent as it sounded, because Hauser himself was enamored of a young lady in the States by the name of Miss Tower. But their objections were overruled, and Langford never could make up his mind who was telling the truth, if anyone.[19]

Not done with naming, they turned their attention next to a grotesquely misshapen column of volcanic breccia, sixty feet tall. They called it the Devil's Hoof, Langford wrote, "from its supposed similarity to the proverbial foot of his Satanic Majesty." Now they had the Devil's Slide and the Devil's Hoof, and many more would follow in the same vein—Devil's Den, the Devil's Thumb, the Devil's Cut, the Devil's Kitchen, and all manner of allusions to Hell.[20] Several of the diarists associated this with the fakelore of Indian superstition. To Doane, the tribes' fear of going near the upper Yellowstone was one reason for his complacency about the risk of hostile encounters. Trumbull linked this explicitly to Christian theology. "I would rather suppose," he wrote, "[the Indian] would give [the thermal features] a wide berth, believing them sacred to Satan."

Later, Langford and Hedges came upon a basin of active springs. The largest, a good twenty feet across, was an unpleasant yellowish-green color and bubbled furiously:

> The spring lying to the east of this, more diabolical in appearance . . . has suggested the name, which Hedges has given, of "Hell-Broth springs;" for, as we gazed upon the infernal mixture and inhaled the pungent sickening vapors, we were impressed by the idea that this was a most perfect realization of Shakespeare's MacBeth [sic]. It needed but the presence of Hecate and her weird band to realize that horrible creation of poetic fancy, and I fancied the "black and midnight hags" concocting a charm around this horrible cauldron.[21]

For the Victorian imagination, however, there was always a fine line between the sublime and the diabolical. "We feel that we have been very near the presence of the Almighty," Langford wrote a couple of days later. And Washburn quoted (inaccurately) from Psalm 8:4, which is devoted to the puniness of man in the face of the infinite: "When I behold the work of Thy hands, what is man that Thou art mindful of him?"[22] In the words of a modern environmental writer, "Satan's home had become God's own creation."[23]

After leaving Tower Fall the previous summer, Folsom and Cook had crossed the Yellowstone at the Bannock Ford and wasted several tedious days slogging across Specimen Ridge and the Mirror Plateau before they reached the Grand Canyon. They had urged Washburn to scout a more direct route that kept to the west side of the river, and while the rest of the group continued to poke around Tower Fall, off he rode, recovered now from his fatigue, beating a path that took him along the densely timbered flank of an imposing mountain. When he finally reached the rocky summit, four or five hundred feet above the snow line, he had a panoramic view of the landscape that lay before them, with the river winding its way northward from the sparkling sheet of Yellowstone Lake, fifteen or twenty miles distant.

A larger group went up the mountain on the 29th, all but Hedges, Everts, and Smith—and Washburn, who had already made the ascent.[24] Hedges was especially frustrated at being left behind. The problem was his horse; the miserable animal had been giving him trouble ever since leaving Helena. It had sore feet. It tired easily. It fell down for no apparent reason. Near the Gardner River, Hedges had become so incensed at the beast that he beat it with a fishing rod.

It had been a cold and uncomfortable night, with the water freezing in camp, but by noon, when they reached the top, it was fifty degrees. As at Tower Fall their estimates of the altitude varied: anything from 9,800 feet (Langford) to 10,700 (Hauser). Doane said 9,966.[25] But there was no disagreement this time over the name, or over the need to break the expedition's no-naming rule: It would be Mount Washburn.

Twenty miles away, through a gap in the rocks, they could see a tall column of steam rising several hundred feet above the trees. "We had all heard fabulous stories of this region and were somewhat skeptical as to appearances," Doane said. A forest fire? But then someone remarked that the steam was rising in regular puffs, and they realized what they were seeing. A rousing cheer went up.

Yet for all the excitement, most of the descriptions they left, with the exception of Doane's, were strangely perfunctory. They wrote down the basic elements of the view—the diagonal slash of the Grand Canyon, the forests, the lake. Perhaps they were simply left speechless. "The view from the summit is beyond all adequate description," said Doane, although he then proceeded to describe it with a mix of emotion and scientific insight that took up several pages of his journal. There were pillars of smoke and steam everywhere. It reminded him of "the view . . . from the Alleghanies [sic], where they overlook iron and coal districts, with all their furnaces in active operation, save that one looks in vain here for the thrifty towns, country villas, steamboats, and railroad depots."

He saw that he was standing on the broken rim of an almost circular plateau. He scanned its mountainous perimeter: the Absarokas, the Tetons, the Madison and Gallatin ranges, a vast chain of rock broken at intervals for the passage of rivers. Alone among the explorers, it seems, he knew exactly what he was seeing. "[A] single glance at the interior slopes of the ranges shows that a former complete connection existed," he reported, "and that the great basin has been formerly one vast crater of a now extinct volcano."[26]

26

NINE NIGHTS WITHOUT SLEEP

August 29–September 3, 1870

How much did Doane actually know about the inner workings of volcanoes, and about the reason for the plumes of steam he saw belching from the ground? Probably very little. In 1870, no one had a clue about continental drift, that the sphere of Earth was formed by a collection of plates slipping and sliding around on a bed of plasticized rock fifty miles or more beneath the surface; or about magma chimneys and chambers, or supervolcanoes.

Doane knew a caldera when he saw one, but he had no idea that this one had been formed by the latest in a long string of major eruptions of the volcanic hot spot that now lies beneath the upper Yellowstone. The first of these occurred about 16.5 million years ago, in northern Nevada and southeastern Oregon. But since then, the North American continent has slipped steadily southwestward, and the "bow-wave" of the hot spot has moved northeast along the Snake River plain.[1] It reached the Yellowstone area a little over two million years ago, since when it has erupted three times. The first of these eruptions, the so-called Huckleberry Ridge event, was probably the biggest volcanic event in the history of the planet, swallowing entire mountain ranges whole and creating the Island Park caldera, to the west of the Yellowstone Plateau. The second, the Mesa Falls eruption, happened about 700,000 years after that and left a smaller caldera on the Henry's Fork of the Snake River. Doane had seen both of these calderas on his ride from Cheyenne to Fort Ellis a year earlier.

The view from the top of Mount Washburn was the result of the third great Yellowstone eruption, the Lava Creek Event, 640,000 years ago, a mere blip in geologic time. Lava Creek had spewed out vast volumes of magma and superheated liquid ash, vaporizing everything that lay in its path. The roof of the crater had imploded, dropping a thousand feet and leaving a smoking pit almost fifty miles wide. Yellowstone Lake was the most visible result. The plateau that stretched away between Doane and the lake, including what would later be called Hayden Valley, was the remnant of a larger original lake, smoothed out over the millennia by continuing flows of volcanic rhyolite and three successive waves of glaciation.

It's been said that geology was the "fashionable science" in the United States in the middle decades of the nineteenth century.[2] Wealthy patrons supported the work of prominent geologists like Ferdinand Vandeveer Hayden, who had tried and failed to reach the upper Yellowstone in 1860. By 1867, when Hayden traveled to Nebraska to launch the new Geological Survey of the Territories, the federal government had thrown its full weight behind the new discipline. People flocked to lectures on the subject in New York, Boston, and Philadelphia. Sophisticated Victorian homes prized display cabinets full of rocks and mineral samples.

However, science was still struggling to break free of religious dogma. When Doane was a schoolboy in the 1850s, it's quite likely that his family Bible would have carried the detailed calculations of the date of the creation by the seventeenth-century Irish Archbishop James Ussher, who established that God had begun his great work on the evening of October 22, 4004 B.C., and completed it on the following day, a Sunday. Until the late eighteenth century, European scientists had generally assumed that all rocks were formed by the precipitation of sediment, perhaps in the wake of Noah's Flood. But by studying the Highland Boundary Fault, the Scottish physician and farmer James Hutton came up with the theory that the interior of Earth was hot, and that the formation of rocks was the result of this intense inner heat. The debate he sparked became known as Plutonism versus Neptunism. Hutton was also the first to advance the notion of deep time, the idea that Earth had taken millions of years to reach its present state. But he was ignorant of volcanoes, geysers, and hot springs, there being none to examine in the Scottish highlands.

The great German naturalist Alexander von Humboldt took matters a step further in the first decade of the nineteenth century. He spent five years in the Americas, burning his leather boots in the ascent of active volcanoes, figuring out that the cause of altitude sickness was the lack of oxygen at high elevations, and evolving his own, sometimes idiosyncratic, theories about volcanism. In 1805, after studying (and naming) the "Avenue of Volcanoes" in Ecuador, Humboldt reported that volcanic eruptions disgorged "an innumerable quantity of fish" (a certain species of bewhiskered catfish, to be exact). "Volcanoes vomiting fish is such a common phenomenon," he wrote, "and so well-known among the local inhabitants, that there can not be the slightest doubt of its authenticity."[3] He did admit, however, that while many people had told him these stories, he had never personally witnessed such a thing.

Catfish aside, Humboldt eventually developed more lasting insights into the nature of volcanoes. These fell naturally into linear groups, he observed, and it could therefore be reasonably surmised that they followed the course of vast subterranean fissures. He also showed conclusively that volcanic rock had igneous origins. Darwin called him "the greatest scientific traveler who ever lived."

Darwin was also hugely impressed by the work of Charles Lyell, the foremost geologist of the middle third of the century, author of the classic *Principles of Geology* and a close and influential friend. Like Hutton, Lyell was a Scot, and he picked up where his compatriot had left off, basing most of his theoretical insights about volcanoes on his study of Etna and Vesuvius. He was much more militant about Plutonism than Hutton had been, announcing that his ambition was "freeing the science from Moses."[4] Darwin took a copy of the first volume of the *Principles* with him on the voyage of the *Beagle* and referred to it constantly.

In the 1840s Lyell traveled widely in the United States, becoming something of a celebrity. An amateur geologist like Doane, or a generally educated man like Langford, would likely have had some passing familiarity with his ideas. Lyell not only confirmed Hutton's idea that Earth was shaped by vast, infinitesimally slow-moving forces; he showed that these were still in operation. The present is the key to the past: That was Lyell's maxim. Looking out over the Yellowstone caldera, Doane had the perfect living illustration. Here was not only the proof of millions of years of titanic subterranean energy, but the steaming, smoking evidence of a continuing process.

The upper Yellowstone had all the right conditions for hydrothermal activity—geysers, hot springs, mud pots, steam vents or fumaroles, and the like—and on a tremendous scale. There was volcanic heat close to the surface; thanks to the high altitude and the surrounding mountain ranges that channeled westerly storm systems to the Yellowstone Plateau, there was plenty of water, mainly in the form of heavy winter snows; and there was a complex underground plumbing system, a labyrinth of fractures and faults that allowed the hot water to percolate and circulate between the surface and the depths.

Yet the geysers that Doane could see from Mount Washburn had been as much of a riddle to early nineteenth-century science as the volcanoes with which they were associated. Small areas of hydrothermal activity were scattered all around the world, but for as long as the upper Yellowstone remained unexplored, the only practicable opportunity for large-scale geyser research had been in Iceland: Not surprisingly, the word *geyser* comes from the Icelandic and Old Norse *geysa,* to gush. European tourists as well as scientists came to the island in droves in the early 1800s, although they put an end to much of the gushing by dumping countless rocks and large quantities of other trash into the mouths of the giant Geysir and the nearby Strokkur ("to churn"). The tales these travelers told made their way across the Atlantic, and a few adventurous Americans went to see the spectacle for themselves. By the time educated men like Langford and Doane heard Jim Bridger's descriptions of waterspouts as high as flagpoles, they immediately had Iceland in their minds as a point of reference.

Whatever Doane knew about geysers, Langford at least seems to have been familiar with the basics—or at least was by the time he wrote his account of the Yellowstone expedition the following year for *Scribner's Monthly*.[5] He reeled off the names of half a dozen European authorities, from the Swedish Bishop Uno von Troil of Uppsala to the great British botanist and explorer Sir Joseph Hooker. Perhaps he had read the most recent edition of Lyell's *Principles,* which had summarized the observations of these and other scientists. Langford wound up his exegesis with a description of the most recent discoveries by the German chemist Robert Bunsen, who was later honored with the name of a mountain near Mammoth Hot Springs and memorialized in every high school science class. Bunsen had gone to Iceland to study volcanoes after the 1845 eruption of Mount Hekla and stayed on to study the island's geysers. His notion was that the temperature of the water in a geyser tube varied at different depths; the longer it boiled, the more its "molecular cohesion" was increased. As the hottest water rose through the column, pressure built up until it was relieved by a sudden explosive release of steam—conditions that Bunsen later reproduced in his laboratory.

All these scientific advances were European in origin. American geologists were more empirical than theoretical, more generalists (or on occasion dilettantes) than specialists. Hayden, a geologist-paleontologist with more than a passing knowledge of medicine, botany, and biology, was the classic type. He did have some major epiphanies (notably a rough recognition of the geological process of uplift now known as the "Exhumation of the Rockies"), but he was mainly a cataloguer, a describer, a popularizer. Much like Langford, and much like the Army Corps of Topographical Engineers, Hayden saw the exploration of the West as a practical matter; the main purpose in understanding its geology was to map its potential for material development. Was there coal? Were there precious metals? Was the topsoil suitable for crops? Was there good grazing land? Would the topography favor a railroad?

At the same time, the Creationists and the Ussherites did not give up without a fight. How could these Western landscapes, with their constant intimations of God's handiwork, be explained by the blind, soulless processes of rock formation? Geologic time made no more sense to them than did Darwin's theory of evolution.

Both schools of thought, no matter how irreconcilable they may sound, were in fact represented in the great explorations of the West. Painters and poets had begun to join these expeditions, striving for a better understanding of the spiritual relationship between man and the wildness of nature. Albert Bierstadt celebrated the glories of Yosemite; Thomas Cole, a deeply religious man, painted ecstatic scenes in which Adam and Eve moved through a shadowed canyon that might have been the approach to Tower Fall.

All of these cultural currents were present in the diaries of the 1870 Yellowstone explorers. Doane described and catalogued what he saw, with never a mention of the divine. Washburn quoted the Psalms; Hedges contemplated the Grand Canyon of the Yellowstone and his heart gave thanks to God; Langford, for all the practicality of his character, wrote, "I can scarcely realize that in the unbroken solitude of this majestic range of rocks, away from civilization and almost inaccessible to human approach, the Almighty has placed so many of the most wonderful and magnificent objects of His creation."[6]

Langford had reckoned that the great falls of the Yellowstone were still two or three days' ride from Mount Washburn, but it turned out to be much less, and by the following evening, August 30, the party had reached an overhanging ledge of black rock at the top of a craggy ravine and were staring down into the Grand Canyon. Splitting up into pairs, as they often did, they spent two full days exploring it. Each man groped for his own way of expressing and encompassing what he was seeing, with the exception of the inimitable Jake Smith, who considered the view for half an hour before declaring, "Well, boys, I have seen all there is, and I am ready to move on."[7]

Doane made the descent twice, once with his orderly, Private McConnell. They marveled at the agility of bighorn sheep, which clambered around on naked pinnacles of rock. McConnell shot one, while the lieu-

EMPIRE OF SHADOWS

305

tenant made his usual meticulous catalogue of geological features, very much in the Hayden manner. Along the bed of Cascade Creek, which tumbles down a steep ravine into the Grand Canyon, he found "an infinite variety of volcanic specimens, quartz, feldspar, mica, granites, lavas, basalts, composite crystals, in fact everything from asbestos to obsidian." He scrutinized the V-shape gash of the canyon itself, cut by the sheer force of the water hammering away at the thermally weakened rock, so different from the broad U of a valley sculpted by glaciers. The walls were gray, white, and shockingly yellow, with streaks of red, black, and green, and jets of steam hissing out of cracks. He and Private McConnell explored downstream for several miles, and it was dark by the time they emerged. Their horses had to flounder through a chest-deep swamp before they finally reached camp at eleven that night, exhausted.

Langford and Hedges, habitual companions, spent much of the time lying flat on a rock at the lip of the canyon. Faced with this "stupendous climax of wonders," Langford wrote, "I realized my own littleness, my helplessness, my inability to cope with or even comprehend the mighty architecture of Nature." Hedges was terrified, as he admitted later in the *Helena Herald:* "I must confess to an uncontrollable shrinking and shaking of limbs that forbade all approach to the verge of these points except by crawling at full length extended." At the Upper Falls, the din of the river inspired wild fancies in him: "The uproar of the waters through this part of the course, reminded me of the wild chant of the Indian before starting out on the warpath. It is the death song before the final leap."[8] Langford calmed him with a line of poetry—"A thing of beauty is a joy forever." (The author slipped his mind, but he looked it up later: It was Keats.)

There was some disagreement over which set of falls was more magnificent. Doane and Hauser preferred the Upper Falls, despite their smaller drop. Doane said that, "In scenic beauty the upper cataract far excels the lower." Hauser declared it "probably the prettiest in the world." Langford and Hedges voted for the Lower Falls, as most visitors probably would today. The Upper Falls were ravishing, Langford acknowledged, but they were "greatly excelled in grandeur and magnificence" by the lower.

The explorers tried to measure both sets of falls, of course; they measured everything. This time there was greater consensus. Everyone agreed that the plunge of the Upper Falls was 115 feet. As for the Lower Falls, the general opinion was 350. Only Langford begged to differ. After three successive lengths of twine had snapped from abrasion against the canyon walls, he finally managed to lower a stone to the bottom. His estimate, more accurate, was 320.[9]

Feet and inches alone could not do justice to the sight of the falls, however, and they also reached for comparisons. For Hedges, it brought back memories of his birthday trip to the Great Falls of the Missouri with Malcolm Clarke and Governor Meagher in 1865. Trumbull tried mathematical calculations of their height and volume relative to the American Falls at Niagara and the Vernal Falls in Yosemite.[10] Doane, meanwhile, strove rather clumsily for metaphors and abstractions.

> Thus the impression on the mind conveyed by Niagara may be summed up as "overwhelming power;" of the Yosemite as "Altitude;" of the Shoshone Fall, in the midst of a desert, as "going to waste." So the Upper Falls of the Yellowstone may be said to embody the idea of "Momentum," and the Lower Fall of "Gravitation."

Whether he had actually seen any of these other great waterfalls is doubtful. Perhaps he had been to Yosemite, one hundred miles or so from his childhood home in California.[11]

For the first time—or at least for the first time in writing—the explorers also sensed the future potential of this wonderland. Langford looked at the Upper Falls and imagined them spanned by a bridge, "crowded with happy gazers from all parts of our country." Hedges predicted that the falls and the canyon were "surely destined at no distant day to become a shrine for a world-wide pilgrimage."

On they rode, and the curiosities continued. Over the next three days, they saw sights that were as much nature's freak show as nature's miracle, the kind of things that would make those future pilgrims laugh as well as gasp. The going was easier, away from the river and over open, rolling country. Doane understood that they were crossing an ancient lake bed, where the clay soil favored meadow vegetation. Large herds of elk browsed in the middle distance. Trumpeter swans and other waterfowl glided along the Yellowstone, which now ran shallow and placid.

Six miles brought them to a collection of ash-colored mounds, dead geysers, which they called the Crater Hills. The form of one reminded Hedges of "Laplanders [sic] snow huts." The ground around them smoked and steamed. Within the space of half a mile there were dozens of bubbling hot springs and burping pools of mud. One sulfurous spring belched out steam with a sound that brought to mind a Missouri riverboat laboring over a sandbar. Some of the springs ran clear; others were tinted blue, pink, yellow, and brown, an indication either of their mineral content or, as we know today, of communities of heat-loving organisms—thermophiles and hyperthermophiles.[12] The kaolinite clay in the mud pots, meanwhile, was composed of rock that had been dissolved by sulfuric acid, and its consistency varied according to how much rain or snow there had been recently. By now, late summertime shading into fall, they were a thick mush that Hedges and Langford—like Folsom and Cook before them—compared to hasty pudding.

It was "a system of nature's chemical works on the grandest scale," Doane wrote. The expanses of ash-white crust around the springs were the first significant deposits the explorers had seen of sinter—dissolved and redeposited volcanic silica, also known as geyserite. There were also vast quantities of pure yellow crystalline sulfur; a man could gather a hundred tons of the stuff without breaking a sweat, Doane said. While Langford and Hedges imagined tourists, he saw a bright industrial future for the Crater Hills, predicting that, "The continuous supply will one day be turned to account in the manufacture of acids on a large scale." (Trumbull wrote later, more tongue-in-cheek, that there was enough brimstone here to supply all the match factories in the world.)

There was a want of good grass for the horses in the Crater Hills, so the explorers rode back toward the river looking for a campsite. For the second night in a row the temperature dipped below zero, but the next day brought a fresh store of exotic sights. Near the riverbank there was a magical grotto, its arched mouth lined with moss and brilliant metallic deposits of green, red, and black, from which waves of clear water pulsed every ten seconds or so. Hauser called it the Cave Spring, but the name didn't stick; it later became the Dragon's Mouth Spring. There was a mud geyser—the first true, active geyser they had seen—and a "mud volcano," evidently formed quite recently, that had spewed mud into the treetops hundreds of feet away.[13] The earth around it shook with subterranean explosions that sounded like distant artillery. Langford was so impressed by it that he and Washburn went back the next morning for a second look.

Several members of the party fell sick that evening. Some said it was from the villainous exhalations of the hot springs and mud pots, which had also tarnished their silver pocket watches. Others ascribed it to the foul, acidic water they had sampled from the streams that meandered across the valley.

The next day, September 3, was less eventful. While Washburn and Langford dallied at the Mud Volcano, the main party scouted for a place where the pack train could ford the river for the first time. After crossing to the east bank, they cut their way through several miles of troublesome timber, waded across a good-size, marshy stream (Pelican Creek), and arrived at last at the shore of Yellowstone Lake, where they pitched camp on a sandy bench about one hundred yards from the water's edge. "It seems to me the most beautiful body of water in the world," wrote Langford.

The expedition was nearing the end of its second week. It had experienced a series of small misadventures, but nothing life-threatening. Truman Everts had succumbed to a twenty-four-hour fever. There had been bouts of nausea. Langford had hit his head on a rotten log. Once or twice the horses had broken through the fragile incrustations around the hot springs and scalded their legs. Both Langford and Hedges had narrowly avoided similar accidents.[14] But Lieutenant Doane now had a much more serious problem.

Ever since leaving Fort Ellis on August 22, he had been troubled by an infection in his right thumb, a felon or whitlow, probably as the result of some puncture wound. Trivial as it may sound, in this wilderness setting, with no doctor for a hundred miles, an infected thumb was potentially life-threatening. For the first few days he had toughed it out, making no complaint, but the pain grew steadily worse. By the 28th, it had "increased to such an extent as to amount to absolute torture." He spent that night pacing around the Tower Fall campsite with a wet bandage wrapped around his hand. Langford offered to lance the infection. For years he had traveled with a scalpel in his pocketbook, but he had unaccountably left it behind in Helena. He poked around at the felon several times with a dull penknife, but Doane was "unwilling to submit to a thorough operation."

By the 30th Langford was seriously worried. Doane had spent the morning in agony, galloping from one spring to another in a desperate effort to keep his bandages wet. That night Langford watched him stagger out of his tent and immerse his forearm in a bowl of ice-cold water. "I am afraid that lock-jaw will set in if he does not consent to have the felon lanced," Langford wrote in his diary. This was not an irrational fear—tetanus was a common complication of such untreated wounds, especially when someone had been digging around in them with a blunt knife—and perhaps Langford knew that lockjaw was what had killed Doane's father.

After several sleepless nights of excruciating pain, Doane's physical and mental stamina was nothing short of astonishing. By the time he made the arduous descent into the Grand Canyon for the first time, he was near-delirious with exhaustion. "I . . . have no distinct recollection how I got to the water's edge," he wrote, "but presently found myself with my arm up to the elbow in the Yellowstone, a few yards below the foot of a graceful cascade." The next day he went down into the canyon again. At three in the afternoon he looked up at the sky: "[S]tars could distinctly be seen; so much of the sunlight was cut off from entering the chasm." This has the ring of an hallucination. Nonetheless, he went on taking his notes and gathering his samples, and as darkness closed in he made the even harder five-hour climb back to his horse. Langford and Washburn sat up with him all night as he writhed in pain.

It went on like this for three more days. The Crater Hills, the Dragon's Mouth, the Mud Volcano: Doane saw them all through a veil of pain and exhaustion, yet recorded them all scrupulously in his journal. Again, Langford insisted that some kind of crude surgery was the only option. "I have in my seamless sack a few simple medicines, including a vial of chloroform," he wrote; "Lieutenant Doane has almost agreed to let me open the felon, provided I put him to sleep with the chloroform." He spent much of that day stropping his penknife against the leather pommel of his saddle.

By the time they reached the shore of Yellowstone Lake, Doane had endured nine days without sleep. His hand was grotesquely swollen. Even ice water could no longer ease the pain. He was so weakened that he could hardly walk. That day he managed to scrawl only three cursory paragraphs in his normally extensive journal. Langford and Washburn conferred and agreed that it would be foolhardy to wait any longer. To improvise an operating table, they used a cartridge box. Hedges pinned the lieutenant's arm flat, and Bean the packer stood by to restrain him if he struggled. "Where is the chloroform?" Doane asked. Langford admitted that he didn't actually know how to use the stuff and didn't feel up to the responsibility. Regardless,

> ... before one could say "Jack Robinson," I had inserted the point of my penknife, thrusting it down to the bone, and had ripped it out to the end of the thumb. Doane gave one shriek as the released corruption flew out in all directions upon surgeon and assistants, and then with a broad smile on his face he exclaimed, "That was elegant!"

Doane soon keeled over like a felled lodgepole, his hand wrapped in a bread poultice, and slept for thirty-six hours straight. But he never did recover the full use of his writing hand.

27

THE DEEP WOODS

September 4-17, 1870

Barometer, 22.50; thermometer, 44° elevation, 7,714 3/5 feet.[1] With Doane once again fit to resume his role as pathfinder, there was a decision to be made: Which way to go? Should they continue along the east shore, or cut back to the west and head for the Madison Valley and Virginia City? Traveling with only thirty days' rations—on the assumption that the lake was their final destination—there was some caution about making the long, laborious circuit through heavily timbered country. They took a vote. Sam Hauser and Jake Smith were for turning back, everyone else for continuing.[2] It was a decision that would have huge consequences, both good and bad.

Walter Trumbull, the wittiest of the diarists, was the first to describe the overall form of Yellowstone Lake as they worked their way round the shore: "Its shape resembles the broad hand of an honest German, who has had his forefinger and the two adjoining shot off at the second joint, while fighting for glory and Emperor William." The changing moods of the lake were an endless fascination. At one moment it was glassy smooth, at the next rippled and sparkling like a field of jewels in the sunlight, then abruptly whipped into whitecaps under a glowering sky. The men lashed together a crude raft to explore the islands, wondering if they would be the first humans to set foot on them, but it was torn apart within an hour by four-foot waves. They caught trout at will, but found many of them wormy—the fish serving as an alternate host for a parasite carried by the lake's abundant population of pelicans.

The expedition's geological journey had now taken them beyond the eastern edge of the caldera. In the course of two days they had passed from the Pleistocene through the Holocene to the early Eocene, crossing over abruptly from the glacial deposits at the mouth of Pelican Creek, barely ten thousand years old, to the fifty-million-year-old rock of the Absarokas. There was a distinct change in the microclimate, too, Doane noted, comparing the dense, dark pine forest with its undergrowth of ferns and berries to "a miniature Oregon in vegetable productions." The shoreline held many points of interest, although no wonders to compare with those of the preceding week. There were alkaline and sulfur springs, a cluster of steam jets that emerged from the rocks with a low roar (Steamboat Springs), and a small bay where the beach was littered with oddly weathered pieces of clay, two of which bore an uncanny resemblance to a human leg and foot. They called this Curiosity Point.

They made fifteen miles that day and another ten the next, despite the tangle of timber. Cornelius Hedges lagged behind, his wretched horse acting up again. But by the second afternoon they had reached the southeast corner of the lake and the swampy mouth of the upper section of the Yellowstone River. They found game trails everywhere and the tracks of elk, mountain sheep, beaver, and bear in the soft mud. But crossing the river was tricky, and they deferred the problem to the following day. Their camp on the Southeast Arm was their poorest yet. The land was either swamp or impenetrable timber, and the night was cold. They were awakened several times by the shrill scream of mountain lions or cougars, which they called California lions according to the usage of the time. This "sound[ed] so like the human voice that I was deceived by it into believing that some traveler in distress was hailing our camp," Langford wrote.

Since the episode of the felon and the penknife, he and Doane seemed to seek out one another's company, taking off on explorations of their own. The previous day it had been a short side trip to the long-dormant sulfur springs of the Brimstone Basin. Now, while Washburn led the advance party in search of a convenient place to ford the Yellowstone, Doane and Langford climbed a peak that rose abruptly from the mouth of the river, looking to measure the height of the surrounding mountains and map the contours of the lake with greater precision.

It was a tough ascent, forcing them to tether the horses partway and proceed on foot, and it took them above the snow line at ten thousand feet. The view from the top was spectacular. Langford sketched a reasonably accurate map, which he later gave to Washburn to be tidied up in the office of the territorial surveyor. It was a great improvement on the earlier renderings by Captain Raynolds and Walter De Lacy. Back in camp that night, Doane suggested to the general that the mountain they had climbed should be named in honor of Langford. Langford returned the compliment; in that case the adjoining peak (which was a few hundred feet higher) should be named for the lieutenant.[3] Both proposals were accepted, another breach of the no-naming rule, although the naming was only temporary.[4]

Langford's journal entry for that day is one of his more relaxed and engaging passages, free of much of his usual bombast. He seemed to relax in Doane's company. To the east of their vantage point, he wrote, the long chain of the Absarokas stretched away for thirty miles, an unbroken series of eleven-thousand-foot peaks "whose jagged slopes were filled with yawning chasms, pine-embowered recesses, and beetling precipices, some hundreds and some thousands of feet in height." He noted that this was the range that had defeated Raynolds, Hayden, and Bridger in 1860 and promised himself that he would reread the Raynolds report more closely on his return home. He went on:

> I have read somewhere (I think in Washington Irving's "Astoria" or "Bonneville's Adventures") that the Indians regard this ridge of mountains as the crest of the world, and that among the Blackfeet there is a fable that he who attains its summit catches a view of the "Land of Souls" and beholds the "Happy Hunting Grounds" spread out below him, brightening with the abodes of the free and generous spirits.[5]

Langford appears to be misremembering his sources. Irving does make scores of references to the Blackfeet, but they reflect the conventional frontier stereotype: "Savage . . . Ruthless . . . The terrible Blackfeet . . . A ruffian horde . . . A restless and predatory tribe . . . Warlike and predatory . . . The most dangerous banditti of the mountains." Not a word about the character of their spiritual beliefs, or even that they had any.

Langford was also confusing his geography. His image of the Blackfeet looking out over the happy hunting grounds from the Absarokas sounds like a bowdlerized version of a myth that refers to the mountains of present-day Glacier National Park, which the tribe called the Backbone of the World. And the destination of dead Blackfeet was the Sand Hills of Saskatchewan; they would have been perplexed to find themselves fetching up in Wyoming.

But Langford's implicit message was that civilization had done its inexorable work. Seven months after the massacre on the Marias, the restless, predatory tribe was now safely reduced to a source of picturesque anecdotes and legends.

On the way back to camp that night, Doane and Langford had their first premonition of later trouble. Washburn had found a way to ford the Yellowstone, but they couldn't find Washburn. They followed their companions' tracks across the river, through a shady forest, and past a couple of small lakes, but then, while scrambling through fallen timber on the slopes of the Two Ocean Plateau, they lost the trail. It was getting dark, and Doane pressed his face to the ground, searching for hoofprints. There was no better tracker in the frontier army, but he found nothing except some freshly disturbed earth. They followed it for some distance, still heading uphill, until Doane concluded that they were mistakenly following a band of elk. They stopped to light a fire, facing the unpleasant prospect of a night on the mountain with neither food nor blankets, then tried to retrace their steps to the lake. Finally they saw the glow of a campfire near the shore a mile away, and reached it just as the others were beginning to grow concerned. It was only a minor scare, but it sent a clear message: This was country in which it was very easy for a man to get lost.

Over the next two days the going got even harder. The south side of the lake was an almost impenetrable morass of downed timber, broken only by sudden ravines and the boggy inlets of small streams. This time it was Hedges who almost got lost. He and Everts struggled up a steep slope of coarse rubble early in the morning of September 8, looking for a better perspective on the path ahead. A huge grizzly rushed out past Hedges, spooking his horse, which snapped its bridle and ran. Hedges eventually recovered the miserable beast and made it back to camp. But the two men became separated, and it took Hedges a long time to regain his bearings.

After these two incidents there was a debate about what should be done if someone became seriously detached from the group. Everts said he would head for the Madison, but everyone else thought it made more sense to make for the lake and try to pick up the main trail.

They labored on, the country growing more treacherous by the hour. On the 8th they zigzagged about twelve miles but covered barely six as the crow flies. Next day they made only half that distance—six miles of zigzagging, three of advance. Downed timber prevented them from keeping to the lakeshore, and they were constantly forced upward. The pines grew so close together, and the gaps between them were so obstructed with deadfalls that the pack animals repeatedly got stuck. Their loads had to be constantly rearranged or hand-carried. Sometimes an animal had to be bodily lifted over some obstacle. Langford and Private Williamson were the ones to take care of this, being the two strongest members of the party, even though Langford by this time had lost twenty pounds or more.

For the first two weeks, other than for the spiky exchanges between Langford and Jake Smith, there had been no serious dissension in the group. But now everyone was fatigued, the daily struggles were Sisyphean, and tempers began to fray. Langford speaks of "fits of sullenness and explosions of wrath which bore no slight resemblance to the volcanic forces of the country itself." There were recriminations over who was to blame for their situation. Presumably the decision to continue round the lake was second-guessed. Langford argued with Hauser. Expletives flew.

The wildlife, too, became more threatening. Reconnoitering alone and unarmed, Washburn and Hauser startled a grizzly sow and her two cubs in the forest—the likeliest of all bear encounters to provoke a serious attack. The rest of the party armed themselves with revolvers, knives, and needle carbines and set off to hunt down the animals, looking as if they were planning to encounter the full Prussian Army. They yelled and roared and crashed about in the undergrowth, but finally abandoned the search and returned to camp, feeling foolish.

With morale so fragile, they tried to extract some humor from the farcical bear hunt and their other travails. "With all the *ore rotundo* I could command," Langford declaimed stanzas from Lord Byron's *Childe Harold's Pilgrimage* ("There is a pleasure in the pathless woods . . .").[6] If nothing else cheered them up, they could always fall back on the unending pratfalls of Hedges's pathetic horse, which was variously nicknamed Little Invulnerable or the Yellowstone Wonder. "This animal, a small cayuse," Doane said, "had been uniformly unfortunate, miring down in marshes, tumbling over log heaps, and rolling endwise down steep banks." On their second day of thrashing through the downed timber, Little Invulnerable disappeared altogether. Langford and the two packers eventually found him a couple of miles back on the trail, wedged firmly between two trees and "evidently enjoying a rest, which he sorely needed."

Worn out by their exertions, the expedition made camp at three in the afternoon of September 9, in a small clearing on Surprise Creek, one of the sources of the Snake River. But there was suddenly no sign of Truman Everts, and when darkness fell he still had not returned.

Even though they fired guns at intervals through the night to signal their location, there was no great anxiety at first. Despite his age and shortsightedness, Everts had proved over the past three weeks to be a surprisingly adept woodsman. At worst he might have an uncomfortable and chilly night in the forest, since he had gone off without a coat, but at least he had matches, a gun and ammunition, and a fishing rod.

On September 10, Gillette and Trumbull retraced their steps to the last camp, taking blankets with them in case they stayed out all night, which in the end they did. They blazed trees and hung bags of rations along the trail, assuming that Everts would eventually find his way back to it. Langford and Hauser, meanwhile, ascended a ridge eight hundred feet above the lake and set a fire that could be seen for miles.

September 11. Doane, Langford, and Hauser rode ahead of the party until they reached the West Thumb of the lake. By now there was real unease about Everts, and Washburn worried that the farther west they went, the greater the risk he would never catch up with them. So a decision was reached: Since the West Thumb offered a good campsite on more open ground, they would stay put there for a few days and organize a more systematic search.

September 12. On the third day since Everts's disappearance, they split up into pairs and fanned out in different directions. Smith and Trumbull kept as close as they could to the lake, where they found footprints in the sand and Smith fancied that he saw six men flitting through the trees like phantoms. Indians? More likely hunters or men with something on their conscience, Doane believed.[7]

Hauser, accompanied by Gillette, thought he heard gunfire, but concluded that it was the cracking and falling of trees in the fire that he and Langford had set two days earlier, which by this time had become a galloping conflagration.

Langford and Washburn rode south toward the reddish hump that members of the party variously (and oddly) called the Brown Mountain or the Yellow Mountain.[8] They found a cluster of hot springs on the way, and Langford's horse broke through the crust and was badly scalded. They came eventually within half a mile of Heart Lake before turning back, dispirited, as everyone was that evening.

September 13. A new enemy now loomed: the weather. A squall of rain and hail started up in the morning, then turned to snow. Hedges stayed in bed, trying to keep warm. Langford did the same. Jake Smith made himself unpopular again by lighting a wet fire that smoked everyone out of the Sibley tent.

Doane ventured out despite the weather, apparently alone. It's not clear whether he was searching for Everts—whom he barely mentioned in his journal—or simply exploring. Whatever the case, he stumbled upon the most striking geothermal features since the Mud Volcano: the pink, green, and blue springs of the West Thumb geyser basin, where he was able to peer deep into craters through water of crystalline clarity.

September 14. By the time they woke, the snow was calf-deep and still coming down. Fifteen inches, some said; others estimated nearer to two feet. Doane again braved the storm and went out to catalogue the bird life on and around the lake—swans, pelicans, Canada geese, brants, many kinds of ducks and dippers, gulls (which he recognized as the same species he had seen overwintering in San Francisco Bay), a mockingbird, two different woodpeckers, two or three varieties of grouse. Later, Private Moore, drawing on Langford's notes, helped Doane catch up on his journal; writing was still difficult. Otherwise the snowstorm paralyzed all further movement. The explorers shivered around the fire and played hands of whist, casino, and seven-up. "Poor Everts, I fear he has perished," Gillette brooded.

September 15. The storm began to abate at last, driven off by a warm wind from the west. Half the snow had melted, although the tethered horses were still unable to forage. "How I pity him, hungry, wet and cold," Gillette wrote of his friend. "I wonder if he killed his mare. I would do it, and dry the meat." Jake Smith, quite out of character, busied himself with the construction of a raft, and even managed to float it out onto the lake. The cougars continued to scream in the night.

September 16. Although the weather had cleared, General Washburn reluctantly decided that it was pointless to resume the search for Everts, who had now been missing for a week. Besides, even with the prodigious numbers of trout that had been brought in by Hedges and Private Williamson,[9] the thirty-day rations were running perilously low. It was now twenty-five days since their departure from Fort Ellis, and they had no idea how much longer it would take them to reach civilization. The decision made, they moved their camp to the west side of West Thumb.

Despite the grim mood of his companions, Langford's mood was strangely upbeat, even manic. He made a detailed inspection of the hot springs that Doane had discovered and was entranced by them. As he contemplated the lake for one last time, his vision of the future burst out in all its fullness:

> How can I sum up its wonderful attractions! It is dotted with islands of great beauty, as yet unvisited by man, but which at no remote period will be adorned with villas and the ornaments of civilized life. . . . It possesses adaptabilities for the highest display of artificial culture, amid the greatest wonders of Nature that the world affords, and is beautified by the grandeur of the most extensive mountain scenery, and not many years can elapse before the march of civil improvement will reclaim this delightful solitude, and garnish it with all the attractions of cultivated taste and refinement.[10]

It was as if all the elements of Langford's life had come triumphantly together—the schoolhouse, the church, the masonic lodge, law and order (established by whatever means necessary), the violent subjugation of the Indian, and the exploration of the last corners of the Western wilderness. All these things formed part of his seamless vision of the civilization of the frontier.

In this exultant mood, Langford's self-regard was on full display. He reported with satisfaction Sam Hauser's opinion "that I have a more correct idea of mountain heights, distances, and directions, and can follow a direct course through dense timber more unerringly than any man he knows, except James Stuart." He prided himself on being the best in the party at cheering up his comrades. He recited more of his *ore rotundo* poetry to raise morale; this time it was "The Task," by William Cowper, a meditation on a difficult journey and an imminent return home.[11]

September 17. On their last morning on Yellowstone Lake, Langford's thoughts about Everts took a darker turn. He considered all the things that might have happened to the Assessor of Inland Revenue. Death by accident? by starvation? by disease? despair and insanity? He decided in the end that, "it is a relief to think that he may have lost his life at the hand of some vagabond Indian." Right to the end, Langford never quite abandoned his morbid anxiety about the red man, even though Doane had told everyone just two days earlier that the only Indians in these parts were the Sheepeaters, "wretched beasts who run from the sight of a white man," repeating the old assurance that, "The larger tribes never enter the basin, restrained by superstitious ideas."[12]

It was time to move on. But Warren Gillette, the best outdoorsman in the party and the man who seems to have been most moved by the plight of Everts, volunteered to remain behind and continue the search if someone else would agree to stay with him. Washburn consulted with Doane, and they decided to detach two men from the escort—Private Moore, the sketch artist, and the rugged and resourceful Private Williamson. They were left with a pack mule and ten days of survival rations. Gillette borrowed a pair of boots from Hedges, for his own were worn through. Hauser tried to make light of the business: Perhaps Gillette's true motive was to go looking for a father-in-law, since he was known to have been paying court to Bessie Everts, the belle of Helena.

And so the rest of them headed west toward the Madison Valley, anticipating a quick return to Virginia City, and having not the least suspicion that the greatest wonders of Wonderland still lay before them.

28

LOST AND FOUND

September–October 1870

Truman Everts was "a man of strong prejudices," said the Englishman "Yellowstone Jack" Baronett. When tempers began to fray over how the explorers were to free themselves from the intolerable timber, the Assessor of Inland Revenue decided that he for one knew *precisely* where to go. So off he went, shouldering his gun, evidently assuming that everyone else would tag along behind. But they didn't, and by the time this dawned on him, he was totally lost.[1]

This is not exactly how Everts himself told it. By his account, he was simply following the usual ground rules: Each man was free to find his own way around the obstacles they encountered. When he realized that he was out of sight and out of hearing range of his companions, he made haste to rejoin them. But he was hampered by his poor eyesight, it was getting dark, and whichever way he turned there was a pine-green wall without a door or window. So he gathered some branches, struck a match, and went to sleep. "This was disagreeable enough," he wrote later, "but caused me no alarm." His reaction, in other words, was much the same as that of his companions back in camp.

Rising at dawn, he saddled up and blundered on for a while until he came to a vantage point. Which way? Leaving his horse untethered for a few moments, he walked off some distance, peering around myopically for clues, at which point the animal decided it wanted no more of his company. It galloped off, taking with it Everts's blankets, his guns, his ammunition, his fishing tackle, and his matches—everything but the clothes he stood up in, two knives (which he soon lost), and a pair of opera glasses. Reaching a clearing, he posted notices on the trees, just as his companions were doing a few miles away, so he must also have had a writing implement of some kind. He wasted half a day looking vainly for the horse.

With no fire in prospect, a second night in the forest was less appealing than the first. But Everts told himself that in a day or two his friends would be laughing about his misadventure and would "incorporate it as a thrilling episode into the journal of our trip." Darkness eclipsed his optimism. "I fully realized the exposure of my condition," he wrote. "The forest seemed alive with the screeching of night birds, the angry barking of coyotes, and the prolonged, dismal howl of the gray wolf." Sleep was impossible.

He was devastated in the morning when he found that his notices were still where he had left them. But he summoned the power of positive thinking again and determined to make a straight line for the lake and overtake the rest of the party before they gave up on him and headed for home. Looking at a map, this doesn't seem an unreasonable ambition. West Thumb was only about three miles away as the crow flies. Everts was not a crow, but even in such dense forest it should have been possible to orient himself by the position of the sun. Unaccountably, though, he struck out to the southwest, not to the north.

At midday, he reached a beautiful forested lake "a full twelve miles in circumference." The woods were filled with birdsong. Otters, natural acrobats, cavorted in the water. There were minks and beavers, swans and other waterfowl. On the far shore, steam rose from a cluster of hot springs at the base of a mountain.[2] Deer, elk, and mountain sheep stood motionless and stared at him. It all sounds like a sketch for the Peaceable Kingdom, but Everts "was in no humor for ecstacy [sic]."

There was one encouraging development, however. He noticed a small, green plant with spiny, dandelion-shaped leaves, pulled it up by the roots, and found that it was "palatable and nutritious," tasting rather like a radish. The first thing he had eaten in three days, it was elk thistle—*Cirsium foliosum*—common in the upper Yellowstone. To celebrate his good fortune, he named the lake for Bessie, "sole daughter of my house and heart." Today it is called Heart Lake, although that refers more to its shape than to the handsome Bessie.[3]

Everts saw a large stream leaving the southeast corner of the lake and entering a deep, rugged canyon. He correctly identified this, the Heart River, as one of the sources of the Snake. He considered following it downstream on its one-hundred-mile journey to Eagle Rock bridge, where Idaho Falls stands today. But he was deterred by the stories he had heard— probably from Walter De Lacy, who had explored the Snake—of its "desolation and elemental upheavals and violent waters." Had he risked it, well before reaching Eagle Rock he would have come to Jackson Hole, and he might have found more to eat along the way. Or at least Langford thought so, having been told by James Stuart that the Snake River Valley was rich in camas root, whose sweet, glutinous, onion-like bulb was highly prized as a staple food ("both flour and potatoes") by the Nez Perce and other northwestern tribes.[4]

Instead Everts circled Heart Lake until darkness fell and he again bedded down under a tree. As on the preceding nights, he was awakened by the screams of a mountain lion, but this time "so alarmingly near as to cause every nerve to thrill with terror." He had no reason to know that cougars are more likely to stalk humans than actually to attack them (although this does happen on occasion). And in any case, anyone meeting a 150-pound predator in the dark is probably not thinking rationally. Instead Everts screamed back and clambered into a tree, tearing off branches and hurling them down at the barely visible cougar as it circled the base of the pine, growling and howling and pawing the ground and lashing its tail. After a time, Everts seems to have decided that making noise was counterproductive. So he fell silent, and after a time the creature gave one last blood-freezing scream and padded off into the forest.

Eventually Everts climbed down and fell asleep with dismal thoughts of death, sure that his family "could never know my fate and would indulge a thousand conjectures concerning it, not the least of which would be that I had been captured by a band of hostile Sioux, and tortured to death at the stake." Although Jim Bridger had said there wasn't a Sioux within a hundred miles, just uttering the name of the tribe was Montana shorthand for saying you were frightened out of your wits.

When the great snowstorm hit on September 13, Everts covered himself in earth and leaves and lay without moving for two days, waiting for it to pass. At some point, he says, a small bird fluttered into range. He snatched it, tore off its feathers, and ate it raw. When the storm finally eased, he soldiered on around the lake until he reached the plumes of steam that rose at the foot of the mountain. He was now standing on the exact spot that Langford and Washburn had reached while searching for him three days earlier. There were thistles here in abundance, and he cooked the roots in one of the springs. Soaked in snow and numb with cold, he sat there and steamed, feeling "parboiled." He built a bower of pine branches and slept with his head by one spring and his feet at another, warm at the extremities at least, although his toes were already frostbitten, with sores that were beginning to fester. But on the third night he rolled over in his sleep, broke through the crust, just as Langford's horse had done in this same spot, and severely scalded his thigh.

His days oscillated between physical agony, mental despair, and bursts of determined optimism. He tried to bolster his morale by telling himself the story of Captain Elisha Kane and his desperate (but in the end successful) fight for survival in the Arctic in 1850–1851, after he went looking for Sir John Franklin, who had disappeared three years earlier while seeking to chart the Northwest Passage. And there was one literal shaft of light that lifted Everts's mood. When the sun at last came out after the storm, he suddenly remembered his opera glasses. "Oh happy, life-renewing thought!" he wrote. He kindled his first fire, and this breakthrough seemed to ignite a fresh burst of creativity. He unraveled a linen handkerchief to make a fishing line, fashioned a hook from a pin that he found in his pocket, sharpened the tongue of a buckle on his vest to replace the lost knives, and used it to cut off his bootlegs to make improvised bags to hold his store of thistles.

After a week at Heart Lake, with a renewed sense of purpose, the Assessor of Internal Revenue for Montana Territory set off again to find his way home.

On the morning of September 17, as Everts still lay at the edge of Heart Lake, boiling his thistles and waiting for his scalded hip to heal, Gillette and the two soldiers left the camp on West Thumb, carrying enough rations for a five-day search and another five days they estimated they would need to return to civilization. With the tacit recognition that this endeavor was hopeless and that they were in effect giving up Everts for dead, the mood of the rest of the party was dismal, with the exception of the irrepressible Langford. Having consigned Everts in his mind to death by Indians, he now wrote that, "I do not know of any day since we left home when I have been in better spirits." While others might think they were lost, Langford declared, "I am sure we are on the right course, and feel no anxiety."

On the first day of what they now knew to be the homeward leg of their journey, they crossed the Continental Divide twice before reaching an acceptable, if cheerless, camping place on the banks of a small stream surrounded by springs. Several hundred feet below them, they saw a large body of water, which would later be known as Shoshone Lake. There was some debate about this. Doane was convinced, mistakenly, that they had reached the source of the river "known in the wretched nomenclature of this region as the Fire Hole."[5] Langford and Hauser believed correctly that they were in the upper watershed of the Snake.

At three in the morning they were woken by a terrific rainstorm that lasted for several hours, but Langford had built a shelter in which he and Hedges bedded down and was feeling very pleased with himself. As everyone else huddled around a damp, smoldering fire, he noted with satisfaction that he was the only one in dry clothes and was feeling "in the best of spirits." His bedmate, however, had managed to position himself under a leak in the roof of Langford's little wickiup, and "felt double disgust."

Langford's smugness must have grated even more on his companions later in the morning, when several of the horses were spooked by some unseen animal and stampeded through the camp, breaking the last two pack saddles that had withstood the rigors of the monthlong expedition. The others were ready to give them up as beyond repair, but Langford came to the rescue. "From my seamless sack of personal baggage," he wrote,

> I produced two gimlets, a screwdriver, a pair of nippers, some wrought nails and two dozens of screws of various sizes . . . It is a matter of surprise to me that I am the only member of our party who has a rubber coat, or a pair of oil-tanned, water-proof boots, or who has brought with him any medicines, tools, screws, etc.; and, except myself, there is but one member of our party (whom I will not "give away" by here recording his name) who had the foresight to bring with him a flask of whiskey.[6]

The saddles were fixed, and the journey continued.

Around midday they came to a small river, some forty feet wide, that tumbled over a beautiful double waterfall—the Kepler Cascades—and into a modest canyon of trachyte lava. "We found ourselves once more in the dominions of the Fire King," Doane wrote. Nothing had prepared Langford for the spectacle; he thought they had already seen "the greatest wonders of the continent," but he was wrong. Spread out before them was a broad valley largely devoid of vegetation and filled with tall columns of steam. Langford wrote, "This entire country is seemingly under a constant and active internal pressure from volcanic forces, which seek relief through the numberless springs, jets, volcanoes, and geysers exhibited on its surface, and which but for these vents might burst forth in one terrific eruption and form a volcano of vast dimensions."

Even as they watched, a great spout of water and steam shot into the air from a mound of sinter on the riverbank. The lieutenant estimated that it rose 125 feet, though others said it was more like 80 or 100. In the course of the day they watched this geyser perform several more times, and timed the interval between its eruptions. You could almost set your watch by them. General Washburn named it Old Faithful.

Even the disconsolate Cornelius Hedges, with his fragile constitution, recalcitrant horse, and damp clothes, said that he "forgot all [his] bad feelings of the morning" as one geyser after another erupted in rapid succession. They saw a dozen in all and named six of the most impressive in addition to Old Faithful. Taking advantage of Sam Hauser's triangulation skills, they also measured the height of their eruptions.

The Fan—one of a pair with what is now called the Mortar, which produced loud underground detonations—had multiple eruptions that lasted anywhere from ten to thirty minutes.

The Grotto threw water sixty feet into the air for half an hour. While it was inactive, the indomitable Private Williamson crawled around in the cavities that perforated its cone. These suggested the geyser's name.

The Castle, which resembled, in Langford's words, "the ruins of some old tower with its broken down turrets," rose to a similar height every two or three hours.

The Giant, which Doane compared to "a huge shattered horn" and Langford to "a miniature model of the Colosseum," erupted repeatedly, its column of water and steam soaring as high as two hundred feet.

On the opposite side of the Firehole, across from their camp, the Beehive, an inconspicuous little bump of sinter that they had ignored on the first day, suddenly put on its display the next morning; it worked like a gigantic firehose, shooting a narrow jet of water 219 feet into the air (Hauser measured this one exactly) for ten minutes or more.

As Langford waded across the river to see the rest of the geysers on the east bank, he felt the lava bed grow warm under his feet. He turned to Hedges and said, "Here is the river which Bridger said was hot at the bottom." Yet another of the mountain man's outlandish stories had turned out to have a basis in fact.

The star of the north bank was the Giantess, which several of the party found the most wondrous of all the geysers. It was certainly the tallest. Five separate jets, each one higher than the last, rose as much as 250 feet.

Doane says it erupted three times in the course of a single afternoon, for twenty minutes at a time.

It was as if the celestial conductor of the geyser orchestra had chosen to put on a special command performance in their honor, an experience no modern visitor could hope to replicate. Today, the Fan goes dormant for long periods, the Castle erupts only once every twelve hours, the Giantess puts on her show only between twice and six times a year, and the Giant, which can remain silent for years at a time, now bursts into life every three to ten days.

Doane devoted several pages of his best, at times almost lyrical descriptive writing to the Upper Geyser Basin, which made "the geysers of Iceland sink into insignificance." He was especially enchanted by the glistening filigree of brightly colored deposits around the cone of Old Faithful—metallic gray, rose-pink, and saffron yellow—all of them gone now, lost to the greedy hands of early tourists. For the first and only time on the trip Doane invoked divinity:

> Those who have seen stage representations of Aladdin's Cave and the Home of the Dragon Fly, as produced in a first class theatre, can form an idea of this wonderful coloring, but not of the intricate frost work of this fairy like yet solid mound of rock. . . . The beauty of the scene takes away one's breath. It is overpowering, transcending the visions of Mosoleum's [Muslim's] Paradise; the earth affords not its equal, it is the most lovely inanimate object in existence.[7]

But then he saw the Giantess, which he declared to be "the grandest, the most majestic, and most terrible fountain in the world." Washburn agreed, though his religious references were of the conventional Christian kind. With the sun at his back, the general watched a rainbow flicker around the head of the column of steam and wrote that it "gives that halo so many painters have vainly tried to give in paintings of the Savior."[8]

They would have stayed longer in the geyser basin, but rations were running perilously low. That afternoon, September 19, they made rapid progress along the flat, grassy valley, pausing only briefly to inspect the rainbow-colored glories of the Grand Prismatic Spring, the Excelsior Spring, and the Opal and Turquoise Pools, before reaching the confluence of the Firehole and the Madison.

From all the accounts they wrote at the time, it seems to have been a quiet and unremarkable evening, a time to reflect quietly on all they had seen and prepare for their return. "Camped at the junction," was all Doane said, "distance 18 miles." Hedges says he slept badly, "thinking of home and business." But Langford, as we shall see later, would turn the conversation at Madison Junction into something much more momentous.[9]

In the morning they headed home. It was a banal business now, and there was nothing left to detain them. Making twenty-five or thirty miles a day over easy country, they came within sight of the first signs of civilization late on September 22. A horseman gave Langford news of the capitulation of the French at Sedan; Napoleon was a prisoner, the republic proclaimed. After raising their tent for the last time, Hedges and Washburn had "quite a confab" about the comparative fighting qualities of the French and the English.

Next day they began to make their farewells, each man setting his own course for home. Langford was gone before dawn, planning to stop over briefly in Virginia City. On the 24th, Washburn, Hauser, Trumbull, and Stickney headed for Helena. Doane rode off alone and was back at Fort Ellis by afternoon. That left only Hedges, Jake Smith, and the indefatigable dog Booby, all of whom jumped aboard a passing wagon bound for Diamond City. By the second of October, Gillette, too, had finally arrived home. Of the fate of Truman Everts, he brought not a word.

By the time Everts abandoned his resting place on Heart Lake, the main party was more than fifty miles away, and Gillette and the two cavalrymen had abandoned their search. Gillette was convinced that the missing man must have perished in the great two-day snowstorm that had hit them at West Thumb.

Everts had already made one attempt to leave the lake, but he quickly returned, disoriented, worried for the first time about his mental state. He began to hallucinate. He thought he saw someone paddling across the lake to rescue him, but it turned out to be only a large pelican. "My mind, though unimpaired in those perceptions needful to self-preservation, was in a condition to receive impressions akin to insanity," he wrote. He spoke of "constantly traveling in dreamland," of "vagaries of the most extravagant character," of "a sort of duality of being," in which his optimistic self and its evil twin debated and fought with one another.

Using the unimpaired part of his brain, Everts drew a map in the sand. For the second time he considered and rejected the Snake. He wondered about retracing his steps around the south side of Yellowstone Lake, but concluded that there was too much risk of going astray again in the deep, dripping timber. That left the third option: to head straight across the mountains to the valley of the Madison. That was the option he selected, although "most unwisely, as will hereafter appear."

After he left Heart Lake, his troubles became Biblical. When there was no sun, he could light no fire. With his hands and feet numb with cold, he spent a long, terrible night walking around and banging them against trees to restore sensation. His scalded hip was badly inflamed, and it caused him such pain that he could sleep only sitting upright, besieged by nocturnal noises, fighting off dream attacks by imaginary cougars and wolf packs. One night he toppled into his campfire and added a burned hand to his litany of miseries.

Eventually he stumbled on the abandoned campsite on West Thumb that the others had used as their base during the search. They had left him no food, but he was slightly cheered by the discovery of an empty can of yeast powder and a fork—a valuable find had he had anything to eat. But he was down to the last of his thistles.

Demoralized, he fell asleep by his campfire on the beach, but was awakened in the night by a great roaring and crackling. He had started a forest fire. For lodgepole pines, this is a good and necessary thing. The seeds of these tall, straight, graceful trees are encased in hard, resin-coated cones that require extreme temperatures to melt; only then can they drop their contents onto the new, fertile bed of ash. For Everts, however, the fire was life-threatening. He now had *two* burned hands, his fingernails were crisped, and his hair was scorched. He lost his buckle-knife, his pin-hook, and his handkerchief–fishing line, not that they had done him any good. He scuttled away from the conflagration and watched in awe as it raged through the forest canopy, leaping from treetop to treetop, driven by fierce gusts of wind. "I never before saw anything so terribly beautiful," he said.

Having picked up the trail of his fellow explorers, he promptly lost it again. He focused instead on the Madison Range and decided to head for its "lowest notch." But in two days of walking, the summits did not get any closer. There seemed to be nothing but "an endless succession of inaccessible peaks and precipices, rising thousands of feet sheer and bare above the plain."

Somehow he worked himself back to the lake, burned, scalded, starved, and sleepless. An old clerical friend now appeared to keep him company as he stumbled on for four more days without food. Everts was cast in the role of Job, and his clerical friend served as proxy for God. I'm going over the mountains, Everts insisted. Don't be ridiculous, the man said; keep to the lake until you hit the Yellowstone River. I can't make it, Everts said. You *must* make it, said the reverend gentleman; put your trust in Heaven. Everts struggled on, buoyed by the encouragement of his new traveling companion, although, he comments cryptically, "his reticence on other subjects both surprised and annoyed me."

The west side of Yellowstone Lake is easier terrain than the south, and at last, on the fourth or fifth day, Everts found himself at the outflow of the big river. He had lost all sense of time by this point, but his ordeal must have been well into its fourth week. Yet the worst of it was still to come.

He took comfort where he could. He found a gull's wing, pounded it between two stones to break the bones, filled his yeast-powder cup with water, and boiled it on his campfire into half a pint of broth. He snatched a few minnows from a stream, wolfed them down, and immediately vomited them up again. He spent half a day catching a grasshopper to eat, but his stomach rejected that also. He wasted hours in fruitless pursuit of trout, this time using a hook he had fashioned from the rim of his broken spectacles.[10] When he slept, he dreamed of banquets in the finest New York restaurants, with oyster stews and succulent pies, or of preparing food himself until "the elegantly furnished tables . . . fairly groaned beneath the accumulated dainties."

Winter tightens its grip rapidly in the upper Yellowstone in October. By the time Everts reached the Upper Falls, and realized that he was back on the party's original trail, he had to contend with a howling gale and a succession of bleak, freezing nights. There was nothing romantic about the falls now; the canyon was no longer grand, but dark and terrifying.

He found that his right arm was partly paralyzed. He was half-blind. He went for days without fire, waiting for the sun to break through the sullen cloud cover. Near Tower Fall he slept in a recently vacated bear's den in a hollow tree—"a most inviting couch." On the Blacktail Deer Plateau it snowed again. He thought of the Bottlers' ranch, but realized that reaching it meant several more days of hard travel in his impossibly weakened condition.

His clerical friend had vanished now, and his new partners in dialogue were his own hands, legs, and stomach, who developed distinct personalities and opinions. The stomach was especially cantankerous. This organ "tormented me with his fretful humors," and "the others would generally concur with him in these fancied altercations," while adding complaints of their own. He retorted that all they did was eat, sleep, and gripe. Why didn't they make themselves useful by gathering firewood? He became so angry with his stomach that he threatened to leave it behind and proceed alone. That shut it up. But by this time Everts had given up all hope. He prepared to die, comforted only by the thought that he was on a well-beaten path now, part of the old Bannock Trail, so his friends would eventually find his body.

Half-walking, half-crawling, in sleet and freezing rain, he made his way across the open country that one of his friends, in the earliest days of the expedition, had called the Valley of Desolation. All of a sudden, he says, "I became . . . sensible of a sharp reflection, as of burnished steel. Looking up, through half-closed eyes, two rough, but kindly faces met my gaze."

"Are you Mr. Everts?" one said.

"Yes—all that is left of him."

"We have come for you."

Cornelius Hedges's law partner, a Mr. Lawrence, had put up a six hundred dollar reward for anyone who could find Everts. "Yellowstone Jack" Baronett, the English-born former "sailor, prospector, soldier-of-fortune, Indian fighter, guide, and much more,"[11] took up the offer, along with a packer and handyman named George Pritchett. Sam Hauser drew them a map, and they enlisted the help of two Crow scouts.

It was Yellowstone Jack's dog who actually found the missing explorer. Baronett himself thought it was a black bear he saw shuffling along the hillside, and perhaps the burnished steel reflection seen by Everts was an indication that his rescuer was readying his gun to shoot the beast. Once he realized that it was not a bear, Baronett couldn't decide what it was— certainly not a human being. Everts "was nothing but a shadow," Baronett said later. "His flesh was all gone; the bones protruded through the skin on the balls of his feet and thighs. His fingers looked like bird claws." He weighed ninety pounds. Baronett pitched camp, lit a fire, and fed him tea from a spoon.

Next day the Englishman carried him to a primitive prospector's shack on Turkey Pen Creek, where he nursed him with "all the care, sympathy, and solicitude of a brother," while Pritchett rode back to Fort Ellis for an ambulance. Colonel Baker was willing enough to help, but there was an excess of red tape, so Pritchett procured a wagon from the livery stable in Bozeman.[12] By the time he got back to Turkey Pen Creek, Everts had rallied, thanks to the idiosyncratic frontier remedy of drinking a pint of oil rendered from the fat of a recently killed bear, which if nothing else dealt with a prodigious case of constipation.

It took Everts almost a month to recover fully. But by the second week of November, General Washburn decided that the Assessor of Internal Revenue was well enough for an official celebration and invited the cream of Helena society to a gala banquet at the Kan-Kan, the fanciest restaurant in town, purveyor of Havana cigars, French cognac, and the celebrated K-K-K ("Kan-Kan Kocktails: Everybody Drinks Them").

The elegantly furnished tables groaned like something out of Everts's

fever dreams. Oysters, raw and roasted; twelve kinds of meat and six vegetables; three pies, three puddings. For dessert, fruitcake, pound cake, jelly
cake, citron cake, jelly roll, jelly tarts, strawberry cream, puff paste, nuts,
raisins, confections, and "rustar tart cream," whatever that might be. Even
the fastidious Cornelius Hedges admitted that he had taken a little too
much champagne.

There were speeches and toasts, of course. Everts himself said a few
words, still a little frail and leaning on a walking stick. And then the
other members of the expedition, all of whom "acquitted themselves in
an oratorical way much to their credit."[13] Only Lieutenant Doane was
absent, off on some unspecified military business.

Afterward, there were mutterings, of the kind that attend any mythol-
ogized event. Everts, "a man of strong prejudices," had rubbed plenty of
people the wrong way over the years. It was said that the skeleton of a
horse had been found by a campsite that showed signs of prolonged occupation. Had Everts's horse really bolted, or had he eaten it? Amid all
the rumors there was at least one hard fact: Everts was less than gra-
cious to his rescuers, and Yellowstone Jack never did receive his promised reward.[14] And the following spring, Hedges grumbled to his diary
that he had been obliged to pay Baronett's expenses, which came to a
total of nine dollars and twenty-five cents.

29

THE PROFESSIONALS

1871

oane's account of the 1870 Yellowstone expedition was compellingly readable, a marvel of clarity, and it brought him a starburst of fame.[1] After perusing it at departmental headquarters in St. Paul the following January, General Winfield Hancock was moved to write the lieutenant a personal note.[2] He conveyed his "warm commendation" and said the report "does you great credit as an officer of intelligence and fidelity in the performance of duty." Doane, never one to hide his light under a bushel, also sent a copy to the Smithsonian Institution, which found its description of the bizarre geology of the upper Yellowstone "very interesting."[3] William Tecumseh Sherman himself, General-in-Chief of the Army, was in the audience that heard Doane's report read at the Philosophical Society of Washington, and recommended that it be printed as an official document of the Senate, which was duly done in March.[4]

But the most extravagant reaction of all came from Ferdinand Hayden, the country's preeminent geologist. "The report is a modest pamphlet of 40 pages," he wrote, "yet I venture to state as my opinion that for graphic description and thrilling interest, it has not been surpassed by any official report made to our government since the times of Lewis and Clark."[5]

Stuck away in a spartan outpost in the wilds of Montana Territory,

Doane had chafed at his obscurity, his unrealized ambitions. Now, in the span of a year, he had been hailed as a conquering hero of the Indian wars and compared to the greatest of all American explorers. But it may be that he also had some faint intuition that Hayden's enthusiasm for his report was also the worm in the bud. Doane was not the only one putting pen to paper that fall and winter. His efforts had been lauded by the military hierarchy and the scientific establishment. But it would fall to others to capture the politicians, the East Coast elites, the financial interests, and the popular imagination.

The *Helena Herald* rushed Langford's first account of the expedition into print on September 26, and quickly followed up with two reports by Washburn and five by Hedges. The paper packaged the Langford and Washburn articles together as a special supplement and promoted it to editors all across the country, starting with the great newspapers of the East. "It reads like the realization of a child's fairy tale," *The New York Times* exclaimed, referring to Washburn's account. "We mean no disparagement, but the reverse," the editors hastened to explain."[6] The *Herald* saw clearly where all this publicity was going, and no doubt Doane did, too: The stir all these reports had created was "almost certain to lead to an early and thorough exploration of those mysterious regions, under the patronage of the General Government and the Smithsonian Institution."[7]

Spring and summer brought a rash of longer narratives. Walter Trumbull published his in the *Overland Monthly,* a journal published in California.[8] The young explorer predicted that as soon as the Northern Pacific Railroad provided easy access to the upper Yellowstone, "probably no portion of America will be more popular as a watering place and resort." Though the journal was obscure, the fact that Trumbull's father was a famous senator surely did no harm in publicizing his conclusions.

But the *Overland Monthly* was small potatoes compared to a new journal called *Scribner's Monthly,* which invited Langford to contribute an extended two-part article on the expedition.[9] *Scribner's* had been launched in New York in November 1870, and within a matter of months it had forty thousand subscribers. The idea was to compete directly with

Harper's Magazine, targeting the same educated readership in the great metropolitan centers of the East. But the subtitle (*An Illustrated Magazine for the People*) indicated that *Scribner's* also had a more populist streak. *Illustrated* was the key word here; in the inaugural issue, the editors promised "to furnish the finest illustrations procurable at home and abroad . . . to meet a thoroughly pronounced popular demand for the pictorial representation of life and truth."[10]

Langford himself realized that one of the shortcomings of the 1870 expedition had been the lack of a professional artist or photographer.[11] *Scribner's* filled the gap by commissioning a promising young English painter, Thomas Moran, the neurasthenic son of Lancashire weavers, to create a series of woodcuts based on Langford's verbal descriptions and the crude sketches executed by Private Charles Moore. Moran contributed more than twenty full-scale illustrations as well as a number of smaller vignettes, and Langford added his own hand-drawn sketch-map of the Upper Geyser Basin.

Not surprisingly, Moran's woodcuts were grotesquely inaccurate. (The Grand Canyon, for example, is a cleft in the earth that looks barely wide enough for a packhorse to squeeze through.) But in a sense that was the point: Yellowstone *was* grotesque and terrifying as well as beautiful, and that was a huge part of its enticement.

If the point had not been made clearly enough, *Scribner's* followed up by bringing the most dramatic narrative of all—Truman Everts's "Thirty-Seven Days of Peril"—to a national audience.[12] It was a perfect genre piece for the occasion, a morally uplifting melodrama of survival in the face of adversity. Langford called it "entertaining and painfully instructive"—just the kind of tale he might have liked to write himself. If Everts had been torn apart and eaten by a cougar, or frozen to death in a blizzard, or boiled alive in a mud volcano, it would have been a different story, and history might have taken a different turn. As it was, the message was that the upper Yellowstone was a gallery of bizarre, often frightening phenomena, enough to cause a frisson of excitement in the reader, but ultimately conquerable, even by a shortsighted, middle-aged assessor of internal revenue. Let the adventurous come and see for themselves. If they did, *Scribner's* predicted in a subsequent issue, Yellowstone would become "verily, a colossal sort of junketing place."[13]

For the nation's political establishment, meanwhile, the most potent publicity tool of all was the spoken rather than the written word. In the weeks after the expedition returned, Langford gave a couple of public talks in Helena and Virginia City. Already there were notions of taking his Yellowstone lecture on the road, although first there were some loose ends to take care of at home. In October, Langford concluded his term as Most Worshipful Grand Master of Montana Masons, handing over the office to Hedges. In December, together with his old friends Sam Hauser and James Stuart, he wrapped up the rights to trade with the Gros Ventres, an attractive business proposition now that these bad-tempered allies of the Blackfeet had been brought to heel.[14]

For the veterans of the Yellowstone expedition, there was only one sorrowful note in all this flurry of activity: the death of their titular leader, General Washburn. On the homeward stretch of the journey, he had come down with a chill. Even so, Hedges remarked in the eulogy, "if he suffered otherwise than the rest, he kept his sufferings to himself and never murmured." Weakened by years of tuberculosis, Washburn lingered through the first half of the bitter Montana winter, but on January 26, 1871, he died, at the age of thirty-eight.

By that time, Nathaniel Langford was already in "the States," and something of a celebrity. His lecture tour grew out of the relationship he had been cultivating with Jay Cooke, financier of the Northern Pacific. Langford was to be one of a number of speakers hired to promote the interests of the railroad, and the initial plan called for him to deliver his Yellowstone talk to audiences up and down the East Coast—as many as twenty appearances altogether.

The first was on January 19, at Lincoln Hall in the nation's capital. He could hardly have asked for a more influential sponsor: House Speaker James G. Blaine, who did the honors at the personal request of Jay

Cooke.[15] "A very fair audience," Langford reported; among the crowd, Ferdinand Hayden. Two days later, Langford went to the podium at Cooper Union in New York City, where Lincoln had given his historic 1860 speech against slavery. Langford's talk was part of the institution's regular program of free Saturday lectures; the previous week's speaker had been Major John Wesley Powell, who described his epic exploration of the canyons of the Colorado in 1869. Again, the hall was "filled to capacity" for the man from Montana.[16] Audiences could not get enough of the wonders of the Yellowstone.

In the end, the rest of the lecture tour never materialized. For several months, Langford went to ground with his family in Utica, New York. Deathly ill, said his sister, Chloe Taylor, who seems to have shared her brother's taste for high drama and underlining. "He had given up his lectures," she wrote to a relative, and had seen "a physician, who says, if he does not get relief from his throat trouble, he is a doomed man in less than three years."[17] Eventually, at the end of May, Langford was well enough to give one final talk at Jay Cooke's mansion, Ogontz. Three lectures: That was all he managed, but three were enough. Wheels had been greased; political energies set in motion.

Back at Fort Ellis, there were no such dramas. If you were politically well-connected, one thing led to another. But for a humble cavalry lieutenant, no matter how talented, battlefield heroics and wilderness explorations were isolated anomalies. Doane's account of the expedition had been masterful, but he was still an amateur, a man without official standing, dependent on his wits, his raw talent, his ability to game the system. He was not part of the military exploring elite. He was not a Frémont, a Gunnison, a George Wheeler, a Clarence King, a Powell.[18] He was not Ferdinand Hayden.

Once Doane's Yellowstone report was written, his life at the fort reverted to its old, dreary routines. Around the turn of the year, a fellow veteran of the Marias, Lieutenant James Batchelder, deserted, making off with two horses and defaulting on almost four thousand dollars worth of bad checks and commissary funds.[19] The problem for Doane was that as property officer he had signed off on some of Batchelder's chits, which made him a de facto accessory to the embezzlement, if only through negligence. Colonel Baker took steps to protect Doane, his favorite officer,[20] but then, in April, the fugitive lieutenant was apprehended in California, and Doane found himself cast in a different role—as star witness for the prosecution. And that meant that he had to report to departmental headquarters in St. Paul and remain there for the duration of the case—which turned out to be more than three months of agonizing frustration.

Brilliant though Doane's report had been, technically he had exceeded Sheridan's orders to conduct a "superficial exploration." Once that was done, the experts would take over, with "a well-equipped expedition . . . to scientifically examine and report upon this strange country."[21] With combat operations in abeyance since the crushing of the Blackfeet, the preparations for this were an urgent priority for the departmental command in St. Paul during the tedious months that Doane was forced to languish there. The resentment felt by the ambitious, thin-skinned lieutenant as these plans proceeded right under his nose can only be imagined.

As head of the eleven-man military expedition Sheridan appointed Captain John W. Barlow, a classmate of Custer's at West Point,[22] veteran of the Atlanta and Nashville campaigns, and now Chief of Army Engineers for the Division of the Missouri. Barlow's deputy was a specialist in astronomical observation, Captain David Porter Heap. To aid in all their mapping and measuring, they loaded up a wagon with two sextants, one artificial horizon, one sidereal chronometer, one mean solar pocket chronometer, two mercurial cistern barometers, one thermobarometer, two aneroids, two prismatic compasses, three pocket compasses, one climometer, two odometers, one pair of odometer wheels, and a box of tools.[23] The 1870 explorers had little more than an unreliable aneroid barometer, a compass, and the two gimlets, screwdriver, nippers, nails, and two dozen screws that Langford carried in his "seamless sack." It seems almost like calculated mockery of their efforts.

. . .

To make matters worse for Doane, the civilian scientific establishment under Ferdinand Hayden had also turned its spotlight on the upper Yellowstone. Hayden might have compared the lieutenant to Lewis and Clark, but now he had the means—and certainly the motive—to eclipse him.

There is debate about whether it was Langford's lecture that inspired the egotistical geologist to seek further glory by exploring the region that summer.[24] It seems more likely that he had already made the decision; he was every bit as ambitious and sensitive to slights as Doane, and he had had plenty of time to brood over his own failure to breach the Absarokas and reach the caldera in 1860. Now he must have felt that some obscure cavalryman had stolen his thunder. In the end, why Hayden made the decision is secondary; the important thing is that he made it, got the government to agree in March to a massive increase in his annual appropriation, from $25,000 to $40,000, and started laying his plans.

Within a week, on the eve of Doane's departure for St. Paul, Colonel Baker received orders from the War Department to provide a large military escort for the Hayden expedition, which can only have further inflamed Doane's jealousy.[25] Each explorer seems to have regarded the other as an upstart.

"I expect to . . . explore the Missouri and the Yellow Stone from their sources down," Hayden wrote to the geologist George Allen, whom he hired to accompany him.[26] He was less concerned with Yellowstone's wonders and geothermal freak shows at this point than he was with solving the persistent topographical conundrum that had puzzled him in 1860: How could it be that the main sources of the Columbia and the Missouri all started from a single plateau, just a few miles from one another?[27]

Like all government explorers since the Corps of Discovery, says William Goetzmann, Hayden was "'programmed' by the knowledge, values, and objectives of the civilized centers from which they depart."[28] Before the Civil War, the task of exploring the West had fallen mainly to the army. But

by 1870 civilians were in the ascendancy. The fulcrum of the government's
effort was the Geological and Geographical Survey of the Territories, and
Hayden, as geologist-in-charge, had shaped that institution (which was
part of the Interior Department) almost single-handedly, starting with his
county-by-county inventory of the resources of Nebraska in 1867.[29] The
next year he expanded his operations farther west, following the future
route of the Union Pacific from Cheyenne to Fort Bridger, and eager to
promote the interests of the railroad in any way he could. Much of this, of
course, was territory he already knew from his travels with Raynolds and
Bridger more than a decade earlier. In 1869 he moved on to Colorado,
looking mainly for mining opportunities: after that, further intensive study
of Wyoming and a side trip into Utah as far as the Great Salt Lake.

As Doane fretted in St. Paul, Hayden assembled his team. By the time
he was done, the party was thirty-two strong; "a small village," Hayden
called it. "I am overwhelmed and fearful, lest I cannot pull through with
what I have," he confided to Allen.[30] Several of them, including his general manager and factotum, James Stevenson, and his chief topographer,
Arnold Schönborn, were veterans of the failed 1860 expedition. From the
Smithsonian, the Academy of Natural Sciences of Philadelphia, and other
learned institutions, Hayden recruited paleontologists and entomolo-
gists, botanists and zoologists, physicians and statisticians, meteorolo-
gists and mineralogists. There were also a number of "general assistants,"
which was a polite way of saying politically connected junketers:

> . . . a half-dozen youths, sons or protégés of men prominent in
> Washington, who were assigned various duties as collectors in
> natural history and as all-round assistants. To these boys,
> however, the whole business at first was very much a lark, and
> the affairs concerning their horses, guns, fishing tackle and
> other equipment were of greater importance than the duties
> assigned to them.[31]

Finally there were four men who came equipped with paintbrushes
and cameras. Largely forgotten are Henry Wood Elliott, Hayden's official

artist, who had executed nice, competent sketches for the geologist on his earlier surveys, and Joshua Crissman, a commercial photographer from Bozeman whose sole moment of celebrity came when his camera was blown into the Grand Canyon of the Yellowstone by a gust of wind as he was photographing the Lower Falls, his "whole outfit gone to Hell a-flunking!"[32]

While Elliott and Crissman are no more than historical footnotes, the other two artists on the 1871 expedition did more than any others to document and celebrate the landscapes of the nineteenth-century West. One was a photographer, one a painter. The new interior secretary, Columbus Delano, insisted on the former; the Northern Pacific Railroad offered the latter, in terms that Hayden could hardly refuse.

The photographer, William Henry Jackson, was a typically footloose young man of the post–Civil War era. In 1866, after a fight with his fiancée, he left his hometown in upstate New York and wandered westward. At first he made paintings of migrants on the Oregon Trail, more descriptive than aesthetic.[33] Then he opened a studio in Omaha, Nebraska, where he worked as a journeyman portraitist for itinerant railroad workers, local businessmen, anyone who wanted a photographic record of the mark they were making on the frontier. He also met Ferdinand Hayden for the first time, briefly.

Jackson's next subjects were Indians of the southern Plains tribes like the Omaha and Pawnee. He placed them in faux-natural studio settings with appropriate props—rocks, branches, blankets—and painted backdrops. They looked noble, exotic, picturesque, suitably subjugated. From the studio he progressed to the reservations, with a traveling darkroom in his wagon, trading tobacco, knives, and items of clothing for the right to make photographs of people who were being morally uplifted by Grant's Peace Policy, learning to build wood-frame houses instead of cutting lodgepoles for tipis. Jackson's Indians were objects for examination and classification—like butterflies safely pinned in a specimen box, says his biographer, Peter Hales.[34]

Like so many young men of his generation, Jackson followed the rails west, until he fetched up in Cheyenne in 1869, at more or less the same time as Doane was passing through town on his way to Fort Ellis. It was a place much like the Montana gold camps had been five or six years earlier, a gaudy strip of saloons, gambling joints, and whorehouses—"a hell on wheels," Jackson said.[35] He still took work where he could find it, including in the whorehouses. He found that the "demi-monde" who frequented the establishment of a certain Madame Cleveland were "hot and heavy for some large portraits to frame and began to count up how many they should want." Delivering the prints later, he was "much surprised to see Dr. Hayden come in with some military friends. He acted like a cat in a strange garret."[36]

The following spring, Hayden showed up in Jackson's studio and looked through some of his recent work. Jackson had moved on to landscapes by this time, and they were remarkable, marrying an appreciation for the pristine qualities of the land with a confidence in their future civilization. Tiny human figures, proxies for the viewer, were dwarfed by the scale but ready to take ownership. Images like these were just what Hayden was looking for, and he hired Jackson on the spot.

In June 1871, already in Utah and well on the way to the upper Yellowstone, Hayden received a letter from Jay Cooke's principal aide, General Alvred Bayard (A. B.) Nettleton. The general begged the privilege of introducing Mr. Thomas Moran, who had just produced the woodcuts to illustrate Langford's articles for *Scribner's*. He wrote, "Mr. Moran is an artist (landscape painter) of much genius, who goes out under the patronage of Messrs. Scribner and Co, Publishers, NY, and our own Mr. Cooke . . . on whom you will confer a great favor by receiving Mr. Moran."[37] The Northern Pacific would cover his costs. How could one say no to Jay Cooke? So Moran joined the expedition on June 30, just as it crossed the Continental Divide into Montana.

An artist of much genius indeed. Moran had come a long way from his humble origins in the woolen mills of Bolton, Lancashire, and his family's emigration to Philadelphia in 1844, when he was seven. A skilled printmaker and watercolorist, he had returned to England in 1862, where he became infatuated with the landscapes of Turner, with their ecstatic swirls of light and color. But, he insisted, "I decided very early that I would be an American painter. I'll paint as an American, on an American basis, and American only."[38]

Moran and Jackson made an odd couple. Jackson was fit, fearless, extroverted. Moran was physically fragile and uncomfortable in the saddle. Yet their personalities meshed painlessly, and they went on to work together for twenty years, evolving a joint aesthetic of the West that was part documentary and part romantic, part promotional and part inspirational. Both men took liberties with the representation of physical reality if it did not fully serve their purpose. Moran in particular made no bones about rearranging the elements of a scene or inventing an imaginary vantage point to convey a sense of the Sublime, just as Bierstadt had done in his paintings of Yosemite.[39] "I place no value upon literal transcripts from Nature," he once said. "My general scope is not realistic; all my tendencies are idealistic." On another occasion, citing Turner, he explained, "Art is not Nature; an aggregation of ten thousand facts may add nothing to a picture, but rather be a destruction of it."[40]

Hayden's basic request of these two artists was that they should create an accurate documentary record of what they saw. What they brought back and showed the world was much more, as far removed from Moran's naïve woodcuts in *Scribner's* as Captain Barlow's sidereal chronometers and artificial horizons were from Langford's bag of screws and nails.

A thousand miles away in St. Paul, the Batchelder court-martial was finally wrapped up with a conviction in early July, and Doane rushed back to Fort Ellis as fast as he could, in such a distracted state that he lost an enlisted man who had been placed in his custody.[41] *How can they leave without me?* But by the time he returned to base on July 28, Hayden, Barlow, and their respective entourages had been gone for nearly two weeks.

Hayden had known nothing about the Barlow expedition when he set out from Cheyenne at the end of May, and he seems to have received the news with bad grace. The fact that Sheridan had also encouraged the captain to make "side surveys" when it pleased him probably did nothing to improve Hayden's mood.[42] Military explorers no longer inspired much reverence in their civilian counterparts, and Hayden's precocious twenty-two-year-old mineralogist, Albert Peale, seems to have seen the two officers as a kind of vaudeville double act: "Col. [sic] Barlow had his umbrella strapped on his saddle and Capt. Heap was the most comical looking man," Peale wrote in his journal. "He has a buckskin suit with fringes and has a lot of traps stuck about his person."[43]

The army engineers had reached Fort Ellis after a dusty, boneshaking, "almost unendurable" ten-day ride from Chicago.[44] Hayden's party, meanwhile, had traveled up through Utah and Idaho, stopping off in Virginia City for the Fourth of July, where they were greeted by an out-of-tune brass band. Jackson wandered around the gulch making photographs of the new and brutally efficient technique of hydraulic mining, which levelled entire hillsides in the search for gold. By the time they all assembled at Fort Ellis, Hayden's small village had become an "Army on the March": eighty-three men in all, a further mockery of the scale of the Washburn-Langford-Doane enterprise.[45] Almost two-thirds were cavalrymen, commanded by a hero of the terrible Battle of the Wilderness in 1864, Captain George Tyler, the full company that had been promised the previous year but had never materialized. There was the usual nonsense in the papers about an imminent Crow uprising, but this was laughed off by the resident Crow agent, who had married into the tribe and knew what he was talking about.[46]

For the first few days the expedition followed the familiar trail: the Bottlers' ranch, Yankee Jim Canyon, the Devil's Slide, the confluence with the Gardner. After that came their first and most significant divergence, turning right instead of left, which brought them to the steaming terraces of Mammoth Hot Springs.[47] Not that this was exactly a "discovery"; they found the place already occupied, a first hint of what unregulated development of the upper Yellowstone might look like.[48] The owner of Chesnut's Folly, a gentleman's club in Bozeman, had opened an embryonic spa called Chesnutville, which served up unlimited amounts of elk, trout, and beef. A certain Jim McCartney had staked a 320-acre claim and was operating a bathhouse right next to a tall, dormant spring cone that Hayden dubbed the Liberty Cap; after that, McCartney said, he planned to nail together a two-story hotel.[49] Happy invalids splashed around in the waters as if they had found Ponce de Leon's Fountain of Youth. The target clientele particularly included soldiers from Fort Ellis, and the springs were pronounced to be especially beneficial in the treatment of syphilis. Perhaps these two things were not unconnected.

Jackson unpacked his wagonload of photographic equipment—cameras, tripods, a dark tent, silver nitrate, collodion for his wet plates, and iron sulfate and potassium cyanide for developing and fixing.[50] He found Mammoth a place of infinite opportunities, both aesthetic and technical. A man usually identified as Moran posed several times for him, striking dramatic attitudes on the stepped travertine terraces. When they were done, Jackson washed his plates in the water that flowed from the springs at 160 degrees Fahrenheit, which cut their drying time by more than half.[51]

After the two-day stopover at Mammoth, the two parties took off in separate directions. Barlow and his soldiers crossed the Yellowstone and picked up the route that Cook, Folsom, and Peterson had taken in 1869. Along the way they found more fresh evidence of commercial activity, crossing a bridge that Yellowstone Jack Baronett had just built across the river to carry supplies to the newly discovered gold mines at the head of Soda Butte Creek, charging two bits per animal—a more efficient passage than the old Bannock Ford, which was only usable at times of low water.

Hayden and his civilians headed for Tower Fall, Mount Washburn, the Grand Canyon, the Mud Volcano, West Thumb, and the geysers, planning to work their way back around the lake counterclockwise. Old Faithful, the Giant, the Fan, and the Grotto all erupted on cue. The Excelsior Pool, Hayden wrote, was "every possible shade of color from scarlet to a bright rose, and every shade of yellow to a delicate cream, mingled with green from minute vegetation."[52] Moran made exquisite watercolors of its enormous pool. Hayden found that "all the descriptions given by Lieutenant Doane and others fall far short of the truth."[53] Was this a slap at his rival? Perhaps it was just an admission that he, like everyone else, was lost for words.

. . .

Riding hard, Doane finally caught up with the expedition on August 6 or 7.[54] No doubt he had done some special pleading with Colonel Baker, but he also came bearing orders that must have given him quiet satisfaction. Captain Tyler's company was to return to base. The reasons were unclear. To protect a group of Northern Pacific Railroad surveyors, some said. To do some Indian fighting, thought the young mineralogist, Peale, though *fighting* was hardly the word for what was going on at Fort Ellis—a bit of galloping around in vain pursuit of a party of hostiles who had raided a ranch, run off some stock, and killed two people. This kind of thing might have been cause for war two years earlier, but after the massacre on the Marias it was just background noise.[55]

Nonetheless, Captain Tyler left for Bozeman per instructions, taking Thomas Moran with him and leaving Doane in command of Hayden's six-man cavalry escort. But before the main body of troops departed, Doane had time to take Moran and Jackson over to the Firehole for some quick photographs and watercolors. He was now back in the role he relished: the explorer, the man in charge. Whatever Hayden may have felt about the new arrangements, he seems to have acted correctly enough at first. Protocol obliged him to invite the lieutenant to share his large wall tent, the only one the survey carried.[56] But that seems to have been as far as politeness extended. Once the two explorers were yoked together by circumstance, each of them appeared to be plagued by his personal green-eyed demons, especially after they left West Thumb and started to make their way to the south side of Yellowstone Lake.

There was something about this terrain that confounded all the early explorers. One of the soldiers in Barlow's party got lost for two days in the dense forests of lodgepole, close to where Truman Everts had gone astray. Once he had been relocated, Barlow and Heap continued on around the lake, counterclockwise. On the way, they observed the 10,000-foot hump that the Washburn party had called Brown Mountain or Yellow Mountain, and Barlow, a loyal military man, named it Mount Sheridan.

Another peak of similar size, to the south of Heart Lake, became Mount Hancock.

Doane and Hayden, meanwhile, accompanied by the topographer Anton Schönborn and one member of the cavalry escort, took off southward on a three-day exploration of the upper Yellowstone River. They went as far upstream as Bridger Lake, although Hayden, bizarrely, later wrote this off as a puddle unworthy of the name.[57] Now Doane was not just angry at being displaced by the professional scientist; he was contemptuous of his rival's ignorance and his ego. "The existence of this lake Hayden denies," he sneered, "but it is there all the same, and more, he has seen it for I showed it to him."[58] But even Doane made his share of mistakes in this difficult country. Having promised to take Hayden to Two Ocean Pass, where Jim Bridger's trout swam in both directions, he too blundered around for six miles in the timber, totally disoriented.

The military and civilian parties eventually met up again on August 20, on the east shore of Yellowstone Lake at Steamboat Springs. They were just in time for a substantial earthquake, which was followed over the next few days by a series of aftershocks. As in 1870, the last few days of the expedition rolled by without real incident, an anticlimax after so many wonders. They traveled north by Pelican Creek, the Lamar, Baronett's Bridge, Mammoth, Emigrant, and Trail Creek. When they finally arrived back at Fort Ellis on the last day of the month, it was to find a group of Northern Pacific surveyors in residence.

"The exploration of the Yellowstone basin is now completed," Hayden wrote. "Our labors have been entirely successful up to this time. No accident has befallen any member of our party. We think no portion of the West has been more carefully surveyed." In Hayden's final report, however, Doane got only a lapidary mention: "We received the benefit of his experience the previous year."[59]

Yet Doane insisted on having the last word, if only in his own mind. A few years later, writing up his army service record, he recorded with bitterness: "In command of escort U.S. Geological Survey through Park. Showed them most of their 'discoveries' that season."

· · ·

So what did the professionals "discover" that Doane had not seen and described a year earlier? In botanical, zoological, and geological terms, quite a lot; huge boxes of specimens collected with passion and sent back for study to the scholarly centers of Washington and Philadelphia. But in terms of new territory explored and accurately documented, in truth, not much. There was Bridger Lake, whose existence Hayden denied—and finding it was Doane's doing anyway. There was Mammoth Hot Springs, but by the time they saw it squatters and claimants were already in residence there. Hayden's barometric readings of altitude, for all his fancy equipment, were full of miscalculations. When he saw Shoshone Lake, he, too, decided it was the source of the Madison, the same mistake Doane had made a year before. His map was riddled with errors, and that part of the survey remained incomplete after his alcoholic topographer, Anton Schönborn, who had a long history of depression, cut his throat in a Philadelphia boardinghouse.[60]

The army engineers accomplished a little more, and Hayden eventually had to rely on Captain Heap's work to present a picture of the upper Yellowstone that tied the details of the landscape to their exact coordinates of latitude and longitude. But even the Barlow party had its disappointments: Less than a month after the engineers returned to Chicago, Mrs. O'Leary's cow kicked over the lantern in its stall, fire swept through the city, and almost all the glass plate negatives that had been made by the army photographer Thomas Hine were destroyed.[61] The Barlow-Heap party was left with no visual record of its doings, and that was where Hayden held his trump card: the paintings of Thomas Moran and the photographs of William Henry Jackson, each one of which was worth a thousand words.

In the end it all came down to power, prestige, and connections. As the educated men of the East digested the reports of the Hayden expedition, *The New York Times* summed it up in a sentence: "The accounts of the Yellowstone country hitherto received, even when brought by authorities as respectable as Lieut. Doane, have been so extraordinary that confirmatory testimony has been anxiously looked for."[62] Again, Doane's reaction can only be imagined. *Respectable authority?* What way was that to talk of the man who discovered Wonderland?

Four days after the *Times* article appeared, Hayden received another letter from Jay Cooke's agent, A. B. Nettleton, who had already sent him Thomas Moran:

> *Dear Doctor:*
>
> *Judge Kelley has made a suggestion which strikes me as being an excellent one, viz.: Let Congress pass a bill reserving the Great Geyser Basin as a public park forever—just as it has reserved that far inferior wonder the Yosemite valley and big trees. If you approve this would such a recommendation be appropriate in your official report?*[63]

The answer was yes.

30

THE FINAL FRONTIER

1872

On March 1, 1872, barely four months after Nettleton had sent his note to Hayden, President Ulysses S. Grant signed the Senate bill setting aside "a certain tract of land lying near the head-waters of the Yellowstone River" as the nation's first national park. Given the avarice, corruption, and cronyism of the time, the speed of its passage and the idealism that drove it (at least in part) were nothing short of astonishing.

Success has many fathers, but in this case Ferdinand Hayden claimed sole rights of paternity. Eight years after his expedition to Yellowstone, at a time when his reputation was in decline, he boasted: "It is now acknowledged all over the civilized world that the existence of the National Park by law, is due solely to my exertions during the sessions of 1871 and 1872."[1]

Baloney, said the territorial delegate William Clagett, a Republican who had been elected in August 1870 on a platform that included the removal of all Indians from Montana. "Since the passage of the bill," he wrote in 1894, "there have been so many men who have claimed the exclusive credit for its passage that I have lived for 20 years suffering from a chronic feeling of disgust whenever the subject was mentioned."[2] Yet some of that disgust should have been directed at the mirror, since he went on to say that, "So far as my personal knowledge goes, the first idea of making it a public park occurred to myself." The notion had first popped into his mind, he said, soon after the return of the Washburn-Langford-Doane expedition, when he heard that two men were chopping down lodgepoles to fence in the major geysers for their personal profit. This, too, has the strong smell of baloney.

Clagett says that he and Langford "probably did two-thirds, if not three-fourths, of all the work connected with the bill's passage." Certainly Langford was one of the prime movers, but a multitude of others also exerted themselves during the epic lobbying effort over those winter months.[3]

With the promotion of a Yellowstone park now a priority for the Northern Pacific, Jay Cooke helped with the preparation of an elaborate show-and-tell in the Capitol, which included Jackson's photographs, Moran's exquisite watercolors, geological specimens both bizarre and beautiful from the hot springs, and copies of Langford's articles and Doane's report (on the desk of every senator). Only Doane himself was absent, relegated once more to the life of soldiering.

The lobbyists put forward a variety of arguments, some altruistic, some pragmatic, some bordering on the cynical.[4] If one didn't work, perhaps another would. Yellowstone's natural wonders should be shielded from settlement by the government; tourism would be an economic bonanza; the government would not suffer any economic loss from protecting the area, since the land was devoid of mineral resources, the soil was too poor for agriculture, and the climate too harsh for stock-raising. Not even an Indian could live there, said Representative Henry Dawes of Massachusetts, dusting off that useful old chestnut.[5]

More important, the upper Yellowstone was a display case of all that was wildest, strangest, and most exotic about the newly conquered West, a unique gallery of wonders that could easily be lost if the government did not step in to protect them. Educated men were painfully aware of the horrors that private ownership had inflicted on Niagara Falls, and many of them would have read Henry James's tirade in the Nation, published in October 1871, just a few weeks before the congressional debate on Yellowstone began. "The spectacle you have come so far to see," the great novelist wrote, is "choked in the horribly vulgar shops and booths and catchpenny artifacts which have pushed and elbowed to within the very spray of the Falls, and ply their importunities in shrill competition with its thunder."[6]

Langford made the comparison explicit. With what seems like genuine passion, he played up the imminent threat to Yellowstone, the unintended outcome of the publicity machine that he, Doane, Hayden, and others had set in motion. Come springtime and the melting of the snows, he wrote, the hucksters and speculators would "enter in and take possession of these remarkable curiosities to make merchandise of these beautiful specimens, to fence in these rare wonders, so as to charge visitors a fee for the right of that which ought to be as free as the air or water (as is now done at Niagara Falls."[7] In the end, the law that Grant signed contained all the provisions that Langford was asking for to protect Wonderland, although how this was to be accomplished or paid for was left to the imagination.

If the idea for the park was not Hayden's or Clagett's, whose was it? Or rather, whose *ideas*—for there were two. The first was the general concept of setting aside a piece of land for permanent federal protection, and the second was the actual "public park and pleasuring-ground" that had now been created in the upper Yellowstone.

To answer the first question, historians have reached far back into antiquity, to the Hanging Gardens of Babylon and the village commons of Saxon England. As far as the American West is concerned, the trail generally leads back to George Catlin, painter of Piegan warriors and the Sun Dance of the Mandans, although it's far from clear what he had in mind when he wrote that sections of the Western wilderness "might in future be seen (by some great protecting policy of government) preserved in their pristine beauty and wildness in a magnificent park . . . A nation's park, containing man and beast, in all the wild and freshness of their nature's beauty."[8] Catlin wanted the native Americans to be part of this idyll, but he was also unsentimental enough to recognize that history was moving in the opposite direction, even in the 1830s, when the tribes of the Northern Plains were already "shrinking from civilized approach, which came with all its vices." In the end, all that would remain would be the empty hunting grounds, and visitors would be left to "contemplate, like Caius Marius on the ruins of Carthage, their splendid desolation."[9]

After Catlin came Henry David Thoreau's yearning for "national preserves . . . for inspiration and our own true recreation"; Frederick Law Olmsted's democratic practicality, which argued that government had a duty to provide its hardworking citizens with "changes of air and habits"; and the California state law of 1864 (which most educated men in Montana would have known about) protecting Yosemite and the big trees for "public use, resort, and recreation." By the time Langford and Doane got their first sight of the geysers in 1870, the park was an idea whose time had come, part of an emergent national identity in the aftermath of the Civil War, along with its companion word, *tourism.* Not that anyone had a very precise idea of what *park* meant—it would be applied indiscriminately to anything from the the faux wilderness of New York's Central Park to the theatrical spookiness of Mammoth Cave in Kentucky and the gimcrack squalor of Niagara.[10] In the West, it was a final affirmation of the conquest and civilization of the frontier. "We stepped out in front of all that surging power and announced that we were in charge," said the Yellowstone historian Paul Schullery.[11] Which was certainly how civilizers like Langford saw it.

As for the second question—whose idea was it to create the world's first national park?—the *who* seems clear in the end, but the *how, why,* and *when* will probably always be murky. Every version of the story was written many years after the fact, and for whatever reasons—the passage of time, the failing memory of old men, or the temptations of self-aggrandizement— none of them can be fully trusted.

For half a century after its birth in 1916, the National Park Service had an unassailable creation myth, celebrated in official histories, memorial plaques, museum displays, dioramas, visitor guides, public lectures by park rangers, and annual reenactments in period costume. It originated in the writings of Nathaniel Langford, who published two separate accounts of the 1870 expedition many years later, in retirement in St. Paul. It was September 19, Langford remembered, their last evening in the geyser basin, and the explorers were making ready to return to the civilized world. Sitting around the campfire at the junction of the Firehole and the Madison, they reflected on their hallucinatory experiences over the preceding month.

Langford told the story twice, with variations. The first, shorter version was in his preface to the journals of David Folsom and Charles Cook, published in 1894.[12] It was Folsom who had first spoken about a national park, Langford said. He had supposedly raised the idea with General Washburn before the 1870 expedition set off, although no one else knew about this until later—which seems odd in itself—and "I do not find that he ever published through the press his ideas on the subject." From there Langford moved on to the campfire at Madison Junction.

> Cornelius Hedges, of Helena, wrote the first articles ever published, urging the withdrawal of this region from public occupancy and dedicating it to the public as a park. I distinctly recall the place and the occasion when he first broached the subject to members of our party. It was in the first camp we made after leaving the Lower Geyser Basin. We were seated round the camp-fire, and one of our number suggested that a quarter section of land opposite the great falls of the Yellowstone would be a source of profit to its owner. Another member of the party thought the Upper Geyser Basin would furnish greater attractions for pleasure-seekers. Mr. Hedges then said that there ought to be no private ownership of any portion of that region, but that the whole of it ought to be set apart as a great national park. The suggestion met with a quick and favorable response from all the members of the party, and, to quote from a recent letter of Mr. Hedges to me, "the idea found favor with all, and from that time we never lost sight of it." On our return Mr. Hedges advocated the project in the public press. I have now in my possession a copy of the Helena *Herald* of Nov. 9, 1870, containing a letter of

Mr. Hedges in which he advocated the scheme; and in my lectures delivered in Washington and New York in January, 1871,
I directed attention to Mr. Hedges' suggestions, and urged the
passage by Congress of an act setting apart that region as a
public park. All this was several months prior to any government exploration. . . . No person can divide with Messrs.
Hedges and Folsom the honor of *originating the idea* of creating the Yellowstone National Park.

The second version appeared in the "diary" of the expedition that
Langford himself published in 1905.[13] There are some changes here, and
a good deal of narrative filigree. This time there were three profit-making
ideas, not two: The third was that "each member of the party should pre-
empt a claim and in order that no one should have an advantage over the
others, the whole should be thrown into a common pool for the benefit of
the entire party."[14] This time Hedges's proposal did not find universal acceptance: There was one dissident, unnamed. Sam Hauser perhaps? Or
Jake Smith? It's easy to imagine either of them succumbing to the allure
of a moneymaking scheme at Old Faithful.

Langford lay awake half that night, he says, turning the idea over in
his head and wondering how it could be turned into a reality: "Our purpose to create a park can only be accomplished by untiring work and
concerted action in a warfare against the incredulity and unbelief of our
National legislators when our proposal shall be presented for their ap-
proval. Nevertheless, I believe we can win the battle."

The first serious questions about Langford's story were raised in the
1960s by Yellowstone's park historian Aubrey Haines; it almost cost him
his career, for creation myths are tenacious things, not willingly surrendered by those who find them useful. Haines's critique fell into three broad
categories: inaccuracy, implausibility, and a general queasiness about Langford's personal integrity.

Langford's main factual error was to suggest that Hedges was proposing a *national park* in his letter to the *Herald*. All Hedges actually said
was that the area around Yellowstone Lake could not be reached from the

Wyoming side, being cut off by "impassable and snow-clad mountains."
Ergo, if anyone was to "secure its future appropriation to public use"
(whatever *public use* might mean), it should be Montana—with all the attendant economic benefits. Since this set up a potential dispute between
two territories, it was an implicit invitation to the federal government to
step in as arbiter. But there's no evidence that Hedges thought things
through that far.[15]

As for implausibility, it's hard to know where to begin. Langford says
that the whole group was enthusiastic about Hedges's radical idea. But if
so, why did none of them ever mention it in their diaries or later publications?[16] Did Langford really bring up the idea in his East Coast lectures?
There's no mention of it in his prepared text.[17] His comments from the
Cooper Union address had been reported in a New York newspaper, he
insisted to a turn-of-the-century historian.[18] But no one has ever found
the article, or the scrapbook in which it was supposedly pasted. Nor for
that matter has anyone found Langford's original journal, which he said
had gone missing for thirty-five years until he dug it out of a trunk of old
papers (after which it supposedly vanished again).

The only diary of Langford's from 1870 that has ever come to light is a
three-by-five-inch pocket book.[19] All this contains are brief notes of business appointments, addresses, travel schedules, sightings of relatives.

> June 4: Met Jay Cooke and went to Ogontz with Mr. Cook.
> July 7: All the folks except Hatty, Lizzie at White Bear Lake.
> July 15: Met Mr. Marshall in Chicago.

But between August 12 ("Coach late left Moriers") and November 18
("Lectured before the Helena Library Association"), there are nothing
but blank pages.

All the signs are that a diary of some kind must have existed. Within
months of the expedition Langford cranked out fifteen thousand words
for *Scribner's* and wrote the text of a lecture of about the same length. The
1905 "diary," although twice as long, contains much of the same lan-

guage.[20] But the most persuasive evidence is a letter that Langford wrote Hedges in that year, after his friend's own diary had been published.

> One thing concerning your diary surprised me, and that is its brevity. I knew that you did not write nearly as much as I did, for in having mine copied, I find repeated references to the fact that I sat up alone away into the "wee sma' hours ayont the twal," [i.e. after midnight] until Jake Smith called to me to quit working and let him get some sleep.[21]

If there had never been a diary, going into this kind of detail would seem risky in the extreme, since Hedges had been Langford's closest companion on the expedition, and he, Hauser, Gillette, and Stickney were all still alive in 1905 and more than likely to read Langford's account.

Haines's verdict was that Langford, in other respects "a literary string-saver," had probably destroyed his original diary to conceal the discrepancies and fabrications in the published version. The fabrications are beyond debate, starting with the photographs that Langford used to embellish his text, three images of himself in boots and buckskins, the very picture of the intrepid explorer. Here is a portrait of the author seated straight-backed on his horse, needle-gun at his side. And another, clearly taken in a photographer's studio, of Langford kneeling to take aim at Jake Smith's hat. And a third in which he is "packing a recalcitrant mule" in preparation for the Yellowstone trip, this time with Langford's head blatantly grafted on to another man's body. The attempt at deception is laughable.

In the end it comes down to what one makes of Langford's character and motives. Pompous, melodramatic, thin-skinned, full of self-regard and false modesty, he is not always the easiest man to like. Haines considered him an outright fraud, "a tireless and unethical self-promoter who left a legacy of shifty dealings and indignant business associates," but that conclusion seems driven more by a kind of pervasive moral animus on Haines's part.[22] The likeliest—or at least more benign—explanation of

the campfire tale is that Langford was, at bottom, a Victorian melodra-
matist, a creature of his time, with all its stylistic tics and ethical incon-
sistencies. All of the writings that he churned out during his long retirement
bear that stamp: the triumph of good over evil in his account of the vigilantes; the various tales of hairsbreadth escapes from ruthless road agents and
marauding Blackfeet; the tragedy and pathos of the murder of Malcolm
Clarke. All of them contain an edifying moral lesson, wrapped up in a rib-
bon. The Madison Junction campfire story is a classic of the type.

B ut Langford's cavalier way with facts did have its limits. For all his
massaging of the legend, he never went as far as to claim that he had
originated the idea of a national park, or even that he was its main promoter. On the contrary, he protested that his role had been inflated.[23]
While David Folsom might have had the glimmering of an idea for a
park,[24] Langford always insisted that Cornelius Hedges was the real intellectual author, and historians generally concur.

This is ironic, because Hedges's role as Yellowstone's founding father is
invariably traced back to a source that is riddled with errors, much shak-
ier than anything in Langford's diary—which those same historians have
ripped to shreds. In 1897, the Belgian Jesuit Father Xavier Kuppens wrote
a brief reminiscence, describing the visit of Hedges, Malcolm Clarke, and
Acting Governor Thomas Meagher to the snowbound St. Peter's mission
in October 1865. According to Kuppens, when he told the visitors of his
trip to the upper Yellowstone with a group of Piegan hunters, Meagher said
that, "if things were as described the government ought to reserve the territory for a national park." More egregiously, Kuppens remembered that the
governor later saw the upper Yellowstone for himself, "and on his return
told me the beauty and grandeur of the place far exceeded his expectations."
But Meagher never went near the place, of course; before he could realize his
plans, he had drowned in the Missouri. Yet oddly, Kuppens's story has been
passed down through generations of eminent Yellowstone scholars without
challenge.[25]

Be that as it may, all roads do still lead eventually to Hedges. By the late 1880s, he was being credited in the Helena press as the first to suggest the idea of a national park.[26] By the mid-1890s, Langford was providing confirmation, and Hedges, by all accounts a modest man, was describing himself as "one who claims the honor of having first proposed constituting this region of wonders into a National Park."[27] By 1904 he was adding an allusion of his own to a campfire discussion of some kind, saying that it was there "that I first suggested the uniting of all our efforts to get it made a National Park, little dreaming that such a thing were possible."[28] And Langford himself appeared to put the final seal on the debate in 1905, when he sent Hedges copies of his own published diary. Gratis, he adds jokingly. "Take them with my love," he wrote, "for no man is more entitled to them than you, who first proposed the creation of the Park."[29]

31

NORTHERN PACIFIC

1872

S o the United States had its first national park, and that meant it needed someone to be in charge of its fortunes. There were rumors that Truman Everts was angling for the job of superintendent,[1] but in May 1872 the Department of the Interior chose Nathaniel Pitt Langford. With no salary, no staff, no budget, and a simultaneous appointment as federal Bank Examiner for the Territories and Pacific Coast States, it was hard to see what Langford was supposed to accomplish. But at least, he joked, his Christian names were fortunate. Friends took to calling him National Park Langford, although cynics might have said that Northern Pacific Langford was more appropriate.

This is the last of the many questions about Langford: that his motives in promoting Wonderland were less than pure, since he was an agent of the railroad, which stood to reap the benefits of the anticipated influx of visitors from the East. But there are at least two counterarguments. First, it's hard to think of anyone in the years after the Civil War (and especially in the West) who was *not* a booster of the railroad. The Northern Pacific was seen as a civilizing agency, rather like the army, the courthouse, or the masonic lodge. It was the guarantor of long-term prosperity for the newly settled territories, tangible proof that they had evolved from rugged pioneer outposts serviced by wagon trains to full members of modern American society. An association with Jay Cooke was an association with a national hero, the man who had just bankrolled the victory of the North in the Civil War. And the ethical code of the postwar years saw no particular contradiction between patriotism and the pursuit of private profit.[2]

Second, who was best equipped to protect the wonders of Yellowstone? Not the government, at least for now; although Langford pleaded for federal funding to build access roads, Congress declined to appropriate a penny for its new creation. Not the unregulated local speculators; they would turn the place into another Niagara. That left only the Northern Pacific, the one private entity capable of providing the infrastructure— rails, wagon roads, hotels—that would foster an orderly, well-mannered kind of tourism.

While Langford was promoting the railroad, Lieutenant Doane was protecting it. He had returned from the Hayden expedition at the end of August 1871 to find a large group of Northern Pacific surveyors cooling their heels at Fort Ellis, ready to take up the work that had been suspended two years earlier after the killing of Malcolm Clarke. The overall head of the survey was William Milnor Roberts, one of the country's most prominent civil engineers. He was a nice man, by all accounts, from an old Philadelphia family, hawk-nosed, black-haired, full of energy, with only one blind spot in an otherwise tolerant nature. This was for alcohol, which was unfortunate, since his chief engineer, Edward Muhlenberg, who was in charge of the party at Fort Ellis, and the commanding officer of the post, "Piegan" Baker, would have cheerfully dumped essential equipment from their saddlebags to make room for an extra bottle of whiskey.[3]

By this time the route of the Northern Pacific had been surveyed from Duluth as far west as Bismarck, and from Tacoma as far east as Bozeman. That left a six-hundred-mile gap, down the Yellowstone and over to the Missouri. This was the most perilous stretch of all, since it would carry the tracks into the heart of the Sioux hunting grounds.[4] Langford, who was spending the summer and fall in Minnesota, was fretful about the risks. He also worried about the enormous cost of the survey and the strain it would put on the railroad's finances, which were already giving him concern for other reasons. "I do not feel as much encouraged as I did," he wrote to Hauser from St. Paul, "and think there is mismanagement"[5]—by which he meant no-bid contracts and blatant cronyism.

From the point of view of the army and the Indian Bureau, the construction of the Northern Pacific was a necessary, even a desirable way of bringing the Sioux to heel once and for all. All the western railroads, of course, had shared this strategic purpose; their completion would be "the solution to the Indian question," Sherman had written in 1867.[6] The Northern Pacific would destroy the buffalo herds on which the Sioux depended and starve the recalcitrant tribe onto the reservations. Colonel David Stanley, commander of the troops who would guard the eastern portion of the survey along the Yellowstone, knew what this meant. He wrote to departmental headquarters in St. Paul, "When the Northern Pacific crosses the Missouri, the entire Sioux question will be brought to a head, and in my opinion will only be served by an Indian War of some magnitude."[7] The name *Custer* would soon start edging its way into this conversation.

The first portion of the 1871 survey was limited, farcical, painful, and very nearly tragic. Muhlenberg and his men set off from Fort Ellis on September 16, escorted by two companies of cavalry with five officers under the command of a well-respected veteran of the Civil War, Captain Edward Ball. Muhlenberg was hitting the bottle, and the surveyors were making less than three miles a day. On hearing this discouraging news, the teetotalling Roberts hastened over from Corinne, Utah, to take matters in hand personally, and Colonel Baker was assigned to escort him. This was a partnership designed by someone with a dark sense of humor.

They finally caught up with Ball and Muhlenberg on November 8, and heard a dismal account of their misadventures, which included a fire that devastated half their camp, burned several soldiers, and sent hundreds of rounds of exploding ammunition zipping in all directions. They had spent more than six weeks struggling over the rugged hills and bluffs on the north bank of the Yellowstone and then fording the river in the evenings to find a campsite on the other side. Roberts took one look at the terrain and decided that the railroad would have to follow the south bank. This was Crow reservation land, but that was just one of those niggling bureaucratic details that could be resolved later.

After Roberts and Baker caught up with Muhlenberg, things didn't improve much. It began to snow. A trooper was trapped beneath his horse in the icy river and almost drowned. Baker had the shakes. No one could get him out of bed in the morning. One whiff of his breath told the story. One day, after Roberts had climbed to the top of a four-hundred-foot hill to examine the lay of the land, he heard bullets pinging off the rocks below him. For some unfathomable reason—alcohol, personal animus, or both?—Baker was taking potshots at him from below. For equally unfathomable reasons, Roberts kept this bizarre incident to himself, although he did decide, after sighting some Indians in the distance and seeing worse weather approaching, that it was time to turn back to Fort Ellis. He left Muhlenberg, Ball, and most of the soldiers behind to continue their work, although they abandoned the effort within a couple of days when a brutal early winter snowstorm moved in.[8]

Baker and Roberts barely outran the weather, but Ball and Muhlenberg were not so fortunate. For a week, laboring upriver, they were lashed by snow and freezing gales. With nothing to eat, the horses began to buckle at the knees. On the fifth day of the storm, Ball and a small detachment of cavalrymen made their way back to Fort Ellis through four feet of snow to fetch rescuers with grain and blankets. Doane seems to have been a member of the relief party.[9] By the time everyone straggled back to the fort, fifty-seven of the soldiers "had their faces, hands, feet, ears, and noses painfully frozen."[10]

Despite these near-disasters, Milnor Roberts viewed the whole exercise with good-natured optimism. He had seen lots of fertile soil, rich grazing land, almost unlimited potential for irrigation and water power, easy fords and bridge sites, evidence of coal. All that was needed was a creative adjustment of the current treaty with the Crows and a couple of forts at the mouths of the Bighorn and Powder rivers, which would have "a most soothing influence on Indian warriors."[11]

The Lakota were not in any mood to be soothed, however. Red Cloud, who had forced the closure of the Bozeman Trail three years earlier, had yielded leadership to the more belligerent Sitting Bull, a man of formidable charisma and intelligence. Joining forces with him were other notable warriors like Gall and Rain-in-the-Face, also Hunkpapas, and the Oglala Crazy Horse. To all of them, the Northern Pacific was an intolerable threat, and Sitting Bull's scouts had kept a wary eye on the surveyors' movements, a fact to which Roberts seems to have been oblivious.

Fort Ellis was a crowded place in July 1872. The railroad surveyors were back in residence, waiting to pick up where they had left off the previous winter. Ferdinand Hayden was also in town again, preparing to embark on another Yellowstone expedition and once more in need of logistical support, although this time his representatives found Colonel Baker befuddled with drink and quite unhelpful.[12] Hayden's party was even bigger than its predecessor—sixty-one men this time—and he split them up into two groups. Hayden himself went straight to the Upper Geyser Basin; he covered little new territory, just dug more deeply into the places he had already seen, this time with a much larger team of scientific specialists. And he made new and better maps, finishing the task that had been interrupted by the suicide of his former topographer, Anton Schönborn.

Langford, meanwhile, teamed up with Hayden's general manager, James Stevenson, to survey the approaches to the park from the Idaho side, planning to meet up with Hayden afterward on the Firehole. This was a convenient arrangement for Langford. He had no money for his superintendency, but Hayden would cover his costs; the geologist could have papered his tent with dollar bills after Congress almost doubled his appropriation for the 1872 survey.

Langford and Stevenson were the survey's true pathfinders, exploring the Snake River Plain and the Tetons, guided by an old Cockney trapper who went by the name of Beaver Dick. They were warned by the local Indian agent that the Bannocks might attack them. "This excited our merriment," Langford recalled. "The poor Bannocks! Many years have elapsed since they ceased to be regarded with any feeling not akin to pity." General Patrick Connor was responsible for that, he went on, having inflicted a terrible punishment on them on the Bear River in 1863, which cleared the way to the Montana goldfields and "entirely broke the courage of the tribe."[13]

William Henry Jackson accompanied Stevenson and Langford and made the first photographs of the three jagged pinnacles, creating a lasting archetype of the unearthly grandeur of the western mountains. Later, when the two parties met up at Camp Reunion in the Upper Geyser Basin, Jackson made the first images the public ever saw of an eruption of Old Faithful.[14] Stevenson suggested possible railroad routes along the Snake and the Madison, while Langford sketched out the rudiments of a wagon road system for the park that closely resembled the modern figure eight layout.[15] In his first (and only) annual report as superintendent, Langford reported that he and Stevenson had been the first men to climb "the loftiest of these singular mountains," the 13,770-foot Grand Teton.[16]

For Doane, this whole sequence of events must have been insult heaped upon insult: There he was at Fort Ellis, forced to watch impotently as Hayden added to his own greater glory and his fellow explorer Langford, the man who had arguably saved his life two years earlier, was given new opportunities for adventure. To make things worse, several of Doane's fellow officers were assigned to guide Colonel John Gibbon, who had taken over from de Trobriand as commanding officer of the District of Montana, on a jaunt to the park, where he sampled the waters at Mammoth Hot Springs (he didn't much care for them) and gave his name to a tributary of the Madison.[17] It's hard not to sympathize with Doane; why a man of his experience and skills should have been bypassed for this job is hard to understand.

Newly promoted to first lieutenant in December and now in command of Company G of the Second Cavalry, Doane instead found himself assigned to the railroad escort. To rub even more salt into his wounded ego, he was not even offered the chance to write another of his exemplary reports about the survey, for Phil Sheridan had chosen Captain—now Major—John Barlow, the umbrella-toting leader of the 1871 military expedition to the upper Yellowstone, as the survey's official scribe.

The escort was massive. Sober or not, Colonel Baker was placed in overall command of four companies of the Second Cavalry and four of infantry from Fort Shaw. There were 376 soldiers in all, even more than had taken part in the march on the Marias River in January 1870. Barely thirty men were left behind to guard Fort Ellis, and many of those were confined to the sick bay.[18]

Baker was to travel west to east. A second party would leave Fort Rice in Dakota Territory and travel east to west. The two groups would meet up at the confluence of the Yellowstone and the Powder River. Like Baker's contingent, the Fort Rice escort packed plenty of whiskey, enough to satisfy the large appetites of its commander, Colonel David Stanley, a humorless, antisocial man, a mean drunk with an Old Testament beard. This military force was even larger and more fearsomely armed than Baker's—586 infantrymen, 114 wagons, two Gatling guns, a gleaming Napoleon 12-pounder—for Stanley had every reason to expect open resistance. In April, he had been personally warned by Spotted Eagle, an emissary from Sitting Bull, that "he would destroy the road and attack any party that tried to build it."[19]

The Sioux did attack Stanley's column a couple of times, though in small numbers. They shot their arrows at the surveyors' marker stakes, with their colored ribbons, apparently regarding them as spirit enemies whose evil power somehow served to attract the hated trains. But it was more defiance and bravado than a serious attempt to stop the survey, and on August 18, a little more than three weeks after leaving Fort Rice, Stanley reached his destination. At the mouth of the Powder River, he and his officers cracked open some bottles of champagne, let off a few rounds from the twelve-pounder in case Baker's party was within hearing distance, and planted a cottonwood trunk on the spot, stripping off the bark and penciling a message "to our delayed friends" on the exposed wood, while angry Sioux warriors splashed about in the water, yelled and yipped, and took shots at the cottonwood.

At length, more Indians appeared, cantering around menacingly while Stanley's infantrymen formed a defensive line. One of them dismounted and walked toward the colonel. He was wearing war paint, a breechcloth, and a silk stovepipe hat. This was the Hunkpapa chief Gall, a handsome, imposing figure of whom Libbie Custer would later write, "I never in my life dreamed that in all the tribes there could be so fine a specimen of a warrior as Gall."[20] Opinions vary as to whether he and Stanley waded across the shallow river to meet in the middle. Stanley says not; Gall declined the invitation. Be that as it may, Gall had a clear message. *Go home.* And after a brief standoff, with his mission accomplished, that is what Stanley did.

Oddly, until Stanley reached the Powder River, Sitting Bull seems not to have been paying much attention to his activities.[21] Most of the Lakota warriors were encamped miles away in a prodigious village of two thousand lodges of Brulé, Hunkpapa, Minneconjou, Oglala, and Sans Arc, and their Northern Cheyenne and Arapaho allies. For the first two weeks of August, the camp was less focused on the railroad than on the Sun Dance ceremony and an impending rampage against the Crows.

Nonetheless, as Sitting Bull, Crazy Horse, and fourteen hundred warriors proceeded upriver toward Crow territory, scouts brought news of the second party of surveyors, which was slogging its way downriver toward them. Baker's contingent had made much slower progress than Stanley's, its progress impeded by mud, thunderstorms, and the colonel's whiskey jar. By August 13, two and a half weeks after leaving Fort Ellis, they had come no farther than the confluence of the Yellowstone and Pryor's Creek, close to present-day Billings. They were still 170 miles short of their rendezvous with Stanley.

The campsite on the north bank of the Yellowstone, encircled by a dry oxbow, was "exceedingly pleasant and quite picturesque," wrote Major

Barlow, dotted with clumps of willow and wild rosebushes. As a defensible position, it had both advantages and disadvantages, which would later be extensively debated. The pros were flat, open ground, proximity to water and forage, and a muddy slough that discouraged the small beef herd from straying. The cons were the surrounding bluffs, an excellent vantage point for attackers, and the nearby cottonwoods, which offered them concealment.

There had been a fair amount of Indian sign along the way—hoofprints, stray horses, dogs. But Baker paid them no mind. He had almost four hundred armed men under his command, and Captain Ball's much smaller contingent had come this far the previous year without being molested. The day passed quietly. The men went trout fishing and did their laundry in the river. In the evening, Baker posted a couple of dozen men to stand guard and retired to his tent with several other officers for a night of poker and whiskey. This went on until the soberest, like Doane, went to bed, and the rest, like Baker, began to doze over their cards.

At about three in the morning, the camp was roused by shouts from the guard. Although the Yellowstone was swollen by the recent rains, several hundred warriors had swum across with their horses and surrounded the camp, in flagrant defiance of the watch-and-wait instructions of Sitting Bull and the Lakota police, the *akicita*. The temptation to make off with some horses and mules was just too great to resist, and even the formidable Sitting Bull could not always exercise full control over his young men.

Captain Charles Rawn, in command of the four infantry companies from Fort Shaw, dashed into Baker's tent to request orders. He found the colonel in bed, "stupefied with drink, skeptical as to the presence of an enemy, and inclined to treat the whole alarm as a groundless fright upon the guard."[22] Rawn, disgusted, took charge himself, drawing up defensive lines and pushing back the attackers. Doane ordered Company G to take up positions on the north side of the camp, where they began firing blindly into the darkness. Baker stumbled around issuing incoherent instructions that no one could make sense of. Cavalry and infantry were "not acting in concert," wrote Major Barlow, a man apparently given to understatement.[23]

Despite the shambles in Baker's camp, the attackers were basically young braves out for personal glory, with no semblance of military tactics or discipline, and they were easily repelled. They made their dare-rides, a reckless practice that must have made more sense in the days before firearms. There were long-distance exchanges of rifle fire for the rest of the night, but to no great consequence. One soldier, Sergeant John McClarren, took a bullet between the eyes. A civilian camp follower named Peeples was mortally wounded. A Hunkpapa with the unhappy name of Plenty Lice went down, and the Indians were incensed when the soldiers tossed his body into a campfire.

Sitting Bull had not come looking for this fight in the first place, and as he watched one dare-rider after another fall wounded, and one horse after another fall dead, he resolved to end it before further damage was done. Even then there were some who ignored his orders, so he decided a more theatrical gesture was called for. He laid down his gun and quiver, clambered down from the bluffs, sat cross-legged on the ground in full view and firing range of the soldiers, got out his pouch and pipe, tamped it full of tobacco, struck his flint, and started puffing away, gesturing for others to join him. Their reaction may be imagined. You want us to do *what?* But four men eventually joined the smoking party—his nephew White Bull, who later gave a long account of the episode,[24] another Sioux named Gets-the-Best-of-Them, and two unidentified Northern Cheyenne. Bullets smacked into the ground all around them, raising puffs of dirt. When the pipe was done, Sitting Bull's four companions scurried back into the cottonwoods. But the chief picked up a stick, scraped out the bowl of the pipe until he was satisfied it was empty, and walked back nonchalantly to the Indian lines. Crazy Horse subjected the soldiers to one last contemptuous dare-ride, resplendent in a white shirt and with his long black hair streaming in the wind, until his horse was shot out from under him, and the encounter was over.

In the annals of warfare, the Battle of Pryor's Creek—or of Poker Flats, as some of the more irreverent soldiers took to calling it—didn't amount to much. But in political terms it was a watershed. Another rail-road survey was aborted,[25] and the most militant factions among the Sioux were emboldened. Sitting Bull and Crazy Horse, both apparently touched by immortality, were confirmed as their supreme war chiefs. Sitting Bull adjusted his military strategy, the anachronistic dare-rides and individual acts of valor giving way to more sophisticated tactics that would allow the Sioux to confront massed military forces on equal terms. Baker's fiasco at Pryor's Creek set the scene for the collapse of the Northern Pacific, a national economic disaster, and eventually Custer's debacle on the Little Bighorn.

The battle also had serious repercussions for Cheyney Doane. Colonel Baker returned to Fort Ellis a virtual pariah, condemned for his blunder in choosing such a vulnerable campsite, his alcoholism, his failure to pursue Sitting Bull.[26] Baker's disgrace robbed Doane of his main patron and protector, putting another big dent in his dreams of being recognized as one of the great American explorers.

"The command returned yesterday," wrote Peter Koch, the young Dane who worked in the sutler's store at Fort Ellis, "and when Col. Baker came up and shook hands with me, I had a great notion to ask him how he dared look any man in the face."[27] In another letter, Koch wrote to his future wife:

> The main cause of this retreat was Col. Baker's drunkenness and incapacity, and unless the affair is hushed up, which I trust it will not be, he will doubtlessly be dismissed from the service. The affair is a disgrace to the army . . . You remember, of course, that he commanded the famous Piegan expedition three years ago; but this time he didn't happen to find the Indians asleep and sick with the smallpox.[28]

Koch need not have worried; the affair was not hushed up. On the contrary, General Hancock placed Baker under arrest on October 15, and convened a court of inquiry. In the end it declined to bring charges, but the colonel was quietly shunted off to a series of low-visibility postings in

Nebraska and Wyoming, where he spent most of the following year purchasing horses and supplying mule trains.

When Baker's transfer to Omaha was announced in January 1873, Montana mourned his passage. The Bozeman paper saluted him as "a true friend to our best interests, and a worthy and accomplished gentleman."[29] And the *Helena Herald* added, without apparent irony, "[his] name is associated with the best memories and most effective achievements of our border defense."[30]

Part Five

TOURISTS

32

TEMPLE OF THE LIVING GOD

1872–1877

I n the summer of 1877 it seemed that all roads led to the national
park. There were visitors of high rank, visitors on a spree, and violent visitors of the most unanticipated kind.

General of the Army William Tecumseh Sherman decided that
it was finally time to see this famous Wonderland that his officers had
talked so much about. He went for two weeks in August, in hot, parched
grasshopper weather, setting out from Fort Ellis with only a four-man
cavalry escort, disdainful of the idea that there was anything to fear from
Indians. He saw the standard sights: Mammoth Hot Springs, Tower Fall,
the Grand Canyon, the lake, the geyser basins. The general's son, Thomas,
who came along on the trip, rode to the top of Mount Washburn with his
father and had an oddly mixed reaction: the familiar awe coupled with
an apprehension at how easily the place could be despoiled. "The view is
simply sublime," he noted in his account of the trip. But at the summit he
found a tin box filled with slips of paper bearing the names of earlier
visitors. *Such vulgarity:* "Society in general goes to the mountains not to
fast but to feast, and leaves their glaciers covered with chicken bones and
eggshells."[1]

On the way home, passing through the Lower Geyser Basin, Sherman
bumped into a party of tourists—one of two in the park at the time—and

reassured them that they had nothing to worry about. He confirmed the advice that they would have read in the first published guidebook: "Dangers from Indians there are none," the geysers being a place where "Manitou displays his anger towards his red children."[2] Langford's successor as superintendent, Philetus Norris, who took up his (still unpaid) office in the spring of 1877, promoted this as official policy: The government would guarantee that Wonderland was Indian-free.[3]

In hindsight, Sherman's complacency is striking. Just days before the two groups of tourists left home, one from Helena and one from nearby Radersburg, Cornelius Hedges made a breathless entry in his journal: "Exciting news . . . More exciting news . . . War meeting."[4] The exciting news was that hundreds of rebellious Indians, Nez Perce, were moving into the Bitterroot Valley after breaking through a militia roadblock at the Lolo Pass, outwitting Captain Edward Rawn, the officer who had taken over from the stuporous Major Baker at Pryor's Creek and was now in command of the small army base in Missoula. It was the fourth time in six weeks that the Nez Perce had made goats of their pursuers, and in a reprise of the panic of 1869, the leading men of Helena gathered at the International Hotel and resolved to form a volunteer company of cavalry.

The Nez Perce, friendly toward the whites since the days of Lewis and Clark, had been subjected to one indignity after another since the Idaho gold rush in 1860. They had been deeply factionalized since the 1863 treaty that had shoved them onto a reservation on the Clearwater River. About a third of the tribe had accepted this miserable arrangement, led by the chief whom the whites called Lawyer. The remainder, the "non-treaty" Nez Perce, split into two bands. One settled on the Salmon River. The other, led by Old Joseph, moved into Oregon and pitched their tipis in the Wallowa Valley. When the peaceable chief died in 1871, he was succeeded by his son, Heinmot Tooyalakekt—Thunder Traveling to Loftier Mountain Heights, or Young Joseph, a man of the same quiet dignity.

President Grant said he would carve out a new reservation in the valley, but that was anathema to the settlers, who had their eyes on the Wal-

Iowa country, too, and Grant backed down. Joseph tried peaceful coexistence, but the sides were too unequal, so the army eventually decided that mediation of some kind was necessary. The officer in charge of the talks was the "praying general," the prideful, spade-bearded, one-armed Oliver Otis Howard (the other one had been torn off by a pair of minié balls at the battle of Fair Oaks in 1862). Evangelist and humanitarian, Howard told the great Indian fighter General George Crook that "the Creator had placed him on earth to be a Moses to the Negro. Having accomplished that mission, he felt satisfied his next mission was with the Indian."[5] Since the Nez Perce had been extensively Christianized, Howard was optimistic that he and they would find common ground.

However, Joseph perplexed "Cut Arm" with strange talk about his people having a spiritual attachment to Earth and their native land, a peculiar concept that Howard found hard to square with his Christian cosmology. It was time for a little coercion. After all, in the words of the missionary Marcus Whitman, who had helped bring the Nez Perce to Jesus in the first place, "When a people refuse or neglect to fulfill the designs of providence, they ought not to complain about the results."[6]

Howard gave Joseph thirty days to move his people back into Idaho. He and the other nontreaty chiefs debated the matter: acquiesce or fight? As happened so often, the headstrong young men took the decision out of their hands. Several of them, inflamed by white man's water, took out their rage on the settlers. The first attack took four lives. Then, in a two-day orgy of violence, they killed fifteen more. Joseph had no option but to flee with eight hundred of his people, and the army gave chase. The government had engaged in hundreds of military encounters with Native Americans since 1776, but this was the first that it officially designated a war.[7]

The Nez Perce made fools of their pursuers. On June 17, cavalry units fell into an ambush in White Bird Canyon, taking dozens of casualties. On July 3, they surprised the Nez Perce at Cottonwood Creek but were forced to retreat, losing another fifteen men to "galling fire." A week later, in a pitched battle on the Clearwater, they were again outwitted and outgunned. When they reached the Lolo Pass, following the rugged, heavily forested trail they had shown Lewis and Clark in 1806, the Nez Perce sailed through Captain Edward Rawn's barricades unmolested. Cut Arm acquired a new nickname: General Day After Tomorrow.

Montana came up with nicknames of its own. People called Rawn's outpost Fort Fizzle. Every newspaper in the territory called his manhood into question. Cornelius Hedges went to his panicky war meeting. At the same time, there had to be an official rationalization of the dog's breakfast Howard had made of the campaign. If Joseph could outwit the U.S. Army, he must be a superhuman military tactician. In fact, Howard's humiliation was the work of half a dozen other Nez Perce leaders, notably Toohoolhoolzote and Allalimya Takanin, or Looking Glass. Joseph himself did not have the mind or the temperament of a warrior. But he was the leader of the band, so people should disregard these other chiefs with the unpronounceable names; Joseph would be the Red Napoleon.

Within a week of the fiasco at Fort Fizzle, however, the "war" quieted down. The Nez Perce rode southward up the Bitterroot without bothering the local settlers, with whom they had no quarrel. For more than a week there was not a sniff of violence. The hysteria in Helena abated, and the two parties of tourists loaded up and set out on their grand Yellowstone adventure.[8]

The Radersburg party left home on August 6. There were ten of them, including a handsome and unusually self-possessed newlywed named Emma Cowan, who had been fascinated by the trappers' tales of the upper Yellowstone ever since arriving in Virginia City as a child in 1864 and had already visited Mammoth Hot Springs in 1873. Even more remarkable, she took her twelve-year-old sister along this time for company. The Helena group, nine strong, all male, set off a week later. They took the old explorers' route up the Yellowstone, past the Bottlers' ranch and the Devil's Slide, and reached Mammoth on August 20.

The Radersburg group had been in the park for five days at that point. They entered the Upper Geyser Basin from the west, traveling up the Madison with a double-seated carriage, a baggage wagon, four saddle horses, and a selection of musical instruments to while away the evenings in camp. "With J. A. Oldham as violinist, my brother's guitar, and two or three fair voices, we anticipated no end of pleasure," Emma Cowan wrote in her lively account of the trip.

Despite her jaunty tone, the fact was that visitors to the national park were still few and far between. The first recorded tourists, in the strict sense of the word, had come to the upper Yellowstone in the late summer of 1871, a party of six men and one tailless dog. Predicting a tourist boom, they raised $2,000 to start up the Virginia City and National Park Free Wagon Road to service it.[9]

But there was no boom, not yet. During the five years of Langford's tenure as superintendent, no more than five hundred visitors came in any single summer. Indians or no Indians, the trip was not for the faint-hearted. There were still no roads and nowhere to stay other than Mc-Cartney's ramshackle hostelry at Mammoth Hot Springs, and Langford's main concern was to keep it that way until development could happen in an orderly fashion. After the jaunt with Hayden in the summer of 1872, he came to the park only once more—briefly, two years later, and apparently for the main purpose of evicting Matthew McGuirk from his 160 squatted acres on the Boiling River, a mile down the hill from Mammoth. Langford's old friend David Folsom, whom he appointed as his deputy superintendent, also made a single visit in 1873.[10]

Langford decided to grandfather in McCartney's claim, since he could personally vouch for the man's integrity, but otherwise his main preoccupation was to turn down applications for leases from Niagara-style hucksters of one flavor or another: people who wanted to build saloons and sawmills, limekilns and landscape gardens, a menagerie, a "race course and observation grounds."[11] Eventually he proposed a formal set of regulations to the Interior Department. Hitherto accepted practices would be redefined as offenses within the boundaries of the park: Setting an untended fire was arson; cutting down a tree was timber theft; fishing and hunting were poaching.[12]

By the summer of 1873, there were much worse abuses to worry about than eggshells and chicken bones. It took only a few boorish visitors to wreak havoc: Many of the most beautiful sinter deposits around Old

Faithful, the Castle Geyser, and the Beehive were already gone, hacked away and carried off as souvenirs.

Hunting in the park was also out of control. European aristocrats like Windham Thomas Wyndham-Quin, 4th Earl of Dunraven and Mount Earl, who came there in 1874, blasted away at anything on four legs.[13] The following year, a visitor estimated that professional hunters had slaughtered four thousand elk in the area around Mammoth Hot Springs during the previous winter, and lamented that "[t]heir carcasses and branching antlers can be seen on every hillside and in every valley."[14] Many were killed for nothing more than their tongues, which everyone from Lewis and Clark to Teddy Roosevelt appreciated as a particular delicacy.

Meanwhile, the military strategy of fragmenting the buffalo herds to starve the Indians onto the reservations had metamorphosed into commerce, entertainment, bloodletting for its own sake. Hide hunters fed a voracious market in the tanneries of the East. "I think it would be wise to invite all the sportsmen of England and America [to the Sioux hunting grounds] for a grand buffalo hunt, and make one grand sweep of them all," said General Sherman.[15] Happy to oblige, said men with names like Shoot-'em-up Mike, Light-Fingered Dick, Texas Jack, Dirty-Face Jones, and Prairie Dog Dave. Phil Sheridan, back from a year of gallivanting around the Old World in the company of kings, queens, emperors, and grand viziers, laid on a gala buffalo hunt on the Nebraska plains in 1871 in honor of the Romanov Grand Duke Alexis, accompanied by Buffalo Bill Cody and George Armstrong Custer. The hoi polloi pitched in cheerfully, poking their Winchesters out of the windows of their Union Pacific pullman cars and taking potshots at the defenseless herds. A semicompetent marksman could bring down sixty buffalo a day, leaving the corpses to rot where they fell. Buffalo bones were ground up and sold for pennies as fertilizer.

The great herds of the West had once numbered more than 30 million, perhaps as much as 70 million. By 1872 they had been reduced to seven million; by 1883 only two hundred survived. According to Blackfeet legend, the buffalo had come originally from a great hole in the ground, but the white man found the hole, drove all the buffalo back into it, and stoppered it shut.

Good wagon roads might bring in more vandals and poachers, Langford acknowledged, but they were also essential if the "wholesale destruction" of the park was to be prevented. Build the roads and "interested and trustworthy persons" could be granted leases to build properly run hotels at the main points of interest—Mammoth, the falls, the lake, the geyser basins—and given powers, even deputed as U.S. marshals if necessary, to enforce the rules.[16]

Langford wrote to Interior Secretary Delano at least six times, appealing urgently for money—$150,000. No response. Well, make it a hundred thousand, then. Nothing.[17] His argument was simple: Congress had laid out the noble goal of protecting this "Temple of the Living God," but without appropriations and enforcement those were just words on paper. In some ways it was worse to have created an unfunded pleasuring ground than to have done nothing: After all the publicity, the park was more likely to attract vandals than if it had remained terra incognita.

Again, the perennial problem arises in judging Langford: Doubt a man's character and you doubt the motives for everything he does. His critics say that the ineffectiveness of his five-year superintendency was deliberate. Beneath the pieties, his denial of leases to the hucksters and speculators was a ploy to advance the interests of the Northern Pacific; keep other commercial players out of the field, and the railroad would reap the whole harvest.[18]

Yet Langford's letters to Delano seem as impassioned as anything he ever wrote. He needs money. He needs it *now*, urgently, without delay. When he tells Delano that the whole vast field of natural wonders is at risk, that "the delicately tinted stucco and arabesque of the borders of the springs" is already vanishing, that "a single break in one of them often destroys the work of years,"[19] there seems no real reason to question his sincerity. Not once does he mention the Northern Pacific. On the contrary, when he talks about railroads—and he does, enthusiastically—it's to describe the easier access routes to the park through the Madison Valley, which was not Northern Pacific territory and would bring it no benefit.

More to the point, when Langford went on pushing the government to create the infrastructure for private development of the park, he could no longer have had the Northern Pacific in mind. For in 1873 the whole scheme had collapsed, taking the rest of the national economy down with it, and there was no prospect of Jay Cooke's enterprise reaching Yellowstone for years.

A lot of Cooke's problems could be traced back to Colonel Baker's embarrassment at Pryor's Creek. The true facts of the case were bad enough, but the jitters of Eastern investors were made much worse by the first exaggerated reports of the encounter. Because of some bureaucratic foul-up, Phil Sheridan's office in Chicago initially said that forty soldiers had been killed or wounded in the "battle" with Sitting Bull and Crazy Horse. The *New York Herald,* always fond of a lurid story and heedless of its consequences, wrote of "20,000 hostile Indians well-armed and ready for the fray."[20] Cooke could have cut his losses right there, and run a perfectly good little railroad from Duluth to Bismarck. But he decided to press on, regardless of the exorbitant cost of more surveys, and in the process changed the history of the West—and indeed of the nation.

The Yellowstone survey party that the Northern Pacific sent out in the summer of 1873 dwarfed those of the preceding year, and those had been huge. This one had thirteen hundred men, with artillery support; infantry troops again under the command of the alcoholic Colonel Stanley; the Seventh Cavalry under George Armstrong Custer. The surveyors were attacked by Hunkpapa within an hour of breaking camp at the start of the journey. On August 4, Gall, Rain-in-the-Face, and Crazy Horse led a more serious assault on Custer's forces. A week later, farther up the Yellowstone near the mouth of the Bighorn, Sitting Bull's warriors attacked again.

Like Pryor's Creek, it was more skirmish than battle, and the casualties were minimal. The real complicating factor was Custer's gift as a narrator, and the platform given to his report by the irrepressible editors of the *New York Tribune*—a savage foe, hideous war cries, gravest danger to life and limb, the enemy beaten back against great odds, heroic cavalrymen, an inspirational commander![21] The more sober *New York Times* offered its own verdict:

> The truth is, we have now struck upon the last and bravest of the old Indian races of the plain. The Sioux beyond the Missouri is a very different Indian from the stupid, peaceful, vagabond creatures who haunt the neighborhood of white settlement in the north-west . . . If several thousand [sic] of our best soldiers, with all of the arms of the service, under some of our most dashing officers, can only hold their ground on the narrow line of march for 150 or 200 miles west of the Upper Missouri, [what] will peaceful bodies of railroad workmen be able to do, or what can emigrants accomplish in such a dangerous region?[22]

The *Times* drew from this an undebatable lesson: There must be total war on the Sioux, commanded by a suitably dashing officer, and the Northern Pacific must be abandoned.

In truth, while Custer's report delivered the coup de grace, the railroad had been grievously wounded for months. Countless investors had been crazed by the lavishness of federal land grants and railroad subsidies after the Civil War, and as a result the economy had overheated, with way too much capital tied up in projects like the Northern Pacific that offered only long-term returns. Jay Cooke found himself saddled with millions of dollars of unmarketable railroad bonds, and rumors swept Wall Street that his credit was no longer good. On September 18, 1873, Cooke declared bankruptcy, and his downfall triggered a cascade of bank failures and a depression from which the United States took six years to recover. Dream had turned to pipe dream. Now the Northern Pacific was mocked as the line that ran "From Nowhere Through No-Man's Land to No Place."[23]

So there was no railroad to Yellowstone in 1877. The only way to get there was by the faint tracks of earlier travelers, and the Cowan party proceeded along them to the Firehole, where they pitched camp for five days near the Fountain Geyser.[24] On the sixth, they moved downriver to the Castle, tired and hungry after two weeks under canvas and ready to make for home. The geyser erupted noisily during the night. "With our heads pillowed on the breast of Mother Earth, one seemed in close proximity to Dante's Inferno," Emma Cowan wrote. But it had been "a delightful time."

As they made ready to leave, a group of riders came in sight: General Sherman and his entourage, on their way back to Fort Ellis. The general had received new intelligence from a courier, although it did not seem to disturb him much. There had been another violent encounter with the Nez Perce, the worst yet. But it had happened more than two hundred miles away to the west, and even though the Indians were now headed in this direction, there was no reason for alarm. Sherman's scout "assured us we would be perfectly safe if we would remain in the Basin, as the Indians would never come into the park," Emma Cowan wrote. But she seems to have wondered slightly about the subtext, and her unease grew as Sherman's party left before nightfall, apparently in some haste. If the general had instructed the tourists to remain near the geysers, what did that say about how close the Nez Perce would come?

33

THE NERVE TO EXECUTE

1874–1876

B y the time Sherman encountered the Cowan party, his commanders in the field had no remaining doubts about the intentions of the Nez Perce. They were headed for the caldera with eight hundred people and a herd of fifteen hundred horses. Whatever the fakelorists might say, the tribe knew the upper Yellowstone well; it was a place of deep spiritual significance for them, and they had traversed it often on their way to the buffalo grounds.[1] They were going in that direction now, looking to join up with their longtime allies, the Crows, another tribe historically friendly to the whites; there was an old saying: "The Crow heart is Nez Perce, and the Nez Perce heart is Crow."[2]

In response, the army was beginning to move troops toward the main exits from the park to close off the refugees' escape route. Potentially the most strategic of these blocking forces would be the smallest: a column of cavalry, armed civilians, and Indian scouts from Fort Ellis, commanded by the officer who knew the upper Yellowstone better than any man alive.

C heyney Doane had followed a tortuous five-year path from the skirmish at Pryor's Creek to command of the cavalry unit that was about to head down the familiar trail that led to Paradise Valley. Sitting Bull and Crazy Horse had cost Doane his patron and protector, Piegan Baker, and those that followed had no interest in playing the same role. Colonel Nelson Sweitzer, Baker's immediate replacement, was a stolid officer of impeccable character, who kept Doane busy with tedious assignments around the fort.[3]

Major James Brisbin, who took command in February 1876, had a varied and impressive background: antislavery orator, organizer of the negro cavalry in the Army of the Potomac, and sometime lawyer, newspaper editor, poet, and essayist. He was a barrel-chested, kindhearted fellow, though tormented by rheumatism. He enjoyed planting vegetable gardens at Fort Ellis and claimed that his men never suffered from scurvy. In later years he would be known as "Grasshopper Jim," a promoter of ranching on the plains and a prolific writer on that topic. His biggest success was a book called *The Beef Bonanza*. But there were shorter works, too: "The Beef Kingdom," "The Beef Supply," "Beef, Beef, Beef." For the reader in search of variety, there was "The Alfalfa Question."[4]

In retirement, Brisbin would become a passionate advocate of Native American rights. Quoting Helen Hunt Jackson, he called the United States' treatment of the Indians since independence "a century of dishonor," and wrote, "We have . . . driven them into desert places where we are now leaving them to starve and die like beasts of the field. It is a wicked thing, a desperately wicked thing that we are doing." He suggested that those who had fought slavery should now "give their attention to the Red Men, who are as deserving of their labors and sympathies as ever were the negroes." His sympathy for the Crows in particular verged on the treasonous. "If I were a Crow Indian instead of a white man," he wrote, "I would go home and get my gun and kill the first white man I met."[5]

Brisbin had no time for Doane, regarding him, not without reason, as arrogant and insubordinate. He especially had no interest in the lieutenant's ambitions to be recognized as America's greatest explorer. The dislike was mutual, and Doane responded in his usual fashion. The more his commanding officers tightened the leash, the more he ignored them and looked for protection in more elevated places.

In late 1871, as Congress was considering the creation of the national park, Henry Stanley of the *New York Herald* had finally found the long-missing Scottish missionary-explorer David Livingstone alive on the shores of Lake Tanganyika. The world had been transfixed by the drama, but Doane was not impressed. For him, the only salient point was that Livingstone had failed in his attempt to locate the source of the Nile. Doane had already been instrumental in solving the greatest geographical conundrum in the United States; now he proposed to solve the greatest geographical conundrum in the world.

In September 1874, Doane wrote at great length to Professor Joseph Henry, secretary of the Smithsonian, who had praised his report on Yellowstone.[6] Let Henry send him to Africa to discover what had eluded Livingstone. "To be qualified to explore one Country, is to be qualified to explore any other," he informed Henry blithely. "The Man who knows what he is aiming at, and has the nerve to execute is invincible."

Doane went on to assert that his exploring instincts were infallible: "I always travel as an Indian does, without guide or compass, and do not know what it is to have the sensation of being lost." The "Great Traveller" was mediocre by comparison, Doane said, his pen dripping contempt. He had wasted fifteen years in Africa "without any intelligent plans of operation," and only toward the end of his life had he understood what Doane knew instinctively—that the key to exploration was not to follow rivers to their source. That was why Livingstone had mistaken the Congo for the Nile. Doane's understanding of the sources of the Yellowstone, the Missouri, and the Snake came from grasping the logic of *watersheds,* not water courses. Climb to the highest summit and the landscape was an open book; a man could see clearly the divides that separated one watershed from another. As for the celebrated newsman who had found Livingstone, he was quickly dismissed. "Stanley lacks calibre," Doane told Henry. "He does well what he is sent to do, but does not rise to the Conception of Great Achievments [sic]."

So much for Livingstone and Stanley. Doane now moved on to Hayden, the man who had stolen his reputation on the upper Yellowstone. This was not a tactic that was likely to get him far, since secretary Henry was a personal friend of the geologist's and had been one of his earliest champions. But Doane plowed ahead. All he needed to find the source of the Nile was a small steam launch, some basic tools and supplies, and a junior army officer as an assistant. Beyond that, "I would hire but two white men, a Photographer and an Engineer, and would qualify myself to dispense with both if necessary." The whole thing could be done for ten thousand dollars plus the salaries of the two officers for two years. Doane's frugal expedition would "solve a great probelm [sic] in Science, and open the water Channels of the heart of a Mighty Continent to the current of Civilization"—and all for "the expenditure of one tenth the cost of the Annual Explorations by Professor Hayden and others."

Henry wrote back two months later, his tone polite but laced with acid: "It is to be regretted that the proprietor of the *New York Herald* was not cognizant of your qualifications and desires since, in connection with the London *Daily Telegraph*, he has just sent out Stanley a second time to carry on African explorations."[7]

Somehow Doane wangled an extended leave so that he could press his case over the winter with others in Washington. This time he went all the way to the top, to General Sherman himself, who had heard enough of the lieutenant's reputation to write a recommendation to his brother, John Sherman, "the Ohio Icicle," who chaired the Senate Committee on Finance. The icicle in turn commended Doane to the Secretary of War, William Belknap, but Belknap's answer was the same as Henry's: thank you, but no thank you.[8]

This did not mean that Belknap saw Doane as a man of no utility. On the contrary, the Secretary of War, like so many other senior officials, was anxious to see this new national park everyone was talking about, and Doane would be the perfect guide. William Strong, a retired

general and Chicago businessman who joined Belknap's party, called
him "a striking officer . . . a superb horseman, a keen and daring hunter,
and a dead shot. We are very fortunate to have him with us on this
trip . . . In this country he is spoken of and pointed out as the man who
'invented Wonderland.'"[9]

They spent a full month in Wonderland in the summer of 1875—Belknap,
Strong, two generals, three colonels, and Captain William Ludlow, head of
the engineering corps in St. Paul. The great Sheridan himself was supposed
to join the junket but had to withdraw at the last minute, sending his personal cook by way of compensation. The legendary army scout and hunter
"Lonesome Charley" Reynolds, who would later perish with Custer at the
Little Bighorn, kept the party well supplied with meat.

Doane led a cavalry escort two dozen strong. His favorite enlisted
man, Daniel Starr, who had carried out his lieutenant's gruesome nocturnal orders on the Marias, served as packer, with Private William White as
his assistant. White idolized Doane, and Doane had a soft spot for White,
whom he described as "a solemn young fellow, useful in any service, full of
romantic ideas, sober, reserved. A man of fearless disposition."[10]

Some of the officers may have thought Doane uncouth, but others
were keen admirers. Ludlow had devoured his writings on the 1870 expedition and praised "their beauty of diction, as well as the clearness of
their descriptions."[11] Doane "seems to have the most magnificent contempt for a trail," Strong wrote, "and will leave it at any moment to dash
straight across the country, no matter how rough and difficult, if he
thinks anything is to be saved in distance."[12] The lieutenant won everyone's praise when he improvised a comfortable mule litter to transport
the ailing General Randolph Marcy, the army inspector general, who had
caught a severe chill after falling into the Yellowstone while trout fishing
and was too weak to ride a horse.[13]

Ludlow thought less highly of Nathaniel Langford. Blaming the absentee superintendent, perhaps unfairly, for the slaughter of game, he believed that "the cure for . . . [these] unlawful practices and undoubted
evils can only be found in a thorough mounted police of the park." Yellowstone should be transferred to the jurisdiction of the War Department,

Ludlow said; cavalrymen could easily be deployed from Fort Ellis and stationed at Mammoth Hot Springs and on the Firehole.[14] This proposal planted a seed that would become Doane's obsession.

Protocol demanded that the lieutenant sleep in one of the lavishly appointed officers' tents, while the enlisted men bedded down under rude shelters of tree limbs. Doane despised his superiors' self-indulgence, Private White says, the empty bottles of champagne and claret dumped at each abandoned campsite. He insisted on eating with the common soldiers, where he could enjoy "plain food and plain companionship" and share his opinions freely. "He was too straightforward in mind and too bluntly outspoken to conceal his contempt for the feather-bed travelers," White says. "He let loose his thoughts in words to us, summed up about like this: 'Brass buttons polished, boots shining, salute all superiors, starve to death if alone on the prairie.'"[15]

After the expedition broke up, "genial Sam Hauser" hosted a lavish party for the participants in Helena,[16] and Belknap presented Doane with an expensive pair of field glasses as a personal gift. His Nile initiative might have failed, but the lieutenant seemed secure in the patronage of the powerful. However, the cesspit of corruption in Washington during President Grant's second term brought Belknap to grief just six months after his Yellowstone trip. The secretary's downfall was a dime-novel scandal that began with the crooked sale of post traderships and grew to embrace "scheming ladies of society, orphaned children, domestic intrigues, journeys to Europe, secret exchanges of money, rumored suicides, hints of illicit sex, flights to Canada, and two sisters wedded to the same husband."[17]

Stripped of support in Washington, and with the unsympathetic Brisbin now in command at Fort Ellis, Doane was like a man with one foot on each of two boats that were drifting apart. He had to choose between ambition and duty. Was he the explorer who had invented Wonderland or the professional soldier at the service of his country? He craved the first identity, but was increasingly hostage to the second. But history presented him with one last opportunity to shine in both fields at the same time. The outcome would be determined by a strange set of circumstances that included Brisbin's rheumatism, accidents of timing, bad weather, and the headstrong arrogance of George Armstrong Custer.

In 1874, less than a year after the collapse of the Northern Pacific, Custer had led a massive and provocative expedition to the sacred Black Hills of Dakota, followed by yet another wave of gold hysteria of the sort that had already torn apart Indian societies from California to Montana.

Just before leaving for Yellowstone in July 1875, Secretary Belknap had taken part in talks with the Sioux chiefs Red Cloud and Spotted Tail, who had been summoned to Washington for a resolution of the Black Hills crisis. Finding them intransigent, government representatives followed up with a visit to Nebraska, bearing a checkbook with lots of room for zeros. They offered six million dollars for outright purchase of the Black Hills, or $400,000 a year for a lease. The chiefs scoffed at the offer; this was sacred land, far more valuable to the Sioux than gold was to the whites. Enough of this nonsense, said inspector E. C. Watkins of the Indian Bureau; time to send in the troops to "*whip* them into subjection."[18]

Sheridan, as usual, favored a Marias-style strike in the depths of winter, to be executed by Custer. But Sitting Bull moved his people out of range, and foul weather prevented the necessary forces from being marshaled in time. So it was springtime before the army was finally ready to attack. Sheridan's battle plan was to envelop the Sioux with troops advancing from three directions simultaneously: northward down the Powder River; westward from Fort Abraham Lincoln in Dakota Territory; and eastward from Fort Ellis. The army would entrap them on the Yellowstone, with each column authorized to attack separately if they encountered hostiles. If everything had gone according to plan, Doane would have either been part of a smashing victory or died at the Little Bighorn.

Doane rode with the smallest of the three forces, the Montana Column, a joint force of 436 officers and men from the Second Cavalry and the Seventh Infantry.[19] Its commanding officer, Colonel John Gibbon, seems an unlikely candidate for the job. A model of rectitude, he enjoyed riding over from Fort Shaw to Fort Ellis to give temperance lectures. The Indians called him No Hipbone, on account of a debilitating pelvic wound sustained at Gettysburg. Under Gibbon's overall authority, the Second Cavalry units were commanded by Major Brisbin, although he spent most of the time grumbling about his aches and pains, was largely confined to an ambulance, and seems not surprisingly to have inspired little confidence in his troops. "One of the political dead-beats who have crowded into the army since the war," wrote Lieutenant John Bourke, who kept a detailed journal of the campaign. "He has never heard a shot fired in a fair fight."[20]

The commander of the one-thousand-man Powder River column, General George Crook, had been Phil Sheridan's roommate at West Point and was his most trusted friend, although the similarities end there. Crook was a ramrod of a man with weather-beaten features and a beard that he wore combed apart symmetrically into the shape of two isosceles triangles. He was frugal and taciturn, mistrustful of fellow officers who were needlessly flamboyant—men like Custer, in other words. He was also an astute fighter who relied on instinct rather than formal written orders; the Apache, who called him Gray Wolf, said he was more Indian than an Indian.[21] Evan Connell says that as an adversary he was worse than a badger in a barrel.[22]

The third column, out of Bismarck, was commanded by Brigadier General Alfred Terry, who had taken over from Hancock in 1872 as commander of the Department of Dakota. *Ostensibly* commanded; everyone knew that it was really Custer's show.[23] The troops rode out of Fort Lincoln on May 17, and Custer's doting wife, Libbie, was unnerved by the freakish atmospheric conditions that prevailed as they left. With the Indian scouts chanting their lugubrious war songs, and the buglers belting out "The Girl I Left Behind Me," an evaporating ground fog somehow imprinted a ghostly reflected image of the Seventh Cavalry on the clouds.[24]

Although Terry's steamboat traveled without incident as far as the mouth of the Powder River, neither Crook nor Gibbon was there to meet him. After picking up a couple of dozen ambivalent scouts at the Crow agency, Gibbon had been ordered to keep to the north side of the Yellowstone to prevent the Indians from escaping in that direction. His chief of scouts had spotted a huge village of Sioux and Cheyenne on the south side, stretching, he estimated, for seven miles up the valley of the Rosebud. Yet with the Yellowstone so swollen with rain and snowmelt, there seemed no danger that the Indians would be bothersome. This was not the first time the army had underestimated them. Somehow a group of warriors sneaked across and killed three soldiers. "Gibbon got mad and said he would go over and give them a fight," Brisbin wrote. But after a dozen horses drowned, Gibbon was forced to abandon the pursuit. Brisbin was no help; crippled by rheumatism, he was unable to walk.

Eventually the Montana Column lumbered its way downstream to the mouth of the Powder River and the rendezvous with Terry. There was no sign of Crook, who was having troubles of his own, having run into a surprisingly large force of Sioux and Cheyenne on the Rosebud on June 17, and lost nine men in nasty hand-to-hand fighting.

It was June 21, before everyone finally assembled on the steamboat *Far West*—Terry, Custer, Gibbon, Brisbin, Crook, and the other officers— and debated what they should do next. The course of action they decided upon would save Doane's life.[25]

Custer was "grave and quiet" at first, Brisbin says, and asked many questions about the numbers and location of the Sioux. He grew excited when he heard the answers, Brisbin goes on: "I could see his eyes sparkle and he said repeatedly, 'We will scoop them. We will scoop them.' " Hearing tales of a village seven miles long, several officers expressed doubts about what exactly Custer meant by "we."

"General," said Brisbin, "Do you think you are strong enough with your regiment alone to whip the Sioux if you should encounter them?" He offered Custer the Second Cavalry. Custer thanked him cordially, but declined the offer. He then turned to a junior officer, apparently making little attempt to lower his voice, and said, "That was clever in the General [sic] to offer me his Cavalry, but I don't want him, this is to be a Seventh Cavalry affair and they are going to have whatever glory is in it."

Terry authorized Custer to go it alone, but left his orders ambiguous. Proceed with the Seventh and do what you deem appropriate according to circumstance. Which led to a debate that has kept historians busy for more than a century: Did Custer disobey orders, or just interpret them in a way that would serve his craving for glory? Whichever it was, off he went on June 22, in a cheerful and chatty mood, heading up the Rosebud in the direction of the Little Bighorn, taking six of Gibbon's Crow scouts with him, riding through the sagebrush in a cold, blustery wind as the buglers sounded "Boots and Saddles."

"Now, Custer, don't be greedy, but wait for us," Colonel Gibbon called out after him. Custer waved and shouted back, "No, I will not."[26] Did Gibbon ponder the ambiguity? No, I will not be greedy? Or, no, I will not wait?

The Montana Column took a different route, also heading for the Little Bighorn to come at the Sioux from a second direction, somewhat to the north, and now under Terry's personal command. "My dear fellow," said the general to Brisbin, "this is too hard for you in your crippled condition." Doane plotted their route of march, and the senior officers deferred to his judgment.[27] But it took them across an alkaline, ravine-cut, rattlesnake-infested wasteland. On June 25, a day of searing heat and dust was followed by a night of thunder, hail, and lashing rain. The column pressed on in pitch darkness, the scouts literally feeling their way through the mud on their hands and knees. An early rendezvous with Custer was now out of the question.

Next day, three of the Crow scouts who had gone with the Seventh— Hairy Moccasin, Goes Ahead, and White Man Runs Him—made contact with the Montana Column. They brought bizarre, awful accounts of what had happened the previous day. The soldiers debated these reports at length, their reactions, says Private William White, passing through "consternation, amusement, bewilderment, finally settling into doubt or utter discrediting of the story."[28] Custer dead? Unthinkable.

But next morning the Montana Column crested the rise overlooking the Little Bighorn. They saw odd shapes scattered across the hillside. Some were dark-colored. Others were light. They took these for skinned buffalo carcasses, but from a closer distance the quantity of arrows in them made them look more like outsize porcupines. The Sioux women had been busy with knives and hatchets. Severed heads were placed in triangular patterns, facing inward. Viscera spilled onto the ground. Dead horses were swollen to bursting. After two days in the sun and rain, the stench was beyond easy description.

In the lovely green valley of the Little Bighorn, which the Indians called the Greasy Grass, nothing stirred. But on a nearby hill there were survivors to evacuate from the units commanded by Major Marcus Reno. Moving fifty-two wounded men on a nineteenth-century Western battlefield was a serious logistical undertaking; in many circumstances, being wounded was tantamount to being dead. The evacuation required ingenuity, and that came from Cheyney Doane and the technique he had used the previous summer to transport the ailing General Marcy in the national park.

To fashion his mule litters, Doane and his men sliced strips of flesh from the dead horses and cut tipi poles from the now-abandoned Indian village, doing a little souvenir-hunting along the way. Doane helped himself to a couple of pairs of moccasins. The Second Cavalry surgeon, Lieutenant Holmes Offley Spaulding, took a particular fancy to an ornately beaded pair, but they were a tight fit over the swollen flesh and the dead Indian's skin sloughed off when the doctor tried to pull them free.[29]

Thanks to Doane, dozens of wounded men made it safely to the *Far West*. It gained him a new kind of celebrity—and the champions he needed to further his exploring ambitions. Gibbon praised him as an officer of "energy, skill, and confidence."[30] Terry even wrote to the great Sheridan himself to say, "I believe that I speak the sentiments of every officer and soldier who served under me in the field during the campaign of last summer, when I say that I feel the most hearty admiration for the

zeal, skill, and energy displayed by this accomplished gentleman and soldier."[31] *Every officer and soldier*—with one exception: Doane's commander
at Fort Ellis, Colonel Brisbin, who couldn't stand him. But with patronage
from the likes of Gibbon and Terry, that seemed of little account.

The Montana Column thrashed around looking for Sitting Bull for
another month or so, but it was fruitless. The Second Cavalry got
back to Fort Ellis on September 3, exhausted.

Doane's thoughts were already being drawn back magnetically to
Wonderland and beyond. What challenges remained for the American
explorer? The main features of the Yellowstone caldera were now known,
thanks largely to Doane himself. John Wesley Powell had conquered the
canyons of the Colorado. Clarence King had crisscrossed the Great Basin
and the High Sierras. Hayden had mapped the high peaks of Colorado.

Doane had read Washington Irving's accounts of the Astorians' and
Captain Bonneville's travels on the Snake, but no one had ever explored
the thousand-mile-long river from its multiple sources in the national
park to its confluence with the Columbia. In 1872, Hayden's topographer,
Gustavus Bechler, had drawn a fairly accurate map of the river from
the tangled pine forests south of Yellowstone Lake to the army base at
Fort Hall, Idaho. There were menacing canyons along that stretch, as
the river horseshoed its way around the southern extension of the Tetons.
But much harsher territory lay downstream, culminating in the wild
whitewater and sheer rockfaces of the mile-deep Hells Canyon, as pro-
found a fissure in the earth as the Grand Canyon of the Colorado. So that
became Doane's objective: to map the Snake. The only problem was his
reckless impatience; he set out to navigate the river in wintertime, and
the winter of 1876–1877 turned out to be an unusually harsh one, even by
the standards of the northern Rockies.

Sheridan authorized the expedition; Brisbin did not even know of its
existence until the order arrived from St. Paul, by which time Doane had
built a boat of his own design in the Fort Ellis carpenter's shop.[32] Twenty
feet long, pine-sided and oak-ribbed, it could be dismantled for transpor-

tation on muleback, then reassembled with screws. Doane handpicked a team of six, including the rambunctious veteran of the Marias, Dan Starr, and the sober private William White as "all around utility man," and they started out for Paradise Valley on October 11, in the balmy sunshine of a Montana autumn.[33]

The first misfortune struck on Friday the 13th, which seems appropriate. Doane's supply wagon overturned in Yankee Jim Canyon, "reducing the body to something resembling kindling wood."

The second misfortune came two weeks later, when the boat was swamped in a storm on Yellowstone Lake. The weather was now abysmal; the ice was an inch thick on the oars and had to be hacked out of the inside of the boat with axes. Doane thought the men onboard had drowned, until he heard "boisterous and double-jointed profanities" echoing across the lake from Private Starr. But most of the flour, sugar, and salt had been reduced to a block of frozen mush.

Two days later they crossed the Continental Divide in a blinding storm. It took them another week to reach Heart Lake, one of the sources of the Snake, laboring through heavy, hard-frozen snow. With almost four weeks gone already, Doane slowed them down further by his insistence on constantly checking the prismatic compass and the aneroid barometer—both bought at his own expense—to tease out any errors he could find in Hayden's mapping of the area.

The third misfortune came on November 21, when the boat slammed into a rock wall on the Snake, smashing all their tipi poles. From this point on they would have to sleep in the open, in temperatures that dipped from fifteen to forty below zero.

With their sixty-day rations running out, they killed the first of the horses on December 2, and ate it boiled and seasoned with gunpowder. It had a spongy texture, Doane reported in his journal, and tasted the way horse sweat smelled.

And so it continued. They coasted across the calm waters of Jackson Lake, hurtled down white-knuckle chutes and churning rapids, slalomed between ice floes. In one fierce eddy, a jagged rock punched a hole in the bottom of the boat. One mule after another keeled over and died. The men ate muskrat and porcupine, parboiled and grilled. They tried river otter, whose flesh had a flavor like fish, but couldn't keep it down. They shot Private White's horse and ate that, too. There was no discernible improvement in the taste.

Private Starr kept up their spirits by bellowing missionary hymns, while Doane wrote ecstatic descriptions of the Tetons by moonlight and took more of his obsessive measurements.[34] In Jackson Hole they chanced on the isolated cabin of a trapper, who fed them a quarter of elk and examined their boat, goggle-eyed. Not surprisingly, he seemed "completely puzzled as to what motives could have induced us to attempt such a trip in such a way and at such a season," Doane wrote.

But somehow they kept going, making it most of the way through the multiple hazards of the Grand Canyon of the Snake—or the Mad River Cañon, as Doane called it—until the river made a near right-angle bend and began to loop back around to the north. They had now been gone for two full months and there was virtually nothing left to eat, so Doane ordered two of his men to strike out westward, try to reach the remote settlements of the Cariboo mining district in Idaho, and bring back supplies. No sooner had they departed than the battered boat capsized in the rapids, dumping all of its contents—weapons, camping supplies, maps, horsemeat, scientific instruments, Doane's journal, Secretary Belknap's $150 field glasses, and the brass-studded mirror that White had taken from a dead Sioux at the Little Bighorn—into the freezing water.

On the morning of December 14 they abandoned the ice-bound boat, gnawed their way through the last of the horsemeat, and began to scale the rugged cliffs that separated them from the Cariboo settlements. They stumbled across ravines and ice ledges, numb with cold, exhausted, delirious from hunger. Suddenly Doane, who had lost more than a third of his normal 190 pounds since leaving Fort Ellis, was "seized with dizziness" and fell to his knees. "I was furious beyond measure," he wrote, "and worked myself into a fever of provocation." White says that he let loose "a successive string of cursings . . . That was the only time in all my association with Lieutenant Doane, past, present, and future, that I ever saw him show any sign of weakening."[35]

Yet somehow they reached the mining settlement of Keenan City on December 18. A store, a saloon, a blacksmith's shop, a livery stable, a post office, a string of ramshackle miners' cabins. A population of two hundred souls, of whom forty were Chinese, busily preparing a feast to celebrate "Melican man Jesus Christ Day."[36]

When they finally reached Fort Hall on January 4, 1877, Doane telegraphed Brisbin: "All well . . . Will refit and proceed at leisure." The indestructible lieutenant proposed not only to continue his exploration of the Snake, but to recover his wrecked boat, which was now encased in ice, repair it, drag it all the way back to Heart Lake, and start the trip all over again, taking fresh measurements along the way to replace those he had lost. Doane's ambition had turned into a kind of madness.

No, you will not refit and proceed anywhere, came the terse reply from Chicago headquarters four days later, after Brisbin had interceded with General Terry.

The Adjutant General for the Division of the Missouri wrote to the commanding officer at Fort Hall: "You will direct Lieut. Doane, Second Cavalry with his escort to rejoin his proper station Fort Ellis, as soon as practicable."[37]

"Lt. Doane was very mad," wrote Sergeant Fred Server in his diary. But the men decided to make the best of things and drown their sorrows in a gallon jug of whiskey.

In the end, Doane had seen nothing that had not been explored and mapped by the Hayden survey four years earlier, and all he could do now was to vent his rage and his delusions of grandeur to his journal. He was still in a different class from the "Engine turned scientists" of the East, Doane fumed, "whose published works are distributed by the ton, through the franks of well intentioned congressmen, and all expenses paid by the government; who are household gods of science in the minds of simple country folk ... The work of such men has degraded the Park district as far as it could be degraded in the estimation of the world at large."[38]

He might as well have nailed a portrait of Ferdinand Hayden to the barracks wall and fired a gun at it.

34

CHIEF OF SCOUTS

July–August 1877

fter the fiasco on the Snake, the army again yanked the leash on Doane, reclaiming him for soldiering. In the spring of 1877 Sitting Bull was safely ensconced on the far side of the Canadian line, but Colonel Nelson Miles, in command of the newly created District of the Yellowstone, continued to scour the country for other bands of hostile Sioux. He looked to the Crows once more for scouts, and asked Doane to recruit and lead them.

The scouting system was an integral part of the Indian wars, going back to at least 1860, when the British explorer Sir Richard Burton recommended it to his hosts during a tour of the West. Imitate the Raj, Burton advised; enlist native regiments.[1] American commanders largely embraced the idea, since their main problem on the Plains had always been finding the enemy—small in numbers, highly mobile, intimately familiar with the vast and forbidding landscape. Scouts, immersed from childhood in perpetual hit-and-run warfare, were a logical response. "A scout is like a lone wolf, that must be looking, looking, looking, all the time," said the Crow Red Wing.[2] In some tribes, the scouts actually dressed in wolf-skins and tied wolf heads on top of their own.

A good scout commander would typically be a lieutenant, one who had long experience in the field yet was held down to modest rank by the tortoise-paced system of promotions in the frontier army, in which ascent was only possible when another officer died or left the service. The job required individuality and self-reliance, a restless and adventurous intelligence, characteristics that Doane had in spades.

But he also had some crippling disadvantages. Although he had spent a lot of time with the Crows, he had never taken the trouble to learn their language. And he basically regarded the tribe with contempt. "Please do not expect too much from them," he wrote to Miles after his appointment, "for they are the greatest of cowards, excepting only all other Indians."[3] The very qualities that made them good scouts—above all their individuality—grated on his nerves. Doane was a fierce disciplinarian, but you could not treat a scout as you would a regular soldier.[4] A scout commander's authority was something like that of a tribal chief, with all its limitations; obedience came from persuasion and example, not from coercion. "It draws terribly on one's patience to deal with these people," Doane wrote—and patience had never been his forte.

He chose a three-man detail to join him on this new assignment. All of them had been with him on the Snake, including the ever-dependable Private White. But this time Doane chose to do without the loud-mouthed Dan Starr. "I don't want him," he said. "He tattles too much." It appears that Starr had dined out once too often on his raucous accounts of Doane's meltdown on the ice, as well as being indiscreet about the killing of the Blood prisoners on the Marias.[5]

D oane found himself responsible for an entire Crow village of three thousand people. For several weeks he shared the lodge of a chief named Iron Bull, who liked to wear a shabby old army uniform and affected a stovepipe hat which he said had been given to him on a visit to Washington to meet the Great Father. Doane called him "an old humbug."[6] The scouts also irritated him, being more interested in hunting buffalo than in hunting the fearsome Sioux.

Doane reached Miles's new headquarters at Fort Keogh on the Tongue River on July 19 and was formally presented to the great General William

Tecumseh Sherman, who was on his way to Wonderland. Here is the man who discovered it, said Miles. This moment was probably the pinnacle of Doane's career, and certainly of his pride.

There was also news from Bozeman: Doane's wife, Amelia had packed up and left him, bound for Chicago. The reasons are unclear. Before moving into Iron Bull's lodge, Doane had spent some time as the guest of a certain Dr. Hunter, formerly the post physician at Fort Ellis. The portly Hunter was an unreconstructed Southerner who had named each of his seven children after a hero of the Confederacy—Stonewall Jackson Hunter, and so forth—though it was the seventeen-year-old Mary Lee (as in Robert E.) who interested Doane the most. Or perhaps Amelia's departure had something to do with the nonmilitary diversions offered by the Crow village. "Here may be seen much love-making, and the little fellow called the god of love—Cupid—on these occasions certainly gets an immense amount of work for a blind boy, for many love affairs are consumated [sic]," wrote one of Doane's white civilian scouts.[7] "Oh, what delightful recollections of that summer!" exclaimed Private White, who was especially attentive to a fifteen-year-old named Yoho-na-ho, who had long black braids and liked to wear a necklace of wildcat claws.[8] So perhaps Doane yielded to the same enticements.

Doane's military orders changed while he was at Fort Keogh. Before leaving for the national park, Sherman had announced that, "I now regard the Sioux Indian problem, as a war question, as solved by the operations of General Miles."[9] Then Miles received word that the fleeing Nez Perce had broken through the army cordon at the Lolo Pass. If they continued to evade the hapless, one-armed General Howard, Miles believed, they would make eventually for the Judith Basin, north of the Yellowstone, which Doane had explored and knew intimately.[10] So he ordered Doane to take his scouts and ride "to the Missouri, at and west of the Musselshell, with instructions to 'intercept, capture or destroy the Nez Perces.'"[11]

This put the Crow scouts in a serious quandary. *The Crow heart is Nez Perce, and the Nez Perce heart is Crow,* said the old adage. But in the thicket of enemy-of-my-enemy alliances that the tribes had forged with the whites since the days of Lewis and Clark, with their muskets and trinkets and peace medals, there was now a major complication. Both these small, vulnerable tribes had made common cause with the new-comers against the terrible Blackfeet. But now the Crows had to choose between two old alliances, and in terms of self-interest there was really no contest. They might be halfhearted about the coming fight with the Nez Perce, but they could not afford to oppose it. If they balked, Doane was authorized by Miles to use his power to hand out large amounts of supplies and ammunition to sweeten the arrangement.

Doane left Fort Keogh on August 3, as Sherman was being welcomed with full ceremonial honors at Fort Ellis on his way to Wonderland. The general of the army had decided to take no personal role in the proceed-ings against the Nez Perce. "I do not propose to interfere, but leave Gib-bon or Howard to fight out this fight," he wrote to Washington. He was much more focused on his coming Yellowstone adventures. "I do not suppose I run much risk," he said, "for we are all armed, and the hostile Indians rarely resort to the park, a poor region for game, and to their su-perstitious minds associated with hell by reason of its geysers and hot springs."[12] With that, Sherman left Fort Ellis on August 4, a day ahead of the Radersburg tourists.

After ascending the Bitterroot and recrossing the divide at Lost Trail Pass, Chief Joseph's exhausted people had encamped on the serpen-tine, willow-choked North Fork of the Big Hole, a place of exceptional beauty under the biggest of skies. With General Howard floundering in pursuit, the army decided to hit the refugees with a column of infantry from Fort Shaw under Colonel Gibbon.

He attacked the Nez Perce camp on August 9. Like the Second Cav-alry on the Marias in 1870, the troops silently took up their positions in the night on the hillside above the camp. Like Doane's men on the Ma-rias, they were to open a massive assault on the sleeping Indians as soon as they heard the first shot fired. On the Marias, the first shot had killed a friendly chief. On the Big Hole, it killed an old, nearly blind man herding horses at first light. Like Doane's company against the Piegans, Gibbon's forces stormed the camp after the initial barrage of fire, shooting promiscuously into the tipis and killing mainly noncombatants. But there the similarities ended. Unlike the Piegans, the Nez Perce fought back effectively. The rout became a siege that lasted into a second day, prolonged by the same adroit counterattacks that had allowed the Indians to escape successive battles during the early stages of their flight through Idaho.

As always, the white casualties were carefully tabulated. Gibbon himself took a bullet in the thigh, which turned him from No Hipbone into One Who Limps Twice.[13] One of the seven officers killed was James Bradley, a sober-sided, well-respected young lieutenant and a distinguished amateur historian. Twenty-one enlisted men also died.

As usual, estimates of the Indian dead varied widely, although the consensus among historians is that the number was between seventy and ninety. As on the Marias, the majority were women and children. No more than thirty-three were men of fighting age.

Some in the territory, as well as Gibbons's superiors, hailed the Battle of the Big Hole as a great victory, but others saw it as yet another example of military ineptitude. One paper ran a piece of doggerel in the form of an imagined exchange of communiqués between the wounded Gibbon and the territorial governor, Benjamin Potts.

GIBBON TO POTTS:
We've had a hard fight
and I'm sorry to say
They've whipped us out quite
And the devil's to pay.

POTTS TO GIBBON:
Your dispatch, trusty soul,
I answer this minute;
If you're near a big hole,
You'd better crawl in it.[14]

Tactically and morally, the Big Hole was further proof of the resilience of the Nez Perce. But it also weakened them and slowed them down, even as the army, having figured out Chief Joseph's ultimate destination, prepared a grand four-sided convergence of forces to entrap them in the national park. The battle had given General Howard, still laboring up the Bitterroot Valley, time to catch up with the refugees. A group of Bannock scouts from Fort Hall rode ahead of him, happy to shoot, scalp, and dismember any Nez Perce they might run across.[15] Although a southward flight was the least likely contingency, General Crook marshaled two groups of cavalry on the Wyoming side, just in case.[16]

Gibbon, who had visited the park himself in 1872, correctly predicted that the likeliest path for the Nez Perce would be to the Crow country, through the Absarokas to the Clarks Fork, crossing Yellowstone Jack Baronett's bridge on the way. In theory, that escape route would be closed off by a contingent of the Seventh Cavalry under Colonel Samuel Sturgis, an odd-looking man with curly hair, a round, cherubic face, and a strangely pendulous goatee. Sturgis's son had died at the Little Bighorn, and the remains of the Seventh had now taken to calling themselves Custer's Avengers. And finally there was Doane, with his cavalrymen and his Crows.

Having first been ordered to ride to the Judith Gap, Doane was redirected by Miles to Fort Ellis. Along the way, he picked up temporary command of a company of the Seventh Cavalry under Lieutenant Carlo Camillo (or Camilius) di Rudio, anglicized in the army rolls as Charles C. DeRudio, and a freshly minted West Point graduate named Hugh Lenox Scott, who came to idealize Doane as the model frontiersman. (Scott would later become chief of staff of the U.S. Army during World War I). Doane had been traveling with only five men of his own company; now he inherited sixty more. It was the largest group of soldiers he had ever commanded.

DeRudio, a forty-five-year-old with finely waxed mustachios and a long goatee that blew about in the breeze, was another of those operatic characters who popped up on the Western battlefields, trailing a résumé

that rivaled that of General Philippe Régis de Trobriand.[17] Fellow cavalrymen derided him as a teller of tall tales, but most of them were in fact
true. Born near Venice, he was the atheist son of Count Ercole Placido
Aquila di Rudio. He fought for Italian independence under Garibaldi and
acquired the nickname *Il Moretto,* the Little Moor, for his dark complexion. Fleeing into exile in Paris, he joined the armed rebellion against
Louis Napoleon's coup d'état.

With the secret police of several countries on his heels, DeRudio fled
again, this time to London, where he worked for a while in the Wapping
docks, impregnated a fifteen-year-old girl who was distantly related to
William Booth, the founder of the Salvation Army, then married her. But
parenthood seems to have had less appeal than violence, and in January
1858 he took part in a failed attempt to assassinate Louis Napoleon—who
by now was Napoleon III—with hand grenades. DeRudio tried to pass
himself off at trial as an innocent Portuguese beer salesman called Da
Selva. His true identity revealed, he was condemned to the guillotine, but
then had his sentence commuted to life imprisonment on Devil's Island,
from which he escaped, predictably enough, to British Guiana—perhaps
in a stolen fishing boat, perhaps in a hollowed-out log. Accounts vary.

Arriving penniless in New York in 1864, the Italian joined the U.S.
Colored Troops and fought with them in Florida, and then, thanks to the
reported intercession of Horace Greeley, obtained a commission with the
Seventh Cavalry; and so to service under Custer, who detested him. By
rights, DeRudio should have died at the Little Bighorn, but like Doane his
life was saved by circumstance, after Custer refused to let him lead Company E, the famous "Gray Horse Troop." DeRudio was assigned instead
to Major Marcus Reno's command, and survived the siege of Reno's positions, hiding in the brush for thirty-six hours and watching as the Lakota
women did the rounds of the battlefield with their sharp implements.[18]
When he learned that Custer himself was among the dead, "He [did] not
hesitate to express his satisfaction," said Captain Samuel Ovenshine of
the Seventh Infantry.[19]

Doane and DeRudio proceeded in pied-piper fashion, picking up more
Crow scouts, losing some to desertion, others to horse-thieving, bumping

into Yellowstone Jack Baronett and adding him to the party, handing out guns to white settlers who wanted to join the fight.[20] By the time Doane reached Fort Ellis, he was in charge of a substantial wagon train laden with rations and ammunition for the campaign.[21]

Sherman had left the fort just a few days earlier, more than satisfied with his adventures in the park. "We saw no sign of Indians and felt at no moment more sense of danger than we do here," he reported to Washington. Now he was heading west to inspect Fort Walla Walla, with a couple of courtesy calls to make along the way, first on the leading men of Helena and then on Colonel Gibbon, who was recovering from his wounds at Fort Shaw. Sherman also decided that it was time for him to take a personal hand in the Nez Perce affair, relieving the wretched Howard of his command and replacing him with Lieutenant Colonel C. C. Gilbert, the undistinguished commander of the small infantry base known as Camp Baker, east of Helena.[22] This was a puzzling choice.

On the way to Fort Shaw, Sherman stopped, as many travelers did, at a welcoming ranch-cum-stage stop at the head of the Little Prickly Pear Canyon. After supper, he went out to take the late summer air. Near the ranchhouse he found an unmarked gravesite and inquired whose it was. The man who lay in the grave, he was told, was a former owner of the ranch named Malcolm Clarke, an old fur trader and pillar of Helena society, murdered by a relative of his Piegan wife some eight years since.

What an extraordinary thing, said Sherman, for "[h]e well remembered Malcolm Clarke, who had been a fellow-cadet with him at West Point and a great favorite there, whom he had then known as a remarkably bright, open-hearted and high-spirited young man, and for whom he had always prophesied a brilliant future." Sadly, however, Sherman said that "he had lost all trace of his schoolmate since their life at West Point until the discovery by him of this sepulchre among the solitudes of the Rocky Mountains."[23]

35

FULL CIRCLE

August–October 1877

T he Nez Perce entered the park on August 23, Howard now trailing more than five days behind them.[1] That night, as they approached the Lower Geyser Basin, their scouts saw the flickering light of a campfire and resolved to investigate the next morning.

As a last-night-of-the-holiday treat, the Radersburg tourists had brought out their musical instruments and put on a minivaudeville show. Emma Cowan's brother Frank and their friend Al Oldham sang songs, dressed up as brigands with rifles, knives, and pistols. Al donned a large sombrero; he had swarthy features and looked quite the part. They were joined by a grizzled old prospector from the Black Hills named John Shively, who was wandering around the park on some solo adventure.

At first light, as the men prepared the campfire, dozens of Indians materialized out of the forest. They were friendly enough at first, but what was on their minds was breakfast—not only what was being prepared at the campfire but all the food that was left in the tourists' wagon. This was too much for Emma's husband, George, a man with a kind of irascible self-righteousness which, she said in later years, was what got them into trouble that day. Frank barred the way with his rifle and said he was d———d if he was going to let some d———d savages steal the last of their supplies.

The mood soured. Some of the Indians were still conciliatory, but others began an angry muttering. They were "double-minded," explained one Nez Perce who had a little English and acted as interpreter.

The Indians marched the group away, not in the direction of the Madison and home, but east, toward the heart of the park, up a quiet creek that now bears the name of the tribe. As they approached the meadow just west of Mary Mountain, there was a sudden burst of gunfire. George Cowan tumbled off his horse, wounded in the leg. Oldham was struck by a bullet that passed through his cheek, knocked out a couple of teeth, tore up his tongue, and exited below the jaw. Emma Cowan flung herself on her husband, but another Indian thrust her aside and fired at him again from point-blank range, hitting him in the forehead. Emma fainted. Another Nez Perce grabbed twelve-year-old Ida Carpenter around the neck, but she bit his hand and wriggled free.

This brief spasm of violence had not been intended, said a Nez Perce named Yellow Wolf: It was the work of "bad boys." But the episode dispersed the prisoners, which only made the bad boys jumpier. George Cowan was left for dead (though remarkably he survived, in a manner worthy of a dime novel, and was picked up four days later by Howard's soldiers).[2] Oldham crawled off into the bushes and hid. Others made a run for it, finding their way eventually to the army lines with useful intelligence about the Indians' movements. Emma, her young sister, and her brother Frank, along with the old prospector, Shively, were taken to a camp on the west side of the Yellowstone, near the Mud Geyser, where a stone-faced chief was seated, clearly dismayed to hear news of the shootings. "Him Joseph," said the translator. Emma Cowan never forgot his face: "The 'noble redman' we read of was more nearly impersonated in this Indian than in any I have ever met," she wrote.

The main body of Nez Perce forded the Yellowstone the next day. On the east side of the river, Joseph and the other chiefs held a council. What to do with the prisoners? They decided eventually to hold on to Shively but let the others go. An interpreter walked them back across the river and pointed them north, toward Mammoth Hot Springs, telling them to travel all night without stopping. This was probably good advice, for several small groups of warriors had already split off from the main column and fanned out in that direction. Some were undoubtedly scouting alternative escape routes. But at least one group was pursuing reports that a second group of tourists had been spotted near the Upper Falls of the Yellowstone.

It had all seemed a bit of a lark to Andrew Weikert, an ebullient young man who wrote the only published account of the experiences of the ten-man party from Helena. Traveling from Bozeman, they reached Mammoth on August 20, and started on the usual circuit—"Soda Mountain," Tower Fall, Mount Washburn, both sets of falls, the Mud Geyser. They sang songs and told tall tales around the campfire, went fishing, teased one another about whose turn it was to do the dishes, had some laughs at the expense of their garrulous black cook, Ben Jones.

On August 25, as the main body of Nez Perce were fording the Yellowstone, the Helena party glimpsed what they thought was a herd of elk in Hayden Valley. But it was a herd of Nez Perce bad boys. The tourists withdrew quietly and made camp on Otter Creek, a mile or so upstream from the Upper Falls. All very frustrating, since they were set on seeing the famous lake. In the morning Weikert and his friend Leslie Wilkie went back to see if the coast was clear and rode straight into an ambush. Somehow they got away, Wilkie unharmed, Weikert with a flesh wound to the shoulder. When they got back to the camp, they found it torn apart and looted, and the horses gone. One of their companions was dead, shot in the head. Another was wounded, but the warriors had spared his life in exchange for the contents of his pockets—$263. Ben Jones, the cook, lay shivering in a creek, playing dead. The others had disappeared.

By convoluted paths, various of the surviving tourists made their way back to Mammoth, where they sought shelter in Jim McCartney's hotel.[3] By the time Weikert, Wilkie, Stewart, and Stone arrived, Emma Cowan and her siblings were already in residence, in the care of Lieutenant Charles Schofield of the Second Cavalry, who had been sent down to the park from Fort Ellis with a handful of men on a scouting mission.[4] After resting up, Weikert and McCartney rode back the forty miles to Otter Creek to collect the body of their friend Charles Kenck. As they left, another member of the party, Richard Dietrich, waved them good-bye. He was a frail young German-born piano teacher, no one's idea of a rugged outdoorsman. Look out for your hair while we're gone, Weikert called out. Dietrich gave a premonitory answer: "Andy, you will give me a decent burial, won't you?"

Meanwhile, a wagon had been sent from Bozeman to pick up Emma Cowan, her sister and brother, and a party of English dudes who had been hunting around the park with Lord Dunraven's celebrated guide, Texas Jack Omohundro. As the wagon bumped its way along Trail Creek, they encountered a contingent of soldiers from Fort Ellis, led by Lieutenant Doane and accompanied, Emma guessed, by seventy or eighty Crow scouts.

It was Doane's sixth trip to the upper Yellowstone; with the single exception of Jim Bridger, no white man had been there more often.[5] He was the man who had invented Wonderland; now he proposed to win a war there.

Doane was operating under a welter of instructions from his commanders that would have confused any normal soldier. But the lieutenant found them conveniently ambiguous, a priceless invitation to do whatever he liked.

"You will use every effort to intercept, capture or destroy the Nez Perces..." Miles had ordered Doane on August 3. If the Nez Perce are defeated, Miles said, they *may* go to the Judith Basin or vicinity. *Or vicinity*: a very elastic concept in a big place like Montana. Then there was an order from Miles for Doane to communicate with Colonel Sturgis of the Seventh Cavalry, who had been ordered to the Judith Gap. *Communicate*: meaning what exactly? Pass messages back and forth? Not a problem.

Sturgis unwittingly gave Doane even greater room for maneuver. Fort Ellis will be sending me dispatches, he said; feel free to open them if you see them first, so you can have timely information about the whereabouts of the enemy. In language that he must have later regretted, he even told

Doane, "Knowing them and their habits etc. as you do, you will be able to guess at their movements better than I can . . . I hope you will exercise your own judgment in scouting."[6] All very helpful.

Doane lost no time in writing to Lieutenant Colonel Gilbert at Camp Baker. "As soon as I heard of General Gibbon's fight [on the Big Hole], I anticipated the movement on the park of the Nez Perce which he has indicated." A few days later, he heard back from Gibbon himself, another message with conveniently vague wording:

> Your letter of twenty first sent me from Baker shows you know exactly what is required to be done. Proceed to do it using your force to obtain early information of the hostiles movements. . . . I believe these hostiles can yet be caught. Let us do our part towards it. These will supersede all other orders you have unless given by some superior on the spot.[7]

There *was* no superior on the spot. Sturgis was on the far side of the Absarokas, anticipating the exodus of the Nez Perce from the park and fretting for Doane to join him. "I fail to see what good can possibly be accomplished by your proposed scouting round the Yellowstone Lake with Company E, 7th Cavalry, marching up the east fork of the Yellowstone," he raged.[8] But Doane was already heading up the familiar trail. Let Sturgis rage. As commander of the District of Montana, Gibbon outranked him.

Even so, Doane had reason for concern now, as well as for excitement: many of his scouts had deserted[9]—at least part of the Crow heart was still Nez Perce—and he saw a dense plume of smoke rising above the river a few miles to his south. Some of the remaining Crows galloped off in their war bonnets to investigate and reported that the Nez Perce were "as thick as grass on the ground." That was not strictly accurate: No one had been killed, and the survivors of the fire, which had consumed James Henderson's ranch, said it had been torched by a small group of eight warriors. Doane's worshipful young lieutenant, Hugh Scott, took ten cavalrymen and pursued their trail to McCartney's hotel at Mammoth, while Doane followed behind with the train. Scott found Richard Dietrich, the young music teacher who had so feared for his scalp, spread out dead on the floor, gunned down by two Nez Perce warriors, Naked-Footed Bull and Shooting Thunder. Andrew Weikert buried him later in an old bathtub from the hotel, there being no timber nearby from which to construct a coffin.

Lieutenant Colonel Gilbert, with a company of cavalry from Fort Ellis, caught up with Doane near the north entrance to the park on September 2. Gilbert had a contradictory reputation: martinet on the parade ground, slug on the battlefield. From Howard's point of view, Gilbert was the most humiliating of replacements—older, junior in rank, a man who inspired little confidence in his men. But Howard was blissfully unaware of Sherman's decision, and the bizarre decisions now taken by Gilbert made sure that he didn't. Instead old Cut Arm would continue to plod through the park, perplexed by the continued absence of Nez Perce but taking time to enjoy his first sight of the geysers.

Doane urged hot pursuit of the Indians, in the direction of Baronett's bridge. He had a better sense than anyone of where the Nez Perce were likely to be found. He was convinced that they had split up into at least two main groups, and that they were probably in the upper Lamar valley. He was correct on both points. But Gilbert was having none of it. The last thing he wanted, he informed Doane, was to be distracted by a fight with the Nez Perce. According to the letter of his instructions, he was to find General Howard and take over his command, and that was what he intended to do. Take over his command to do what exactly? would be a reasonable question.

In a war of many stupidities, Gilbert's was the most clownish of all. Even if his goal was to find Howard, he could have accomplished this with a two- or three-day journey up the Yellowstone, guided by Doane. Instead, he told the troops to turn around and head back fifteen or twenty miles downriver, turn left at Tom Miner Creek, and hack their way over the mountains to the valley of the Gallatin until eventually they struck the Madison, outside the western edge of the park—which was where the last reports had placed Howard. Unfortunately those reports were the better part of a week old.

Doane pleaded with him; this was absolute folly. Gilbert refused to listen, and this time there was nothing Doane could do to ignore or deliberately misconstrue his orders, since they came directly from Sherman.

The lieutenant wept tears of frustration, his second public breakdown in nine months.[10] All his ambitions lay in ruins now, first as an explorer and now as a war hero. Yet Gilbert was not entirely to blame. Lieutenant Hugh Scott—a man who idolized Doane—said "I admired his knowledge more than his discretion."[11] Even though Sturgis was right that Doane understood the movements of Indians better than anyone, his rush to the park was an ill-considered (if typical) drive for personal glory. Gilbert's stupidity simply made sure that a high risk of failure became an unmitigated disaster.

So, over the mountains and faraway they went, following a hideous apology for a trail, full of ravines and downed timber and with no forage for the animals. Most of the supplies had to be sent back to Fort Ellis, being too cumbersome to carry. By the time Gilbert and Doane reached the Gallatin, the horses were grievously weakened by hunger. The colonel "had no idea of marching cavalry," wrote Hugh Scott.[12] When they finally got to the Madison, Howard's trail was stone cold. At an abandoned Nez Perce encampment, one of Doane's scouts bent down and picked up a pair of baby's moccasins. "I could not repress a wish," he wrote later, "that the fleeing, hunted creatures would get through all right."[13]

But of course they did not. Whether or not the fight with the Nez Perce had ever had any real strategic significance, the credibility of the U.S. Army was now at stake. The frustrations of the campaign brought out all of Sherman's most brutal tendencies. The Nez Perce had to surrender "without terms," he ordered, "else other tribes alike situated may imitate their example." Their chiefs should be executed.

After releasing the Radersburg tourists on August 25, the refugees had worked their way down to Yellowstone Lake, passing the point where Langford had performed his penknife operation on Doane, and then making their way up the broad, lush valley of Pelican Creek, where the horse herd could graze to its heart's content. After that, as Doane surmised, they had split up. Their war chief, Looking Glass, and their spiritual leader, Joseph, had made separate camps.

Some historians believe that emissaries were sent out over the mountains to assess the welcome the Nez Perce would receive in the Crow lands, and came back with discouraging reports. Scouts and freelance raiders had ridden out to assess the options for escape. After attacking the Helena tourists and Henderson's ranch, and partially burning Baronett's bridge, they must have reported back that the trails to the north had been closed off by the army.

Precious days were lost. Perhaps the Nez Perce were undecided about which route to take. Perhaps the good grazing detained them too long. Perhaps they were hungry, and the abundance of elk was too great a temptation. Perhaps they were simply exhausted after two and a half months of running and fighting, and simply needed to rest. Yet somehow they still drove hundreds of people and two thousand horses across the forbidding Absarokas, through an obscure pass overhung by the unearthly eroded rock pinnacles of the Hoodoo Basin.[14]

On the east side of the divide, traveling down the canyon of the Clarks Fork, they somehow managed to outflank Colonel Sturgis's Seventh Cavalry, which was waiting to head them off. They crossed the Yellowstone, Sturgis and Howard still flailing along behind, trailed by the hapless Gilbert, who had described a huge and futile circle back to Fort Ellis. Roused to passion by Doane's insubordination, Grasshopper Jim Brisbin made sure that his insolent lieutenant took no further part in the proceedings. The whole adventure ended in bathos. Instead of winning military glory, Doane was ordered to take five men and bury a load of potatoes that had been left behind by a supply boat on the Yellowstone.[15]

On September 13, the Nez Perce held off the army again at Canyon Creek, on the north side of the big river. They reached the Missouri ten days later, and fought yet another skirmish, at Cow Island. At this point they were less than a hundred miles from the Canadian line and sanctuary in the camps of Sitting Bull. But they were traveling more slowly now, through the badlands of the Missouri Breaks, and the weather was turning bleak, the ground frozen.

The army had one final card to play. Realizing he would never catch the fleeing Indians, Howard sent a dispatch to Colonel Nelson A. Miles on the Tongue River, urging him to send reinforcements. Miles, whose middle initial stood for Appleton but might as well have stood for ambition,[16] saw an excellent opportunity to advance his career. His troops were fresh and they rapidly closed the distance, commandeering a steamboat along the way. They caught up with the Nez Perce at last in the Bear Paw Mountains, entrapping them in a coulee bottom. Canada was less than fifty miles away.

The camp was ultimately indefensible, but the fighting spirit of its occupants was still not extinguished. Joseph's people held out for five days. Twenty-five Nez Perce died in the fight, including Looking Glass, and thirty-six soldiers. But on October 5, Joseph surrendered to Miles with perhaps the most famous words ever spoken in the course of the Indian Wars: "Hear me, my chiefs. I am tired; my heart is sick and sad. From where the sun now stands I will fight no more forever."

Looking back on the episode many years later, Emma Carpenter Cowan, who had seen her husband shot and left for dead in the national park, wrote, "Truly a quality of mercy was shown to us during our captivity that a Christian might emulate, and at a time when they must have hated the very name of the white race."[17]

In the end, the government shipped the survivors off to a reservation in the alien "hot place" of Oklahoma Territory. The Nez Perce quickly built a cemetery there, filling up a hundred graves, most of them containing infants. But they buried old people, too. One was a man with unusually fair skin and sandy gray hair. They called him Halahtookit, or Daytime

Smoke. Nathaniel Langford had once taken his photograph in Helena; he was the man who had pounded his chest and said "Me Clark!," conceived more than seventy years earlier during the prolonged sojourn of the Corps of Discovery in the camps of the Nez Perce, a people whose kindness those first explorers of the West never forgot.

{ *Epilogue* }

THE MAN WHO INVENTED WONDERLAND

Fort Bowie, Arizona Territory, January 1891. He was Captain Gustavus Cheyney Doane now, but the promotion had done nothing to soften his bitter sense of injustice. The only thing that kept him stable was a happy second marriage, to Mary Lee Hunter, daughter of the Confederate doctor who had once attended the troops at Fort Ellis.

Doane had joined an expedition to the Arctic in 1880, one last shot at the kind of celebrity that would have come from discovering the sources of the Nile. But it ended, like the exploration of the Snake River, in disaster, the ship crushed in a storm off the west coast of Greenland and Doane again fortunate to survive.[1] Then, in 1882–1883, he spent two dull years at the wind-blasted Fort Assiniboine, about as far north as one could go in Montana Territory. A man falling over drunk—and there was little else to do there—might land with his head in Saskatchewan. There were no more Indian troubles to speak of on the Northern Plains, other than those caused by hunger. From the sacred Sweetgrass Hills above the Marias River to the Bear Paw Mountains where Chief Joseph had surrendered, the buffalo herds were gone. The so-called Starvation Winter of 1883–1884 had stamped the last spark out of the once proud and militant Piegans. A chief called Almost-a-Dog kept track of the deaths by cutting notches in a willow stick. He is said to have stopped when he reached 555.[2]

Doane traveled around the country for a while, training new recruits. His weight ballooned to 250 pounds; people took to calling him "Fatty."[3] He spent most of 1886 in Arizona Territory—"the most hideous desert wilderness in the world"—a bit player in the pursuit of Geronimo, serving again under Nelson Miles, who was now a general. Doane saw no action, other than the whiskey-sodden cavorting of his soldiers with prostitutes from the local doggeries.[4] After that, he took command of a cavalry company at the Presidio in San Francisco, where there was little for him to do but drill his soldiers up and down on the parade ground.

He remained close to Miles and to Colonel Gibbon, his old commander during the Sioux campaign. Colonel Eugene Baker, meanwhile, Doane's patron and protector during his moments of glory on the Marias and the Yellowstone, had been shunted from one backwater posting to another, always protected by General Sheridan, until he finally succumbed in 1884 to cirrhosis of the liver. West Point gave him a discreetly worded obituary: "Believing that nothing could injure his constitution, [he] neglected such precautions as he might have taken and broke down sooner than he had the slightest idea he could."[5]

Always Doane listened for news of Yellowstone, though there is no indication that he kept in touch with any of his fellow explorers. The man he resented for usurping his fame, Ferdinand Vandeveer Hayden, had fallen victim to tertiary syphilis, contracted no doubt in the brothels of the frontier. But years before his death in 1887, Hayden had already been eclipsed by rivals of his own. Having been seen as the first of the midcentury professional scientists, he was now viewed as the last of its amateurs, and anyway there was nothing left to explore in the West.

Cornelius Hedges had become one of the most revered figures in the new state of Montana, which was admitted to the Union in 1889—probate judge, state senator, dean of freemasons, two terms as superintendent of public instruction, universally considered a man of sterling integrity. Sam Hauser had accumulated vast wealth and served a term as governor, with Hedges writing some of his speeches.[6] Truman Everts, a vigorous old man of seventy-five, had recently fathered a child. Warren Gillette was a successful sheep farmer. Ben Stickney was running a general store in Craig, a few miles down the Missouri from Malcolm Clarke's old ranch. Young Walter Trumbull had gone into the diplomatic service and died in Africa. No one seems to have kept much track of Jake Smith.

The driving force behind the great Yellowstone expedition, Nathaniel Langford, had returned to St. Paul in 1876, just before the end of his five-year term as the park's absentee superintendent. He had married late in life, but his wife, Emma, did not live long; after her death, he married her sister, Clara. Langford, his thick, black beard now turned to white, was a pillar of Minnesota society, active in business, politics, and good works. He devoted much of his time to writing about the violence and derring-do of the frontier in the 1860s, from the mass hangings of the road agents to the salutary punishment of the Indians, and the role he had been per-sonally privileged to play. "An empire has sprung up as if by enchant-ment," he wrote of the West, made possible by the decision of principled men to use violence as "[t]he necessity of the hour." The capstone of this new career as an author would be his epic memoir of the early gold camps, *Vigilante Days and Ways,* published in 1890.

The Northern Pacific Railroad, revived by new investors, was finally completed in the summer of 1883. Triumphal arches were erected in Langford's hometown of St. Paul, and the streets were decorated with flags and fir trees. At Bismarck, Sitting Bull, who had laid down his arms two years earlier, signed autographs for the gawkers at $1.50 apiece. President Chester Arthur rode one of the Gold Spike Specials to Mon-tana, in the company of ex–President Grant and a bevy of generals, gov-ernors, senators, congressmen, titans of business, English and German noblemen—"the most remarkable aggregation of unadultered greatness that we have ever seen," said the newspaper in the new railroad town of Livingston, at the mouth of Paradise Valley.[7]

The Crows were given an important role in ushering in the new age of Yellowstone tourism. Chief Iron Bull, whose tipi Doane had shared during the summer of the Nez Perce campaign, made a speech under a banner that read "Livingston, the Gate to Wonderland," telling the crowd,

> There is a meaning in my part of the ceremony, and I under-stand it. The end of our lives is near at hand. The days of my people are almost numbered; already they are dropping off like rays of sunlight in the western sky. Of our once powerful nation there are now few left—just a little handful, and we, too, will soon be gone.[8]

His warriors dressed up in their feathers, paint, and bear grease and danced at the celebration, and many of the guests, soused on barrels of German beer, danced along with them. As a special treat, the Crows served dog soup.

Within a short time, the Northern Pacific had completed a spur line to the national park, which took passengers as far as the Devil's Slide. A few miles upriver, where Henderson's ranch had burned, the new boom-town of Gardiner offered visitors six restaurants, five general stores, two hardware stores, two fruit stands, two barber shops, two dance halls, a newsstand, a billiard hall, a blacksmith shop, one milkman, twenty-one saloons, and four brothels.[9] Guidebooks like *Wonder-Land Illustrated* and the *Great American Wonderland* laid out recommended circuits of the park, beginning at Mammoth Hot Springs and designed to maximize the emotional impact of "objects of interest, seen in their natural order." All of them certified that Yellowstone was now Indian-free.

President Arthur went to the park as part of his Northern Pacific jun-ket, accompanied by Phil Sheridan, who had just replaced Sherman as general-in-chief of the army. It was Sheridan's third visit in as many summers. He had come for the first time in 1881, guided by Yellowstone Jack Baronett. In 1882, his party blazed the first trail into the park from the south, traveling from Jackson Hole up the Lewis River to the West

Thumb of the lake, where Langford, Doane, and their companions had camped during the futile search for Truman Everts.

Little Phil's views had mellowed over the years. Now that the buffalo were close to extinction, he was determined to preserve a few, as symbols of a West that no longer existed. Now that the Plains Indians were silenced, he became almost sentimental about the idea of the noble red man in his natural paradise.[10] Civilization was an unstoppable force, but Sheridan wondered if perhaps the army had been too harsh. "We took away their country and their means of support, broke up their mode of living, their habits of life, introduced disease and decay among them, and it was for this and against this that they made war," he said in 1878. "Could anyone expect less?"

With each visit to the park, he grew angrier at the mindless destruction of the delicate geyser deposits, the wanton slaughter of game, and the impotence of the federal government to prevent these abuses. He was disgusted by the Interior Department's decision to grant a monopoly to a shady new consortium of investors, cronies of the Northern Pacific, who called themselves the Yellowstone National Park Improvement Company and had been charged only a peppercorn rent for leasing prime land around the geyser basins, the hot springs, the falls, and the lake. Sheridan pressed the Senate to pass a bill quashing the monopoly, and Langford wrote a letter of support from St. Paul, a further sign that while he might once have represented the interests of the railroad he had never intended it to exercise this kind of stranglehold over the park's development.

Sheridan's proposed remedy was to place Yellowstone under military control. Initially he suggested that the army could use troops from Fort Ellis, but with the plains at peace and the wars won, that fort no longer served any strategic purpose. In 1886, with its barracks rotting away and overrun by gophers, Fort Ellis was closed. Instead, Company M of the First Cavalry, under Captain Moses Harris, arrived in August of that year from Fort Custer, inaugurating thirty-two years of army protection of the park. They built a base at Mammoth Hot Springs, which the army named Camp Sheridan.

· · ·

Doane watched all this from a resentful distance until the end of 1890, when word came that it was time for the cavalry detail at Yellowstone to be rotated out. At the same time, there was one final spasm of war. Amidst the mystical frenzy of the Ghost Dance, which the defeated Lakota saw as a pathway to eternal bliss with their friends and family, the great Hunkpapa chief Sitting Bull was killed in a brawl with Indian police. Two weeks later, on December 29, 1890, five hundred soldiers surrounded a Sioux camp on Wounded Knee Creek in South Dakota. By the time the vicious hand-to-hand combat was over, more than 150 Indians lay dead, along with 25 officers and soldiers.

The two great currents in Doane's life, violence and exploration, now flowed together for one last time. His path and Langford's might never have crossed, but for an act of violence whose roots stretched all the way back to Lewis and Clark. Together the cavalryman and the tax collector had become explorers. For Langford the connection was implicit: Violence created the conditions for peace and prosperity, and once the frontier was civilized in this way, its leading men could cap their careers by exploring its last unmapped corners. For Doane, however, who had dreamed for so long of being the American Livingstone, exploration was the direct reward for violence.

On January 7, 1891, a week after Wounded Knee, Doane wrote a long letter—a screed would be more accurate—to Wilbur Fisk Sanders, the old vigilante prosecutor and intimate friend of Langford, Hedges, and Malcolm Clarke. Montana had finally achieved statehood a year earlier, and Sanders was one of its first two senators.

Doane's letter began:

> I write to ask you to work for me in this matter on a double headed proposition—1st. To get ordered to the Park with my Troop.—2nd. To get ordered to General Miles' command in the field, for "general slaughter" and work the Park business afterward. For me all roads lead to the Park that are worth traveling.

He raged to Sanders that the park's regulations had been "drawn by someone who knew nothing of its conditions and there does not appear to have been anyone sent there in charge who has known enough or had interest enough or nerve enough to even suggest a correction," then went on:

> I want no brevets, no staff nor feather bed promotions, no foreign court details, no pilgrimages to distant shrines, after military knowledge, on full pay and allowances, I have never & never will ask for such things, nor yearn for the same . . . I want command of the Yellowstone National Park. If I have not deserved it, justice is a mockery, merit a scandal, gratitude a farce and liberty a lie. I remember the day when we slaughtered the Piegans, how it occurred to me, as I sat down in the bank of the Marias & watched the stream of their blood, which ran down on the surface of the frozen river over half a mile, that the work we were then doing would be rewarded, as it has been. It has always been to me a question which is the more acceptable in the long run, a suitable & just reward for services rendered or the conscientiousness of unmerited neglect & the sustaining elements engendered therefrom of undying hatred & supreme contempt. . . .
>
> Ever yours very truly,
> G. C. Doane
> Capt. 2d. Cavalry

Doane still had influential supporters and patrons, and they deluged the government with letters of endorsement. The entire Montana legislature signed a petition. Generals added their voices: John Schofield, who had replaced Sheridan after his death in 1888 as general-in-chief of the army, and whose son had served with Doane at Fort Ellis; John Gibbon, Doane's old commander in the District of Montana; Samuel Sturgis, who had so bitterly condemned his conduct during the pursuit of the Nez Perce; and Nelson Miles, who wrote that Doane had rendered very good service both during the war and since on the frontier. He was the first to thoroughly explore the Yellowstone Park and make known that wonderful country to the world. He is anxious to be assigned to the military charge of the National Park, and I do not think any better selection could be made.[11]

But it all came to nothing. All the government said, in a form letter to Doane's sponsors, was that his transfer to Yellowstone was "not deemed advisable."[12] The post went instead to a man who was Doane's very antithesis: Captain George Anderson of the Sixth Cavalry, a veteran Indian fighter and professor of natural philosophy at West Point, a man known for his urbane and gentlemanly manners.

Captain Gustavus Cheyney Doane died barely a year later, on May 5, 1892, at the age of fifty-one. The death certificate said that his heart had failed, but it may not be a stretch to say that it was broken. He was laid to rest in Bozeman with full honors, and the Military Order of the Loyal Legion of the United States mourned him as "the beau ideal of a sabreur." The funeral was the largest procession the town had ever seen, with a line of carriages that stretched for half a mile.

DRAMATIS PERSONAE

Eugene Baker, Brevet Lieutenant Colonel: Doane's alcoholic commanding officer of Fort Ellis, 1869–1872, removed after the Sioux attack on the Northern Pacific Railroad survey party at Pryor's Creek.

Jack Baronett ("Yellowstone Jack"): English-born adventurer, prospector, Indian fighter, and guide, who found Truman Everts alive after his separation from the 1870 expedition; built "Baronett's Bridge" across the Yellowstone, which was partly burned by the Nez Perce in 1877.

X. Beidler: Vigilante enforcer in the gold camps in 1863–1864 and later in Helena; close associate of Nathaniel Langford.

John Bozeman: Pioneer, prospector, explorer, and entrepreneur, who opened the Bozeman Trail from the North Platte to the Yellowstone River in 1863 and subsequently founded the town of Bozeman, as well as working briefly for Nathaniel Langford. Murdered in mysterious circumstances in 1867.

Albert Brackett, Brevet Colonel: Sometime poet, ethnographer, and ornithologist, who led the Second Cavalry to Fort Ellis in July 1869 and commanded the post ineffectually until his replacement by Eugene Baker.

Jim Bridger: One of the most celebrated of the mountain men, an early pioneer of the beaver trade, and the most important early explorer of Yellowstone, known for his tall tales about what he had seen there. The Bridger Trail, which he opened in 1863, served as an alternative route to the Bozeman Trail.

James Brisbin ("Grasshopper Jim"): Third commanding officer of Fort Ellis (from 1872 to 1876), known for his antipathy to Doane, his expertise on agriculture and cattle raising, and the arthritis that made him an ineffective leader of the Montana Column during the 1876 Custer campaign against the Sioux.

William Clark: Former army officer and co-captain with Meriwether Lewis of the Corps of Discovery, which explored the route from St. Louis to the mouth of the Columbia, 1804–1806.

Malcolm Clarke: Renowned trader for the American Fur Company, related by marriage to the All Chiefs band of Piegans and known to them as Four Bears. After retiring from the fur trade and moving to a ranch close to Helena, he became a close friend of Nathaniel Langford, Cornelius Hedges, and other members of the 1870 Yellowstone expedition. His murder by a Piegan relative in 1869 precipitated the crisis that culminated in the Marias River massacre.

John Colter: Member of the Corps of Discovery and renowned hunter who explored the upper Yellowstone in the winter of 1807–1808, and was the first white man to see the area of the future national park.

Charles Cook: Maine-born pioneer who arrived in Montana in 1864, and childhood friend of David Folsom, with whom he led the 1869 expedition to the upper Yellowstone.

Jay Cooke: Head of the banking house of Jay Cooke and Co. in Philadelphia, known as "the financier of the Civil War," and promoter of the Northern Pacific Railroad; enlisted Nathaniel Langford's help to promote the interests of the railroad and the creation of the national park.

Alexander Culbertson: Close friend and associate of Malcolm Clarke and the leading figure in the operations of the American Fur Company at Fort Pierre and Fort Union; married to a Blood woman.

Walter De Lacy: Mapmaker and explorer who stumbled upon the Yellowstone geyser basins in the course of a prospecting trip in 1863; subsequently worked in the office of the surveyor general of Montana Territory and produced the most accurate maps used by the 1869 and 1870 Yellowstone expeditions.

Pierre-Jean De Smet: Jesuit priest who befriended Jim Bridger and created a map of the upper Yellowstone based on the mountain man's descriptions; first missionary to succeed in baptizing members of the Piegan tribe, and left Montana in 1869 after Blackfeet attacks on the St. Peter's mission.

Philippe Régis de Trobriand, Brevet Major General: Aristocratic Frenchman who came to the United States in 1861; was commanding officer of Fort Shaw during the Piegan crisis of 1869–1870.

Gustavus Cheyney Doane: Lieutenant in the U.S. Second Cavalry with ambitions to be the greatest American explorer; in command of troops who stormed the Piegan camp on the Marias River and leader of the military escort in the 1870 Yellowstone expedition. Known thereafter as "the man who invented Wonderland."

Truman Everts: Assessor of Internal Revenue for Montana Territory and member of the 1870 expedition, best remembered for becoming separated from the rest of the party and being lost in the Yellowstone wilderness for thirty-seven days.

David Folsom: New Hampshire Quaker who came to Montana with Nathaniel Langford on the 1862 Fisk wagon train from Minnesota and remained his close personal friend; joint organizer with Charles Cook of the 1869 Yellowstone expedition.

Warren Gillette: Helena merchant and operator of the toll road through the Little Prickly Pear Canyon, close to Malcolm Clarke's ranch; member of the 1870 expedition and stayed behind to search unsuccessfully for Truman Everts.

Winfield Hancock, General: Civil War hero known as "Hancock the Superb," and commanding officer of the Department of Dakota during the Blackfeet crisis of 1869–1870; later was Democratic presidential nominee in the 1880 election.

Samuel Hauser: Friend and business partner of Nathaniel Langford and member of the 1870 Yellowstone expedition; later became governor of Montana.

Ferdinand Vandeveer Hayden: Head of the U.S. Geological Survey of the Territories and the most renowned geologist-explorer of his time; led surveys of the upper Yellowstone in 1871 and 1872 and was instrumental in the creation of the national park.

Heavy Runner: Piegan chief, friendly to the whites, whose camp on the Marias River was attacked by the Second Cavalry on January 23, 1870; killed during the attack.

Cornelius Hedges: Harvard- and Yale-educated lawyer, who walked from Iowa to Montana Territory in 1864 and later set up a law office in Helena, where he became Nathaniel Langford's closest friend; his clients included Malcolm Clarke; leading member of the 1870 Yellowstone expedition.

William Henry Jackson: One of the pioneering landscape photographers of the nineteenth century; documented the 1871 Yellowstone expedition and accompanied Ferdinand Hayden on several other surveys of the West.

Joseph: Chief of the "non-treaty" Nez Perce, who fled from Idaho in 1877 and were pursued by the army through Yellowstone National Park before finally being defeated by forces under General Nelson Miles.

Francis X. Kuppens: Young Jesuit at St. Peter's Mission, who accompanied a Piegan hunting party to the upper Yellowstone and later wrote of discussing the idea of a national park with Cornelius Hedges and Governor Meagher as early as 1865.

Nathaniel Langford: Born in upstate New York, came to Montana on the Fisk wagon train in 1862; sympathizer and chronicler of the 1863–1864 vigilante campaign and later member of the executive committee of the reformed vigilantes in Helena while working as federal collector of internal revenues; principal organizer of the 1870 Yellowstone expedition and leader of the campaign to create the national park, of which he was the first supervisor.

Meriwether Lewis: Co-captain with William Clark of the Corps of Discovery; his clash with a group of Piegans on the Two Medicine River was the only violent encounter during the two years of the expedition.

Thomas Francis Meagher: Colorful Irish freedom fighter who served two terms as acting governor of Montana and hoped to explore the upper Yellowstone; drowned in the Missouri River in 1867.

Thomas Moran: Great nineteenth-century landscape painter who accompanied the 1871 Hayden expedition to Yellowstone, and whose paintings were instrumental in persuading Congress to create the first national park.

Mountain Chief: Militant Piegan leader of the All Chiefs band; the intended target of the January 1870 attack on the Marias River.

Owl Child (Ne-tus-che-o, aka Peter or Pete): Young Piegan renegade and murderer of Malcolm Clarke in a family quarrel; died of smallpox soon after the Marias River massacre.

William Raynolds, Captain: Leader of the failed attempt to reach the upper Yellowstone in 1860, guided by Jim Bridger and accompanied by Ferdinand Hayden.

Phil Sheridan, General: Civil War hero and architect of the doctrine of total war against civilian populations; commander of the Division of the Missouri in 1870, when he ordered the cavalry attack on the Marias River; later became an active defender of the Yellowstone National Park, eventually placing it under military control.

William Tecumseh Sherman, General: Commander of the U.S. Army during the Piegan campaign, who subsequently exonerated Major Eugene Baker.

Alfred Sully, General: Former military hero disgraced after his failed campaign against the Cheyenne; as Superintendent of Indian Affairs for Montana, sidelined during the Blackfeet crisis of 1869–1870.

Gouverneur Kemble Warren, Lieutenant: Explored the Northern Plains for the Army Corps of Topographical Engineers during the late 1850s, accompanied by Ferdinand Hayden.

Jake Smith, Benjamin Stickney, Walter Trumbull: Members of the 1870 Yellowstone expedition.

NOTES

PROLOGUE: THE VIEW FROM MOUNT WASHINGTON

1. The contemporary names are, respectively, the Ruby River, Willow Creek, and the Big Hole.
2. Langford's account of the expedition was published only in 1905, under the title *The Discovery of Yellowstone National Park, 1870*. Whether it constitutes a genuine transcript of an original diary or a later reconstruction has been the subject of intense debate for many years. For the sake of convenience, I use the word *diary* throughout. For a detailed discussion of the controversy, see below pp. 354–61.
3. The brevet system was a system of promotions, generally for meritorious conduct, that was widely used during the Civil War. Most famously, George Armstrong Custer was breveted major general at the age of twenty-three. After the war, "Colonel" Brackett reverted to plain Lieutenant Colonel—as did Custer—but like most officers he retained his brevet rank as an honorific. I have generally used officers' brevet titles, since these were the ones commonly applied to them at the time.
4. Others have disputed this, arguing that Washburn's transfer to Montana was the result of an internecine feud in the Republican Party.
5. The name of the mountain remains the same, but all of them were wrong about the altitude, which is now established as 10,243 feet.
6. Doane, "Personal Recollections—Two Yellowstone Expeditions," in Theodore F. Rodenbough, *From Everglade to Cañon with the Second Dragoons,* New York: D. Van Nostrand, 1875, 405–19.

1: "A KNOLEDGE OF THESE PEOPLE"

1. Reprinted in full in Frank Bergon, ed., *The Journals of Lewis and Clark*, New York: Penguin, 1989, xxiii–xxvii.

2. Stephen Ambrose, *Undaunted Courage: Meriwether Lewis, Thomas Jefferson, and the Opening of the American West*, New York: Simon and Schuster, 1997, 168–75; James P. Ronda, *Lewis and Clark Among the Indians: Centennial Edition*, Lincoln: University of Nebraska Press, 1984, 27–41.

3. Ambrose, *Undaunted Courage*, 354–58; Ronda, *Lewis and Clark*, 219.

4. Clark journal, March 31, 1805, in Bernard De Voto, ed., *Journals of Lewis and Clark*, Boston: Houghton Mifflin, 1953, 90.

5. Ambrose, *Undaunted Courage*, 359. Lewis journal, May 1, 1806.

6. Ambrose, *Undaunted Courage*, 285. Lewis journal, August 19, 1805.

7. Ronda, *Lewis and Clark Among the Indians*, 157.

8. George Bird Grinnell, *Blackfoot Lodge Tales: The Story of a Prairie People*, Lincoln: University of Nebraska Press, 1962, 257.

9. Journal, June 14, 1806, in Ambrose, *Undaunted Courage*, 370.

10. William H. Goetzmann, *Exploration and Empire: The Explorer and the Scientist in the Winning of the American West*, New York: Alfred A. Knopf, 1966, 16.

11. Aubrey L. Haines, *The Yellowstone Story*, Vol. 1. Yellowstone Library and Museum Association, in collaboration with Colorado Associated University Press, 1977, 5, citing Clarence E. Carter, ed., "The Territories of Louisiana-Missouri, 1803–1806," in *The Territorial Papers of the United States*, Vol. 13. Washington, D.C.: Government Printing Office, 1948, 243; also Richard A. Bartlett, *Nature's Yellowstone*, Tucson: University of Arizona Press, 96.

12. This note may not actually refer to the Yellowstone per se. Clark actually locates the phenomenon "on a west branch of Tongu river (a branch of the Rochejhone) . . . This river is called by the Indians Min-na-e-sa (or big water)." Clark "Miscellaneous Memoranda," in Reuben Gold Thwaites, ed., *Original Journals of the Lewis and Clark Expedition, 1804–1806*, Vol. 6, 266–7.

2: THE TERRIBLE PAHKEES

1. Ronda identifies the Pahkees as the Siksika, in *Lewis and Clark Among the Indians*, 144. John C. Jackson, in *The Piikani Blackfeet: A Culture Under Siege*, Missoula, Montana: Mountain Press Publishing Company, 1999, x, says it refers to the Piegans.

2. John C. Ewers, *The Blackfeet: Raiders on the Northwestern Plains*, Norman: University of Oklahoma Press, 1958, 5.

3. Jackson, *Piikani*, 111.

4. David Lavender, *The Way to the Western Sea: Lewis and Clark Across the Continent*, New York: Anchor, 1990, 376–7.

5. Gary Moulton, ed., *The Journals of the Lewis & Clark Expedition*, Lincoln: University of Nebraska Press, 1988, 113.

6. Ben Bennett, *Death, Too, for The-Heavy-Runner*, Missoula, Montana: Mountain Press Publishing Company, 1982, 1–2.

7. Peter Nabokov and Lawrence Loendorf, *Restoring a Presence: American Indians and Yellowstone National Park*, Norman: University of Oklahoma Press, 2004, 92. Ibid., 94, citing Walter McClintock, *The Tragedy of the Blackfoot*, Los Angeles: Southwest Museum, 1970, 435, says they traveled to "the country inhabited by a people with dark skin, and long hair falling over their faces"—presumably Mexico.

8. Haines, *The Yellowstone Story*, Vol. 1, 21.

9. The reputation of the Blackfeet as a particularly violent people extended well into the twentieth century. In the 1941 Powell and Pressburger film *49th Parallel*, which deals with a group of Nazi saboteurs in Canada, the writer-explorer played by Leslie Howard compares them to the Nazis: "From the earliest age, their small boys were trained in the arts of war, which they regarded as the only pursuits worthy of a man. But they preferred to attack by night rather than by day and wherever possible to shoot the enemy in the back. Their smaller neighbors lived in constant danger from them. They also believed in first terrorizing their opponent by covering themselves in war paints and beating loudly on their tribal arms. Well, doesn't that sound familiar to you? . . . Well, what price Goebbels, eh? And listen to this . . . When a tribal leader really desired to drive a point home, he used that most terrible of all public speaker's weapons—repetition, constant and unutterably wearisome repetition. Old man Hitler himself."

10. Despite their distinct territories, the three Blackfeet tribes shared a common Algonkian language and similar rituals. Nabokov and Loendorf, *Restoring a Presence*, 91; Ewers, *The Blackfeet*, 4–5.

11. J. P. Dunn, *Massacres of the Mountains: A History of the Indian Wars of the Far West*, New York: Harper Brothers, 1886, 309 ff.; Ewers, *The Blackfeet*, 37–8.

12. Ewers, *The Blackfeet*, 60. One estimate is that 9,000 of these could be classed as warriors; see Nabokov and Loendorf, *Restoring a Presence*, 93 and 314, notes 28 and 29. Catlin in 1832 estimated the total population as 16,500. Prince Maximilian von Wied, who came a year later, said 18,000.

13. Ewers, *The Blackfeet*, 30, 40; Richard Lancaster. *Piegan: A Look from within at the Life, Times, and Legacy of an American Indian Tribe*, New York: Doubleday, 1966, 121.

14. The Rocky Mountain Front, including present-day Glacier National Park.

15. The characterization certainly fits the Piegans, but at this stage, perhaps because Drouillard was not on hand to translate, Lewis took the Indians to be "Minnetares of Fort de Prairie." In other words, Gros Ventres, also known as Atsina—the only real allies of the Blackfeet. Lavender speculates that the Indians may have misidentified themselves with sign language as Gros Ventres, and their real identity was established only later when Canadian traders heard reports of the encounter. See Lavender, *Western Sea*, 348.

16. Blackfeet sources say the victim of the shooting was about twelve years old. Author interviews.

17. Lavender, *Western Sea*, 351, 377. Lavender identifies the probable recipient of the letter, which is dated September 29, 1806, and exists only in partial replica, as John Hay, postmaster of Cahokia, Illinois.

18. *Journals*, ed. Moulton, 136, note 2, citing James H. Bradley, "Affairs at Fort Benton from 1831 to 1869," *Contributions to the Montana Historical Society* 3 (1900), 201; Olin Dunbar Wheeler, *The Trail of Lewis and Clark, 1804–1904*, Vol. 2, New York: The Knickerbocker Press, 1904, 311–2 (which cites the account of a member of the Piegan party named Wolf Calf). There is also a certain dark irony in reading the account of the incident in John A. Hawgood's *America's Western Frontier*, New York, Knopf, 1967, which reports that, "Lewis's encounter with an Indian war party . . . resulted in no casualties." But Hawgood's account is immediately followed by a lengthy extract from Lewis's journal describing the deaths of the two Piegans, which presumably did not count. Cited in Michael P. Malone

and Richard B. Roeder, *The Montana Past: An Anthology,* Missoula: University of Montana Press, 1969, 29–30.

19. James H. Bradley, "Account of the Drowning of Governor Thomas Francis Meagher," *Contributions to the Historical Society of Montana* 8 (1917): 131–6.

20. Paul Russell Cutright, "Lewis on the Marias, 1806," *Montana the Magazine of Western History*, 18, 3 (Summer 1968), 30–43.

3: ALL FOR A BEAVER HAT

1. The classic early account of the fur trade is Hiram Chittenden's two-volume *The American Fur Trade of the Far West*, Stanford: Academic Reprints, 1954. An excellent recent work is Eric Jay Dolin, *Fur, Fortune, and Empire: The Epic History of the Fur Trade in America*, New York: W. W. Norton, 2010.

2. Merrill J. Mattes, *Colter's Hell and Jackson Hole*, Washington, D.C.: National Park Service, 1962, 17, citing Thomas James, *Three Years Among the Indians and Mexicans*, Lincoln: University of Nebraska Press, 1984; see also Mark H. Brown, *Plainsmen of the Yellowstone: A History of the Yellowstone Basin*, Lincoln: University of Nebraska Press, 1961, 37.

3. Stallo Vinton, *John Colter, Discoverer of Yellowstone Park*, New York: Edward Eberstadt, 1926, 17.

4. Burton Harris, *John Colter: His Years in the Rockies*, New York: Charles Scribner's Sons, 1952, 39.

5. Goetzmann, *Exploration and Empire*, cited in Robert H. Utley, *A Life Wild and Perilous: Mountain Men and the Paths to the Pacific*, New York: Henry Holt, 1997, 317.

6. See the description by Rotten Tail (Arapooish) in Brown, *Plainsmen*, 17.

7. Following is drawn from Nabokov and Loendorf, *Restoring a Presence*, 48–9; Peter Nabokov, *Where the Lightning Strikes: The Lives of American Indian Sacred Places*, New York: Viking, 2006, 188, 197–200; Fred W. Voget, *The Shoshone-Crow Sundance*, Norman: University of Oklahoma Press, 1974, 7; and Charles Bradley, *The Handsome People: A History of the Crow Indians and the Whites*, Billings, Montana: Council for Indian Education, 1991, 42.

8. Thomas H. Leforge and Thomas B. Marquis, *Memoirs of a White Crow Indian (Thomas H. Leforge, as told to Thomas B. Marquis)*, Lincoln: University of Nebraska Press, 1974, 184. As the author argues, "Eyes Yellow" may be more accurate, since the first three syllables of the Crow name mean "eyes" and the last two "yellow." See also Evan S. Connell, *Son of the Morning Star: General Custer and the Battle of the Little Bighorn*, New York: North Point Press, 1984, 208.

9. Goetzmann, *Exploration and Empire*, 17–25; Bartlett, *Nature's Yellowstone*, 1974, 97–100; Haines, *Yellowstone Story*, Vol. 1, 35–8; Utley, *A Life Wild*, 11–5. The most detailed source on Colter specifically is Harris, *John Colter*.

10. Haines is close to categorical that Colter must have crossed the river just above Tower Fall, using what later became known as the Bannock Ford. He describes this as the only place where a practicable winter crossing coincided with evidence of volcanism. But Bartlett makes the reasonable point that this description could also apply to the so-called

Nez Perce Ford, which is close to the Mud Volcano, a few miles below Yellowstone Lake. In that case, Colter may well not have seen the falls of the Yellowstone Canyon. Bartlett, *Nature's Yellowstone*, 100. Historians continue to debate the details of Colter's route. See, for example, Robert Betts, *Along the Ramparts of the Tetons: The Saga of Jackson Hole, Wyoming*, Boulder: Colorado Associated University Press, 1978; Paul Lawrence, *John Colter: Journey of Discovery*, Ogden, Utah: Uinta Press, 1978; and Lillian Ruth Colter-Frick, *Courageous Colter and Companions*, Washington, Missouri: L. R. Colter-Frick, 1997.

11. The similarity of the names is coincidental; Coulter Creek was named for John Merle Coulter, a botanist attached to Ferdinand Vandeveer Hayden's 1872 Yellowstone expedition. Aubrey Haines discredits this account, concluding that the "JC" carving was probably left by Coulter, not Colter. See Haines, *Yellowstone National Park: Its Exploration and Establishment*, Washington, D.C.: National Park Service, 1974, 5. The account of Woody's find is taken from Vinton, *John Colter*, 61–2.

12. William Beard and his son, who dug up the rhyolite stone, had never heard of John Colter. See Mattes, *Colter's Hell*, 32–3.

13. Vinton ignored the fact that Hiram Chittenden had recanted his earlier theory in the 1903 revised edition of his *The Yellowstone National Park: Historical and Descriptive*, Cincinnati: Stewart & Kidd Company.

14. James, *Three Years Among the Indians*, and John Bradbury, *Travels in the Interior of America in 1809, 1810 and 1811*, Lincoln: University of Nebraska Press, 1986. Harris finds James's version the more convincing of the two. See Harris, *John Colter*, 127–31.

15. Utley, *A Life Wild*, 19, citing James, *Three Years Among the Indians*, 65 and 80.

4: THE BIG KNIVES

1. See Langford's account of conversation with Doane about the Tetons, *The Discovery of Yellowstone Park: Journal of the Washburn Expedition to the Yellowstone and Firehole Rivers in the Year 1870*, foreword by Aubrey L. Haines. Lincoln: University of Nebraska Press, 1972, 52–3.

2. J. Cecil Alter, *James Bridger, Trapper, Frontiersman, Scout and Guide: A Historical Narrative*, Salt Lake City: Shepard Book Co., 1925, 6–7.

3. Ibid., 110.

4. Grenville M. Dodge, "Biographical Sketch," in Ibid., 522. See Utley, *A Life Wild*, 324, note 10.

5. This description is by David L. Brown, who met Bridger at the 1837 trappers' rendezvous. Brown, *Three Years in the Rocky Mountains* (1845), Fairfield, Washington: Ye Galleon Press, 1982. See Utley, *A Life Wild*, 352, note 4.

6. Stanley Vestal, *Jim Bridger, Mountain Man*, New York: Morrow, 1936, 108.

7. In Joe Meek's words, "When the pie was opened, the birds began to sing." Utley, *A Life Wild*, 136.

8. Mae Reed Porter and Odessa Davenport, *Scotsman in Buckskin: Sir William Drummond Stewart and the Rocky Mountain Fur Trade*; http://home.att.net/~mman/StewartWilliam Drummond.htm.

9. The scene was captured by Alfred Jacob Miller, the artist traveling with the Stewart party. See Utley, *A Life Wild*, 167.

10. See Ewers, *The Blackfeet*, 45–71.

11. Fort Piegan itself did not last long. Kipp's men were too nervous to remain there over the winter of 1831–1832, and during their absence the post was burned down—perhaps by Assiniboines, perhaps by Bloods. Ewers, *The Blackfeet*, 57–8; François A. Chardon, *Journal at Fort Clark, 1834–1839*, Anne Heloise Abel, ed. Lincoln: University of Nebraska Press, 1997, 253.

12. Lesley Wischmann, *Frontier Diplomats: Alexander Culbertson and Natoyist-Siksina' Among the Blackfeet*, Norman: University of Oklahoma Press, 2004, 38, citing Chardon, *Journal*, 253.

13. Chittenden, *American Fur Trade*, Vol. 1, 87.

14. Reprinted in full in Haines, *The Yellowstone Story*, Vol. 1, 42. Complete Potts letters are in *Yellowstone Nature Notes*, 21, no. 5 (September–October) 1947: 49–56.

15. Warren Angus Ferris, *Life in the Rocky Mountains: A Diary of Wanderings on the Sources of the Rivers Missouri, Columbia, and Colorado, 1830–1835*, Denver: Old West Publishing Company, 1983, 257–60.

16. Le Roy R. Hafen, ed., *The Mountain Men and the Fur Trade of the Far West*, Glendale, California: Arthur A. Clark Co., 1966, Vol. 2, 154, cited in Bartlett, *Nature's Yellowstone*, 104.

17. Mrs. Frances A. Fuller Victor, *The River of the West: Joe Meek in the Rocky Mountains*, Hartford: R. W. Bliss and Co., 1870, 75–6, cited in W. Turrentine Jackson, "The Early Exploration and Founding of Yellowstone National Park," doctoral dissertation, University of Texas, 1940, 50–1.

18. Quoted in Harvey Lewis Carter, *"Dear Old Kit": The Historical Christopher Carson*, Norman: University of Oklahoma Press, 1990, 67.

19. A useful brief account of each of the rendezvous, with photographs of each site, can be found at www.thefurtrapper.com/rendezvous_sites.htm. This includes a summary of the various accounts of the battle and their considerable discrepancies.

20. Ferris, *Life in the Rocky Mountains*, 175–9; the attack is described in Utley, *A Life Wild*, 141.

21. Edgeley W. Todd, ed., Washington Irving, *The Adventures of Captain Bonneville, U.S.A., Digested from His Journals*, Norman: University of Oklahoma Press, 1961, 91–5.

22. After this operation Whitman's medical skills were in great demand from the Nez Perce and other northwestern tribes. Bridger later sent his daughter Mary Ann, the first of his three children by his Flathead wife, Cora Insala, to the Whitmans' mission school at Walla Walla; Joe Meek also sent his daughter Helen to study there. In 1847 Whitman and his wife Narcissa, together with twelve other white settlers, were murdered by Cayuse Indians, who held him responsible for failing to stem an epidemic of measles. The victims of the Whitman Massacre, which sparked the so-called Cayuse War, included Mary Ann Bridger and Helen Meek.

23. William T. Hamilton and E. T. Sieber, *My Sixty Years on the Plains: Trapping, Trading and Indian Fighting*, New York: Forest and Stream, 1905, 94–5. See Bartlett, *Nature's Yellowstone*, 112 and 225, note 39.

24. Estimates of the numbers who died in the Fort McKenzie massacre vary widely, from

three to twenty-one (the figure reported by Alexander Culbertson). See Wischmann, *Frontier Diplomats*, 112, note 22.

25. James H. Bradley, manuscript, *Contributions to the Montana Historical Society* 8 (1917): 134, cited in Ewers, *The Blackfeet*, 65.

26. For an excellent short account of the 1837 epidemic, see Wischmann, *Frontier Diplomats*, 67–74. The Crows were the only tribe in the region to remain unaffected. See also T. C. Tessendorf, "Red Death on the Missouri," *American West* 14 (January–February 1977), 52.

27. Tessendorf, "Red Death," 52.

28. Victor, *River of the West*, Vol. 1, 264.

5: BRIDGER'S FORT

1. Contemporary documents and close friends such as Nathaniel Langford and Cornelius Hedges generally refer to him as Clark. However, the final "e" was always used by members of his family, and I have kept to that spelling throughout. For more details, see James H. Bradley, "Affairs at Fort Benton: From Lieut. Bradley's Journal," *Contributions to the Historical Society of Montana*, 3 (1900) 232.

2. Isaac I. Stevens, Senate Exec. Doc. 1 746, 33rd Cong., 2nd Sess., 403, Washington, D.C.: Government Printing Office, 1853. See also John C. Ewers, *Indian Life on the Upper Missouri*, Norman: University of Oklahoma Press, 1968, 62. Natoyist-Siksina' was actually Culbertson's second wife. He had already married a Piegan woman in 1833, but her name is not recorded.

3. Wischmann, *Frontier Diplomats*, 103.

4. Adolf Hungry Wolf, *Blackfeet History and Culture: Native Life on the Northern Plains*, Vol. 4, 1041, Skookumchuck, British Columbia: Good Medicine Cultural Foundation, 2007. See also Nancy M. Peterson, *Walking in Two Worlds: Mixed-Blood Indian Women Seeking Their Own Path*, Caldwell, Idaho: Caxton Press, 2006. Peterson renders Nellie's Piegan name as Piotopowaka, or The Bird That Comes Back.

5. Helen P. Clarke, "Sketch of Malcolm Clarke. A Corporate Member of the Historical Society of Montana," *Contributions to the Historical Society of Montana*, 2 (1896): 255–68; Charlotte Ouisconsin Van Cleve, "A Sketch of the Early Life of Malcolm Clarke: A Corporate Member of the Historical Society of Montana," *Contributions to the Historical Society of Montana* 1 (1876): 90–8; Nathaniel Pitt Langford, "A Frontier Tragedy," undated typescript, Yellowstone National Park Archives.

6. Clarke, "Sketch of Malcolm Clarke." The incident is also described in Charles Larpenteur, *Forty Years a Fur Trader on the Upper Missouri*, Elliot Coues, ed. New York: Francis P. Harper, 1896, 352–3. Larpenteur, who also worked for the American Fur Company, quarreled mightily with Clarke. "He thought himself a king," Larpenteur writes. "I knew him to be very unpopular with both whites and Indians." Ibid., 317, 319.

7. Helen Clarke, application for enrollment on the Blackfeet Census, Helen P. Clarke Papers, SC 1153, Montana Historical Society Archives.

8. James Welch and Paul Stekler, *Killing Custer: The Battle of the Little Bighorn and the Fate of the Plains Indians*, New York: Penguin, 1994, 27.

9. Hungry Wolf, *Blackfeet History and Culture*, Vol. 1, 191–2.

10. Horace Clarke, biography, undated typescript, SC 540, Montana Historical Society Archives.

11. John Wesley Powell, *Exploration of the Colorado River and Its Canyons*, New York: Penguin Classics, 2003, 72. The combative Yale paleontologist Othniel Marsh brought a party here in 1872. His finds included a giant mastodon which he named *Uintatherium*. On Marsh's fossil-hunting competition with his archrival, Edward G. Cope, see James Cassidy, *Ferdinand V. Hayden: Entrepreneur of Science*, Lincoln: University of Nebraska Press, 2000, 183–9.

12. There are numerous books on these events. The most recent is Ethan Rarick, *Desperate Passage: The Donner Party's Perilous Journey West*, New York: Oxford University Press, 2008.

13. From the journal of William Clayton, Brigham Young's secretary; see Alter, *James Bridger*, 225–6.

14. Gunnison, *The Mormons, or, Latter-Day Saints, in the Valley of the Great Salt Lake: A History of Their Rise and Progress, Peculiar Doctrines, Present Condition, and Prospects, Derived from Personal Observation, During a Residence Among Them*, Philadelphia, Lippincott, Grambo, & Co., 1852, 151. See also Goetzmann, *Exploration*, 278–9.

15. William F. Wheeler, "The Late James Gemmell," *Montana Historical Society Contributions*, 2 (1896): 331–2. Cited in Jackson, "Early Exploration," 77.

16. Eugene Sayre Topping, *The Chronicles of the Yellowstone: An Accurate, Comprehensive History*, St. Paul, Minnesota: Pioneer Press, 1888, 16.

6: FAKELORE

1. Gunnison, *The Mormons*, 150.

2. Hubert Howe Bancroft and Alfred Bates, *History of Utah 1540–1886*, San Francisco: History Publishing Company, 1889, 309.

3. Pierre-Jean De Smet, with Hiram M. Chittenden and Alfred Talbot Richardson, *Life, Letters and Travels of Father Pierre-Jean de Smet, S. J.*, New York: F. P. Harper, 1905, 1012.

4. Jackson, *Piikani*, 141. On the Small Robes and the Jesuits, see Ewers, *The Blackfeet*, 185–7.

5. Ewers, *The Blackfeet*, 188–91. Another priest, a reputedly unstable individual named Nicholas Point, wrote to De Smet: "I could have baptized a great number of adults; they even seemed to desire it ardently; but these desires were not yet sufficiently imbued with the true principles of religion. I could not content myself with the persuasion generally existing among the savages, that when they had received baptism they can conquer any enemy whatsoever. . . . This explains why some wretches, who seek only to kill their neighbors, were the first to petition for baptism." De Smet, *Life, Letters and Travels*, 953–4.

6. Edwin T. Denig, *Indian Tribes of the Upper Missouri*, Bureau of American Ethnology, 46th Annual Report, 551–2, cited in Ewers, *The Blackfeet*, 188.

7. The present-day Yellowstone National Park in fact stretches from 44°08' to 45°07'N and from 109°48' to 111°10' W.

8. *De Smet: Life, Letters and Travels*, 660–1. The reference is to the English archaeologist Richard Chandler (1738–1810), who described the hot springs at Hieropolis in his *Travels in Asia Minor*, 287–90. Pambuk Kalassi, or "Castle of Cotton," refers to the famously

snow-white calcareous deposits there. It's also clear from this passage that De Smet knew that Colter's Hell and the upper Yellowstone were two different places.

9. The best discussion of Bridger's Yellowstone stories is in Haines, *Yellowstone Story*, Vol. 1, 53–9. Paul Schullery makes the point that many of his tall tales may have originated with other trappers but were increasingly attributed to Bridger as his reputation grew. See Schullery, *Searching for Yellowstone: Ecology and Wonder in the Last Wilderness*, Boston: Houghton Mifflin, 1997, 38.

10. See p. 21.

11. De Smet, *Life, Letters, and Travels*, 661.

12. This idea is comprehensively debunked by Joseph Weixelman, "The Power to Evoke Wonder: Native Americans and the Geysers of Yellowstone National Park," M.A. Thesis, Montana State University, 1992, copy in Montana State University Libraries Special Collections, Bozeman. Weixelman also cites a later letter from De Smet describing how, in the Indians' view, the warring spirits of Yellowstone were "continually at the anvil forging their weapons."

13. See the extended discussion of "fakelore"in Nabokov and Loendorf, *Restoring a Presence*, 21–8, citing such works as Mary Earl Hardy, *Little Ta-Wish-Indian Legends from Geyserland* (1914); LaVerne Fitzgerald, *Black Feather: Trapper Jim's Fables of Sheepeater Indians in Yellowstone* (1933); and Dr. and Mrs. N. W. Christensen, *A Trip Through Yellowstone Park: Interesting Events Portrayed in Music* (1953), which includes lyrics "too insultingly stereotyped to bear repeating." On Bridger's and De Smet's roles, see Weixelman, "Power to Evoke Wonder," 12–3.

14. See Nabokov and Loendorf, *Restoring a Presence*; Weixelman, "Power to Evoke Wonder"; Åke Hultkrantz, "The Fear of Geysers Among Indians of the Yellowstone Park Area," in Leslie B. Davis, ed., *Lifeways of Intermountain and Plains Montana Indians*, Bozeman: Montana State University Press, 1979; Hultkrantz, "The Indians in Yellowstone Park," *Annals of Wyoming* 29, 2 (1957): 125–49. Much of this work is well summarized in Lee H. Whittlesey, *Storytelling in Yellowstone: Horse and Buggy Tour Guides*, Albuquerque, New Mexico: University of New Mexico Press, 2007, 11–23. Whittlesey suggests that one theory for the early ignorance of the park area among whites is that few white men were even told of its existence, for fear they might come there and form alliances with local spirits against the Indians. This makes sense in view of the well-known tendency of most tribes to keep quiet about matters of religious significance.

15. Richard A. Bartlett, *Great Surveys of the American West*, Norman: University of Oklahoma Press, 1962, 37–8; and Chris J. Magoc, *Yellowstone: The Creation and Selling of an American Landscape, 1870–1903*, Albuquerque: University of New Mexico Press, 1999, 140–1.

16. Nabokov and Loendorf even cite evidence that the Kiowa passed through the future national park area at the beginning of their great southward migration, which eventually took them to Oklahoma. For a map of their possible migration route, see *Restoring a Presence*, 69. There is even a Kiowa belief that the tribe was conceived and born in Yellowstone Park at the Dragon's Mouth Spring. I am indebted to Lee Whittlesey for this point.

17. Obsidian from Yellowstone has been found as far away as Ohio and Ontario, indicating the extent of the trading network. See Schullery, *Searching for Yellowstone*, 13–5. Nabokov and Loendorf, *Restoring a Presence*, 162–4. Despite their "Approach-the-rocks" theory,

Nabokov and Loendorf do acknowledge a variety of oral accounts from Nez Perce and Kootenai sources that lend weight to the "neutral ground" theory.

18. Photographer Edward S. Curtis, interview with Mountain Crow warrior Hunts to Die, in Nabokov and Loendorf, *Restoring a Presence*, 56–7.

19. Nabokov and Loendorf, *Restoring a Presence*, 173 and 323, note 215.

20. *Autobiography of George Washington Bean: A Utah Pioneer of 1847*, Salt Lake City: Utah Publishing Company, 1945, cited in Nabokov and Loendorf, *Restoring a Presence*, 280.

21. Patricia Roberts Clark, *Tribal Names of the Americas: Variant Spellings and Alternative Forms, Cross-Referenced*, Jefferson, North Carolina: McFarland & Company, 2009, 34; Haines, *Yellowstone Story*, Vol. 1, 22, 25.

22. Aubrey L. Haines, "The Bannock Indian Trails in Yellowstone National Parks," speech before the 4th Annual Meeting of the Montana Archaeological Society, Lake Hills Country Club, Billings, Montana, April 15, 1961, typescript in Yellowstone National Park Archives. Since then, debate has continued over which of these pathways was actually used by the Bannock, which by other tribes, and which by hunters, miners, and other visitors.

7: MAN PICKING UP STONES RUNNING

1. Roy Morris Jr., *Sheridan: The Life and Wars of General Phil Sheridan*, New York: Vintage, 1992, 19–20.

2. Cassidy, *Entrepreneur of Science*, 33–5; Mike Foster, *Strange Genius: The Life of Ferdinand Vandeveer Hayden*, Niwort, Colorado: Roberts Rinehart Publishers, 1994, 22, 31–2, 35–6.

3. See Goetzmann, *Exploration and Empire*, 181–4.

4. Cassidy, *Entrepreneur of Science*, 41.

5. Jackson, "Early Exploration," 215, attributes it to Louis C. Cramton, *Early History of Yellowstone National Park and Its Relation to National Park Policies*, U.S. Department of the Interior, National Park Service, 1932. Foster, *Strange Genius*, 60–1, casts doubt on its veracity and discusses how the myth was subsequently embellished by Hayden himself and then cemented into history in later accounts, including by John McPhee, *Annals of the Former World*, New York: Farrar, Straus and Giroux, 2000, 383–4.

6. Wischmann, *Frontier Diplomats*, 173–4.

7. Goetzmann, *Exploration and Empire*, 328.

8. Paul Norman Beck, *The First Sioux War: The Grattan Fight and Blue Water Creek, 1854–1856*, Lanham, Maryland: University Press of America, 2004, 79–80.

9. Brown, *Plainsmen of the Yellowstone*, 106–9. Randolph B. Marcy, *Thirty Years of Army Life on the Border*, New York: Harper Brothers, 1866, 364–6.

10. Hayden, *Preliminary Report of the United States Geological Survey of Montana and Portions of Adjacent Territories: Being a Fifth Annual Report of Progress*, Washington, D.C.: Government Printing Office, 1872, cited in Jackson, "Early Exploration," 216.

11. Quoted in Foster, *Strange Genius*, 80.

8: TERRA INCOGNITA

1. This time Hayden was paid $120 a month plus expenses, a handsome increase over what Warren had paid him. My basic source for the account of the Raynolds-Hayden-Bridger expedition is William F. Raynolds, "Report on the Exploration of the Yellowstone and Country Drained by That River," 40th Congress, 2nd. Sess., Sen. Exec. Doc. 77 (July 17, 1868).

2. http://www.ldshistory.net/fbridger.htm.

3. Author's correspondence with Marlene Merrill and Tom Turiano. See Marlene and Daniel Merrill, *Up the Winds and over the Tetons: Descriptions and Images from the 1860 Raynolds Expedition*, Albuquerque: University of New Mexico Press, 2011.

4. Raynolds and Bridger never came closer than twenty-five miles from the southern boundary of the national park. See Schullery, *Searching for Yellowstone*, 41. On the way north to the Three Forks, however, Hayden and the topographer J. D. Hutton reached the Targhee Pass, barely ten miles from the present-day town of West Yellowstone.

5. This may not be strictly accurate; Bridger had gone to Yellowstone with Kit Carson for the second time in 1850, traveling from Fort Bridger and taking a route between the Green and Snake rivers that led to Yellowstone Lake. Topping, *The Chronicles of the Yellowstone*, 62.

6. The name "Burnt Hole" is confusing, since later it was often applied to the Firehole Geyser Basin—a logical-sounding name, which makes it seem as if Raynolds and Bridger should have realized that the river Hayden saw from the Targhee Pass would lead straight to the geysers. However, "Burnt Hole" was actually an old fur-trapper's name for the Madison Valley, going back to the accounts of Warren Ferris and Osborne Russell in the 1830s; it apparently refers to a major forest fire at that time. According to Haines, the Firehole acquired the name only later in the 1860s. See Haines, *Yellowstone Story*, Vol. 1, 340, note 7, and 341, note 27.

7. Two further ironies here: First, Maynadier was delayed and kept Raynolds waiting for four days at the rendezvous point. Then, after the entire party had reassembled, Raynolds received fresh orders to abandon the trip to the Canadian border to observe the eclipse.

9: SAVAGERY, BARBARISM, CIVILIZATION

1. Wilbur Fisk Sanders, "The Pioneers," *Contributions to the Historical Society of Montana* 4 (1903), 122–48.

2. Cited in Merrill G. Burlingame, *The Montana Frontier*, Helena, Montana: State Publishing Company, 1942, 221.

3. Mullan to Governor Isaac Ingalls Stevens, governor of Washington Territory, November 18, 1853. House Misc. Docs. 59, 33rd Cong., 1st. Sess., 741, cited in Wischmann, *Frontier Diplomats*, 232.

4. Cited in Haines, *Yellowstone Story*, Vol. 1, 60.

5. Bruce Hampton, *Children of Grace: The Nez Perce War of 1877*, New York: Henry Holt, 1994, 26–32.

6. Cited in Hampton, *Children of Grace*, 29.

7. George Washington had watched this same pernicious dynamic at work in the East, seventy years earlier. "Unless we can restrain the turbulence and disorderly conduct of our own borders, it will be in vain to expect peace with the Indians, or that they will govern their own people better than we do ours." It maddened Washington to see that "a lawless set of unprincipled wretches . . . can infringe the most solemn treaties, without receiving the punishment they so richly deserve." In the end he concluded despairingly that, "Scarcely anything short of a Chinese Wall or a line of troops will restrain land jobbers and the incroachment of settlers upon the Indian Territory." Cited in Joseph J. Ellis, *American Creation: Triumphs and Tragedies in the Founding of the Republic*, New York: Knopf, 2007, 159.

8. The Superintendent of Indian Affairs reported with satisfaction to his superiors in Washington that the settlers had come out of the proceedings with "very nearly six millions of acres . . . at a cost not exceeding eight cents per acre." The Nez Perce were left with 800,000 acres. See Hampton, *Children of Grace*, 32.

9. Chief Joseph, "An Indian's View of Indian Affairs," *North American Review* (April 1879): 412–33, cited in Hampton, *Children of Grace*, 34.

10. Phyllis Smith, *Bozeman and the Gallatin Valley: A History*, Helena, Montana: Twodot, 1997, 38.

11. Granville Stuart's journals, published as *Forty Years on the Frontier*, Cleveland: Arthur H. Clark and Company, 1925, are an invaluable record of life in Montana in the mid to late 1800s. See also Clyde A. Milner and Carol A. O'Connor, *As Big as the West: The Pioneer Life of Granville Stuart,* New York: Oxford University Press, 2009.

12. Langford to Doolittle, from St. Paul, June 29, 1857, Nathaniel Pitt Langford and Family Papers, 1707–1942, Minnesota Historical Society.

13. Goetzmann and Goetzmann make this point well. "The men and women who were engaged in this movement West . . . knew somehow that they were part of one of the largest mass migrations in history. So those that could write or remember—from the mountain men in the vanguard, to the builders of railroads and towns and cities—kept a record, a memory of their experiences which has become the shared inheritance of the American people." William H. Goetzmann and William N. Goetzmann, *The West of the Imagination*, New York: W. W. Norton, 1986, ix.

14. Langford to Doolittle from Pepin, Minnesota, January 12, 1855, Langford Papers, Minnesota Historical Society.

15. Langford to Doolittle, June 22, 1855, Langford Papers, Minnesota Historical Society.

16. Langford to Doolittle, July 4, 1855, and December 16, 1855, Langford Papers, Minnesota Historical Society.

17. Langford to Doolittle, January 25, 1857, Langford Papers, Minnesota Historical Society.

18. Main biographical sources for Langford's early life include Olin D. Wheeler, "Nathaniel Pitt Langford," *Collections of the Minnesota Historical Society* 15 (1915), 631–88; A. W. Orton, "Some Scattered Thoughts on the Early Life of Nathaniel P. Langford," unpublished typescript, Yellowstone National Park Archives; Grand Lodge, Anaconda, "Nathaniel Pitt Langford: Past Grand Master," January 1, 1911; and Langford's correspondence, most of which is in the Minnesota Historical Society Archives. See also Paul Schullery and Lee H. Whittlesey, *Myth and History in the Creation of Yellowstone National Park*, Lincoln: University of Nebraska Press, 2003, 104–5, note 2.

19. See Alvin M. Josephy Jr., *The Civil War in the American West*, New York: Alfred A. Knopf, 1991, 237–54; and Robert G. Athearn, "The Civil War and Montana Gold," *Montana the Magazine of Western History* (Spring 1962): 62–73.

20. Years after his Montana adventures, Fisk became deeply embroiled in the financial scandals of the Gilded Age, a co-conspirator with the financier Jay Gould in the attempt to corner the gold market in 1869, and a central figure in the collapse of the corrupt Erie Ring. See Dee Brown, *Bury My Heart at Wounded Knee*, New York: Henry Holt, 1970, 175, 191, and Dee Brown, *Year of the Century: 1876*, New York: Scribners, 1975, 75.

21. James McClellan Hamilton, *History of Montana: From Wilderness to Statehood*, Portland, Oregon: Binfords and Mort, 1957, 148–52; "Diary of Nathaniel P. Langford, January to December, 1863," Langford Papers, Minnesota Historical Society.

22. Langford to Doolittle, March 22, 1855, Langford Papers, Minnesota Historical Society.

23. Nathaniel Pitt Langford, *Vigilante Days and Ways: The Pioneers of the Rockies, The Makers and Making of Montana, Idaho, Oregon, Washington, and Wyoming*, 1890, reprint with an introduction by Dorothy M. Johnson, Missoula: Montana State University Press, 1957, 90.

24. Nathaniel Pitt Langford, "Address Delivered Before the Grand Lodge of Montana at its Third Annual Communication in the Town of Virginia, Oct. 8, A.D. 1867." The painting is in the Grand Lodge's Museum and Library in Helena.

25. James Fergus, "Early Mining Life in Bannack and Alder Gulch," *Rocky Mountain Magazine* 1, No. 4: 265–69.

26. Langford, *Vigilante Days and Ways*, 93.

10: ROADS PAVED WITH GOLD

1. *Contributions to the Historical Society of Montana* 1 (1876), 334–54.

2. Michael P. Malone, Richard B. Roeder, and William L. Lang, *Montana: A History of Two Centuries*, Seattle: University of Washington Press, 1976, 52–3, estimates that the settlements along Alder Gulch, which included the gold camps of Virginia City, Nevada City, Circle City, and Central City, produced between $30–40 million; Last Chance Gulch $19 million; and Confederate Gulch anything from $10–30 million.

3. Ibid., 69, 72.

4. The most infamous of these was the 1861 "Almo Massacre," in which 294 members of a wagon train were supposedly slaughtered in Almo, Idaho. The myth, which gathered steam in the 1920s and 1930s, is demolished in Brigham Madsen, "The 'Almo Massacre' Revisited," *ID Yesterdays*, 37, no. 3 (Fall 1993). The fictitious incident is well summarized in James W. Loewen, *Lies Across America: What Our Historic Sites Get Wrong*, New York: Touchstone, 2000, 75–8.

5. Josephy, *Civil War in the West*, 254–60.

6. The following account is drawn from Brigham Madsen, *The Shoshoni Frontier and the Bear River Massacre*, Salt Lake City: University of Utah Press, 1985; Kass Fleisher, *The Bear River Massacre and the Making of History*, Albany: State University of New York Press, 2004, which gives special attention to violence against women; and Josephy, *Civil War*, 237–46. See also Scott R. Christensen, *Sagwitch: Shoshone Chieftain and Mormon Elder*,

1822–1887, Salt Lake City: Utah State University Press, 1999; Gregory Michno, *The Deadliest Indian War in the West: The Snake Conflict 1864–1868*, Caldwell, Idaho: Caxton Press, 2007.

7. McGarry was also a notorious alcoholic, who was finally brought up on charges in 1864 after his men complained of his violent, drunken rages. Madsen, *Shoshoni Frontier*, 166.

8. To be fair, the miners did make one final attempt at peace. In November, around the time of McGarry's mass executions, they held a council with "about five hundred warriors," who said they were not inherently opposed to the passage of gold seekers; what they refused to accept was the permanent loss of their lands. Madsen, *Shoshoni Frontier*, 159, citing Brigham Madsen and Betty M. Madsen, *North to Montana*, Salt Lake City: University of Utah Press, 1980.

9. The following is based on Brigham Madsen, *The Northern Shoshoni*, Caldwell, ID: Caxton Press, 2000, 181–99, Fleisher, *Bear River Massacre*, 54–66.

10. Brigham Madsen, *Glory Hunter: A Biography of Patrick Edward Connor*, Salt Lake City: University of Utah Press, 1990, 80–2.

11. From the account of Mae T. Barry, the granddaughter of the Shoshone Chief Sagwitch. Cited in Madsen, *Northern Shoshoni*, 234.

12. Fleisher, *Bear River Massacre*, 63.

13. Cited in Madsen, *Northern Shoshoni*, 17. Madsen himself, the principal authority on the Bear River Massacre, estimates that 250 died. Whether we accept his figure or Connor's, Bear River was almost certainly the single largest mass killing of the Indian Wars by military forces.

14. Others formulated the thought with greater eloquence. "[Connor] has shown that he knows how to fight the kind of Indians that God made, but I suppose the humanitarians want somebody to fight the Indians that J. Fenimore Cooper made. There is just where the mistake is. The Cooper Indians are dead—died with their creator. The kind that are left are of altogether a different breed, and cannot be successfully fought with poetry, and sentiment, and soft soap, and magnanimity." This, rather surprisingly, from a newspaper column by Mark Twain, who had something close to a personal vendetta against Cooper. Cited in Madsen, *Northern Shoshoni*, 209.

15. William J. Trimble, "The Mining Advance in the Inland Empire," *Bulletin of the University of Wisconsin History Series* 3, 2 (1914), 112; Dorothy M. Johnson, *The Bloody Bozeman*, New York: McGraw Hill, 1971, xxx–xxxi.

16. These distinctive characteristics of the frontier economy are discussed in Richard Slotkin, *The Fatal Environment: The Myth of the Frontier in the Age of Industrialization, 1800–1890*, Norman: University of Oklahoma Press, 1998, 40.

17. William G. Robbins, "The Deconstruction of a Capitalist Patriarch," *Montana the Magazine of Western History* (42:4, Autumn 1992), 20–33. See also John W. Hakola, "Samuel T. Hauser and the Economic Development of Montana," Ph.D. thesis, Indiana University, 1961, copy in Montana Historical Society Archives.

18. Hauser diary, in Montana Historical Society Archives, cited in Frederick Allen. *A Decent, Orderly Lynching: The Montana Vigilantes*, Norman: University of Oklahoma Press, 2004, 64.

19. The following account is drawn from Stuart, "The Yellowstone Expedition of 1863,"

Contributions to the Montana Historical Society I (1876): 80–9. See also Johnson, *The Bloody Bozeman*, 25–47; Brown, *Plainsmen of the Yellowstone*, 129–32.

20. Aubrey Haines, who takes a generally dim view of Nathaniel Pitt Langford's integrity, charges him with making false claims about having taken part in the Stuart-Hauser trip. He cites a letter written by Langford to Hauser in 1865, when the latter was on the way east to meet Langford's family. "Hauser, you remember that I told you of 'blowing' to my nephews and nieces in Utica about <u>our</u> Yellowstone trip. Now don't you for the world say a word about it, as if I wasn't there, for I would not have them know that I was <u>gassing</u>, for anything. It was a piece of foolishness that I'll never repeat, but not a word from you. So be careful: and don't let this letter be seen. Burn it up." Haines, *Yellowstone Story*, Vol. 1, 67–8, citing Langford to Hauser, May 18, 1865, Montana Historical Society Archives. Whether or not Haines's interpretation is correct, the letter gives interesting insight into Langford's character; his professed embarrassment about "gassing" and "blowing" is strikingly similar to his January 25, 1857, letter to Will Doolittle; see, p. 101.

21. The only significant Crow-on-white military attack was the siege of Fort McKenzie in 1834, but even that was intended only to keep trade guns out of the hands of the hated Blackfeet. Wischmann, *Frontier Diplomats*, 61–4.

22. Johnson, *Bloody Bozeman*, 34–6.

23. Ibid., 327–8.

24. On the foundation and early history of the town, see Smith, *Bozeman and the Gallatin Valley*, 51–4.

25. Bartlett, *Nature's Yellowstone*, 122.

26. William F. Wheeler, "Walter Washington De Lacy," *Contributions to the Montana Historical Society* 2 (1896): 241–51; Bartlett, *Nature's Yellowstone*, 121.

27. Following account is drawn from Walter De Lacy, "A Trip Up the South Snake River in 1863," *Contributions to the Montana Historical Society* 1 (1876): 113–43.

28. Now known as Shoshone Lake. The stream that flows into it is still called De Lacy Creek.

29. Davis, *Louisville Courier* interview, 1884. See Bartlett, *Nature's Yellowstone*, 125, note 10.

11: A NOOSE PENDANT

1. Allen, *A Decent, Orderly Lynching*, 114, 132.

2. From an article in *Anaconda Ltd.* by "T.B.E.," who describes himself as a pupil of Dimsdale's in Millbrook, Ontario. Burlingame papers, Montana State University Libraries, Bozeman, Special Collection 2245/2.

3. Cited in Johnson, *Bloody Bozeman*, 172.

4. Langford, *Vigilante Days and Ways*, 3.

5. "Lecture presented by Nathaniel Pitt Langford (during the winter of 1870–71): A verbatim transcription from the original notebook in the manuscript collection of the Yellowstone Park reference library," Aubrey L. Haines, Bozeman, Montana, July 17, 1970.

6. David J. Bailey, "Diary and Reminiscences of David J. Bailey: His Journal from Indiana to Montana, 1865," 68. Local History Archives, Fort Collins Museum, Fort Collins, Colorado. Copy in Montana State University Libraries, Bozeman.

7. Burlingame, *The Montana Frontier*, 86–7. Dorothy M. Johnson, introduction to Langford, *Vigilante Days and Ways*, xxx.

8. Thomas J. Dimsdale, *The Vigilantes of Montana, or Popular Justice in the Rocky Mountains*, Norman, University of Oklahoma Press, 1982, 8–9.

9. Ibid., 11.

10. Quoted in Larry Barsness, *Gold Camp: Alder Gulch and Virginia City, Montana*, New York: Hastings House Publishers, 1962, 232–34, 239.

11. Langford, *Vigilante Days and Ways*, 6–12, 36.

12. Dimsdale, *Vigilantes of Montana*, 218–20.

13. Langford, *Vigilante Days and Ways*, 122.

14. James Fergus diary, January 21, 1863.

15. Langford, *Vigilante Days and Ways*, 106.

16. The account of the trial is drawn from Langford, *Vigilante Days and Ways*; Dimsdale, *Vigilantes of Montana*; Allen, *A Decent, Orderly Lynching*; and Barsness, *Gold Camp: Alder Gulch and Virginia City, Montana*, Winter Park, Florida: Hastings House, 1962. A second botched trial occurred in June 1863, when three of Plummer's men were sentenced to hang by a miners' court but freed from the gallows in a mob scene. The two trials gave the road agents a sense of total impunity and set the stage for the wave of violent crime during the fall, which led in turn to the formation of the vigilantes.

17. *Vigilante Days and Ways*, 131.

18. Conceivably these facts may have come out during the interrogation and "trial" of those who were subsequently tracked down and hanged by the vigilantes. There are some discrepancies between the two accounts of the events described here, some of which may be explained by the passage of time (Dimsdale's book was published in 1866, Langford's not until 1890). Allen, who has written the best single account of the Montana vigilantes, finds the identification of Plummer in the aborted attack on Langford and Hauser unpersuasive and sees it as another example of Langford's taste for melodramatic narrative. See Allen, *A Decent, Orderly Lynching*, 151.

19. Langford's intercession with Lincoln on behalf of the non-Mormons of Utah is described in an undated document, titled only "Letter from N. P. Langford," in the files of the Montana State Historical Society. Langford says that, "I called one day at the 'White House' and through the courtesy of the Rev. E. D. Neill, of St. Paul, one of Mr. Lincoln's secretaries, I was accorded an interview with the President." The Langford-Hauser-Stuart meeting with Lincoln is described in Allen, *A Decent, Orderly Lynching*, 290–1.

20. And, as Paul Schullery and Lee Whittlesey have pointed out, a position that would place Langford "next to the till." Author's conversations and correspondence with Schullery and Whittlesey.

21. Bailey, "Diary," 70–1.

22. Dimsdale, *Vigilantes of Montana*, 102.

23. The best account of the formation of the Vigilance Committee is Allen, *A Decent, Orderly Lynching*, 195 ff.

24. Reproduced in Ibid., 195.

25. Hauser's role is confirmed in a 1908 speech by Montana Senator Thomas Carter, who hailed him as "Trail Blazer, Explorer, Vigilante, Banker." Cited in Robbins, "Deconstruction of a Capitalist Patriarch."

26. Dimsdale says that "X" was "a letter of the alphabet having singular terrors for evil doers in Montana, being calculated to awaken the idea of crime committed and punishment to follow, more than all the rest of the alphabet, even if the enumeration were followed by the repetition of the Ten Commandments." *Vigilantes of Montana*, 209.

27. Daniel Sylvester Tuttle, *Reminiscences of a Missionary Bishop*, New York: Thomas Whittaker, 1906, 223, in Merrill G. Burlingame Special Collection 2245/71, Montana State University Libraries, Bozeman. Interestingly, in later years, Beidler served as a tour guide in Yellowstone National Park. Author's conversation with Lee Whittlesey.

28. *Vigilante Days and Ways*, 388.

29. See chapter 13, pp. 150–53.

30. Slotkin, *The Fatal Environment*, 125, compares the vigilante to the Indian-hater: "[B]y exercising a privilege of violence that goes beyond legal or conventional prohibitions . . . [he] shares some of the 'dangerous' characteristics of the criminal he pursues—just as the Indian-hater shares the traits of the 'savage.'" See also Richard White, *"It's Your Misfortune and None of My Own": A New History of the American West*, Norman: University of Oklahoma Press, 1993, 333–4.

31. Montana historians Ruth E. Mather and F. E. Boswell have written extensively on the subject, questioning the guilt of Sheriff Henry Plummer. See Mather and Boswell, *Hanging the Sheriff: A Biography of Henry Plummer*, Salt Lake City: University of Utah Press, 1987; *Vigilante Victims: Montana's 1864 Hanging Spree*, Oklahoma City: History West Publishing Company, 1991; and *Gold Camp Desperadoes: Violence, Crime, and Punishment on the Mining Frontier*, Norman: University of Oklahoma Press, 2000. These authors trace the persecution of Plummer to partisan politics: As a Democrat, he had supposedly aroused the hostility of two leading Republicans, future governor Sidney Edgerton and vigilante prosecutor Wilbur Fisk Sanders.

32. Dimsdale, *Vigilantes of Montana*, 12–4.

12: TALES OF THE CHIEF GUIDE

1. Vivian Paladin and Jean Baucus, *Helena: An Illustrated History*, Helena: Montana Historical Society Press, 1983, especially 13–25.

2. White, *It's Your Misfortune*, 305; Haines, *Yellowstone Story*, Vol. 1, 347; Kim Allen Scott, *Yellowstone Denied: The Life of Gustavus Cheyney Doane*, Norman: University of Oklahoma Press, 2007, 180.

3. Hauser has been compared to the fictional nineteenth-century character Captain Simon Suggs of Tallapoosa, the creation of the writer Johnson Jones Hooper: "It is good to be shifty in a new country." See Malone, Roeder, and Lang, *Two Centuries*, 66.

4. Nash is the essential source on the evolution of the idea—and the ideal—of wilderness in the nineteenth century. See Roderick Nash, *Wilderness and the American Mind*, New Haven, Connecticut: Yale University Press, 1967.

5. Langford, *Discovery*, xxxvi.

6. Lieutenant John Mullan, *Report on the Construction of a Military Road from Fort Walla Walla to Fort Benton*. For the full text, see http://www.narhist.ewu.edu/mullan_report/

mullan_report_home.html. Langford, *Discovery*, xxviii–xxix; Bartlett, *Nature's Yellowstone*, 144.

7. Donnelly, a year older than Langford, was a colorful character: a populist, advocate of women's suffrage, and in his spare time a theorist of the lost city of Atlantis and the author of a book on Bacon's putative authorship of the plays of Shakespeare. The letter, which exists in the form of a later typescript in the Montana Historical Society Archives, seems to have been written a short time after Langford's arrival in the East in early 1864, at about the same time he met with President Lincoln, to advocate for the creation of Montana Territory and to discuss the Mormon question. Langford refers at one point to the 1862 Fisk wagon train and having "spent the intermediate time of a year and a half in the mines," which would date the letter to the first quarter of 1864.

8. Langford also makes it clear in this letter that he holds the Crows responsible for the attack on the Stuart-Hauser prospecting party the previous summer.

9. According to Dimsdale's *Montana Post*, April 18, 1865, Langford's company had merged with the Bozeman City and Fort Laramie Wagon Road and Telegraph Company. Other sources refer to it as the Broad Gauge Wagon Company, a barbed reference to the amount of territory it proposed to control. See Topping, *Chronicles*, 29. The company's ferry on the Bighorn River was operated by Mitch Buoyer, the celebrated half-Sioux guide and scout who later died with Custer at the Little Bighorn.

10. Langford to Hauser, March 25, 1865, Montana Historical Society Archives. The letter is dated 1864 in Langford's hand, but the references to his work as Collector of Internal Revenues make it clear that it must have been written in 1865. The *Montana Post* article, loc. cit., says that, "Messrs. Bridger and Bozeman have joined their interests in their respective roads, with this Company, and have been employed to conduct the emigration from Fort Laramie."

11. Biography of David Folsom, unpublished typescript, Yellowstone National Park Archives.

12. Ned Buntline was the pseudonym of Colonel Edward Zane Carroll Judson (1821–1886), who at various times was a navy officer, a New York gang leader, a temperance lecturer, and a traveling companion of Buffalo Bill Cody.

13. Langford, *Discovery*, xxviii.

14. Langford actually wrote two different accounts of his conversations with Bridger in Virginia City, which differ slightly in their details and chronology. In one he dates their first meeting to 1865; in the other to 1866. The first date is almost certainly the correct one, since we know he was doing business with Bridger by March 1865 at the latest. See letter to Hauser, March 25, 1865. Also Brown, *Plainsmen of the Yellowstone*, 189–90, and Haines, *Yellowstone Story*, Vol. 1, 53.

15. Langford to Bozeman, May 25, 1866, and Bozeman to Langford, June 26, 1866 (describing the difficulties of that spring's migration), Montana Historical Society Archives.

16. Chivington was also regarded as a hero of the Union Army because of his defiance at Glorieta Pass of a Confederate attack on the Colorado goldfields. The standard accounts of Chivington and Sand Creek are Stan Hoig, *The Sand Creek Massacre*, Norman: University of Oklahoma Press, 1964; and Duane P. Schultz, *Month of the Freezing Moon: The Sand Creek Massacre, November 1864*, New York: St. Martin's Press, 1990.

17. The systematic mutilation of the victims of the Sand Creek Massacre, including the shipment of skulls and other body parts for anthropological study at the Army Medical Museum in Washington, D.C., is discussed in David Hurst Thomas, *Skull Wars: Kennewick*

Man, Archaeology, and the Battle for Native American Identity, New York: Perseus, 2001.

18. General Grenville Dodge, telegraphed message to General John Pope, cited in Brown, *Plainsmen of the Yellowstone*, 142.

19. Cited in Ibid., 143.

20. Brown, *Plainsmen of the Yellowstone*, 128–9. The hostilities between the Crows and the Sioux are discussed at length in Ewers, *Plains Indians*, and Leforge and Marquis, *Memoirs*.

21. Ewers, *Plains Indians*, 139; Thomas W. Dunlay, *Wolves for the Blue Soldiers: Indian Scouts and Auxiliaries with the United States Army, 1860–90*, Lincoln: University of Nebraska Press, 1982, 43.

22. Ibid., 148.

23. Leigh R. Freeman, *Fort Kearny Herald*, January 6, 1866, cited in Alter, *James Bridger*, 316.

24. Before returning to the Bozeman Trail in June 1866, Bridger served two brief spells—in January, and again in March—under the command of an old fellow explorer, Colonel Henry E. Maynadier, who, as a lieutenant, had accompanied Captain William Raynolds in the abortive expedition to the upper Yellowstone. Maynadier was now commanding officer of the army's western subdistrict of Nebraska. See Vestal, *Jim Bridger*, 318.

25. Margaret I. Carrington, *Ab-sa-ra-ka: Home of the Crows*, Lincoln: University of Nebraska Press, 1983, 113–5, cited in Alter, *James Bridger*, 332.

26. Carrington, *Ab-sa-ra-ka*, 114.

27. Ibid., 92.

28. Quoted in Vestal, *Jim Bridger*, 271.

29. Two recent works have questioned many of the central elements of the Fetterman episode: Shannon Smith Calitri, " 'Give Me Eighty Men': Shattering the Myth of the Fetterman Massacre," *Montana the Magazine of Western History* 54 (Autumn 2004): 44–59; and John H. Monnett, *Where a Hundred Soldiers Were Killed: The Struggle for the Powder River in 1866 and the Making of the Fetterman Myth*, Albuquerque: University of New Mexico Press, 2008.

30. Carrington, *Ab-sa-ra-ka*, 1, 61, and Frances C. Carrington, *My Army Life and the Fort Phil Kearny Massacre, With an Account of the Celebration of "Wyoming Opened,"* Philadelphia: Lippincott, 1910, 61–2.

31. Carrington report, January 3, 1867, quoted in Johnson, *Bloody Bozeman*, 345, note 35.

32. Merrill J. Mattes, *Indians, Infants, and Infantry: Andrew and Elizabeth Burt on the Frontier*, Lincoln: University of Nebraska Press, 1988, 134, cited in Alter, *James Bridger*, 333.

33. Paul Hutton, *Phil Sheridan and His Army*, Lincoln: University of Nebraska Press, 1985, 35, citing De B. Randolph Keim, *Sheridan's Troopers on the Borders: A Winter Campaign on the Plains*, New York: George Routledge and Sons, 1870, 58.

13: THE LEADING MEN

1. Hedges's early biography is drawn from Thomas Edward White, "Cornelius Hedges: Uncommon Hero of the Common Life," unpublished MSC thesis, Montana State College, Bozeman, August 1863, copy in Montana State University Libraries, Bozeman; and Wyllys A. Hedges, "Cornelius Hedges," *Contributions to the Montana Historical Society* 7 (1910): 181–96.

2. *Montana Herald* obituary, Cornelius Hedges Papers, 1831–1907, MC 33, Montana Historical Society Archives.
3. "Brief Sketch of the Life of Wyllys A. Hedges," unpublished manuscript, Montana Historical Society Archives.
4. Clyde A. Milner II, "The View from Wisdom: Four Layers of History and Regional Identity," in William Cronon, George Miles, and Jay Gitlin, eds., *Under an Open Sky: Rethinking America's Western Past*, New York: Norton, 1992.
5. Hedges, "Early Masonry in Montana," *Rocky Mountain Gazette*, 1.1, 1900, 14, cited in White, "Uncommon Hero," 15.
6. Wyllys A. Hedges, "Cornelius Hedges."
7. Hedges, letter to his parents, April 18, 1865, Hedges Papers, Montana Historical Society Archives.
8. Hedges, letter to his parents, May 24, 1865, Hedges Papers, Montana Historical Society Archives.
9. Hedges, masonic biography, Yellowstone National Park Archives.
10. Hedges, letter to his parents, August 24, 1869, Montana Historical Society Archives.
11. According to Horace Clarke, his father was also an emissary to the Sioux during the Minnesota uprising of 1862, but with less success. David Hilger, 1924 interview with Horace Clark, Montana Historical Society Archives.
12. The other founders included the brothers James and Granville Stuart and the former vigilante prosecutor Wilbur Fisk Sanders.
13. Helen P. Clarke, "Sketch of Malcolm Clarke."
14. The child's name may have been Judith, though the records are unclear. According to Langford's "Frontier Tragedy," another younger daughter, Mollie, had died recently. All we know of Clarke's second wife is that she was the daughter of an American Fur Company trader named Isidro Sandoval, who had been murdered by the irascible Alexander Harvey—the man in whose skull Clarke had implanted a tomahawk. Wischmann, *Frontier Diplomats*, 321, citing Jack Holterman, *King of the High Missouri: The Saga of the Culbertsons*, Helena, Montana: Jack Holterman with the Falcon Press, 1987, 173.
15. Langford, "Frontier Tragedy."
16. The photograph is in the Montana Historical Society Archives.
17. E. B. Nealley, "A Year in Montana," *Atlantic*, July 1866. The magazine lists him as "Nealy," but contemporary Montana records generally prefer Nealley.
18. Letter to Alvina Hedges, July 28, 1865, Hedges Papers, Montana Historical Society Archives. Hedges did at least note in lawyerly fashion that, "This country where we are has never been bought of the Indians yet & we are all trespassers," which seemed to recognize, at least implicitly, that the Blackfeet had some rational grounds for "making trouble." That was certainly the view of his friend Malcolm Clarke. Hedges was hardly more tolerant of other non-whites than he was of Indians. "I cannot really say that I am in favor of letting all the negroes at the south vote," he wrote to his father. "It is letting in too much ignorance. . . . I don't know that I have a much better opinion of the negroes than formerly, but I think they are better than rebels. I wish all the negroes could be returned to Africa, if they are not they will soon die out in this country. . . . I shall not mourn over the result." Hedges letter, September 9, 1867. The Chinese were similarly unappealing to him,

and he later wrote to territorial senator Seth Bullock to demand a bar on their immigration, calling them "a degraded class of cheap laborers." Hedges memorandum to Bullock, December 1871, Montana Historical Society Archives. Hedges remained an unreconstructed racist until the end of his life. In a speech in 1902 on the U.S. occupation of the Philippines, he said, "Filipinos in the mass are pretty hard subjects for civilization. Besides being ignorant, they are the most accomplished liars in the world, naturally cruel, treacherous, and unreliable and without the industry of the Chinese." *Proceedings of the Grand Lodge of Ancient Free and Accepted Masons of Montana, 38th Communication,* 1902, cited in White, "Uncommon Hero," 74.

19. Langford to Hauser, May 10, 1865, Samuel Thomas Hauser Papers, MC 37, Montana Historical Society Archives.

20. Langford, *Vigilante Days and Ways,* 437; Langford to Will Doolittle, January 1, 1884, Minnesota Historical Society Archives; Langford to J. W. Taylor, Commissioner, Internal Revenue Service, Describing the Organization and Operation of the U.S. Internal Revenue District of Montana Territory, by N. P. Langford, May 20, 1866, typescript copy, Minnesota Historical Society Archives. Despite the ethical questions about his conduct as a tax collector, the IRS itself continues to cite Langford's letter to Taylor as a seminal document in its own institutional history.

21. Ibid.

22. Langford to Doolittle, November 24, 1865, and Langford to Taylor, May 20, 1906. Langford Papers, Minnesota Historical Society. At the end of his account of the confrontation with seceshes and road agents, Langford told Taylor with characteristic false modesty, "To any one who knows me less intimately than you do, what I have written might savor of self-laudation. But I have none of this feeling of conceit, as I believe you will know."

23. Ibid.

24. "Biographical Sketch of Hezekiah L. Hosmer, First Chief Justice of the Territory of Montana," revised by his son J. H. Hosmer, *Contributions to the Historical Society of Montana* 3 (1900): 288–9. See also Barsness, *Gold Camp,* 51.

25. Hedges diary, June 7, 1865, Hedges Papers, Montana Historical Society Archives.

26. *Proceedings of the Grand Lodge, A.F. & A.M,* Butte, Grand Lodge, A.F. & A.M., 1914, 164, cited in Smith, *Bozeman and the Gallatin Valley,* 60.

27. Oscar O. Mueller, correspondence with W. Turrentine Jackson, cited in Jackson, "Early Exploration," 75–6. Mueller was Charles Cook's son-in-law and thus can be considered a reliable source on this point.

28. Hedges, *Art Work of Montana: Published in Twelve Parts,* Chicago: W. H. Parish Publishing Company, 1896, 15.

29. Hedges, "Reminiscences of Early Days in Helena," undated typescript, Hedges Papers, Montana Historical Society Archives.

30. Lyman Munson, "Pioneer Life in Montana," *Contributions to the Montana Historical Society* 5 (1904), 209. Munson's recollection of events, written almost forty years after the fact, is confused in many respects. He writes that he arrived in Helena on July 9, 1865, and that on that day "there was suspended to the limb of a tree, a man hung by the Vigilance Committee the night before, which was the eighth specimen of similar fruit encased in leather boots that tree had borne in so many months." The reference seems to

be to the hanging of James Daniels on July 29, 1865, which was the first vigilante killing since that of Jack Keene seven weeks earlier. Before Keene, no one had been hanged by the vigilantes since October 1864, in Bannack. For a full list of all fifty-seven of the vigilantes' victims from 1864–1870, see Allen, *A Decent, Orderly Lynching*, 365–6.

31. In a letter to Hauser dated January 14, 1866, Langford mentions the hanging of an un-named man for robbing the Salt Lake stagecoach in Portneuf Canyon, and says, "I was collecting money to ferret out this matter, when you were here." See also Allen, *A Decent, Orderly Lynching*, 338.

32. Langford to Doolittle, November 24, 1865, Langford Papers, Minnesota Historical Society Archives. This passage comes after Langford mentions his enclosure of the latest install-ment of Thomas Dimsdale's vigilante memoir in the *Montana Post*, but the wording seems odd, since we know that Langford was traveling in the East when the majority of the hang-ings in Bannack and Virginia City took place. So either Langford is in self-aggrandizing mode again or he is conflating the events of 1863–1864 with the renewed vigilante activities in 1865. Interestingly, he uses exactly the same phrase—"all of which I saw, and part of which I was"—in his January 1867 letter to Doolittle, in which his personal role with the vigilantes is set forth unambiguously. Langford's count of "fifteen to twenty" hangings is somewhat inaccurate. In fact, since the lynching of Jack Keene on June 9, 1865, thirteen men had been hanged by the time Langford wrote—two of them just the day before, on November 23.

33. Langford to Doolittle, January 16, 1867. The executive committee of the Helena vigilantes met almost monthly. See Oscar O. Mueller to W. Turrentine Jackson, January 6, 1938, cited in Jackson, "Early Exploration," 143, note 94.

34. Cited in Barsness, *Gold Camp*, 53.

35. Hedges, "Historical Sketch of Lewis and Clark County, Montana, July 4, 1876, Hedges Papers, Montana Historical Society Archives.

36. Langford, *Vigilante Days and Ways*; Chicago, A. C. McClurg and Company, 1912, intro-duction, xiv. The introduction does not appear in the 1957 reprint edition from which other references are taken.

14: MISSION IN THE SNOW

1. Quoted in Ewers, *The Blackfeet*, 208.
2. Culbertson to Stevens, undated letter, ca 1853, Indian Office Records.
3. Ewers, *The Blackfeet*, 215–21.
4. "Major Vaughan was a jovial old fellow, who had a very fine paunch for brandy, and when he could not get brandy, would take almost anything which would make drunk come." Larpenteur, *Forty Years a Fur Trader*, 417–8.
5. Report of the Commissioner of Indian Affairs, 1863, 179, cited in Ewers, *The Blackfeet*, 237.
6. Ewers, *The Blackfeet*, 88–108.
7. Francis M. Thompson, *A Tenderfoot in Montana: Reminiscences of the Gold Rush, the Vigilantes, and the Birth of Montana Territory*, Helena: Montana Historical Society Press, 2004, 215–6; Wischmann, *Frontier Diplomats*, 309.

8. Joe was the son of James Kipp and Earth Woman, a Mandan. He spoke Piegan, Crow, Gros Ventre, Sioux, Mandan, and Arikaree. Raven Quiver was not a conventional Indian name, but a nickname given to Kipp by his wife. Peter Sloan, "Joseph Kipp (Kipah)," unpublished manuscript, Montana Historical Society Archives; and James Arthur, *Retracing Kipp Trails*, Lewiston, Montana: Central Montana Publishing Company, 1999.

9. Burlingame, *Montana Frontier*, 39–43; Ewers, *The Blackfeet*, 238–44; Arthur, *Kipp Trails*, 51.

10. Paul R. Wylie, *The Irish General: Thomas Francis Meagher*, Norman: University of Oklahoma Press, 2007, 239.

11. Munson, "Pioneer Life in Montana."

12. Robert Ege, *Tell Baker to Strike Them Hard! Incident on the Marias, Jan. 23, 1870*, Bellevue, Nebraska: Old Army Press, 1970, 6; Wischmann, *Frontier Diplomats*, 321, citing Helen Clarke, "Sketch of Malcolm Clarke," 256. Calf Shirt was believed by the Blackfeet to be immortal, after a dream in which the bear spirit told him that he could not be harmed by any bullet, arrow, or knife. Some whiskey traders, reportedly led by Joe Kipp, finally disposed of him by shooting him sixteen times, then dumping his body into the frozen Oldman River through a hole in the ice. It took three tries to keep him down. Even then, legend has it that his frozen body was partially revived the next day by a medicine man who administered more whiskey to the corpse. See Hugh A. Dempsey, *The Amazing Death of Calf Shirt and Other Blackfoot Stories: Three Hundred Years of Blackfoot History*, Saskatoon, Saskatchewan: Fifth House Publishers, 1994, 47–58.

13. Hedges, *Rocky Mountain Gazette*, and diary entry. Hedges Papers, Montana Historical Society Archives.

14. Gillette biography, Yellowstone National Park Archives. Gillette had attended Oberlin, where he overlapped with Ferdinand Vandeveer Hayden, three years his senior. Gillette had arrived at Fort Benton on the steamship *Shreveport* in 1862; the first man he met was Malcolm Clarke. From there he made his way to Bannack, where he befriended Langford; after that, the well-trodden progression from Bannack to Virginia City, and finally to Last Chance Gulch. He also invested heavily in the placer mines at Diamond City, where the Mainer Charles W. Cook had made his fortune. By the summer of 1866 his tollgate at the entrance to the Little Prickly Pear Canyon was turning a brisk profit. He was also a client of Hedges's law firm. Gillette's own account of his early days in Montana is contained in Robert Vaughn, *Then and Now, or Thirty-Six Years in the Rockies*, Minneapolis: Tribune Printing, 1900.

15. Thomas F. Meagher, "A Journey to Benton," *Montana the Magazine of Western History*, 1.4 (October 1951): 46–58.

16. Wilfred P. Schoenberg, "Historic St. Peter's Mission: Landmark of the Jesuits and the Ursulines Among the Blackfeet," *Montana the Magazine of Western History* 11.1 (Winter 1961), 68–85. Kuppens's own history of St. Peter's, written in 1914, is in the Oregon Province Archives of the Society of Jesus.

17. Munson, "Pioneer Life in Montana"; Cornelius Hedges, "An Account of a Trip to Fort Benton in October, 1865, with Acting Governor Thomas H. Meagher to Treat with the Blackfeet Indians," *Rocky Mountain Magazine* 1, 3 (November 1900), 155–8.

18. Wylie, *The Irish General*, 242, note 63.

19. Hedges, "An Account of a Trip."

20. Anne McDonnell, "The Catholic Indian Missions in Montana," in Merrill G. Burlingame and K. Ross Toole, eds., *A History of Montana*, Vol. 1, New York: Lewis Historical Publishing Company, 1957; Burlingame, *The Montana Frontier*, 298; Bartlett, *Nature's Yellowstone*, 144–5. The Birdtail Butte mission was anything but permanent, as it turned out. See also Howard L. Harrod, *Mission Among the Blackfeet*, Norman: University of Oklahoma Press, 1971, 53–4.

21. *The Jesuit Bulletin*, biographical note accompanying the reprint of Kuppens, "On the Origin of the Yellowstone National Park," *The Woodstock Letters*, XXVI, 3 (September 3, 1897), 400–3.

22. De Smet, *Life, Letters and Travels*, 333, notes 96–7. The Bridger-De Smet maps are reproduced in Haines, *Exploration and Establishment*, 188–9.

23. By "the narrator," Kuppens may mean either the Piegan chief, Big Lake, or the fur trader Baptiste Champaigne. On Champaigne, see Dan L. Thrapp, *Encyclopedia of Frontier Biography*, Lincoln: University of Nebraska Press, 1991, 249.

24. Kuppens, "On the Origin."

25. Ibid.

26. Ibid. It is worth noting that Yosemite had been granted to the state of California by the federal government in March 1864 "upon the express conditions that the premises shall be held for public use, resort, and recreation." It is reasonable to suppose that educated men like Hedges, Meagher, and Munson would have heard something about Yosemite by this time.

27. His brief account, written in 1897, is rife with inaccuracies. First of all, it is of little help in establishing when he went to the upper Yellowstone with the Piegans. He suggests that it was in the spring of 1866, but that has to be taken with a grain of salt because he dates Meagher's visit to the spring of 1867. More egregiously, he writes that Meagher himself later visited the upper Yellowstone "and on his return told me that the beauty and grandeur of the place far exceeded his expectations." In fact, Meagher died before his plans to organize an expedition came to fruition. Although some historians have inferred that Kuppens's trip to Yellowstone must have been in the spring of 1865, Jesuit authorities have established that he spent the winter and spring of 1864–1865 doing the rounds of the mining camps and visiting Helena, where he laid out the site of the first Catholic church. See L. B. Palladino, S. J., *Indian and White in the Northwest: A History of Catholicity in Montana, 1831–1891*, Lancaster, Pennsylvania: Wickersham Publishing Company, 1922, 318. It seems safe to conclude, then, that since Kuppens was ordained in July 1863, his trip with the Piegan hunting party almost certainly took place in the spring of 1864. It's also hard to credit that none of the Meagher party had ever heard of "the wonderful place," especially in the case of Clarke, a well-read and widely traveled man who had lived among the Blackfeet for a quarter of a century and had known Father De Smet for most of that time. So can Kuppens be trusted? Probably not.

28. Quoted in Ambrose, *Undaunted Courage*, 239.

29. Hedges letter to his parents, November 6, 1865, Hedges Papers, Montana Historical Society Archives.

30. *Rocky Mountain Gazette*, 156. Hedges says he remained at Fort Benton for "about ten days," but in fact it must have been less than a week, because the letter he wrote to his parents on his return to Helena said that his entire trip had taken sixteen days. Hedges

letter, November 6, 1865, Montana Historical Society Archives. He says that "those of us who had business at home felt constrained to depart," but it isn't clear who else he means, since Meagher, Munson, Clarke, and Sheriff Howie are all recorded as being present when the treaty was eventually signed on November 16. Of the original party, that leaves just the former vigilante X. Beidler and Captain George Wood, a hero of Gettysburg who had chaired the committee that gave the town of Helena its name.

31. James Doty, who acted as secretary to Isaac Stevens at the 1855 "Lame Bull" treaty, estimated the 1864 population at 7,630. Cited in Ewers, *The Blackfeet*, 212. Hamilton, *History of Montana*, 184, estimates the population at the time of the Fort Benton treaty at between 8,000 and 10,000.

32. Munson, "Pioneer Life in Montana."

33. Bradley, "Account of the Drowning of Governor Thomas Francis Meagher."

34. Charles J. Kappler, ed., *Indian Affairs: Laws and Treaties,* Vol. IV, Washington, D.C.: Government Printing Office, 1929.

15: CALL TO ARMS

1. Morgan had already become embroiled in tribal politics by offering to arrange a settlement with Calf Shirt's faction of Bloods after the killing of Langford's assistant, Frank Angevine, and his fellow woodcutters the previous spring. Tradition called for some form of restitution in these situations, and the Bloods offered some horses. Malcolm Clarke, who had agreed to play his time-honored role as interpreter and mediator, is said to have deliberately mistranslated the offer, telling Morgan that the horses were intended as a personal gift to him, as the only white man Calf Shirt trusted. This seems to contradict Langford's view of Clarke as a man of the highest honor, but we have it on the authority of Lieutenant James Bradley, a sober-sided young officer who came to Montana in 1870 and became one of the territory's best-regarded early historians. See Bradley, "Sun River Stampede" and "Blackfoot War," *Contributions to the Historical Society of Montana* 9 (1966): 251–2.

2. De Smet, *Life, Letters and Travels,* Vol. II, 785, 858.

3. The Crows were divided into two main bands. The more numerous Mountain Crows occupied the territory along the upper Yellowstone and the Bighorn and Absaroka mountains, and were traditionally closest to the whites. The poorer River Crows, with about half that number, were concentrated in the Musselshell and Judith rivers. A third, smaller band went by the name of Kicked-in-the-Belly Crows. See Frederick E. Hoxie, ed., *Encyclopedia of North American Indians,* Boston: Houghton Mifflin, 1996, 146–8. According to Brown, *Plainsmen of the Yellowstone*, 430, in January 1874 the Mountain Crows had 233 lodges, or 2,200–2,400 people, and the River Crows had 110 lodges, with 1,000–1,200 people. Brown says that the latter "were the more dissipated of the two groups," whereas the Mountain Crows "still looked with disfavor on the use of liquor and sometimes punished those who transgressed with a heavy hand."

4. Wischmann, *Frontier Diplomats*, 313–6. See also M. A. Leeson, ed., *History of Montana, 1739–1885*, Chicago: Warner, Beers and Company, 1885, 118.

5. Smith, *Bozeman and the Gallatin Valley*, 2; Montana Commission on Conservation, *Report of the Commission*, January 14, 1911, 132.

6. Sarah J. Tracy [sic], "Life in Early Bozeman," unpublished manuscript, June 1957, and Sarah J. Bessey Tracey (Mrs. William H. Tracey), Diary, 1869, Montana Historical Society Archives.

7. Thomas C. Rust, "Settlers, Soldiers, and Scoundrels: Economic Tension in a Frontier Military Town," *Military History of the West* 31, 2 (Fall 2001): 117–38.

8. The history of scalping is brilliantly summarized in Connell, *Son of the Morning Star*, 162–65.

9. Ewers, *Plains Indians*, 200–1.

10. Anthony McGinniss, *Counting Coup and Cutting Horses: Intertribal Warfare on the Northern Plains, 1738–1889*, Evergreen, Colorado: Cordillera Press, 1990, 116–7. Again, there is nothing intrinsically Native American about the practice, as anyone who has studied the late twentieth-century wars in Vietnam, Central America, and the former Yugoslavia, among others, can attest. Captivity narratives, of course, added another layer to this complicated weave of sexually driven anxieties. One of the most famous was that of Fanny Kelly, who was abducted by 250 Oglala Sioux warriors on the Bozeman Trail in July 1864. Although Kelly's account was not published until 1871, some of the details would certainly have reached Montana long before then. During her five-month captivity, Kelly describes seeing women and children killed, and on one occasion a warrior bringing back the bloody scalp of a woman with luxuriant chestnut tresses four feet long. Kelly also speaks of seeing children taught to torture small animals and birds, as entertainment. Fanny Kelly, *Narrative of My Captivity Among the Sioux Indians*, Hartford: Mutual Publishing Company, 1871. See also William M. Osborne, *The Wild Frontier: Atrocities During the American-Indian War from Jamestown Colony to Wounded Knee*, New York: Random House, 2001.

11. William A. Bell, *New Tracks in North America*, London: Chapman and Hall, 1869, cited in Connell, *Son of the Morning Star*, 160–1.

12. George Catlin, *North American Indians: Being Letters and Notes on their Manners, Customs, and Conditions, Written During Eight Years' Travel Amongst the Wildest Tribes in North America, 1832–1839*, New York: Penguin Nature Classics, 1989, Letters 21 and 22, 165–9.

13. Goetzmann and Goetzmann, *West of the Imagination*, 23.

14. The *Helena Herald* was edited by James Liberty Fisk, who had guided the Minnesota wagon train on which Nathaniel Langford had traveled to the goldfields in 1862, and subsequently by Fisk's brother Robert. James Fisk subsequently became one of the main figures in Acting Governor Meagher's Montana militia.

15. His name was also variously rendered as Sa-Pi's-To-Cos or S-pis-ti-Cos. See Horace Clarke, biography, Montana Historical Society Archives. For convenience, I generally refer to him as Owl Child, except when quoting directly from army documents.

16. Mountain Chief actually signed the unratified 1865 Fort Benton Treaty, one of eleven Piegans to do so. But by 1867 he was openly hostile to the whites after they reneged on its terms.

17. The murder was over a dispute about which man had the right to count coup on an Assiniboine enemy. James Willard Schultz, *Blackfeet and Buffalo: Memories of Life Among the Indians*, Norman: University of Oklahoma Press, 1962, 294, quotes the Piegan Bear Head's description of Ne-tus-che-o as "a man of terrible temper." Welch and Stekler, *Killing Custer*, 27, says that he lived off and on with Mountain Chief's band but mainly roamed

on his own, railing against the Piegan chiefs who had signed the Fort Benton treaty in 1865 and "stealing animals, destroying houses and property, occasionally killing a settler or miner."

18. Langford, "Frontier Tragedy."

19. Bear Head's version is recounted in Schultz, *Blackfeet and Buffalo*, 299. The story of Horace Clarke's altercation with Owl Child is in the Horace Clarke biography, Montana Historical Society Archives. The suggestion of rape is in Hungry Wolf, *Blackfeet History and Culture*, 1041.

20. William S. McKinzie, "John M. Bozeman," *Bozeman Avant Courier*, December 19, 1891; George W. Irwin II, "Overland to Montana in 1863," *Butte Miner*, January 1, 1888. Both cited in Smith, *Bozeman and the Gallatin Valley*, 51.

21. J. Bruce Putnam, "The Evolution of a Frontier Town: Bozeman, Montana, and Its Search for Economic Stability, 1864–1877," M.A. Thesis, Montana State University, 1973, copy in Montana State University Libraries, Bozeman.

22. Testimony of George Reed Davis and W. S. McKenzie, in Grace R. Hebard and E. A. Brininstool, *The Bozeman Trail*, Glendale, California, 1922. See also Merrill G. Burlingame, *John M. Bozeman: Montana Trailmaker*, Bozeman, Montana: Museum of the Rockies, rev. ed., 1983, 37. The questions about Cover's version of Bozeman's death are summarized in Smith, *Bozeman and the Gallatin Valley*, 102–4.

23. *Helena Herald*, May 2, 1867.

24. Putnam, *Evolution of a Frontier Town*, 13.

25. Ewers, *The Blackfeet*, 244; Wylie, *The Irish General*, 299. Chapman may be regarded as a tainted source, however, since Meagher had removed him from his post on suspicion of stealing from his charges.

26. Robert H. Utley, *Frontier Regulars: The United States Army and the Indian, 1866–1891*, New York: Macmillan, 1973, 125.

27. Sherman, May 7, 1867, cited in Wylie, *The Irish General*, 291.

28. In fact, Sherman later accused Meagher of having altered the wording of his telegram from "enter" to "threaten." Wylie, Ibid.

29. According to one man in Helena, Montana, merchants, realizing that many of the recently arrived settlers were in dire economic straits, decided to "Get up an Indian Excitement and Let the Goverment [sic] pay the Bill." William J. Snavely to Ulysses S. Grant, cited in Wylie, *The Irish General*, 298. See also, generally, James L. Thane Jr., "The Montana 'Indian War' of 1867," *Arizona and the West*, 10 (1968), 153–70.

30. Hubert Howe Bancroft, *History of Washington, Idaho and Montana, 1845–1889*, San Francisco: The History Company, 1890, 699–702.

31. Wylie, *The Irish General*, 298, note 58.

32. Quoted in Ibid., 305.

33. Haines, *Yellowstone Story*, Vol. 1, 91.

34. Langford, *Discovery*, xxxi; Jackson, "Early Exploration," 106–8; Bartlett, *Nature's Yellowstone*, 147 (although this identifies Samuel Hauser as part of the group, not Hezekiah Hosmer).

35. *Montana Post*, June 29, 1867.

36. Meagher's death remains a mystery. Some said he committed suicide, despondent over his mounting debts, others that he was murdered—either by Helena vigilantes, who

never forgave him for the pardon of James Daniels, or by one of the Indian agents with whom he had crossed swords: the Flathead agent Augustus Chapman or the Blackfeet agent George Wright. Most likely it was an accident, the result of drink and perhaps the opiates he had taken to relieve his dysentery. The various theories are reviewed in Wylie, *The Irish General*, 301–18.

16: PATHS OF GLORY

1. Sources for the account of Doane's early life to 1869 are Scott, *Yellowstone Denied*, 6–63; Orrin H. Bonney and Lorraine Bonney, *Battle Drums and Geysers: The Life and Journals of Lt. Gustavus Cheyney Doane, Soldier and Explorer of the Yellowstone and Snake River Regions*, Chicago: Sage-Swallow Press, 1970, 3–18; and Merrill G. Burlingame, notes for unpublished biography of Doane, Montana State University Libraries, Bozeman, Burlingame Special Collection 2245/18.
2. Alfred A. Doane, *The Doane Family and Their Descendants*, 1902, Third Edition, 1976. Boston: The Doane Family Association of America, Vol. I, 1–2.
3. Scott, *Yellowstone Denied*, 8–9.
4. Years later Doane claimed that, while a student at the University of the Pacific, he had applied for admission to West Point, but had been turned down because of his strong antislavery opinions. Scott concludes that this claim is "highly suspect." Ibid., 10.
5. University of the Pacific Web site, http://web.pacific.edu.
6. Doane, "Oration: California," and essay, "The Present Condition of Our Nation." In the first of these, he also deplores "the listless Mexican" and "the barbarous and repulsive Chinese and Malays." Montana State University Libraries, Bozeman, Burlingame Special Collections 2211/3.
7. Doane, "Familiar Lecture on Geology, Connected with Political Science," Montana State University Libraries, Bozeman, Burlingame Special Collections 2211/3. This paper is also a good example of Doane's scathing, over-the-top wit. In a bizarre satire on the supposed scientific justifications for slavery, he writes about "geology, and its connection with the 'Nigger Question.'" Discussing "those peculiarly rounded boulders found in mountain streams, and usually denominated Niggerheads," he writes, "These after a careful examination we have discovered to correspond as regards their structure and density with the African cranium, in a remarkable degree. Prof. Guttersnipes, a learned friend of ours, has recently discovered upon some of these boulders unmistakeable traces of fossil wool; thus confirming beyond a doubt their <u>niggeriferous</u> origins."
8. Doane, "Oration: The Eloquence of Solitude," Montana State University Libraries, Bozeman, Burlingame Special Collections 2211/3.
9. Frémont's third expedition to the West, accompanied by Kit Carson, morphed from an exploration of the sources of the Arkansas and a winter crossing of the Sierra Nevada into a wild series of military adventures that included a massacre of Klamath Indians, the execution of three Mexican *Californios* by Carson—on Frémont's orders—and the capture of Santa Barbara. See Hampton Sides, *Blood and Thunder: An Epic of the American West*, New York: Doubleday, 2006, especially 68–73, 77–81, 85–8, 92–101.

10. Rodenbough, *From Everglade to Cañon*, 405–6.

11. Jessie Frémont was the daughter of Senator Thomas Hart Benton of Missouri, one of the leading advocates of Manifest Destiny and Western expansion.

12. George Washington Towle, "Some Personal Recollections of George Washington Towle," unpublished typescript, Bancroft Library, Manuscript Collection, University of California at Berkeley, cited in Scott, *Yellowstone Denied*, 20.

13. Scott, Ibid., 25–8; Bonney and Bonney, *Battle Drums and Geysers*, 6–8.

14. Doane's service with the Mississippi Marine Brigade is described in Scott, *Yellowstone Denied*, 30–40.

15. Doane's credentials as justice of the peace were challenged by a former Missouri infantry officer, Joshua W. Bourne. The affair, which involved legalistic quibbles, displays of bombast, and missed appointments, is detailed in Ibid., 48–50.

16. Ibid., 53.

17. The recommendation came from California Senator John Conness. The Secretary's son, Charles B. Schofield, also joined the Second Cavalry and served with Doane at Fort Ellis, Montana.

18. Revised United States Army Regulations of 1861 and Articles of War, to June 25, 1863, cited in Don R. Rickey Jr., *Forty Miles a Day on Beans and Hay: The Enlisted Soldier Fighting the Indian Wars*, Norman, University of Oklahoma Press, 1963, 31.

19. Bonney, *Battle Drums and Geysers*, 15–7, citing Doane, letter to Smithsonian Institution, September 1, 1874.

20. From annual report of Brevet Brigadier General George D. Ruggles, October 17, 1868, Montana State University Libraries, Bozeman, Burlingame Special Collection 2245/18.

21. Scott doubts Doane's account of this episode, noting that Powell had announced his intention to explore the Colorado in December 1867 and had officially requested permission from General Ulysses S. Grant on April 2, 1868, before Doane had even reenlisted. Scott found no corroboration of Doane's request in army records. See Scott, *Yellowstone Denied*, 58–63.

17: THE LOST TRIBES OF THE SECOND CAVALRY

1. *Montana Post*, April 2, 1869, cited in William S. Phillips, "Total Warfare on the Marias," M.A. thesis, Wake Forest University, 1996, copy in Montana State University Libraries, Bozeman.

2. Hutton, *Sheridan*, 142–5.

3. As his troops prepared to march to Montana, Brackett was at work on a history of Fort Bridger. His diary does not record whether he made the twelve-mile ride to the fort from Carter's Station. His unpublished manuscript, "Fort Bridger," dated 1870, is in the special collections of the Harold B. Lee Library, Brigham Young University, Utah.

4. Brackett believed that the Shoshone language was a kind of lingua franca that could be understood by any Indian from the Columbia to Mexico. This kind of scholarship by army officers was not uncommon, and it included some of the pioneering works on Native

American anthropology. General Hugh Lenox Scott, who served with Doane and later became army chief of staff, was a renowned ethnologist and an expert on the sign language of the Plains Indians. John G. Bourke, an aide to the legendary Indian fighter General George Crook, published a number of papers for the Bureau of Ethnology, as did the Signal Corps officer Garrick Mallery, who wrote the first book to be published on Indian sign language. See Dunlay, *Wolves for the Blue Soldiers*, 97.

5. Cited in M. Constance Guardino III and Rev. Marilyn A. Riedel, "Sovereigns of Themselves: A Liberating History of Oregon and Its Coast," http://ftp.wi.net/~census/lesson34.html.

6. William White, *Custer, Cavalry, and Crows, Being the Thrilling Account of the Western Adventures of William White: The Story of William White as Told to Thomas Marquis*, Fort Collins, Colorado: Old Army Press, 1975, 38.

7. Ibid.

8. Burlingame unpublished manuscript, Burlingame Special Collection 2245/18.

9. Albert Brackett, "A Trip Through the Rocky Mountains," *Contributions to the Historical Society of Montana* 8 (1917), 329–44; J. P. Peters, "The March of the Montana Battalion," *Montana the Magazine of Western History*, 15, 2 (Spring 1965): 38–51; Scott, *Yellowstone Denied*, 62–3.

10. See Allen, *A Decent, Orderly Lynching*, 244.

11. Peters, "March of the Montana Battalion," 49.

12. Letter, A. G. Brackett, Lt. Col., 2nd Cav., to Brevet Brig. Gen. Geo D. Ruggles, Asst. Adj. Gen., Dept. of the Platte, July 6, 1869. Record group No.98 B17 and 58 (OQMG Series), National Archives and Records Service, cited in Peters, "March of the Montana Battalion," 51.

13. Hancock was at Fort Ellis on June 18, 1869. "The town seems nearly full of Indians," a local resident wrote at the time. "About two miles from here there are eighteen lodges of Crows . . . a very rough-looking set." Diary of Sarah J. Bessey Tracey (Mrs. William H. Tracey), 1869, Montana Historical Society Archives.

14. The best general accounts of mining in the upper Yellowstone are Haines, *Yellowstone Story*, Vol. 1, 127–39, and Bartlett, *Nature's Yellowstone*, 117–42. Henderson's diary is in the Collection of Western Americana (the "Coe Collection"), Beinecke Library, Yale University. Henderson is said to have been the first man to give Yellowstone the name of "Wonderland," in a diary entry in 1871, though Paul Schullery is not entirely convinced of this. See Schullery, *Searching for Yellowstone*, 287, note 1.

15. Quoted in Bartlett, *Nature's Yellowstone*, 130.

16. *Montana Post*, August 18, 1867, quoted in Jackson, "Early Exploration," 115.

17. According to one historian, Henry was only a half-brother, Henselbecker by name, and the brothers were Dutch, not German. Marlene Deahl Merrill, *Yellowstone and the Great West: Journals, Letters, and Images from the 1871 Hayden Expedition*, Lincoln: University of Nebraska Press, 1999, 258, note 5.

18. Schullery, *Searching for Yellowstone*, 68 and 72. Fred Bottler in particular was a killing machine to rival St. George Gore; his shooting of elk, Schullery says, amounted to an "ecological holocaust."

19. Folsom diary, Yellowstone National Park Archives.

20. Langford, *Discovery*, xxxi.

21. *Montana Post*, May 28, 1869, cited in Bennett, *Death, Too, for The-Heavy-Runner*, 17.

22. *Montana Post*, June 4, 1869.

18: THE FORT AT THE END OF THE WORLD

1. Later, when Doane became property officer at Fort Ellis, William White said, "I never heard any insinuation of corrupt intent on his part. Universally it was known that he was not that kind of man." Leforge, *Memoirs*, 35.

2. Ibid., 46. Another cavalryman who served under Doane gave a similar account, describing the lieutenant as a "big stalwart man" with "long black hair," who "appeared to have no fear." Fred F. Munn, as told to Robert A. Griffen, "Fred Munn, Veteran of Frontier Experiences, Remembered the Days He Rode with Miles, Howard, and Terry," *Montana the Magazine of Western History* 16, 2 (Spring 1966), 50–64.

3. The survey was commanded by Captain E. W. Clift of the 13th Infantry, operating out of Fort Shaw. The map of its route is included in *Annual Report, Department of Dakota, 1870,* Adjutant General's Office, No. 1869, National Archives, and reproduced in Bonney and Bonney, *Battle Drums and Geysers*, 135.

4. Burlingame, unpublished notes, "Life at Fort Ellis," Montana State University Libraries, Bozeman, Burlingame Special Collection 2245/18.

5. Ibid. This description probably comes from an account by Mary Hunter Doane, the lieutenant's second wife, who gave Burlingame exclusive access to his private papers.

6. Doane, Snake River Expedition report, in Bonney and Bonney, *Battle Drums and Geysers*, 455.

7. The following depiction of the frontier army is based largely on Rickey, *Forty Miles a Day*; Utley, *Frontier Regulars* and *The Indian Frontier of the American West, 1846–1890*, Albuquerque: University of New Mexico Press, 1984; and Jack D. Foner, *The United States Soldier Between Two Wars, 1865–1898*, New York: Humanities Press, 1970.

8. The classic account of a soldier's everyday life on a frontier post is Rickey, *Forty Miles a Day*. On Fort Ellis specifically, see Thomas C. Rust, ed., *Fort Ellis: A Documentary History*, Bozeman, Montana: Gallatin County Historical Society, 2004; Rust, "Settlers, Soldiers, and Scoundrels"; James M. Hamilton, "History of Fort Ellis," Special Collections, Montana State University Libraries, Bozeman, 1926; Kim Allen Scott, ed., *"Splendid on a Large Scale": The Writings of Hans Peter Gyllembourg Koch, 1869–1874*, Helena, Montana: Drumlummon Institute and Bedrock Editions, 2010; and, for an ordinary soldier's firsthand account, White, *Custer, Cavalry and Crows*, 21–35.

9. Rickey, *Forty Miles a Day*, 27, 50; Koch to Laurie, January 21, 1871, in Scott, ed., *"Splendid on a Large Scale,"* 115.

10. One infamous box of hardtack shipped to the troops in 1890, the year of Wounded Knee, was date-stamped with its year of production—1863. Rickey, *Forty Miles a Day*, 249.

11. Ibid., 125–33, 169–70; David A. Clary, "The Role of the Army Surgeon in the West: Daniel Weisel at Fort Davis, 1868–1872," *Western Historical Quarterly*, 3 (1972), 53–66.

12. Rust, "Settlers, Soldiers, and Scoundrels," gives the population of Bozeman in 1870 as ninety-three—sixty-nine men and twenty-four women. Another scholar cites a higher number of 150 in 1868. See Putnam, "The Evolution of a Frontier Town."

13. White, *Custer, Cavalry and Crows*, 27–8.

14. Rickey, *Forty Miles a Day*, 189, 208.

15. Ibid., 200–4.

16. White, *Custer, Cavalry and Crows*, 27–8.

17. The Indian Bureau was still part of the Department of the Interior.

18. The total military force stationed in the Department of Dakota in 1869 numbered 2,368. The following year, after the conflict with the Blackfeet, it was increased to 3,721, though it was reduced again to 2,978 in 1871. *Annual Reports of the Secretary of War*, cited in M. John Lubetkin, *Jay Cooke's Gamble: The Northern Pacific Railroad, the Sioux, and the Panic of 1873*, Norman: University of Oklahoma Press, 2006, 50. See also Hutton, *Sheridan*, 395, note 6, citing P. H. Sheridan, *Record of Engagements with Hostile Indians within the Division of the Missouri from 1868 to 1882*, Washington, D.C.: Government Printing Office, 1882.

19. By way of comparison, Utley notes that the population of the United States was around 20 million. By 1860, 1.4 million of these people were living in the West. By the last spasm of the Indian Wars at Wounded Knee in 1890 that number had grown to nine million. Utley, *Indian Frontier*, 4. Elsewhere, Utley estimates that by 1866 the total number of Indians had declined to around 270,000, divided into 12 main population groups. *Frontier Regulars*, 4.

20. Brown, *Plainsmen of the Yellowstone*, 85.

21. Report to the President of the Indian Peace Commission, January 7, 1868, in House Exec. Doc. 97-2, 17. Cited in P. E. Byrne, *Soldiers of the Plains*, New York: Minton, Balch and Company, 1926, 211.

22 *The New York Times*, October 16, 1868, cited in Utley, *Indian Frontier*, 125.

23. "For operations in the open country of Pennsylvania, Maryland, and Northern Virginia, cavalry is much better than infantry." Roy Morris Jr., *Sheridan: The Life and Wars of General Phil Sheridan*, New York: Vintage, 1992, 184.

24. Morris, *Sheridan*, 154.

25. Grant went on, "It is desirable that nothing should be left to invite the enemy to return. Take all provisions, forage, and stock wanted for the use of your command. Such as cannot be consumed, destroy . . . [T]he people should be informed that so long as an army can subsist among them recurrences of these raids must be expected, and we are determined to stop them at all hazard." U.S. War Department, *The War of the Rebellion: A Compilation of the Official Records of the Union and Confederate Armies*, 43.1, 628, cited in Morris, *Sheridan*, 184.

26. *War of the Rebellion: Official Records*, 36.1, 801, cited in Morris, *Sheridan*, Ibid.

27. Goetzmann, *Exploration and Empire*, 328–9. For Sheridan, close contact with the natives extended as far as taking the daughter of a Klikitat chief as his mistress in 1857. But that was just a year after he had led a punitive attack on a force of Yakimas who had assaulted some white settlements on the Columbia River in Oregon. A bullet killed his orderly in this action, grazing Sheridan's nose on the way. After a cursory trial, he hanged nine Yakima and said this had "a most salutary effect." See Morris, *Sheridan*, 33–4. The following year, Sheridan desecrated a Flathead burial ground.

28. Senate Ex. Docs., 40th Congress, 3rd session., No.18, Pt. 1, 3–5, cited in Utley, *Frontier Regulars*, 150–1.

29. The Canyon de Chelly attack is described in Sides, *Blood and Thunder*, 349–57.

30. Hutton, *Sheridan*, 54–5.

31. The standard histories are Stan Hoig, *The Battle of the Washita: The Sheridan-Custer Indian Campaign of 1867–69*, Lincoln: University of Nebraska Press, 1979; and Jerome A. Greene, *Washita: The U.S. Army and the Southern Cheyenne, 1867–1869*, Norman: University of Oklahoma Press, 2004.

32. Hutton, *Sheridan*, 98, citing *Annual Report of the Secretary of War, 1869*, 1:47.

33. Surprisingly, there is no modern book on Grant's Peace Policy. For good, concise analyses, see Utley, *Indian Frontier*, 129–55, and *Frontier Regulars*, 195–224.

34. Hancock compensated for his failure by court-martialing Custer, Sheridan's favorite, for visiting his wife without permission while on combat duty. Hutton, *Sheridan*, 30–3.

35. Lubetkin, *Jay Cooke's Gamble*, 23.

36. Baker's formal rank was major, but his honorific was invariably used during his tenure at Fort Ellis, and I use it throughout.

19: A DEATH IN THE FAMILY

1. Cornelius Hedges Diary, Hedges Papers, Montana Historical Society Archives.

2. David E. Folsom, with a preface by Nathaniel P. Langford, "The Folsom-Cook Exploration of the Upper Yellowstone in the Year 1869," *Contributions to the Historical Society of Montana* V (1904): 349–69.

3. W. A. Clark is listed in the 1868 *Helena General City Directory* as involved in "business/banking" on Main Street. He went on to make a fortune in the Butte mines and was the bitter rival of the most legendary of all the mining barons, Marcus Daly. He also served for six years in the U.S. Senate. When he died in 1925, Clark left an estate worth $47 million. See Joseph K. Howard, *Montana: High, Wide and Handsome*, New Haven, Connecticut: Yale University Press, 1943, 58–68.

4. Hedges eulogy for Washburn, Hedges Papers, Montana Historical Society Archives.

5. The two men were less than a month apart in age: Gillette was born on March 10, 1832, and Washburn on March 28. Like Gillette, Washburn may have overlapped at Oberlin with Ferdinand Vandeveer Hayden.

6. Grand Lodge, Anaconda, Montana, "Nathaniel Pitt Langford: Past Grand Master," obituary, January 1, 1911, Yellowstone National Park Archives.

7. See Burlingame, *The Montana Frontier*, 150–69; and Clark C. Spence, "The Territorial Officers of Montana, 1864–1889," *Pacific Historical Review*, Vol. 30, No. 2, May 1961, 123–36.

8. *Congressional Globe: Containing the Debates and Proceedings of the Second Session, Fortieth Congress*, 1868, at 2638. The "dead Indian" aphorism is usually attributed to General Phil Sheridan, but the honor seems to belong to Cavanaugh. Sheridan's remark was differently phrased. In January 1869 he was approached by a Comanche chief who is reported to have said, "Me Tosawi; me good Indian." To which Sheridan responded, "The only good Indians I ever saw were dead." Morris, *Sheridan*, 328. The origins of the phrase are fascinatingly discussed in Wolfgang Mieder, *The Politics of Proverbs*, Madison: University of

Wisconsin Press, 1997, 138–59. "Nits make lice" has also been attributed to a number of officers serving in the Indian Wars, most notably Colonel John Chivington, author of the 1864 Sand Creek Massacre.

9. Langford claimed later that he could have taken up the post regardless, had he chosen to return to Montana rather than staying in Washington. Langford to "Toby," January 27, 1909, Langford Papers, Minnesota Historical Society.

10. Langford to Hauser, March 24, 1867, Langford Papers, Minnesota Historical Society.

11. The best source on Cooke's railroad schemes is Lubetkin, *Jay Cooke's Gamble*. See also Ellis P. Oberholtzer, *Jay Cooke: Financier of the Civil War*, Philadelphia: George W. Jacobs and Company, 1907, 226–36.

12. John L. Harnsberger, *Jay Cooke and Minnesota: The Formative Years of the Northern Pacific Railroad, 1868–1873*, New York: Arno Press, 1981, 69.

13. Lubetkin, *Jay Cooke's Gamble*, 167.

14. Langford, *Discovery*, xxxii.

15. *Helena Weekly Herald*, August 19, 1869.

16. Langford, "The Blackfoot Treaty," unpublished typescript, Yellowstone National Park Archives.

17. Ewers, *The Blackfeet*, 246, citing *Reports of the Commissioner of Indian Affairs*, 1868, at 215.

18. Helen Clarke, "Sketch of Malcolm Clarke"; Langford, "Frontier Tragedy."

19. Langford, "Frontier Tragedy." On the killings in Fort Benton, see Ege, *Tell Baker to Strike Them Hard!*, 27; Bennett, *Death, Too, for The-Heavy-Runner*, 21.

20. Sully to Ely Parker, August 3, 1869, in *Piegan Indians: Letter from the Secretary of War in Answer to a Resolution of the House, of March 3, 1870, in Relation to the Late Expedition Against the Piegan Indians, in the Territory of Montana*, Washington, D.C., House Committee on Indian Affairs, May 11, 1870, House Exec. Doc. No. 269, 41st Congress, 2d Session.

21. Bennett, *Death, Too, for The-Heavy-Runner*, 37.

22. The account of the Clarke murder and its immediate aftermath is based on Helen Clarke, "Sketch of Malcolm Clarke"; Langford, "A Frontier Tragedy"; and Langford to Doolittle, September 14, 1869, Langford Papers, Minnesota Historical Society.

23. For some reason, Helen Clarke's initial thought was that the murder had been committed by Pend d'Oreille Indians, which makes no sense since that tribe was friendly to the whites. Clarke, "Sketch of Malcolm Clarke."

24. Langford, "Frontier Tragedy."

25. Langford to Doolittle, September 14, 1869, Langford Papers, Minnesota Historical Society.

20: THE WORLD OF LETTERS AND THE WORLD OF ARMS

1. This account of the Folsom-Cook-Peterson expedition is drawn from Cook, Folsom, and Peterson, *The Valley of the Upper Yellowstone*, Aubrey L. Haines, ed., Norman: University of Oklahoma Press, 1965; Folsom and Langford, "The Folsom-Cook Exploration of the Upper Yellowstone in the Year 1869"; Cook, "Remarks of C. W. Cook, Last Survivor of the Original Explorers of the Yellowstone Park Region, on the Occasion of His Second Visit to the Park in 53 Years, During the Celebration of the Park's Golden Anniversary," official transcript, July 14, 1922, Yellowstone National Park Archives. The best general

summaries of the expedition are Haines, *Yellowstone Story*, Vol. 1, 91–101; Bartlett, *Nature's Yellowstone*, 152–63; and W. Turrentine Jackson, "The Cook-Folsom Exploration of the Upper Yellowstone, 1869," *Pacific Northwest Quarterly* 32 (1941), 307–22.

2. Peterson diary, Yellowstone National Park Archives.

3. *Helena Herald*, July 29, 1869. The "Mysterious Mounds" presumably refers to the terraces at Mammoth Hot Springs.

4. Haines, *Yellowstone Story*, Vol. 1, 94.

5. With the exception of a handful that were named by the early trappers and prospectors, very few of the natural features of the upper Yellowstone and the future national park had been given names by the time of the Folsom-Cook-Peterson expedition. For the sake of convenience I have used the names that are commonly in use today.

6. The "Chemical Works" were probably the southern portion of today's Coffee Pot Hot Springs. Personal communication with Lee H. Whittlesey.

7. Lecture presented by Nathaniel Pitt Langford.

8. The complicated story of the Folsom and Cook diaries, and how they were amalgamated and revised, is told in Jackson, "Early Exploration," 137–41.

9. "Remarks of C. W. Cook."

10. Ibid.

11. Unaccountably, there is no satisfactory single source on the Piegan crisis and the Baker Massacre on the Marias River, which remains perhaps the most underreported incident in the history of the Indian Wars in the West. Many works on the period include cursory chapters on the event, but there are only two book-length studies, neither of which received wide circulation. These are Ege, *Tell Baker to Strike Them Hard!* and Bennett, *Death, Too, for The-Heavy-Runner*. Ege's is by far the more detailed analysis of the event, and has a useful appendix that includes many key military documents. However, its value is greatly diminished by its polemical tone, which ignores or distorts significant pieces of evidence and equates critics of Colonel Baker's actions with critics of the Vietnam War. Bennett's account, meanwhile, is written largely from the Piegan point of view, and its analysis is interspersed with lengthy imagined dream sequences and "visions" involving Heavy Runner, Mountain Chief, General Sully, and General de Trobriand.

    Of the many other primary and secondary sources I consulted, it's worth singling out the two effective accounts of the massacre by James Welch—one fictionalized, in his superb novel, *Fools Crow*, New York: Viking Penguin, 1986, and the other in Welch and Stekler, *Killing Custer*, 25–47. The most important military correspondence is collected as *Piegan Indians: Letter from the Secretary of War*. A collection of eye-witness accounts by Piegan survivors is available in Stan Gibson and Jack Hayne, "Witnesses to Carnage: The 1870 Marias Massacre in Montana," at www.dickshovel.com/parts.html. Several of these are drawn from testimonies to the Indian Claims Commission, 1913–1914, copies in the Montana Historical Society Archives. Among shorter accounts, the most useful are probably Paul Hutton, "Phil Sheridan's Pyrrhic Victory: The Piegan Massacre, Army Politics, and the Transfer Debate," *Montana the Magazine of Western History* 32 (Spring 1982), 32–43; and Ewers, *The Blackfeet*, 236–53.

12. Schultz, *Blackfeet and Buffalo*, 299–300.

13. *New North West*, Deer Lodge, Montana, August 27, 1869.

14. *Helena Daily Herald*, August 19, 1869.

15. *Helena Daily Herald* and *Helena Weekly Herald*, August 26, 1869.

16. Custer's remarks are cited in Bennett, *Death, Too, for The-Heavy-Runner*, 47.

17. Culbertson to Sully, September 1869. The acting Blackfeet agent, F. D. Pease, concurred, even though he had only been in the job for three months: "In fact, by what I can learn, there is so far only a small band of the Piegans that are or that have been interested in the depredations lately committed." Pease to Sully, August 31, 1869. Both in *Piegan Indians: Letter from the Secretary of War*.

18. Cited in Athearn, "Frontier Critics of the Army," *Montana the Magazine of Western History* 5.2 (Spring 1965), 16–28.

19. Lucille M. Kane, ed. and trans., *Military Life in Dakota: The Journal of Philippe Régis de Trobriand*, Lincoln: University of Nebraska Press, 1951, xxi–xxv.

20. One of the more interesting passages in de Trobriand's diaries is his fulsome praise for the way in which Indian women handled childbirth. They were up the next day and back to work, he wrote, in contrast to the "long torture, medical attendance, intervention of chloroform, puerperal fever, two weeks in bed, 30 days in the bedroom, and such precaution" that "physically and morally . . . corrupted the work of nature" in their white sisters. See Kane, *Military Life in Dakota*, 157.

21. Ibid.

22. Sherry Lynn Smith, *The View from Officers' Row: Army Perceptions of Western Indians*, Tucson: University of Arizona Press, 1991, 21.

23. Kane, *Military Life in Dakota*, 96.

24. De Trobriand to Hancock, September 9, 1869, in *Piegan Indians: Letter from the Secretary of War*.

25. Morse's Store was another name for the now-vanished town of Hamilton, between the Three Forks and Bozeman. Tuttle, *Reminiscences*, 438.

26. There has been some speculation that Quail—answering to the nickname "Grouse"— may have been one of the men involved in the shooting of Mountain Chief's brother in July. See Ege, *Tell Baker to Strike Them Hard!*, 28.

27. Sully to Parker, September 27, 1869, in *Piegan Indians: Letter from the Secretary of War*.

28. *Helena Daily Herald*, September 30, 1869.

29. To General R. P. de Trobriand, Commanding District of Montana, Fort Shaw, October 1, 1869. The other signatories were A. P. Simmons (chairman), who had accompanied Langford and X. Beidler to the Clarke ranch on the day after the murder; H. P. A. Smith, a flamboyant, alcoholic lawyer who had defended several of the road agents hanged by the Bannack and Virginia City vigilantes; and Martin Maginnis, who was later elected as Montana's Democratic delegate to the U.S. Congress. On Smith and the vigilantes, see Allen, *A Decent, Orderly Lynching*, 105 ff.

30. Ege, *Tell Baker to Strike Them Hard!*, 22–3.

31. Based on affidavits from a number of citizens, U.S. Court Commissioner S. V. Clevenger also named another fourteen Indians accused of "depredations": Big Horn, Big Rain, Big Snake, Big White Buffalo, Black Eagle, Crow Foot, Cut Hand, Mountain Chief, Old Bull's Head, Red Horn, Star, Three Sun, Under Bull, and White Man's Dog. *Piegan Indians: Letter from the Secretary of War*, 67–70. In asking for the indictments, U.S. Marshal William F. Wheeler accused the Blackfeet of killing a total of fifty-six people and stealing more than

one thousand horses in 1869. See Ewers, *The Blackfeet*, 247. For his own account, see Wheeler, "The Piegan War of 1870," *Helena Daily Herald*, January 1, 1880.

32. De Trobriand to citizens' committee, October 6, 1869, in *Piegan Indians: Letter from the Secretary of War.*

33. The date of his departure is recorded in Cornelius Hedges's diary. Hedges Papers, Montana Historical Society Archives.

34. "Letter and Notes by N. P. Langford on the Cullen Treaty with the Blackfoot Indians, September 1, 1868," Fort Benton, Montana, © 1901, typescript in Yellowstone National Park Archives.

35. Sheridan to Brevet Major General E. D. Townsend, Adjutant General, U.S. Army, October 21, 1869, in *Piegan Indians: Letter from the Secretary of War.*

36. Townsend to Sheridan, November 4, 1869, in Ibid.

21: FORTY-FOUR BELOW

1. Sheridan to Hancock, November 15, 1869, in Ibid.

2. Description cited in Lubetkin, *Jay Cooke's Gamble*, 84.

3. Peter Cozzens, *Eyewitnesses to the Indian Wars, 1865–1890, Vol. 2, The Wars for the Pacific Northwest*, Mechanisburg, Pennsylvania: Stackpole, 2002, 4–7.

4. Quoted in White, *Custer, Cavalry and Crows*, 32.

5. Koch went on to become a prominent figure in late nineteenth-century Montana, and a street in Bozeman is still named after him. All quotes are taken from Scott, ed., "*Splendid on a Large Scale.*"

6. White, *Custer, Cavalry and Crows*, 24.

7. "Men wore overalls, jumpers, irregular boots or shoes, irregular hats or caps, or one might go bareheaded or barefooted," recalled Private White. "In the field might be seen among us all kinds of hats, except I never observed a stovepipe or a derby." Ibid., 25.

8. Koch to Laurie, February 21, 1871. Scott, ed., "*Splendid on a Large Scale,*" 115.

9. De Trobriand to Brevet Brigadier General O. D. Greene, Assistant Adjutant General, Department of Dakota, November 22, 1869, in *Piegan Indians: Letter from the Secretary of War.*

10. De Trobriand to Greene, November 26, 1869.

11. Life in winter camp is described, in somewhat romanticized terms, in Bennett, *Death, Too, for The-Heavy-Runner*, 109–11.

12. Ewers, *The Blackfeet*, 76.

13. According to Blackfeet legend, Napi, the Old Man, had fashioned the Sweetgrass Hills from rocks he laid out to trace the shape of his own body. Grinnell, *Blackfoot Lodge Tales*, 137.

14. The source of Hardie's assertion was probably a deposition by one John R. Wren, taken by U.S. Court Commissioner S. V. Clevenger in Fort Benton, January 8, 1870: "[T]he Blackfeet declare that if any cases of small-pox occur they will kill every white man on the prairie, or words to that effect," in *Piegan Indians: Letter from the Secretary of War.*

15. De Trobriand to Greene, December 21, 1869, in Ibid.

16. De Trobriand to Greene, December 18, 1869, in Ibid.

17. Sully to Ely Parker, January 3, 1870, in Ibid.

18. Sully to Hardie, January 13, 1870, quoted in Ege, *Tell Baker to Strike Them Hard!*, 110–1.
19. Hardie to Sheridan, January 13, 1870, in *Piegan Indians: Letter from the Secretary of War*.
20. Sheridan to Hardie, January 15, 1870, in Ege, *Tell Baker to Strike Them Hard!*, 32–3.
21. The language of these justifications is often strikingly similar to modern arguments about the inevitability of "collateral damage" in situations where "terrorists use the civilian population as a shield."
22. On de Trobriand's redactions, see Bennett, *Death, Too, for The-Heavy-Runner*, 108.
23. Kane, *Military Life in Dakota*, 64–5.
24. Kipp also reported that "if Pete were killed, no one would care, as he is a sort of renegade and does not always sleep in the same tent, from fear of being attacked at night." Hardie to Hartsuff, January 29, 1870, cited in Phillips, "Total Warfare," 74.
25. Captain Oliver Ormsby G. Robinson was charged for a minor offense committed during the August survey of the route to the Musselshell River. See Bonney and Bonney, *Battle Drums and Geysers*, 21–2.
26. They were, respectively, Captain Seneca H. Norton (Company G), Captain Edward Ball (Company H), and Brevet Major Lewis Thompson. See Rodenbough, *Everglade to Cañon*, 401; Brian M. Best, Letter to the Editor, *Montana* 35.2 (Spring 1985), 83; John Y. Simon, ed., *Papers of Ulysses S. Grant*, Vol. 27. Carbondale: University of Southern Illinois Press (2005), 256.
27. De Trobriand to Baker, January 16, 1870, in *Piegan Indians: Letter from the Secretary of War*.
28. Descriptions are from General Nelson Miles's 1876–1877 Fifth Infantry campaign against the Sioux. Rickey, *Forty Miles a Day*, 256. See also Walter F. Beyer and Oscar Frederick Keydel, *Deeds of Valor from Records in the Archives of the United States Government: How America's Heroes Won the Medal of Honor*, Detroit: The Perrien-Keydel Company, 1906, 221.

22: A CASE OF MISTAKEN IDENTITY

1. Aristotle, *The Poetics*, translated by G. M. A. Grube, Indianapolis: Bobbs-Merrill, 1958, 11–38.
2. Bonney and Bonney contrast the march of the Second Cavalry with the distintegration of Napoleon's army in his advance on Moscow, the thousands of Russian soldiers who died in the 1939–1940 winter campaign against the Finns, and the ten thousand American troops put out of action in the winter of 1944–1945. *Battle Drums and Geysers*, 441.
3. For a sketch-map of Baker's line of march, see Ege, *Tell Baker to Strike Them Hard!*, front endpapers.
4. Doane's March 21, 1874, report, the most complete account written by the army, says there was only a single lodge; Ponsford, handwritten notes, © 1910, reproduced in *Witnesses to Carnage*, speaks of a camp with several tipis; Scott, *Yellowstone Denied*, 66, mentions "a small cluster of five lodges," but cites no source for this. Presumably this is from Ege, *Tell Baker to Strike Them Hard!*, 42, but his book offers no footnotes at all.
5. Even at this age, Bear Head was a celebrated figure among the Piegans; if his own account is to be believed, he counted his first coup at the age of eight, seizing an enemy's gun and scalping him, and at twelve was known as an accomplished buffalo hunter. His is the

most detailed eyewitness account from a Piegan point of view. It appears in Schultz's *Blackfeet and Buffalo*, 282–304. However, some of the details should be taken with a grain of salt: Bear Head's account was given when he was an old man, in his late seventies, and Schultz's highly colored writings gave him the nickname of "Lard Oil Jim." Bear Head gave a separate account of the events to the Indian Claims Commission in 1915, which is included in *Witnesses to Carnage*.

6. The topography of the site has changed somewhat since 1870. The cottonwoods are long gone, and the course of the river has altered many times, with the outlines of old meanders and silted oxbows clearly visible. Some of this is the result of the construction of the Tiber Dam in the 1950s, which backed up the river as Lake Elwell for more than twenty miles. Bennett, *Death, Too, for The-Heavy-Runner*, 113, names one of the buttes as Black Robe Butte (presumably referring to the Jesuits), and Schultz, *Blackfeet and Buffalo*, 302, says the camp was to the north of Goosebill Butte. Neither of these names appears on contemporary maps.

7. Some sources say that in addition to the Piegans, a small number of whites were in the camp that day. White, *Custer, Cavalry and Crows*, 33, mentions some whiskey traders, and also a nineteen-year-old "White Crow" named Tom Leforge. Born in Ohio in 1850, Leforge and his family had settled in Virginia City in 1864, and Jim Bridger lived with them for a spell. But the following year, Leforge ran away and attached himself to a group of Mountain Crows known as the Kick-in-the-Belly band. He joined General Meagher's volunteer militia in 1867 and hunted and sold meat to Fort Ellis. When Doane cleared the camp after the January 23 massacre, he is said to have found a quilt that had been stolen from Leforge's home by the Piegans the previous year. See Leforge, *Memoirs*, vi, 16, 21, 31.

8. White, *Custer, Cavalry, and Crows*, 32.

9. Welch and Stekler, *Killing Custer*, 31.

10. Hungry Wolf, *Blackfeet History and Culture*, 1209–10.

11. Ege, *Tell Baker to Strike Them Hard!*, 43, and others say that it was Joe Kipp's shouted warning that alerted the camp, but it seems clear from Doane's account, which says that "[t]he other companies came up in a few minutes," that F Company's encirclement of the camp happened first.

12. The accounts of Heavy Runner's actions vary slightly in their details. Mrs. Frank Monroe, a Piegan who later married a white man, says that the idea of showing the safe-conduct pass was suggested by someone else. Good Bear Woman says that the chief actually gave his paper to the commanding officer (unidentified), who tore it up. This is not substantiated by other witnesses. Indian Claims Commission testimonies. Another Piegan source, also without substantiation, says that it was not Heavy Runner who went outside with the paper but another man named Packing-Tail-Feathers-Coming-Over-the-Hill, who was also supposedly carrying a peace medal he had been given in the 1850s by Governor Isaac Stevens. Lancaster, *Piegan*, 123. Unfortunately this version of the story is rife with factual errors and cannot be relied upon.

13. Ege, *Tell Baker to Strike Them Hard!*, 43. The irony of Baker's drunkenness is almost unbearable, since one of the arguments General Sully had been making for months was that the main use of the army in Montana should be to crack down on the whiskey traders who had turned the Blackfeet into a nation of alcoholics.

14. Martha Edgerton Plassman Papers, 1863–1839, MC 78, Montana Historical Society Archives.

15. See Lloyd James Dempsey, *Blackfoot War Art: Pictographs of the Reservation Period, 1880–2000*, Norman: University of Oklahoma Press, 2007, 242, plate 14.

16. Baker himself reported the distance as sixteen miles. Baker to de Trobriand, February 18, 1870, in *Piegan Indians: Letter from the Secretary of War*. However, Robert Ege, who conducted the most extensive archaeological research into the location of the massacre site, identified the location of Mountain Chief's camp as the mouth of Dead Indian Coulee, about eight miles east of the Big Bend. Ege, *Tell Baker to Strike Them Hard!*, 62–3.

17. For details of burial customs, see Ewers, *The Blackfeet*, 106–8.

18. Joseph Kipp, Deposition to Indian Claims Commission, February 8, 1913.

19. Kim Allen Scott also comes to this conclusion. See *Yellowstone Denied*, 68.

20. White, *Custer, Cavalry and Crows*, 33.

23: HEROES OF THE HOUR

1. Sherman to Sheridan, January 29, 1870, in *Piegan Indians: Letter from the Secretary of War*, 8.

2. Quoted in Bennett, *Death, Too, for The-Heavy-Runner*, 144.

3. Quoted in Ibid., 123.

4. Quoted in Milo Milton Quaife, ed., *Army Life in Dakota: Selections from the Journal of Philippe Régis Denis de Keredern de Trobriand*, Whitefish, Montana: Kessinger Publishing, 2007, 368–71.

5. A placard on the victim's back read, "Ah Chow, the murderer of John R. Bitzer [sic]. Beware! The Vigilantes still live!" Interestingly, the *Helena Herald* condemned this killing, despite having no sympathy for Ah Chow. "There was a time in Montana when vigilante justice was essential to the protection of the lives and property of peaceable citizens. But . . . the hanging of Ah Chow without trial before a legal tribunal was a grave wrong . . . The death of that Chinaman, guilty or guiltless . . . is a disgrace and a crime. Chinaman, alien, pagan, depraved as he may have been; his blood-clots stain deep on the record of Montana." *Helena Herald*, January 28, 1870.

6. Kipp deposition to Indian Claims Commission, February 1913, Montana Historical Society Archives.

7. De Trobriand to Sully, February 3, 1870.

8. Pease to Sully, February 8, 1870, in *Reports of the Board of Indian Commissioners, 1870*, 89, cited in Dunn, *Massacres of the Mountains*, 30.

9. Quoted in *Witnesses to Carnage*.

10. *Chicago Tribune*, February 3, 1870.

11. Quoted in Robert Winston Mardock, *The Reformers and the American Indian*, Columbia: University of Missouri Press, 1971, 69.

12. Ibid.

13. Bennett, *Death, Too, for The-Heavy-Runner*, 132.

14. *New North West*, February 25, 1870, cited in Bennett, *Death, Too, for The-Heavy-Runner*, 135.

15. Sheridan to Sherman, February 28, 1870, in *Piegan Indians: Letter from the Secretary of*

War. New North West also invoked the Washita in supporting Sheridan's attack on Colyer, saying that, "The Indian Ring failed in its efforts for a Head after Wachita [sic], because Sheridan stood by his faithful subordinates. We have not less confidence in his manliness now, and the vindication of Baker."

16. See Bennett, *Death, Too, for The-Heavy-Runner*, 142–3.

17. Baker to Assistant Acting Adjutant General Brevet Major J. T. McGinnis, District of Montana, February 18, 1870. Ege, *Tell Baker to Strike Them Hard!*, 133–5.

18. *Chicago Tribune*, March 3 and March 5, 1870.

19. *Piegan Indians: Letter from the Secretary of War.*

20. It is impossible to know what de Trobriand is referring to here. No other source mentions any evidence of papers belonging to Clarke being found in Heavy Runner's camp.

21. Citing military documents selectively in Baker's defense, Robert Ege omits any reference to the exchange between Hardie and de Trobriand. It is discussed in Bennett, p. 149. On March 18, de Trobriand had written to his daughter, "In my correspondence, my disposi-tions, and my instructions to Colonel Baker, there is not one word to form a basis for criticism. Sustained by the testimonials which I received in Helena on this matter, my attitude remains serenely amused and unmoved." This exchange does not appear in the government's official compilation of military documents, *Piegan Indians: Letter from the Secretary of War,* but is included in Bennett, *Death, Too, for The-Heavy-Runner,* 152, which unfortunately does not cite a source.

22. *Piegan Indians: Letter from the Secretary of War,* 70–1.

23. Ibid., 72.

24. Ibid., 73.

25. Ibid., 74.

26. The reference is to Langford's assistant, Frank Angevine, murdered with nine others by Blood Indians under Calf Shirt at the mouth of the Marias in 1865. Borhees is not fur-ther identified.

27. *Chicago Tribune,* March 29, 1870. The meeting was held in the courthouse on March 25. The preamble to the resolution read, "It is with no little degree of pleasure that we lay before the country [the proceedings] as they will have a tendency to open the eyes of all persons not wilfully blind to Indian atrocities in Montana.... Certain Congressmen, editors and professional philanthropists of the East have taken it upon themselves to deny or pervert facts which justified the chastisement of the Indians by the soldiers." The other signatories to the resolution, with Hedges, were lawyer Warren Toole and H. L. Warren, otherwise unidentified.

28. Lieutenant W. B. Pease, the Blackfeet agent, was also concerned that, "It is hardly reason-able to expect that they will be satisfied without the revenge that an Indian's nature craves." Bennett, *Death, Too, for The-Heavy-Runner,* 131. Dee Brown suggests that other northern plains tribes responded to news of the massacre by burning agencies, chasing government employees off reservations, and denouncing the Great Father in Washington as "a fool and dog, without ears or brains." But there was no hint of such a response from the Blackfeet. Brown, *Bury My Heart,* 178, citing U.S. Department of Interior, Report 1870, 672–82. U.S. Congress 41st, 3d Session, Senate Ex. Doc. 39, 2.

29. Bennett, *Death, Too, for The-Heavy-Runner,* 162–3. On April 12, Sully wrote to Indian Commissioner Ely Parker summarizing a letter he had received from the Jesuit Father

John B. Imoda. The Piegans were "frightened at the lesson they got, and have no wish for any further movement of troops this spring, or any more such severe punishment."

30. Jackson, *Piikani*, 178.

31. Arthur, *Kipp Trails*, and Ewers, *The Blackfeet*, 259–60, on Kipp's reputed role in killing the supposedly indestructible Blood chief Calf Shirt in Fort Benton.

32. Mountain Chief survived only another two years. He was shot dead in 1872 while trying to break up a fight between two drunken Piegans.

24: THE SPOILS OF WAR

1. Another library fund-raiser the following month featured a benefit performance by Jack Langrishe's traveling troupe. See Hedges diary, May 16 and June 24, 1870, Hedges Papers, Montana Historical Society Archives.

2. Sunderlee, "A Thrilling Event on the Yellowstone," *Helena Herald*, May 18, 1870. National Park historian Lee Whittlesey has found this legend further embroidered in a couple of classic works of fakelore: Charles M. Skinner, "A Yellowstone Tragedy," in *Myths and Legends of Our Own Land* (1896), 204–6; and Ella Clark, *Indian Legends of the Northern Rockies* (1966), 361–2. Both add the toothsome detail that the Crows committed suicide because they were being pursued and fired on by the U.S. Army; the soldiers supposedly stood on the riverbank and watched in awe as the raft swirled around in the rapids before vanishing in the spray, with the warriors staring back defiantly at their pursuers and singing their death song. Since there was no particular animosity between the Crows and the military, all this is even more implausible than the original elements of Sunderlee's story. Whittlesey implies, in fact, that the entire tale is an invention, since none of the four companions named by Sunderlee appears in the 1870 Montana census. Lee H. Whittlesey, *Storytelling in Yellowstone: Horse and Buggy Tour Guides*, Albuquerque: University of New Mexico Press, 2007, 21.

3. In 1877, Norris would become the second superintendent of Yellowstone National Park. See below, p.TK.

4. Haines, *Yellowstone Story*, Vol. 1, 103–4.

5. *Personal Memoirs of P. H. Sheridan, General, United States Army*, 550. On meeting with Folsom, Cook, and Peterson, see Robert E. Hartley, *Saving Yellowstone: The President Arthur Expedition of 1883*, Westminster, Colorado: Sniktau Publications/Exlibris, 2007, 15, note 11.

6. Langford, *Discovery*, 24. Hancock's interest in the upper Yellowstone for reasons of national defense echoes a peculiar suggestion that General Sherman had made three years earlier. At the same time as Acting Governor Meagher was raising his militia, and plans were being laid for the establishment of Fort Ellis and Fort Shaw, Sherman had proposed building a military post on Yellowstone Lake as a bulwark against the Sioux. What he knew of this remote location, and why he thought it would serve any strategic purpose, is a mystery, and despite all its normal enthusiasm for a military presence, the *Montana Post* had poured scorn on the idea. An editorial dated May 18, 1867, said: "By the way, that is where Sherman proposes to send his regulars, going up there to build a fort at the lake, probably to keep the trout from catching the blue-tailed flies. There has not been a

Sioux on the headwaters of the Yellowstone for 30 years, that Bridger affirms he knows from personal observation, and that none of the living Sioux have ever been there." Cited in Haines, *Yellowstone Story*, Vol. 1, 339, note 43.

7. Lubetkin, *Jay Cooke's Gamble*, 11.

8. Haines, *Yellowstone Story*, Vol. 1, 105; on Cooke's interest in Yellowstone, see Oberholtzer, *Jay Cooke*, Vol. 2, 226–36, and Henrietta M. Larson, *Jay Cooke: Private Banker*, Cambridge: Harvard University Press, 1936, 236 ff.

9. Langford, *Discovery*, xxxvii.

10. See pp. 112–13.

11. The letter is reproduced in Langford, *Discovery*, xxxvii–xxxviii.

12. Ibid., xxxix.

13. Ibid.

14. Cited in Hiram M. Chittenden, *The Yellowstone National Park*, Cincinatti, Robert Clarke Company, 1895, 69.

15. Hedges, "Eulogy for Henry D. Washburn," Hedges Papers, Montana Historical Society Archives.

16. According to Walter De Lacy, who was now working with Washburn, the general's enthusiasm for the expedition had grown after he heard stories of the geysers in Iceland from a friend in St. Louis who had visited them, and then was regaled with accounts of similar phenomena on the upper Yellowstone from a former miner named Collins Jack Baronett ("Yellowstone Jack"), who later became a fixture in the national park as guide and assistant superintendent and builder of a bridge across the river that still bears his name. See De Lacy, "A Trip Up the South Snake."

17. Haines believes that the potential profits to be made from a future Northern Pacific spur line to the upper Yellowstone was a primary motive for Hauser's decision to join the expedition. Introduction to Langford, *Discovery*, x.

18. It seems that there was no love lost between Everts and Langford when both men were working for the Department of Internal Revenue. A letter from Langford to Hauser, dated February 27, 1866, details a bitter dispute between the two men and mentions a petition to remove Everts from office. Hauser Papers, Montana Historical Society Archives.

19. Looking back on the expedition thirty-five years later, Langford took a less jaundiced view, saying that, "Jake has more wit and philosophy than I have given him credit of possessing." *Discovery*, 119.

20. Original in Montana Historical Society Archives.

21. Bartlett, *Nature's Yellowstone*, 165.

22. This raises the intriguing possibility that one of the packers may have been "Lonesome Charley Reynolds," Custer's favorite scout, who died at the Little Bighorn. From 1868 to 1872, before joining the Seventh Cavalry, Reynolds worked as a hunter and trapper, based at Fort Berthold in Dakota Territory. In 1875, he guided an expedition to Yellowstone National Park headed by Captain William Ludlow, but even before this, according to John S. Gray, "Charley had guided other expeditions and met other scientists"— including one of the 1872 Northern Pacific Railroad surveys of the Yellowstone Valley. Also, in his account of Truman Everts's experiences in 1870, Aubrey L. Haines refers to the packer on that expedition as "Charley" Reynolds, not "Charles." See Gray, "Last Rites for Lonesome Charley Reynolds," *Montana the Magazine of Western History* 13, 3 (Summer

1963), 40–51, and Haines, "Lost in the Yellowstone," *Montana the Magazine of Western History* 22, 3 (Summer 1972), 31–41. The evidence remains inconclusive, however.

23. Langford, "The Wonders of the Yellowstone," *Scribner's Monthly* II, 1 (May 1871): 2.

24. "Departure of the Expedition," *Helena Herald*, August 18, 1870, quoted in Haines, *Yellowstone Story*, Vol. 1, 108.

25. Smith, *Bozeman and the Gallatin Valley*, 113.

26. Ibid., 89.

27. Warren Gillette diary, Yellowstone National Park Archives.

28. Langford says that Hancock telegraphed this order to Baker on August 14. See *Discovery*, xxxviii–xxxix.

29. Langford, *Scribner's Monthly* II, 1 (May 1871), 3, and "Lecture presented by Nathaniel Pitt Langford." Doane's first biographers present a fanciful scene, source not given, in which the telegraphed order from General Hancock lay "almost crumpled" on Baker's desk and an empty whiskey bottle rattled around on the floor. Washburn, by this account, pulled rank and invoked reasons of national security; the army knew nothing of the territory to the south of Fort Ellis, and Baker had to understand the importance of sending out an experienced officer to conduct a reconnaissance. Bonney and Bonney, *Battle Drums and Geysers*, 201.

30. Langford, *Scribner's Monthly* II, 1 (May 1871), 3.

31. "Lecture presented by Nathaniel Pitt Langford."

32. Haines, introduction to *Discovery*, xvi–xvii.

33. Langford, *Discovery*, 5.

34. De Lacy, "A Trip Up the South Snake." Langford also says that Yellowstone Lake was "the proposed object of our visit." See "Lecture presented by Nathaniel Pitt Langford." De Lacy would have been an obvious candidate to join the 1870 expedition, especially since he was now working for Washburn. But he had been assigned to survey a possible Northern Pacific Railroad route through the valley of the Salmon River in Idaho, which set out in August at the same time as the Yellowstone explorers.

25: GRAND, GLOOMY, AND TERRIBLE

1. The principal journals are *Report of Lieutenant Gustavus C. Doane upon the So-called Yellowstone Expedition of 1870*, 41st Cong., 3d sess., Senate Exec. Doc. 51. Washington, D.C.: U.S. Government Printing Office, 1932, 113–48; Nathaniel P. Langford, *Diary of the Washburn Expedition to the Yellowstone and Firehole Rivers in the Year 1870*, St. Paul, Minnesota: F. J. Haynes, 1905, reprinted as *The Discovery of Yellowstone Park*, Lincoln: University of Nebraska Press, 1972; "Excerpts from the Diary of Samuel T. Hauser (August 17, 1870 to September 4, 1870)," transcribed by Aubrey L. Haines, Manuscript no. 249, Yellowstone Park Archives; "Journal of Judge Cornelius Hedges, *Contributions to the Montana Historical Society* 5 (1904), 370–94; "Manuscript Diary Kept by Warren Caleb Gillette During 1870 Expedition in Yellowstone Park Region," typescript copy in Yellowstone National Park Archives, acc. no. 919; and Henry D. Washburn, diary of 1870 expedition to Yellowstone. The Washburn diary remains in private ownership and has not been placed in any public archive; its contents were summarized by Lee Parsons, In-

dianapolis, Indiana, at "People and Place: The Human Experience in Greater Yellowstone," Fourth Biennial Conference on the Greater Yellowstone Ecosystem, October 12–15, 1997, Mammoth Hot Springs, Yellowstone National Park. Paul Schullery and Lee Whittlesey, *Myth and History in the Creation of Yellowstone National Park*, Lincoln: University of Nebraska Press, 2003, 99–102, give an exhaustive list of 40 published and unpublished accounts of the 1870 expedition, including later journalistic versions by Hedges in the *Helena Herald*, Langford in *Scribner's Monthly* and Trumbull in the *Rocky Mountain Daily Gazette* and the *Overland Monthly*.

2. At the very least, Langford has a serious tendency to exaggerate. He describes Bozeman as a thriving town of seven hundred (in fact, its population in 1870 was around one hundred); and the broad, fertile Gallatin Valley as larger than any of the New England states (in reality, it covers 325 square miles—Rhode Island is nearly four times that size). Later, he gives the maximum depth of the Grand Canyon of the Yellowstone as five thousand feet (it is twelve hundred) and estimates that it is fifty miles long (it is twenty).

3. "Report of Lieutenant Gustavus C. Doane," in Bonney and Bonney, *Battle Drums and Geysers*, 203–4. For ease of reference, future citations will use this source.

4. Langford saw this as his first opportunity to put the bumptious Smith in his place. "While several members of our party were blazing away with indifferent success, with the result that Jake was adding to his exchequer without damage to his hat, I could not resist the inclination to drop quietly out of sight behind a clump of bushes, where from my place of concealment I sent from my breech-loading Ballard repeating rifle four bullets in rapid succession, through the hat, badly riddling it. Jake inquired, 'Whose revolver is it that makes that loud report?' He did not discover the true state of the case, but removed the target with the ready acknowledgment that there were members of our party whose aim with a revolver was more accurate than he had thought. I think that I will make confession to him in a few days. I now wish that I had brought with me an extra hat. My own is not large enough for Jake's head." Langford, *Discovery*, 7–8.

5. Ibid., 6.

6. A good brief summary of Yellowstone geology and its relationship to the soil, vegetation, and ecology is Mary Meagher and Douglas B. Houston, *Yellowstone and the Biology of Time: Photographs Across a Century*, Norman: University of Oklahoma Press, 1998. See especially 217–22.

7. Langford, *Discovery*, 10. Trumbull treated the threat of Indian attack almost as a joke. Commenting on the variety of weapons carried by the explorers, he wrote, "We intended to hunt for all sorts of large game, Indians only excepted." He approved of posting a night guard on the camp, "in order to keep the Indians from breaking the Eighth Commandment" and said that the military escort, riding out ahead of the main group as "skirmishers," was "much commended by parties who had had experience in our 'late unpleasantness.'" Trumbull, "The Washburn Yellowstone Expedition," *Overland Monthly*, Vol. 6, Nos. 5, 6 (May–June 1871), 1.

8. Langford, *Scribner's Monthly* II, 1 (May 1871), 4. This does not square with Doane's August 12 letter to Washburn, cited at pp. 282–83, which suggests that the general was already seen as the official head of the expedition several days before it left Helena.

9. There were seven authors and seven variant spellings. Doane rendered it as Butler;

Langford said Boteler; Gillette preferred Bottler; Washburn opted for Botelier; Trumbull, Botteller. Hauser's version was Buttler; Hedges started with Boteler but then shifted to Boutelier.

10. The canyon got its name from "Yankee Jim" George, who operated a toll road there from 1873 to 1893, by which time the Yellowstone National Park spur line of the Northern Pacific Railroad, reaching as far as Cinnabar station, below the Devil's Slide, had made it redundant. The final portion of the railroad, from Cinnabar to the town of Gardiner, was completed in 1903.

11. Langford, *Discovery*, 14. In fact, the Devil's Slide is predominantly sandstone. Trumbull suggests that the name was probably chosen because it had already been given to a similar, smaller rock formation in Echo Canyon (Weber Canyon) in Utah, on the route of the Union Pacific Railroad. *Overland Monthly*, 2.

12. The route of the expedition on August 26, was across the northern flank of what would later be called Mount Everts.

13. Langford's group camped in a meadow by a stream, which he called Antelope Creek. Hauser called it Lost Trail Creek. In the end it acquired the name of Rescue Creek, after Truman Everts was found there by Jack Baronett.

14. Bonney and Bonney, *Battle Drums and Geysers*, 244–5.

15. Other diarists refer to it as Warm Springs Creek, and Trumbull says this name had been given to it by "early prospectors." *Overland Monthly*, 3.

16. The mineralogist who accompanied Ferdinand Vandeveer Hayden's 1871 Yellowstone expedition, Albert Peale, made the same mistake. See Merrill, *Yellowstone and the Great West*, 137 and 263, note 10.

17. "Camp Comfort" is now the site of the large parking lot and gift shop at the head of the Tower Fall trail.

18. This is the figure both Hauser and Doane give in their journals; Langford's reconstructed diary says 110. *Discovery*, 19. None of the estimates was very accurate; the actual height of Tower Fall is 132 feet.

19. In *Discovery*, 22, Langford says, "The weight of testimony was so evenly balanced that I shall hesitate long before I believe either side of this part of the story." This seems odd, since he and Hauser were close friends and business partners. The whole affair is actually very confusing, since Trumbull himself wrote that, "Another of the party"—not himself evidently—"was in favor of the name Minaret (Minne Rhett); but that was too apparent, and he was outvoted." *Overland Monthly*, 3.

20. Yellowstone National Park historian Lee H. Whittlesey enumerates more than fifty features with diabolic names of this kind. See Whittlesey, *Yellowstone Place Names*, Helena: Montana Historical Society, 1988.

21. Langford, *Discovery*, 24. The area on the south side of Mount Washburn is now known as Washburn Hot Springs. The stream that flows through it is Sulfur Creek.

22. Psalms 8:3 reads, "When I consider thy heavens, the work of thy fingers, the moon and the stars, which thou hast ordained;" and verse 4 continues, "What is man, that thou art mindful of him? and the son of man, that thou visitest him?"

23. William Cronon, "The Trouble With Wilderness," in Cronon, ed., *Uncommon Ground: Toward Reinventing Nature*, New York: W. W. Norton, 1995, cited in Schullery, *Searching for Yellowstone*, 17, note 1.

24. The group that rode to the summit of Mount Washburn included Langford, Hauser, Gillette, Stickney, Trumbull, and Doane. Richard Bartlett says that Doane did not accompany them. For such a scrupulous historian, this is a bizarre assertion. He ascribes the lieutenant's absence to the excruciating pain he was suffering from his infected thumb, but this is implausible given the many activities, much more arduous than this, that Doane took part in over the next few days after several more sleepless nights. And on several occasions he went exploring with only his orderly, Private O'Connell, or another member of the military escort. Although none of the other diarists mentions Doane by name, his description of the view from the top is by far the most detailed, and unlike Langford there is no reason to suspect him of misstating or exaggerating the facts. See Bartlett, *Nature's Yellowstone*, 173.

25. The actual height of Mount Washburn is 10,243 feet.

26. For Doane's full description, see Bonney and Bonney, *Battle Drums and Geysers*, 262–5.

26: NINE NIGHTS WITHOUT SLEEP

1. The authoritative work on the subject is Robert B. Smith and Lee J. Siegel, *Windows into the Earth: The Geologic Story of Yellowstone and Grand Teton National Parks*, New York: Oxford University Press, 2000.

2. See Rebecca Bedell, *The Anatomy of Nature: Geology and American Landscape Painting*, Princeton: Princeton University Press, 2002.

3. Humboldt, *"Mémoire sur une nouvelle espèce de Pimelode, jetée par les volcans du Royaume de Quito"* (1805). See Alexander von Humboldt and Aimé Bonpland, *Essay on the Geography of Plants*, Chicago: University of Chicago Press (2008), 28.

4. Cited in McPhee, *Annals of the Known World*. For more on Hutton and Lyell, see Ibid., 72–9 and 95–8.

5. However, Langford did not know of the geysers in New Zealand or other parts of Asia. He says that other than Yellowstone, the phenomenon is only found in "Iceland and Thibet." *Scribner's Monthly*, II, 2 (June 1871), 127.

6. Langford, *Discovery*, 37.

7. Ibid., 29. By this time, ten days into the trip, Langford was ready to strangle Smith, who had almost set fire to the camp a couple of days earlier. "Jacob is indolent and fond of slumber," Langford wrote, "and I think he resents my remark to him the other day that he could burn more and gather less wood than any man I ever camped with. He has dubbed me 'The Yellowstone Sharp.' Good! I am not ashamed to have the title."

8. *Helena Herald*, October 15, 1870.

9. In fact, the Lower Falls of the Yellowstone measure 109 feet, and the Upper Falls 308.

10. *Overland Monthly*, 5. He reckoned that the Lower Falls carried half as much water as the American Falls but were twice as high; they were the same height as the Vernal Falls, but the volume of water was five times greater.

11. Doane, "Report," in Bonney and Bonney, *Battle Drums and Geysers*, 277.

12. Doane knew nothing about thermophiles, of course. There was no serious understanding or study of these exotic organisms until almost a century after the 1870 expedition. The molecular biologist Kary Mullis was awarded the 1993 Nobel Prize for chemistry for his

use of the Taq polymerase enzyme from Yellowstone thermophiles to develop a gene-replicating procedure known as polymerase chain reaction (PCR), which has been called the "Swiss Army knife of molecular biology." See Schullery, *Searching for Yellowstone*, 1.

13. According to Langford, "Mr. Hauser, whose experience as an engineer and with projectile forces entitles his opinion to credit, estimates from the particles of mud upon the high trees, and the distance to which they were thrown that the mud had been thrown, in this explosion, to the height of between 300 and 400 feet. By actual measurement we found particles of this mud 186 feet from the edge of the crater." *Discovery*, 44. Today's Mud Volcano is only a shadow of what was seen by the 1870 expedition. Even by the time Langford returned to Yellowstone with the 1872 Hayden survey, the "volcano" had exploded, leaving only a small, ragged crater.

14. Hedges had thrown himself clear of a blinding cloud of steam. Langford's mishap, by his own account, was yet another of his near-death experiences. On September 3, he says, "as I was unconcernedly passing by [a] spring, my weight made the border suddenly slough off beneath my feet. General Washburn noticed the sudden cracking of the incrustation before I did, and I was aroused to a sense of my peril by his shout of alarm, and had sufficient presence of mind to fall suddenly backwards at full length upon the sound crust, whence, with my feet and legs extended over the spring, I rolled to a place of safety. But for General Washburn's shout of alarm, in another instant I would have been precipitated into this boiling pool of alum." *Discovery*, 46–7.

27: THE DEEP WOODS

1. Doane, "Report," Bonney and Bonney, *Battle Drums and Geysers*, 304–5.

2. Langford records the vote as six for, three against, which suggests that only the civilians, and not Doane, had a say in the decision. *Discovery*, 55.

3. While these two peaks were marked as Mount Langford and Mount Doane on the Langford-Washburn map, the mountains that bear those names today are in a different location, ten miles or so to the north. The change was made by Ferdinand Hayden during his 1871 Yellowstone expedition. The Mount Langford of 1870 is now Colter Peak (10,683 feet). The original Mount Doane is now Mount Schurz (11,139 feet), named for the Union Army general who became Secretary of the Interior in 1877. See Bonney and Bonney, *Battle Drums and Geysers*, 312–3.

4. See p. 295.

5. Langford, *Discovery*, 60–1.

6. There is a pleasure in the pathless woods,
   There is a rapture on the lonely shore,
   There is society, where none intrudes,
   By the deep sea, and music in its roar:
   I love not man the less, but Nature more,
   From these our interviews in which I steal
   From all I may be, or have been before,
   To mingle with the Universe, and feel
   What I can ne'er express, yet cannot all conceal.

7. Three days later, after remaining behind to continue the search for Everts, Warren Gillette ran into a man in the woods who said he was one of a group of four who had come up the Snake River. Gillette said that "from his illy repressed nervous manner took him for a man who was fleeing justice." Gillette diary, September 17, 1870. Yellowstone National Park Archives.

8. Present-day Mount Sheridan.

9. Hedges noted that he caught 41 two-pound trout in a single session on September 12. Doane reported that on the 10th Private Williamson brought in an even more staggering catch—52 trout in less than an hour.

10. Langford, *Discovery*, 96–7. This passage does not appear in Langford's 1871 articles for *Scribner's Monthly*, in which his predictions of a mass influx of visitors are much more tied up with the future interests of the Northern Pacific Railroad.

11. Cited in Ibid., 98.

    As one who long in thickets and in brakes
    Entangled, winds now this way and now that,
    His devious course uncertain, seeking home,
    Or having long in miry ways been foiled
    And sore discomfited, from slough to slough
    Plunging, and half despairing of escape,
    If chance at length he finds a green-sward
    Smooth and faithful to his foot, his spirits rise.
    He chirrups brisk his ear-erecting steed,
    And winds his way with pleasure and with ease.

12. Hedges, undated memoir, "Lost in the Wilderness," Hedges Papers, Montana Historical Society Archives.

28: LOST AND FOUND

1. The Baronett interview appears in Theodore Gerrish, *Life in the World's Wonderland*, Biddeford, Maine: Press of the Biddeford Journal, 1887, 236–40, cited in Bartlett, *Nature's Yellowstone*, 184. Otherwise the story of Everts's ordeal is based on his own account, "Thirty-Seven Days of Peril," *Scribner's Monthly*, 7.1 (November 1871), 1–17, reprinted in *Contributions to the Montana Historical Society* 5 (1904), 395–427.

2. He refers to this mistakenly as "Mount Everts," which was the name Cornelius Hedges had given three days earlier to another, smaller mountain they had climbed together several miles back along the trail. See Hedges diary, September 8, 1870, Hedges Papers, Montana Historical Society Archives. The mountain Everts saw across the lake was actually Mount Sheridan, named the following year by the Barlow-Heap party.

3. Aubrey Haines says this was the name given to it years earlier by Hart Hunney, one of Captain Bonneville's trappers, who was reputedly killed by the Crows in 1852. Haines, *Yellowstone Place Names: Mirrors of History*, Boulder, University Press of Colorado, 1996, 35.

4. Langford discusses the camas root (which he calls "both flour and potatoes for several wandering nations") and its close relative, the yampa, in "The Ascent of Mount Hayden, Grand Teton 1872: A New Chapter of Western Discovery," *Scribner's Monthly* VI, 2 (June

1873), 129–57. See especially 135. This lengthy passage is repeated verbatim in his "diary" of the 1870 expedition, a good illustration of how this much later composite text is drawn from a variety of earlier sources.

5. The depiction of the lakes that lie to the southwest of Yellowstone Lake is one of the few major inaccuracies in Doane's map of the expedition, as rendered later by Lieutenant Edward Maguire, chief engineer for the Department of Dakota. Shoshone Lake, which Doane calls Madison Lake, is much too small, and completely the wrong shape. Lewis Lake and Heart Lake appear to be a single connected body of water, while Jackson Lake appears to be seven or eight miles west of Lewis/Heart Lake. In fact it lies about twenty miles farther south. The Doane-Maguire map is reproduced as a large foldout insert in Bonney and Bonney, *Battle Drums and Geysers*, 198–9. See also the discussion of the Doane-Maguire and Washburn maps in Ibid., 399–403.

6. Langford, *Discovery*, 105.

7. Doane, "Report," in Bonney and Bonney, *Battle Drums and Geysers*, 344.

8. Washburn, "The Yellowstone Expedition," *Helena Herald*, September 28, 1870.

9. See pp. 355–58.

10. One Samuel W. Langhorne published two highly colored reports in the *Helena Herald* after interviewing Everts several times during his recovery at Fort Ellis. By these accounts, Everts also spent two days chasing a toad and frequently ate fish raw, including two large ones, which he caught on a line made of strips of canvas tied together. It is hard to tell which one of them, Everts or Langhorne, is embroidering the facts. *Helena Herald*, October 26 and October 28, 1870.

11. Haines, *Yellowstone Story*, Vol. 1, 132.

12. *Helena Herald*, September 28, 1870.

13. *Helena Herald*, November 14, 1870.

14. When Baronett visited Everts many years later in New York, he got a cold reception, and declared that "he wished he had let the son-of-a-gun roam." R. C. Wallace, *A Few Memories of a Long Life* (privately printed, 1900), cited in Bartlett, *Nature's Yellowstone*, 187.

29: THE PROFESSIONALS

1. Oddly, Doane dated his report December 15, 1875, though he obviously meant 1870.

2. Hancock to Doane, February 9, 1871, cited in Bonney and Bonney, *Battle Drums and Geysers*, 211.

3. "We are happy to announce that this paper was received and its account of the geological and physical character of the remarkable section of which it treats is very interesting. We were about having it printed when an ascertainment [was made] that a . . . copy . . . had been ordered published by Congress." Cited in Bonney and Bonney, 211.

4. Foster, *Strange Genius*, 225. Doane's report was published as Senate Executive Document No. 51, 41st Congress, 3rd Session.

5. Hayden, *Preliminary Report*, 8.

6. *The New York Times*, October 15, 1870. The *Herald* told its readers that, "We have spared neither pains nor expense in giving the world these descriptions. . . . These articles have been largely copied by the press, and have furnished the basis for numerous and exten-

sive leading editorials." *Helena Herald*, October 26, 1870. Cited in Jackson, "Early Exploration," 207.

7. *Helena Herald*, November 14, 1870.

8. *Overland Monthly*, 431–7 and 489–96.

9. Langford, *Scribner's Monthly*, 2, 1 (May 1871), 1-17, and 2, 2 (June 1871), 113–28. One letter to the editor called Langford "the greatest liar in the Northwest," but this kind of reaction, which had undermined the publication of Cook and Folsom's diary a year earlier, was now rare, given the standing and credibility of the 1870 explorers and the comprehensiveness of their reports. Langford letter to Miller, 1906.

10. *Scribner's*, cited in Bonney and Bonney, *Battle Drums and Geysers*, 405–6, note 1.

11. According to Langford, the explorers had tried to recruit a photographer in Helena, but were unable to find one with the necessary talent—or one willing to brave the hazards of the expedition or make such a long trip without proper compensation. *Discovery*, 184.

12. *Scribner's Monthly*, 3, 1 (November 1871), 17.

13. *Scribner's Monthly*, 4, 1 (May 1872), 120.

14. In a characteristic note to Hauser, Langford wrote, "On the principle that one good turn deserves another, I will suggest that, should your operations prove lucrative, and extend to other posts, a finger in the pie would not come amiss." Undated handwritten document in Montana Historical Society Archives.

15. The speaker's brother, John E. Blaine, took Washburn's place as surveyor general of Montana after his death.

16. *The New York Times*, January 22, 1871.

17. Cited in Haines, *Yellowstone Story*, Vol. 1, 140. Haines also speculates that the Northern Pacific may have decided to curtail the lecture series because it did not want to provoke a tidal wave of emigration to Montana. See Ibid., 348, note 120. Langford himself wrote to Jay Cooke from Utica on March 4, saying that he was in better health and ready to come to New York and Philadelphia for more lectures, but Ogontz was the only one that ever materialized.

18. Powell is a partial exception to this rule, in that his famous exploration of the Colorado was not officially endorsed by the army. But he was many things that Doane was not: a hero of the Civil War, a renowned anthropologist and geologist, and a noted professor at Illinois Wesleyan University. When the Chief of Army Engineers learned of Powell's Colorado trip, he willingly suspended the military's own plans. In his annual report for 1869, he said, "The continuation of the exploration of this river above Callville, Utah, has been postponed in view of the enterprise now in progress under the direction of Professor Powell." Report of the Chief of Army Engineers, in "Annual Report of the Secretary of War," 41st Cong., 2nd sess., H.R. Exec. Doc. 1, Pt. II (1869), 68, cited in Goetzmann, *Exploration and Empire*, 397, note 5.

19. E. M. Baker to Lieutenant Colonel E. M. Elliot, 1st Cavalry, Beneria [Benicia], California, February 12, 1871. Montana Historical Society Archives.

20. Baker to Assistant Adjutant General, Department of Dakota, February 12, 1871; Fort Ellis, Letters Sent, 1867–1886, RG 393, NARA, cited in Scott, *Yellowstone Denied*, 86–7 and 273, note 3.

21. See pp. 345–46.

22. Barlow graduated 14th in the class, Custer last. See Ralph Kirshner and George A.

Plimpton, *The Class of 1861: Custer, Ames, and Their Classmates After West Point*, Carbondale: Southern Illinois University Press, 1989.

23. J. W. Barlow and David P. Heap, *Report of a Reconnaissance of the Upper Yellowstone in 1871*, 42nd. Cong., 2nd Sess., Senate Exec. Doc. 66, SN-1479, Vol. E., 4–5.

24. Haines says that it was "an idea that came to him that evening. . . . What Hayden got from that lecture was . . . the idea to capitalize upon the current interest in the Yellowstone region by asking Congress for funds to explore it officially." *Yellowstone Story*, Vol. 1, 138. Both of Hayden's biographers take issue with this. Cassidy says that, "contrary to traditional opinion it is doubtful that Langford's lecture sent Hayden to Yellowstone the following summer." *Entrepreneur of Science*, 117. Foster concludes that the only sources that support the idea of Hayden's epiphany are Chittenden's 1895 book, *The Yellowstone National Park*, which Foster thinks succumbed to the turn-of-the-century notion of Hayden as an impulsive publicist rather than a serious scientist, and the memoir of the photographer William Henry Jackson, which was written in 1936. In fact, not even the Chittenden book goes as far as Foster asserts. All it says is that Hayden heard Langford's Washington lecture, and that, "The direct result of the expedition of 1870 was to cause the U.S. Geological [and Geographical] Survey to change its program for the season of 1871." Chittenden, 74, 75. Not quite the same thing.

25. Baker, "Report of Operations, 1871." The order was reaffirmed by the headquarters of the Department of Dakota on May 26.

26. Hayden to Allen, March 17, 1871, in Merrill, *Yellowstone and the Great West*, 28.

27. Hayden also had the secondary purpose of exploring a possible railroad route through Two Ocean Pass and the Grand Canyon of the Snake River, "at the instigation of Jay Cooke & Co., who contemplate running a branch road through this Pass to connect with the Central Pacific, if practicable." See Foster, *Strange Genius*, 201, 207.

28. Goetzmann, *Exploration and Empire*, 199. This is in fact the central thesis of Goetzmann's masterful work.

29. The purpose of the Nebraska survey was transparently political, to encourage settlement and map the suitability of the territory for farming, mining, ranching, and other economic activities. To his later embarrassment, Hayden identified himself with the bizarre "rain-follows-the-plow" theory of agriculture, which originated in Europe and was widely accepted in the mid-nineteenth century but totally discredited by 1890. See Foster, *Strange Genius*, 181–2, ff., and Goetzmann, *Exploration and Empire*, 496.

30. Hayden to Allen, April 13, 1871, in Merrill, *Yellowstone and the Great West*, 15. In the event it was Allen, fifty-eight years old, frail and neurotic, who failed to pull through, withdrawing before the expedition left Fort Ellis.

31. William Henry Jackson with Howard R. Driggs, *The Pioneer Photographer: Rocky Mountain Adventures with a Camera*, Yonkers, New York: World Book Company, 1929, 100–1. These young men included William B. Logan, son of one of Hayden's most powerful patrons, Senator John A. ("Black Jack") Logan of Illinois, and Chester M. Dawes, son of Representative Henry L. Dawes of Massachusetts. Hayden said that he had taken on six men because of their political connections and turned away another fifty. See Foster, *Strange Genius*, 227.

32. Jackson lent Crissman one of his own cameras as a replacement. See *Pioneer Photographer*, 114–5; Merrill, *Yellowstone and the Great West*, 259, note 8. On Crissman's work

generally, both during the 1871 expedition and later, see Steven B. Jackson, "Joshua Crissman: Yellowstone's Forgotten Photographer," *Montana the Magazine of Western History*, 49 (Summer 1999), 24–37.

33. Goetzmann and Goetzmann call Jackson's wagon train images "probably our most accurate surviving visual renditions of the experience." *West of the Imagination*, 116.

34. Peter B. Hales, *William Henry Jackson and the Transformation of the American Landscape*, Philadelphia: Temple University Press, 1988, 37.

35. Jackson himself did not coin the phrase, although there is no evidence to show who did. See Stephen Ambrose, *Nothing Like It in the World: The Men Who Built the Transcontinental Railroad, 1863–1869*, New York: Simon & Schuster, 2000, 351.

36. Hales notes that Jackson mentioned this incident only in his diaries and later expurgated it from his two volumes of memoirs, *Time Exposure* and *Pioneer Photographer*, in which he says only that he met Hayden in Omaha.

37. Nettleton also mentioned the possibility of the famous painter Albert Bierstadt joining the Hayden survey, but that idea never materialized.

38. Fritiof Fryxell, *Thomas Moran, Explorer in Search of Beauty,* East Hampton, New York: East Hampton Free Library, 1958, 69.

39. For an excellent discussion of how painters like Moran and Bierstadt saw the Western landscape, see Nash, *Wilderness and the American Mind*, 78–83.

40. Stephen Pyne, *How the Canyon Became Grand: A Short History*, New York: Viking, 1998, 89, citing G. W. Sheldon, *American Painters* (1879), 124–5. Pyne describes this approach as "landscape as opera."

41. Scott, *Yellowstone Denied*, 87.

42. Hayden learned of Sheridan's plans only when he arrived at Fort Hall, Idaho, on June 21. Hayden to Spencer Baird, Report no. 4, June 22, 1871, in Merrill, *Yellowstone and the Great West*, 85. On Barlow's orders, see Sheridan to Captain D. P. Hancock, Senate Exec. Doc. 66, 42nd Cong., 2nd Sess., 1, cited in Jackson, "Early Exploration," 224–5.

43. Peale journal, July 18, 2010, in Merrill, *Yellowstone and the Great West*, 122.

44. Barlow, *Reconnaissance*, 3.

45. Merrill, *Yellowstone and the Great West*, 18.

46. Extravagant reports of danger appeared in the *Bozeman Avant Courier.* The agent, "Major" F. D. Pease (the rank was honorific, not military), "There is not the slightest foundation to these rumors, and they must have been put in circulation by some evil disposed person or persons, for the sake of creating excitement among the citizens. . . . Such conduct is to say the least villianous [sic] and its consequence liable to lead to very serious results." Cited in Brown, *Plainsmen of the Yellowstone*, 430.

47. Hayden referred to Mammoth as White Mountain Hot Springs; Barlow called it Soda Mountain.

48. Just two days after Hayden's arrival, one Helena paper carried a detailed report from a party of visitors from Bozeman. They not only hailed the healing powers of Mammoth Hot Springs but spoke of Chesnut's description of other "curiosities and sights, many of which the Washburn party are ignorant of." "The Mineral Springs of the Yellowstone—Wonderful Health Restoring Qualities," *Rocky Mountain Gazette*, July 24, 1871. Hayden himself wrote, "Around these springs were gathered, at this time, a number of invalids, with cutaneous diseases, and they were most emphatic in their favorable expressions in

regard to the sanitary effects. The most remarkable effect seems to be on persons afflicted with syphilitic disease of long standing." Hayden, *Preliminary Report*, 5.

49. Immediately after Hayden's visit, one Matthew McGuirk filed a 160-acre claim under the Homestead Act to operate "McGuirk's Medical Springs" on the Boiling River, which flows into the Gardner below Mammoth Hot Springs. He was subsequently evicted. Haines, *Yellowstone Story*, vol. 1, 144, 198, 218.

50. Hales says that Jackson had brought along two new cameras—a $6\frac{1}{2} \times 9$ and an 8×10 that allowed him to shoot deeper and more dramatic images than his old 5×8 half-plates. *William Henry Jackson*, 61. Goetzmann, *Exploration and Empire*, 604–5, provides a detailed list of Jackson's equipment on the 1870 survey, citing Robert Taft, *Photography and the American Scene*, New York: Dover Publications, 1964.

51. William Henry Jackson with Karl Brown, *Time Exposure*, New York: G. P. Putnam's Sons, 1940, 198.

52. Hayden, *Preliminary Report*, 107. There was no indication yet of the huge eruptions of the Excelsior Geyser that would excite later tourists; see Lee H. Whittlesey, "Monarch of All These Mighty Wonders: Tourists and Yellowstone's Excelsior Geyser, 1881–1890," *Montana the Magazine of Western History* 40 (Spring 1990), cover and 2–15.

53. Hayden to Baird, Report No. 7, August 8, 1871, in Merrill, *Yellowstone and the Great West*, 153.

54. See Merrill, *Yellowstone and the Great West*, 269, note 26, on the conflicting accounts in the diaries and memoirs of members of the Hayden party on the first encounter with Doane. She concludes that Doane did not actually meet Hayden until August 9.

55. E. M. Baker to Assistant Adjutant General, Deptartment of Dakota, St. Paul, Minnesota, Report of Operations 12/31/71. Baker notes sardonically that Hayden could release the escort because he "was not travelling in a country frequented by Hostile Indians." His report makes no mention of the Northern Pacific survey; that story comes from the *Philadelphia Inquirer*, August 5, 1871, cited in Merrill, *Yellowstone and the Great West*, 269.

56. Everyone else in the party used "dog tents" small enough to be folded and carried in a knapsack. Jackson, *Pioneer Photographer*, 106–7.

57. Hayden wrote that the lake was "not more than one or two hundred yards in width" and "has no real existence." In fact, Bridger Lake is more than a mile wide. Haines says, "one suspects the geologist of not wanting the lake to exist," perhaps because of his bitterness at Jim Bridger's failure to take him to the upper Yellowstone in 1860. *Yellowstone Story*, vol. 1, 149 and 350, note 140.

58. Doane, Service Record, Montana State University Libraries, Bozeman, Burlingame Special Collection 2211.

59. Hayden to Secretary of the Interior Columbus Delano, August 28, 1871, reprinted in *Helena Herald*, September 23, 1871; on Doane's role, Hayden, *Preliminary Report*, 9. To add insult to injury, Hayden ignored the Washburn party's naming of Mount Doane and Mount Langford, and attached those names to other peaks in the Absarokas, about ten miles farther north.

60. Merrill, *Yellowstone and the Great West*, 204.

61. For more than a century, it was believed that only sixteen of Hine's prints had survived, but another seven stereographs were discovered in 1999, and five more turned

up later. The stereographs included the first image ever recorded of the eruption of Old Faithful.

62. Cited in Scott, *Yellowstone Denied*, 86.

63 Record Group 57, National Archives, Records of the Department of the Interior, Geological Survey, letters received by F. V. Hayden, 1871. The reference is to Republican Congressman and Northern Pacific booster William D. "Pig Iron" Kelley of Pennsylvania.

30: THE FINAL FRONTIER

1. Hayden to Secretary of the Interior Carl Schurz, February 21, 1879, in U.S. Congress, House Exec. Doc. 75, 45th Cong., 2nd Sess.

2. Clagett to William R. Marshall, Secretary of Minnesota Historical Society, July 14, 1894, cited in Langford, *Discovery*, xliv–xlviii.

3. In addition to Hayden, Langford, and Clagett, William Henry Jackson, Sam Hauser, Truman Everts, Walter Trumbull (now working as secretary of the Senate Committee on the Judiciary), Senator Samuel Pomeroy of Kansas, Representative Mark Dunnell of Minnesota, and Representative Henry Dawes of Massachusetts (whose son, Chester, had been one of the young fishermen-junketers on the Hayden expedition), all left their fingerprints on the legislation. David Folsom and Cornelius Hedges may also have played some role. Hedges's diary suggests that he did not leave Montana, at least during 1871, but it seems likely that he conferred with Langford about the legislative strategy before Langford left for Washington in December.

4. The debate over the bill is described in detail in Haines, *Exploration and Establishment*, 110–28.

5. Dawes said that, "[T]he Indians can no more live there than they can on the precipitous sides of the Yosemite Valley." House *Congressional Globe*, 42nd Cong. 2nd Sess., February 27, 1872, 1243. In fact, the Miwoks lived perfectly successfully in Yosemite, just as the Sheepeaters did in the upper Yellowstone. See Nabokov and Loendorf, *Restoring a Presence*, 64.

6. *The Nation*, October 12, 1871. For more on the nineteenth-century commercialization of the Falls, see Ginger Strand, *Inventing Niagara: Beauty, Power, and Lies,* New York: Simon and Schuster, 2008, especially 59–73.

7. Langford, "Notes on the Yellowstone National Park Bill," undated manuscript, Yellowstone National Park Archives. Hayden made much the same argument, warning of squatters "taking possession of the springs and destroying the beautiful decoration." See Hayden, "The Wonders of the West," *Scribner's Monthly*, February 1872.

8. Peter Matthiesen, "Introduction," in Catlin, *North American Indians*, 7.

9. George Catlin, *Letters and Notes on the Manners, Customs, and Condition of the North American Indians*, New York: Wiley and Putnam, 1841, vol. 2, 156–7; and Harold McCracken, *George Catlin and the Old Frontier*, New York: The Dial Press, 1959, 15–6.

10. The best survey of tourism and parks during the period is John F. Sears, *Sacred Places: American Tourist Attractions in the Nineteenth Century*, New York: Oxford University Press, 1989.

11. Schullery, *Searching for Yellowstone*, 247.

12. "The Folsom-Cook Exploration," *Contributions to the Montana Historical Society* 5 (1904).

13. It has been suggested that Langford's decision to locate and publish his original diary was motivated by a visit in 1903 from General Washburn's daughter, Lelia de Motte. Parsons, "People and Place."

14. In fact, no member of the party did stake a claim to any land in the upper Yellowstone, even though many others tried to do so after the expedition returned. This suggests at least circumstantially that some more altruistic scheme was discussed before the end of the expedition. I am grateful to Paul Schullery for this point. Author's conversation with Schullery, July 2010.

15. *Helena Herald*, November 9, 1870.

16. Hedges's own journal entry for September 20, 1870, says only, "Didn't sleep well last night—got to thinking of home and business." See "Journal of Judge Cornelius Hedges," *Contributions to the Historical Society of Montana* 5 (1904), 370–94.

17. "Lecture presented by Nathaniel Pitt Langford."

18. Langford wrote to Hiram Chittenden that the January 23, 1871, edition of the *New York Tribune* cited his comment that, "This is probably the most remarkable region of natural attractions in the world; and, while we already have our Niagara and Yosemite, this new field of wonders should be at once withdrawn from occupancy, and set apart as a public National Park for the enjoyment of the American people for all time." However, Chittenden pointed out to him that the article did not appear in the *Tribune* on that date. Chittenden, *Yellowstone National Park*, 92. This led Aubrey Haines to conclude that Langford fabricated the article. For an extended discussion, see Schullery and Whittlesey, *Myth and Creation*, 16–9.

19. Langford Papers, Minnesota Historical Society. An entry for August 9—"Dr. Hayden 915 "L" Street (office), 919 "L" Street (boards)—raises the intriguing question of whether Langford and Hayden may have met before the Hayden expedition. Hayden did have an office in Washington at this time, although it is not registered at this address.

20. It also has passages that strongly echo the language in Doane's report, as well as others that are lifted verbatim from Langford's 1872 article in *Scribner's Monthly* on the second Hayden survey of Yellowstone, which he accompanied. There are also extended direct quotations from members of the expedition, which seems implausible in a bona fide diary, but that may be more a question of poetic license.

21. Langford to Hedges, February 26, 1905, copy in Hedges Papers, Montana Historical Society Archives.

22. Among the many points Haines cites as evidence of Langford's moral turpitude are a May 8, 1865, letter to Sam Hauser discussing the personal income that could be made by the collection of taxes over and above the modest target set by the federal government. This was a common practice in territories where the writ of the authorities was limited. Allowing the tax collector to keep a percentage on additional revenues served as an incentive that benefited both him and the government. Haines also points to Langford's insistence that after reading the letter Hauser should "burn it up." But this has nothing to do with the tax-collecting issue. It's about Langford's embarrassment after boasting to his family that he had accompanied Hauser on "<u>our</u> Yellowstone trip"—which Haines takes to mean the gold-hunting expedition that Hauser made with James Stuart in 1863.

Haines also says that Langford and Hauser's ability to set up the First National Bank in Helena was an indication of dirty dealing, since "both were poor men when they arrived." This is debatable. As a young banker in the 1850s, Langford became a partner in the firm of William Marshall, who later became governor of Minnesota, investing heavily in lucrative land and real estate deals in St. Paul (which was fast becoming a boomtown), and in railroad stock in Kansas. Haines condemns Langford as "a weak character . . . a coattail rider, dependent on family and friends for the influence which got him jobs and favors." He certainly benefited from the influence of others—but that is precisely why his business career in St. Paul prospered. See Haines, letter to Robert Utley, February 3, 1972, citing Orton, "Some Scattered Thoughts." Orton himself does not even reach an especially damning conclusion about Langford. He simply says that there is an "implication by ommission [sic]" that Langford's early career was advanced by family connections—which is indisputably true. His last word is simply that, "N. P. Langford did his best and it was quite well."

23. *New North West*, January 27, 1872. Langford credited Clagett as the person most responsible for the movement to create a national park.

24. This was also suggested many years later by Charles Cook, who even told of having a similar campfire discussion with David Folsom near the junction of the Madison and the Firehole at the end of their 1869 expedition. According to this version, Folsom said, "'The government ought not to allow anyone to locate here at all.'—'That's right,' I [Cook] said, 'It ought to be kept for the public in some way.'—We knew that as soon as the wonderful character of the country was generally known outside, there would be plenty of people hurrying in to get possession unless something were done." But Cook was eighty-three when he said this—and his memory of events fifty years earlier may well have been distorted by age and the passage of time. "Remarks of C. W. Cook."

25. Kuppens, "On the Origins of the Yellowstone National Park." Meagher's mention of a national park and Hedges's presence when the idea was articulated are accepted without comment in, for example, Bartlett, *Nature's Yellowstone*, 147; Bonney and Bonney, *Battle Drums and Geysers*, 371; Haines, *Yellowstone Story*, Vol. 1, 90, 103, 163; Haines, foreword to *Discovery*, xix; Schullery, *Searching for Yellowstone*, 59; Schullery and Whittlesey, *Myth and History*, 56. Haines also unquestioningly accepts Cook's 1922 recollections of his campfire discussion with Folsom, an equally fragile source so long after the event.

26. Writing in response to a reader's letter, the *Helena Herald* said, "It was on the way home from [the 1870] expedition that Mr. Hedges first suggested the propriety of making a national park of it." The phrase *on the way home* lends credence to the idea that there was some kind of a discussion at the time, whether or not it took place around a campfire at Madison Junction. This brief article, entitled "Who Were the Discoverers of Wonderland?" was found by the author, tattered and torn in half, in the Montana Historical Society Archives. It is undated, but three advertisements for local businesses appear on the reverse of the page—Reeder and Helmick, Mineral Surveyors; Chris Mockel's Atlantic Hall; and R. L. Scott's Novelty Carriage Works. From an examination of their addresses in city directories, the date of publication can be narrowed down to 1885–1890—when Hedges was a special correspondent for the paper. The *Herald*, in other words, and by inference Hedges himself, is alluding to the idea of a campfire discussion, or something resembling it, at least four years before it was mentioned by Langford.

27. Hedges, "Lost in the Wilderness." From references in the text ("Twenty-six years ago this region was a pathless wilderness"), this appears to have been written in 1896.

28. "Journal of Cornelius Hedges." This raises further questions about the extent to which Langford was really guilty of fabrication, since Hedges's journal was published a year earlier, and the language ("the uniting of all our efforts") is strikingly similar to Langford's "untiring work and concerted action." Writing to Hedges on February 26, 1905, having already read his friend's diary, Langford says that his own has just been transcribed. So while Langford may not have made any reference to a campfire discussion or a national park in his original field journal, he was not necessarily inventing the episode out of whole cloth thirty-five years later.

29. Langford to Hedges, November 24, 1905. Copy in Hedges Papers, Montana Historical Society Archives.

31: NORTHERN PACIFIC

1. Haines, *Yellowstone Story*, Vol. 1, 180.

2. Schullery and Whittlesey, who generally share Haines's negative view of Langford, acknowledge this point. Although they say that "the glow of altruism is tarnished by the corrosion of commerce" in his promotion of the railroad, they also concede that he was a man of his time, when "boosterism was regarded as good citizenship." See *Myth and History*, 31.

3. Roberts had initially refused to hire Muhlenberg, but had to bow to pressure from the engineer's influential friends in Washington. Roberts's doubts about Muhlenberg deepened after it took him almost three weeks to get from the Three Forks of the Missouri to Fort Ellis—a thirty-mile ride over flat, easy country with several saloon stops along the way to tempt the thirsty horseman. Lubetkin, *Jay Cooke's Gamble*, 82.

4. Article XVI of the 1868 Fort Laramie Treaty said, "The United States hereby agrees and stipulates that the country north of the North Platte river and east of the summits of the Big Horn mountains shall be held and considered to be unceded Indian territory, and also stipulates and agrees that no white person or persons shall be permitted to settle upon or occupy any portion of the same." The northern boundary of the "unceded Indian territory" was left undefined.

5. Langford to Hauser, September 3, 1871, Hauser Papers, Montana Historical Society Archives. Langford sounds peevish and frustrated in many of his letters during this period, complaining of the lack of business opportunities in St. Paul and repeatedly urging Hauser to use his influence to get their friend David Folsom a lucrative contract with the Northern Pacific.

6. Hutton, *Sheridan*, 41.

7. Stanley to Assistant Adjutant General, Department of Dakota, July 30, 1871, cited in David Eckroth, *Baker's Battle*, Billings, Montana: privately published, n/d, 27.

8. The survey reached a point twenty miles west of Pompey's Pillar, the sandstone butte on which Captain William Clark had carved his name in 1806—the only physical sign that remains of the journey of the Corps of Discovery. The signature was discovered by James Stuart, during his 1863 trip down the Yellowstone with Sam Hauser.

9. The biographical sketch that Doane prepared later for the Society of California Pioneers says that he took part in the 1871 Northern Pacific survey, although he is not named in the original reports on the expedition by Ball or Roberts. Logically, then, if he did take part it must have been as part of the rescue party sent out from Fort Ellis. *Yellowstone Denied*, 89, and author's correspondence with Kim Allen Scott.

10. Captain Edward Ball, "Report on the 1871 Yellowstone Surveying Expedition from Fort Ellis, Montana," December 10, 1871. MF-339, Reel 1, Montana Historical Society Archives, cited in Lubetkin, *Jay Cooke's Gamble*, 92.

11. Lubetkin, loc. cit. Roberts was totally complacent about the security situation since the crushing of the Blackfeet, writing that, "It is certain that at this time the people of Montana have about as little molestation from Indians as we have in New York or Pennsylvania."

12. William Logan (son of Senator "Black Jack" Logan of Illinois), who was Hayden's general assistant on the 1872 expedition, wrote to Hayden on July 1, to complain about Baker's drunkenness. See Goetzmann, *Exploration and Empire*, 514. Langford gave pro forma thanks to Baker for his "kindness in furnishing camp equipage and guns." Langford, "Report of the Superintendent of the Yellowstone National Park for the Year 1972," 42nd Cong. 3rd Sess., Senate Exec. Doc. No. 35, February 4, 1873.

13. Langford, "Hayden Party Under Stevenson—1872," undated typescript ("copied by McN"), Yellowstone National Park Reference Library and Archives.

14. The army photographer Thomas Hine had in fact made images of an eruption the previous year, but these were lost for more than a century. See chapter 29, note 61. Because of the long time exposures required, Jackson could not render the full effect of the spray from the eruption, so later added white streaks to his image by hand.

15. Stressing that it was much easier to approach the park from the west, Langford proposed a road that would follow the Madison, turn south along the Firehole to the Upper Geyser Basin, cut across to Yellowstone Lake, then follow the lakeshore and the river to the Grand Canyon and Tower Fall, and from there to Mammoth Hot Springs and the northern boundary of the park. A second road would go directly from Mammoth to the confluence of the Madison and the Firehole, a route that he said had been taken in the summer of 1872 by a tourist group from Bozeman. With the exception of the short connecting road between the Norris Geyser Basin and the Grand Canyon and the stretch from Canyon to Tower Junction, this is essentially the outline of the present-day Grand Loop Road. Langford, "Report of the Superintendent."

16. Langford's claim was challenged in 1898 by a group of six members of the Rocky Mountain Climbing Club of Denver that reached the summit. One of them, William Owen, charged that Langford and Stevenson had gotten no higher than a secondary peak known as the Enclosure, named for a row of upright rocks that is generally believed to have been a Shoshone vision quest site. The most exhaustive analysis of the competing claims was made by Doane's first biographers, Orrin H. Bonney and Lorraine G. Bonney, in *The Grand Controversy: The Pioneer Climbs in the Teton Range and the Controversial First Ascent of the Grand Teton*, New York: American Alpine Club Press, 2000. Having examined all the evidence, they concluded that Langford was indeed telling the truth and that he and Stevenson had been the first to make it to the top.

17. Gibbon wrote an enthusiastic account of his visit in "The Wonders of the Yellowstone," *Journal of the American Geographical Society of New York* 5 (May 1873), 112–37.

18. *Bozeman Avant Courier*, July 30, 1872.
19. Stanley to Rosser, April 4, 1872, cited in Lubetkin, *Jay Cooke's Gamble*, 114–5.
20. Cited in Lubetkin, 126.
21. Modern accounts of the attack on the Baker party include David Eckroth's painstaking reconstruction, *Baker's Battle*; Robert Utley, *Sitting Bull: The Life and Times of an American Patriot*, New York: Henry Holt, 1993, 107–10; Lubetkin, *Jay Cooke's Gamble*, 131–47; and Scott, *Yellowstone Denied*, 90–5. See also Robert W. Larson, *Gall: Lakota War Chief*, Norman: University of Oklahoma Press, 2007, 82–3. The fullest contemporaneous military account is "The Report of Major J. W. Barlow, Who Accompanied a Surveying Party of the Northern Pacific Railroad, in Relation to Indian Interference With That Road," Senate Exec. Doc. 16, 42nd Cong., 3rd Sess., January 6, 1873.
22. John W. Ponsford, "Reminiscences," Montana State University Libraries, Bozeman, Burlingame Special Collection 659.
23. Eckroth, a defender of Baker against his critics, disagrees with this, insisting that, "The entire force opposed the Indians in an orderly and effective manner, with strict adherence to U.S. military tactics and doctrine." Eckroth, *Baker's Battle*, 74.
24. White Bull's account is quoted in Ibid., 55.
25. At first Baker said that they had turned back because the railroad surveyors were too nervous to proceed, which was probably correct. Later he said that it was because the land along the Yellowstone was impassable. This was blatantly untrue, since a new survey party under Colonel Stanley and George Armstrong Custer covered the ground in two weeks the following summer. See Lubetkin, *Jay Cooke's Gamble*, 144–6.
26. Phil Sheridan, who had defended Baker against all his critics after the massacre of the Piegans, continued to support him, writing that, "To protect the surveying party is the object of his expedition, and I am glad that Baker has not allowed himself to be diverted from this object to follow the Indians who attacked." Baker to Hancock, August 20, 1872, cited in Eckroth, *Baker's Battle*, 75.
27. Koch to Laurie, September 28, 1872, in Scott, ed., *"Splendid on a Large Scale,"* 223.
28. Koch to Laurie, September 7, 1872, in Ibid., 219. Lieutenant James H. Bradley, the gifted young amateur historian of Montana in the 1860s and 1870s, added, "Baker's star as an Indian fighter shone out brilliantly on the Marias River in January 1870, but suffered a great diminuation (sic) of luster on the Yellowstone August 1872." Cited in Bonney and Bonney, *Battle Drums and Geysers*, 41.
29. *Bozeman Avant Courier*, January 10, 1873.
30. *Helena Daily Herald*, cited in Lubetkin, *Jay Cooke's Gamble*, 147.

32: TEMPLE OF THE LIVING GOD

1. Thomas Ewing Sherman, "Across the Continent, II—the National Park," *Woodstock Letters*, 11 (1882), 27–8. Sherman's account is included in Lee H. Whittlesey and Elizabeth A. Watry, eds., *Ho! for Wonderland: Travelers' Accounts of Yellowstone, 1872–1914*. Albuquerque: University of New Mexico Press, 2009.
2. Harry J. Norton, *Wonder-Land Illustrated, or Horseback Rides Through the Yellowstone National Park*, Virginia City, Montana: Harry J. Norton, 1873, 31.

3. The irony of Norris's superintendency is that while energetically propagating the idea that Native Americans had always stayed away from the park, he was an enthusiastic amateur archaeologist who found a rich trove of sites and artifacts in the park that gave the lie to this hoary myth. Modern historians have pointed out that Norris saw the park as "a place where tourists should be free of worry and annoyance, not to mention 'molestation' by local American Indian tribes. Thus, while he marveled at his discoveries of various Sheepeater haunts, he was also grateful for the regional military presence that kept local native inhabitants under a watchful eye." Kiki Leigh Rydell and Mary Shivers Culpin, *Managing the "Matchless Wonders": A History of Administrative Development in Yellowstone National Park 1872–1965*, Yellowstone National Park Historic Resource Study, Vol. III, Park Administrative History, Part 1, Yellowstone Center for Resources, YCR-2006-03.

4. Journal, July 29, 1877, Hedges Papers, Montana Historical Society Archives.

5. Cited in Hampton, *Children of Grace*, 41.

6. Cited in White, *It's Your Misfortune*, 72.

7. Nabokov and Loendorf, *Restoring a Presence*, 223. Oddly, the only other conflict to receive this designation was the minor skirmish with the Bannock tribe in 1878, part of which also took place in the national park.

8. The account of the tourists' encounters with the Nez Perce in the park is based on Heister Dean Guie and Lucullus McWhorter, eds., Frank D. Carpenter, *Adventures in Geyser Land*, Caldwell, Idaho, Caxton Printers, 1937; Mrs. George F. (Emma) Cowan, "Reminiscences of Pioneer Life," *Contributions to the Historical Society of Montana* 4 (1903), 155–86; S. G. Fisher, "Journal of S. G. Fisher," *Contributions to the Historical Society of Montana* 2 (1896), 269–82; and Andrew J. Weikert, "Journal of the Tour Through the Yellowstone National Park in August and September 1877," *Contributions to the Historical Society of Montana* 3 (1900), 154–74.

9. Clawson, reports in the *New North West*, reprinted as Eugene Lee Silliman, ed., *A Ride to the Infernal Region: Yellowstone's First Tourists*, Helena, Riverbend Publishing, 2003.

10. Haines, *Yellowstone Story*, Vol. 1, 212; Langford to Delano, November 7, 1873, Minnesota Historical Society Archives.

11. Magoc, *Yellowstone*, 43.

12. Langford to Delano, February 17, 1874. The only exception Langford recommended was to grant a limited timber concession that would bring in revenues to offset the government's expense in protecting the park. In his first and only annual report to Delano, he wrote, "With roads such as I have recommended, the business might be extended to reach the settlements of Montana, in most of which lumber commands a high price."

13. Like many early visitors to the park, Lord Dunraven found it ugly and freakish. In a memoir of his travels in the Rockies, he wrote that the valley of the Firehole "appeared somewhat like a steaming canal cut through a country composed entirely of limekilns, slagheaps, and the refuse of old smelting works." Earl of Dunraven (Windham Thomas Wyndham-Quin, Fourth Earl of Dunraven), *The Great Divide: Travels in the Upper Yellowstone in the Summer of 1874*, London: Chatto and Windus, 1886, 270. Elsewhere, Dunraven links images of Dickensian industrial squalor with the familiar theme of Hell: "You fancy you can hear the rattle of the loom, the whirl of wheels, the clang and clatter of machinery; and the impression is borne upon the mind that you are in the manufacturing

department of Inferno, where the skilled hands and artisans doomed to hard labour are employed." (*Great Divide*, 263)

14. William E. Strong, *A Trip to the Yellowstone National Park in July, August, and September 1875*, Norman: University of Oklahoma Press, 1968, 28, 92–3.

15. Utley, *Indian Frontier*, 170, citing William G. Athearn, *William Tecumseh Sherman and the Settlement of the West*, Norman: University of Oklahoma Press, 1957, 197.

16. Langford to Delano, February 6, 1874, Minnesota Historical Society Archives.

17. Langford says that friends in Congress tried to get him a salary, but he refused: "I requested them to make no effort in this behalf, saying that I feared that some successful applicant for such a salaried position, giving little thought to the matter, would approve the applications for leases; and that as long as I could prevent the granting of any exclusive concessions I would be willing to serve as superintendent without compensation." *Discovery*, i.

18. See especially Haines, *Yellowstone Story*, Vol. 1, 214.

19. Langford to Delano, November 7, 1873, and February 6, 1874, Minnesota Historical Society Archives.

20. Cited in Lubetkin, *Jay Cooke's Gamble*, 171.

21. As Lubetkin notes, Ibid., 276, "With unerring instinct Custer understated his role, credited subordinates . . . and left the reader with the knowledge—without ever stating it—that victory had been achieved only through exceptional leadership: his."

22. *The New York Times*, September 11, 1873, cited in Lubetkin, Ibid., 277.

23. Magoc, *Yellowstone*, 23, citing Richard A. Bartlett, *Yellowstone: A Wilderness Besieged*, Tucson: University of Arizona Press, 1987, 121. Lubetkin, Ibid., 287, ascribes a similar remark to Cornelius Vanderbilt—"Building railroads from nowhere to nowhere at public expense is not a legitimate undertaking."

24. Cowan, "Reminiscences," 194–5.

33: THE NERVE TO EXECUTE

1. The Nez Perce historian Adeline Fredin wrote to the historian Joseph Weixelman, "[The] geysers/hot springs were a ceremonial and religious part in our history/prehistory. . . . It was one place where the Great Spirit existed and we could bath [sic] the body and spirit directly." Weixelman, "The Power to Evoke Wonder," 53.

2. Dunlay, *Wolves for the Blue Soldiers*, 120–1.

3. Scott, *Yellowstone Denied*, 95.

4. In later years, ironically, Brisbin acquired the concession to operate a steamboat on Yellowstone Lake and wrote a short book, *The Great Yellowstone Valley Described*, St. Louis: Commercial Printing Company, 1882.

5. Undated letter to the editor of the *New York Herald*, Brisbin Papers, Montana Historical Society. However, like General O. O. Howard, and like most military humanitarians for that matter, Brisbin felt that the ultimate solution was to educate and Christianize the Indians, especially the younger generation. He reasoned that, "The children are like blank sheets of paper upon which we can write any kind of impression."

6. The letter to Henry, dated September 1, 1874, is reproduced in full in Bonney and Bonney, *Battle Drums and Geysers*, 149–57.

7. Ibid., 46.

8. Doane also tried vainly to get support for the Nile expedition from the American Geographical Society and from private funders in New York and Philadelphia. Ibid., 46–7.

9. Strong, *A Trip to the Yellowstone National Park*, 43.

10. Scott, *Yellowstone Denied*, 112.

11. Ibid., 41.

12. Doane's instincts did, however, tax some members of the party. Strong says that, "[Belknap] and General [James William] Forsyth were annoyed and disgusted at the way Doane led us, but said little." Strong, *A Trip to the Yellowstone National Park*, 54.

13. It's not entirely clear whether Doane actually invented this contraption. According to Strong, Marcy himself had described something similar in his 1859 book, *The Prairie Traveler*. See Strong, *A Trip to the Yellowstone National Park*, 85.

14. H. Duane Hampton, *How the U.S. Cavalry Saved Our National Parks*, Bloomington: Indiana University Press, 1971, 41. Belknap made a similar suggestion that the army "could station one or two companies of troops in or near the park for the purpose of preventing spoliation." He also saw no reason why army engineers should not build roads into the interior of the park for "a modest sum." *Report of the Secretary of War for 1875*, I, 27–8.

15. White, *Custer, Cavalry, and Crows*, 39.

16. Strong, *A Trip to the Yellowstone National Park*, 117.

17. *New York Herald*, n/d, cited in Brown, *Year of the Century*, 92.

18. Utley, *Frontier Regulars*, 254.

19. There are a number of firsthand accounts of the march of the Montana Column and their role in the aftermath of the Little Bighorn. I have relied particularly on James H. Bradley, *The March of the Montana Column: A Prelude to the Custer Disaster*, Norman: University of Oklahoma Press, 1961; James Sanks Brisbin, handwritten notes, Brisbin Papers, Montana Historical Society Archives; Edward J. McClernand, *On Time for Disaster: The Rescue of Custer's Command*, Lincoln: University of Nebraska Press, 1989; and White, *Custer, Cavalry, and Crows*.

20. Cited in Brown, *Plainsmen of the Yellowstone*, 288.

21. Byrne, *Soldiers of the Plains*, 360.

22. Connell, *Son of the Morning Star*, 83.

23. Custer had angered President Grant by testifying in the impeachment proceedings against Secretary of War Belknap. Grant at first planned to punish Custer by excluding him from the campaign against the Sioux. He eventually yielded to Custer's pleading, but stipulated that Terry would have overall command of the Dakota Column. Utley, *Frontier Regulars*, 259.

24. Elizabeth Bacon Custer, *Boots and Saddles: Life in Dakota with General Custer*, New York: Harper, 1899, 263.

25. The description of the conversation aboard the *Far West* is drawn principally from Brisbin's account.

26. Welch and Stekler, *Killing Custer*, 127.

27. Bonney and Bonney, *Battle Drums and Geysers*, 57. Lieutenant Bradley seems to offer a different interpretation. "A worse route could not have been chosen, but destitute of a

guide as we were, it is not to be wondered that we entangled ourselves in such a nest of physical obstacles." Cited in Byrne, *Soldiers of the Plains*, 83.

28. White, *Custer, Cavalry, and Crows*, 66.

29. Richard G. Hardorff, *Hokahey! A Good Day to Die! The Indian Casualties of the Custer Fight*, Lincoln: University of Nebraska Press, 1999, 111.

30. Scott, *Yellowstone Denied*, 112–3. Doane had already befriended Gibbon on the march to the Little Bighorn. Having come up with a design for a "Centennial Tent," an improvement on the army's standard-issue model, he suggested that the two men go into business together to make their fortunes from marketing it. Like so many of Doane's dreams, this one came to nothing. See Ibid., 198–201.

31. Bonney and Bonney, *Battle Drums and Geysers*, 62–3.

32. Brisbin protested to Gibbon but was overruled. Bonney and Bonney, *Battle Drums and Geysers*, 451–2; Scott, *Yellowstone Denied*, 113–4. Given that the first section of the Snake, as far downstream as Fort Hall, Idaho, had already been explored, it would have made much more sense to start from there. But Fort Hall was in a different military jurisdiction, the Division of the Columbia.

33. My account of the Snake River expedition is drawn largely from Doane's own undated "Expedition from Fort Ellis, Montana, to Fort Hall, Idaho, October 11, 1876, to January 4, 1877," Montana State University Libraries, Bozeman, Burlingame Special Collection 2211/3, Doane Papers, reproduced in full in Bonney and Bonney, 451–78, supplemented by details from Sergeant Fred E. Server, "Diary, 1876–1877," typescript in Montana State University Libraries, Bozeman, Burlingame Special Collection 507; and White, *Custer, Cavalry, and Crows*, 100–13. Doane's journal, like his account of the 1870 Yellowstone expedition, remains wonderfully readable.

34. Doane described the scene this way: "The wide valley in front seamed with rocky channels and heaped with moraines, is a grim ruinous landscape. There are no foothills to the Tetons. They rise suddenly in rugged majesty from the rock strewn plain. Masses of heavy forests appear on the glacial débris and [the] general field of vision is glittering glaciated rock. The soft light floods the great expanse of the valley, the winding silvery river and the resplendent deeply carved mountain walls. The vast masses of Neve on the upper ledges from their lofty resting places, shine coldly down and stray masses of clouds, white and fleecy, cast deep shadows over lake and terrace, forest and stream.

    And later on when the moon had gone down in exaggerated volume behind the glorified spire of the Grand Teton, the stars succeeded with their myriad sparkling lights, and these blazed up the setting on the sharp cut edges of the great serrated walls like Indian signal fires in successive spectral flashes, rising and dying out by hundreds as the hours pass on." Doane Journal, Friday, December 1, 1876, in Bonney and Bonney, *Battle Drums and Geysers*, 523–4.

35. White, *Custer, Cavalry, and Crows*, 107.

36. Ibid., 109.

37. Bonney and Bonney, *Battle Drums and Geysers*, 571.

38. Dated December 10, but obviously written sometime after the fact, Doane's tirade is reprinted in Bonney and Bonney, Ibid., 532–3.

34: CHIEF OF SCOUTS

1. Dunlay, *Wolves for the Blue Soldiers*, 24.

2. Leforge, *Memoirs*, 297.

3. Doane to Assistant Adjutant General, Yellowstone Command, July 13, 1877, Doane Papers, Montana State University Libraries, Bozeman.

4. General George Crook, a strong advocate of the scout system, believed that, "The first principle is to show that we trust them . . . they are quick to note any lack of confidence. . . . They appreciate the situation, and understand thoroughly what is expected of them, and know how best to do their work. They know this business better than we do. . . . We cannot expect them to act automatically as drilled soldiers do. Their best quality is their individuality, and as soon as this is destroyed their efficiency goes with it." C. S. Roberts to W. E. Shopp, August 14, 1885, cited in John Bigelow, *On the Bloody Trail of Geronimo*, New York: Tower Books, 1958, 43–4.

5. White wrote in his memoirs, "I knew that my regular companion had enjoyed himself in telling our Fort Ellis people about the leader's temporary breakdown at the time we were on our way out of the Snake River Canyon. I had reason to believe that the Lieutenant also was annoyed by Starr's too promiscuous references to various ugly happenings during the campaign against the Piegans on the Marias river." *Custer, Cavalry, and Crows*, 116.

6. Ibid., 128; Scott, *Yellowstone Denied*, 135.

7. Mary Allen Phinney, *Allen-Isham Genealogy: Jirah Isham Allen, Montana Pioneer*, Rutland, Vermont: Tuttle Publishing Company, 1946, 90.

8. Yoho-na-ho was the daughter of a Crow named Crooked Foot, who told White, "At any time you may want her for a wife she belongs to you." *Custer, Cavalry, and Crows*, 130.

9. Sherman to Secretary of War George W. McCrary, July 17, 1877, in *Reports of Inspection Made in the Summer of 1877 by Generals P. H. Sheridan and W. T. Sherman of Country North of the Union Pacific Railroad*, Washington, D.C.: Government Printing Office, 1878.

10. Doane had carried out an extensive survey of the Judith Basin in 1873. See Doane, "Report to the Commissioner of Indian Affairs, Department of the Interior, February 19, 1874," Records of the Bureau of Indian Affairs, Record Group 75, NARA, transcript in Doane Papers, Montana State University Libraries, Bozeman.

11. Report of the Secretary of War, 1877, 540, cited in Bonney and Bonney, *Battle Drums and Geysers*, 71.

12. Sherman to McCrary, August 4, 1877, in *Reports of Inspection*.

13. Brown, *Bury My Heart*, 325.

14. *The Weekly Missoulian*, October 5, 1877, cited in Hampton, *Children of Grace*, 190–1.

15. "Journal of S. G. Fisher." In the event, the Bannock scouts found only one Nez Perce, an old, sick woman left behind on the trail to die. They duly shot her, scalped her, and held a celebratory dance.

16. Captain William Jones of the Corps of Engineers entered the park from the Wyoming side in 1873, discovering the Togwotee Pass—which had eluded Raynolds, Hayden, and Bridger in 1860—and a smaller pass to the east of Yellowstone Lake (Jones Pass) that cut

through the Absarokas and led to the South Fork of the Shoshone, known in those days as the Stinkingwater. Presumably these are the possible escape routes to Wyoming that Gibbon and Crook had in mind. On the Jones expedition, see Haines, *Yellowstone Story*, Vol. 1, 201–3.

17. Cesare Marino and Ken Comery, "Carlo de Rudio: A Survivor of the Little Bighorn," www.derudio.co.uk. Connell, *Son of the Morning Star*, 383–5.

18. De Rudio's survival on Reno Hill is described by Sergeant Thomas O'Neill, who was with him, in E. A. Brininstool, *Troopers with Custer: Historic Incidents of the Battle of the Little Big Horn*, Lincoln: University of Nebraska Press, 1989, 125–52.

19. Jerome A. Greene, *Yellowstone Command: Colonel Nelson A. Miles and the Great Sioux War, 1876–1877*, Lincoln: University of Nebraska Press, 1994, 37.

20. "I have 65 white men and 100 Indians, with more coming." Doane to commanding officer, Camp Baker, August 21, 1877. Doane Papers, Montana State University Libraries, Bozeman.

21. There are colorful descriptions of Doane's journey from Fort Keogh to Fort Ellis in White, *Custer, Cavalry and Crows*, 137; Phinney, *Allen-Isham Genealogy*, 96–7; and Scott, *Yellowstone Denied*, 52–60.

22. Camp Baker, which lies on the Smith River about fifteen miles east of Diamond City, was established in November 1869 as an additional buffer against the Blackfeet. It was named for Major Eugene M. Baker—although he openly questioned the need for its existence. See Burlingame, *Montana Frontier*, 213. Later in 1877, it was renamed Fort Logan, in honor of Captain William Logan, who died at the Battle of the Big Hole.

23. Note by W. E. S. (sic, presumably Wilbur Fisk Sanders), *Contributions to the Historical Society of Montana* 2 (1896), 268.

35: FULL CIRCLE

1. My account of the pursuit of the Nez Perce in the national park is based on several sources, including: Cowan, "Reminiscences of Pioneer Life"; Carpenter, *The Wonders of Geyser Land*; and Weikert, "Journal of the Tour." Jerome A. Greene, *Nez Perce Summer, 1877: The U.S. Army and the Nee-Me-Poo Crisis*, Helena: Montana Historical Society Press, 2000, 165–201; Elliott West, *The Nez Perce Story*, New York: Oxford University Press, 2009, 214–29; Hampton, *Children of Grace*, 223–37; and Haines, *Yellowstone Story*, Vol. 1, 216–39. Lucullus McWhorter also published two accounts based on Nez Perce sources: *Yellow Wolf: His Own Story*, Caldwell, Idaho: Caxton Press, 1948, and *Hear Me, My Chiefs!* Caldwell, Idaho: Caxton Press, 1952.

2. When he recovered consciousness, Cowan found that the bullet, presumably defective, had flattened itself against his skull. As he came to, another Indian shot him in the thigh and again left him for dead. When that Indian had left, Cowan spent four days crawling back toward the Firehole before being rescued by Howard's forces. Instead of sending him back to the settlements for medical treatment, Howard insisted on taking Cowan along on his continued futile pursuit of the Nez Perce. Near Fort Ellis, the wagon carrying him tipped over and threw him into a canyon. When he finally reached Bozeman, three weeks after being shot, he was put to bed in a hotel. While his wounds were being

dressed, the bed collapsed, pitching him onto the floor. If you can't kill me any other way, he suggested, why don't you try artillery? *Adventures in Geyserland*, 228.

3. Seven of the nine survivors from the Helena party reached Mammoth. The other two, August Foller and Joe Roberts, went in the opposite direction and were later found by Howard's troops. Of the Radersburg party, all except Emma Cowan and Ida and Frank Carpenter—and George Cowan, when he was eventually evacuated—left the park via the Madison.

4. Ironically, Schofield, a West Point graduate and brother of former Secretary of War General John M. Schofield, had been rumored in Bozeman to be romantically involved with Doane's wife, Amelia. See Scott, *Yellowstone Denied*, 89.

5. Doane's best documented visits were in 1870, with the Washburn-Langford-Doane expedition; in 1871, as head of the escort to the Hayden party; in 1875, with the Belknap party; and in 1876, on his way to the Snake. But he also visited the park in 1874, when he explored the rugged backcountry in the Tower Creek Basin with one other man and two mules. He includes a brief description in his report on the Snake River expedition. See Bonney and Bonney, *Battle Drums and Geysers*, 471–3.

6. Sturgis to Doane, August 17, 1877, Doane Papers, Montana State University Libraries, Bozeman.

7. Gibbon to Doane, August 27, 1877, Doane Papers, Montana State University Libraries, Bozeman.

8. Sturgis to Doane, August 29, 1877, Doane Papers, Montana State University Libraries, Bozeman. Scott discusses Doane's creative interpretation of his orders in *Yellowstone Denied*, 160–5. But there is another possibility: that Doane was doing exactly what Gibbon wanted. Gibbon's final report on the Nez Perce campaign says that, "Lieutenant Doane was ordered by telegraph to push up the Yellowstone to the bridge at the mouth of the East Fork [i.e. Baronett's Bridge at the confluence with the Lamar], cross that, and feel for the Indians up the right bank of the Yellowstone. . . . Lieutenant Doane, in obedience to his orders, proceeded with his command up the Yellowstone." Since none of the field communications at the time go into this detail, Gibbon's motives for doing so in his final report are open to speculation. By October 18, when Gibbon wrote his report, Doane was in trouble with both Sturgis and Brisbin for his irregular behavior during the Nez Perce campaign, and it is possible Gibbon was trying to shield him from criticism. *Report of the Secretary of War, 1877*, Vol. 2.

9. "In reality," said Thomas Leforge, an adopted member of the tribe, "their warlike operations were restricted to the capture of ponies." Leforge, *Memoirs*, 128–9; Dunlay, *Wolves for the Blue Soldiers*, 120–1.

10. Hugh Scott, *Some Memories of a Soldier,* New York: Century Company, 1928, 68.

11. Hugh Scott, "Remarks at the 1929 Bear Paw Battlefield Monument Dedication," *Chinook Opinion* (Chinook, Montana), October 3, 1929, cited in Scott, *Yellowstone Denied*, 162.

12. Scott, *Some Memories*, 68.

13. Phinney, *Isham-Allen Genealogy*, 99.

14. William L. Lang, "Where Did the Nez Percés Go in Yellowstone in 1877?" *Montana the Magazine of Western History* 40 (Winter 1990), 14–29. Lang convincingly refutes the opinion of many earlier historians that the Nez Perce were lost at this point. See also Lee H. Whittlesey, "The Nez Perce in Yellowstone," *Montana the Magazine of Western*

History 57, Spring 2007, 48 55. Some of the route taken by the Nez Perce is also described by S. G. Fisher, chief of the Bannock scouts under General Howard. See "Journal of S. G. Fisher," and Shively's account of his captivity, *New North West*, September 14, 1877.

15. Brisbin's vindictiveness toward Doane is described in Scott, *Yellowstone Denied*, 175–7.

16. Sherman found Miles insufferable. He wrote to Sheridan, "I have told him plainly that I know of no way to satisfy his ambitions but to surrender to him absolute power over the whole Army with President and Congress thrown in." Cited in Hampton, *Children of Grace*, 283. Miles did in fact become Commanding General of the United States Army in 1895. His own account of the Nez Perce campaign is in *Personal Recollections & Observations of General Nelson A. Miles,* Vol. 1, Lincoln: University of Nebraska Press, 1992, 259–80.

17. Cowan, "Reminiscences of Pioneer Life," 169–70. In the same passage, she also showed enormous compassion for the injustice that had been visited on the Nez Perce: "[A] tribe of Indians is located on a reservation. Gold is discovered thereon by the prospector. A stampede follows. The strong arm of the government alone prevents the avaricious pale face from possessing himself of the land forthwith. Some negotiations are pending with as little delay as a few yards of red tape will admit. A treaty is signed, the land is ceded to the government and opened to settlers, and 'Lo, the poor Indian' finds himself on a tract of a few degrees more arid, a little less desirable than his former home. The Indian has few rights the average white settler feels bound to respect." Cornelius Hedges also had second thoughts about the army's Indian policy after the crushing of the Nez Perce, "sens[ing] that bad handling and even injustice against the Nez Perce had contributed to the confrontation." Rex C. Myers, "The Settlers and the Nez Perce," *Montana the Magazine of Western History* 27 (October 1977), 20–9.

EPILOGUE: THE MAN WHO INVENTED WONDERLAND

1. On the Howgate expedition to the Arctic, see Scott, *Yellowstone Denied*, 202–20.

2. Ewers, *The Blackfeet*, 294.

3. Scott, *Yellowstone Denied*, 228.

4. Ibid., 230.

5. Lubetkin, *Jay Cooke's Gamble*, 84.

6. Hedges Journal, January 12, 1887, Hedges Papers, Montana Historical Society Archives.

7. *Livingston Enterprise*, August 29, 1883, cited in Haines, *Yellowstone Story*, Vol. 1, 260.

8. *Livingston Enterprise*, March 28, 1884, cited in Nabokov and Loendorf, *Restoring a Presence*, 67.

9. *Livingston Enterprise*, n.d., quoted in Thornton Waite, *Yellowstone by Train: A History of Rail Travel to America's First National Park*, Missoula, Montana: Pictorial History Publishing Company, 2006, 34.

10. Sheridan also sponsored some serious scholarly work on Native American ethnography, including a book on Indian sign language by Captain William P. Clark, who had served

on General Crook's staff during the Great Sioux War. See Paul A. Hutton, "Phil Sheridan's Crusade for Yellowstone," *American History Illustrated*, 19, 10 (1985), 14.

11. Miles to Republican Senator of Pennsylvania (and Secretary of War in 1876–1877) Donald Cameron, March 11, 1889. Yellowstone National Park Archives.

12. Secretary of War Redfield Proctor to William W. Morrow et al., January 29, 1891, quoted in Scott, *Yellowstone Denied*, 252.

BIBLIOGRAPHY

BOOKS

Allen, Frederick. *A Decent, Orderly Lynching: The Montana Vigilantes*. Norman: University of Oklahoma Press, 2004.

Alter, James Cecil. *James Bridger, Trapper, Frontiersman, Scout and Guide: A Historical Narrative*. Salt Lake City: Shepard Book Co., 1925.

Ambrose, Stephen A. *Crazy Horse and Custer: The Parallel Lives of Two American Warriors*. New York: Doubleday, 1975.

——— *Undaunted Courage: Meriwether Lewis, Thomas Jefferson, and the Opening of the American West*. New York: Simon and Schuster, 1997.

Armstrong, James, ed. *Wonders of the Yellowstone*. New York: Scribner, 1889.

Arthur, James. *Retracing Kipp Trails*. Lewiston, Montana: Central Montana Publishing Company, 1999.

Athearn, Robert G. *Thomas Francis Meagher: An Irish Revolutionary in America*. Boulder: University of Colorado Press, 1949.

——— *William Tecumseh Sherman and the Settlement of the West*. Norman: University of Oklahoma Press, 1956.

Ballantine, Betty and Ian Ballantine, eds. *The Native Americans: An Illustrated History*. Atlanta: Turner Publishing Company, 1993.

Bancroft, Hubert Howe and Alfred Bates. *History of Utah 1540–1886*. San Francisco: History Publishing Company, 1889.

Barbour, Barton H. *Fort Union and the Upper Missouri Fur Trade*. Norman: University of Oklahoma Press, 2001.

Barsness, Larry. *Gold Camp: Alder Gulch and Virginia City, Montana*. New York: Hastings House Publishers, 1962.

Bartlett, Richard A. *Great Surveys of the American West*. Norman: University of Oklahoma Press, 1962.

—— *Nature's Yellowstone.* Albuquerque: University of New Mexico Press, 1974.

—— *Yellowstone: A Wilderness Besieged.* Tucson: University of Arizona Press, 1985.

Beal, Merrill D. *"I Will Fight No More Forever": Chief Joseph and the Nez Perce War.* Seattle: University of Washington Press, 1963.

—— *The Story of Man in Yellowstone.* Caldwell, Idaho: Caxton Printers, 1949.

Beck, Paul Norman. *The First Sioux War: The Grattan Fight and Blue Water Creek, 1854–1856.* Lanham, Maryland: University Press of America, 2004.

Bennett, Ben. *Death, Too, for The-Heavy-Runner.* Missoula: Mountain Press Publishing Company, 1982.

Bergon, Frank, ed. *The Journals of Lewis and Clark.* New York: Penguin, 1989.

Binnema, Theodore. *Common and Contested Ground: A Human and Environmental History of the Northwestern Plains.* Norman: University of Oklahoma Press, 2001.

Bonney, Orrin H. and Lorraine Bonney. *Battle Drums and Geysers: The Life and Journals of Lt. Gustavus Cheyney Doane, Soldier and Explorer of the Yellowstone and Snake River Regions.* Chicago: Sage-Swallow Press, 1970.

—— *The Grand Controversy: The Pioneer Climbs in the Teton Range and the Controversial First Ascent of the Grand Teton.* New York: American Alpine Club Press, 1992.

Bradbury, John. *Travels in the Interior of America in the Years 1809, 1810, and 1811.* Lincoln: University of Nebraska Press, 1986.

Bradley, Charles. *The Handsome People: A History of the Crow Indians and the Whites.* Billings, Montana: Council for Indian Education, 1991.

Bradley, James H. *The March of the Montana Column: A Prelude to the Custer Disaster.* Norman: University of Oklahoma Press, 1961.

Brown, Dee. *Bury My Heart at Wounded Knee.* New York: Henry Holt, 1970.

—— *The Fetterman Massacre.* Lincoln: University of Nebraska Press, 1973.

—— *Year of the Century: 1876.* New York: Scribner, 1975.

Brown, Mark H. *The Flight of the Nez Perce.* New York: Putnam, 1967.

—— *Plainsmen of the Yellowstone: A History of the Yellowstone Basin.* Lincoln: University of Nebraska Press, 1961.

Brown, David L. *Three Years in the Rocky Mountains.* Fairfield, Washington: Ye Galleon Press, 1982.

Burlingame, Merrill G. *John M. Bozeman: Montana Trailmaker.* Bozeman, Montana: Museum of the Rockies, rev. ed., 1983.

—— *The Montana Frontier.* Helena, Montana: State Publishing Company, 1942.

—— and K. Ross Toole, eds. *A History of Montana,* 3 vols. New York: Lewis Historical Publishing Company, 1957.

Burns, Robert Ignatius, S. J. *The Jesuits and the Indian Wars of the Northwest.* Moscow: University of Idaho Press, 1966.

Byrne, P. E. *Soldiers of the Plains.* New York: Minton, Balch and Company, 1926.

Callaway, Colin G. *Our Hearts Fell Down to the Ground: Plains Indians Views of How the West Was Lost.* New York: Bedford Books, St. Martin's Press, 1996.

Callaway, Lew L. *Montana's Righteous Hangmen: The Vigilantes in Action.* Norman: University of Oklahoma Press, 1982.

Carpenter, Frank D., ed., Hester D. Guie and L. V. McWhorter. *Adventures in Geyserland.* Caldwell, Idaho: Caxton Printers, 1935.

Carrington, Margaret I. *Ab-sa-ra-ka: Home of the Crows*. Lincoln: University of Nebraska Press, 1983.

Cassidy, James. *Ferdinand V. Hayden: Entrepreneur of Science*. Lincoln: University of Nebraska Press, 2000.

Catlin, George. *North American Indians: Being Letters and Notes on Their Manners, Customs, and Conditions, Written During Eight Years' Travel Amongst the Wildest Tribes in North America, 1832–1839*. New York: Penguin Nature Classics, 1989.

Chaffin, Tom. *Pathfinder: John Charles Frémont and the Course of American Empire*. New York: Hill and Wang, 2004.

Chardon, F. A. *Journal at Fort Clark, 1834–1839*. Lincoln: University of Nebraska Press, 1997.

Chittenden, Hiram M. *The American Fur Trade of the Far West*, 2 vols. Stanford, California: Academic Reprints, 1954.

—— ed. Richard A. Bartlett. *The Yellowstone National Park: Historical and Descriptive*. Norman: University of Oklahoma Press, 1964.

Clarke, Charles G. *The Men of the Lewis and Clark Expedition: A Biographical Roster of the Fifty-one Members and a Composite Diary of Their Activities from All Known Sources*. Lincoln: Bison Books Reprint Edition, 2002.

Connell, Evan S. *Son of the Morning Star: General Custer and the Battle of the Little Bighorn*. New York: North Point Press, 1984.

Cook, Charles, David E. Folsom and William Peterson, Aubrey L. Haines, ed. *The Valley of the Upper Yellowstone*. Norman: University of Oklahoma Press, 1965.

Cozzens, Peter. *Eyewitnesses to the Indian Wars, 1865–1890, Vol. 2, The Wars for the Pacific Northwest*. Mechanicsburg, Pennsylvania: Stackpole, 2002.

Cramton, Louis C. *Early History of Yellowstone National Park and Its Relation to National Park Policies*. Washington, D.C., Government Printing Office, 1932.

Cronon, William. *Changes in the Land: Indians, Colonists, and the Ecology of New England*. New York: Hill and Wang, 1983.

Cutler, Bruce. *The Massacre at Sand Creek*. Norman: University of Oklahoma Press, 1995.

Deloria, Vine, Jr. *Custer Died for Your Sins: An Indian Manifesto*. Norman: University of Oklahoma Press, 1988.

Dempsey, Hugh A. *The Amazing Death of Calf Shirt and Other Blackfoot Stories: Three Hundred Years of Blackfoot History*. Saskatoon, Saskatchewan: Fifth House Publishers, ca. 1994.

Denig, Edwin T. *Five Indian Tribes of the Upper Missouri: Sioux, Arickaras, Assiniboines, Crees, Crows*. Norman: University of Oklahoma Press, 1961.

De Smet, Pierre-Jean, with Hiram M. Chittenden and Alfred Talbot Richardson. *Life, Letters and Travels of Father Pierre-Jean de Smet, S. J.* New York: F. P. Harper, 1905.

De Voto, Bernard. *Across the Wide Missouri*. Boston: Houghton Mifflin, 1947.

—— *The Journals of Lewis and Clark*. Boston: Houghton Mifflin, 1947.

Dimsdale, Thomas J. *The Vigilantes of Montana, or Popular Justice in the Rocky Mountains*. Norman, University of Oklahoma Press, 1982.

Dippie, Brian. *The Vanishing American: White Attitudes and U.S. Indian Policy*. Middletown, Connecticut: Wesleyan University Press, 1982.

Doane, Alfred A. *The Doane Family and Their Descendants*, Vol. 1. Boston: The Doane Family Association of America, 1976.

Dolin, Eric J. *Fur, Fortune and Empire: The Epic History of the Fur Trade in America*. New York: W. W. Norton, 2010.

Doyle, Susan Badger. *Journeys to the Land of Gold: Emigrant Diaries from the Bozeman Trail, 1863–1866*. Helena: Montana Historical Society Press, 2000.

Dunlay, Thomas W. *Wolves for the Blue Soldiers: Indian Scouts and Auxiliaries with the United States Army, 1860–90*. Lincoln: University of Nebraska Press, 1982.

Dunn, J. P. *Massacres of the Mountains: A History of the Indian Wars of the Far West*. New York: Harper Brothers, 1886.

Dunraven, Earl of (Windham Thomas Wyndham-Quin, Fourth Earl of Dunraven). *The Great Divide: Travels in the Upper Yellowstone in the Summer of 1874*. London: Chatto and Windus, 1886.

Eckroth, Dave. *Baker's Battle*. Billings, Montana: privately published, n.d.

Ege, Robert. *Tell Baker to Strike Them Hard! Incident on the Marias, Jan. 23, 1870*. Bellevue, Nebraska: Old Army Press, 1970.

Ewers, John C. *The Blackfeet: Raiders on the Northwestern Plains*. Norman: University of Oklahoma Press, 1958.

—— *The Horse in Blackfoot Indian Culture, with Comparative Material from Other Western Tribes*. Honolulu: University Press of the Pacific, 2001.

—— *Indian Life on the Upper Missouri*. Norman: University of Oklahoma Press, 1968.

—— *Plains Indian History and Culture: Essays on Continuity and Change*. Norman: University of Oklahoma Press, 1998.

Fahey, John. *The Flathead Indians*. Norman: University of Oklahoma Press, 1974.

Ferris, Warren Angus. *Life in the Rocky Mountains: A Diary of Wanderings on the Sources of the Rivers Missouri, Columbia, and Colorado, 1830–1835*. Denver: Old West Publishing Company, 1983.

Fleisher, Kass. *The Bear River Massacre and the Making of History*. Albany: State University of New York Press, 2004.

Folsom, David E. *The Folsom-Cook Expedition of the Upper Yellowstone in the Year 1869*. St. Paul, Minnesota: H. L. Collins, 1894.

Foner, Jack D. *The United States Soldier Between Two Wars, 1865–1898*. New York: Humanities Press, 1970.

Foster, Mike. *Strange Genius: The Life of Ferdinand Vandeveer Hayden*. Niwort, Colorado: Roberts Rinehart Publishers, 1994.

Fryxell, Fritiof. *Thomas Moran, Explorer in Search of Beauty*. East Hampton, New York: East Hampton Free Library, 1958.

Gerrish, Theodore. *Life in the World's Wonderland*. Biddeford, Maine: N.P., 1887.

Goetzmann, William H. *Army Exploration in the American West, 1803–1863*. New Haven, Connecticut: Yale University Press, 1959.

—— *Exploration and Empire: The Explorer and the Scientist in the Winning of the American West*. New York: Alfred A. Knopf, 1966.

—— *New Lands, New Men: America and the Second Great Age of Discovery*. New York: Viking, 1986.

—— and William N. Goetzmann. *The West of the Imagination*. New York: W. W. Norton, 1986.

Gowans, Fred R. and Eugene E. Campbell. *Fort Bridger: Island in the Wilderness*. Provo, Utah: Brigham Young University Press, 1975.

Greene, Jerome A. *Nez Perce Summer, 1877: The U.S. Army and the Nee-Me-Poo Crisis.* Helena: Montana Historical Society Press, 2000.

—— *Washita: The U.S. Army and the Southern Cheyenne, 1867–1869.* Norman: University of Oklahoma Press, 2004.

—— *Yellowstone Command: Colonel Nelson A. Miles and the Great Sioux War, 1876–1877.* Lincoln: University of Nebraska Press, 1994.

Grinnell, George Bird. *Blackfoot Lodge Tales: The Story of a Prairie People.* Lincoln: University of Nebraska Press, 1962.

Hafen, LeRoy R., ed. *The Mountain Men and the Fur Trade of the Far West,* 4 vols. Glendale, California: Arthur A. Clark Co., 1966.

Haines, Aubrey L. *Yellowstone National Park: Its Exploration and Establishment.* Washington, D.C.: National Park Service, 1974.

—— *The Yellowstone Story,* 2 vols. Yellowstone Library and Museum Association, in collaboration with Colorado Associated University Press, 1977.

—— ed. *Osborne Russell: Journal of a Trapper.* Portland: Oregon Historical Society, 1955.

Hales, Peter B. *William Henry Jackson and the Transformation of the American Landscape.* Philadelphia: Temple University Press, 1988.

Hamilton, James McClellan. *History of Montana: From Wilderness to Statehood.* Portland, Oregon: Binfords and Mort, 1957.

Hamilton, William T. and E. T. Sieber. *My Sixty Years on the Plains: Trapping, Trading and Indian Fighting.* New York: Forest and Stream, 1905.

Hampton, Bruce. *Children of Grace: The Nez Perce War of 1877.* New York: Henry Holt, 1994.

Hampton, H. Duane. *How the U.S. Cavalry Saved Our National Parks.* Bloomington: Indiana University Press, 1971.

Harnsberger, John L. *Jay Cooke and Minnesota: The Formative Years of the Northern Pacific Railroad, 1868–1873.* New York: Arno Press, 1981.

Harper, Frank B. *Fort Union and Its Neighbors on the Upper Missouri.* Great Northern Railway, n.d.

Harris, Burton. *John Colter: His Years in the Rockies.* New York: Charles Scribner's Sons, 1952.

Harrod, Howard L. *Mission Among the Blackfeet.* Norman: University of Oklahoma Press, 1971.

Hartley, Robert E. *Saving Yellowstone: The President Arthur Expedition of 1883.* Westminster, Colorado: Sniktau Publications/Exlibris, 2007.

Hebard, Grace R. and E. A. Brininstool. *The Bozeman Trail.* Glendale, California: Arthur H. Clark Co., 1922.

Hedges, Cornelius. *Art Work of Montana: Published in Twelve Parts.* Chicago: W. H. Parish, 1896.

Hoig, Stan. *The Sand Creek Massacre.* Norman: University of Oklahoma Press, 1980.

—— *The Battle of the Washita: The Sheridan-Custer Indian Campaign of 1867–69.*

Holterman, Jack. *King of the High Missouri: The Saga of the Culbertsons.* Helena, Montana: Jack Holterman with the Falcon Press, 1987.

Howard, Joseph K. *Montana: High, Wide and Handsome.* New Haven, Connecticut: Yale University Press, 1943.

Hoxie, Frederick E. *The Crow (Indians of North America).* Philadelphia: Chelsea House Publishing, 1989.

—— *Parading Through History: The Making of the Crow Nation in America, 1805–1935*. Cambridge: Cambridge University Press, 1995.

—— ed. *Encyclopedia of North American Indians*. Boston: Houghton Mifflin, 1996.

Hungry Wolf, Adolf. *Blackfeet History and Culture: Native Life on the Northern Plains*, 4 vols. Skookumchuk, British Columbia: Good Medicine Cultural Foundation, 2007.

—— *The Blood People: A Division of the Blackfoot Confederacy*. New York: Harper and Row, 1977.

Hutton, Paul. *Phil Sheridan and His Army*. Lincoln: University of Nebraska Press, 1985.

Irving, Washington., ed. Edgeley W. Todd. *The Adventures of Captain Bonneville, U.S.A., Digested from His Journals*. Norman: University of Oklahoma Press, 1961.

—— *Astoria; or Enterprise Beyond the Rocky Mountains*. Norman: University of Oklahoma Press, 1964.

Jackson, John C. *The Piikani Blackfeet: A Culture Under Siege*. Missoula, Montana: Mountain Press Publishing Company, 1999.

Jackson, William Henry, with Karl Brown. *Time Exposure*. New York: G. P. Putnam's Sons, 1940.

—— with Howard R. Driggs. *The Pioneer Photographer: Rocky Mountain Adventures with a Camera*. Yonkers, New York: World Book Company, 1929.

Jacoby, Karl. *Crimes Against Nature: Squatters, Poachers, Thieves, and the Hidden History of American Conservation*. Berkeley: University of California Press, 2001.

James, Thomas. *Three Years Among the Indians and Mexicans*. Lincoln: University of Nebraska Press, 1984.

Janetski, Joel. *Indians of Yellowstone Park*. Salt Lake City: University of Utah Press, 1987.

Johnson, Dorothy M. *The Bloody Bozeman*. New York: McGraw Hill, 1971.

Josephy, Alvin M., Jr. *The Civil War in the American West*. New York: Alfred A. Knopf, 1991.

—— *Lewis and Clark Through Indian Eyes: Nine Indian Writers on the Legacy of the Expedition*. New York: Vintage, 2007.

—— *The Nez Perce Indians and the Opening of the Northwest*. New Haven, Connecticut: Yale University Press, 1965.

—— ed., and David Lavender. *The Great West*. New York: American Heritage Publishing, 1965.

Kane, Lucille M., ed. and trans. *Military Life in Dakota: The Journal of Philippe Régis de Trobriand*. Lincoln: University of Nebraska Press, 1951.

Keim, de B. Randolph. *Sheridan's Troopers on the Borders: A Winter Campaign on the Plains*. New York: George Routledge and Sons, 1870.

Kelly, Fanny. *Narrative of My Captivity Among the Sioux Indians*. Hartford, Connecticut: Mutual Publishing Company, 1871.

Kinsey, Joni Louise. *Thomas Moran and the Surveying of the American West*. Washington, D.C., Smithsonian Press, 1992.

Kittredge, William and Annick Smith. *The Last Best Place: A Montana Anthology*. Seattle: University of Washington Press, 1991.

Koury, Michael J. *Gibbon on the Sioux Campaign of 1876*. Bellevue, Nebraska: Old Army Press, 1970.

Lancaster, Richard. *Piegan: A Look from Within at the Life, Times, and Legacy of an American Indian Tribe*. New York: Doubleday, 1966.

Langford, Nathaniel Pitt. *Diary of the Washburn Expedition to the Yellowstone and Firehole Rivers in the Year 1870*. St. Paul, Minnesota: F. J. Haynes, 1905.

—— *The Discovery of Yellowstone Park, 1870*. St. Paul, Minnesota: J. E. Haynes, 1923.

—— *The Discovery of Yellowstone Park: Journal of the Washburn Expedition to the Yellowstone and Firehole Rivers in the Year 1870*, foreword by Aubrey L. Haines. Lincoln: University of Nebraska Press, 1972.

—— *Vigilante Days and Ways*. Boston: J. G. Cupples, 1890.

—— *Vigilante Days and Ways*, reprint with an introduction by Dorothy M. Johnson. Missoula: Montana State University Press, 1957.

Larpenteur, Charles, ed. Elliott Coues. *Forty Years a Fur Trader on the Upper Missouri*, 2 vols. New York: Francis P. Harper, 1896.

Larson, Henrietta. *Jay Cooke, Private Banker*. Cambridge, Massachusetts: Harvard University Press, 1936.

Larson, Robert W. *Red Cloud: Warrior-Statesman of the Lakota Sioux*. Norman: University of Oklahoma Press, 1997.

Lavender, David. *Let Me Be Free: The Nez Perce Tragedy*. New York: Harper Collins, 1992.

—— *The Way to the Western Sea: Lewis and Clark Across the Continent*. New York: Anchor, 1990.

Leeson, M. A., ed. *History of Montana, 1739–1885*. Chicago: Warner, Beers and Company, 1885.

Leforge, Thomas H. and Thomas B. Marquis. *Memoirs of a White Crow Indian (Thomas H. Leforge, as Told to Thomas B. Marquis)*. Lincoln: University of Nebraska Press, 1974.

Limerick, Patricia Nelson. *The Legacy of Conquest: The Unbroken Past of the American West*. New York: W. W. Norton, 1987.

Lubetkin, M. John. *Jay Cooke's Gamble: The Northern Pacific Railroad, the Sioux, and the Panic of 1873*. Norman: University of Oklahoma Press, 2006.

McClernand, Edward J. *On Time for Disaster: The Rescue of Custer's Command*. Lincoln: University of Nebraska Press, 1989.

—— *With the Indian and the Buffalo in Montana, 1870–1878*. Glendale, California: Arthur H. Clarke Company, 1969.

McClintock, Walter. *The Old North Trail or Life, Legends, and Religion of the Blackfeet Indians*. Lincoln: University of Nebraska Press, 1968.

—— *The Tragedy of the Blackfoot*. Los Angeles, California: Southwest Museum, 1970.

McGinniss, Anthony. *Counting Coup and Cutting Horses: Intertribal Warfare on the Northern Plains, 1738–1889*. Evergreen, Colorado: Cordillera Press, 1990.

McMurtry, Larry. *Oh What a Slaughter: Massacres in the American West, 1846–1890*. New York: Simon and Schuster, 2005.

McPhee, John. *Annals of the Former World*. New York: Farrar, Straus and Giroux, 2000.

McWhorter, Lucullus V. *Hear Me, My Chiefs: Nez Perce Legend and History*. Caldwell, Idaho: Caxton Printers, 1952.

—— *Yellow Wolf: His Own Story, as Told to Lucullus Virgil McWhorter*. Caldwell, Idaho: Caxton Printers, 1940.

Madsen, Brigham D. *The Bannock of Idaho*. Moscow: University of Idaho Press, 1996.

—— *Glory Hunter: A Biography of Patrick Edward Connor*. Salt Lake City: University of Utah Press, 1990.

—— *The Northern Shoshoni*. Caldwell, Idaho: Caxton Printers, 1980.

—— *The Shoshoni Frontier and the Bear River Massacre*. Salt Lake City: University of Utah Press, 1985.

Madsen, Betty M. and Brigham D. Madsen. *North to Montana*. Salt Lake City: University of Utah Press, 1980.

Magoc, Chris J. *Yellowstone: The Creation and Selling of an American Landscape, 1870–1903*. Albuquerque: University of New Mexico Press, 1999.

Malone, Michael P. and Richard B. Roeder. *The Montana Past: An Anthology*. Missoula: University of Montana Press, 1969.

Malone, Michael P., Richard B. Roeder and William L. Lang. *Montana: A History of Two Centuries*. Seattle: University of Washington Press, 1976.

Marcy, Randolph B. *The Prairie Traveler: A Handbook for Overland Expeditions*. New York: Harper Brothers, 1859.

—— *Thirty Years of Army Life on the Border*. New York: Harper Brothers, 1866.

Mardock, Robert. *The Reformers and the American Indian*. Columbia: University of Missouri Press, 1971.

Marks, Paula Mitchell. *In a Barren Land: American Indian Dispossession and Survival*. New York: William Morrow, 1998.

Marquis, Thomas. *Custer, Cavalry and Crows: The Story of William White*. Fort Collins, Colorado: Old Army Press, 1975.

Mather, Ruth E. and F. E. Boswell. *Hanging the Sheriff: A Biography of Henry Plummer*. Salt Lake City: University of Utah Press, 1987.

—— *Vigilante Victims: Montana's 1864 Hanging Spree*. Oklahoma City: History West Publishing Company, 1991.

Mattes, Merrill J. *Colter's Hell and Jackson Hole*. Washington, D.C.: National Park Service, 1962.

—— *Indians, Infants, and Infantry: Andrew and Elizabeth Burt on the Frontier*. Lincoln: University of Nebraska Press, 1988.

Meagher, Mary and Douglas B. Houston. *Yellowstone and the Biology of Time: Photographs Across a Century*. Norman: University of Oklahoma Press, 1998.

Merrill, Marlene Deahl. *Yellowstone and the Great West: Journals, Letters, and Images from the 1871 Hayden Expedition*. Lincoln: University of Nebraska Press, 1999.

Miles, Nelson A. *Personal Recollections & Observations of General Nelson A. Miles*, Vol. 1. Lincoln: University of Nebraska Press, 1992.

Millard, Candice. *The River of Doubt: Theodore Roosevelt's Darkest Journey*. New York: Doubleday, 2005.

Miller, Don and Stan B. Cohen. *Military Forts and Trading Posts of Montana*. Missoula, Montana: Pictorial History Publishing Company, 1978.

Milner, Clyde A. and Carol A. O'Connor. *As Big as the West: The Pioneer Life of Granville Stuart*. New York: Oxford University Press, 2009.

Monnett, John H. *Where One Hundred Soldiers Were Killed: The Struggle for the Powder River in 1866 and the Making of the Fetterman Myth*. Albuquerque: University of New Mexico Press, 2008.

Morgan, Dale L. *Jedediah Smith and the Opening of the West*. Lincoln: University of Nebraska Press, 1964.

Morris, Roy, Jr. *Sheridan: The Life and Wars of General Phil Sheridan*. New York: Vintage, 1992.

Moulton, Gary E., ed. *The Lewis and Clark Journals: An American Epic of Discovery*. Lincoln, Nebraska: Bison Books, 2004.

Murray, Robert A. *The Bozeman Trail: Highway of History*. Boulder, Colorado: Pruett Publishing Company, 1988.

Nabokov, Peter. *Where the Lightning Strikes: The Lives of American Indian Sacred Places*. New York: Viking, 2006.

—— and Lawrence Loendorf. *Restoring a Presence: American Indians and Yellowstone National Park*. Norman: University of Oklahoma Press, 2004.

Nash, Roderick. *Wilderness and the American Mind*. New Haven, Connecticut: Yale University Press, 1967.

Nerburn, Kent. *Chief Joseph and the Flight of the Nez Perce*. New York: Harper, 2005.

Norris, Philetus. *The Calumet of the Coteau and Other Poetical Legends of the Border*. Philadelphia: Lippincott & Co., 1883.

Norton, Harry J. *Wonder-Land Illustrated, or Horseback Rides Through the Yellowstone National Park*. Virginia City, Montana Territory: Harry J. Norton, 1873.

Oberholtzer, Ellis Paxson. *Jay Cooke: Financier of the Civil War*. Philadelphia: George W. Jacobs and Company, 1907.

Olson, James C. *Red Cloud and the Sioux Problem*. Lincoln: University of Nebraska Press, 1965.

Osborne, William M. *The Wild Frontier: Atrocities During the American-Indian War from the Jamestown Colony to Wounded Knee*. New York: Random House, 2001.

Ostler, Jeffrey. *The Plains Sioux and U.S. Colonialism from Lewis and Clark to Wounded Knee*. New York: Cambridge University Press, 2004.

Paladin, Vivian and Jean Baucus. *Helena: An Illustrated History*. Helena: Montana Historical Society Press, 1983.

Parkman, Francis, Jr. *The Oregon Trail*. Oxford: Oxford University Press, 1996.

Phillips, P. C., ed. *W. A. Ferris: Life in the Rocky Mountains (Diary of the Wanderings of a Trapper in the Years 1831–1832)*. Denver: Old West Publishing, 1940.

Phinney, Mary Allen. *Allen-Isham Genealogy: Jirah Isham Allen, Montana Pioneer, Government Scout, Guide, Interpreter and Famous Hunter, During Four Years of Indian Warfare in Montana and Dakota*. Rutland, Vermont: The Tuttle Publishing Company, 1946.

Pomeroy, Earl. *In Search of the Golden West: The Tourist in Western America*. New York: Alfred A. Knopf, 1957.

Powell, John Wesley. *Exploration of the Colorado River and Its Canyons*. New York: Penguin Classics, 2003.

Progressive Men of the State of Montana. Chicago: A. W. Bowen & Co., 1902.

Pyne, Stephen J., *How the Canyon Became Grand: A Short History*. New York: Viking, 1998.

Quaife, Milo Milton, ed. *Army Life in Dakota: Selections from the Journal of Philippe Régis Denis de Keredern de Trobriand*. Whitefish, Montana: Kessinger Publishing, 2007.

Rickey, Don, Jr. *Forty Miles a Day on Beans and Hay: The Enlisted Soldier Fighting the Indian Wars*. Norman: University of Oklahoma Press, 1963.

Rister, Carl C. *Border Command: General Phil Sheridan in the West*. Lincoln: University of Nebraska Press, 1944.

Rodenbough, Theodore F. *From Everglade to Cañon with the Second Dragoons.* New York: D. Van Nostrand, 1875.

Roe, Frances M. *Army Letters from an Officer's Wife.* New York: D. Appleton and Co., 1909.

Ronda, James P. *Lewis and Clark Among the Indians: Centennial Edition.* Lincoln: University of Nebraska Press, 1984.

Runte, Alfred. *National Parks: The American Experience.* Lincoln: University of Nebraska Press, 1979.

Russell, Osborne, ed. Aubrey L. Haines. *Journal of a Trapper.* Lincoln: University of Nebraska Press, 1964.

Rust, Thomas C. *Fort Ellis: A Documentary History.* Bozeman, Montana: Gallatin County Historical Society, 2004.

Sanders, Helen Fitzgerald and William H. Bertsche Jr., eds. *X. Beidler: Vigilante.* Norman, Oklahoma: University of Oklahoma Press, 1957.

Schofield, Brian. *Selling Your Father's Bones: America's 140-Year War Against the Nez Perce Tribe.* New York: Simon and Schuster, 2009.

Schullery, Paul. *Searching for Yellowstone: Ecology and Wonder in the Last Wilderness.* Boston: Houghton Mifflin, 1997.

—— and Lee H. Whittlesey. *Myth and History in the Creation of Yellowstone National Park.* Lincoln: University of Nebraska Press, 2003.

Schultz, Duane P. *Night of the Freezing Moon: The Sand Creek Massacre, November 1864.* New York: St. Martin's Press, 1990.

Schultz, James Willard. *Blackfeet and Buffalo: Memories of Life Among the Indians.* Norman: University of Oklahoma Press, 1962.

—— *My Life as an Indian.* Boston: Dover Books, 1997.

Scott, Hugh. *Some Memories of a Soldier.* New York: Century Company, 1928.

Scott, Kim Allen. *Yellowstone Denied: The Life of Gustavus Cheyney Doane.* Norman: University of Oklahoma Press, 2007.

—— ed. *"Splendid on a Grand Scale": The Writings of Hans Peter Gyllembourg Koch, 1869–1874.* Helena, Montana: Drumlummon Institute and Bedrock Editions, 2010.

Sears, John. *Sacred Places: American Tourist Attractions in the Nineteenth Century.* New York: Oxford University Press, 1989.

Sheridan, Philip H. *Personal Memoirs of Philip Henry Sheridan, General, United States Army: New and Enlarged Edition, with an Account of His Life from 1871 to His Death, in 1888,* 2 vols. New York: D. Appleton and Company, 1904.

Sides, Hampton. *Blood and Thunder: An Epic of the American West.* New York: Doubleday, 2006.

Slotkin, Richard. *The Fatal Environment: The Myth of the Frontier in the Age of Industrialization, 1800–1890.* Norman: University of Oklahoma Press, 1998.

—— *Gunfighter Nation: The Myth of the Frontier in Twentieth-Century America.* Norman, Oklahoma: University of Oklahoma Press, 1998.

—— *Regeneration Through Violence: The Mythology of the American Frontier, 1600–1860.* Norman: University of Oklahoma Press, 2000.

Smith, Henry Nash. *Virgin Land: The American West as Symbol and Myth.* Cambridge, Massachusetts: Harvard University Press, 2007.

Smith, Phyllis, *Bozeman and the Gallatin Valley: A History.* Helena, Montana: Twodot, 1997.

———— and William Hoy. *The Northern Pacific Railroad and Yellowstone National Park*. Helena, Montana: Riverbend Publishing, n.d.

Smith, Sherry Lynn. *The View from Officers' Row: Army Perceptions of Western Indians*. Tucson: University of Arizona Press, 1991.

Spence, Clark C. *Territorial Politics and Government in Montana, 1864–1889*. Urbana: University of Illinois Press, 1975.

Stanley, Edwin J. *Rambles in Wonderland; or, Up the Yellowstone and Among the Geysers and Other Curiosities of the National Park*. New York: D. Appleton and Co., 1878.

Stannard, David E. *American Holocaust: The Conquest of the New World*. New York: Oxford University Press, 1992.

Stegner, Wallace. *Beyond the Hundredth Meridian: John Wesley Powell and the Second Opening of the West*. Lincoln: University of Nebraska Press, 1982.

Strand, Ginger. *Inventing Niagara: Beauty, Power, and Lies*. New York: Simon and Schuster, 2008.

Strong, William E. *A Trip to the Yellowstone National Park in July, August, and September 1875*. Norman: University of Oklahoma Press, 1968.

Stuart, Granville. *Forty Years on the Frontier*. Cleveland, Ohio: Arthur H. Clark and Company, 1925.

Sunder, John E. *The Fur Trade on the Upper Missouri, 1840–1865*. Norman: University of Oklahoma Press, 1965.

Thomas, David Hurst. *Skull Wars: Kennewick Man, Archaeology, and the Battle for Native American Identity*. New York: Basic Books, 2000.

Thompson, Francis M. *A Tenderfoot in Montana: Reminiscences of the Gold Rush, the Vigilantes, and the Birth of Montana Territory*. Helena: Montana Historical Society Press, 2004.

Thrapp, Dan L. *Encyclopedia of Frontier Biography*. Lincoln: University of Nebraska Press, 1991.

Toole, K. Ross. *Montana: An Uncommon Land*. Norman: University of Oklahoma Press, 1959.

Topping, Eugene Sayre. *The Chronicles of the Yellowstone: An Accurate, Comprehensive History*. St. Paul, Minnesota: Pioneer Press, 1888.

Tuttle, Daniel Sylvester. *Reminiscences of a Missionary Bishop*. New York: Thomas Whittaker, 1906.

Utley, Robert H. *Frontier Regulars: The United States Army and the Indian, 1866–1891*. New York: Macmillan, 1973.

———— *Frontiersmen in Blue: The United States Army and the Indian, 1848–1865*. New York: Macmillan, 1967.

———— *The Indian Frontier of the American West, 1846–1890*. Albuquerque: University of New Mexico Press, 1984.

———— *The Lance and the Shield: The Life and Times of Sitting Bull*. New York: Ballantine, 1994.

———— *A Life Wild and Perilous: Mountain Men and the Paths to the Pacific*. New York: Henry Holt, 1997.

———— and Wilcomb E. Washburn. *Indian Wars*. Boston: Houghton Mifflin, 1977.

Vaughn, Robert. *Then and Now; or, 36 Years in the Rockies*. Minneapolis: Tribune Printing, 1900.

Vestal, Stanley. *Jim Bridger, Mountain Man*. New York: Morrow, 1936.

—— *Mountain Men*. Boston: Houghton Mifflin, 1937.

Victor, Mrs. Frances A. Fuller. *The River of the West: Joe Meek in the Rocky Mountains*. Hartford: R. W. Bliss and Co., 1870.

Vinton, Stallo. *John Colter, Discoverer of Yellowstone Park*. New York: Edward Eberstadt, 1926.

Voget, Fred W. *The Shoshone-Crow Sundance*. Norman: University of Oklahoma Press, 1974.

Waite, Thornton. *Yellowstone by Train: A History of Rail Travel to America's First National Park*. Missoula, Montana: Pictorial History Publishing Company, 2006.

Welch, James. *Fools Crow*. New York: Penguin, 1987.

—— and Paul Stekler. *Killing Custer: The Battle of the Little Bighorn and the Fate of the Plains Indians*. New York: Penguin, 1994.

Wheeler, Olin Dunbar. *The Trail of Lewis and Clark, 1804–1904*. New York: The Knickerbocker Press, 1904.

White, G. Edward. *The Eastern Establishment and the Western Experience: The West of Frederic Remington, Theodore Roosevelt, and Owen Wister*. New Haven, Connecticut: Yale University Press, 1968.

White, Richard. *"It's Your Misfortune and None of My Own": A New History of the American West*. Norman: University of Oklahoma Press, 1993.

White, William. *Custer, Cavalry and Crows, Being the Thrilling Account of the Western Adventures of William White: The Story of William White as Told to Thomas Marquis*. Fort Collins, Colorado: Old Army Press, 1975.

Whittlesey, Lee H. *Storytelling in Yellowstone: Horse and Buggy Tour Guides*. Albuquerque: University of New Mexico Press, 2007.

—— *Yellowstone Place Names*. Helena: Montana Historical Society, 1988.

Wilkins, Thurman. *Thomas Moran: Artist of the Mountains*. Norman: University of Oklahoma Press, 1966.

Wischmann, Lesley. *Frontier Diplomats: Alexander Culbertson and Natoyist-Siksina' Among the Blackfeet*. Norman: University of Oklahoma Press, 2004.

Wooster, Robert. *The Military and United States Indian Policy, 1865–1903*. Lincoln: University of Nebraska Press, 1988.

—— *Nelson A. Miles and the Twilight of the Frontier Army*. Lincoln: University of Nebraska Press, 1996.

Worster, Donald. *A River Running West: The Life of John Wesley Powell*. New York: Oxford University Press, 2002.

Wylie, Paul R. *The Irish General: Thomas Francis Meagher*. Norman: University of Oklahoma Press, 2007.

Wylie, W. W. *Yellowstone National Park, or The Great American Wonderland*. Kansas City, Missouri: Ramsey, Millett and Hudson, 1882.

ARTICLES, PAPERS, ETC.

Antrei, Albert. "Father Pierre Jean DeSmet." *Montana the Magazine of Western History* 13, 2 (Spring 1963): 24–42.

Athearn, Robert G. "The Civil War and Montana Gold." *Montana the Magazine of Western History* 12, 2 (Spring 1962): 62–73.

—— "Frontier Critics of the Army." *Montana the Magazine of American History* 5, 2 (Spring 1955): 16–28.

"Biographical Sketch of Hezekiah L. Hosmer, First Chief Justice of the Territory of Montana." *Contributions to the Historical Society of Montana* 3 (1900): 288–308.

Brackett, Colonel A. G. "A Trip Through the Rocky Mountains." *Contributions to the Historical Society of Montana* 8 (1917): 329–44.

Bradley, James H. "Adventure on the Upper Missouri." *Contributions to the Historical Society of Montana* 1 (1876): 80–9.

—— "Affairs at Fort Benton: From Lieut. Bradley's Journal." *Contributions to the Historical Society of Montana* 3 (1900): 201–87.

—— "Bradley Manuscript Book II: Miscellaneous Events at Fort Benton." *Contributions to the Historical Society of Montana* 8 (1917): 127–96.

—— "Bradley Manuscript: Yellowstone Expedition of 1874, Book 4 and 5." *Contributions to the Historical Society of Montana* 8 (1917): 105–26.

Brayer, Herbert O. "Exploring the Yellowstone with Hayden, 1872." *Annals of Wyoming* 14, 4 (October 1942): 253–98.

Brown, Mark H. "Yellowstone Tourists and the Nez Perce." *Montana the Magazine of Western History* 16, 3 (July 1966): 30–43.

Clarke, Helen P. "Sketch of Malcolm Clarke, A Corporate Member of the Historical Society of Montana." *Contributions to the Historical Society of Montana* 2 (1896): 255–68.

Cockhill, Brian, ed. "The Quest of Warren Gillette." *Montana the Magazine of Western History* 22, 3 (Summer 1972): 12–30.

Cowan, Mrs. George F. "Reminiscences of Pioneer Life." *Contributions to the Historical Society of Montana* 4 (1903): 155–86.

Cronon, William. "The Trouble with Wilderness," in Cronon, ed., *Uncommon Ground: Toward Reinventing Nature*. New York: W. W. Norton, 1995.

Cutright, Paul Russell. "Lewis on the Marias, 1806." *Montana the Magazine of Western History* 18, 3 (Summer 1968): 30–43.

Davidson, Stanley R. and Dale Tash. "Confederate Backwash in Montana Territory." *Montana: The Magazine of Western History* 17, 4 (Autumn 1967): 50–8.

De Lacy, Walter W. "A Trip up the South Snake River in 1863." *Contributions to the Historical Society of Montana* 1 (1876): 113.

Everts, Truman C. "Thirty-Seven Days of Peril." *Scribners Monthly* 3, 1 (November 1871): 1–17.

Ewers, John C. "Self-Torture in the Blood Indian Sun Dance." *Journal of the Washington Academy of Sciences* Vol. XXXVIII, No. 5 (1948): 166–73.

Farr, William E. "Going to Buffalo: Indian Hunting Migrations Across the Rocky Mountains, Part 2, Civilian Permits and Army Escorts." *Montana the Magazine of Western History* 54, 2 (Spring 2004): 26–43.

Fergus, James. "Early Mining Life in Bannack and Alder Gulch." *Rocky Mountain Magazine* 1, No. 4: 265–69.

Fisher, Captain S. G. "Journal of S. G. Fisher, Chief of Scouts to General O. O. Howard During the Campaign Against the Nez Perce Indians, 1877." *Contributions to the Historical Society of Montana* 2 (1896): 269–82.

Folsom, David E., with a preface by Nathaniel Pitt Langford. "The Folsom-Cook Exploration of the Upper Yellowstone in the Year 1869." *Contributions to the Historical Society of Montana* 5 (1904): 346–69.

Gibbon, General John. "The Wonders of the Yellowstone." *Journal of the American Geographical Society of New York* 5 (May 1873): 112–37.

Greenfield, Charles D. "Little Dog, Once-Fierce Piegan Warrior, Was Wise and Just Beyond His Time." *Montana the Magazine of Western History* 14, 1 (Winter 1964): 23–33.

Haines, Aubrey L. "The Bannock Trails of Yellowstone National Park." *Archaeology in Montana*, 4 (1962): 1–8.

—— "The Bridge That Jack Built." *Yellowstone Nature Notes* 21, 1 (1947): 1–4.

—— "Lost in the Yellowstone." *Montana the Magazine of Western History* 22, 3 (Summer 1972): 31–41.

Harvey, J. H. "Historic Luster Glorifies Dingy House." *St. Paul Pioneer Press*, April 9, 1939.

Hayden, Ferdinand Vandeveer. "The Wonders of the West II: More About the Yellowstone." *Scribner's Monthly* 3 (February 1872): 388–96.

—— and Albert Charles Peale. "Wonders of the Rocky Mountains: The Yellowstone Park, How to Reach It," in Henry T. Williams, ed. *The Pacific Tourist: Williams Illustrated Trans-Continental Guide of Travel*. New York: Henry Williams, 1876: 277–92.

Hedges, Cornelius. Articles on the 1870 expedition from the *Helena Herald*, October 8–November 9, 1870, collected and reprinted in Cramton, *Early History of Yellowstone National Park*, 97–110.

—— "An Account of a Trip to Fort Benton in October, 1865, with Acting Governor Thomas H. Meagher to Treat with the Blackfeet Indians." *Rocky Mountain Magazine* 1, 3 (November 1900): 155–58.

—— "Journal of Judge Cornelius Hedges." *Contributions to the Historical Society of Montana* 5 (1904): 370–94.

Hedges, Wyllys A. "Cornelius Hedges." *Contributions to the Historical Society of Montana* 7 (1910): 181–96.

Henderson, A. Bart. "Journal." Coe Collection, Beinecke Library, Yale University, portions on Yellowstone reprinted in *The Yellowstone Interpreter*, Vol. 2 (1964).

Hosmer, J. H. "Biographical Sketch of Hezekiah L. Hosmer." *Contributions to the Historical Society of Montana* 3 (1900): 297–98.

Hultkrantz, Åke. "The Fear of Geysers Among Indians of the Yellowstone Park Area," in Leslie B. Davis, ed., *Lifeways of Intermountain and Plains Montana Indians*. Bozeman: Montana State University Press, 1979.

—— "The Indians in Yellowstone Park." *Annals of Wyoming* 29, 2 (1957): 125–49.

—— "The Shoshones in the Rocky Mountain Area." *Annals of Wyoming* 33, 1 (1961): 19–41.

Hutton, Paul A. "Phil Sheridan's Pyrrhic Victory." *Montana the Magazine of Western History* 32, 2 (Spring 1982): 32–43.

—— "Phil Hutton's Crusade for Yellowstone." *American History Illustrated* XIX (February 1985), 10–16.

Koch, Peter. "A Historical Sketch of Bozeman, Gallatin Valley and the Bozeman Pass." *Contributions to the Historical Society of Montana* 2 (1896): 126–39.

—— "Discovery of the Yellowstone National Park: A Chapter of Early Exploration in the Rocky Mountains." *Magazine of American History* 11, 6 (1884): 497–512.

Kuppens, Francis X. "On the Origin of the Yellowstone National Park." *The Woodstock Letters* XXVI No. 3 (1897): 400–2, reprinted in *The Jesuit Bulletin* 41 (1962): 6–7, 14.

Lang, William L. "Where Did the Nez Perce Go in Yellowstone in 1877?" *Montana the Magazine of Western History* 40, 1 (Winter 1990): 14–29.

Langford, Nathaniel Pitt. "The Ascent of Mount Hayden, Grand Teton, 1872: A New Chapter of Western Discovery." *Scribner's Monthly* VI (1873): 129–57.

—— "The Wonders of the Yellowstone." *Scribner's Monthly* II, 1 (May 1871): 1–17, and II, 2 (June 1871): 113–28.

McClure, Colonel A. K. "Wilbur Fisk Sanders." *Contributions to the Historical Society of Montana* 8 (1917), 25–36.

Meagher, Thomas F. "A Journey to Benton." *Montana the Magazine of Western History* 1, 4 (October 1951): 46–58.

Munson, Lyman E. "Pioneer Life in Montana." *Contributions to the Historical Society of Montana* 5 (1904): 200–33.

Myers, Rex C. "The Settlers and the Nez Perce." *Montana the Magazine of Western History* 27, 4 (Fall 1977): 20–9.

Osgood, Ernest S. "The Fiery Ordeal of Cornelius Hedges." *Montana the Magazine of Western History* 25, 3 (Summer 1975): 68–75.

Peters, J. P. "The March of the Montana Battalion." *Montana the Magazine of Western History* 15, 2 (Spring 1965): 38–51.

Reeves, Thomas C. "President Arthur in Yellowstone." *Montana the Magazine of Western History* 19, 3 (Summer 1969): 18–29.

Robbins, William G. "Samuel T. Hauser: The Deconstruction of a Capitalist Patriarch." *Montana the Magazine of Western History* 42, 4 (Fall 1992): 20–33.

Ronan, Peter. "Discovery of Alder Gulch." *Contributions to the Historical Society of Montana* 3 (1900): 143–52.

Rust, Thomas C. "Settlers, Soldiers, and Scoundrels: Economic Tension in a Frontier Military Town." *Military History of the West* 31, 2 (Fall 2001): 117–38.

Sanders, Wilbur Fisk. "The Pioneers." *Contributions to the Historical Society of Montana* 4 (1903): 25–36.

Schullery, Paul and Lee H. Whittlesey. "Yellowstone's Creation Myth: Can We Live with Our Own Legends?" *Montana the Magazine of Western History* 53, 1 (Spring 2003): 2–13.

Silliman, Lee. "A Ride to the Infernal Regions: An Account of the First Tourist Party to Yellowstone." *Yellowstone Nature Notes* 8, 1 (Winter 2000): 8–14.

Stuart, Granville. "A Memoir of the Life of James Stuart." *Contributions to the Historical Society of Montana* 1 (1876): 36–79.

Stuart, James. "An Adventure on the Upper Missouri." *Contributions to the Historical Society of Montana* 1 (1876): 80–9.

—— "The Yellowstone Expedition of 1863." *Contributions to the Historical Society of Montana* 1 (1876): 149–233.

Thane, James L., Jr. "The Montana 'Indian War' of 1867." *Arizona and the West* 10 (1968): 153–70.

Trumbull, Walter. "The Washburn Yellowstone Expedition." *Overland Monthly* 6, 5–6 (May–June 1871): 431–7, 489–96.

Van Cleve, Charlotte Ouisconsin. "A Sketch of the Early Life of Malcolm Clarke. A Corporate

Member of the Historical Society of Montana." *Contributions to the Historical Society of Montana* 1 (1876): 90–8.

Walter, Dave. "The Baker Massacre." *Montana the Magazine of Western History* 37, 2 (March–April 1987): 61–8.

Weikert, Andrew J. "Journal of the Tour Through the Yellowstone National Park in August and September, 1877." *Contributions to the Historical Society of Montana* 3 (1900): 153–74.

Wheeler, Olin D. "Nathaniel Pitt Langford, the Vigilante, the Explorer, the Expounder, and First Superintendent of the Yellowstone Park." *Minnesota Historical Society Collections* 15 (1919): 630–68.

Wheeler, William F. "Walter Washington De Lacy: A Brief Biography as Given by Him in Several Conversations and from Other Sources." *Contributions to the Historical Society of Montana* 1 (1876): 241–51.

Whittlesey, Lee H. "The Nez Perce in Yellowstone in 1877." *Montana the Magazine of Western History* (Spring 2007): 48–55.

Wilson, Wesley. "The U.S. Army and the Piegans: The Baker Massacre of 1870." *North Dakota History* 32 (January 1965): 40–58.

GOVERNMENT DOCUMENTS

Baker, Eugene M. "Report of the Operations of the Escort to Surveyors of the N.P.R.R. Company down the Yellowstone," typescript, n.d., Montana Historical Society Archives.

Ball, Edward. "Report on the 1871 Yellowstone Surveying Expedition from Fort Ellis, Montana." December 10, 1871, MF-339, reel 1, Montana Historical Society Archives.

Barlow, John Whitney. *Indian Interference with the Northern Pacific Railroad.* 42nd Cong., 3rd Sess., Senate Exec. Doc. 16, 1872. Washington, D.C., Government Printing Office, 1872.

—— *Journey Down the Yellowstone from Fort Ellis.* 42nd Cong., 3rd Sess., Senate Exec. Doc. 12, 1873. Washington, D.C., Government Printing Office, 1873.

—— and David P. Heap. *Report of a Reconnaissance of the Basin of the Upper Yellowstone in 1871.* 42nd Cong., 2nd Sess., Senate Exec. Doc. 66, 1872. Washington, D.C., Government Printing Office, 1872.

De Trobriand, Régis. Incoming Correspondence, September 2, 1869–March 16, 1870, and Outgoing Correspondence, September 9–December 29, 1869. Copies in Montana Historical Society Archives.

Doane, Gustavus Cheyney. Army Records, Record Group 94, 2422 AGO 1876, Records of the War Department, Office of the Adjutant General, National Archives.

—— *Report of Lieutenant Gustavus C. Doane on the Socalled Yellowstone Expedition of 1870.* 41st Cong., 3rd Sess., Senate Exec. Doc. 51. Washington, D.C., Government Printing Office, 1871, reprinted in full in Bonney and Bonney, *Battle Drums and Geysers*, 215–388.

Doane, Captain G. C., 2nd Cavalry. Record of Service, Presidio, San Francisco, February 16, 1889, typescript copy, Burlingame Special Collections, Montana State University Libraries, Bozeman.

Doane, Lieutenant G. C., 2nd Cavalry et al. Field correspondence, Sioux and Nez Perce campaigns, 1876–1877, Burlingame Special Collections, Montana State University Libraries, Bozeman.

Hayden, Ferdinand Vandeveer. *Final Report of the United States Geological Survey of Nebraska and Portions of the Adjacent Territories.* 42nd Cong., 1st Sess., 1871, House Exec. Doc. 19. Washington, D.C., Government Printing Office, 1872.

—— *Report on the Proposed Yellowstone National Park.* Washington, D.C., Government Printing Office, 1872.

Jones, W. A. *Report on the Reconnaissance of Northwestern Wyoming, Including Yellowstone National Park, Made in the Summer of 1873.* 43rd Cong., 1st Sess., House Exec. Doc. 285. Washington, D.C., Government Printing Office, 1875.

Langford, Nathaniel Pitt. *Annual Report of the Superintendent of the Yellowstone National Park for the Year 1872.* 42nd Cong., 3rd Sess., Senate Exec. Doc. 35, 1873. Washington, D.C., Government Printing Office, 1873.

Ludlow, William. *Report of a Reconnaissance from Carroll, Montana Territory, on the Upper Missouri to the Yellowstone National Park, and Return, Made in the Summer of 1875.* Washington, D.C., Government Printing Office, 1876.

Norris, Philetus W. *Report upon the Yellowstone National Park, to the Secretary of the Interior, for the Year 1877.* Washington, D.C., Government Printing Office, 1877.

Raynolds, W. T. *The Report of Brevet Brigadier General W. T. Raynolds on the Exploration of the Yellowstone River and the Country Drained by That River.* 40th Cong., 1st. Sess., Senate Exec. Doc. 77. Washington, D.C., Government Printing Office, 1868.

Sheridan, P. H. *Record of Engagements with Hostile Indians within the Division of the Missouri from 1868 to 1882.* Washington, D.C., Government Printing Office, 1882.

—— and W. T. Sherman. *Reports of Inspections Made in the Summer of 1877.* Washington, D.C., Government Printing Office, 1878.

—— et al. *Report of an Exploration of Parts of Wyoming, Idaho, and Montana in August and September 1882, with the Itinerary of James F. Gregory.* Washington, D.C., Government Printing Office, 1882.

United States, *Proceedings of the Great Peace Commission of 1867–1868.* Washington, D.C., Institute for the Development of Indian Law, 1975.

United States Army. Records of Posts, 1820–1940, Fort Ellis, Montana, 1867–1886, Records Group 393, National Archives and Records Administration, Washington, D.C.

United States, Joint Special Committee. *Condition of the Indian Tribes: Report of the Joint Special Committee Appointed Under Joint Resolution of March 3, 1865, with an Appendix.* 39th Cong., 2nd Sess., Senate Report No. 156. Washington, D.C., Government Printing Office, 1867.

United States Secretary of War. *Annual Report of the Secretary of War, 1870.* 41st Cong., 2nd Sess., Doc. No. 185, Vol. 1418. Washington, D.C., Government Printing Office, 1870.

—— *Annual Report of the Secretary of War, 1871.* 42nd Cong., 2nd Sess., House Exec. Doc. 1, Part 2. Washington, D.C., Government Printing Office, 1871.

—— *Annual Report of the Secretary of War, 1872.* 42nd Cong., 3rd. Sess., House Exec. Doc. 1, Part 2. Washington, D.C., Government Printing Office, 1872.

—— *Annual Report of the Secretary of War, 1877.* 45th Cong., 2nd. Sess., House Exec. Doc. 1, Part 2. Washington, D.C., Government Printing Office, 1877.

—— *Piegan Indians: Letter of the Secretary of War in Answer to the Late Expedition Against the Piegan Indians, in the Territory of Montana.* 41st Cong., 2nd. Sess., 1870, House Exec. Doc. 269. Washington, D.C., Government Printing Office, 1870.

United States Senate. *"The Chivington Massacre," Reports of the Joint Special Committees on the Condition of the Indian Tribes,* 39th Cong., 2nd Sess., Senate Report 156, 1867. Washington, D.C., Government Printing Office, 1867.

—— *Claims of the Heirs of Chief Heavy Runner,* microfilm copy in Montana Historical Society Archives.

United States War Department. *Record of Engagements with Hostile Indians within the Military Division of the Missouri from 1868 to 1882, Lieutenant General P. H. Sheridan Commanding.* Chicago: Headquarters of the Military Division of the Missouri, 1882.

Warren, Gouverneur Kemble. *Preliminary Report of Explorations in Nebraska and Dakota in the Years 1855–'56 –'57.* 35th Cong., 2nd Sess., 1858, Senate Exec. Doc. 1. Washington, D.C., Government Printing Office, 1858.

Washburn, Henry Dana. "The Yellowstone Expedition." *Mining Statistics West of the Rocky Mountains,* March 21, 1871. 42nd Cong., 1st Sess., House Exec. Doc. 10. Washington, D.C., Government Printing Office, 1871.

"Yellowstone Park, Letter from the Secretary of the Interior Transmitting a Draught of a Bill Amendatory of and Supplementary to the Act Entitled 'An Act to Set Apart a Certain Tract of Land, Lying Over the Head-Waters of the Yellowstone River, as a Public Park.'" February 21, 1874, 43rd Cong. 1st Sess., House Exec. Doc. 147. Washington, D.C., Government Printing Office, 1874.

UNPUBLISHED WORKS

"Benjamin F. Stickney." Biographical note, typescript, n/d, Yellowstone National Park Archives.

Berg, Ben, Jr. "Our No. 1 Judge [Hezekiah L. Hosmer]." Typescript, October 1986, Montana State University Special Collections, Bozeman.

Brackett, Albert, "Fort Bridger," unpublished manuscript, 1870, special collections, Harold B. Lee Library, Brigham Young University, Utah.

Brisbin, James S. "Sketches of Noted Frontiersmen." Manuscript, Montana Historical Society Archives.

Burlingame, Merrill G. *Gustavus C. Doane.* Manuscript and notes, Montana State University Special Collections, Bozeman.

"Cornelius Hedges." Biographical note, typescript, n/d, Yellowstone National Park Archives.

Grand Lodge, Anaconda. "Nathaniel Pitt Langford: Past Grand Master." Obituary, January 1, 1911.

Grand Lodge of Montana. "Cornelius Hedges." Obituary, 1907.

Hamilton, James M. "History of Ft. Ellis." Typescript, 1926 (?), Yellowstone National Park Archives.

"Henry Dana Washburn." Biographical note, typescript, n/d, Yellowstone National Park Archives.

Hilger, David. "Interview with Horace Clarke, September 27, 1924." Typescript, Montana Historical Society Archives.

"Horace Clarke." Biographical note, typescript, n/d, Montana Historical Society Archives.

"Jacob Ward Smith." Biographical note, typescript, n/d, Yellowstone National Park Archives.

Jackson, W. Turrentine. "The Early Exploration and Founding of Yellowstone National Park." Doctoral dissertation, University of Texas, June 1940.

Logan, Brett. "Sieben Ranch." Research paper, Montana Historical Society Archives.

"Nathaniel Pitt Langford." Biographical note, typescript, n/d, Yellowstone National Park Archives.

Orton, A. W. "Some Scattered Thoughts on the Early Life of Nathaniel P. Langford," unpublished typescript, Yellowstone National Park Archives.

Phillips, William S. "Total Warfare on the Marias." M.A. thesis, Wake Forest University, 1996, copy in Montana State University Libraries.

Putnam, J. Bruce. "The Evolution of a Frontier Town: Bozeman, Montana, and Its Search for Economic Stability, 1864–1877." M.A. thesis, Montana State University, 1973, copy in Montana State University Libraries, Bozeman.

"Samuel Thomas Hauser." Biographical note, typescript, n/d, Yellowstone National Park Archives.

Server, Fred E. "Diary of a Trip Through Yellowstone National Park, down the Snake River to Fort Hall and Back to Fort Ellis, 1876–1877." Typescript, Montana State University Libraries, Bozeman.

Sloan, Peter. "Joseph Kipp (Kipah)." Typescript, March 14, 1963, Montana State University Special Collections, Bozeman.

"Truman C. Everts." Biographical note, typescript, n/d, Yellowstone National Park Archives.

"Walter Trumbull." Biographical note, typescript, n/d, Yellowstone National Park Archives.

"Warren Caleb Gillette." Biographical note, typescript, n/d, Yellowstone National Park Archives.

White, Thomas Edward. "Cornelius Hedges: Uncommon Hero of the Common Life." Master's thesis, Montana State College, Bozeman, copy in Montana State University Libraries special collections.

PRIMARY SOURCES

Bailey, David J. "Diary and Reminiscences of David J. Bailey: His Journal from Indiana to Montana, 1865." Montana State University Libraries, Special Collections, Bozeman.

Bozeman, John and Nathaniel Pitt Langford, Correspondence, May–June 1866, Montana State University Special Collections, Bozeman.

Brisbin, James Sanks, Papers, 1850–1891, Manuscript Collection 39, Montana Historical Society Archives.

Burlingame, Merrill G., Papers, 1880–1980, Collection 2245, Burlingame Special Collections, Montana State University Libraries, Bozeman.

Clarke, Helen P. Papers, Small Collection 1153, Montana Historical Society Archives.

Cook, Charles W. "Remarks of C. W. Cook, Last Survivor of the Original Explorers of the Yellowstone Park Region, on the Occasion of His Second Visit to the Park in 53 Years, During the Celebration of the Park's Golden Anniversary." July 14, 1922, transcript in Yellowstone National Park Archives.

Doane, Gustavus Cheyney, Military and Personal Papers, 1860–1939, Burlingame Special Collection 2211, Montana State University Libraries, Bozeman.

—— "American Progress." Undated essay, Pacific University, Burlingame Special Collection 2211/3, Montana State University Libraries, Bozeman.

——"The Beauties of Nature." Undated essay, Pacific University, Burlingame Special Collection 2211/3, Montana State University Libraries, Bozeman.

—— "Expedition from Fort Ellis, Montana, to Fort Hall, Idaho, October 11, 1876, to January 4, 1877." Reprinted in full in Bonney and Bonney. *Battle Drums and Geysers*, 433–578.

—— "Exploration of the Judith Basin." Report to the Secretary of the Interior, Commissioner of Indian Affairs, February 19, 1874, in Montana Historical Society Archives.

——"The Fabulous Ages." Undated essay, Pacific University, Burlingame Special Collections 2211/3, Montana State University Libraries, Bozeman.

—— "Familiar Lecture on Geology, As Connected with Political Science." Undated essay, Pacific University, Burlingame Special Collection 2111/3, Montana State University Libraries, Bozeman.

—— Letter to Senator Wilbur Fisk Sanders, January 7, 1891, typescript copy, Burlingame Special Collection 2211/1, Montana State University Libraries, Bozeman.

—— "Oration on the Eloquence of Solitude." Pacific University, December 3, 1860, Burlingame Special Collection 2211/3, Montana State University Libraries, Bozeman.

—— "The Present Condition of Our Nation." Undated essay, Pacific University, Burlingame Special Collection 2211/3, Montana State University Libraries, Bozeman.

—— "Salutatory Oration." Pacific University, Commencement Day, June 13, 1861, Burlingame Special Collection 2211/3, Montana State University Libraries, Bozeman.

Doane, Mary Hunter, Papers, 1860–1952, Burlingame Special Collection 2417, Montana State University Libraries, Bozeman.

—— Papers 1881–1950, Burlingame Special Collection 292, Montana State University Libraries, Bozeman.

Fort Ellis and Gustavus C. Doane, Military and Personal Papers, 1865–1930, Burlingame Special Collection 851, Montana State University Libraries, Bozeman.

Gillette, Warren Caleb. "Diary of Warren Caleb Gillette (1870)." Original in the collection of the Montana Historical Society.

Haines, Aubrey L., Letter to Gary B. Wetterberg on the retreat of the Nez Perce through Yellowstone National Park, February 15, 1965, Yellowstone National Park Archives.

Hauser, Samuel Thomas, Papers, 1864–1914, Manuscript Collection 37. Montana Historical Society Archives.

—— Papers, 1862–1910, Burlingame Special Collection 283, Montana State University Libraries, Bozeman.

—— "Diary of Samuel T. Hauser, August 17 to September 4, 1870." Coe Collection, manuscript no. 249, Beinecke Library, Yale University, typescript copy in the Yellowstone National Park Archives.

Hayden, Ferdinand Vandeveer, Correspondence, RG 57, National Archives.

Hedges, Cornelius, Papers 1831–1907 and Family Papers, 1828–1945, Manuscript Collection 33, Montana Historical Society Archives.

—— Papers, 1864–1865, Maureen and Mike Mansfield Library, University of Montana, Missoula, MSS 373.

—— "An Address Delivered by Cornelius Hedges on Sunday Evening, Jan. 29, 1871, Eulogistic of Hon. Henry D. Washburn." Typescript, Montana Historical Society Archives.

——— "Diary of Cornelius Hedges, July 6, 1870, to January 29, 1871." Original manuscript in Montana Historical Society Archives.

——— "Diary of Cornelius Hedges on Journey to Montana from Iowa, 1864." Typescript, Montana Historical Society Archives.

——— "Historical Sketch of Lewis and Clark County, Montana." Typescript, July 4, 1876, Montana Historical Society Archives.

——— "Lost in the Wilderness." Undated typescript, Montana Historical Society Archives.

——— "Reminiscences of Early Days in Helena." Undated typescript, Montana Historical Society Archives.

Joyner, Newell F. "Mrs. Mary L. Doane." Memorandum for Historical File, October 15, 1930, Yellowstone National Park Archives.

Langford, Nathaniel Pitt and Family, Papers, 1707–1942, manuscript collection of the Minnesota Historical Society.

Langford, Nathaniel Pitt, Papers, Manuscript Collection 215, Montana Historical Society Archives.

——— "Address Delivered Before the Grand Lodge of Montana at Its Third Annual Communication in the Town of Virginia, Oct. 8, A. D. 1867." Montana Historical Society Archives.

——— "Account of a Journey Down the Missouri River, 1866." Undated typescript, Yellowstone National Park Archives.

——— "Blackfoot." Undated typescript, Yellowstone National Park Archives.

——— "A Frontier Tragedy." Undated typescript, Yellowstone National Park Archives.

———"Hayden Party Under Stevenson, 1872." Undated typescript, Yellowstone National Park Archives.

——— "Helena, 1865." Undated typescript, Yellowstone National Park Archives.

——— "History and Description of Montana, 1870." Undated typescript, Yellowstone National Park Archives.

——— "Letter, May 20, 1866, to J. W. Taylor, Commissioner Internal Revenue Service, Describing the Organization and Operation of the U. S. Internal Revenue District of Montana Territory." Langford Papers, Minnesota State Historical Society.

——— "Letter and Notes by N. P. Langford on the Cullen Treaty with the Blackfoot Indians, Sept. 1, 1868, Fort Benton, Montana." Undated typescript, Yellowstone National Park Archives.

——— "Notes of Lectures Given by N. P. Langford During the Winter of 1870–71." Undated typescript in Yellowstone National Park Archives.

——— "Shade Colyer." Undated typescript, Yellowstone National Park Archives.

——— "Stage Drivers." Undated typescript, Yellowstone National Park Archives.

Lewis, Reuben. "Letter to His Brother Meriwether," April 21, 1810. Copy in Montana State University Special Collections, Bozeman.

Plassman, Martha Edgerton, Papers, Manuscript Collection 78, Montana Historical Society Archives.

——— "Notes on Interview Taken with Horace Clarke." Undated typescript, Montana Historical Society Archives.

Ponsford, John W. "Account of the Baker Battle." Undated typescript, Small Collection 659, Montana Historical Society Archives.

Server, Fred E., Diary, Burlingame Special Collection 507, Montana State University Libraries, Bozeman.

Virginia City Vigilantes, Collection 953, Montana Historical Society Archives.

Weixelman, Joseph. "The Power to Evoke Wonder: Native Americans and the Geysers of Yellowstone National Park." M.A. thesis, Montana State University, 1992, copy in Montana State University Libraries Special Collections, Bozeman.

NEWSPAPERS

Bozeman Avant Courier (Bozeman, Montana)

Helena Herald (Helena, Montana)

Helena Weekly Herald (Helena, Montana)

Livingston Enterprise (Livingston, Montana)

Montana Post (Virginia City, Montana)

New North West (Deer Lodge, Montana)

Pick and Plow (Bozeman, Montana)

INDEX